LECTURES IN SYSTEMATIC THEOLOGY
Volume I

Doctrine of God

GREG NICHOLS

Copyright © 2017 by Greg Nichols
ALL RIGHTS RESERVED

No part of this publication may be reproduced, stored in a retrieval system, or transmitted in any form or by any means, electronic, mechanical, photocopying, recording, or otherwise, without prior permission.

Printed in the United States of America

Scripture taken from the NEW AMERICAN STANDARD BIBLE ®, Copyright © 1960, 1962, 1963, 1968, 1971, 1972, 1973, 1975, 1977, 1993, 1995 by The Lockman Foundation. Used by permission.

The Greek and Hebrew fonts in this work are available from www.linguistsoftware.com.

ISBN:
ISBN-13: 978-1540773036
ISBN-10: 1540773035

Contact Information:

Grace Immanuel Reformed Baptist Church
860 Peachcrest Ct NE, Grand Rapids, MI 49505
Office: 616-249-7336

The book can be purchased at:
www.amazon.com

Credits:
Cover design and formatting for print by Cameron Porter

I have waited for 20 years to see these lectures finally delivered to us in book form. Though Greg Nichols has evidently interacted with the great Systematic theologians of the past, the contents of these pages are no mere echoes of a bygone era. He has used his gifts and applied his mind in his vintage years to build on this historic foundation and bequeathed to the church a Systematic Theology that is both biblically based and historically fresh. If these are the first fruits, I wonder what the other volumes will be like!

—Dr Conrad Mbewe, Chancellor of the African Christian University and Principal of the Lusaka Ministerial College in Lusaka, Zambia

In a day full of light books, Greg Nichols has given us a treatment on the attributes of God in a manner so thoroughly Biblical as to establish the adoration of our Lord upon the firmest of foundations. Here we find gems worth mining. Here is solid nourishment for the head and heart of every hungry believer.

—John Snyder, Christ Church, New Albany, Mississippi, Authored 'Behold Your God', PhD. Trinity St. David's, University of Wales

Table of Contents

ACKNOWLEDGMENTS 7
PREFACE 9
ABBREVIATIONS 11
OUTLINE 13
PROLOGUE: Introduction to Systematic Theology 15
Introduction: *Overview of the Doctrine of God* 81
Part 1: The Existence of God 91
Part 2: The Knowledge of God 127
   Section 1. The Knowability of God 127
   Section 2. The Incomprehensibility of God 147
Part 3: The Nature of God 169
   Introduction to Part 3: Overview of God's Nature: *Simple, Supreme, and Spiritual* 169
   Division 1: God's Supreme Being: God's Existential Attributes 203
     Section 1. God's Ideal Being: *Ideality* 204
     Section 2. God's Self-Existent Being: *Aseity and Independence* ... 213
     Section 3. God's Infinite Being: *Spatial Supremacy* 223
     Section 4. God's Eternal Being: *Temporal Supremacy* 233
     Section 5. God's Unchangeable Being: *Immutability* 249
   Division 2: God's Supreme Spirituality: God's Spiritual Attributes .. 265
     Section 6. God's Incorporeality: *The Majestic Form of God* 265
     Section 7. God's Animacy: *The Vivacity and Omnipotence of God* 277
     Section 8. God's Faculty 303
       Unit 1. God's Supreme Mind: *The Omniscience of God* 304
       Unit 2. God's Supreme Will: *The Sovereignty of God* 325
       Unit 3. God's Supreme Affection: *The Emotivity of God* 369
     Section 9. God's Morality: The Supreme Virtue of God 415
       Introduction: God's Moral Capacity and Character: *Overview of God's Supreme Virtue* 415
       Unit 1. The Goodness of God 425
       Unit 2. The Holiness of God 475
       Unit 3. The Justice of God 505
       Unit 4. The Faithfulness of God 525
       Conclusion: God's Self-Esteem: *God's Consciousness of his Supreme Virtue* 543
     Section 10. God's Personality: The Trinity 549
Part 4: The Names of God 579
Part 5: The Decree of God 661
Conclusion to the Doctrine of God 675

ACKNOWLEDGMENTS

I wish to express my appreciation to all who helped with this publication. I especially acknowledge my wife, Ginger, for her unfailing love and encouragement, my late mother, Blanche Nichols, for her prayers, the pastors and people of Grace Immanuel, for their support, and my spiritual grandson and friend, Rob Ventura, whose vision and hard work brought this book into existence.

PREFACE

This book stems from my lectures in systematic theology. It has been my stewardship to teach systematics since 1979. Over the years this instruction has included courses on the doctrine of God, of man, of Christ, of the church, of the Christian life, of the Holy Spirit, and of the last things. The format of these courses has varied widely, everything from Sunday school classes, to modules of various lengths, to semester length seminary courses. The content has condensed or expanded to fit these many formats. Now at last the time has come to attempt to conserve in print the fruit of these studies.

This book contains the substance of my course on the Doctrine of God. Since the doctrine of God is the first of my systematics courses, the prologue consists of an introduction to systematic theology.

This book, God willing, is the first volume in a series of systematics studies that I hope to publish over the next several years. The plan includes volumes on the doctrines of man (Volume 2), of Christ (Volume 3), of the church (Volume 4), of the Christian life (Volume 5), of the Holy Spirit (Volume 6), and of the last things (Volume 7).

In this book quotations from Scripture come mostly from the 1901 American Standard Version and sometimes from the New American Standard Version. I also use other translations or my own translation occasionally in the interest of clarity.

This book retains the flavor of my lectures. Although the written page can never fully capture the interaction of live instruction, I aim to assist readers to study the major themes of the Bible comprehensively as in systematics class. My hope and prayer is that as you study the existence, knowledge, nature, names, and decree of God, you will be moved to love, revere, and praise him.

Greg Nichols
Grand Rapids, Michigan
January, 2017

ABBREVIATIONS

ASV   The Bible, American Standard Version. Thomas Nelson & Sons, 1901.

BAG   *A Greek-English Lexicon of the New Testament.* Translation by William F. Arndt and F. Wilbur Gingrich of Walter Bauer's *Griechisch-Deutsches Wörterbuch.* Chicago: University of Chicago Press, 1957.

BDB   *A Hebrew and English Lexicon of the Old Testament.* Francis Brown, S.R. Driver, and Charles A. Briggs. Oxford: Oxford University Press, 1978.

BLC   The Belgic Confession

CSD   The Canons of the Synod of Dort

HC   The Heidelberg Catechism: The version of BEL, CSD, and HC cited is from "Doctrinal Standards of the Christian Reformed Church consisting of the Belgic Confession, the Heidelberg Catechism, and the Canons of Dort." In the *Psalter Hymnal.* Grand Rapids: The Publication Committee of the Christian Reformed Church, 1959.

LCF   The 1689 London Confession of Faith: The version of LCF cited was published as *The Baptist Confession of Faith & The Baptist Catechism.* Birmingham and Carlisle: Solid Ground Christian Books & Reformed Baptist Publications, 2010.

LXX   *The Septuagint Version of the Old Testament and Apocrypha.* Grand Rapids: Zondervan, 1978.

WCF   The Westminster Confession of Faith: The version of WCF cited was published as *The Confession of Faith, The Larger and Shorter Catechisms.* The Publications Committee of the Free Presbyterian Church of Scotland, 1970.

OUTLINE

PROLOGUE: Introduction to Systematic Theology

INTRODUCTION: Overview of the Doctrine of God

PART 1: THE EXISTENCE OF GOD

Unit 1 The Fact of God's Existence
Unit 2 The Revelation of God's Existence
Unit 3 The Uniqueness of God's Existence
Unit 4 The Denial of God's Existence
Unit 5 The Practical Importance of God's Existence

PART 2: THE KNOWLEDGE OF GOD

Section 1 The Knowability of God
Section 2 The Incomprehensibility of God

PART 3: THE NATURE OF GOD

Introduction: The Spiritual, Supreme, and Simple Nature of God

Division 1: The Existential Attributes of God: God's Supreme Being

Section 1. God's Ideal Being: Ideality (Absolute Perfection): Inexhaustibility and Impeccability
Section 2. God's Self-Existent Being: Aseity: The Independence of God
Section 3. God's Infinite Being: The Immensity and Omnipresence of God
Section 4. God's Eternal Being: The Eternity and Ever-presence of God
Section 5. God's Unchangeable Being: Immutability: The Incorruptibility of God

Division 2: The Spiritual Attributes of God: God's Supreme Spirituality

Section 6. God's Incorporeality: The Majestic Form of God
Section 7. God's Animacy: The Vivacity and Omnipotence of God:
Section 8. God's Faculty: The Incorruptible Metaphysical Capacaties of God

    Unit 1. The Infinite Mind of God: *Omniscience*
    Unit 2. The Unlimited Will of God: *Sovereignty*
    Unit 3. The Absolute Affection of God: *Emotivity*

Section 9 Divine Morality: God's Impeccable Virtue

    Introduction: God's Moral Capacity and Character
    Unit 1. Goodness
    Unit 2. Holiness
    Unit 3. Justice
    Unit 4. Faithfulness
    Conclusion: God's Self-Esteem: God's Consciousness of his Impeccable Virtue

Section 10 Divine Personality: The Triune Personality of God: *The Trinity*

PART 4: THE NAMES OF GOD

PART 5: THE DECREE OF GOD

CONCLUSION

PROLOGUE:
INTRODUCTION
TO
SYSTEMATIC
THEOLOGY

Introduction:

This prologue puts into perspective a series of presentations that expound and apply the major themes of the Bible. What are its major themes? How should we study them? These questions introduce us to *systematic theology*. Accordingly, in this prologue I unfold *the essential features* of systematic theology, the *biblical mandate* for systematic theology, and *the content and development* of systematic theology. I conclude by underscoring the tremendous importance of systematic theology. I commend its value for all Christians, Christian leaders, and Christian churches.

Unit 1. The Essential Features of Systematic Theology

We begin with the distinctive features or primary principles of systematic theology. We consider three essential features: the concept, method, and goals of systematic theology.

I. The Concept of Systematic Theology

First, we define this concept. Second, we identify its major designations. Third, we consider the relation of systematic theology to local church dogma.

A. Definition

Systematic theology is:

> Topical teaching that presents and applies the comprehensive testimony of the Bible, on the major themes of the Bible, in biblical categories and proportions.

1. Topical teaching

Systematic theology is topical teaching. It zeros in on themes. It posits and expounds biblical doctrine.

2. The major themes of the Bible

What topics does systematics address? Systematic theology traffics in the sound doctrines of Scripture. Systematic theology isn't, however, completely exhaustive. It doesn't present and apply everything the Bible says about everything. Rather, its focus is its *major* themes, topics, doctrines, issues, and concerns.

3. *The comprehensive testimony of the Bible*

Once systematics identifies crucial issues, it aims to present them comprehensively. A systematic theology should never present merely one side of what Scripture teaches about any major theme. Rather, it should present all sides of every topic. It should do justice to each facet of the biblical witness. Therefore, it should teach what Scripture calls "the faith," "the truth," and the "whole counsel of God." Thus, it must strive for balance and completeness. It must walk boldly on the razor's edge of truth.

4. Biblical categories and proportions

A teacher of systematics should also labor to present the major themes of the Bible in a biblical manner. Systematics should use biblical categories. It should not import categories of thought that are foreign to Scripture. It should also honor biblical proportions. Our theology should reflect the weight that Scripture places on its various themes, and on each aspect of each theme. Theology should not distort such things. Rather, systematics should show sensitivity to the categories and proportions of God's Word.

5. Presents and applies

Systematic theology should also apply its formulations to the practical concerns and religious life of God's people. Unless a theological concept has practical relevance to the spiritual needs of God's people, it has no business in systematic theology. Systematics receives criticism because some teach doctrine as though it had no relevance to the pressures that confront Christians, or to the struggles they face. Teachers of systematics must be careful to avoid this danger. By expressing this concern, I echo the warning of men like the late Professor John Murray. We must labor to present a systematic theology that passes through the sieve of usefulness, practicality, and applicability to everyday Christianity.

Is this concept of systematic theology something novel that I have concocted? Absolutely not. Kersten sets forth this concept, which he designates. "dogmatics," in similar words:[1]

> *Dogmatics is the systematic description of the contents and mutual connection of the truths (dogmata) revealed in the Word of God.*

Consider also how Cornelius Van Til defines systematics:[2]

> It is well to point out the relation of Systematic Theology to the other theological disciplines. The name *systematic theology* does not imply that the other disciplines do not do their work systematically. It means, rather, that systematics alone seeks to offer the truth about God as revealed in Scriptures as a *whole*, as a unified system.

---

[1] G. H. Kersten, *Reformed Dogmatics*, Translator Joel R. Beeke (2 Vols.; The Netherlands Reformed Book and Publishing Co., 1980), 1:xiii

[2] Cornelius Van Til, *Introduction to Systematic Theology*, editor William Edgar (Phillipsburg, NJ: P&R Publishing, 2007), 17.

Exegesis takes the Scriptures and analyzes each part of it in detail. Biblical theology takes the fruits of the exegesis and organizes them into various units and traces the revelation of God in Scripture in its historical development. It brings out the theology of each part of God's Word as it has been brought to us at different stages, by means of various authors. Systematic Theology then uses the fruits of the labors of exegetical and Biblical theology, and brings them together into a concatenated system. Apologetics seeks to defend this system of truth against false philosophy and false science. Practical theology seeks to show us how to preach and teach this system of biblical truth, while church history traces the reception of this system of truth in the course of the centuries.

Again, consider how the Baptist theologian Augustus Strong defines systematics:[3]

> Systematic Theology takes the material furnished by Biblical and by Historical theology, and with this material seeks to build up into an organic and consistent whole all our knowledge of God and of the relations between God and the universe, whether this knowledge be originally derived from nature or from the Scriptures.
> Systematic Theology is, therefore, theology proper of which Biblical and Historical theology are the incomplete and preparatory stages . . .

Hodge,[4] Shedd,[5] Gill,[6] and Murray[7] define the concept similarly. Thus, widely respected men who have labored as systematic theologians with God's blessing affirm this same concept clearly.

B. Designations: Systematics and Dogmatics

The term, *"systematics,"* stresses the idea of a *"system or body"* of truth. This term emphasizes that systematics seeks to present the whole set of biblical doctrines comprehensively. Thus, it emphasizes their "wholeness" and "inter-relatedness," as an integrated, cohesive, body of truths. The term "dogmatics," stresses that biblical doctrine is authoritative. It highlights the

---

[3] Augustus Strong, *Systematic Theology*, (Valley Forge, PA: The Judson Press, 1962), 41

[4] Charles Hodge, *Systematic Theology* (3 Vols.; Grand Rapids, MI: Wm. B. Eerdmans Publishing Co., 1989), 1:18

[5] W. G. T. Shedd, *Dogmatic Theology* (3 Vols.; Grand Rapids, MI: Zondervan Publishing Co., n.d.), 1:11

[6] John Gill, *Body of Divinity* (2 Vols.; Grand Rapids, MI: Baker Book House, 1978), 1:8, 16-17

[7] John Murray, *The Collected Writings of John Murray* (4 Vols.; Edinburgh: The Banner of Truth Trust, 1982), 4:19

fact that the entire set of biblical and apostolic doctrines binds the conscience of the Christian church. Thus, theologians designate this same concept both "dogmatics" and "systematics."

C. Relation to Local Church Dogmatics

Systematics is another name for biblical dogmatics. Symbolics is another name for local church dogmatics. Strong explains the difference between local church dogmatics and systematics:[8]

> Systematic Theology is to be clearly distinguished from dogmatic theology. Dogmatic theology is in the strict usage, the systematizing of the doctrines as expressed in the symbols of the church together with the grounding of those in the Scriptures, and the exhibition so far as may be of their rational necessity. Systematic Theology begins, on the other hand, not with the symbols, but with the Scriptures. It asks first not what the churches believed, but what is the truth of God's Revealed Word?

These different uses of the term "dogmatics" can be confusing. The biblical concept of "dogma" provides the clue we need to fit these pieces of the puzzle together. Apostolic dogma binds the whole church. Their inspired dogmata constitute the faith, the sum of sound doctrine. Systematics presents and applies these apostolic dogmata comprehensively. In this respect, systematic theology *is* dogmatic theology. Systematics is "biblical" dogmatics. Kersten features this connection in his definition.

Yet notice a crucial distinction between *inspired* and *uninspired* dogma. Uninspired dogma also order the church. These consist of the creeds and confessions by which the churches confess their understanding of and commitment to the "faith once delivered to the saints." Thus, with these local church dogmata, churches bind themselves *relatively* and *voluntarily*. I stress "relatively and voluntarily" to emphasize the limits of church confessions and creeds. I say "orders" and "binds" to emphasize the important role of these symbols. Reformed Baptist Seminary,[9] for example, is a ministry of "confessional" churches. The 1689 London Confession defines the "things most surely believed among us." It orders our churches. We stand committed to it. Yet it is not our Word of God. It is not infallible, and therefore, it does not *absolutely* bind our consciences. Rather, it expresses conscientiously the confession of our faith. The study of these uninspired "church dogmata" is also a branch of dogmatics. Thus, the study

---

[8] Strong, *Systematic Theology*, 41.
[9] For information on Reformed Baptist Seminary (RBS) visit their website at rbseminary.org.

of these uninspired dogmata is, strictly speaking, distinct from systematics. Shedd confirms this twofold significance of the word, dogma:[10]

> the term 'dogma' has two significations: 1. It denotes a doctrinal proposition that has been derived exegetically from the Scriptures. 2. It denotes a decree or decision of the church. The authority of the dogma, in the first case, is divine; in the latter, it is human. Dogmatic theology, properly constructed, presents dogmas in the first sense; namely, as propositions formulated from inspired data."

This leads to the insight of Van Till about the close relation between apostolic dogma, the Christian faith, and local church dogma.[11]

> Some theologians prefer the name *dogmatic theology*, while others prefer to speak of *systematic theology*. This is not a matter of great importance. The reason why some prefer the term *dogmatics* is that it seems better than the term *systematics* to express the idea that we deal in this discipline with the dogmas or the truths of the church. This brings up the question of the relation of systematics to the confessions of the church. Does systematics deal primarily with these confessions? Or should we say that systematics deals primarily with the *dogmas* or truths of Scripture? Basically there is agreement among all leading Reformed theologians on this point. All agree that the dogmas of the church have been derived from the Scripture. Hence, it is true that ultimately systematics seeks to expound the system of truth as given in the Scriptures.

The churches by their creeds and symbols express their uninspired, but nonetheless illumined, understanding of and commitment to apostolic dogma. Therefore, a systematic theology is similar to a church symbol. Both involve uninspired confession of the Christian faith. Yet they are also dissimilar. In a systematic theology a Christian teacher confesses comprehensively the major tenets of the Christian faith. Yet no churches stand commited to it. Whereas in a church creed a society or societies of Christians confess relevant tenets of their Christian faith, not necessarily comprehensively. And, these Christians commit themselves voluntarily and relatively to that confession.

Therefore note well this distinction. In their uninspired dogmata, the churches often address issues and doctrines while engaged in controversy. Thus, local church dogmata do not aim, usually, to present "all" the major themes of the Bible "in biblical proportions." The necessities of the day, as a rule, set the focus and proportions of church symbols. Current errors that

---

[10] Shedd, *Dogmatics*, 1:11
[11] Van Til, *Introduction to ST*, 19

threaten the peace and health of the churches, or their perceived spiritual needs, influence and determine their proportions. The Canons of Dort serve as a striking example of this fact. Conversely, Scripture, not some present controversy, sets the proportions of systematics.

In sum, comprehensive teaching of sound doctrine is both "systematic" and "dogmatic" theology. Either term is acceptable, as long as we know what we mean by it. Especially, we must keep in mind the distinction between inspired and uninspired dogma. I use *systematics* to avoid ambiguity and confusion because *dogmatics* has more than one meaning. In my systematics I seek to present and apply the whole set of biblical and inspired dogmata in biblical categories and proportions. I acknowledge a close association with local church symbols because these confessions and creeds display their grasp of various aspects of revealed truth. This leads us to consider the most prudent method of conducting systematics.

II. The Proper Method of Conducting Systematic Theology

I use "proper" to depict that which is most prudent and most likely to achieve a God-honoring result. The proper method involves two components, "*biblical exegesis*" and "*historical theology*." I use "biblical exegesis" to refer to careful exposition of every key biblical text that addresses a given topic. I use "historical theology" to depict diligent study of church creeds and theological and exegetical works that address a given topic. Systematics must couple these two things. Consider now with me why it is so important to use both aspects of this proper method.

A. The Importance of Biblical Exegesis

Why is exegesis necessary? Professor Murray explains this necessity:[12]

> Biblical Theology is indispensable to Systematic Theology. This proposition requires clarification. The main source of revelation is the Bible. Hence, the exposition of Scripture is basic to Systematic Theology. Its task is not simply the exposition of particular passages, that is the task of Exegesis. Systematics must coordinate the teaching of particular passages and systemize this teaching under the appropriate topics. There is thus a synthesis that belongs to Systematics that does not belong to Exegesis as such.

Exegesis dwells on specific passages, individually. Systematics combines the contributions of many specific passages. Having expounded the major texts, systematics collates the major emphases in categories that those texts supply. Teachers of systematics should never simply impose their own ideas

---

[12] Murray, *Collected Writings*, 4:16-17

on Scripture and then list a few proof texts in support. We must behave humbly, as men totally dependent on exegesis both for our categories of thought and our doctrinal concepts. Again, hear Professor Murray:[13]

> But to the extent to which Systematic Theology synthesizes the teaching of Scripture, and this is its main purpose, it is apparent how dependent it is upon the science of Exegesis. It cannot coordinate and relate the teaching of particular passages without knowing what that teaching is.

In other words, systematics can't put the puzzle together unless it properly grasps the teaching of each piece of the biblical witness to a topic. Thus, exegesis is basic to the aim and method of systematics. On the same page Murray goes on to observe:[14]

> Systematic theology has gravely suffered and indeed has deserted its vocation when it has been divorced from meticulous attention to biblical Exegesis. This is one reason why the charge mentioned has so much to yield support to the indictment. Systematics becomes lifeless and fails in its mandate just to the extent to which it has become detached from Exegesis. Exegesis keeps Systematics not only in direct contact with the Word but always imparts to Systematics the power it derives from the Word which is living and powerful.

This is why concordance tools expedite systematic theology. They facilitate discovering the epitomizing passages on a theme. This lays the foundation of expounding each thoroughly in order to analyze them all carefully. Only then can one hope to put the whole puzzle together accurately. This also explains why systematics often necessitates "speed-reading" the Bible repeatedly, searching for the rich and wide variety of terms in which the Bible may present any given topic. Sometimes important pieces of the puzzle are hidden under an obscure word or two, or in figurative language. No little part of the difficulty of systematics consists in the finding all the ways in which the Bible addresses a topic. For example, consider the radical spiritual and moral change that occurs at conversion. The Bible presents this transformation as calling, re-birth, emancipation, re-creation, resurrection, crucifixion and resurrection, circumcision of heart, a heart transplant, washing, and etc. We must consider all these descriptions in a comprehensive presentation of "the new birth." We uncover these descriptions by reading through the Bible and noting every passage that somehow describes the radical moral change associated with conversion.

---

[13] Ibid., 4:17
[14] Ibid.

Then we must collate all that material after we study each text that presents each description. That kind of work is essential to teach systematics accurately to a group of men preparing for the ministry, or to a Sunday School class, or in a sermon on Sunday morning. Without this kind of labor systematics will lack clarity, or accuracy, or spiritual vibrancy. We should beware of just picking up a theology book and rehashing its contents. If we do, we foster results that are dry and lifeless. This underscores the weight of the admonition, "*be not many of you teachers*" (James 3:1).

B. The Importance of Historical Theology

Exegesis is a crucial part of the story, but it is not the whole story. We must not act like we are the first person who ever examined his Bible on the topic in question. We must also seek counsel from the insights of others who have received illumination from the Holy Spirit, whether respecting the exegesis of a given text, or respecting the identity of the key texts on a topic, or respecting the categories or teaching of Scripture on a given topic. It's not enough unilaterally to exegete every passage in the Bible that deals with a topic. Why? Because, God has given important light, by illumination, to many who have gone before. If we despise that light and go it alone as a theological maverick and "lone ranger," we will surely err. Sooner or later our novelties will introduce serious error. Professor Murray also stresses this aspect of a proper method. He explains the development of systematic theology. He notes that today's theology, if sound, does not exist in a vacuum. This, he says, is due to the presence of the Holy Spirit with the church, giving illumination to God's servants over the past 2000 years. Thus, he says:[15]

> He has also been present in the church in all the generations of the church's history, endowing the church in its organic unity as the body of Christ with gifts of understanding and expression. It is the ceaseless activity of the Holy Spirit that explains the development throughout the centuries of what we call Christian doctrine. Individual theologians are but the spokesmen of this accumulating understanding which the Spirit of truth has been granting to his church. Christ as the Head of the Church must not be thought of apart from the Spirit or the Spirit apart from Christ. Hence, it is to state the same truth in terms of Christ's presence when we say that he is walking in the midst of the churches and the angels of the churches are in his right hand. In him are hid all the treasures of wisdom and knowledge and from this fullness that resides in him he communicates to the church so that the church organically and corporately may increase and grow up into

---

[15] Murray, *Collected Writings*, 4:6

knowledge to the measure of the stature of the fullness of Christ. It is this perspective that not only brings to view but also requires the progression by which Systematic Theology has been characterized.

This warns us never to think that we have the final word in systematic theology. Illumination did not start with us. It will not end with us. The history of doctrine demonstrates progressive development. This progression will reach its finale when Christ returns and expels every last vestige of error from his church. Therefore, if we regard the 1689 Confession as the Word of God, spiritual stagnation and theological decline will mar Reformed Baptists. Presbyterianism too will decay, if our brethren treat the Westminster standards as Scripture. Dutch Calvinism will also shrivel, if our brethren act like the Three Forms of Unity are inspired. Listen to Murray's warning about this clear and present danger:[16]

> When any generation is content to rely upon its theological heritage and refuses to explore for itself the riches of divine revelation, then declension is already underway and heterodoxy will be the lot of the succeeding generation. The powers of darkness are never idle and in combating error each generation must fight its own battle in exposing and correcting the same. It is light that dispels darkness, and in this sphere light consists in the enrichment which each generation contributes to the stores of theological knowledge.
>
> It is true, however, that the presentation of the gospel must be pointed to the needs of each generation, so it is with theology. A theology that does not build on the past ignores our debt to history and naively overlooks the fact that the present is conditioned by history. A theology that relies upon the past evades the demands of the present.

Do not misunderstand me. I neither oppose creeds, nor despise the rich heritage we have received from the documents mentioned. Rather, I intend to say that we must proceed with balance and caution. On the one hand, we must honor the insights of the past. Surely, this implies that there must be some branch of historic and confessional Christianity where each of us may comfortably hang our theological hat. Beware of any teacher of doctrine who claims to have no "home," no heritage theologically. As for me, I am thoroughly committed to every doctrinal distinctive of the 1689 London Confession of Faith. I make no bones about it. That is my home, my heritage. I am not ashamed of it, nor do I feel uncomfortable with it. On the other hand, we must not turn our confession into Scripture. We must, with

---

[16] Ibid., 4:8-9

grateful acknowledgment of our large debt to our forefathers, build on their insights and contributions, following them as they follow Christ. This doesn't mean, however, that we must share in their greatness in order so to build. No, says the Professor, even ordinary men like us may at times contribute a little to the wealth of our theological heritage:[17]

> The progressive correction and enrichment which theology undergoes is not the exclusive task of great theologians. It often falls to the lot of students with mediocre talent to discover the oversights and correct the errors of the masters. In the orthodox tradition we may never forget that there is much land yet to be possessed and this is both the encouragement and the challenge to students of the wonderful works of God and particularly of his inscripturated Word to understand that all should address themselves to a deeper understanding of these unsearchable treasures of revelation to the end that God's glory may be made more fully manifest and his praise declared to all the earth.

What a precious and encouraging statement. Anyone can contribute. Possibly even Professor Murray at times learned things from his students. I know for sure that I have learned much from the questions and constructive criticisms of my students. Many times they have raised an important issue that I had neglected to address, or challenged me to reconsider my understanding of a text, or to restructure my presentation of a topic.

Finally, observe that Reformed theologians have rightly stressed the tremendous importance of historical theology for systematics. Take for examples: Berkhof,[18] Hoeksema,[19] Kersten,[20] and Charles Hodge.[21]

III. The Goals and Designs of Systematic Theology

First, I summarize the general purposes and designs of systematics, and then conclude by explaining, specifically and explicitly, my additional goals for my systematics courses and lectures.

A. The General Goals and Designs of Systematics

In general, systematic theology aims to build up God's people in their faith, to unify them, and to aid in their sanctification. Respecting the world,

---

[17] Ibid., 4:9
[18] Louis Berkhof, *Introduction to Systematic Theology* (Grand Rapids, MI: Baker Book House, 1979), 35.
[19] Herman Hoeksema, *Reformed Dogmatics* (Grand Rapids, MI: Reformed Free Publishing Association, 1976), 3.
[20] Kersten, Dogmatics, 1:13-15.
[21] Hodge, *Systematic Theology*, 1:18-19.

systematics aims to convict them of their sin and convert them to Christ and the Christian faith. Finally, systematics ultimately aims to glorify and extol God, to honor his Word, to proclaim his name, and to further his cause in the world. Now we focus on each briefly.

1. Systematics aims to build up God's people in their faith, unify them, and aid in their sanctification.

To support this I appeal to Ephesians 4:13-14. Paul defines clearly and explicitly the goals of teaching sound doctrine: "till we all attain the unity of the faith." We want God's people to understand and confess revealed truth about Scripture, about God, about all God's works, and about all man's duties. That's the positive design of systematics. Negatively, systematics aims to guard God's people from error: "that we may be no longer children, tossed to and fro, and carried about with every wind of doctrine." Commitment to the whole body of sound doctrines inoculates God's people against the many errors that threaten their souls. Truth dispels error. Thus, we inculcate truth to protect God's people from error.

Let me clarify this. The structure and proportions of systematics should follow the proportions and structure of Scripture. Systematics should not be primarily polemical in its structure. We must keep a clear sense of focus. We must remember that systematics aims to present the comprehensive teaching of the Bible, on the major themes of the Bible, in biblical categories and proportions. It must not dwell exclusively or excessively on those aspects of truth which are today most denied or threatened. That's a noble and needful work. But it is the aim and task of apologetics, polemics, and local church dogmatics.

Thus, systematics aims to achieve greater unity and communion among the people of God. It aims at greater spiritual unity in each church and among all true churches. It also aims to assist each Christian to grow in grace. Truth is "according to godliness." As error produces sin, truth produces holiness. Accordingly, Strong reminds us that our aim must always be to apply truth, not merely to present it:[22]

> I make no apology for the homiletical element in my book. To be either true or useful, theology must be a passion. *Pectus est quod theologum facit.* And no disdainful cries of 'Pectoral Theology!' shall prevent me from maintaining that the eyes of the heart must be enlightened in order to perceive the truth of God, and that to know the truth it is needful to do the truth. Theology is a science

---

[22] Strong, *Systematic Theology*, xi

which can be successfully cultivated only in connection with its practical application. I would therefore, in every discourse of principles, point out its relation to Christian experience, and its power to awaken Christian emotions and lead to Christian decisions. Abstract theology is not really scientific. Only that theology is scientific which brings the student to the feet of Christ.[23]

To this I say, "Amen." We aim always to assist God's people in their pursuit of godliness. Remember, if it has no practical relevance, it has no place in systematics.

2. Systematics aims to convict the world of sin and convert them to Christ and the Christian faith.

When we thus design the good of God's people, we also aim to convict the gainsayers and convert them to Christ and Christianity. This indeed is the special province of apologetics. As we saw, polemics, not systematics, focuses on and emphasizes convicting the gainsayers. Nevertheless, exhorting in the sound doctrine, in its very nature, inherently convicts gainsayers. The truth, as a body, exposes error and proclaims the way of salvation to lost sinners.

3. Systematics aims ultimately to glorify God and honor his Word.

At the end of the day, we aim to honor God. He is worthy that we should study his Word carefully, present its doctrines comprehensively and clearly, and apply them faithfully and experimentally. The riches of God's creation are worthy of painstaking investigation with a view to glorifying him for what men discover thereby. How much more does God's Word deserve painstaking study and analysis with a view to blessing him for the riches of truth contained therein? Therefore, ultimately, we pursue systematics because we love God, love his Word, and love to explore and learn about him. We do all this because we aim to praise him for who he is and for what he has done.

B. The Additional and Special Goals and Designs of these Lectures

In these lectures I aim at everything that I just mentioned. The three goals that I am about to specify are in addition to the former ones, not replacements for them.

---

[23] Strong quotes a favorite motto of Augustus Neander, a German theologian who lived from 1789-1850. Neander believed that sound theology only thrives in a soul devoted to God. Neander's motto: "pectus est quod theologum facit," is literally, "chest is that theologian makes." It could be translated, "it is the heart that makes a theologian." Thus, "pectoral theology" probably signifies "chest" or "heart" theology in contrast with "head theology."

1. I especially aim to reach and address the people in the pews.

In Ephesians 4:13-15 Paul nurtures all Christians: "till *we all* attain." Jude speaks of "the faith once delivered *to the saints*," not "the seminary students," or "the bishops and elders." Now I'll tell you a secret. Over the years the quality control of my systematics lectures has been the secretary who typed them. Soon after I began teaching systematics in 1979 the Lord provided as my secretary a recently converted, single young woman. Being a new convert, she was especially hungry to learn. She typed many transcripts of those early lectures. Though I didn't tell her this at the time, she was my quality control. If, after she typed the transcript of a lecture, she said, "Pastor Nichols, I really got blessed by that." Then I said to myself, "that material passes the test." If, however, she came to me scratching her head, saying: "Pastor Nichols, I didn't understand that. It didn't make any sense. It went over my head." Then I said to myself, "that's not good yet, I must edit and clarify it. I must try to present it so that she can benefit from it." That's how I approach systematics. I refuse to be ashamed of it or intimidated away from it. Systematics is for secretaries. It is for housewives. It is for Christian young people in high school and college. It is for mechanics. It is for fishermen and carpenters. Should that shock us? The Master was a carpenter. He chose some fishermen as apostles. Some may despise that if they like. They can scream that it is unscholarly until they are blue in the face. I refuse to be impressed. I make no bones about it. My special design is to produce a systematic theology that I address to all church members.

2. I especially aim to present and apply fresh and comprehensive exposition of the Scriptures.

My second specific design is to feature exposition of Scripture. Dagg also expresses this concern:[24]

> Any one who may desire to see a history of religious opinions, will not find it in this work . . . It has been my aim to lead the mind of the reader directly to the sources of religious knowledge, and incite him to investigate them for himself, without respect to human authority. He may learn, from the help I am proffering him, what my views are, but I will here give him the caution, once for all, not to adopt any opinion which I may advance, farther than it is well sustained by the word of God. Had I wished him to fix his faith on human authority, I should have adduced quotations from writers of celebrity in support of my opinions; but I have chosen not to do so. It is my desire that the reader should see, in

---

[24] J. L. Dagg, *Manual of Theology* (Harrisonburg, VA: Gano Books, 1982), v-vi.

the doctrine here presented, so far as respects human authority, nothing but the mere opinion of a fallible worm; but that so far as it is sustained by the word of God, he should receive it as the truth of God.

Dagg probably knew more in his little pinkie about what the celebrated writers and safe guides in theology wrote than most of us will ever know in all our fingers, toes, and head. Arrogance or a love for novelty didn't motivate him. Rather, he wanted to ground the minds of his readers in the faith by direct contact with God's Word. That's why he did it. That's why I'm committed to do it. Thus, these lectures major on biblical exposition, not on salting abstractions drawn from the "rabbis of theology" with a few proof texts. Do not misunderstand me. We must always be sensitive to the input of "historical theology." Certain doctrines, like God's covenants, call for a more thorough presentation of historical theology than others. Even when I must spend considerable time with historical theology, my special design is always, on every issue, to stress comprehensive and fresh exposition of every relevant portion of God's Word.

3. I especially aim to highlight and stress every doctrinal distinctive of the 1689 Confession.

I have a third special purpose and design. Some may think that what I now say completely contradicts what I just said. Not so. In my judgment, there is no contradiction whatsoever between fresh and careful exegesis of Scripture and the doctrinal distinctives of the 1689 Confession. My concern to present and apply fresh exegesis does not mean that I have no Confession of Faith or religious tradition. To the contrary, I love my Reformed Baptist heritage. I adhere to the 1689 Confession. I am very grateful for it, and thoroughly committed to its distinctive doctrines. It is high time that a Baptist systematic theology endeavored to stress and expound every doctrinal distinctive of our 1689 Confession. These distinctives include orthodox Christianity, covenant theology, Calvinistic soteriology, Puritan experimental religion, and Baptist and independent ecclesiology. Boyce and Strong, for example, make no mention whatsoever of God's covenants. Dagg has only a brief statement, no exposition. Only Gill even attempts to address all the distinctives. Yet, as we shall see, he departs from the 1689 doctrine of a covenant between God and men. Therefore, I am very concerned to address each and every doctrinal distinctive of the 1689 Confession, in its proper place, and in due proportions. I also aim to demonstrate that the doctrines of the 1689 are biblical and edifying. I want to highlight the richness of our heritage, yet without departing from biblical proportions or categories. I hope that no one mistakenly thinks I am equating the 1689 with Scripture. I assure you I intend no such thing.

Finally, I hope that when I elucidate and present these distinctive doctrines of the 1689, it will encourage deeper fellowship, closer cooperation, and edifying dialogue among all those who confess the Christian faith. I intend to highlight how our Confession agrees with the other Reformed standards, especially with the Westminster Confession and the Canons of Dort. I especially intend to acquaint Reformed Baptists with the rich heritage we have received both from Dutch Calvinism and from the English Puritans.

These goals, over the years, have crystallized in my mind and heart. They drive my pursuit of this enormous task. Brethren, please pray for me.

Unit 2: The Mandate for Systematic Theology

After long wrestling over how to establish the biblical grounds for systematic theology, I have settled on three epitomizing texts: Acts 16:4, 20:27; Eph. 4:13-15. These texts unfold a threefold mandate for systematic theology. This mandate springs from: (1) The responsibility of Christian churches to obey apostolic dogma (Acts 16:4); (2) The stewardship of gospel ministers to proclaim the sum of Christian faith and duty (Acts 20:27); (3) The duty of every Christian to affirm the Christian faith and reject false doctrine (Eph. 4:13-15).

I. The Responsibility of Christian Churches to Obey Apostolic Dogma[25]

The word translated "decrees" is δογματα (dogmata). Its singular is δογμα (dogma), "a decree." Our English words "dogma" and "dogmatic" are transliterations of the singular and plural forms of this Greek word. The word, dogma, occurs four other times in the New Testament: Luke 2:1; Acts 17:7; Eph. 2:15; Col. 2:14. In Luke 2:1 it refers to the decree of Caesar concerning the enrollment, "*in* those days there went out *a decree* from Caesar Augustus, that all the world should be enrolled." In Acts 17:7 it refers to the Roman ordinances regarding the supreme authority of the emperor: "these all act contrary to the *decrees* of Caesar, saying that there is another king, one Jesus." In Ephesians 2:15 it describes the ordinances of the ceremonial law: "having abolished in his flesh the law of commandments contained in *ordinances.*" In Colossians 2:14 the specific reference is somewhat ambiguous, but the general notion is plain enough: "having blotted out the bond written in *ordinances* that was against us, which was contrary to us: and he has taken it out of the way, nailing it to the cross." Only Acts 16:4 employs the word in a church setting. Those in authority, "the apostles and elders that were at Jerusalem," issue this order. It binds all those under their authority: "they gave them the decrees to keep." Conscience constrains all the Gentile churches to "*keep,*" that is, to obey this directive that came from the apostles. It is not advisory, or suggestive, but authoritative. Thus, *dogma* depicts a formal, authoritative, and binding regulation, order, or decision. A decree always comes from someone in authority and binds those under that authority. G. H. Kersten conducts a similar survey of the word, *dogma.*[26] Then he says: "Each time the word *dogma* is used the authority of those who make the decree or give the

---

[25] *Acts 16:4*: And as they went on their way through the cities, they delivered them the decrees [dogmata] to keep which had been ordained of the apostles and elders that were at Jerusalem. So, the churches were strengthened in the faith, and increased in number daily.

[26] Kersten, *Dogmatics*, 1:xiii

command is shown, whether it be Caesar, or the church, or the Holy Spirit himself."

What then prompted the apostles to issue these decrees? In Acts 15 Luke tells the story of the religious controversy that necessitated this formal doctrinal statement. These apostolic decrees settled the heated dispute that threatened to split the infant church. The doctrinal controversy concerned whether or not Gentile believers must be circumcised and charged to keep the ceremonial law in order to enter the church on earth and the company of the saints in heaven. Some said yes: "Except you be circumcised after the custom of Moses, you cannot be saved" (15:1, 5). Others, like Paul and Barnabas, said no (15:2). The church in Antioch sent them to Jerusalem in order that the apostles and elders might address this burning doctrinal issue and settle the dispute (15:2-3, 6). They thoroughly debated the matter, until, on the basis of the Old Testament (15:13-19) and New Testament (15:7-12), the apostles and elders eventually reached oneness of mind and heart (15:7, 25). They formulated a written statement that expressed their mind on the issue (15:23-29). It specifically addressed the ecclesiastical (15:24-27), doctrinal (15:28), and ethical (15:29) aspects of the matter. It carried with it the expectation and requirement that the churches would submit to this formal statement of the mind of the apostles on the subject. Thus the issue was settled, the matter closed. Each specific statement in this formal document is a decree (dogma). Luke calls the sum of them "the decrees" (dogmata).

How exactly does this relate to systematic theology? Shedd helps us to uncover this relationship:[27]

> the term 'dogma' has two significations: 1. It denotes a doctrinal proposition that has been derived exegetically from the Scriptures. 2. It denotes a decree or decision of the church

Some church decrees and decisions arise from illumination. They are neither inspired nor infallible. Local churches, often acting in concert, issue these decisions and declarations. They are not binding on the church universal. Local churches adopt them conscientiously. They regulate those churches that adopt them voluntarily and relatively. Often controversy occasions their formulation and determines their emphases. An example of such dogmata would be the Canons of the Synod of Dort.

However, some decrees or decisions of the church have arisen from inspiration. They are infallible. Only the Holy Spirit and apostles issue such decrees: "it seemed good to *the Holy Spirit, and to us*, to lay upon you no

---

[27] Shedd, *Dogmatics*, 1:11

greater burden than these necessary things" (Acts 15:28). They have authority over the church universal, which includes all true churches in every generation. Our text furnishes an example of such apostolic dogmata. As with uninspired church dogmata, controversy occasioned these apostolic decrees and regulated their emphasis. Therefore, these inspired dogmata form a bridge that connects Shedd's two uses of dogma.

As Shedd observes, every doctrinal proposition contained in Scripture is in a generic sense a dogma because it has divine authority and binds the consciences of every Christian and every Christian church. Thus following Shedd, I offer the following definition of a *biblical dogma*:

> A *biblical dogma* is a doctrinal proposition contained in Scripture, which orders the faith and practice of every Christian and every Christian church.

Therefore, biblical dogmata play a vital role for God's people. They settle all religious controversy. They expose error and expel it from the churches. Accordingly, *Biblical Dogmatics* proclaims the whole set of biblical dogmata. Thus, I define it as follows:

> *Biblical Dogmatics* collates comprehensively, presents biblically, and applies practically the whole system of biblical dogmata.

Therefore, biblical dogmatics thus defined is systematic theology. It pursues its noble vision because God has preserved the Scriptures of the Old and New Testaments. The whole Bible, interpreted by the apostles, is the church's rule of faith and practice. The apostles confirm the inspiration of the Old Testament.[28] They teach us how the Old Testament, especially its set of dogma addressed to the Jewish nation under the old covenant, applies to God's people under the new covenant.[29] Thus, the preservation of the Scriptures, by God's singular care and providence in every generation, is the true "apostolic succession." Biblical dogmata, properly understood, do not come from bishops or church councils, but from God's Word. Kersten confirms this: "Theological dogma derives its authority from the Holy Scriptures, and shows that which God has determined and made known to us in His Word."[30] This supports his definition of dogmatics and displays its biblical warrant: *"the systematic description of the contents and mutual connection of the truths (dogmata) revealed in the Word of God."*

In conclusion, this is why the peace and stability of the Christian church mandate systematic theology. Only when we study and grasp the set of

---

[28] 2 Pet. 3:16
[29] Acts 15:13-18; 1 Cor. 9:8-10, 10:11; Eph. 2:14; Heb. 9:8-10; 1 Pet. 1:10-12
[30] Kersten, *Dogmatics*, 1:xiii

doctrinal propositions by which Scripture binds all Christians and churches can we obey these dogmata. Only then can churches repel the cancerous doctrinal errors that now, even as they did then, threaten to decimate their memberships. Only this can strengthen Christians and Christian churches in their faith. Though it may seem ironic, when churches embrace biblical dogmata, they not only tend to grow spiritually, they also tend to grow numerically. Those very churches "increased in number daily." Modern "experts" might be skeptical of Paul's "church growth" program because it included rigorous instruction in sound doctrine, designed to bring the churches, not only to grasp, but also to implement each biblical and apostolic regulation.

II. The Stewardship of Gospel Ministers to Proclaim the Sum of Christian Faith and Duty[31]

The word, βουλη (boule) translated "counsel," sometimes refers to men's guidance, or advice.[32] When applied to God, it refers to the desires, decisions, and designs of his will. Sometimes it describes his sovereign or decretive will, whereby he ordains whatsoever comes to pass.[33] Sometimes it refers to his revealed will, whereby he prescribes what men should believe and practice.[34] God executes all his sovereign will in providence, and discloses all his revealed will in Scripture.

Here Paul refers to God's revealed will. He means that he declared to them comprehensively what God prescribes for them to believe and practice; not that he declared to them the whole substance of God's secret and eternal decree. Over three years, at night and during the day (20:31), publicly and privately (20:20), Paul proclaimed the sum and substance of Christian faith and duty. Especially, he stressed God's plan concerning the issues most vital for their eternal welfare. He featured the gospel and its implications. Context confirms his evangelical and experiential emphasis.[35] Thus, Paul features God's message of salvation from sin through Christ. He stresses repentance and faith, the duty of obedience to the gospel. He highlights the

---

[31] *Acts 20:27*: For I shrank not from declaring unto you the whole counsel [boule] of God.
[32] Acts 27:12, 42
[33] Acts 2:23, 4:28; Eph. 1:11
[34] Luke 7:30; Heb. 6:17
[35] *Acts 20:20, 24-25*: How I shrank not from declaring unto you anything that was profitable, and teaching you publicly, and from house to house, testifying both to Jews and to Greeks, repentance toward God, and faith toward our Lord Jesus Christ . . . 24 I hold not my life of any account as dear unto myself, so that I may accomplish my course, and the ministry which I received from the Lord Jesus, to testify the gospel of the grace of God. 25 And now behold I know that you all, among whom I went about preaching the kingdom.

kingdom of God, the society of those who believe and obey the gospel. The Christian church is God's kingdom, his theocracy, which does his will in evangelical obedience.[36]

God's people need authoritative guidance and direction from the Lord. Left to themselves, they are confused. They don't know what to do, or how to act or respond. Thus, they inquire of the Lord, and seek specific answers about pressing issues from his Word. Under the old covenant, the Lord ordained prophets and priests from whom his people could obtain special direction about important issues and decisions. For example, when Joshua neglected to seek such counsel from God, he erred respecting the Gibeonites.[37] Conversely, Israel sought God's counsel about continuing the battle with the Benjaminites, and prevailed.[38] However, when Christians face difficult issues and come to inquire of God, we do not have living prophets or special priests to give us direct revelation about the topic, question, or decision facing us. Where then do we turn? We turn to the *"whole counsel of God"* revealed in Scripture. It is sufficient to guide us through every crisis of faith or duty.

Accordingly, Paul kept a good conscience by faithfully discharging his stewardship of a comprehensive teaching ministry: "Wherefore I testify to you this day, that I am pure from the blood of all men, For I shrank not from declaring unto you the whole counsel of God" (Acts 20:26-27). This underscores why gospel ministers must teach God's people the whole counsel of God. This is why it is so important that the saints grasp the sum and substance of what God requires them to believe and to practice. It also underscores that when God's people come to their pastors for counsel about pressing and perplexing concerns, God's servants must direct them with God's counsel revealed in Scripture. Brethren, only when God's servants declare the sum and substance of faith and duty to their congregations, are they "pure from the blood" of their hearers. We must not shrink in cowardice from comprehensive teaching. We must not leave out the unpopular issue of sin and repentance, or downplay the demands derived from the fact that the church is a theocracy, run according to God's will. A comprehensive teaching ministry takes time. It isn't completed in a day. It could require teaching at night, or in people's homes. We must not shrink from this enormous task, or from the self-denial and hard work needed to complete it. Here is ample warrant for the pursuit of systematic theology. We can faithfully discharge this stewardship only when we declare all God

---

[36] Matt. 21:43; Rev. 1:5-6, 1 Pet. 2:5, 9
[37] Josh. 9:14
[38] Judg. 20:18, 23

requires us to believe on every major subject and to practice in every situation.

III. The Duty of Each Christian to Affirm the Christian Faith and Reject False Doctrine[39]

We expound this key text under three headings. *First*, we examine its *general context and concern*. *Second*, we expound its *fourfold summons* regarding the faith, the knowledge of Christ, doctrine, and the truth. *Third*, and finally, we summarize *the conclusion* it mandates about systematic theology.

A. The General Context and Concern: Spiritual Unity

In Ephesians 4:1-16 the apostle expresses concern over spiritual unity and peace among God's people. Verse 3 epitomizes his concern: "giving diligence to keep the unity of the Spirit in the bond of peace." God's people must maintain this peace and unity. Each Christian must try to prevent, minimize, and avoid division, strife, and warfare among his fellow Christians. We must pursue peace with "diligence." The maintenance of unity is hard work. It requires arduous effort. Conversely, it is easy to be divisive. It doesn't take great skill to cause trouble and dissension in a church or among the churches. Thus, the maintenance of peace requires a clear grasp of the things necessary for spiritual unity. Peace isn't maintained by accident. A shot in the dark approach doesn't work well. Thus, Paul outlines the essentials of spiritual peace and unity. Unity requires three things: a gracious disposition of love and humility (4:1-2); a religious experience of God's salvation (4:4-6); and a comprehensive commitment to biblical and apostolic doctrine (4:7-16). Nothing can easily break this threefold cord of spiritual unity.

1. Spiritual unity requires a gracious disposition.

Paul begins by identifying and enjoining the disposition essential to unity and peace. He introduces this attitude as the only disposition worthy of the Christian experience (4:1). Then in 4:2 he describes the attitude essential for unity: "with all lowliness and meekness, with longsuffering, forbearing one another in love." Peace and unity among the people of God spring from a demeanor of humility, longsuffering, and love. Carnal pride, the opposite

---

[39] *Eph. 4:13-15*: Till we all attain unto the unity of the faith, and of the knowledge of the Son of God, unto a full-grown man, unto the measure of the stature of the fullness of Christ: 14 that we may be no longer children, tossed to and fro and carried about with every wind of doctrine, by the slight of men, in craftiness, after the wiles of error; 15 but speaking truth in love, may grow up in all things into him, who is the head, even Christ.

of lowliness and meekness, produces an incessant fountain of contention.[40] It is the taproot of carnal controversy, division, and strife in the Christian church. Similarly, carnal anger and vengeance are the very antithesis of longsuffering and forbearance. Therefore, a wrathful man creates constant tension among Christians with his intolerant, judgmental, and hypercritical spirit.[41] Again, hatred, disaffection, and malice, the opposites of love, stir up strife and warfare among God's people.[42] Disaffection often arises from the sins of jealousy and envy in the heart (James 3:14-16), as in the case of the hatred of the Pharisees for the Lord Jesus Christ. It also springs at times from the insidious influence of false reports and lies. These work best when men listen to backbiting and spread slander.[43] Whatever their source, disaffection and hatred are incompatible with peace and unity among Christians. If we are to maintain the unity of the Spirit in the bond of peace, we must cultivate and walk in love, longsuffering, and humility. This demeanor is absolutely essential.

2. Spiritual unity requires a religious experience of God's salvation.

Next, Paul identifies the experimental bond or glue of Christian unity. He says in essence in 4:4-6 that spiritual unity and peace require spiritual compatibility. What is spiritual compatibility? It is the compatibility that results from a common experience of the grace of God in the application of redemption. Genuine conversion, saving grace, and reality in experimental religion bind Christian unity. These spring from the saving power of the triune God, from experimental communion with the Spirit, the Lord, and the Father: "There is one body, and one Spirit . . . One Lord, one faith . . . one God and Father of all."

The first strand of experimental union relates to God the Spirit: "There is one body, and one Spirit, even as you were also called in one hope of your calling" (4:4). The Holy Spirit regenerates and indwells each of God's true people. Thus, effectual calling, moral renewal, and the transformation of the heart unite the people of God. Thus also, the common hope and joy implanted in their hearts unite God's people. God plants this hope in them when he summons them out of the world, encourages and indwells them with his Spirit, and accompanies them with his special presence throughout the journey of the Christian life.

---

[40] Prov. 13:10
[41] Prov. 15:18, 29:22
[42] Prov. 10:12
[43] Prov. 26:22, 28; Acts 14:2, 19

The second strand of experimental union relates to God the Son: "One Lord, one faith, one baptism" (4:5). Each of God's true people has saving faith in the same Lord, Jesus Christ, God the Son. Thus, personal reliance upon Christ alone, as their only ground of acceptance with God, unites his people. Public confession of that faith in the ordinance of Christian baptism, whereby they openly join the society of Christ's disciples, also unites God's people.

The third and final strand of experimental union relates to God the Father: "one God and Father of all, who is over all, and through all, and in all" (4:6). God adopts each of his people into his family. He gives each Christian the privileges and blessings of adoption. Each, with the same disposition of adoption, cries "Abba Father" to the same God. Each enjoys filial communion with God the Father as part of the same spiritual family. Each lives as an obedient child in submission to the will of the same Father.

In conclusion, these three bonds of experiential unity are essential for peace among Christians. Whatever notions men have in their heads, they can't live together in the same church in peace unless they have this root of the matter in their hearts (2 Cor. 6:14-18). The regenerate righteous, living in God's special presence, can never walk in spiritual harmony with the unregenerate wicked, who live without hope and without God in the world. Unbelievers who trust in their own virtue cannot peacefully coexist in the same fellowship with believers who rely solely on the virtue of Jesus' perfect life and atoning death. The ungodly children of the devil who know not the Lord and don't call on God can never walk together in agreement in the same society of disciples with God's holy children who daily cry, "Abba Father." What shall we say then, is love all we need for unity? Is experimental reality all we need for peace? Absolutely not! If that were the case, this paragraph would have stopped at Verse 6. Even though both a disposition of love and humility, and experimental reality, are crucial and fundamental, they are not the whole story. More is needed. This leads us directly to the basis for systematic theology.

3. Spiritual unity requires a comprehensive commitment to biblical doctrine.

In 4:7-16 the apostle features the importance of grounding God's people in the Christian faith. Instruction in sound theology and adherence to apostolic doctrine are vital for spiritual unity. Yet, Paul doesn't divorce adherence to a sound creed from spiritual life and grace. Verses 1-6 proclaim this crucial lesson. Every advocate of sound theology must take this warning to heart. Sound theology alone without love and humility and without genuine Christian experience cannot maintain spiritual unity. Good theology must never be wrenched from its inspired setting. This is its womb, the source of its life. This is its atmosphere, the air it breathes. Theology extracted from its experiential habitat is like a fish out of water. It soon dies, yea it stinketh, and the stench of its decay rises to the third heaven. Small wonder then that whenever godless and unbelieving men motivated by pride and ambition devise and teach religious doctrines, they dream up subtle and dangerous errors and heresies ruinous to men's souls. With their errors they import the unbelief of the world into the Christian community. The stench of such error abounds in our day. Its smell points our spiritual noses to the vital connection between grace and truth.

In 4:7-11, Paul begins his commendation of sound theology with the fact that the Lord Jesus Christ gives gifts to his church, namely, teachers of the sound doctrines of the Christian faith. In 4:11 he enumerates these gifts. He starts with the extraordinary teachers of the church, the apostles and prophets, whose inspired teaching, forever preserved in Scripture, serves as the foundation of the church. He concludes with the ordinary and enduring gifts of Christ to his church, pastors and teachers, who expound and apply the Scriptures, not by inspiration, but by illumination.

In 4:12, he confirms the important and permanent place that Christ entrusts to pastors and teachers in the life of God's people. Their role is "the perfecting of the saints, unto the work of ministering, unto the building up of the body of Christ." Christ assigns shepherds to bring his sheep to the maturity that promotes spiritual unity and peace. How must they fulfill their commission to bring Christians to spiritual maturity? This question directly introduces our text. They must instruct his sheep in Scripture. This pastoral ministry of the Word has both a positive and a negative design.

In 4:13, he states its positive design: "till we all attain unto the unity of the faith, and of the knowledge of the Son of God, unto the full-grown man." Theological soundness marks the "full-grown man." He has attained "the unity of the faith." He stands committed to that system of doctrine known as the Christian faith. This body of doctrines focuses on Christ. Its core is "the knowledge of the Son of God." This refers to understanding with the mind and receiving in the heart the entire set of propositional truths that Scripture reveals about Christ. This is essential to Christian growth and maturity. As God's people develop in their grasp of and commitment to the teachings of the Bible, especially its teachings about Christ, they grow closer to each other. They become more stable, more unified, and more at peace.

In 4:14, he states its negative design: "that we may be no longer children tossed to and fro and carried about with every wind of doctrine, by the slight of men, in craftiness, after the wiles of error." Pastoral ministry of God's

Word also aims to prevent and correct false doctrine, which is a grave evil detrimental to spiritual peace and maturity. Thus Paul introduces the concept of *"doctrine."* A religious doctrine is a verbal proposition on a religious topic or issue. False doctrines contradict *"the faith"* and *"the knowledge of the Son of God."* He multiplies terms: *"slight," "craftiness," "wiles,"* to stress that theological errors always betray devilish subtlety. False teachers are always hard to pin down. My friend and colleague, the late RBS professor Dr. Bob Martin, expressed this well when he said that exposing them was like "nailing Jell-O to the wall." False teachers are crafty, sneaky, clever, underhanded, and wily. To prevent their insidious influence we must express the truths of the Christian faith plainly. We must openly expose their clever ambiguities and explicitly condemn their subtle departures from biblical teaching.

In 4:15-16, Paul stresses the important role that the whole church plays in the development of Christian maturity and unity: "But speaking truth in love, may grow up in all things into him, who is the head, even Christ, from whom all the body . . . makes the increase of the body unto the building up of itself in love." Pastoral instruction in sound doctrine must take place in a climate of congregational nurture and love. Paul envisions the church, not as a "preaching station," but as a close-knit, caring, spiritual organism. Yet, he envisions this loving church committed to the *"truth." "Speaking truth,"* means articulating the sound doctrines that constitute the Christian faith. Thus, Paul combines love with the truth. Many today, however, pit love against sound doctrine. They tell us that doctrine divides but love unifies. But brethren, according to this text, not the body of sound doctrine, but theological ignorance and doctrinal error divide God's people. When Christian people remain ignorant of major aspects of the Christian faith, they are vulnerable to wiles the error and susceptible to division. Truth and love are friends, not enemies.

Therefore, these verses provide ample warrant for systematic theology. They issue a compelling mandate for formulating sound doctrine in words and propositions that expose the errors of clever and evil men. They extol the wisdom of grounding all God's people in the whole body of sound doctrines that constitute the Christian faith. This is precisely the noble aim systematic theology.

B. *The Fourfold Summons: the faith, the knowledge of Christ, doctrine, the truth*

I featured this passage as our primary text because it employs four major terms and concepts that constitute the biblical foundation of systematic theology: *"the faith," "the knowledge of the Son of God," "doctrine,"* and "*the truth.*" Many portions of God's Word expound and elucidate these terms and ideas. We now survey and summarize this biblical witness. We expound its fourfold summons regarding the faith, the knowledge of Christ, doctrine, and the truth.

1. The summons to grasp and affirm the sum of the Christian faith

The goal of pastoral instruction issues a summons that compels every Christian: "Till we all attain unto the unity of *the faith.*" What is "the faith"? The word πιστις (pistis), translated "faith" in this verse, occurs some 243 times in the New Testament. It most frequently depicts the grace of personal trust in God and Christ. For example, Paul speaks of: "testifying both to Jews and Greeks repentance toward God, and *faith* toward our Lord Jesus Christ" (Acts 20:21). Sometimes, as in this text, it denotes the entire collection of verbal propositions about the things of God that Christ and the apostles taught and that true Christians confess. These two uses stand closely connected. Clearly Christ is the special focus and object of saving faith: "*faith toward our Lord Jesus Christ.*" Saving faith has three essential elements: knowledge, assent, and trust. It is knowing the story of Jesus, affirming that story to be true, and trusting, personally and exclusively, in the living Jesus of that story, for acceptance with God and deliverance from sin. This knowledge and assent consist in commitment to the set of apostolic assertions concerning the person, life, and work of Jesus of Nazareth. Saving faith involves not only knowing this body of apostolic doctrines, but also affirming that they are true. Thus, even when *pistis* primarily signifies the grace of saving faith, the body of Christian doctrine is always implicitly in view, because saving faith includes knowing and affirming that body of sound doctrine to be true. We use "faith" this way in our doctrinal statements and hymns. We call a compendium of our doctrines a confession "of faith." When we entitle it, "the things most surely *believed* among us," we recognize that our doctrines express the content of our faith. Similarly, we sing of allegiance to "*the faith* of our fathers." Therefore, we shouldn't balk at the idea that the biblical term for the body of sound doctrines is "the faith." From a thorough survey of this biblical testimony, I have culled out 21 texts in which *pistis* explicitly depicts the body of Christian doctrine: Acts 6:7, 13:8, 14:22, 16:5, 24:24; 2 Cor. 13:5; Gal. 1:23; Eph. 4:13; Phil. 1:27; Col. 1:23; 1 Tim. 1:19, 3:9, 13, 4:1, 6, 5:8, 6:10, 21; 2 Tim. 3:8; Titus 1:13; Jude 3. Observe that almost 50% (10/21) of these occur in the Pastoral Epistles. This shouldn't shock us, due to the teaching role of gospel ministers. I do not claim that this list is exhaustive. I have not included ambiguous texts (Luke 18:8; Heb. 12:2). We collate and survey this testimony in seven segments.

a. The witness in Acts (Acts 6:7, 13:8, 14:22, 16:5, 24:24)

(1) Acts 6:7[44]

Disciples of Christ are persons obedient to the faith. People become obedient to the faith when God's Word increases and bears fruit in their hearts. Thus, sound doctrine is crucial to true religion. Genuine conversion involves both exposure and obedience to apostolic doctrine.

(2) Acts 13:8[45]

Sergius Paulus, a Roman proconsul, wanted to hear Paul expound God's Word (13:7). A sorcerer objected to Paul's preaching. He tried to refute his propositions about God, sin, Christ, repentance, faith, and the world to come. Sadly, some not only reject Christian doctrine, they attempt to poison the minds of others. The faith always faces opposition. Its avid opponents eventually find that they, like the sorcerer, avail little, manifest their own villainy, and bring on themselves the Lord's judgment (13:9-12).

(3) Acts 14:22[46]

Someone could argue that in this text *pistis* depicts saving faith. Even if it does, the body of Christian doctrine, which disciples believe at conversion, is still in view implicitly. Paul was moved with concern for the eternal welfare of his converts. He returned to the churches he planted. He exhorted them to remain committed to sound doctrine in spite of their afflictions. Saving faith is enduring faith, which remains committed for life to the Christian faith. Apostasy from the faith is a grave danger. Jesus warned that apostasy typically stems from tribulation that arises because of commitment to the gospel.[47]

---

[44] *Acts 6:7*: And the word of God increased; and the number of the disciples multiplied in Jerusalem greatly; and a great company of the priests were obedient to the faith.

[45] *Acts 13:8*: But Elymas the sorcerer (for so is his name by interpretation) withstood them, seeking to turn aside the proconsul from the faith.

[46] *Acts 14:22*: confirming the souls of the disciples, exhorting them to continue in the faith, and that through many tribulations we must enter the kingdom of God.

[47] *Matt. 13:21*: yet he does not have root in himself, but endures for a while; and when tribulation or persecution arises because of the word, straightway he stumbles; *Luke 8:13*: And those on the rock *are* they who, when they have heard, receive the word with joy; and these have no root, who for a while believe, and in time of temptation fall away.

(4) Acts 16:5[48]

Again, someone could say that "the faith" denotes saving faith. Again, even if it does, a growing grasp of the body of sound doctrine is a major element of a growing faith. This text closely connects apostolic doctrine (16:4) with the Christian faith (16:5). Their teaching regulates the substance of the faith. Further, this text displays the vital role of sound doctrine as the foundation of healthy church growth: "the churches were strengthened in the faith, and increased in number daily." Thus, when church members hunger for instruction in sound doctrine, their church is on the path of spiritual and numerical growth. Therefore, don't let yourself be enticed or intimidated by any theory of church growth that minimizes sound doctrine, and features entertainment, recreation, clever gimmicks, or anything else.

(5) Acts 24:24[49]

Paul proclaimed Christ to Felix "the faith that is in Christ Jesus." He declared three essentials of the faith: "And as he reasoned of righteousness, and self-control, and the judgment to come." First, Paul proclaimed "*righteousness*," the necessity and method of justification. He declared that sinners get right with God because of grace alone, on ground of Christ alone, by means of faith alone. Second, he proclaimed "*self-control*," the necessity and substance of sanctification. He declared that true Christians display their faith by mortifying sin and putting on Christ. Third, he proclaimed that divine judgment is certain, impartial, and eternal. God through Christ will hold every person accountable. He will commend the righteous with eternal blessedness and life. He will condemn the wicked to eternal torment. Felix responded with great fear: "Felix was terrified." Yet he didn't repent and believe. Paul's inspired sermon reproves modern church growth "gurus" who condemn "scare tactics" and urge us only to present Christ in a "positive and non-threatening way." The faith Paul preached in its very essence threatens the wicked. No one can make it "non-threatening" unless he dismembers and eviscerates it.

---

[48] *Acts 16:4-5*: And as they went on their way through the cities, they delivered them the decrees [dogmata] to keep which had been ordained of the apostles and elders that were at Jerusalem. 5 So the churches were strengthened in the faith, and increased in number daily.

[49] *Acts 24:24-25*: But after certain days, Felix came with Drusilla, his wife, who was a Jewess, and sent for Paul, and heard him concerning the faith in Christ Jesus. 25 And as he reasoned of righteousness, and self-control, and the judgment to come, Felix was terrified, and answered, Go thy way for this time; and when I have a convenient season, I will call thee unto me.

b. Gal. 1:23[50]

Paul reports how the news of his striking conversion spread among the churches. Once he made havoc of the faith he now proclaims. Clearly, "the faith" denotes the content of Paul's preaching. It is a body of truth, a body of divinity. What does Paul preach? He preaches verbal propositions about Scripture, God, creation, sin, Christ, salvation, and the world to come. He calls the sum of these doctrines, "the faith."

c. Col. 1:23[51]

The apostle asserts the necessity of perseverance in sound doctrine. He says that the Colossians stand truly reconciled to God, and will stand before Christ blameless, if and only if, they continue firm in their commitment to the Christian faith throughout their lives.

Almost all who have been on the journey to the celestial city for a decade or more can relate sad tales of those who once confessed orthodox faith who now repudiate evangelical doctrines. Sometimes they depart from the truth suddenly, with a shocking scandal. It is not always so. Sometimes they shed apostolic doctrines gradually, one at a time. We watch their souls shrivel and die as if infested with a steadily growing spiritual cancer. They oft accompany their rejection of sound doctrine with wounded protests that they are still Christians, and that our concern for their eternal welfare springs, not from love, but from our own intolerance and narrowness. Their apostasy takes root when they jettison the doctrine of Scripture. Once they reject its inerrancy and infallibility, they undermine every tenet of the faith, for all rests on that foundation. Therefore, beware brothers and sisters. Let none of you so grieve our hearts.

d. The witness in 1 Timothy (1 Tim. 1:19, 3:9, 13, 4:1, 6, 5:8, 6:10, 21)

(1) 1 Tim. 1:19[52]

Paul stresses the close tie between conscientious living and sound doctrine. He explains that apostasy from the faith has experimental roots. It springs from a throwing away a good conscience. Those who indulge sin act as

---

[50] *Gal. 1:22-24*: I was still unknown by face to the churches of Judea which were in Christ: 23 but they only heard say, he that once persecuted us now preaches the faith of which he once made havoc; 24 and they glorified God in me.

[51] *Col. 1:22-23*: yet now has he reconciled in the body of his flesh through death, to present you holy and without blemish and unreproveable before him: 23 if so be that you continue in the faith, grounded and steadfast, and not moved away from the hope of the gospel which you heard

[52] *1 Tim. 1:19*: holding faith and a good conscience; which some having thrust from them made shipwreck concerning the faith: 20 of whom is Hymenaeus and Alexander; whom I delivered unto Satan, that they may be taught not to blaspheme.

though they don't need to rely on Christ's virtue and strength. Self-righteousness doesn't feel the need to keep short accounts about sin, either with God or with fellow human beings. Therefore, walk conscientiously in the fear of God, for through hypocrisy people depart from the faith.

(2) 1 Tim. 3:9[53]

Paul informs Timothy that to qualify to be a deacon a man must conscientiously embrace the set of apostolic doctrines. Not only elders, but also deacons, must be doctrinally "literate" and orthodox. They must be well versed in sound theology and committed to it. A deacon must conscientiously comply with the moral demands of the faith he professes. This has many and mighty implications. When churches appoint deacons successful in business who see little value in sound doctrine, or worse, who hold it in contempt, we shouldn't wonder why such congregations chop up one minister after another, or spend years mired in squabbling and power struggles, or grieve the souls of the godly with scandal and schism.

The phrase, "*the mystery of the faith*," indicates that the Christian faith is a body of revealed truth. Its exclusive source is special divine revelation. Unless God unveiled it in his Word, humans could never have known it. They never could or would have devised it. The faith originates, not from human philosophy or human reason, but from God and his Word alone.

(3) 1 Tim. 3:13[54]

This text encourages those who serve as deacons with the promise of great confidence in the veracity of the Christian faith. Here is striking irony. Serving others faithfully and compassionately in labor that is often unheralded becomes the root of great courage in embracing and affirming the Christian faith. This furnishes strong incentive to persevere in the difficult service of diaconal ministry among God's people.

(4) 1 Tim. 4:1[55]

Paul predicts the apostasy of some from sound doctrine. He contrasts "the faith" with false doctrines that stem from demons: "giving heed to seducing

---

[53] *1 Tim. 3:8-9*: Deacons in like manner must be grave, not double-tongued, not given to much wine, not greedy of filthy lucre; 9 holding the mystery of the faith in a pure conscience.

[54] *1 Tim. 3:13*: For they that have served well as deacons gain to themselves a good standing, and great boldness in the faith which is in Christ Jesus.

[55] *1 Tim. 4:1-3*: But the Spirit says expressly, that in later times some shall fall away from the faith, giving heed to seducing spirits and doctrines of demons, 2 through the hypocrisy of men that speak lies, branded in their own conscience as with a hot iron; 3 forbidding to marry, *and commanding* to abstain from meats, which God created to be received with thanksgiving by them that believe and know the truth.

spirits and doctrines of demons." Thus, clearly, "the faith" is the entire body of sound doctrine that Scripture reveals and that Christians believe. Again, apostasy from the faith stems from moral hypocrisy, dishonesty, and a bad conscience: "through the hypocrisy of men that speak lies, branded in their conscience as with a hot iron." This text connects this widespread apostasy with forced celibacy and asceticism: "forbidding to marry and commanding to abstain from meats, which God created to be received with thanksgiving by them that believe and know the truth." This features an important truth: the right of all Christians to partake in marriage and all kinds of meats.

(5) 1 Tim. 4:6[56]

Paul relates the success of a good gospel minister to the Christian faith. Observe the close connection between the faith and sound doctrine: "the words of the faith and of the good doctrine." The Christian faith consists in "*words*." Specifically, it consists in verbal propositions that constitute its tenets. Its good doctrines have the capacity to benefit, edify, and feed the soul: "nourished in the words of the faith." Sound theology is "soul food" of the richest variety both for those who sit in the pews and for those who stand in the pulpits. Thus, Paul reminds Timothy that a minister too needs to have his soul fed. A good minister never ceases to hunger for the truth. He studies the Bible not only for others, but also for his own spiritual welfare. A good minister, whose soul is nourished on the truth, does not shrink from putting "the brethren in mind of these things." He warns of soul-withering doctrines (4:1-5). He focuses the people's minds on Christ (3:16). He inculcates prayer and biblical order in the house and church of God (2:1-3:15). He does all this when he pays careful attention to good doctrine, so that his own mind and heart are saturated with the sound words of the Christian faith.

(6) 1 Tim. 5:8[57]

Paul warns Timothy about any professing Christian who refuses to care financially for his own offspring.
When any man forsakes and despises his domestic responsibilities, his profession of Christianity has no credibility. Some say they believe Christian doctrine, but their domestic neglect betrays that these claims are false: "if any provides not for his own . . . he has denied the faith." This

---

[56] *1 Tim. 4:6*: If you put the brethren in mind of these things, you will be a good minister of Jesus Christ, nourished in the words of the faith, and of the good doctrine which you have followed until now

[57] *1 Tim. 5:8*: But if any provides not for his own, and especially his own household, he has denied the faith, and is worse than an unbeliever.

teaches a valuable lesson about the faith and lifestyle. The way a man lives at home displays what he really believes. Men who truly believe sound doctrine behave responsibly as husbands and fathers. They aren't "deadbeat dads." They nurture and provide for their children. Stable families and a wholesome society stem from sound doctrine, embraced from the heart. When society is full of the fatherless, a deeper moral malady lies beneath the surface. Irresponsible men that neglect domestic responsibility produce this tragedy and its baneful fruits. Such men may claim to believe in God, but their actions speak louder than their words.

(7) 1 Tim. 6:10[58]

Paul warns that materialism can lead people away from the sound doctrines of the Christian faith. Greed opposes truth and promotes error. How? Greed harm souls in many different ways: "the love of money is the root of all kinds of evil." Some may formulate popular doctrines suited to fill their pews and coffers and repudiate sound doctrine because it holds little prospect of popularity or the material gain that oft goes with it. Others may compromise with heresy because they place greater value on job security than on doctrinal integrity. Others may repudiate the faith to avoid religious persecution and spoiling of their goods. Others may cheat or steal because they value treasure on earth more than treasure in heaven.

(8) 1 Tim. 6:21[59]

Paul's urges Timothy to watch out for those whose doctrines are a hybrid of the Christian faith and the so-called "insights" of worldly science and philosophy. Few things pose greater danger to the modern church than this. Unless we turn away from the "*profane babblings*" of those who try to marry the Christian faith and the tenets of godless science and secular philosophy, we will gravely err.

Modern science confidently applauds its atheistic "insights" into the origin and nature of the cosmos. Some theologians tremble in their boots. They dread the labels "obscurantist" or "reactionary." They must "save the credibility of Christianity." So they struggle and wrestle, and at last, eureka, they find a way to remain "Christian" and embrace the tenets of secular humanism. Some "discover" the preposterous concept of "theistic evolution." Others concoct the faithless notion that the first eleven chapters

---

[58] *1 Tim. 6:10*: For the love of money is the root of all kinds of evil: which some reaching after have been led astray from the faith, and have pierced themselves through with many sorrows.

[59] *1 Tim. 6:20-21*: O Timothy, guard that which is committed unto you, turning away from the profane babblings and oppositions of the knowledge which is falsely so called; 21 which some professing have erred concerning the faith.

of Genesis are "primeval mythology." They tell us that even though creation, the fall, and the flood never actually happened, we must still "believe" in the values that these legends picture. Others invent the serpentine notion that biblical ethics are "culturally bound." They pretend that Paul's unwillingness to allow women to rule the church indicates that he took the feminist cause as far as he could in his culture. He permitted women to learn. Thus they claim to apply his "progressive attitude toward women" to our culture and ordain women as bishops and elders. How slippery their doctrine is. They suppose that they honor Paul while they disobey his direct orders!

Such novelties would be ludicrous if they weren't so dangerous. But this is no joke. They lead many astray. Unless we master the timidity that spreads them, we too will "*err concerning the faith.*"

e. 2 Tim. 3:8[60]

Paul again warns Timothy about false teachers. They oppose the truth adamantly. He furnishes Timothy with detailed picture of their character, influence, and end. They lack grace and goodness (3:2-5). They prey on vulnerable women: "For of these are they that creep into houses, and take captive silly women laden with sins, led away by divers lusts" (3:6). Eventually they will be exposed: "But they shall proceed no further. For their folly shall be evident unto all men" (3:9). Thus Paul teaches us to do pastoral work with patience and realism. We won't convince everybody, for some are "*corrupted in mind.*" Sound doctrine will always have opponents. Thus we must not be shocked or disillusioned when we encounter such persons. We must press on diligently, always abounding in the Lord's work, knowing that our labor is not in vain in the Lord.

Observe that Paul closely associates "the faith" with "the truth." Those who thus "*withstand the truth*" are "*reprobate concerning the faith.*" Thus, the faith is a series of verbal propositions, which articulate the truth that Scripture reveals about the whole gamut of religious topics.

f. Titus 1:13[61]

Titus must labor conscientiously so that the Cretans may be "sound in the faith." Paul contrasts soundness in the faith with believing "Jewish fables"

---

[60] *2 Tim. 3:8*: And even as Jannes and Jambres withstood Moses, so did these withstand the truth; men corrupted in mind, reprobate concerning the faith.

[61] *Titus 1:12-14*: One of themselves, a prophet of their own, said, Cretans are always liars, evil beasts, idle gluttons. 13 This testimony is true. For which cause reprove them sharply, that they may be sound in the faith, 14 not giving heed to Jewish fables, and commandments of men who turn away from the truth.

and following "the commandments of men that turn away from the truth." Those who reject Scripture often make dogmatic religious pronouncements. Paul prescribes an inspired remedy, pointed reproof: "wherefore reprove them sharply." Titus must take the bull by the horns. He must call for repentance from culturally acceptable sins. He must pointedly oppose the twisted thinking that tolerates and even justifies such behavior. That will promote spiritual health.

g. Jude 3[62]

Jude is concerned because evil persons have infiltrated the Christian community and are *"turning the grace of God to lasciviousness."* Such deny the apostolic doctrine of Christ. Thus, he feels constrained to contend for the faith. He must expose their error. He exhorts Christians to contend for the body of apostolic doctrines. He affirms that God has entrusted "the faith," the entire set of biblical doctrines, to his people as a stewardship of sacred trust: "the faith once delivered to the saints." God hasn't entrusted the faith only to "the seminaries," or to "the clergy," but his "saints." He entrusted it to the whole society of Christ's disciples. He has tailor made it for all Christians. He entrusted Scripture, not to a select few sequestered from society in a seminary or monastery, but to the whole church of Christ.

Summary: "The faith" is the entire body of biblical doctrines, expressed in verbal propositions, which God reveals in Scripture, which Christ proclaims through his apostles. These sound doctrines feed men's souls. All God's people should be versed in the faith, committed to it, and prepared to confess and defend it: "till we all attain unto the unity of the faith." This is why systematics pertains to God's people in the pews. This is why it must be expository and suitable to be preached. Here is its abundant warrant.

2. The summons to grasp and affirm the knowledge of Christ

We return now to Ephesians 4:13 to consider the second aspect of this fourfold summons: "Till we all attain unto the unity of the faith and of *the knowledge of the Son of God.*" Paul uses the word, ἐπίγνωσις (epignosis), translated "knowledge." Observe the close association between "the faith" and the knowledge of Christ. Like the faith, the knowledge of Christ is also doctrinal in its substance. It involves the whole set of verbal propositions that Scripture reveals about the Son of God. The biblical doctrine of Christ

---

[62] *Jude 3-4*: Beloved, while I was giving all diligence to write unto you of our common salvation, I was constrained to write unto you exhorting you to contend earnestly for the faith that was once delivered to the saints. 4 For there are certain men crept in privily, *even* they who were of old written of beforehand unto this condemnation, ungodly men, turning the grace of our God into lasciviousness, and denying our only Master and Lord, Jesus Christ.

is the hub and preoccupation of the Christian faith. It is summed up in him, revolves around him, and leads to him.[63] The doctrine of Christ is the very core of the Christian faith. Thus, the heart of preaching the Christian faith is preaching Christ. The apostles' doctrine of Christ addresses two crucial issues: (1) the identity of Christ and (2) the work of Christ.

a. The knowledge of Christ includes the apostolic doctrine of Christ's Person.

The apostles' doctrine of the personal identity of Christ has two focal points. First, they identify the Christ by name. Second, they affirm the Christ's divine personage.

(1) The apostles affirm that Jesus of Nazareth is the Christ.

They identify by name the one true Christ from the many who falsely claim to be the promised Messiah. They affirm that Jesus of Nazareth is the Messiah, the Christ. This apostolic doctrine is the foundation of the Christian church.[64] Their writings and proclamations aim to bring men to believe that Jesus is the Messiah.[65] The apostles repeatedly muster unanswerable arguments to prove this point.[66] They appeal to the "signs" Jesus did, to his bodily resurrection, and to his fulfillment of everything Scripture predicts about Christ.[67] In John 5:30-47 Jesus unfolds five categories of evidence to prove that he is the Christ.[68]

(2) The apostles affirm that the Christ, Jesus of Nazareth, is God the Son incarnate.

Their doctrine is that Jesus of Nazareth, the Christ, is God incarnate. According to them, the Christ is one Person, God the Son, who ever is and

---

[63] *Col. 2:2-3*: ... that they may know the mystery of God, *even* Christ, 3 in whom are all the treasures of wisdom and knowledge hidden

[64] Mtt. 16:15-18

[65] *John 20:30-31*: Many other signs therefore did Jesus in the presence of the disciples, which are not written in this book: 31 but these are written, that you may believe that Jesus is the Christ, the Son of God; and that believing you may have life in his name.

[66] *Acts 9:22*: But Saul increased the more in strength, and confounded the Jews that dwelt at Damascus, proving that this is the Christ

[67] *Acts 18:28*: for he powerfully confuted the Jews, *and that* publicly, showing by the scriptures that Jesus was the Christ.

[68] [1] Jesus personally testifies that he is the Christ (5:31, with 4:25, 5:18, 46-47, 10:33-39); [2] John the Baptist testifies that Jesus is the Christ (5:32-35); [3] the miraculous works that Jesus does testify that he is the Christ (5:36); [4] God the Father, with an audible voice from heaven, testifies that Jesus is the Christ (5:37-38, with Matt. 3:17); and [5] the Old Testament Scriptures testify that Jesus is the Christ (5:39-40, 46-47).

always was divine, the true God, and who became human, a true man, with a human body and soul. Their affirmation of Christ's deity is the wonder, glory, and zenith of the apostolic doctrine of the person of Christ. Jews stumble at this.[69] Heretics and false teachers deny it.[70] The Christian church, however, fixes its gaze on this glorious mystery, confesses it, and defends it against all its foes and detractors. John especially features this perspective.[71] He declares two primary propositions. His first tenet is the deity of Christ: *"the Word was God."* Christ is a divine Person, God the Word, God the Son. His second tenet is the incarnation of Christ: *"and the Word became flesh."* God the Son became human. Without relinquishing his deity, he took a human nature, both body and soul. These two propositions are the marrow of the Christian faith respecting the person of Christ.[72]

Summary: the knowledge of Christ is knowledge of his Person, of who he is. The apostolic doctrine of his person is that the Christ is Jesus of Nazareth, God the Son incarnate.

b. The knowledge of Christ includes the apostolic doctrine of Christ's work.

Christ does what he does, because Christ is who he is. Matthew highlights this: "you shall call his name JESUS; for he it is that shall save his people from their sins" (Matt. 1:21). His name, "Jesus," signifies "Jehovah is salvation," or "Jehovah our salvation." This pinpoints the mission that brought God the Son from heaven to earth. His work focuses on the salvation of his people.[73] He came to earth to save. His work is remedial and redemptive.[74] It establishes intimate fellowship between Redeemer and redeemed.[75] The apostles feature the accomplishment, application, and completion of Christ's work. These correspond with three phases of his life: his two comings and the heavenly session between them.

---

[69] John 5:18, 8:57-58, 10:30-33

[70] 1 John 2:22-23; 2 John 7-10

[71] *John 1:1-3, 14*: In the beginning was the Word, and the Word was with God, and the Word was God. 2 The same was in the beginning with God. 3 All things were made through him; and without him was not anything made that has been made . . . 14 And the Word became flesh and dwelt among us (and we beheld his glory, glory as of the only begotten of the Father), full of grace and truth.

[72] *John 20:28-29*: Thomas answered and said unto him, My Lord and my God. 29 Jesus says to him, Because you have seen me you have believed: blessed are they that have not seen and yet have believed.

[73] *1 Tim. 1:15*: Faithful is the saying, and worthy of all acceptation, that Christ Jesus came into the world to save sinners.

[74] Gal. 3:13; Titus 2:14

[75] 1 Cor. 6:19-20; Titus 2:14; 1 Pet. 1:18-19

(1) Christ, in his first coming, has accomplished redemption for his people.

Christ in his earthly humiliation accomplished redemption for his people.[76] Paul writes: "But now apart from the law God's righteousness has been manifested, being witnessed by the law and the prophets" (Rom. 3:21). What Paul calls, "God's righteousness," is the active ingredient of the gospel.[77] God bestows Christ virtue by means of faith.[78] When a believing sinner receives Christ's virtue, he is justified, right with God. God constitutes him legally righteous and declares him so.[79] This virtue stems from the obedience of Jesus Christ.[80] God's righteousness is the virtue, in God's eyes, of Christ's perfect life and atoning death. Christ accomplished this virtue, completely and perfectly, by his perfect life and propitiatory death on the cross. It stands finished and manifested. Christ's perfect life is all the merit any sinner needs for acceptance with God. Christ's propitiatory death is all the atonement any sinner needs for pardon from God. Christ has forever, finally, accomplished the ground of salvation from sin.

(2) Christ, in his heavenly session, now applies redemption to his people.

Second, in the heavenly exaltation of his session, he applies redemption to his people.[81] When Christ had accomplished the ground of redemption, God highly exalted him, by resurrection, ascension, and session in heaven at God's right hand. Christ is still now seated in heaven, reigning as Lord. In this exalted posture and capacity he is undertaking the second phase of his redemptive work. He is now applying redemption to his people from every kindred, tribe, and tongue, and thus building and governing his body, the church. Paul explicitly affirms that the application of salvation is an essential part of the knowledge of Christ.[82] Christ applies salvation to his people through the gospel.[83] For this purpose he sent the Holy Spirit

---

[76] Luke 1:68; Gal. 3:13; Heb. 9:12
[77] Rom. 1:16-17
[78] Rom. 3:22
[79] Rom. 3:24, 5:16-17
[80] Rom. 5:18-19
[81] Rom. 3:24; Eph. 1:7, 2:8; Col. 1:14; Tit. 3:5-6
[82] Eph. 1:17-19
[83] Matt. 11:27-28; Rom. 1:16-17; 2 Thess. 2:13-14

Prologue: Introduction to Systematic Theology | **53**

to earth.[84] To this end he intercedes on behalf of his people to his Father.[85] In answer to Christ's prayers, the Father sends his Word and the Spirit, as the means and Agent, to apply redemption.[86]

(3) Christ, at his second coming, will complete the redemption of his people.

Christ in the eternal consummation of his second coming will complete the redemption of his people.[87] He will complete the redemption of his people both individually and corporately. He will "present the church to himself a glorious church, not having spot, or wrinkle, or any such thing" (Eph. 5:27). He will redeem the body of each dead Christian by resurrection.[88] Then he will judge all the enemies of his people. Then he will vindicate and avenge his people and forever deliver them from the presence of sin and sinners.[89] He will cast the wicked, along with the devil, into the lake of fire. Then God's people will shine forth as the sun in the kingdom of their Father.[90] For all eternity they will enjoy the new heavens and earth wherein righteousness dwells.[91]

Summary: the knowledge of Christ is the centerpiece of the Christian faith. Its substance is the biblical doctrine of salvation from sin through Christ's person and work. All true Christians begin to attain the knowledge of Christ at conversion. They continue to attain it throughout the Christian life on earth, in the intermediate state in heaven, and in the eternal state of resurrection glory. The Christian life involves growth and development in experiential knowledge of Christ: "that I may know him, and the power of his resurrection, and the fellowship of his sufferings" (Phil. 3:10). Christ's perfect life is the standard and example of Christian obedience.[92] Personal communion with Christ is the spiritual life and joy of every Christian.[93] Conformity to Christ's resurrection and perfection is the

---

[84] Acts 2:33
[85] Heb. 7:25
[86] Rom. 8:29-30; Phil. 1:29; Titus 3:4-6
[87] Rom. 5:9, 8:23; Eph. 1:14, 4:30; Heb. 9:28; 1 Pet. 1:5
[88] Rom. 8:23
[89] 2 Thess.1:7-10; Matt.25:31-46; Heb.9:28
[90] Matt. 13:40-43; Rev. 20:10, 14-15
[91] 2 Pet. 3:4-13
[92] Phil. 2:1-5; 1 Pet. 2:19-24
[93] Phil. 1:21-23

Christian hope.[94] Any systematic theology that honors God features these themes. This abundantly displays the mandate for systematics.

3. The summons to reject false doctrines

We return now again to our key text: "that we may be no longer children tossed to and fro and carried about with every wind of doctrine, by the slight of men, in craftiness, after the wiles of error." The word translated "doctrine," διδασκαλια (didaskalia) signifies "what is taught." It depicts both the act and content of teaching. It occurs 21 times in the New Testament. Fifteen of those, over 75%, are "crammed" into the Pastoral Epistles. A similar word for doctrine, διδαχη (didache), occurs 30 times in the New Testament, twice in the Pastoral Epistles. This shift in emphasis is interesting. Combined, these words occur 51 times, 17 in the Pastoral Epistles. That shouldn't shock us. Christ gave pastors and teachers to edify his saints and bring them to the unity of the faith. How fitting that the lion's share of their use occurs in letters addressed to pastors. Below I catalogue the uses of *didaskalia* and *didache*:

didaskalia: Matt. 15:9; Mark 7:7; Rom. 12:7, 15:46; Eph. 4:14; Col. 2:22; 1 Tim. 1:10, 4:1, 6, 13, 16, 5:17, 6:1, 3; 2 Tim. 3:10, 16, 4:3; Titus 1:9, 2:1, 7, 10.

didache: Matt. 7:28, 16:12, 22:33; Mark 1:22, 27, 4:2, 11:18, 12:38; Luke 4:32; John 7:16, 17, 18:19; Acts 2:42, 5:28, 13:12, 17:19; Rom. 6:17, 16:17; 1 Cor. 14:6, 26; 2 Tim. 4:2; Titus 1:9; Heb. 6:2, 13:9; 2 John 9(2), 10; Rev. 2:14, 15, 24

The word, *didaskalia*, always refers to the act or content of religious teaching. It always depicts the conveyance of verbal propositions about religious topics. The word, *didache*, often also denotes the act or content of religious teaching. Occasionally, however, it takes on an additional meaning. It sometimes seems to denote the power or impact of religious teaching (Mark 1:27; Acts 13:12). This difference possibly explains the prominence of didaskalia in the Pastoral Epistles. Perhaps Paul featured *didaskalia* because it emphasizes the substance of doctrine. Consider now a survey of ten aspects of this witness.

a. Matt. 16:12, with 15:9[95]

Christ exposes false doctrine. He counteracts the influence of those who make false assertions about religion. He envisions specific persons and errors. He depicts false teaching as leaven. Pharisees and Sadducees had distinctive doctrines. Pharisees held well-defined ideas about religious

---

[94] 1 John 3:2-3

[95] *Matt. 16:12*: Then understood they that he bade them not beware of the leaven of bread, but of the teaching [didache] of the Pharisees and Sadducees; 15:9: But in vain do they worship me, Teaching *as their* doctrines [didaskalia] the precepts of men.

tradition and ceremonies, marital ethics, and the Sabbath. These doctrines distinguished them as a religious movement. Similarly, Sadducees held specific tenets about angels, life after death, and Scripture. Both groups held well-defined ideas on religious topics that distinguished them as sects.

In Matthew 15:9 the Lord discloses the source of their false teachings: "in vain do they worship me, teaching as their doctrines the precepts of men." In this text he uses the synonym, *didaskalia*. Clearly, their doctrines are verbal assertions and propositions about religious topics. Again, these doctrines, when considered as a body, distinguish them as a group. In 15:2 Scripture identifies the specific concern with which the Scribes and Pharisees confront Jesus: "Why do your disciples transgress the tradition of the elders? For they wash not their hands when they eat bread." They have a doctrinal problem with Christ. Jesus responds they have a problem with him because they draw their doctrines from the wrong source. Their doctrines come from men's traditions, rather than from God's Word. He calls the source of their teaching "the precepts of men." In 15:6 he says: "and you have made void the Word of God because of your tradition." Similarly, he asks in 15:3, "Why do you also transgress the commandment of God because of your tradition?" The Pharisees regard the "traditions of the elders" as the proper source of authoritative religious teaching, binding on the conscience. Jesus has a different doctrine of religious authority. He asserts that the Word of God, not the traditions of men, furnishes the sole source of authoritative and sound doctrine. He says boldly that no religious movement can ever honor God, or bring him acceptable worship, as long as it formulates its distinctive doctrines from the poverty of human tradition, rather than from the riches of Scripture: "This people honors me with their lips; but their heart is far from me. But in vain do they worship me, teaching as their doctrines the precepts of men."

Summary: "doctrine" is a biblical idea. Systematic theology has not imposed on Scripture the idea of well-defined concepts, in verbal propositions, concerning religious topics and issues. Jesus condemns false doctrines, derived from the wrong source, human traditions. He teaches that Scripture is the only proper source of religious doctrine.

b. *Acts 2:42*[96]

The Bible also speaks about true doctrine. This text identifies its source. On the day of Pentecost the apostle Peter preaches and proclaims the gospel.

---

[96] *Acts 2:41-42*: Then they that received His word were baptized: and there were added unto them in that day about three thousand souls. 42 And they continued steadfastly in the apostles' teaching [didache] and fellowship, in the breaking of bread and the prayers.

Thus we read that with many other words he testified and exhorted them saying: "Save yourselves from this crooked generation" (Acts 2:40). Then many became Christians and continued steadfastly in the Christian church and in the teaching of the apostles. Thus, the apostles also teach religious doctrine. They make pronouncements about religious topics. They propound a distinctive set of ideas about religious themes. Apostolic teaching, considered as a body, distinguishes the society of Christ's disciples: "they continued steadfastly in the apostles' doctrine." Thus, sound theology is apostolic. Topical teaching is biblical only to the degree that it agrees with apostolic teaching preserved for us as Scripture (2 Pet. 3:15-16). Sound theology never departs from apostolic teaching, contradicts it, adds to it, or subtracts from it, but rather, continues steadfastly in it.

c. *Rom. 6:17*[97]

Paul depicts the conversion of the Roman Christians. The phrase, "form of teaching," could be translated, "pattern of doctrine." The topic in view here is the gospel. The body of doctrine that they obey is about the topic of salvation from sin. It constitutes a body of verbal propositions and assertions that the apostles proclaimed about God, about sin, about Christ, and about repentance and faith. Their conversion consisted of their obedience to this body of apostolic doctrine. Therefore, people that reject, deny, and disobey the apostolic gospel have not been truly converted. Those who reject the apostles' verbal pronouncements about God, sin, Christ, repentance, and faith are lost. They are still in their sins. Evangelical doctrine marks all true conversion and saving religion. God delivers people from hell and wrath only by adherence to the Christ of apostolic teaching. What more commendation of sound theology do we need? The welfare of men's souls hinges upon sound doctrine about the topic of salvation.

d. *Rom. 16:17-18*[98]

Paul asserts that false doctrines cause schisms and scandals in the church. His inspired cure for this may shock some and offend others. Paul prescribes church discipline! The church should name and avoid those who cause divisions and overthrow men's faith by their false doctrines. Such are not servants of Christ but self-serving. They are smooth, clever, deceptive, and dangerous. They present soul-destroying errors in an appealing and pleasant

---

[97] *Rom. 6:17*: But thanks be to God, that, whereas you were servants of sin, you became obedient from the heart to that form of teaching [didache] whereunto you were delivered.
[98] *Rom. 16:17-18*: Now I beseech you, brethren, mark them that are causing the divisions and occasions of stumbling, contrary to the doctrine [didache] which you learned: and turn away from them. 18 For they that are such serve not our Lord Christ, but their own belly; and by their smooth and fair speech they beguile the hearts of the innocent.

way. They fool the less discerning among Christians. Some well-meaning brethren are duped by them and defend them. Thus, it is very important to ground God's people in their Christian faith. It is doubly important that the teachers and watchmen of the church are alert to see through and expose such deceivers and bold to summon the church to label them publicly and avoid them. This alone can demolish their insidious influence over the minds of vulnerable Christians.

e. *The testimony in 1 Timothy: 1:3, 10, 4:1, 6, 5:17, 6:1, 3*

(1) 1 Tim. 1:3[99]

Here Paul uses the compound verb, ἑτεροδιδασκαλειν, (heterodidaskalein), which means, "to teach something different." It depicts departing from the religious doctrines of the apostles. Evidently, some associated with the churches were making "heterodox" pronouncements about religious themes. Their doctrines differed from the "orthodox" doctrine of the apostles. Timothy must confront those who propound in the church novel ideas that contradict the apostles. He must insist that they cease and desist.

(2) 1 Tim. 1:10-11[100]

Here Paul uses *didaskalia*. He speaks about ethics, right and wrong behavior. He asserts the incompatibility of an immoral life with the sound doctrine that accords with the gospel. He defines various aspects of immoral living (1 Tim. 1:9-10). He includes murder, fornication, homosexuality, and dishonesty. Such living, he says, is contrary to sound doctrine and incompatible with the Christian faith.

(3) 1 Tim. 4:1[101]

We considered this text when we surveyed "the faith." Note well the contrast of the faith with false doctrine. Some will fall away from the faith when they embrace "doctrines of demons." What doctrines of demons will distinguish this apostasy? Paul tells us: "forbidding to marry, and commanding to abstain from meats" (1 Tim. 4:3). The doctrines of a celibate clergy and asceticism are demonic. Paul predicts that these errors will mark a religious sect composed of those who have apostatized from the faith.

---

[99] *1 Tim. 1:3*: As I exhorted you to tarry at Ephesus when I was going into Macedonia, that you might charge certain men not to teach a different doctrine [heterodidaskalein].

[100] *1 Tim. 1:10-11*: . . . if there be any other thing contrary to the sound doctrine [didaskalia], 11 according to the gospel of the glory of the blessed God, which was committed to my trust.

[101] *1 Tim. 4:1*: But the Spirit says expressly, that in the latter times some shall fall away from the faith, giving heed to seducing spirits and doctrines [didaskalia] of demons

(4) 1 Tim. 4:6[102]

Notice the close connection between sound doctrine and the faith. The Christian faith consists in *"words."* More specifically, it consists in verbal propositions that constitute its doctrines. The faith is *"good"* doctrine. It has the capacity to benefit, edify, and feed the soul. Paul reminds Timothy that truth nourishes souls. A minister too needs to have his soul fed. A good minister never ceases to hunger for the truth. He studies the Bible not only for others, but also for the welfare of his own soul. Sound theology is "soul-food" of the richest variety for those who sit in the pews and stand in the pulpits. A good minister, whose soul is nourished on the truth, puts "the brethren in mind of these things." He warns of soul-withering errors (1 Tim. 4:1-5). He focuses the saints on Christ (1 Tim. 3:16). He inculcates prayer and biblical order in the house of God (1 Tim. 2:1-3:15). He does so only when he pays careful attention to good doctrine and saturates his mind and heart with the sound words of the faith.

(5) 1 Tim. 5:17[103]

Some elders labor as their calling in life in the sound doctrines of God's Word. These provide for themselves and their families by exposition and application of the Scriptures. Peter includes himself with such when he says: "but we will continue steadfastly in prayer, and in the ministry of the word" (Acts 6:4). Therefore, those whose work focuses on God's Word can ill afford to be ignorant of or unskilled in the sound doctrines of the Christian faith. Therefore, ministers of the Word must take care to keep our labors in proper focus. We must never forsake the priority of feeding our own souls, or the souls of our people on sound doctrine. The focal point of our work must be feeding our flocks with the truth. We must not neglect labor in the word for church administration, or building programs, or fund-raising, or civic involvement, or social concerns. If a gospel minister neglects the word and prayer, and keeps "busy, busy, busy" with everything and everyone else, he has lost sight of the primary focus of his calling.

(6) 1 Tim. 6:1[104]

Paul observes that men judge both our God and our doctrines by our behavior. When Christian servants show disrespect for their masters, he

---

[102] *1 Tim. 4:6*: If you put the brethren in mind of these things, you will be a good minister of Jesus Christ, nourished in the words of the faith, and of the good doctrine [didaskalia] which you have followed until now

[103] *1 Tim. 5:17*: those who labor in the word and teaching [didaskalia].

[104] *1 Tim. 6:1*: Let as many as are servants under the yoke count their own masters worthy of all honor, that the name of God and the doctrine [didaskalia] be not blasphemed.

says, people malign God and the Christian faith. We must take to heart that people are watching us. This should motivate us to live circumspectly at all seasons, and in every company, in such a way that we commend and honor our God and the teachings of his Word.

(7) 1 Tim. 6:3[105]

The phrase, "teaches a different doctrine," translates the same verb, *heterodidaskalein*, found in 1 Timothy 1:3. Paul contrasts heterodox doctrines with "*sound words*": "and consents not to sound words." Note again that doctrine consists of verbal assertions about the things of God. Observe that Christ himself is the author of Christian doctrine: "words of our Lord Jesus Christ." Christ is the Teacher, whose words form the sound doctrine that produces our Christian way of life. The apostles formulate sound doctrines with wholesome words in verbal propositions that are true and biblical. Observe that sound doctrine produces holy living: "doctrine which is according to godliness." Observe that carnal pride drives men to reject sound doctrine and the morality that always grows out of it: "he is puffed up." Similarly, Paul exhorts Timothy to: "hold the pattern of sound words which you have heard from me" (2 Tim. 1:13). The Greek word, ὑποτύπωσις (hupotuposis), is translated, "pattern." Arndt and Gingrich say that it depicts a standard, norm, or model.[106] The exact words that Paul taught Timothy are the infallible standard and norm of the sound doctrines of the Christian faith. Apostolic doctrine comes in inspired words that must be believed and preserved.

f. The testimony in 2 Timothy: 3:16, 4:3-4

(1) 2 Tim. 3:16[107]

The apostle identifies Scripture as the exclusive, complete, and sufficient source of sound doctrine. It is profitable for verbal propositions about every religious issue and theme. It thoroughly furnishes the man of God for every good work. Additional revelation is not required. Tradition is not required. God's Word furnishes the whole set of sound doctrines which constitute the

---

[105] *1 Tim. 6:3*: If any man teaches a different doctrine [heterodidaskalein], and consents not to sound words, even the words of our Lord Jesus Christ, and to the doctrine [didaskalia] which is according to godliness; he is puffed up.

[106] William Arndt and F. Wilbur Gingrich, *A Greek-English Lexicon of the New Testament* (Chicago: The University of Chicago Press, 1967), 856.

[107] *2 Tim. 3:16*: Every Scripture is inspired of God and profitable for teaching [didaskalia], for reproof, for correction, for instruction which is in righteousness, that the man of God may be complete, furnished completely unto every good work.

faith. Thus, sound Christian doctrine is expository, because Christians derive and formulate it by exposition of the Scriptures.

(2) 2 Tim. 4:3-4[108]

Paul equates sound doctrine with "the truth." The truth is the opposite of "fables," which are false assertions and myths about the ways and things of God. Paul predicts a day when more than a few in the society of professing Christians will have no heart for sound doctrine. They will hate it and refuse even to listen to it. It will "turn them off." Such will find a "heap" of religious teachers to tell them what they want to hear. Paul prescribes his remedy for this impending loss of spiritual hunger: "preach the word; be urgent in season, out of season; reprove, rebuke, exhort, with all longsuffering and teaching [didache]" (2 Tim. 4:2). We must not cave in before spiritual declension. We must prepare for an evil day with the preventive medicine of biblical teaching. The Christian faith, proclaimed in the power of the Holy Spirit, is the best antidote for the loss of spiritual hunger. Paul stresses four features of such preaching.

(a) Biblical preaching of sound doctrine is expository in its content: "*preach the word.*" This grows out of the sufficiency of Scripture (2 Timothy 3:16). We must expound and apply only the words and concepts of Scripture, because Scripture alone is the complete and infallible source of sound doctrine.

(b) Biblical preaching of sound doctrine is earnest in its manner: "*be urgent.*" We must not present sound doctrine blandly. We must expound and apply it with animation and zeal. If we serve up good theology dispassionately, half asleep on our feet, in mumbled monotones, we ourselves are to blame for the resultant boredom and spiritual apathy. We shouldn't wonder if God's people gag on our doctrine if we serve it cold, and forget to cook it in the oven of experimental reality.

(c) Biblical preaching of sound doctrine is pointed and bold in its address: "*reprove, rebuke, exhort.*" It comes from the heart to the heart. It uses great plainness of speech. We shouldn't wonder why people sleep or daydream through our sermons, if our terminology sends archangels confused to their dictionaries, or if our structure exhausts men's minds in a seemingly endless maze of words and thoughts. It also "meddles" boldly with specific sins. We shouldn't wonder if men miss the point, if in cowardice we "leave the application to the Holy Spirit," and only speak about sin in generalities so

---

[108] *2 Tim. 4:3-4*: For the time will come when they will not endure sound doctrine [didaskalia]; but, having itching ears, will heap to themselves teachers after their own lusts; 4 and will turn away their ears from the truth, and turn aside unto fables.

vague that even Sherlock Holmes couldn't trace them to the offenders. Do not misunderstand. I do not condone hiding cowardly malice behind a pulpit and using sermons to snipe at brethren over personal offenses that love would address privately. I commend Peter's courage at Pentecost (Acts 2:36-38), not violating Christ's due process for resolving private offenses (Matt. 18:15-18).

(d) Biblical preaching of sound doctrine is steadfast ("sticktuitive") and systematic in its method: *"with all longsuffering and teaching."* We shouldn't think, "Why don't you people get it; I said that once six years ago." We must hammer the essentials of the faith over and over, until we drive the nails of truth deep into the souls of our people. A biblical ministry covers *all* the essentials of the faith, in an orderly manner, over a realistic period of time, to establish God's people in the whole body of sound doctrine.

g. Titus 1:9[109]

This text clearly displays that *didache* and *didaskalia* can be synonyms. Paul sets before Titus the qualifications for elders. He requires an elder to have a firm grasp on the whole body of Christian theology. This alone will enable him both to present and apply the apostolic doctrines, and to discern, expose, and refute the errors of those who oppose the teaching of the apostles.

h. Heb. 6:2[110]

The writer addresses specific apostolic pronouncements about religious themes. He singles out issues associated with becoming a Christian. The apostles address, in verbal propositions, topics basic to Christian experience, such as resurrection and judgment, initiatory rituals, and repentance and faith. Thus, their verbal propositions about each of these issues constitute their "doctrine" of that issue.

i. 2 John 9-10[111]

John points out the crucial role of doctrine in assessing character and spiritual state. The apostles affirm Christ's deity, true humanity, perfect life,

---

[109] *Titus 1:9*: holding to the faithful word which is according to the teaching [didache], that he may be able both to exhort in the sound doctrine [didaskalia], and to convict the gainsayers.

[110] *Heb. 6:1-2*: Wherefore leaving the doctrine [logos] of the first principles of Christ, let us press on unto perfection; not laying again a foundation of repentance from dead works, and of faith toward God, 2 of the teaching [didache] of baptisms, and of laying on of hands, and of resurrection of the dead, and of eternal judgment

[111] *2 John 9-10*: Whosoever goes onward and abides not in the teaching [didache] of Christ has not God: he that abides in the teaching [didache], the same has the Father and the Son. 10 If any one comes to you, and brings not this teaching [didache], receive him not into your house, and give him no greeting.

atoning death, bodily resurrection, heavenly session, and second coming. We shouldn't regard as a genuine Christian anyone that rejects these apostolic pronouncements. Orthodox doctrine is a dividing line. It divides false from true, real from phony, who is of Christ from who is of anti-Christ, and who is a brother from who is a deceiver. Thus, we need discernment. The devil's messengers don't have horns, pitchforks, tails, and red capes. Some of them stand in seminary classes with white hair and saintly smiles, gently proclaiming that Jesus was a good man, but not truly God, or that Jesus' resurrection is meaningful but not historical. John warns us not to let a winning smile, gentle demeanor, or scholarly reputation fool us. "Whosoever," he says, denies the doctrine of Christ has not God. We shouldn't extend distinctly Christian greeting or hospitality to such. If we violate his warning, we are accomplices in their evil works. This may sound narrow, bigoted, and intolerant. Thus, this underscores just how desperately the churches need to be grounded in the faith.

j. Rev. 2:14-15[112]

The Lord addresses the church at Pergamum. The word, *didache*, translated "teaching," depicts specific doctrinal errors that infected that society of disciples. Christ threatens to make war against those who hold these false doctrines unless they repent. This war does not consist in physical or military combat, but in spiritual combat that he wages with the sword of his mouth, the Word of God. Scripture doesn't reveal the details of these errors that Jesus stands committed to fight. Yet it teaches us that this theological controversy was of the Lord. Christ takes a stand against those errors. He threatens to start a spiritual battle over them. The Lord here rebukes those who think and teach that doctrine doesn't matter. It should matter to us, because it matters to him.

Summary: Now we draw together the implications of this biblical summons to reject false doctrine. Brethren, in the light of this overwhelming witness, how can anyone seriously entertain the notion that systematic theologians have forced the concept of topical teaching on the Bible? Scripture presents a religious doctrine as verbal propositions about a religious topic or theme. Doctrines can be either true and sound, or false and demonic. Their final arbiter is Scripture, which alone is the sufficient source of all sound doctrine.

---

[112] *Rev. 2:14-16*: But I have a few things against you, because you have there some that hold the teaching [didache] of Balaam, who taught Balak to cast a stumblingblock before the children of Israel, to eat things sacrificed to idols, and to commit fornication. 15 So you also have some that hold the teaching [didache] of the Nicolaitans in like manner. 16 Repent therefore; or else I come to thee quickly, and I will make war against them with the sword of my mouth.

Prologue: Introduction to Systematic Theology | 63

False doctrine produces an evil way of life. Christian maturity results when the saints reject false doctrines. False doctrine harms men's souls, brings reproach on God's name, and engenders strife in the church. Churches should mark teachers of false doctrine by name and avoid them. They should never tolerate or coddle them. Rejection of the apostolic doctrine of Christ is "heresy." It is incompatible with being saved and going to heaven. All this demonstrates, clearly and emphatically, the mandate for systematic theology.

4. The summons to grasp and affirm the sum of revealed truth

We return for the fourth and final time to our key text: "but *speaking truth in love, may grow up in all things into him who is the head, even Christ.*" The verb, ἀλεθευω, (aletheuo), is translated "speaking truth." It has only one other use in the New Testament (Galatians 4:16): "am I become your enemy by telling you the truth?" In general, telling the truth, or being truthful, means speaking words that accurately express and reflect reality. Conversely, telling lies, or being dishonest, means knowingly speaking words that distort or misrepresent reality. Our text contrasts "speaking truth" with "the wiles of error." Here "error" is false teaching. John similarly depicts doctrinal error (1 John 2:22): "Who is the liar but he that denies that Jesus is the Christ?" Thus, in this context, "speaking truth" signifies speaking words that accurately express biblical reality. Conversely, *"error"* signifies verbal propositions that contradict what Scripture affirms. Similarly, Jesus prays: "Sanctify them in the truth: your word is truth" (John 17:17). He refers to God's Word as "truth," ἀληθεια (aletheia). He calls its teachings, *"the truth,"* ἡ ἀληθεια (he aletheia). Similarly, Paul calls the entire body of biblical doctrine, *"the truth"*: "men who concerning the truth [aletheia] have erred, saying that the resurrection is past already, and overthrow the faith of some . . . the time will come when they will not endure the sound doctrine: but . . . will turn away their ears from the truth [aletheia], and turn aside unto fables" (2 Tim. 2:18, 4:4). In these texts Jesus and Paul use a noun, *aletheia*, which belongs to the same word family as the verb in our text. This noun occurs some 109 times in the New Testament. From a survey of its use, I catalogue these 53 times in which "truth" probably means "biblical doctrine" and "the truth" is "the entire body of biblical doctrines":

John 1:17, 8:32(2), 16:13, 17:17, 19, 18:37(2); Rom. 2:8, 20, 15:8; 1 Cor. 13:6; 2 Cor. 4:2, 6:7, 13:8(2); Gal. 2:5, 14, 3:1, 5:7; Eph. 1:13, 4:21; Col. 1:5; 2 Thess. 2:10, 12, 13; 1 Tim. 2:4, 3:15, 4:3, 6:5; 2 Tim. 2:15, 18, 25, 3:7, 8, 4:4; Titus 1:1, 14; Heb. 10:26; James 3:14, 5:19; 1 Pet. 1:22; 2 Pet. 2:2; 1 John 2:21(2), 3:19, 4:6; 2 John 4; 3 John 3(2), 4, 8, 12

I do not claim that this list is exhaustive or infallible. I found it difficult to classify quite a few uses. One text, Galatians 3:1, contains a variant reading. Observe that twelve of these uses, over 22%, occur in the Pastoral Epistles. This underscores the stewardship of Christian teachers to present biblical doctrines accurately. These texts feature the significance, redemptive focus, and moral relevance of the truth.

a. The significance of the truth

The truth signifies the entire set of religious doctrines revealed in the Scriptures.[113] The Holy Spirit, the Spirit of truth, reveals the truth comprehensively to the apostles,[114] so that their writings, the New Testament, set forth all its essential tenets.[115] Accordingly, Scripture closely associates "the truth" with the faith,[116] with sound doctrine,[117] and with the doctrine of Christ.[118] Like the faith, the truth refers to the entire body of biblical doctrine. Each, however, has a distinct emphasis. *The truth* emphasizes the divine origin, disclosure, and authority of that body of doctrines. *The faith* emphasizes the believing reception and confession of that body of doctrines by God's people.

b. The redemptive focus of the truth

Like the faith, the principal substance of the truth is God's gospel, the message about salvation from sin in Jesus Christ.[119] The preeminent object and focus of the truth is God the Son incarnate, Jesus Christ.[120]

c. The religious and moral impact of the truth

The truth sets apart God's people, who believe it, from the world, which rejects it.[121] Men are saved when they hear and believe the truth.[122] Men hear and reject the truth because they delight in their sins.[123] The truth produces a godly lifestyle.[124] The indulgence of sin often eventuates in doctrinal error

---

[113] John 17:17; 2 Tim. 2:15, 18, 4:2-4
[114] John 16:13
[115] 1 John 4:6
[116] 1 Tim. 4:1, 3; 2 Tim. 3:7-8; Titus 1:1
[117] 1 Tim. 6:3, 5; 2 Tim. 4:3-4
[118] 2 John 4:6-9
[119] Gal. 2:5, 14; Eph. 1:13; Col. 1:5; 2 Thess. 2:13-14; 1 Tim. 2:4; 3 John 8
[120] Eph. 4:21
[121] John 17:17, 19; 1 John 3:19
[122] Eph. 1:13-14; 2 Thess. 2:13-14; 1 Tim. 2:4
[123] 2 Thess. 2:10, 12
[124] Titus 1:1; James 3:14; John 17:17, 19; 1 John 3:19

contrary to the truth.[125] Some who know the truth and profess to believe it eventually repudiate it. To their eternal ruin they return to a lifestyle of highhanded sinning against God.[126]

Conclusion: two practical implications of the summons to affirm the truth

(1) First, God's servants should study the truth diligently and proclaim it graciously.[127]

Some err grievously concerning the truth. Their false doctrine is a spiritual cancer. It leads those who imbibe it to apostasy from the faith and ruin. Paul mentions two such teachers by name. These heretics spiritualized the resurrection and denied the future resurrection of dead Christians. They destroyed the hope and imperiled the souls of those who believed them. God's servants must shun the profane babblings of false teachers. They should focus on God's Word. They should study it diligently and present it accurately. They must handle it honorably to avoid embarrassment that stems from ignorance of the Scriptures. Only careful study of biblical doctrines equips God's servants to diagnose and treat the spiritual cancers that threaten the health of the churches. Spiritual cancer spreads with frightening speed through churches with unskilled spiritual doctors who fail to recognize its telltale symptoms. In one generation it can destroy the orthodoxy of whole denominations of churches. Therefore, we must prepare diligently to stand against every error that threatens the spiritual life and peace of God's people.

Further, we must fight error with love in our hearts for those whose spiritual life is in danger. We must correct "with meekness" those who oppose themselves. We must never lose hope. The cure is all of God, not of us. All things are possible with him. He may yet grant them "repentance unto the knowledge of the truth."

---

[125] 2 Tim. 2:25; James 5:19

[126] Heb. 10:26

[127] *2 Tim. 2:15*: Give diligence to present yourself approved unto God, a workman that needs not to be ashamed, handling aright the word of truth. But shun profane babblings: for they will proceed further in ungodliness, and their word will eat as does a gangrene: of whom is Hymenaeus and Philetus; men who concerning the truth have erred, saying that the resurrection is past already, and overthrow the faith of some; *2 Tim. 2:24-25*: the Lord's servant must not strive, but be gentle to all, apt to teach, in meekness correcting them that oppose themselves; if peradventure God may give them repentance unto the knowledge of the truth

(2) God's people should embrace the truth comprehensively and support it conscientiously.[128]

Paul equates *"the faith of God's elect"* with *"the truth which is according to godliness."* God's elect must embrace all the truth. Every aspect of the truth plays an important part in the maintenance and development of godliness. Again, he calls the church of Christ *"the pillar and ground of the truth."* The entire society of Christ's disciples has this vital function. Therefore, it is essential that God's people hunger for the truth, be fed on the truth, and assimilate the truth. How else can they support it? This underscores the great need of the people in the pews for systematic theology.

C. The Conclusion Mandated by Eph. 4:13-15

We have expended considerable time expounding the biblical setting and fourfold summons of this key text. We have considered the call to embrace the Christian faith and reject false doctrine. We have labored to expound and apply each important aspect of this key text. Our survey mandates the conclusion that systematic theology is essential for the spiritual health and peace of God's people. The biblical witness concerning the faith, the knowledge of Christ, doctrine, and the truth, presses this conclusion on our consciences repeatedly with many practical implications. Doctrines are verbal propositions about a religious topic or theme. The faith, the truth, is the entire set of biblical and apostolic doctrines. Its heart is the biblical doctrine of Christ. Thus, this key text emphatically mandates systematic theology.

Conclusion to Unit 2: *Summary of the Biblical Warrant for Systematics*

Systematic theology presents and applies *biblical dogmata*. It declares *the faith* comprehensively. It expounds *the truth* in biblical categories and proportions. It features *the knowledge of Christ*. The propriety of systematics rests on a solid and biblical foundation. Its warrant stems from the responsibility of the churches to embrace apostolic dogma (Acts 16:4-5), from the stewardship of pastors to proclaim the whole counsel of God (Acts 20:26-27), and from the duty of every Christian to embrace the Christian faith and repudiate false doctrines (Eph. 4:13-15). This abundantly displays the propriety of systematics. Why did I go to these lengths? Today some have little use for systematics. Disaffection to Christian doctrine is

---

[128] *1 Tim. 3:15*: that you may know how men ought to behave themselves in the house of God, which is the church of the living God, the pillar and ground of the truth; *Titus 1:1*: according to the faith of God's elect, and the knowledge of the truth which is according to godliness.

nothing new. Antipathy to systematics was in vogue over two centuries ago when Gill wrote his *Body of Divinity*:[129]

> Systematical Divinity, I am sensible, is now become very unpopular. Formulas and articles of faith, creeds, confessions, catechisms, and summaries of divine truths, are greatly decried in our age.

If people berated systematics then, should we be shocked that it is not popular today? Some actually go so far as to condemn it as unbiblical. They allege that topical teaching, per se, distorts the Bible. They claim that it imposes man-made, and thus unbiblical, patterns of thought on God's Word. Therefore, they conclude that systematics itself, the very concept, is illegitimate. We must stand up to this false doctrine of Christian doctrine. We must derive all our religious ideas from Scripture, even our concept of Christian doctrine. We have seen that the Bible has a "doctrine" of Christian doctrine. We have seen that this witness is neither skimpy nor obscure. It is abundant, patent, yes, massive. Perhaps I have wearied some by showing you the mammoth scope of the biblical materials on the topic of Christian doctrine. I make no apology. The assault on Christian doctrine, and the malice behind it, are too bold and too influential. Their error must be exposed. In the light of this overwhelming biblical testimony, let the adversaries of systematics convince the consciences of sincere students of Scripture that it is wrong to confess Christian doctrine. Let them support, from Scripture, their doctrine of Christian doctrine. Make no mistake about it, the adversaries of systematic theology also teach a doctrine of Christian doctrine! But, they derive their false doctrine of Christian doctrine, not from God's Word, but from their own preconceived imaginations. Thus, in a striking and stinging piece of irony, they commit the very folly of which they accuse the teachers of systematics. They impose on Scripture their false doctrine of Christian doctrine. Where do they get their notion of doctrine? How can they support their assertions on that topic from Scripture? If they seek to support their doctrine of doctrine from Scripture, then they are guilty of topical teaching and proof-texting. Thus, they condemn themselves the minute they open their mouths to defend themselves. If they refuse to appeal to Scripture for support, then they openly display that their doctrine is indefensible and unbiblical. Worse, they display that they have abandoned using the Bible as the authority for their religious ideas. This convoluted mess in which they entangle themselves displays the folly of their doctrine that Christian doctrine itself is unbiblical.

---

[129] Gill, *Body of Divinity*, 1:viii

Contrary to such nonsense, the Bible mandates topical teaching. Systematic theology addresses the topics that the Bible itself portrays as its major concerns. If pastors should teach God's people about topics of lesser importance, how much more should they teach God's people clearly and comprehensively about those topics to which the Bible assigns the greatest importance? Thus, those who teach systematics must especially face the pressure of James 3:1: "Be not many of you teachers, my brethren, knowing that we shall receive heavier judgment." Surely God reserves the heaviest judgment for those who teach God's people about the weightiest matters that Scripture addresses. If heavier judgment awaits the teachers of systematics because it is so vital, then what woe awaits those who reject systematics? What woe awaits those who condemn teaching Christians what God's Word presents as its most important issues?

I have gone to great lengths to expose the folly of rejecting systematics. Yet this does not excuse cold formalism or philosophical speculation in systematics. Thus, I conclude with Murray's cogent comments in his article, "*Systematic Theology*," where he ably defends the warrant for systematics:[130]

> In some cases the present day interest in Biblical Theology springs from, or at least is related to, an antipathy to Systematics. Or, as it is sometimes called, Dogmatics. The latter (Systematics) is charged with being abstract and philosophical, and therefore devoid of the dynamic realism and force which ought to characterize any reproduction of the Bible's witness. Now this charge is not to be dismissed as without any ground or warrant. Systematic Theologies have too often betrayed a cold formalism that has been prejudicial to their proper aim and have not for that reason and to that extent promoted encounter with the Living God of the Living Word.
>
> But, two observations require to be made with reference to this charge and to the corresponding admission. First, there are certain phases of the truth with which Systematic Theology must deal and certain Polemics which it must conduct that call for the type of treatment which to many people seems cold and formal. The painstaking analysis and exacting research which the pursuit of faithful dogmatics requires must not be abandoned because some people have no interest in or patience with such studies. This would mean that areas of investigation necessary to the wide range of the theologian's mandate would be abandoned to the enemy. We must appreciate how diversified are the tasks and interests that come within the orbit of Systematic Theology. A

---

[130] Murray, *Collected Writings*, 4:15-16.

biblical scholar's product may have to be sometimes as dry as dust, but dust has its place, especially when it is gold dust.

Second, the charge insofar as it is warranted, is not the fault of Systematic Theology but of the theologian or of the milieu of which his product is the reflection. Systematic Theology by its nature must have logical divisions because it is topical.

Therefore, let us not be ashamed of systematics, or shaken by the attacks leveled upon it. On the other hand, let us always conduct topical studies in such a way as to be free from just reproach. Let us avoid unprofitable speculations and vain reasoning. Let us not impose man-made doctrines on God's Word. O that the Lord would establish our hearts firmly in commitment to be true to the faith, and arouse our appreciation for the tremendous value of systematic theology, so that we would study it with hunger, enthusiasm, and diligence. We turn now to the content and development of systematic theology.

Unit 3: The Content and Development of Systematic Theology

We look now at the content and development of systematic theology. We focus on its positive task, *"to exhort in the sound doctrine"* rather than on its negative task in "polemics" or "apologetics," which is to *"convict the gainsayers"* (Titus 1:9). What major doctrines, topics, and themes does the Bible address? This is a weighty question. Yet, to be faithful to the stewardship of systematics, we must answer it. What is the Bible all about? In a word, the Bible is all about God. It focuses on who and what he is, on what he does, and on what he requires of us. The Bible is not man-centered, but God-centered. How can we best present and develop this burden and focus of the Bible?

The Shorter Catechism furnishes a superb model for this presentation. Question Two asks, "What rule has God given to direct us how we may glorify and enjoy him?" They answer, "The Word of God, the Scriptures of the Old and New Testaments." The Greek word for "rule" is κανων (kanon), from which we get "canonics." Thus, systematics begins with the doctrine of the Word of God, the inspired and only rule of faith and duty. The doctrine of Scripture grounds the rest of systematics. The next question in the Shorter Catechism is: "What do the Scriptures principally teach?" They answer, "The Scriptures principally teach what man is to believe concerning God, and what duty God requires of man." This pivotal answer regulates the structure of the rest of the Catechism. Questions 4-38 expound the first part of their answer, questions 39-107, the second part.[131] First they mention: "what man is to *believe concerning God*." In a narrower sense this is the sum of the Christian faith. It includes the doctrine of God and his works. It encompasses the heart and core of systematics. Second they mention: "what *duty God requires* of man." This defines the sum of Christian duty, the doctrine of God's revealed will. The Greek word for what is expected, required, or proper, is ἐθος (ethos), which we transliterate, "ethics." Thus, Christian ethics declares the sum of Christian duty as the conclusion or capstone of systematics.

Now I must clarify this. In its broadest sense, the Christian faith includes what we believe about God's Word (canonics) and his revealed will (ethics). Thus, it is useful to have a word that describes the core of the faith, "what we are to believe concerning God." Following the footsteps of our fathers, we return to Greek terms in search for a word. Recall that the major biblical terms for "the faith" are "the truth," "doctrine," and "dogma." Thus, I could use, "dogmatics," for this purpose. But another significance for dogma

---

[131] A detailed outline of this appears in *The Shorter Catechism: A Baptist Version*, (Simpson Publishing Co, 1991)

could engender even more confusion. Therefore, using the Greek word, διδαχη (didache), "doctrine," I call the core of systematics, *"didactics."* Thus, in sum, systematics, includes an introduction (canonics), a core (didactics), and a conclusion (ethics). The Shorter Catechism commends this overall development of the major branches of systematics. I present an overview of the content and development of systematic theology on the following page.

THE CONTENT OF SYSTEMATIC THEOLOGY: BIBLICAL DOGMATICS

INTRODUCTION: THE DOCTRINE OF GOD'S WORD: *CANONICS*
(THE RULE OF FAITH AND DUTY)

CORE: THE DOCTRINE OF GOD AND HIS WORKS: *DIDACTICS*
(WHAT WE BELIEVE CONCERNING GOD)

FIRST: THE DOCTRINE OF GOD

Part 1 - The Existence of God
Part 2 - The Knowledge of God
Part 3 - The Nature of God
Part 4 - The Names of God
Part 5 - The Decree of God

SECOND: THE DOCTRINE OF THE ORIGINAL CREATION

Part 1 - Formation of the Original Creation: The Doctrine of Creation
Part 2 - Preservation of the Original Creation: The Doctrine of Providence
Part 3 - Culmination of the Original Creation: The Doctrine of Man
Part 4 - Devastation of the Original Creation: The Doctrine of Sin
Part 5 - Benevolence to the Original Creation: The Doctrine of Common Grace

THIRD: THE DOCTRINE OF SALVATION

Part 1 - The Plan of Salvation: The Doctrine of Predestination
Part 2 - The Promise of Salvation: The Doctrine of God's Covenants
Part 3 - The Accomplishment of Salvation: The Doctrine of Jesus Christ
Part 4 - The Application of Salvation:

   Section 1 The Community Formed: The Doctrine of the Church
   Section 2 The Blessings Bestowed: The Doctrine of the Christian Life
   Section 3 The Personal Agent: The Doctrine of the Holy Spirit

Part 5 - The Completion of Salvation: The Doctrine of the Consummation

CONCLUSION: THE DOCTRINE OF GOD'S REVEALED WILL: *ETHICS*
(WHAT DUTY GOD REQUIRES OF US)

Now we briefly review the content and development of each branch of systematics.

I. *The Introduction to Systematics:* Canonics

Canonics, the doctrine of Scripture, introduces systematic theology. Some call it "prolegomena," which is a transliteration of a Greek participle that means, "the things being said beforehand." That's just a fancy way to say, "introduction." Therefore, systematics begins with what the Bible says about itself. It has never been my province to teach Canonics. Reformed Baptist Seminary (RBS) does not neglect canonics. It is simply not part of my stewardship.

II. *The Core of Systematics:* Didactics

We first consider the content and presentation of Didactics. This is the scope of my stewardship at RBS and the substance of this series of lectures in systematic theology.

A. *The Content of Didactics*

What are we to believe concerning God? We are to believe what the Bible says about who and what God is, and about what God does. The core of systematics, of our faith, is the biblical teaching about God and his works. This core of systematics has three focal points, usually called "loci." The first focal point is the doctrine of God. The second is the doctrine of the original creation. The third is the doctrine of salvation. When you boil it all down to these basics, its core is very simple: God, creation, and salvation.

1. The first focus is on God himself.

Now, in a sense, all systematics is about God. The Bible is God's Word. God is the Creator and Savior. The law and gospel are God's revealed will. I mean, however, that we focus explicitly on who and what he is. Why do we start with God? The Bible begins with God: "in the beginning God." We start with him because the Bible does. We organize our first focal point around God's eternal existence, because God existed before he ever formed the earth and the world.

2. The second focus is on the original creation.

The Bible opens with the work of creation: "in the beginning God created the heavens and the earth." God brought everything that exists, both in the material and spiritual world, into existence.

We expound the doctrine of God's work of creation in five parts. In this we follow the biblical story of the original creation. Scripture begins with *the formation* of the original creation (Gen. 1:1-2:3). Many passages confirm and elucidate the witness of this key passage. Scripture continues with *the preservation* of the original creation, the doctrine of providence. The God who made everything sustains and rules everything he made. Scripture is replete with assertions respecting God's role in history. The first of the ten histories in Genesis (Gen. 2:4-4:26) displays the close connection between creation and providence. Scripture next features *the culmination* of creation, the final creature that God made, man. God gave him dominion over all his other creatures. He alone, of all the creatures, is *"the image of God"* (Gen. 1:26-28). Then Scripture relates the sad story of the key event that steered the course of the history of the original creation, namely, the fall of man (Gen. 3:6; Rom. 5:12-21). Thus, we next take up *the devastation* of the original creation, the doctrine of sin. Finally, Scripture features God's forbearance and *benevolence* to the original creation, even after the fall. Even when God judges for sin, he acts with great forbearance toward sinners. He is kind to the unthankful and to the evil (Gen. 3:21, 8:22-9:17; Rom. 2:4). Therefore, we conclude the doctrine of creation with the doctrine of common grace.

This is the story of the original creation in biblical categories. I have not imposed this story on the Bible. Rather, the Bible has "imposed" this story on us. We couldn't have dreamed it up in a "million years." This "story," as I have dubbed it, is biblical dogma. It is an essential part of the Christian faith.

3. The third focus is on salvation from sin.

Blessed be God, that's not the whole story. If the tragic tale of the creation were the whole story, we wouldn't have a Christian faith to expound! The glory of the Bible, its major purpose, is to proclaim that God has done a work even more glorious than creation, the work of salvation from sin.

a. The eternal plan of salvation

First, the Bible tells us that God planned salvation from sin in eternity before he created the world: "even as he chose us in him before the foundation of the world" (Eph. 1:3). It teaches that from all eternity God chose some sinners for salvation in Jesus Christ, while he destined other sinners to be hardened in their sins unto eternal ruin: "so then he has mercy on whom he will, and whom he will he hardens" (Rom. 9:18). God's plan to save discloses the mystery of election and reprobation. Thus, we begin with *the plan* of salvation, the doctrine of predestination.

b. The solemn promise of salvation

Passing from eternity into history, we first encounter God's stated purpose to save sinners immediately after the fall (Gen. 3:15). God did not accomplish his saving work immediately after this announcement. Rather, with greater light and solemn promises, called covenants, he prepared a solid framework in which to perform salvation from sin in Christ. Thus, we next expound *the solemn promise* of salvation, the doctrine of God's covenants.

c. *The accomplishment of salvation*

Then in the fullness of time God sent his Son into the world to accomplish this great work of salvation from sin. Matthew explains the purpose of his mission: "you shall call his name Jesus, for he it is that shall save his people from their sins" (Matt. 1:21). The story of Jesus Christ and what he came to do is the very heart of salvation from sin. Thus, we expound *the accomplishment* of salvation, the doctrine of the person and work of Jesus Christ.

d. *The application of salvation*

When the Lord returned to heaven, having accomplished the work he came to do, he poured forth his Spirit upon his people. He sent his servants to proclaim his salvation to sinners from every kindred, tribe and tongue. He gathered them together into his saved society. These things constitute *the application* of salvation. They encompass the doctrines of the Christian church, the Christian life, and the Holy Spirit. Scripture affirms this distinction between the accomplishment and application of salvation (Rom. 3:21-22, 8:3-4; 2 Cor. 5:21). The Spirit dwells in the heart of each individual Christian and in the midst of each true Christian church, so that each Christian is a temple of God, and each church is a temple of God. The Holy Spirit spiritually unites the resurrected and exalted Christ to every true Christian and to every true Christian church. This shows us the close connection between the Christian life and the Christian church. We expound the blessings and graces bestowed in the Christian life on every true Christian. Yet, these very blessings are the blessings of the new covenant, and thus, the distinctive possession of the Christian church. The person and work of the Holy Spirit unites these three aspects of the doctrine of the application of salvation.

e. *The completion of salvation*

Finally, salvation is not complete in this life. After death the souls of the righteous, freed from sin, enter the presence and joy of Christ in heaven (Phil. 1:21-23). The final consummation of salvation, however, occurs when Christ comes again (2 Thess. 1:7-10). Then he will present the church to himself a glorious church, without blemish or fault (Eph. 5:27). Then death and the grave will be swallowed up in the victory of the resurrection body (1 Cor. 15:23, 50-58; 1 Thess. 4:13-18). Then, we will dwell in a new heavens and earth wherein dwells righteousness (2 Pet. 3:8-13). Then the wicked will go away to everlasting torment and punishment, but the righteous to eternal life (Matt. 25:31-46). Thus, we conclude the story of God's work of salvation with *the completion* of salvation, the doctrine of the consummation, commonly called the doctrine of the last things, or eschatology.

This is the glorious core of our faith. We confess and proclaim the biblical doctrines of God, creation, and salvation. The Reformed confessions of faith and theologians all recognize the importance of these three primary themes and focal points of Scripture.

B. *The Presentation of Didactics*

Widespread agreement exists concerning the identity of these topics and their order of presentation. The amount of biblical material for each topic and the constraints of time are the primary factors that regulate how I present didactics. I have typically used seven courses, each contained in a separate syllabus:

1. Theology: the Doctrine of God
2. Anthropology: the Doctrine of Man
3. Christology: the Doctrine of Christ
4. Ecclesiology: the Doctrine of the Church
5. Soteriology: the Doctrine of the Christian Life
6. Pneumatology: the Doctrine of the Holy Spirit
7. Eschatology: the Doctrine of the Completion of Salvation

The name of each of these courses is derived from two Greek words. The Greek word for "a discourse," λογος (logos), is combined with the Greek word for each topic. For example, the term "theology" combines the Greek for "God," θεος (theos), with logos. Thus, "theology" means "a discourse about God." I wish briefly to explain how each of these courses relates to the major themes and topics that we expound in systematics.

The Theology course expounds the first focal point, God himself. The Anthropology course expounds the second focal point, the original creation. We often call it the "Doctrine of Man" because man is the apex of the original creation. We could also call it the Doctrine of the Original Creation. Five courses expound the third and final focal point, salvation from sin. The Christology course expounds the plan, promise, and accomplishment of salvation. Three courses cover the application of salvation. The Ecclesiology course expounds the corporate application of salvation in the Christian church. The Soteriology course expounds the individual application of salvation in the Christian life. The Pneumatology course expounds personal agent of the application of salvation, the person and work of the Holy Spirit. The Eschatology course expounds the completion of salvation.

III. The Conclusion to Systematics: *Ethics*

The conclusion of systematics is Christian ethics, the doctrine of God's revealed will. The Shorter Catechism sums this branch of systematics with the phrase, "what duty God requires of man." Further, it furnishes us with an excellent treatment of the sum and substance of Christian ethics. It expounds man's duty of obedience to God's gospel and to God's law. The first pillar of Christian duty is obedience to the gospel. This consists of repentance toward God and faith in the Lord Jesus Christ (Acts 20:21). The second pillar of Christian duty is evangelical obedience to God's law, the Ten Commandments.

The Shorter Catechism begins its exposition with God's law. In redemptive history God first *emphatically* disclosed his law at Sinai when he entered into the old covenant with his people. Afterward, through the person and work of Christ, he emphatically disclosed his gospel, when he entered into the new covenant with his people. Thus, the Shorter Catechism adopts this covenantal order of redemptive history (law→gospel). Even though I speak of the "emphatic" disclosure of law and gospel in redemptive history, I do not mean that God never revealed the gospel at all before the incarnation (Gal. 3:8), or that he never disclosed the substance of the decalogue in any sense until Sinai (Rom. 2:14-15).

The Heidelberg Catechism also expounds these two aspects of Christian duty. However, it first expounds God's gospel. It adopts the order in which Christians experience them in the Christian life (gospel→law). First, Christians obey the gospel, exercising repentance and faith. Afterward, we obey God's law, with gospel obedience to the decalogue in the power of the indwelling Holy Spirit. Disaster results if we attempt to reverse this order. Sinners cannot first obey the law so that they can obey the gospel. Further, all individuals who experience salvation, whether under the old or new covenant, first obey the gospel, then the law. God never required legalistic obedience from his people. Even under the old covenant, he required evangelical obedience.

The doctrine of ethics is also outside the scope of my present stewardship to teach systematics.

Conclusion to Prologue: *A Vision for Systematic Theology*

Scripture commends the superlative value of sound doctrine for every church, every pastor, and every Christian. This commendation shapes my vision for systematic theology.

Every Church Needs Systematics

Sound doctrine promotes ecclesiastical peace, health, and preservation: "they delivered them *the decrees* [dogmata] to keep which had been ordained of the apostles and elders that were at Jerusalem. So the churches were strengthened in *the faith*, and increased in number daily" (Acts 16:4-5). Apostolic "dogma" settles religious controversy. It prevents heresy from eating through the churches like a cancer. Accordingly, it strengthens churches in the Christian faith: "so the churches were strengthened in the faith." It preserves the churches by numerical growth: "and increased in number daily." Thus, Scripture views the whole body of revealed truth from different perspectives. It is both the sum of the doctrines that Christians believe and of the regulations that order the Christian church. Therefore, systematics is of great importance. It prevents doctrinal cancer from consuming the churches. It promotes the peace, strength, unity, and numerical growth of the churches. This is why every church should be grounded in systematic theology.

Every Pastor Needs Systematics

Sound doctrine promotes a good conscience for pastors: "I am pure from the blood of all men, for I did not shrink from declaring unto you the whole counsel of God" (Acts 20:26-27). The Bible reveals everything Christians need to know to live a godly life and to make wise choices about religion and eternity. A gospel minister must have the courage to declare every aspect of God's revealed will. He must proclaim faithfully the sum of Christian faith and duty. Then he will maintain a good conscience: "for I did not shrink." How can gospel ministers declare the whole counsel of God unless they are well grounded in the Christian faith? How else can they exhort in the sound doctrine and convict the gainsayers (Titus 1:9)? This is why it is so important for every gospel minister to learn and be proficient in systematic theology.

Every Christian Needs Systematics

Sound doctrine promotes spiritual unity and maturity: "till we all attain unto the unity of the faith . . . that we may no longer be children . . . carried about with every wind of doctrine" (Eph. 4:13-14). The Christian faith is the whole set of inspired doctrines, the body of biblical and apostolic divinity. Christians attain *"the unity of the faith"* when they grasp and confess what the Bible says about the most important religious topics. Ignorance of sound doctrine splinters Christians and inhibits conformity to Christ. Apathy about sound doctrine is no virtue or asset. It is a vice, liability, and problem. Sound doctrine separates the men from the boys: *"that we may no longer be children."* Thus, topical teaching pertains to all Christians and church members: "till *we all attain* unto the unity of the faith." Sound doctrine prevents division and chronic immaturity, fosters spiritual growth and unity, and promotes God's honor and glory. Therefore, since every Christian should strive to attain "*the unity of the faith*," every Christian needs systematic theology.

This fuels my vision for a systematic theology that does not confuse or discourage Christians hungering to learn sound doctrine. I envision topical teaching that Christians sitting in the pews can readily follow and grasp, which edifies them and feed their souls. I envision a systematics that directly addresses their hearts, not one zooming over their heads in the "theological stratosphere." Thus, I aim to ground Christians in the sound doctrines of the Christian faith. When those in the pews stand committed to the whole body of revealed truth, they insist that those who stand in their pulpits preach sound doctrine. Herein lies our only hope to see our rich theological heritage transmitted unimpaired to succeeding generations of our spiritual heirs.

For this reason, I behold with dismay the apathy and antipathy to systematic theology that defile, it seems, almost every part of religious life in modern America. Some tell us that all topical teaching distorts and misrepresents the Bible, because it imposes our way of thinking on God. Others tell us that theology itself is sinful, because God can only be known by "spiritual contact and experience," which, they say, theology hinders. Others add that what we need today is love, not doctrine. They tell us that doctrine merely divides Christians. Others go even further—if that were possible—and assure us that it doesn't matter what men believe. Such simply can't be bothered with Christian doctrine. They ask, "Who cares?" They lack hunger to learn about the things of God.

We must not allow all this apathy and antipathy to dim our vision. Every church, pastor, and Christian needs systematic theology, even if relatively few realize the superlative value of sound doctrine. Therefore, I aim to inoculate you against insidious attacks on systematics that may threaten your minds and hearts. I aim to establish you in the Christian faith. My hope and prayer is that love for systematics will burn in your hearts as it does in mine, to the end that God will receive greater glory in the church and in Christ in every generation until Jesus comes.

Topic 1. Introduction to the Doctrine of God
"Show me, I pray you, your glory" (Exod. 33:18)

Introduction: *Overview of the Doctrine of God*

This first topic sets these lectures in perspective. Moses' prayer, "Show me, I pray you, your glory," comes from a heart filled with God. Few things are more needful in our day than men who are God-centered. We live in an age especially enthralled with man and his works. Godless humanism and self-absorption pollute the waters of every branch of human study and endeavor. Nothing smells worse than the stench of their insidious influence on religion and theology. Nothing cures these maladies better than permeating our minds and hearts with the biblical teaching about God. Nothing is better for our spiritual health than fixing our gaze on God's glory. Nothing honors God more than a God-centered approach to every aspect of life. We desperately need more of God, less of man, in everything. We need more of God in the churches. We need more of God in worship. We need more of God in preaching. We need more of God in evangelism. We need more of God in our doctrines. We need more of God in our devotions. We need more of God in our families, schools, government, laws, and society. If we would have more of God in our lives, then we must contemplate who and what he really is until our hearts are lost in wonder, love, and praise. Our souls must be humbled and ravished with his majesty.

Therefore, we need to learn and embrace, from our hearts, what the Bible teaches about God. Nothing will make us godlier as Christians and as churches. Nothing will be more conducive to bringing him the praise that he infinitely deserves. Herein abides the value of the doctrine of God. This is why a biblical concept of God should permeate the soul of every church member, every grandparent, every breadwinner, every wife and mother, every teenager, every school teacher, every civil servant, everyone. We all need the biblical doctrine of God. It is not only for ministers, seminary students, philosophers, and scholars. Therefore brethren, we have strong incentive to labor ardently to master the biblical doctrine of God.

We now consider, *first*, the overall content and development of the doctrine of God; *second*, the requirements for the doctrine of God; and *third*, a wholesome attitude toward the doctrine of God.

I. The Content and Development of the Doctrine of God

With this end in view, let's survey the content and development of the doctrine of God.

First, in Part 1 we address *the existence of God*. We consider the fact that God is. The Bible presupposes God's existence: "*In the beginning God created.*" Indeed, all sound theology rests on the dual assumption that one true God exists and that the Bible is his Word. In other words, we presuppose that the God of the Bible is the one and only true and living God. We presuppose this because Scripture does. Thus, we think biblically. Someone may say, "You reason in circles." Yes, biblical circles. Our whole approach to systematic theology assumes that the God of the Bible exists, and that the Bible is the Word of God. This is why we study what the Bible says about God and his works. We never try to prove by human reason these assumptions on which our faith rests, because our faith does not rest on human reason. The Bible, not human logic or wisdom, is our ultimate authority for systematic theology.

Second, in Part 2 we consider *the knowledge of God.* Here the question is: can we know the true and living God? If so, how can we know him? Scripture teaches that we can know God truly, accurately, and personally, even though we can never know him exhaustively. Thus, we study the knowledge of God in two units: the *"knowability"* and *incomprehensibility* of God.

Third, in Part 3 we expound *the nature of God.* Who and what is God? What is he like? What does Scripture tell us about his nature? The nature of God embraces his being, attributes, form, and personality, all he essentially is. Thus, it shouldn't shock you that our study of God's nature constitutes the bulk of this course. The pillars of God's nature are his spirituality, supremacy, and simplicity. God is one, the Supreme Being, the Supreme Spirit. In deference to God's simplicity we treat God's nature as a single part of the course, composed of ten sections. In deference to God's supremacy and spirituality, we arrange these ten sections in two divisions. The first division, sections 1-5, unfolds his supremacy, the second, sections 6-10, his spirituality. These divisions correspond to what Reformed theologians have called God's "incommunicable" and "communicable" attributes. The "incommunicable" attributes especially relate to God's supremacy (sections 1-5), the "communicable" to his spirituality (sections 6-10). Accordingly, we develop God's nature as follows: Section 1, his ideality, infinite and absolute perfection; Section 2, his self-existence, aseity and independence; Section 3, his infinity, especially with respect to space, his omnipresence; Section 4, his eternity, especially with respect to time, his ever-presence; Section 5, his immutability; Section 6, his incorporeality, his majestic form; Section 7, his animacy, unoriginated and unlimited life and power, omnipotence; Section 8, his faculty, metaphysical capacity, his infinite mind (omniscience), unlimited will (sovereignty), and absolute affection (emotivity); Section 9, his morality, impeccable moral character, his goodness, holiness, justice and faithfulness; Section 10, his personality, triunity, the mystery of the Trinity. We approach God properly only when we think of him biblically.

Fourth, in Part 4 we consider *the names of God*. How does God denominate himself? What names describe him? How does God want his worshippers to address him? We answer such crucial questions.

Fifth, in Part 5 we consider *the decree of God.* In eternity, before creation, God planned everything he would do: "who works all things after the counsel of his own will" (Eph. 1:11). In eternity, he decided to create: "because of your will they were, and were created" (Rev. 4:11). In eternity, he decided to save: "even as he chose us in him before the foundation of the world" (Eph. 1:3). God's decree, determined and fixed in eternity, is the ultimate cause and foundation of all his works. It unifies and certifies them. Therefore, God's decree serves as the bridge to our study of God's works of creation and salvation.

In conclusion, here is the heart of the doctrine of God. First, Is there a God? Yes. Second, Can we truly know God? Yes, but not exhaustively. Third, Who and what is God? God is one, the Supreme Being, the Supreme Spirit. Fourth, How should we address God? We should use the names he gives us in his Word. Fifth, What has God planned? God in eternity decided whatever happens in history. I close with the perspective that opens and governs the Shorter Catechism: "What is the chief end of man?" "Man's chief end is to glorify God, and to enjoy him forever." We never fulfill our primary purpose and privilege as human beings more than when we contemplate and adore God. We can never experience greater joy than when we gaze on the living God and commune with him by his Word and Spirit.

II. The Requirements for the Doctrine of God (for students)

It seems right to publish these requirements. We require three things of students: (1) reading or hearing all the lectures; (2) completing the assigned reading; (3) mastering the final exam.

A. Attendance to all the Lectures

The reason for this requirement is simple. Regarding the right way to prepare men for the ministry, Paul said: "these things *commit* to faithful men." Thus, we labor to *commit* the doctrine of God as a sacred trust to faithful men. Each lecture addresses an important aspect of that sacred trust.

B. Completion of the Assigned Reading[1]

Paul also exhorted Timothy to give himself to reading. Reading is a necessary part of a systematics course. It supplements the lectures and establishes their theological framework. It taps into the riches of illumination that the Holy Spirit has shined upon the servants and church of God. The two primary textbooks come from the circle of Dutch Calvinism. I select Bavinck because of his thoroughness, theological acumen, and breadth of scriptural materials. I select Berkhof because of his clarity of structure and concise definitions. I assign sections of Calvin's *Institutes* because of his significant insights, especially respecting the knowledge of God and the Trinity. I assign those sections of Gill's *Body of Divinity* in which he expounds God's emotive life, because his treatment is both singular and superb. I assign Warfield's article on the Trinity because he masterfully shows how the biblical testimony develops. I also recommend to students books that I think will be useful over the long haul. Charnock's exposition of God's existence and attributes is a classic. Two other books that I strongly recommend are, *The Sovereignty of God*, by A. W. Pink, and, *Knowing God*, by J. I. Packer. As a young Christian I read more than a few books; yet no book by a modern author blessed my soul as much as these two. Finally, I recommend pertinent sections in five systematics works because they furnish a good handle on the best insights of Reformed theology.

C. Mastery of the Final Exam

Paul urged Timothy to study to show himself approved. Students must demonstrate mastery of the doctrine of God. A comprehensive exam is simply a means to that end. The exam has no trick questions. My stewardship is not to trick students, but to commit these truths to them as a sacred trust.

I hope that relating what I require of students benefits your souls. Yet I do not wish to end with the mundane; so I conclude with the wholesome attitude with which we should study the doctrine of God.

III. A Wholesome Attitude Toward the Doctrine of God

Note well the demeanor with which we should study God's existence, knowledge, nature, names, and decree. We discern this from key texts that describe how God's servants approach God and behold the disclosure of his

---

[1] I have attached as an appendix to this topic a list of the reading that I assign and recommend for the doctrine of God.

nature, attributes, and glory. Consider five aspects of this wholesome disposition.

A. Reverent Hunger

> And Jehovah said to Moses, I will do this thing also that you have spoken; for you have found favor in my sight, and I know you by name. And he said: show me, I pray you, your glory. And he said, I will make all my goodness pass before you, and will proclaim the name of Jehovah before you (Exod. 33:17-18).

Moses hungered to see God's glory. He pleaded: "Show me, I pray you, your glory." This should be our prayer as we study the doctrine of God. Reverent hunger to see God's glory should motivate us. We must hunger to see the glory of his existence, knowledge, nature, names, and decree. We must hunger to know God and thirst after the knowledge of God. Further, the Lord promised to give Moses the desire of his heart: "I will make all my goodness pass before you, and will proclaim the name of Jehovah before you." God also fulfilled this promise.[2] When we come to God with reverent hunger, he will fill our hearts with the knowledge of himself. He will not disappoint us. He will surely show us his glory, and satisfy us with the display of his Name. Further, Moses drew near with *reverent* hunger, for when God answered his prayer we read: "And Moses made haste, and bowed his head toward the earth, and worshipped." We should not approach the doctrine of God with a critical spirit, or as a philosophical quest with a hunger for speculation. If any study in systematic theology should evoke spiritual hunger, this one should. The doctrine of God should never be dull, or dry, or speculative, or philosophical. It should pulse with spiritual life and hunger. Let's approach this study with Moses' disposition.

B. Contrite Humility

> In the year that king Uzziah died I saw the Lord sitting upon a throne, high and lifted up; and his train filled the temple. Above him stood the seraphim: each one had six wings; with twain he covered his face, and with twain he covered his feet, and with twain he did fly. And one cried to another, and said: holy, holy, holy, is Jehovah of hosts: the whole earth is full of his glory. And the foundations of the thresholds shook at the voice of him that cried, and the house was filled with smoke (Isa. 6:1-4).

In this work we see no prophetic vision. Rather, with our spiritual eye we see the Lord in his Word. Thus, we should gaze on God's glory with the

---

[2] *Exod. 34:6-7*: And Jehovah passed by before him, and proclaimed, Jehovah, Jehovah, a God merciful and gracious, slow to anger, and abundant in lovingkindness and truth; keeping lovingkindness for thousands, forgiving iniquity and transgression and sin; and that will by no means clear the guilty, visiting the iniquity of the fathers upon the children, and upon the children's children, upon the third and upon the fourth generation.

same demeanor that marked Isaiah. What glory did Isaiah see? He saw the glory of God's supremacy and holiness: "And one cried to another, and said: holy, holy, holy is Jehovah of hosts: the whole earth is full of his glory." John tells us that Isaiah saw Jesus' glory, and spoke of him (John 12:41). He saw Christ exalted, seated at God's right hand. How did he respond? "Then said I, Woe is me! For I am undone; because I am a man of unclean lips, and I dwell in the midst of a people of unclean lips: for mine eyes have seen the King, Jehovah of hosts" (Isa. 6:5). When he saw the Lord's majesty, he felt his own wretchedness. He was undone. He felt his lips unclean and unsuitable to speak for God. Isaiah wasn't living in gross sin. Rather, when he saw the glory of God the Son, he became acutely aware of his own remaining corruption.

Job had a similar experience. When he attained a better grasp on God's power and his sovereignty over his suffering, he also attained a deeper sight of his own remaining corruption.[3] Job was already aware of God's power and sovereignty. Still, he confessed that suffering brought him to a deeper experience of them: "I know that you can do all things," [the omnipotence of God], and, "that no purpose of yours can be restrained," [the sovereignty of God]. What did that deeper insight into God's glory produce? It created a deeper experience of his remaining sin: "Wherefore I abhor myself, and repent in dust and ashes." Calvin (*Institutes*: 1:1:2) also saw this connection:[4]

> man never achieves a clear knowledge of himself unless he has first looked upon God's face, and then descends from contemplating him to scrutinize himself. For we always seem to ourselves righteous and upright and wise and holy—this pride is innate in all of us—unless by clear proofs we stand convinced of our own unrighteousness, foulness, folly, and impurity. Moreover we are not thus convinced if we look merely to ourselves and not also to the Lord, who is the sole standard by which this judgment must be measured.

Our study of God should increase our sense of our own smallness and sinfulness. In this class our spiritual eyes will see the King, Jehovah of hosts, high and lifted up. We will see him in his supremacy, sovereignty, omnipotence, holiness, majesty, splendor, and glory. When we see more of

---

[3] *Job 42:2-6*: I know that you can do all things, and that no purpose of yours can be restrained. Who is this that hides counsel without knowledge? Therefore have I uttered that which I understood not, things too wonderful for me, which I knew not. Hear, I beseech you, and I will speak; I will demand of you, and you declare unto me. I had heard of you by the hearing of the ear; but now mine eye sees you: wherefore I abhor myself, and repent in dust and ashes.

[4] John Calvin, *Institutes of the Christian Religion*, translator Ford Lewis Battles (2 Vols.; Philadelphia, PA: The Westminster Press, 1967), 1:37.

the wisdom of God, we see more of our own ignorance. When we see more of God's power, we see more of our own impotence. When we see more of God's holiness, we see more of our own wretchedness and uncleanness. When we see more of his supremacy and independence, we see more of our own dependence. When we see more of his love and justice, we see more of our own selfishness and prejudice. The more we behold his glory, supremacy, sovereignty, and purity, the more we sense how small, weak, ignorant, and wretched we really are.

C. Saving Faith

> And without faith it is impossible to be well pleasing to him. For he that comes to God must believe that he is, and that he's the rewarder of those that diligently seek him (Heb. 11:6).

Just as speculation and arrogance have no place in our study of God, so also Scripture banishes unbelief. If any study should be conducted in faith, it's the study of God. How can we pray: "Show me your glory," without faith? How can we seek him without faith? Unbelief can never contemplate and approach God acceptably, because: "without faith it is *impossible* to be well pleasing to him." Thus, no study of God that is conducted in a spirit of "higher" criticism and skepticism can possibly please God or profit men. Thus I assign no such reading. Some may scoff at this. Others may call it "unscholarly" or "obscurantist." So be it. Godless "scholarship" is too abundant in our day, and greatly overrated. Saving faith is too rare, and undervalued. I prefer to expose you to the edifying writings of believers, not to subject you to the spiritual poison of unbelievers who falsely label their skeptical speculations as "Christian theology."

D. Imitation of God's Virtues

> But you are an elect race, a royal priesthood, a holy nation, a people for God's own possession, that you may show forth the excellences of him who called you out of darkness into his marvelous light (1 Pet. 2:9).

We should be committed to imitate God's virtues. When we attain increased appreciation for who he is, we should endeavor to be more like him. We are the image of God as his beloved children. Thus we should strive to reflect the perfection of our heavenly Father (Matt. 5:48). We study his love so that our love may reflect his more accurately. We study his holiness, justice, and faithfulness, so that we may show forth these virtues more consistently in our lives. We should not resist the pressure exerted by any moral implication of who and what God is. Rather, the desire of our hearts should be to see his glory so that we can more faithfully, by his grace and power, display his virtue in our lives. Our study of God should cause us more and more to see him as he is and be like him.

E. Grateful Adoration to God

We return to the account with which we began. When, in answer to his prayer, Moses saw all God's goodness: "Moses made haste, and bowed his head to the earth, and worshipped." Similarly, when John saw the Lord in his glory, he fell at his feet as one dead. Again, when those who surround the throne contemplate the glory of God the Creator and Redeemer, they fall down and worship (Rev. 1:17, 4:11, 5:14, 11:16). We should do likewise. When we see the glory of God's existence, knowledge, nature, name, and decree set before us in the Word of God, we must make haste, bow our heads, and worship. We should approach each aspect of the doctrine of God with a disposition of grateful adoration. Any other attitude would be sacrilege. This syudy must not be merely an academic or intellectual exercise. It must never deteriorate into a venture in philosophical speculation. Such an approach to the doctrine of God would be insulting to God and disgraceful. Therefore, let us remember always to return thanks to God for all we learn about him in this course. He is infinitely worthy of our sincere praises.

In sum, we should hunger to see his glory. We should recognize our own remaining sin. We must come in faith, believing whatever God says in His Word. We should strive to be more like him. We should bow before him in grateful adoration. This is the only proper attitude with which to study the doctrine of God. May the Lord be pleased to produce this demeanor in abundance in our hearts as we pursue these studies together, to the end that he may be pleased and glorified, and to the end that we may know him better, enjoy him more, and through this material experience greater measures of communion with him.

APPENDIX TO TOPIC 1: REQUIRED READING

Primary Textbooks: Required Reading: 813 pages

Louis Berkhof, *Systematic Theology*
Herman Bavinck, *The Doctrine of God*

John Murray, *Collected Writings*, Vol. 4: Berkhof, *Introduction to Systematic Theo* 15-89 Strong, *Systematic Theology*, p. 1-51 Hodge, *Systematic Theology*, Vol. 1: p. 1- Kersten, G. H., *Reformed Dogmatics*, Vol xiii-xviii Van Til, *Defense of the Faith*, p. 3-22	**INTRODUCTION TO SYSTEMATIC THEOLOGY**
Bavinck, p. 65-80 Berkhof, p. 19-28	**THE EXISTENCE OF GOD**
Berkhof, p. 29-40 Bavinck, p. 13-64 Packer, *Knowing God*, Ch. 3, p. 29-37 Calvin, *Institutes*, 1:1-5, p. 35-69 (Battles Edition)	**THE KNOWLEDGE OF GOD**
Bavinck, p. 113-251 Berkhof, p. 41-46, 52-81 Gill, *Body of Divinity*, p. 71-84; 112-148; 175	**THE NATURE OF GOD** God's Attributes
Bavinck, p. 255-334 Berkhof, p. 82-99 Warfield, *Biblical and Theological Studie* 22-59 Calvin, *Institutes*, 1:13, p. 120-159 (Battle Edition)	**THE NATURE OF GOD** The Trinity
Bavinck, p. 83-110 Berkhof, p. 47-51	**THE NAMES OF GOD**
Bavinck, p. 337-407 Berkhof, p. 100-108	**THE DECREE OF GOD**

Recommended Additional Reading: Pages

Charnock, *The Existence and Attributes of God*, p. 11-802   792
Pink, *The Sovereignty of God*, p. 13-301   289
Packer, *Knowing God*, p. 1-158   158
Gill, *Body of Divinity*, Vol. 1, Book 1: p. 1-245   245
Kersten, *Reformed Dogmatics*, Vol. 1: p. 3-118   116
Strong, *Systematic Theology*, p. 243-370   128
Hodge, *Systematic Theology*, Vol. 1: p. 191-441   251
Dabney, *Lectures in Systematic Theology*, p. 5-144   140

Total Recommended Reading: 2119

Topic 2. The Existence of God

"Look unto me, and be saved, all the ends of the earth; for I am God, and there is none else" (Isa. 45:22);

"The fool has said in his heart, there is no God" (Ps. 14:1)

Part 1: The Existence of God

Introduction to Part 1: These "epitomizing texts" display the structure of the biblical witness to God's existence. They embody the primary categories in which Scripture presents it. The Lord never promises a teacher of theology that one text will provide the best handle on all the categories of revelation on any topic. Yet the Lord is merciful, and as it turns out, he often provides his servants with a few texts that epitomize his mind on a subject. These key texts serve as guides who lead us safely away from the pitfall of imposing our predispositions on Scripture. They enable us more readily to think God's thoughts after him. Consider the contribution of Isaiah 45:22 to this topic. The heart of the text is: "I am God." This phrase exposes the foundation of biblical thinking. It affirms that God's existence is *a fact*. This phrase also reveals the identity of the God who in fact exists, for it says: "*I* am God." Thus, the Bible furnishes an account of the self-disclosure, or *revelation*, of God's existence. The text also asserts the *uniqueness* of God's existence, for it says: "for I am God, *and there is none else.*" Finally, the text presses the moral and religious relevance of God's existence, for it says: "*Look unto me and be saved all the ends of the earth, for* I am God." Yet, I can't readily deduce from this text every major category of biblical revelation about God's existence. Even if I could force the poor text to introduce every major category, my presentation would be contrived.

This brings us to the important contribution that Psalm 14:1 makes to this topic. This text epitomizes an additional category of thought. It asserts plainly that foolish men deny God's existence: "The fool has said in his heart, there is no God." This text also makes moral applications. It reveals that the denial of God's existence in the heart always leads to moral degeneracy in the life: "The fool has said in his heart, There is no God. *They are corrupt, they have done abominable works.*" It reveals that the denial of God's existence in the heart is universal among sinners: "*There is none that does good.*"

Stephen Charnock recognized the importance of this text. He built his exposition of God's existence on it. He derives three major lessons from the text:[1]

---

[1] Stephen Charnock, *The Existence and Attributes of God* (Minneapolis, MN: Klock and Klock, 1977 reprint), 13.

I. It is great folly to deny or doubt of the existence or being of God; or, an atheist is a great fool. II. Practical atheism is natural to man in his corrupt state . . . III. A secret atheism, or a partial atheism, is the spring of all the wicked practices in the world.

We develop this topic accordingly in five units. *First*, in Unit 1 we consider *the fact* of God's existence. We demonstrate that Scripture both presupposes and asserts God's existence. *Second*, in Unit 2 we take up *the revelation* of God's existence. We demonstrate that Scripture describes the effective manner in which God reveals his existence certainly to all men. *Third*, in Unit 3 we address *the uniqueness* of God's existence. We show that Scripture insists that God is unique, that only one God exists, the God of the Bible. *Fourth*, in Unit 4 we address *the denial* of God's existence. Scripture plainly admits that some deny God's existence and exposes the real reasons for that denial. *Fifth* in Unit 5 we address the *practical relevance* of God's existence. God's Word presents his existence, not as a matter for philosophical speculation, but rather as the foundation of life, morality, and religion. It emphasizes its moral and experiential import.

Finally, suffer a brief word about philosophical speculation. Too much speculation surrounds this subject, as your assigned reading confirms. Theologians too often present God's existence philosophically, rather than in an expository, experiential, and devotional way. Their reasoning belongs in a course on philosophy, or historical theology, or apologetics, not in lectures that purport to convey scriptural testimony. Little they say would ground a godly mind in the Word, or nourish a hungry soul with truth.

Nonetheless, it is important to acquaint students with what they say. Thus, I assign my students reading that covers the so-called theistic proofs and the history and development of various schools of philosophy. My class lectures focus on biblical exposition. Rational arguments emit dim light. Merely presenting God's existence philosophically would abandon the stewardship of systematic theology. This is why I labor to unfold the biblical witness to God's existence in biblical categories. I aim to honor God's mind above man's mind. Let God have the preeminence. To him alone be glory.

Unit 1: The Fact of God's Existence

It is beneficial to distinguish the *being* of God from his *existence*. The existence of God dwells on the fact *that* God is. The being of God defines *who* and *what* God is. This lecture focuses on the biblical assertion *that* God is. Subsequent lectures expound the biblical witness to *who* and *what* God is. God's existence is a fact objective to us and independent of us. God does not need man to exist. His existence does not depend upon human awareness of it, belief in it, or confession of it. Whether men embrace God's existence or deny it, they don't alter it in the least. Our existence does not support God's; to the contrary, his existence is the ground of our existence (Acts 17:25). Now consider with me how Scripture both presupposes and asserts God's existence.

I. Presupposition of God's Existence

Scripture implicitly assumes, or presupposes, the fact that God exists. The first line of the Bible presupposes his existence: "In the beginning God created the heavens and the earth." Scripture simply assumes that God exists from the first line of Genesis to the last line of Revelation. The Bible does not begin with questions like, "Does God exist?" or "Is there a God?" It never questions or doubts God's existence. The evil doubts that men call "neutral objectivity," the Bible calls lies and folly. It never confers the honors of legitimacy or intellectual honesty on the notion that men don't know or can't know for certain that God exists. It never caters to agnosticism. Rather, it says that agnostics are liars and that atheists are fools.[2] For this reason the Bible doesn't begin with an attempt to prove by reason and logic that God exists. It doesn't start with an agnostic or atheistic perspective and attempt to coax the reader by empirical or rational evidence to believe in God's existence. It nowhere attempts such a feat. It never adopts agnosticism in order to reason its way to theism. Such an effort is futile, for Scripture asserts that men already know that God exists.[3] That philosophical quest, beyond futile, is unbiblical. In sum, the Bible begins by presupposing God's existence. It always maintains this posture. Thus, to be biblical, we must do likewise. Bavinck rightly begins on this note. He says: "For example, the Bible never makes any attempt to prove the existence of God but assumes this; and it presupposes all along that man has an ineradicable idea of that existence, and that he has a certain knowledge of the being of God."[4]

II. Assertion of God's Existence

Scripture explicitly asserts the fact of God's existence in two major ways. First, God asserts his existence personally in the first person. Second, God's people explicitly assert his existence.

A. Divine Assertion

God affirms his existence directly in the first person: "I am God, and there is none else." He asserts that he alone is the Supreme Being. He gives his

---

[2] Rom. 1:18, 19, 25; Ps. 14:1
[3] Rom. 1:18-23, 25, 28
[4] Herman Bavinck, *The Doctrine of God* (Edinburgh: The Banner of Truth Trust, 1977), 14.

personal testimony. This allows no neutrality. Our response to his testimony is intensely personal and moral. It exposes our personal relationship with him and our heart attitude toward him. It isn't a theoretical matter, or an innocent intellectual exercise. It demonstrates whether we love or hate God, whether we reject or receive him, whether we have or lack confidence in him, whether we are loyal or disloyal to him. Therefore, questioning his existence maligns his veracity. It discredits his Word. It insults God, calls him a liar, and declares war against him. If we grant that doubting God's existence is objective, or morally neutral, or intellectually legitimate, we reject the authority of the Bible. We can no longer cite it as decisive or binding. We set ourselves adrift, without anchor or compass, on a sea of confusion where the ultimate authority is the prejudicial reasoning of God's enemies. Can such a voyage land us anywhere but in shipwreck concerning the faith?

B. Human Assertion[5]

God's people assert his existence by the public confession of their faith. These confessions of faith have a common thread. They contrast the true God with idols. Idols do not exist in fact, but only in the delusions of those who create them. Only the God of the Bible exists in fact. Thus, the faith of God's people is not polytheistic, but monotheistic and exclusive. Confessing him to be a god among many gods is not faith, but unbelief and idolatry.

The affirmation of God's existence is an aspect of faith: "and without faith it is impossible to be well-pleasing unto him, for he that comes to God *must believe that he is*, and that he is a rewarder of them that diligently seek him" (Heb. 11:6). In order to come to God, a person must "*believe that he is.*" The text doesn't say: "must prove scientifically that he is," or, "must discover by experiment that he is." Faith is conviction regarding things that *cannot* be seen.[6] God is invisible; no man has seen him.[7] When we assert his existence, we declare a conviction about invisible and spiritual things. A word of qualification is in order. The text does not present belief in God's

---

[5] *Ps. 115:1-4*: Not unto us, O Lord, not unto us, but unto your name give glory, for your lovingkindness, and for your truth's sake. Wherefore should the nations say, where is now their God? But our God is in the heavens; He has done whatsoever he pleased. Their idols are silver and gold, the work of men's hands; *1 Cor. 8:4*: Concerning therefore the eating of things sacrificed to idols, we know that no idol is anything in the world, and that there is no God but one; *1 John 5:20*: This is the true God, and eternal life. Little children, guard yourselves from idols.

[6] Heb. 11:1

[7] John 1:18; Col. 1:15

existence as infallible proof of *saving* faith: "You believe that God is one; you do well: the demons also believe and shudder" (James 2:19). Sadly, some who believe in God's existence are not saved, for even demons believe that God exists.

In sum, Scripture both *assumes* and *asserts* the existence of God. It never adopts an agnostic perspective in order to prove God's existence by rational evidence. Therefore, no teacher of apologetics or systematics should adopt agnosticism as valid and intellectually honest and then try to coax men with theistic proofs from agnosticism to theism. Van Til powerfully employs a fictitious conversation to correct such a misguided compromise. He clearly exposes and illustrates its futility.[8] Take to heart that you cannot reason biblically unless you presuppose God's existence. If you are ever tempted to compromise this truth, flee from such compromise. It is dangerous and potentially ruinous to your souls.

Unit 2: The Revelation of God's Existence

Scripture teaches that God reveals his existence both in *general* and *special* revelation. The entire cosmos, man included, furnishes the general revelation of God's existence. God's Word provides its enhanced and special revelation. Since the Bible addresses both the general and the special revelation of God's existence, we consider both aspects of its testimony.

I. The General Revelation of God's Existence

Most teachers of systematics cite five key texts.[9] The testimony of these passages has two focal points, the general revelation of God's existence in *the creation* and in *the conscience*. We now consider each

A. General Revelation of God's Existence in the Creation

Three texts focus on the disclosure of God's existence from without, from the heavens and earth.[10] We now consider the testimony of each passage.

1. Ps. 19:1-4[11]

These verses describe how everything in the heavens discloses God's glory. The sky displays his skillful labor. Creation *"declares* and *"shows"* his

---

[8] Cornelius Van Til, *The Defense of the Faith* (Philadelphia, PA: Prebyterian and Reformed, 1967), 248-259.

[9] Ps. 19:1-4; Acts 14:17; Rom. 1:19-23; 1:32; 2:14-15

[10] Ps. 19:1-4; Acts 14:17; Rom. 1:19-23

[11] *Ps. 19:1-4*: The heavens declare the glory of God; and the firmament shows his handiwork. Day unto day utters speech, and night unto night shows knowledge. There is no speech nor language; their voice is not heard. Their line is gone out through all the earth, and their words to the end of the world. In them has he set a tabernacle for the sun.

existence. "*Day unto day*" delivers a message about him. The passing of time is regular, ordered, reliable, and predictable. The expanse of the heavens, the sun, the moon, and the stars speak and teach, even without words, eloquently of their Maker. Further, their message does not reach only one continent or nation. Their instruction is universal: "gone out through all the earth." Do fallen men perceive this display of God's existence? The text doesn't explicitly say. Scripture answers elsewhere.

2. Acts 14:17[12]

Paul teaches that the Living God discloses himself to men in his kind providence. The bounties of the earth and man's enjoyment of its abundance testify on behalf of his existence. The ocean, the sun, the wind, and the clouds carry the rain to the earth. The watered earth brings forth food abundantly so as to sustain, nourish, and satisfy man. This displays the goodness of our Creator. Do men perceive from their blessings the Creator who gave them? We now come to the answer of Scripture.

3. Rom. 1:19-20[13]

Since this passage furnishes the most complete and clear treatment of this topic in the Bible, we exegete it in greater detail. Consider its context. Paul launches an exposition of God's gospel (Rom. 1:16-32). He addresses man's greatest problem, namely, the wrath of God revealed against his sin.[14] He proclaims God's wrath to show men why they need Christ and the salvation that is in him. He asserts that men are under wrath because they suppress what they know to be true. Then he supports his assertion that men suppress truth (1:19-23). First, he declares that men are exposed to and perceive truth (1:19-20). Then he describes their blatant rejection of that truth (1:21-23). What truth do men perceive, blatantly reject, and suppress? Our text gives a clear answer. Men suppress and reject the revelation of their Creator that they perceive by means of his creation. Paul describes their exposure to the general revelation of God's existence: "Because that which is known of God is manifest among them; for God manifested it unto them." Then Paul goes further. He asserts that this exposure is effective. It is effective because it results in their perception of God's existence: "for the invisible things of him

---

[12] *Acts 14:17*: And yet he left not himself without witness, in that he did good and gave you from heaven rains and fruitful seasons, filling your hearts with food and gladness

[13] *Rom. 1:19-20*: because that which is known of God is manifest in them; for God manifested it unto them. 20 For the invisible things of him since the creation of the world are clearly seen, being perceived through the things that are made, even his everlasting power and divinity; that they may be without excuse.

[14] *Rom. 1:18*: for the wrath of God is being revealed from heaven upon all ungodliness and unrighteousness of men, who suppress the truth in unrighteousness.

are clearly seen, *being perceived* through the things that are made." Paul insists that even pagans recognize God's "invisible things." They perceive God's existence. In that limited sense they know God through his creation (1:21). Thus, they are "without excuse." Now let that sink in. Consider its weighty implication. Either Paul's right, or he's wrong. If he's wrong, the Bible is not inspired, and our whole religion is false and vain! If he's right, and he is, then no man needs to have God's existence proved to him. He already knows it. Anyone who denies this is a liar. Agnosticism is a lie.

Therefore, we examine the content of Romans 1:20 in detail. The heart or skeleton of the passage is the assertion: "the invisible things of him are clearly seen." It could be translated: "his invisible attributes are being noticed." All men, even pagan idolaters, observe the existence of the invisible God. Paul uses a synonymous word translated, "*being perceived*," to enhance this concept in the next phrase. He embellishes the idea even more by describing this perception in the next verse as "*knowing God*." All men know God through creation. They notice his invisible attributes. They are aware of the fact that God exists. Notice how the apostle develops this universal awareness of God's existence. He specifies four features: its origin and duration; its vehicle, instrument, or means; its content or substance; and its result or design. In this verse, Paul answers four basic questions: How long have men recognized God's existence and attributes? How, by what means, do men recognize these things? What things do all men recognize about God? And, So what? Or, what results from this awareness?

a. The origin and duration of this awareness: "since the creation of the world"

From the creation of the world even lost men have always known about God's existence. Human perception of God by means of creation began at the dawn of human history and has continued unaltered and uninterrupted until this day.

b. The means or vehicle of this awareness: "through the things that are made"

This perception began when creation began, precisely because the creation itself is the means by which men perceive God's existence. Paul conveys this with a common grammatical construction, the dative of means. The entire creation described in Genesis 1:1-31 serves as the instrument of this perception. The whole visible world displays the glory of the invisible God who made it, because God himself designed it that way. The material world was never inherently evil or sinful. Its dignity and goodness rest on the fact that God made it to display his glory. Further, it effectively fulfills this intention, so that men actually notice God's invisible attributes through this light of nature.

c. *The content or substance of this awareness:* "even his everlasting power and deity"

What do men notice? What invisible things of God do all men perceive through nature? Paul says: "his eternal power and deity." What are God's eternal power and deity? How do men perceive these things from creation? Is this the sum of what all men know about God from creation? If not, why single these things out?" Now we attempt to answer these four questions biblically and briefly.

What are God's eternal power and deity? Both his power and deity are modified by the adjective, "eternal." The word has a dual significance. It can mean either *always existing* or *unoriginated*. These nuances both pertain here. The creation reveals God's always existing and unoriginated power and deity. It displays that God's power and deity have neither beginning nor source. They are not derived, but always existent. The power of God is his ability to perform whatever his holy will decides. This ability is infinite. This infinite ability to accomplish anything he wills to do is his *omnipotence*. Paul calls God's omnipotence "unoriginated" and "underived." He asserts that creation displays this unoriginated power and that all men perceive it through creation. The word translated "*deity*" is used nowhere else in the New Testament. In general, it conveys that which pertains to the Supreme Being, or to the supernatural. Thus, it signifies his personal identity as the Supreme Being. Paul also calls his personal identity as the living God "underived" and "unoriginated." God is the uncreated Creator. Paul asserts that God's unoriginated life as the Supreme Being is both displayed in creation and perceived by all men through creation. In sum, all men know and perceive by the light of nature that God is, and that his deity and power are underived and unoriginated. This prompts the second question.

How are these things perceived from creation? God stamped creation from top to bottom with the labels: "*energy*" and "*design.*" Men can and do read these labels. They are visible and evident. From this energy and design, men perceive what is invisible, but equally evident. They perceive the existence of the unoriginated and living God, who is the cause and source of the energy and design they see in creation. Men know by looking at the world that it was made by an eternal, personal, and powerful Designer, by the uncreated Creator. This enters the orbit of the so-called theistic proofs. Bavinck says that two of the arguments, the cosmological (based on cause) and teleological (based on design), stem from the nature of the universe.[15] He then affirms in detail that these arguments are cogent when considered

---

[15] Bavinck, *Doctrine of God*, 68.

in combination.[16] Then sums up the point of his discourse: "Everything depends upon the presence of purpose in the universe. If that is established, the existence of the Highest Being and the fact that he possesses consciousness are thereby given."[17] Similarly, Charnock appeals to Romans 1:20 to show the folly of an atheist.[18] He asserts it is folly for an atheist to deny what all things in the world manifest. He then enlarges upon how all things created declare the existence of their Creator in their production, harmony, preservation, and answering their several ends. Accordingly, he asserts:[19]

> Who ever saw statues or pictures, but presently thinks of a statuary [*sculptor*] and limner [*painter*]? Who beholds garments, ships, or houses, but understands there was a weaver, a carpenter, an architect? Who can cast his eyes about the world but must think of that power that formed it, and that the goodness which appears in the formation of it hath a perfect residence in some being? [*Contemporary sense of archaic terms supplied.*]

Then he shows how God's production of the world declares his existence. He reasons as follows:[20]

> The world and every creature had a beginning . . . (Prop. 1) No creature can make itself . . . (Prop. 2) No creature could make the world . . . (Prop. 3) From hence it follows that there is a first cause of things, which we call God.

Then Charnock demonstrates at length how the creation declares its Creator by means of its harmony, order, and design.[21] He concludes by observing:[22]

> From all this it follows, if there be an order and harmony, there must be an orderer, one that 'made the earth by his power, established the world by his wisdom, and stretched out the heavens by his discretion' (Jer. 10:12). Order being the effect, cannot be the cause of itself. Order is the disposition of things to an end, and is not intelligent, but implies an intelligent orderer; and therefore it is as certain that there is a God as it is certain there is order in the world.

---

[16] Ibid, 68-72
[17] Ibid, 72
[18] Charnock, *Existence and Attributes*, 28-46
[19] Ibid, 29
[20] Ibid, 29-36
[21] Ibid, 36-43
[22] Ibid, 43

Charnock doesn't adopt an agnostic attitude. He merely applies the assertions of Romans 1:20. He never grants for a moment that agnosticism is anything other than a lie. Rather, his whole purpose is to expose the folly of atheism. He properly fulfills the biblical injunction to "answer a fool according to his folly, lest he be wise in his own conceits," and he does so without becoming like him.

Does this exhaust what people know about God from creation? The answer is, no. Scripture affirms that men know even more about God from the light of nature. It indicates that creation also displays God's goodness.[23] Paul appeals to men's awareness of his goodness. He confronts their impenitence in the face of his goodness. He says it indicates that they despise his goodness.[24] It also indicates that men perceive God's justice and judgment through creation.[25] This provokes the last question.

Why did Paul single out God's power and deity? I think the best clue comes from the context. The polytheistic idolatry that Paul condemned was a frontal assault on the power and deity of the one true God. Possibly for this reason he featured these two divine attributes.

d. The result or design of this awareness: "that they may be without excuse"

The phrase literally reads: "unto the to be them without excuse." This grammatical construction, the articular infinitive, could express either purpose or result. The precise nuance is a moot point, because God's purpose necessarily results. Their idolatry is inexcusable because they perceived God's power and deity through creation. They have no excuse for their sin because they suppressed and denied the truth that they clearly perceived from creation about the existence of God. We pause a moment to apply these things. All perceive that an intelligent, powerful Creator made the world. Yet, many refuse to face this truth and live in the light of it. They hate their Creator. They suppress and deny what they know to be true about him, because they have no heart to serve him. They pretend not to know what they know, and not to see what they see. They don't want to admit that they suppress what they know to be true or that they hate their Maker. Evidently, such persons are without excuse. Paul does not paint agnosticism in innocent and neutral colors. He never claims that innocent people must somehow reason from agnosticism to theism. To the contrary, he affirms that lies and suppression of truth lead people from theism to agnosticism, in spite of what they know about God through his creation. Paul asserts that

---

[23] Ps. 19:1-6; Acts 14:17
[24] Rom. 2:4
[25] Rom. 1:32

they "refused to have God in their knowledge" and that they "exchanged the truth of God for a lie." Thus, he teaches that any religious systems or philosophies that deny the Creator's existence are dishonest shams. Thus, he makes no attempt to reason pagan idolaters to theism. This is how we too should respond to agnostic pretensions and lies. When an agnostic protests that he doesn't know if God exists, we must not credit him with honesty. That would be a naive and dangerous compromise. It would excuse the inexcusable. It would fall short of faithful dealings with his soul and imperil the health of our own. Worse yet, it would credit and value man's word over God's Word. It would treat God, not man, as the liar. For example, several years ago someone asked me how I could prove to him that God existed. I said it was pointless to try to prove it to him since he already knew it. Then I said, "Why are you asking me to prove to you what you already know? Do you want to be honest? Why don't you want to admit that God exists? What are your reasons?" Some may say that this is too simplistic. Rather, it is the simple truth.

B. The Revelation of God's Existence in the Conscience

We now consider two texts that focus on its disclosure from within, from the heart and conscience.[26]

1. Rom. 1:32[27]

Here Paul draws his exposition of divine abandonment to a close. With the thrice-repeated phrase, "God gave them up," he paints a sad picture of pagan society abandoned by an angry God.[28] He explains that God gave them up because they refused to have him in their knowledge, exchanged his truth for a lie, and suppressed what they knew about him from creation. He affirms that their sexual promiscuity[29], sexual perversion[30], and reprobate ["unapprovable," or worthless] disposition[31] are living monuments to the wrath of God. This wrath is presently being revealed against ungodly men who deny what they know about God's existence. Then he reports the shocking response to this God-forsaken way of life that prevailed in that pagan society. What reaction prevailed? Their prevalent response was, "live and let live." They openly practiced and tolerated a shameful way of life.

---

[26] Rom. 1:32, 2:14-15

[27] *Rom. 1:32*: Who knowing the ordinance of God that they that practice such things are worthy of death, not only do the same but also consent with those that do them.

[28] Rom. 1:24, 26, 28

[29] Rom. 1:24-25

[30] Rom. 1:26-27

[31] Rom. 1:28-31

Their toleration was brazen because it disregarded what they knew about God's ordinance. This introduces the focus of the text, *"the ordinance of God."* Paul specifies three things about this divine ordinance or determination. He identifies its content, asserts that even pagans are aware of it, and exposes their brazen disregard for it.

a. The content or substance of God's determination: "that they that practice such things are worthy of death"

When Paul says, *"such things,"* what things does he mean? He refers to the things that he just labeled as manifestations of divine abandonment. These are sexual promiscuity, sexual perversion, and a reprobate mind. He says that God has determined that all persons who live like that deserve to die. They are "worthy of death." God decided that death is just punishment for the fornicator, the homosexual, and the reprobate. This is the content of God's ordinance.

b. The universal awareness of God's determination: "Who knowing the ordinance of God"

It may appear shocking, but the truth is that such persons did not live wantonly because of their ignorance of God's determination, but in spite of their knowledge of it. People know that sexually promiscuous men and women are under divine sentence of death. They know that he condemns lesbians and gays. They know that he consigns to death those whose hearts are greedy, brutal, dishonest, and self-worshipping. Paul furnishes a remarkable insight into the nature of fallen humanity. People don't say this about themselves. Modern psychology doesn't admit this. Nevertheless, it is true. This exposes secular humanism as hypocritical and phony. It reveals that notorious sinners are self-destructive. Even the most brazen human beings know that God condemns them for gross wickedness.

This prompts the question, "How do they know?" It is possible that the Mosaic Law had some impact even on pagan society. The primary factor, however, cannot be the Law of Moses, for Paul describes these pagans as "without the law."[32] Paul depicts sinners who were without the benefit of formative exposure to Scripture. It is possible that remnants of the revelation received from their ancestor Noah somehow survived and played a role in this understanding. Yet this is unlikely. Paul does not even mention it in the context. Rather, the basic source of this understanding is the testimony of their conscience. Paul affirms that conscience is active in these pagans and assures us that its activity is the means by which God will condemn them on judgment day (Rom. 2:13-16). I conclude that fallen mankind perceives

---

[32] Rom. 2:12-15

that God exists, from creation without and also from the voice of conscience within. Creation emphasizes his power and deity; conscience stresses his disfavor and condemnation of sin.

c. Brazen disregard for God's determination: "not only do the same but also consent with those who practice them"

The "live and let live" attitude flagrantly rejects conscientious living. Men condone and do what they know God regards as a capital offense. Conscience within them says that God is not pleased with such things, that those who do them deserve to die, and that God has determined to punish such with death. In spite of this testimony from their own hearts, they tolerate, encourage, and even justify sexual uncleanness, sexual perversion, and a lack of common decency. What shall we say? Isn't God provoked to visit with wrath for such things? Don't be deceived when modern sinners confidently pronounce that in their process of moral maturation they have outgrown God. They are not being honest. Though outwardly they mock and laugh, inwardly they cringe with dread, because they know that God regards them as worthy to die. They know his assessment of such evil ways. It stands impressed on their hearts. They too carry his label, "made in heaven, property of the Creator." No matter how hard sinners try, they can never remove or eradicate their consciences. Never forget this fact. We must beware lest we be carried away with the error of the wicked. We must beware lest flagrant toleration of sin seep into the cellar of our own hearts. May God help us to proclaim this truth with courage and compassion.

2. Rom. 2:14-15[33]

This text clearly asserts the presence and action of conscience in persons in the state of sin. Paul explains how God will condemn Gentiles in the judgment. Note that all people, even idolaters, have a conscience, for Paul says: *"their conscience* bearing witness." Note also that the conscience of all people affirms the authority and justice of God's law: "these, not having the law, *are the law for themselves*; in that they show the work of the law written in their hearts, *their conscience bearing witness therewith.*" Now consider the *fact* and *witness* of conscience.

a. The fact of conscience: "their conscience"

Paul asserts plainly that all men have a conscience, a faculty or capacity of moral awareness, obligation, and judgment: "commending ourselves to

---

[33] *Rom. 2:14-15*: for when the Gentiles that have not the law do by nature the things of the law, these, not having the law, are the law unto themselves; in that they show the work of the law written in their hearts, their conscience bearing witness therewith, and their thoughts one with another accusing or else excusing them

every man's conscience in the sight of God" (2 Cor. 4:2). Paul speaks about gaining approval in the court of mankind's moral standards, sense of duty and propriety, and judgment. He calls this capacity, "conscience." Conscience judges not only others but also ourselves: "and their thoughts one with another accusing or else excusing them." Even people living in sin judge and condemn themselves. This links present acts of conscience with its role on judgment day.

b. *The witness of conscience:* "their conscience bearing witness therewith"

Paul explains exactly how God will employ conscience on judgment day as the instrument with which he will condemn lost Gentiles. Their conscience affirms the authority and justice of God's law. Paul expresses this strikingly with the phrase, "they are the law." They function like the law does. Their souls perform the same job that the Decalogue performs. What function or work does the law of God perform? First, the law defines right and wrong. Second, the Decalogue urges and commands men to do right and forbids men to do wrong. Third, the law commends men when they do right and condemns them when they do wrong. For example: "You shall not take the name of the Lord your God in vain, for the Lord will not hold him guiltless that takes his name in vain." And again: "Honor your father and mother, that it may be well with you and that your days may be long upon the earth." Paul asserts that this is precisely how conscience functions here on earth, and exactly why it will be the instrument that God uses to condemn sinners in judgment. First, conscience discerns right and wrong. Second, conscience obliges us to do right and forbids us to do wrong. Third, conscience excuses us when we do right and accuses and condemns when we do wrong. Thus conscience functions like the law. God has stamped this function on every human heart. He thundered from Mount Sinai with the voice of conscience. On Sinai he codified, amplified, and purified that voice. Thus, when God's law thunders from without, conscience from within whispers, "amen." Therefore, the aim of conscience, even as of the Decalogue, is that "every mouth be stopped, and the entire world may be brought under the judgment of God" (Rom. 3:19). Each man's conscience assures him that he is under God's authority, accountable to God. In that way it furnishes a general revelation of God's existence. Before we press the implications of all this, an important word of qualification is in order. The conscience of fallen mankind is not exempt from the ravages of sin. Paul affirms this when he says of the unbelieving: "both their mind and their conscience are defiled" (Titus 1:15). He even describes some sinners as: "branded in their own conscience as with a hot iron" (1 Tim. 4:3). A sinner's discernment of right and wrong is defiled. They often call evil good, and good evil. Their sense of moral obligation is defiled. Their accusations and exonerations are defiled. Conscience is defiled by sin, but not erased. It is twisted and confused by sin, but still testifies to the authority and rightness of God's law. It is muffled, stifled, denied, and hated, but still echoes the will of the God who created man in his image.

Charnock establishes that conscience displays God's existence. He lays his foundation with two principles that he derives from this text: "(1) There is a law in the minds of men which is a rule of good and evil . . . (2) From the transgression of this law of nature fears do arise in the consciences of men."[34] He then builds his case with four assertions about the working of conscience that Scripture and history support:[35] "(1) This operation of conscience hath been universal . . . (2) These operations of conscience are when the wickedness is most secret . . . (3) These operations of conscience can not be totally shaken off by man . . . (4) We may add, the comfortable reflections of conscience." He concludes that man, through his conscience, clearly displays God's existence.

Summary: Now let's summarize and apply the testimony of Romans 1:32 and 2:14-15. All men have a conscience. They discern, albeit imperfectly, right and wrong. They know themselves obligated to God to do right, and condemned by God for doing wrong. They know his disfavor upon their wrongdoing, and his determination that for their wrongdoing they deserve to die. Nevertheless, they persist in doing, condoning, and justifying the very things for which they know God condemns them. You may say to me, "You are mad; how can such things be?" Moral madness is here indeed, but I speak words of soberness and truth. Such is the twisted and tragic state of men who live in rebellion against their Creator. They are filled with self-contradiction and deceit. They inwardly deny what outwardly they affirm, and inwardly affirm what outwardly they deny and mock. They know from their own conscience that God exists and that they are accountable to him and guilty before him. Thus far, but no further, the general revelation of God's existence brings men. Fallen humans are fearful and inexcusable before God.

Accordingly, it is no surprise that every branch of the human race practices some form of religion. It is also no surprise that humans confess their perception of some "moral principle" operating in the world. Yet many are unwilling openly to admit all they inwardly know about it. This returns us to the orbit of the so-called theistic proofs. Two of these, *the moral argument* (based on perceived morality) and *the argument from universal*

---

[34] Charnock, *Existence and Attributes*, 51, 52.
[35] Ibid, 52, 53, 54

consent (based on the proliferation of religions), are closely tied to these operations of conscience. Conscience explains the universal sense of moral imperative and the proliferation of religion among men. Defiled conscience explains men's perversion of biblical morality and the proliferation of false religion. Man's sense of moral accountability to God and his practice of religion, though defiled by sin, dimly display that fallen men know that God exists. However, this "sense of divinity" and "seed of religion," as Calvin called them, don't paint a pretty picture. Fallen men worship and serve many grotesque gods. They labor in pursuit of sundry false hopes of deliverance from their inner dread, guilt, and shame.

The general revelation of God's existence in creation and conscience is sufficient to condemn men but insufficient to save them. They know that they are accountable and guilty before their uncreated Creator. They see his goodness, wisdom and power, but inwardly they dread him, for they know that by his standard they deserve to die. Yet they do not have from general revelation either instruction, inclination, or ability to get right with him or to enjoy fellowship with him.

II. The Special Revelation of God's Existence

Scripture discloses two general features of this special revelation that make it distinct from and superior to general revelation. Special revelation of God's existence is *verbal* and *personal*: "I am God."

First, the special revelation of God's existence is *verbal*, made by his Word. Before the fall of man God revealed his existence by his Word. God verbally gave direction to Adam (Gen. 2:16-17) and blessing to Adam and Eve (Gen. 1:28-30). Even after the fall God communicated his existence verbally to men. Adam and Eve still heard his voice in the garden (Gen. 3:8-19). He even spoke to Cain after he murdered Abel (Gen. 4:9-12). In this world that sin defaced God's Word has furnished an unspoiled testimony to his existence. This testimony is superior to the muffled and defiled testimony of conscience. Yet, throughout history God's Word has come to men piecemeal (Heb. 1:1). God has not distributed these pieces of spiritual bread equally among men (Matt. 4:4; Acts 14:16). He has meted them out according to his sovereign prerogative. Now finally, he has collected, summarized, comprehended, and published his Word in Scripture, which is the sole and complete Word of God for mankind on earth today.

Second, the special revelation of God's existence is *personal*. It declares his name. Special revelation is also superior in this respect. God does not merely reveal that some God, or a God, exists, but that *he* exists. General revelation discloses a Creator, who is the Designer and Judge of men. In special revelation the Creator (Isa. 45:18) tells us that his name is Jehovah

(Isa. 45:21). He calls men to personal communion with himself: "Look unto me, and be saved, all the ends of the earth; for I am God." Special revelation is the essential foundation of all true religion.

Having examined these two general features with a narrow focus lens, now we spy out the specific elements of this special revelation with a broad focus lens. Surveying the whole landscape of Scripture, we note that the special revelation of God's existence stands closely united to public displays in history of his *supernatural power*, of his *special presence*, and of his *secret purposes*. God especially reveals his existence in inspired words that surround, accompany, and explain those public displays. Theologians usually refer to special events in which God openly manifests his supernatural power as *miracles*. They usually call a visible or audible display of God's special presence a *theophany*, which literally means, "a visible manifestation of God." They usually refer to public disclosure of God's secret purposes prior to their fulfillment as *prophecy*. These are the categories in which we study this special revelation. Time does not permit an exhaustive survey of the events recorded in Scripture in which God specially reveals his existence (Heb. 11:32). We examine a few of the most striking examples in each category.

A. *Display of God's Supernatural Power: Miracle*

God specially reveals his existence by miraculous intrusions of supernatural power. The Scripture records and explains numerous occasions in which the Lord has affirmed his existence by the open exercise of his supernatural power. We focus only on the miracles associated with the exodus of Israel from Egypt. Scripture records the history of the exodus in Exodus 3-12. The first confrontation with Pharaoh epitomizes the issue: "Who is Jehovah, that I should hearken to his voice and let Israel go? I know not Jehovah, and moreover I will not let Israel go" (Exod. 5:2). This statement explains plainly how these miracles relate to God's existence. Pharaoh says in so many words: "as far as I'm concerned your god doesn't exist": "Who is Jehovah . . . I know not Jehovah." Jehovah designs all the plagues and judgments that follow to demonstrate certainly, both to his enemies and to his people, that he does indeed exist, and that he alone is God.[36] Similarly, even the periods of respite from the plagues served this end: "And he said,

---

[36] *Exod. 7:4-5*: But Pharaoh will not hearken unto you, I will lay my hand upon Egypt, and bring forth my hosts, my people out of the land of Egypt with great judgments. *And the Egyptians shall know that I am Jehovah*, when I stretch forth my hand upon Egypt, and bring out the children of Israel from among them; *Exod. 7:17*: Thus says Jehovah, in this *you shall know that I am Jehovah*: behold, I will smite with the rod that is in my hand upon the waters which are in the river, and they shall be turned to blood.

Be it according to your word; that *you may know that there is none like unto Jehovah our God*. And the frogs shall depart from you" (Exod. 8:10). Nevertheless, the Egyptians were not easily convinced that Jehovah alone was God. The magicians replicated the initial plagues with their enchantments.[37] But this didn't last: "And the magicians did so with their enchantments to bring forth lice, but they could not: and there were lice upon man and upon beast. Then the magicians said unto Pharaoh, *This is the finger of God*" (Exod. 8:18-19). The Lord further underscored the point with the plague of flies.[38] The Lord's reproof of Pharaoh summed up his revelatory design in these miracles: "For I will this time send all my plagues upon your heart, and upon your servants, and upon your people; *that you may know that there is none like me in all the earth* . . . but in very deed for this cause have I made you to stand, to show you my power, and *that my name may be declared throughout all the earth*" (Exod. 9:14-16). Further, these miracles furnished the Israelites ground for a perpetual testimony that Jehovah is God.[39] Thus, these miraculous plagues reveal profoundly that God exists, and emphatically, that Jehovah is God. They also show that the special revelation of God's existence is superior to its general revelation.

Time would fail to tell how God displayed his existence in the supernatural power that parted the Red Sea for Israel, or that toppled the walls of Jericho, or that held the sun in its place for Joshua, or that reversed the dial for Hezekiah, or that turned water into wine, or made loaves of bread multiply, or raised Jesus from the dead. Scripture provides an inspired record of these supernatural events from those who witnessed them personally.

Now let's apply what we have just seen. Some say that if they could only see Jehovah perform a miracle, then they would believe that he is God and serve him: "If only I could see the Red Sea supernaturally opened, or behold the resurrected Christ with my own eyes, then I would believe that the God of the Bible exists."

What should we say to those who claim that they would believe in the existence of the God of the Bible if he performed a miracle for them? *First*, they should beware of being deceived by lying signs and wonders (2 Thess. 2:9-12). Satan and the demons also sometimes exercise supernatural power.

---

[37] Exod. 7:10-12, 22, 8:7

[38] *Exod. 8:22*: And I will set apart the land of Goshen, in which my people dwell, that no swarms of flies shall be there; to the end *that you may know that I am Jehovah* in the midst of the earth.

[39] *Exod. 10:2*: . . . that you may tell in the ears of your son, and of your son's son, what things I have wrought upon Egypt, and my signs I have done among them; *that you may know that I am Jehovah*.

What would such do if Pharaoh's magicians turned their rods into snakes? Would they serve the gods of Egypt as well as Jehovah because Pharaoh's magicians could also make the waters become blood? They would be hard pressed to tell the difference between the power of Satan and the power of God without God's Word. *Second*, even if they saw a miracle, it would not guarantee that they would get right with God. The Israelites of the wilderness generation are a tragic monument to this. They saw all the miraculous plagues that God inflicted on Egypt. They saw the Red Sea open supernaturally. Yet most of them perished in the wilderness in their unbelief. Jesus confirms this in Luke 16:30-31. With this same misconception the rich man says to Abraham: "but if one go to them from the dead they will repent." But Abraham isn't convinced. He replies: "If they hear not Moses and the prophets, neither will they be persuaded, if one rise from the dead." Jesus' point is clear. If men don't believe the Bible, miracles won't persuade them either. God has given us his Word. His Word is sufficient to bring people to saving faith. They do not need to witness miracles personally. As the Lord said to Thomas: "Blessed are they who have not seen and yet have believed."

B. Display of God's Special Presence: Theophany

God specially reveals his existence by audible and visible displays of his special presence. God is present everywhere always. Nevertheless, God is also present in a special sense in some places at some times. This is his *special presence*. God at times is pleased to display his special presence audibly or visibly with striking displays that reveal his existence. Scripture records many theophanies. Again time would fail to consider in detail how he displayed his existence to Moses in the burning bush, or how he spoke the ten commandments from heaven with an audible voice to the whole nation of Israel, or how the pillars of cloud and fire accompanied Israel in the wilderness, or how the glory of the Lord filled the tabernacle, and later the temple, or how God's glory shined above the cherubim in his house, or how he appeared visibly to Joshua and others as the angel of Jehovah, or how the Father spoke from heaven with an audible voice to Jesus, or how the Holy Spirit descended with fire at Pentecost. In these many ways, and more, God has specially revealed his existence.

Consider with me one such display in greater detail. On this occasion the nation of Israel publically contested God's existence. God ended the debate with a profound display of his special presence. This confrontation took place on Mount Carmel. The contestants were Jehovah and Baal. Scripture records the story in 1 Kings 18:20-40. Elijah, the lone prophet of the Lord, gives a challenge. He concludes this challenge saying: "And you call on the name of your god, and I will call on the name of Jehovah: and the God that answers by fire, let him be God" (1 Kings 18:24). Men prepared the sacrifices and placed them on the wood, but God would need to supply the fire. He would need to manifest visibly that he was present and existed. Who would "answer by fire"? Would it be Jehovah or Baal? Or would neither be able to answer? This open and public challenge would decide the question for all the people and steer the course of the nation. The prophets of Baal had the first chance to call on their god. They called on Baal from morning till noon, saying, "O Baal, hear us" (18:26). The response, to their dismay, was silence: "But there was no voice, nor any that answered." They had lost the first round, so they fought even harder. All afternoon they shouted for Baal to respond. They pleaded with him for a display of his presence. They even cut themselves until blood gushed from their wounds. Yet at the end of the day all their shenanigans prevailed nothing: "but there was neither voice, nor any to answer, nor any that regarded" (18:29). Now they were done. It was Elijah's turn to call on Jehovah. First he made an altar of stones. Then he laid the sacrifice upon it. He made the people pour water all over the sacrifice and the altar. They poured so much water that it overflowed and filled the trench that surrounded the altar. Now things were ready. This would be no cheap magician's trick. Only a supernatural display of the presence of God could ignite that sacrifice. Then Elijah cried to Jehovah and said: "let it be known this day that you are God in Israel . . . hear me, that this people may know that you, Jehovah, are God." Then it happened: "the fire of Jehovah fell, and consumed the burnt-offering, and the wood, and the stones, and the dust, and licked up the water that was in the trench" (18:38). God manifested his special presence and his existence. The people clearly understood this. They fell on their faces and said: "Jehovah, he is God; Jehovah, he is God." That settled the issue.

Let's consider the application of this. I can almost hear someone say: "if only I could have been on Carmel that day, then I would know for sure whether Jehovah, the God of the Bible, exists. Then I would believe in him. If only he would appear to me, as he did to Joshua, or speak audibly with me from heaven, then I would believe in him and serve him."

How should we respond to those who say they would believe in the existence of Jehovah if only they saw or heard a theophany? *First*, those who seek a theophany should beware, for all supernatural appearances are not theophanies. Even Satan presents himself as an angel of light (2 Cor. 11:14). *Second*, they should consider that a theophany would not guarantee their salvation. The entire nation heard God's voice audibly on Mount Sinai. Yet most of them perished in unbelief even after they heard the Ten Commandments with their own ears. Jesus' words, "If they hear not Moses and the prophets," apply both to theophanies and miracles. *Third*, God gives us the ultimate display of his special presence in Jesus Christ. Jesus is superior to all theophanies. He is more than a mere theophany. He is God manifested in the flesh, God incarnate. If men truly have Christ, they will no longer want theophanies. Therefore, I say to such, receive Christ through the gospel. *Fourth*, God is especially present by his Spirit, now and always, with all who believe in Christ. To those who seek a theophany I say, repent, and you will receive the gift of the Holy Spirit. This is how God manifests his special presence on earth today. Searching for a theophany is futile. If you seek Christ by faith with all your heart, you will find him, and he will satisfy your soul with his presence by his Spirit.

C. *Display of God's Secret Purpose: Prophecy*

God specially reveals his existence by predicting and fulfilling his secret purposes. Prophecy rests on the fact that God knows the future. God knows the future because God planned and decided the future. God alone knows the future, because he alone determined it (Deut. 29:29). In prophecy God discloses his decisions before he implements them. This teaches us the distinctive mark of a true prophet. A true prophet speaks God's Word about the future. All his predictions come true, without exception. Conversely, from this we also learn how to spot a false prophet. The false prophet speaks his own words from his own heart. Therefore, he cannot possibly predict the future either with clear specificity or with perfect accuracy (Deut. 18:20-22). Scripture contains many instances of fulfilled prophecy. Consider a few examples. God disclosed the exodus to Abraham long before it happened (Gen. 15:12-16). Joshua predicted the exact evils that would befall the man who rebuilt Jericho, hundreds of years before they happened to him (Josh. 6:26; 1 Kings 16:34). God's Word predicted the demise of the altar at Bethel centuries before it was ruined, and even named the man, Josiah, who would ruin it (1 Kings 13:1,2; 2 Kings 23:15-18). Isaiah named the man who would rebuild Jerusalem, Cyrus, over one hundred years before the city was even besieged (Isa. 44:28, 45:1). These fulfilled prophecies reveal in a most profound and special way that God exists, and that Jehovah is God.

Scripture does not make us reach this conclusion by inference alone. In Isaiah 41:23 the Lord challenges idols to prove their deity by prophecy: "Declare the things that are to come hereafter, that we may know that you are gods." Then, in Isaiah 48:4-5 the Lord explicitly explains why he makes known specific things that will happen long in the future. His reason is that men have hard hearts. God intends to prevent and discredit any claim that their idols brought those things to pass. He is determined to leave them no credible way to pretend that he didn't do them. He is determined to display before them in a most profound way that he exists. Hear the Word of God: "Because I knew that you are obstinate, and your neck is an iron sinew, and your brow brass; therefore I have declared it to you from of old; before it came to pass I showed it to you; lest you should say, Mine idol has done them." Several pages after these words Isaiah penned the most profound of prophecies. He told the story of the most important events in the history of the world over seven hundred years before they happened. He pictured those events with detail so graphic that it is as if he were an eyewitness to them. Simply listen to the words of Isaiah. I am sure you will recognize the events he saw and described long before they occurred:

> *Isa. 53:3-12:* He was despised and rejected of men; a man of sorrows, and acquainted with grief: and as one from whom men hide their face he was despised; and we esteemed him not. Surely he has borne our griefs and carried our sorrows; yet we did esteem him stricken, smitten of God, and afflicted. But he was wounded for our transgressions, he was bruised for our iniquities; the chastisement of our peace was upon him; and with his stripes we are healed. All we like sheep have gone astray; we have turned every one to his own way; and Jehovah has laid on him the iniquity of us all. He was oppressed, yet when he was afflicted he opened not his mouth; as a lamb that is led to the slaughter, and as a sheep that before its shearers is dumb, so he opened not his mouth. By oppression and judgment he was taken away; and as for his generation, who among them considered that he was cut off out of the land of the living for the transgression of my people to whom the stroke was due? And they made his grave with the wicked, and with a rich man in his death; although he had done no violence, neither was any deceit found in his mouth. Yet it pleased Jehovah to bruise him; he has put him to grief: when you shall make his soul an offering for sin, he shall see his seed, he shall prolong his days, and the pleasure of Jehovah shall prosper in his hand. He shall see of the travail of his soul, and shall be satisfied: by the knowledge of himself shall my righteous servant justify many; and he shall bear their iniquities. Therefore will I divide him a portion with the great, and he shall divide the spoil with the strong; because he poured out his soul unto death, and was numbered with the transgressors: yet he bare the sin of many, and made intercession for the transgressors.

This preview of the sufferings of Jesus Christ and his resurrection glory that follows them is the epitome of prophecy. God reveals his existence this way because the hearts of sinners are as hard as iron. Our consideration of the revelation of God's existence ends on this note. How fitting that the most profound disclosure of the existence of Jehovah leads us to Jesus Christ.

Unit 3: The Uniqueness of God's Existence

We return again to Isaiah 45:22: "for I am God, *and there is none else.*" These words set forth the uniqueness of God's existence. There is only one God, who made the world, who revealed himself in Scripture. Jehovah is his name. Consider with me two principles that apply in concrete terms the uniqueness of God's existence: the *non-existence* and *impotence* of other gods.

I. The Non-Existence of Other Gods: "and there is none else"

Since only the God of Scripture exists, all other so-called gods are non-entities, and the religions by which men serve them are false. God's people should declare his glory among the nations. They should publish his name abroad. They should call all the peoples of the world to fear the true God and to serve him by true religion. This is because the gods of the nations are "*things of nothing.*" Other gods do not exist in fact.[40] They are man-made. They only exist in the imagination of those who fabricate them (Ps. 115:1-4). Nevertheless, men serve them. This service is false religion. I do not deny the existence of evil spirits. Demons indeed exist. Some in their blindness even worship them.[41] According to Paul all religions are not created equal. They do not all worship the same being. They do not merely address him by a different name. The Gentiles offer their sacrifices to "*demons and not to God.*" The mentality in vogue today, however, is that the major religions of the world are all really in touch with the true God. According to this modern notion, Animism, Hinduism, Buddhism, Confucianism, Taoism, Shinto, and Islam are merely alternate forms of the religion of the Bible. They are biblical religion dressed in a different costume. The nations merely address the true God by a name suitable to their language and approach him in ways indicative of their culture. This popular notion contains an element of truth. All men know from creation and conscience that God exists, that he created the world, that they are answerable to him, and that they are guilty before him. Indeed, this knowledge of God is the common foundation of all the religions in the world. As for this modern notion, however, nothing could be further from the truth. Even as the Scripture teaches that in one sense all men know God, it also teaches that in another sense some men do not know him: "for some have no

---

[40] *Ps. 96:3-5*: Declare his glory among the nations, his marvelous works among all the peoples. For great is Jehovah, and greatly to be praised: He is to be feared above all gods. For all the gods of the nations are idols; But Jehovah made the heavens.

[41] *1 Cor. 10:19-20*: What say I then? that a thing sacrificed to an idol is anything, or that an idol is anything? But I say, that the things which the Gentiles sacrifice, they sacrifice to demons, and not to God.

knowledge of God" (1 Cor. 15:34). All men do not know him with saving knowledge or approach him acceptably. All men are not already saved through their religions, but need to be saved by Jehovah: "Look unto me, and be saved, all the ends of the earth; for I am God, and there is none else." Again, Acts 4:12 says: "And in none other is there salvation: for neither is there any other name under heaven, that is given among men, wherein we must be saved." Indeed, ignorance of God is the common root of all the false religions in the world. In this respect the modern nations are much the same as the extinct nations mentioned in Scripture. The modern nations no more worship the true God than the ancient nations did. As the idols of ancient nations were molten images graven with hands, so the idols of modern mankind are mental images fashioned with the mind. Modern man prides himself in his sophistication and advancement. Yet a candid survey of the major religions of mankind exposes the truth that man has not progressed very far in the field of religion. In fact, the false gods worshipped today are not vastly different from the idols of long ago. These modern idols misrepresent God as badly as the gods of the ancient Egyptians, Babylonians, Greeks, and Romans.

Soper conducts a candid survey of the religions of mankind.[42] Archer and Purinton conduct a similar survey in *Faiths Men Live By*.[43] Both books objectively present a fair account of the major religions of the modern world. I cannot now delve into the details. That properly belongs in a course on comparative religions. I want to present enough to demonstrate the error of this modern notion that all religions are essentially the same. To begin, Animism and Hinduism are polytheistic. Suffice it to say that Animism's many gods are idols. The gods and lords of Hinduism are idols. These false religions do not enable men to know and worship Jehovah, the one true God. We may say of them, as Paul said of the pagans of his day: "the things which the Animists and Hindus sacrifice they sacrifice to demons, and not to God." As for the Buddha (*"enlightened one"*), I do not attack his sincerity in his desire to relieve his fellow men in their suffering. Still the question remains, what light has he seen? He does not claim to lead men to Jehovah to be saved from their sins. He claims to lead men to a place of peace and fulfillment without God, a place called "Nirvana." Regarding him Soper writes: "He was not an atheist. He took the gods of India for granted, but it made no difference to him whether they were real beings or not . . . Why should anyone look to them? They could give no assistance which man

---

[42] Edmund Soper, *The Religions of Mankind* (New York: The Abington Press, 1925)
[43] John Clark Archer and Carl E. Purinton, *Faiths Men Live By* (New York: The Ronald Press Company, 1958)

could not render himself. They were in possession of no powers man did not have at his disposal. The result was that the Buddha constructed a system in which no god was needed."[44] Any such system is not light but darkness. Buddhism is not biblical religion in another costume, but false religion in the nakedness of human blindness and pride. As for Confucius, let us concede that he was a man of considerable wisdom in the fields of law and politics. Soper reports that polytheism, ancestor worship, and animistic superstition marked the religion of his day. He records his reaction to that religion:[45] "He did not condemn it, he did not criticize it, he did not add to it- he simply took it for granted. His temper of mind was essentially practical; he seemed always to be averse to any discussion of spiritual or purely philosophical matters. He claimed to be agnostic concerning the next life and the world of the gods." Surely following this man in his agnosticism is not biblical religion dressed in a costume of Chinese culture. Taoism is based on a vague philosophical treatise written between 500 and 600 B.C. by an elderly man named Laocius. The treatise is called the "Tao Teh King," or, "the writing of the way of duty." According to Soper "the Way" is that of quiet placidity, of self-effacement, of freedom from effort. The great Tao hope is to absorb good from nature in order to live a long life and even possibly enter the company of the gods. This hope is achieved by embracing a gospel of inactivity. Clearly, this is not "the way of the Lord," but a false way, which leads to perdition. What of Shinto (the way of the good spirits), or, as it is called in Japanese, "*Kami-no-Michi*," "*the way of the gods*"? Shinto is not true religion in another garb, but Animism in another garb. Shinto does not lead men to venerate the Lord, but their ancestors. Shinto does not inculcate allegiance to Jesus Christ, but to an Emperor. As for Judaism and Islam, these both profess to serve the God of Scripture, who revealed himself to Abraham. Yet we must say with Paul: "for I bear them witness that they have a zeal for God, but not according to knowledge. For being ignorant of God's righteousness and seeking to establish their own, they did not subject themselves to the righteousness of God" (Rom. 10:2-3). Neither Judaism nor Islam is biblical religion robed in the culture of the Middle East. Both religions are founded, not upon the virtue and blood of Jesus, but upon human virtue. They have in common that they reject the deity and final authority of Jesus Christ. If anyone rejects the deity of Jesus, he rejects the true God. Jesus said: "I am the way, the truth, and the life. No man comes to the Father but by me" (John 14:6). John said of Christ: "This is the true God and eternal life. Little children guard yourselves from idols"

---

[44] Soper, *Religions*, 189-190.
[45] Ibid, 222.

(1 John 5:20). I hope that you have not forgotten or missed the point of this brief display of the major religions of modern man. My point is that Jehovah Jesus alone is God. All religions do not lead to the true God or serve him acceptably.

II. The Impotence of Other Gods

Since only the God of Scripture exists, no other so-called god can either help or harm men. This second principle comes from the immediate context of Isaiah 45:22: "they have no knowledge that carry the wood of their graven image, and pray to a god that cannot save" (Isa. 45:20). The Psalmist also pictures the impotence of idols in Psalm 115:5-7. They have eyes, but they can't see; ears, but they can't hear; feet, but they can't walk. They can't do anything. Therefore, it is vain superstition to be afraid of them. Non-entities cannot make anything happen. They cannot purpose and perform evil. Thus, the Lord challenges false gods: "Declare the things that are to come hereafter, that we may know that you are gods: yea, do good, or do evil, that we may be dismayed and behold it together" (Isa. 41:23). Again, I don't deny that Satan and demons at times afflict and harm men. Yet even they are under God's power and control.[46] Thus, it is futile for men to seek help from other gods, or to depend on them for protection and deliverance. Isaiah describes this futility in graphic detail in Isaiah 44:9-20. It is futile because idols are "gods that cannot save." People practice such futility when they seek help from non-entities.

One striking example of this is the 12-Step Method of deliverance from addiction. This method, heralded by many, is growing in popularity and credibility in America. Although it originated in the treatment of alcohol abuse, it is now employed in the treatment of addictions of every kind. Some even proclaim it as the panacea for all the psychological and behavioral ills of men. You may ask, what does this have to do with the uniqueness of God's existence? The connection is this. The 12-Step Method instructs men to cast themselves on some "higher power" for deliverance from their addiction. They must give over control of their lives to this "higher power." You may ask, on what "higher power" does the recovery industry call men to depend? Dr. William Playfair documents their answer: "God as we understand Him."[47] They allow any concept of a higher power. They call men to depend on any god they like. Playfair exposes this sham: "If we say any god will do as long as he is greater than you, we may open the door for Satan himself. Why is it so easy for us to call Hinduism, Buddhism,

---

[46] Job 1:12, 22, 2:3-6, 10

[47] William L. Playfair M.D., *The Useful Lie* (Wheaton, IL: Crossway Books, 1991), 89-98

Mormonism, or Shintoism false religion and not the religion of AA or the recovery industry? AA and the recovery industry's doctrine of God is clearly just as false."[48] The only "higher powers" that exist are the true God and demons. Higher powers that men invent are non-entities. Such gods cannot deliver men from addiction or any other evil. In this way the recovery industry promotes false religion. Men hope in vain that impotent gods of their own invention will emancipate them. Only the true God can set people free from the enslaving power of sin. They must "look unto him" alone to deliver them, because he is God, "and there is none else."

Unit 4: The Denial of God's Existence

Ps. 14:1-4: The fool has said in his heart: There is no God. They are corrupt, they have done abominable works; there is none that does good. Jehovah looked down from heaven upon the children of men, to see if there were any that did understand, that did seek after God. They are all gone aside; they are together become filthy; there is none that does good, no, not one. Have all the workers of iniquity no knowledge, who eat up my people as they eat bread, and call not upon Jehovah?

This passage focuses on heart atheism. It begins with a fundamental lesson about it. Then it paints a sordid picture of its practical and moral implications. Observe in this text: (1) the concept of heart atheism, "The fool has said *in his heart*"; (2) the folly of heart atheism, "*the fool* has said"; (3) the moral fruits of heart atheism, "They are corrupt, they have done abominable works"; (4) the universal spread of heart atheism, "there is none that does good . . . there is none that does good, no, not one"; and (5) the telltale signs of heart atheism, "Who eat up my people as they eat bread, and call not upon Jehovah." We now expound these five observations.

I. ***The Concept of Heart Atheism:*** "said in his heart: There is no God"

Atheism is avowed disbelief in the existence of God. It involves open denial of his existence. This text discloses something about the human heart that is neither obvious nor freely acknowledged. It discerns that open atheism is not the only kind of atheism in the world. A more subtle form of atheism exists. I call this type of atheism, "*heart atheism*," because it resides in the heart. Men guilty of heart atheism profess with their mouths that they believe in God, but in their hearts they say, "*There is no God.*"

The state of every person's heart defines his moral and spiritual condition. Thus, a person does not need to embrace atheism openly; heart atheism is

---

[48] Ibid, 93

sufficient to ruin the soul. The Lord confirms this crucial role of the heart.[49] Therefore, we should guard our hearts above all else (Prov. 4:23). To avoid heart atheism, we must understand it. Thus, consider its *core* and its *roots*.

A. The Core of Heart Atheism: *no fear of God*

The core of heart atheism is: "There is no fear of God before their eyes." The fear of God is the awareness of his eye upon you, even in secret. It is recognizing your primary accountability to him at all times, in all circumstances (Lev. 19:14). Thus, heart atheism is the absence of the fear of God.

B. The Roots of Heart Atheism: carnal pride and desires: "all his thoughts are there is no God"[50]

Psalm 10 identifies two primary taproots of heart atheism, carnal pride and carnal desires.

1. Carnal pride: "the wicked, in the pride of his countenance, says, He will not require it"

Carnal pride is the first taproot of heart atheism. Those infected with heart atheism think: "I can sin and get away with it." They reason that there must be no recompense for wicked deeds, because lightning doesn't strike those who commit them (Eccles. 8:11). They imagine that God has forgotten, or that somehow, at the end, they will escape his wrath no matter how they live (Rom. 2:3-5). They ignore God's purpose for delaying the punishment of sin, which is to "lead them to repentance." Such persons think too highly of themselves. They despise God. They dare God to damn them. Yet God does nothing. Thus they think, "What kind of God is this? Why should I be afraid of the likes of him?"

2. Carnal desires: "the covetous renounces, yea contemns Jehovah"

The carnal desires of lost persons are the second taproot of heart atheism. Those in the state of sin despise and renounce God because they covet. Coveting is indulging lusts. Lusts are inordinate or forbidden desires. When

---

[49] *Luke 6:45*: The good man out of the good treasure of his heart brings forth that which is good; and the evil man out of the evil treasure brings forth that which is evil: for out of the abundance of his heart his mouth speaks

[50] *Ps. 10:3-7*: the wicked boasts of his heart's desire, and the covetous renounces, yea, contemns Jehovah. The wicked, in the pride of his countenance, says, He will not require it. All his thoughts are, there is no God. His ways are firm at all times; Your judgments are far above out of his sight: As for all his adversaries, he puffs at them. He says in his heart, I shall not be moved; To all generations I shall not be in adversity. His mouth is full of cursing and deceit and oppression: Under his tongue is mischief and iniquity.

people indulge lust, they deny God's existence in their hearts. Inordinate desires for power, fame, sexual pleasure, possessions, or cheer, drive people to heart atheism. Therefore, atheism is not objective or impartial. It doesn't engage in honest investigation. Rather, it generates a lifestyle hateful to God and attempts to justify its hope to get away with it. Heart atheism does not come from intellectual difficulties, but from moral decadence. It doesn't start in the head, but in the heart. Let me put this in concrete terms. When I was in college, I had a pat answer for my engineering classmates when they lamented to me that they had intellectual problems with the existence of God. I used to quip, "Oh, you have intellectual problems, what's her name?" Intellectual problems are a smoke screen. The underlying problems are pride and indulged lust. Don't be naive brethren. Deal faithfully in love with those that espouse it. Call them to repentance from the taproot sins of heart atheism. Do they indulge sexual lust? Are they bitter against God? Do they blame God because tragedy hit them or someone they love? Is it money? Is it popularity? Heart atheists don't search for God sincerely and fail to find him. They challenge God brazenly and succeed in suppressing what they know to be true about him.

II. The Foolishness of Heart Atheism: "the fool has said in his heart"

The fundamental lesson of our text is: *heart atheism makes a person a spiritual fool.* If it is foolish to deny God's existence secretly in the heart, how much more foolish is it to deny his existence openly with the mouth? What is folly? Scripture contrasts foolishness with wisdom and prudence. Folly involves "a lack of good sense, or a failure to use good judgment." This text depicts a moral folly that relates to spiritual reality. A person can be wise in the things of the world and yet be foolish in the things of God. A spiritual fool lacks good sense in relation to God, his soul, spiritual things, and the world to come. Why is a heart atheist spiritually foolish? Consider with me a biblical exposé of this folly. In this exposé I follow the trail that Charnock blazed. Charnock enlarges upon four things that uncover this folly: universal knowledge, creation, conscience, and Scripture.[51]

A. Universal Knowledge Exposes the Foolishness of Atheism

Charnock appeals to what he calls "universal consent," as his first reason that atheism is great folly: "It is folly to deny or doubt of that which has been the acknowledged sentiment of all nations, in all places and ages."[52]

---

[51] Charnock, *Existence and Attributes*, 13-58.
[52] Ibid, 17. He expounds this first reason that atheism is great folly on pages 17-27.

Everyone knows that God exists. To deny what everyone, including you, knows to be true shows a significant lack of good sense.

B. Creation Exposes the Foolishness of Atheism

Second, Charnock appeals to the revelation of God's existence in creation as his second reason that atheism is folly: "It is folly to deny that which all creatures, or all things in the world manifest."[53] He argues convincingly that the world cannot be eternal. He observes that generations propagating after their kind necessitate a first generation of each kind. He concludes that an eternity of generations without a beginning makes no sense. Then he appeals to the harmony, design, and preservation of the material world. The realities of creation clash with atheism—and every atheist knows it. Clearly it lacks good sense to deny what you know creation clearly displays to you.

C. Conscience Exposes the Foolishness of Atheism

Third, Charnock appeals to the operations of conscience: "It is a folly to deny that which a man's own nature witnesseth to him."[54] The conscience of every person tells him that God condemns those who live in gross sin. Conscience tells every person that God obliges and commends doing right, and condemns doing wrong. Yet no atheist openly admits what his own heart tells him inwardly. It plainly lacks good sense to deny what your own conscience tells you.

D. Scripture Exposes the Foolishness of Atheism

Fourth, Charnock appeals to special revelation: "it is a folly to deny the being of God, which is witnessed unto by extraordinary occurrences in the world."[55] He then lists three categories of such events to which Scripture bears witness: (1) extraordinary judgments, (2) miracles, and (3) accomplishments of prophecies. Special revelation records many miracles, theophanies, and fulfilled prophecies that attest God's existence. Sadly, some have the privilege of seeing this clear attestation of God's existence, yet like Pharaoh, they refuse to humble themselves and acknowledge it. This displays a lack of good judgment in spiritual things.

In sum, it is foolish to deny God's existence because everyone knows it, the whole world displays it, men's own consciences declare it, and Scripture attests it. Further, it is brazen folly to deny openly what you know to be true. Everyone knows that God exists from creation and from conscience.

---

[53] Ibid, 27. He expounds this second reason that atheism is great folly on pages 27-46
[54] Ibid, 46. He expounds this third reason that atheism is great folly on pages 46-56
[55] Ibid, 56. He expounds this fourth reason that atheism is great folly on pages 56-58

Therefore, when a man says that he doesn't believe that God exists, this really means that he refuses outwardly to admit what he inwardly knows to be true. That indeed displays a profound lack of good sense.

III. The Moral Fruits of Heart Atheism: "They are corrupt, they have done abominable works"

Heart atheism breeds a wicked way of life. Men do what they do because men are what they are: "They have done abominable works" precisely because "they are corrupt." Heart atheism is the epitome and foundation of corrupt nature. Heart atheism can only give rise to a wicked way of life. It cannot bear edible fruit because it is a poisonous plant. The moral fruits of atheism in the heart are manifold. It produces carnal behavior toward other men in every conceivable respect. It spreads its folly like the wind scatters seeds. It holds nothing sacred. It despises every requirement of God's law. The proverbs expose these manifold fruits. Spiritual fools despise the sanctity of proper authority,[56] of human life,[57] of marriage,[58] of private property,[59] and of truth.[60] Atheism in men's hearts produces every kind and degree of wickedness in men's lives. It produces disrespect, insolence, rebellion, anarchy and tyranny; hatred, enmity, railing, strife, and murder; promiscuity, adultery, rape, incest, and homosexuality; ingratitude, greed, laziness, theft, and extortion; lying, deceit, cheating, slander, and perjury. This is why an atheistic society cannot sustain moral decency. Godlessness breeds crime and man's inhumanity to man (Prov. 19:29). Conversely, only the fear of God can breed and sustain a decent society. When a society forsakes God, it begins to disintegrate and destroy itself. Sadly, this process is already at work in America. Yet, men remain adamant that we can have a decent and peaceful society without the theistic values on which America was built. This text exposes the error of a humanistic view of morality.

IV. The Universal Spread of Heart Atheism "There is none that does good"

All fallen human beings are not overt atheists, but all in the state of sin are atheists in their hearts. Heart atheism is the tragic folly of all men in Adam. The text depicts heart atheism in still darker colors. This moral virus not only produces all manner of wicked behavior, it infects everyone in Adam. The passage highlights this truth. This section of the passage begins and ends with the assertion: "There is none that does good." Everything in

---

[56] Prov. 14:16, 15:5, 20
[57] Prov. 14:29, 18:6, 20:3
[58] Prov. 6:32, 9:13-18
[59] Prov. 10:5, 21:25, 26
[60] Prov. 10:18, 11:9, 14:8

between confirms the universality of heart atheism. All human beings (Jesus Christ excepted) contracted this moral virus from our father Adam. We are all conceived with it. We all die with it, and are damned by it, unless the gospel cures us from it. Conversion is the only cure for heart atheism. God in mercy spares us from facing the unbridled fury of this spiritual virus. If the heart atheism of every sinner on earth were totally unleashed, if God allowed it to run rampant without restraint, life in society would not even be possible. God restrains this virus with conscience, with the desire to live, with marriage, with parental nurture, with civil government, and with other means. These restraints prevent heart atheism from producing as much of its fruit as it would otherwise bear. Even a spiritual fool has a conscience. At times conscience restrains such fools from doing all the folly in their hearts (Rom. 2:14-15). Even a moral fools want to live. The fear of venereal disease is sometimes all that prevents acts of perversion. Even moral fools have parents who trained them not to express all their inward folly outwardly (Prov. 22:15). Even moral fools have sexual lust restrained to some degree by marriage (Prov. 5:15-19; 1 Cor. 7:1, 2). Even moral fools sometimes refrain from crime because they fear going to jail (Prov. 19:29; Rom. 13:4). Ironically, spiritual fools assume that they are wise because God in such ways restrains their folly. In pride and self-righteousness they proclaim their own virtue. Yet in Adam there are no exceptions, "there is none that does good."

V. *The Telltale Signs of Heart Atheism:* "Who eat up my people as they eat bread, and call not upon Jehovah?"

Heart atheism makes men hostile to God's people, "who eat up my people as they eat bread," and prayer-less before God, "And call not upon Jehovah." Disaffection to the people of God has always marked the workers of iniquity. God himself has initiated this enmity between the children of the devil and his own children (Gen. 3:15). He has ordained that it shall continue until the end of the world. Thus, this enmity is an indelible mark of people infected with heart atheism. Those who have this virus hate to go to church or be with true Christians. They say they hate to be with hypocrites, but they really hate to be with saints. If they really hate hypocrites, why are they willing to spend eternity with them in hell? The other telltale sign of heart atheism is disaffection to God. Those infected with this virus live as though God did not exist. They have no dealings with him. They are not on speaking terms with him. Thus, those who have this virus do not truly pray. They do not "call on Jehovah." To "*call on Jehovah*" means to address him by faith, in a posture of trust and submission, in accordance with his gospel (Acts 22:16). Whatever those infected with heart atheism may appear to be in public, in secret they never truly pray. Even some who profess to believe in

God *never* call on God in secret. They affirm confidently that all is well with their souls. They say they have assurance that they are going to heaven. They excuse prayerlessness in a thousand ways. They downplay its significance. In truth, it is a symptom of heart atheism. It betrays that they are "workers of iniquity." It testifies against them that they are yet in their sins. I stress the word *never* because I do not mean that all who struggle with consistency in secret prayer are lost.

Unit 5: The Practical Importance of the Existence of God

God's existence is of great importance *morally*, *remedially*, and *existentially*.

I. The Moral Import of God's Existence

Psalm 14:1-4 displays its moral impact. Heart atheism stems from pride and lust. It breeds wickedness. It destroys moral decency and promotes decadence. It prevents prayer. Thus, it destroys devotion and promotes irreverence. All those in the state of sin deny God's existence in their hearts. Therefore, heart atheism is the fountain of human depravity and the spring of all the decadence and irreverence in the world. Conversely, God's existence is the great nemesis of human depravity, and the foundation of all the moral decency and true religious devotion in the world. Here is its moral import.

II. The Remedial Import of God's Existence

God's existence gives mankind hope of deliverance from sin and death. In Unit 3 we saw that other gods do not exist. Such gods cannot save anybody from anything. The religions by which people look to them for help are futile. Therefore, if deliverance from sin must come from the gods of this world and the religions that appeal to them, then mankind has no hope, no remedy for sin. In Unit 4 we learned that heart atheism breeds only decadence and irreverence and that it infects everyone in Adam. Therefore, if deliverance from sin must come from sinners, then mankind has no hope, no remedy for sin. Therefore, then, unless the true God intervenes on man's behalf to save people from sin and death, mankind has no hope, no remedy for sin. Human beings want to be clothed in virtue and honor, but cannot escape their self-reproach and shame before their fellow humans. If there is no God, then mankind is wandering aimlessly in the maze of its own self-condemnation, guilt, and shame. Human beings want to live in comfort and safety, but cannot escape danger and suffering. If God does not exist, then mankind is permanently trapped in its present state of misery. Above all, human beings want to live. They dread death and what lies beyond it. Yet they have no power over death. They are its slaves (Heb. 2:15). If there is no God, then mankind has no hope of overcoming death. All this leads us back to Isaiah 45:22. Blessed be God, there is a remedy because God does exist. Mankind does have hope of deliverance from sin and death. This is the glorious message of this text. God in the gospel publishes this hope of divine deliverance. He personally calls sinners to experience his salvation. Consider the *substance* and *scope* of this call.

A. *The Substance of God's Call:* "Look unto me, and be saved"

God himself delivers human beings from sin, misery, death, and damnation, through the person and work of his only Son, Jesus Christ. In the gospel he calls mankind to experience his deliverance (2 Thess. 2:14). Thus, the substance of this call is that people should exercise repentance toward God and faith in our Lord Jesus Christ (Mark 1:15; Acts 20:21). This is what it means to look to God for salvation.

B. *The Scope of God's Call:* "all the ends of the earth"

God's call extends to all mankind. He commands all human beings everywhere to repent and believe (Acts 17:30-31, 20:21). This is because all people everywhere need to be saved from the wrath of God against their sins (Rom. 1:18, 3:9-20). Shame, misery, and fear drive lost sinners to find a way to deliver themselves. Sadly, their search ends in futility and failure, because through false religions they call on gods that cannot save. Jehovah himself, the true God, appeals to all peoples to put a stop to this foolishness and futility once and for all. He pleads with them to stop looking for help to gods that don't exist. He appeals to them to look to him for help.

III. The Existential Import of God's Existence

God's existence is the basis for the existence of the universe. His existence grounds the existence of everything that exists. Divine creation, preservation, and intention demonstrate this.

A. *Divine Creation* (Gen. 1:1)

God brought into existence the universe and everything in it: "In the beginning God created the heavens and the earth." Before God created everything he already existed: "*In the beginning* God created." Thus, God's existence is the rationale for the existence of the universe. God always existed. God made everything. Everything that is exists because God made it. Man exists because God exists. Angels exist because God exists. The earth exists because God exists. The universe exists because God exists.

B. *Divine Preservation* (Acts 17:25; Col. 1:17; Heb. 1:3)

God keeps everything in existence. The Creator is also the Sustainer. He sustains all life. We do not sustain his life; he sustains ours. He doesn't depend on us for existence. We depend on him.[61] The Triune God keeps everything, not just men, in existence.[62] He sustains it all, just like he made it all, by his Word.[63] Therefore, God's existence is the ground of the existence of the universe.

C. Divine Intention (Rev. 4:11)

God wants everything in existence for a reason: "for you did create all things, and *because of your will* they were, and were created" (Rev. 4:11). God has a purpose for everything he made. The Creator and Sustainer also is the Sovereign. His will gives meaning to everything that exists. Because he exists, everything else that exists has meaning. It has meaning because he decided the reason for its existence. The earth has meaning because God exists. The heavens have meaning because God exists. Man has meaning because God exists. Life has meaning because God exists. Everything has meaning because God exists. This is the import of God's existence.

Conclusion to Part 1: In conclusion I sum up the content of this lecture. *God's existence is a fact.* Scripture assumes and asserts that fact. *God's existence is revealed.* God reveals his existence generally to all mankind in creation and conscience. He reveals it in a special way in Scripture in conjunction with supernatural intrusions in history, theophany, and prophecy. *God's existence is unique.* All other so-called gods are non-entities. The religions by which men serve them are false. None of them has any power to save or to harm men. *God's existence is denied.* Spiritual fools deny it. Heart atheism produces great wickedness and infects all mankind in Adam. It produces disaffection to God's people. It stifles prayer. *God's existence is important.* It is important morally. Its denial is the spring of all the decadence and irreverence in the world. It is important remedially. It affords mankind the hope of deliverance from sin and death. It is important existentially. It is the basis for the existence of the entire universe. Everything rests on God's existence. May the Lord engrave these truths, by the power of his Spirit, upon our hearts.

---

[61] *Acts 17:25*: neither is he served by men's hands, as though he needed anything, seeing he gives to all life, and breath, and all things.

[62] *Col. 1:17*: and in him all things hold together.

[63] *Heb. 1:3*: and upholding all things by the word of his power.

Topic 3. The Knowability of God

"neither does any know the Father, save the Son, and he to whomsoever the Son wills to reveal him" (Matt. 11:27);
"And this is life eternal, that they should know you the only true God" (John 17:3)

Part 2: The Knowledge of God

Introduction to Part 2: *God's knowability and incomprehensibility*

In Part 2 our theme is men's knowledge of God. Our epitomizing texts certify that it is possible for men to have true and personal knowledge of God. The two texts that introduce God's incomprehensibility[1] confirm with equal clarity that it is impossible for men to have *exhaustive* knowledge of God. Finite men can have accurate knowledge of the infinite God, but never exhaustive knowledge. God's knowability indicates that men can and do know God truly. God's incomprehensibility indicates that men can never know God completely and exhaustively. Perhaps no single text draws these two aspects of truth together as ably as Ephesians 3:19: "and to know the love of Christ that passes knowledge." Paul prays that God would strengthen Christians in their souls by his Spirit to know the love of Christ. The love of Christ is knowable. Yet, this love of Christ, even though it is knowable, is also incomprehensible: "*that passes knowledge.*" We unfold God's knowability in Section 1 and God's incomprehensibility in Section 2.

Section 1. The Knowability of God

The Bible presents two distinct ways in which people can and do know God. As a result, Scripture speaks of two distinct types of knowledge of God. The first is the *damning* knowledge, which gives rise to God's "*universal knowability.*" The second is *saving* knowledge, which gives rise to his "*evangelical knowability.*" The knowability of God rests on this distinction. We now consider each aspect.

Unit 1. The Universal Knowability of God

The Bible describes a sense in which all in Adam can and do know God. We could call this knowledge general, universal, creative, or damning. All men know that God exists, because all men know the Creator through general

---

[1] Ps. 145:3; Rom. 11:33

revelation in creation[2] and conscience.[3] We first review what we have already learned about God's universal knowability; second, look its radical inadequacy; and third, consider an important lesson about its limited role and proper use.

I. Review of the Universal Knowledge of God

We now summarize the prominent features, sinful response, and damning impact of this knowledge.

A. The Prominent Features

We noted three prominent features. First, we observed *the source* of God's universal knowability. God is knowable through general revelation in creation and conscience (Rom. 2:14-15). Second, we observed the *scope* of God's knowability as Creator. All men in Adam, even agnostics and atheists, know their Creator. Third, we observed *the substance* of universal knowledge. All men through creation perceive the Creator's eternal power and deity (Rom. 1:20). Further, all men through conscience know that they are accountable to their Lord and Judge who regards them worthy of death (Rom. 1:32, 2:14-15).

B. The Sinful Response

We observed that evil men hate, distort, and suppress this knowledge. Some even openly deny that they know God (Rom. 1:18, 25, 28). Yet human beings can never completely erase this knowledge from their hearts, even if they openly hate and deny God and refuse to serve him (Rev. 16:9).

C. The Damning Impact

We have also studied the damning impact of this universal knowledge of God on all in Adam. This knowledge doesn't restore men to fellowship with their Maker. Rather, it leaves them no excuse for sin and condemns them before their Lord and Judge: "that they may be without excuse: because that, knowing God, they glorified him not as God, neither gave thanks." In Adam, it always has a condemning impact. Thus, I call it *damning* knowledge.

---

[2] *Rom. 1:19-21*: Because that which is known of God is manifest in them; for God manifested it unto them. For the invisible things of him since the creation of the world are clearly seen, being perceived through the things that are made, even his everlasting power and divinity; that they may be without excuse: because that, knowing God, they glorified him not as God, neither gave thanks; but became vain in their reasonings, and their senseless heart was darkened.

[3] *Rom. 1:32*: who, knowing the ordinance of God, that they that practice such things are worthy of death, not only do the same, but also consent with them that practice them.

II. The Radical Inadequacy of the Universal Knowledge of God

Universal knowledge of God through creation and conscience is inadequate to save sinners. Thus, Scripture affirms repeatedly and clearly that those in the state of sin *do not know* God. Jesus affirms that the world doesn't know God.[4] Paul asserts that lost Gentiles don't know God.[5] Scripture asserts that lost nations have no knowledge of God.[6] Even among those born under the Old Covenant, many didn't know God.[7] Even some priests, like Eli's sons, didn't know him.[8] Jesus confirmed this unpopular truth. He courageously told some of his countrymen that they didn't know God because they rejected God's Son.[9] He accurately predicted that some sinners, because they didn't know God, would persecute his disciples.[10] Even some who profess the Christian religion don't know God. Jesus told some who professed to be his disciples (John 8:31) that they didn't know God.[11] John warned professing Christians that men who say they know God, yet live wickedly, are liars.[12] Even those who now know God have not always known him. The Galatians only came to know him after they turned from their idols.[13]

Indisputably then, the Bible speaks about knowing God in two completely different respects or ways. Men in the state of sin simultaneously know God in one sense and do not know him in another. Lost sinners know God as Creator, with damning knowledge obtained from general revelation. Yet

---

[4] *John 17:25*: O righteous Father, the world knew you not, but I knew you

[5] *1 Thess. 4:5*: not in the passion of lust, even as the Gentiles who know not God; *1 Cor. 15:34*: Awake to soberness righteously, and sin not; for some have no knowledge of God: I speak this to move you to shame

[6] *Ps. 79:6*: Pour out your wrath upon the nations that don't know you; *2 Thess. 1:8*: rendering vengeance to them that know not God, and to them that obey not the gospel of our Lord Jesus

[7] *Jer. 9:3, 6*: they are grown strong in the land, but not for truth: for they proceed from evil to evil, and they don't know me, says Jehovah ... 6 through deceit they refuse to know me, says Jehovah

[8] *1 Sam. 2:12*: Now the sons of Eli were base men, they knew not Jehovah

[9] *John 8:19*: They said therefore to him, Where is your Father? Jesus answered: You know neither me, nor my Father: if you knew me, you would know my Father also

[10] *John 16:3*: And these things will they do, because they have not known the Father, nor me

[11] *John 8:54-55*: it is my Father that glorifies me; of whom you say, that he is your God; and you have not known him: but I know him; and if I should say, I know him not, I shall be like you, a liar

[12] *1 John 2:3-4*: And hereby we know that we know him, if we keep his commandments. He that says, I know him, and keeps not his commandments, is a liar

[13] *Gal. 4:8-9*: Howbeit at that time not knowing God, you were in bondage to them that by nature are no gods: but now that you have come to know God, or rather to be known by God

they do not know him with saving knowledge. They do not have that knowledge of God that is eternal life (John 17:3). Creation and conscience alone are impotent in this respect. They cannot give sinners saving knowledge of God. If sinners had only general revelation, God would be unknowable in this most profound way. Only God's Word conveys saving knowledge of God. That is its glory. Thus, the Bible is remedial. It is God's means to save men from sin. In this respect universal knowledge of God by itself without God's Word is futile and vain. Here is its radical inadequacy.

III. The Limited Role and Use of the Universal Knowledge of God

Thus, it would be wrong to major on universal knowledge. It would dishonor the prominence Scripture assigns to evangelical knowledge. This highlights an important lesson about the limits of human wisdom. The apostle teaches this philosophy lesson to the Corinthians. He affirms that human insight unaided by Scripture has always failed to attain saving knowledge of God: "the world through its wisdom knew not God."[14] He explains that God deliberately engineered this failure: "has not God made foolish the wisdom of the world?"[15] All the insight of men devoid of God's Word can never meet the desperate need of a human soul to know God. The reasoning of the world can never bring true solace to those in the state of sin. Rather, the world's wisdom leads lost men around in circles back to the pit where they started. It leaves them without excuse and without an effective remedy for their sin. Ironically, all their insight adds up to ignorance of God. Thus, such wisdom is foolish. Paul calls their collected knowledge: *"the wisdom of the world."* Theologians call it *"Natural Theology."* Natural Theology attempts philosophically to display man's knowledge of God comprehensively through logic and reason alone.

Here is the lesson. We should keep the universal knowledge of God in the place the Lord has assigned to it. If God has made Natural Theology foolish, can Christian theologians make it wise? If God has made it unprofitable for salvation, what benefit can come from filling books of Christian theology with it? Dear brethren, take this lesson to heart. Never forget it. Let it regulate your approach to theology. Any theology composed of philosophical speculations can neither help men nor honor God. It won't humble men before God, but inflate them with a false sense of their own profundity: "Professing themselves to be wise, they became fools" (Rom. 1:22). It won't enlighten men in spiritual blindness, but further entangle them in the maze of their own ignorance: "they became vain in their

---

[14] 1 Cor. 1:21
[15] 1 Cor. 1:20

reasonings, and their senseless heart was darkened" (Rom. 1:21). It won't lead men to worship God with thanksgiving, but harden them in the worship of their own minds: "they did not glorify him as God, neither gave thanks; but became vain in their reasonings" (Rom. 1:21). Like pagan philosophers of old, modern secular philosophers have "exchanged the truth of God for a lie, and worshipped and served the creature rather than the Creator, who is blessed forever" (Rom. 1:25). Such have formulated an idolatrous religion in which man is god, reason and investigation are his prophets, and human intellect is their divine word, their final authority. We should not do anything to encourage this self-worship. We should not formulate sacred theology with the methods of secular philosophy. We should reject their way of thinking and think God's thoughts after him. Fallen human reason, walking by the dim light of general revelation alone, can never lead men to saving knowledge of God. Thus I would be an unfaithful steward if I filled your heads with Natural Theology. Only God's Word, unalloyed with human speculations, presented and applied by the light and power of the Holy Spirit, can teach men to know God. Thus, a teacher of systematic theology must aim to expound the riches of God's Word with the perspective Paul expressed in 1 Corinthians 2:1-14. He must not act as a philosopher devoid of Scripture. He must not come "with excellency of speech or of wisdom" in order that men's faith "should not stand in the wisdom of men, but in the power of God."

Unit 2. The Evangelical Knowability of God

The Bible also depicts a sense in which all in Christ, and only those in Christ, know God. I call this knowledge, "evangelical," "experimental," or "saving." Under the Old Covenant some of God's people had saving knowledge of God. This knowledge was to be their chief delight and boast.[16] Yet the prophets foretold a better day for God's people. Under the new covenant saving knowledge of God would distinguish and mark them as a society.[17] In that day "the people that know their God" would do exploits.[18] In that day God himself would come to dwell among his people.[19] It would be the day of Immanuel,

---

[16] *Jer. 9:24*: But let him that glories glory in this, that he has understanding, and knows me, that I am Jehovah who exercises lovingkindness, justice, and righteousness, in the earth: for in these things I delight, says Jehovah.

[17] *Jer. 31:34*: and they shall teach no more every man his neighbor, and every man his brother, saying, Know Jehovah; for they shall all know me, from the least of them unto the greatest of them, says Jehovah: for I will be merciful to their iniquity, and their sin will I remember no more.

[18] *Dan. 11:32*: And such as do wickedly against the covenant shall he pervert by flatteries; but the people that know their God shall be strong, and do exploits

[19] Isa. 7:14, 9:6-7, 11:2-9

"God with us." Immanuel would fulfill these blessed promises personally. Through him the knowledge of God would "cover the earth as the waters cover the sea" (Isa. 11:9). Blessed be God that day has come. Jesus Christ is Immanuel,[20] God incarnate.[21] Accordingly, Immanuel Jesus is the epitome of God's evangelical knowability. Only through him can men know God evangelically.[22] To know him is to know God.[23] Thus, Christ's words epitomize biblical thought about saving knowledge of God. Thus, I glean categories of thought regarding saving knowledge from his pronouncements.

Some may scoff at deriving categories of thought from Jesus' words. They could call this a "red letter" theology. It is a sad day when a teacher of theology must justify following trails of thought blazed by Christ. Who can categorize our thought about knowing God better than Immanuel? Which is a better model, the inspired mindset about the knowledge of God championed by heavenly Immanuel Christ, or the agnostic mindset about it peddled by worldly Immanuel Kant? I would rather dress my soul in a "red letter" theology cut from the thought patterns of God incarnate, than play the naked and unashamed fool in a "no clothes" theology of knowing God cut from the pretensions of "emperor" reason.

First, Christ unfolds three *major features* of saving knowledge: its source, scope, and substance.[24] Second, Christ depicts two *distinguishing characteristics* of saving knowledge: its complete sufficiency and momentous significance.[25] Third, Christ affirms the *practical application* saving knowledge. He reveals its telltale signs and presses its moral summons.[26] We expound saving knowledge accordingly.

I. Three Major Features of the Evangelical Knowledge of God

Notice with me its source, scope, substance.

A. The Source of the Evangelical Knowledge of God: special revelation

How can finite men on earth have experiential knowledge of the infinite God of heaven? The source is special revelation. This special revelation has two

---

[20] Matt. 1:21-23

[21] John 1:1, 14

[22] *Matt. 11:27-28*: All things have been delivered unto me of my Father: and no one knows the Son, save the Father; neither does any know the Father, save the Son, and he to whomsoever the Son wills to reveal him. Come unto me, all you that labor and are heavy laden, and I will give you rest

[23] John 8:19, 14:7-9

[24] Matt. 11:27-28

[25] John 17:3

[26] John 8:54-55, 17:26

aspects. *First*, God the Son conveys saving knowledge to sinners in the gospel. *Second*, God the Spirit conveys it to saints in the Scriptures. These harmonize completely. God the Son sends God the Spirit to reveal saving knowledge to his apostles (John 16:12-13). They in turn publish it to the church in Scripture (Acts 2:33; 1 Cor. 2:10-14). When the church proclaims the gospel, Christ by his Spirit reveals God to sinners (Rom. 10:14-15).

1. God the Son conveys saving knowledge to sinners through the gospel (Matt. 11:27-28).

We consider the necessity, sufficiency, and methodology of his conveyance of saving knowledge.

a. The absolute necessity of the Son's conveyance of saving knowledge[27]

Human beings know God evangelically only through special revelation from Christ himself. Thus, evangelical knowledge is "*special*," since people can only attain it through special revelation. Everyone in Adam needs this saving knowledge of God the Father.[28] Special revelation from God the Son is the only way any human being can ever attain this saving knowledge. No man, religion, or philosophy can reach God without Christ. Any person, religion, or philosophy that does not have Christ, God the Son, does not and cannot know God the Father.[29]

b. The unique sufficiency of the Son's conveyance of saving knowledge[30]

Christ alone, because he is God the Son, has complete and intimate knowledge of God the Father. Only he can accurately and effectively convey saving knowledge. His deity grounds his unique ability to make God known experimentally.

c. The gospel methodology of the Son's conveyance of saving knowledge[31]

Jesus Christ conveys saving knowledge of God through the gospel. God the Son sincerely calls lost men indiscriminately to come to him to receive saving knowledge of the Father. Reformed theologians name this the "general call," or "free offer," of the gospel. Yet this well-meant offer is only part of the story. In conjunction with it, Jesus bestows saving knowledge on men according to the good pleasure of his will: "he to

---

[27] neither does any know the Father, save the Son, and he to whomsoever the Son wills to reveal him

[28] John 1:10-13, 8:19, 8:54-55, 16:3, 17:25

[29] John 14:6; 1 John 2:23, 5:20; 2 John 9

[30] neither does any know the Father, save the Son

[31] he to whomsoever the Son wills to reveal him. Come unto me, all you that labor and are heavy laden, and I will give you rest. Take my yoke upon you, and learn of me

whomsoever the Son wills to reveal him." Reformed theologians name this the "effectual call" of the gospel. The LCF associates this gospel method with "the covenant of grace" (7:2). In sum, sinners can come to know God only because God the Son knows God the Father and makes him known through the general and effectual call of the gospel.

2. God the Spirit conveys saving knowledge to saints through the Scriptures (1 Cor. 2:10-14).[32]

The focus of this text is "the deep things" God reveals to Christians. Paul also calls them, "the things of the Spirit of God," "the things of God," and, "the things that were freely given to us by God." They are God's gracious thoughts and purposes toward those in Christ. Only by knowing them, can we know him intimately. Consider five observations from the text regarding this saving knowledge of God.

a. God has complete knowledge of himself, even of his deepest thoughts and purposes (1 Cor. 2:10).

If God were ignorant of himself, men couldn't know him. If he lacked self-awareness, or the ability to understand his thoughts, he would be unknowable. The foundation of his knowability is that he knows himself. Whereas the Holy Spirit is the Supreme Being, he searches and knows all the things of God. The Spirit's deity explains his ability to reveal evangelical knowledge of God.

b. God can only be known intimately through self-disclosure (1 Cor. 2:11).

God can only be known through self-disclosure because God alone knows his hidden thoughts and purposes. In this respect knowing God is like knowing a man. The Creator designed man as his image to be a living visible picture of the invisible God. Here is one facet of that picture. An analogy exists between the "things of God" and "the things of a man." The "things of a man" are the secret thoughts and purposes of his heart. He alone knows the secrets of his inner life. Other men cannot know him intimately unless he discloses his heart. Even so, self-disclosure is essential to the knowledge of God. Without it God would be unknowable.

---

[32] *1 Cor. 2:10-14*: for the Spirit searches all things, yea, the deep things of God. For who among men knows the things of a man, save the spirit of the man, which is in him? even so the things of God none knows, save the Spirit of God. But we received, not the spirit of the world, but the Spirit that is from God; that we might know the things that were freely given to us of God. Which things also we freely speak . . . Now the natural man does not receive the things of the Spirit of God: for they are foolishness unto him; and he cannot know them, because they are spiritually judged.

c. God is willing and able to reveal himself to human beings (1 Cor. 2:12).

God is willing and able to reveal himself to men, because he himself has deliberately enabled Christians to know him. God would be unknowable if he were unwilling or unable to disclose his hidden thoughts to men. If God were aloof, or opaque, no one could know him. If he were distant, reclusive, or "anti-social," he would be unknowable. If he were autistic, completely absorbed in self-centered mental activity, he would be unknowable. If he could not communicate, no one could know him. If, like some men of genius, he could not communicate intelligibly on the level of creatures of lesser intellect, he would be unknowable. Therefore, the notion that God cannot or will not communicate effectively with men insults God. Even a deaf and blind mute can communicate. Even a retarded child can communicate. Is God of lesser ability than they? Should we think of God as a heavenly hermit? Is the Lord an "egghead" genius? Beyond ludicrous, such notions are blasphemous. Men who posit an unknowable God are pitiable, for they testify against themselves that they don't know him. Contrary to this delusion of some lost men, Paul declares that God is willing and able to reveal himself. He goes out of his way to be knowable. God, not man, has taken the initiative. He has enabled Christians to know him. This conclusion is valid whether the "spirit" that Paul says we received from God is the Holy Spirit given at conversion upon faith,[33] or the new spirit given at conversion in regeneration.[34] In either case, this enablement demonstrates God's willingness to be known.

d. God has revealed his deep thoughts and purposes in the Scriptures (2:13).

Christians are morally and experientially capable of knowing God. Yet he would still be unknowable unless he declared his thoughts to men in language they could comprehend. A silent God would be unknowable. An alien God speaking in some foreign tongue spoken only in heaven would be unknowable. Yet God has declared his deep things in Scripture. The Scriptures are the Word of God conveyed through inspired men. They are the words of God in the language of men. The apostles spoke the Word of God.[35] Paul's writings are Holy Scripture.[36] Scripture publishes "the deep things of God" in human language. Where did Paul learn God's thoughts and purposes? Paul tells us: "Things which eye saw not, and which entered not into the heart of man, whatsoever things God prepared for them that love

---

[33] Ezek. 36:27; Acts 2:38; Rom. 8:8-9
[34] Ezek. 36:26; Eph. 4:23-24
[35] 1 Thess. 3:13
[36] 2 Pet. 3:15-16

him. But unto us God revealed them through the Spirit: for the Spirit searches all things, yea the deep things of God" (1 Cor. 2:9-10). God is knowable because he has revealed his secret things to inspired writers who have declared them in Scripture.

e. Sinners can only know God through Scripture when he converts them by supernatural power (1 Cor. 2:14).

Fallen men are incapable of knowing God unless he saves them by a supernatural work of his grace. Scripture does not bring all men to know God. The fault is not in Scripture, but in fallen men. Unconverted men do not and cannot know the things of the Spirit of God. All human beings enter this world in the state of sin. Therefore, no man can know God by nature apart from grace (Rom. 3:9-20). The deep things of God are "foolishness" to lost sinners. They can read the Bible. They can understand its grammar and vocabulary. Yet they cannot know God through the Bible because they are spiritually blind and dead in sin. Their inability to know God is moral (Rom. 8:7). It is total. Sin pollutes and enslaves their entire soul (Titus 1:15). It is insurmountable by human strength alone. They are dead in sin. They cannot emancipate themselves from it (Eph. 2:1-3). Unless God changes their hearts through grace, they can never come to know him (Acts 16:14).

In sum, God is knowable because he knows himself, because he is willing and able to disclose himself to men, because he has disclosed himself perspicuously in the Scriptures, and because he has enabled Christians to know him by regenerating their hearts and placing his Spirit within them. In this way God the Spirit reveals saving knowledge of God to saints through the Scriptures.

B. The Scope of the Evangelical Knowledge of God (Matt. 11:27; 1 Cor. 2:14)

All those in Christ, but only those in Christ, know God. Our Lord affirms this limited scope of saving knowledge: "neither does any know the Father, save the Son, and he to whomsoever the Son wills to reveal him." Therefore, saving knowledge of God is *"Christian,"* or *"evangelical."* Lost sinners come to know God only through a supernatural work of sovereign grace. God takes the initiative. He draws them effectually to Christ.[37] He gives them a new heart capable of knowing him and places his Spirit within that new heart.[38] He thus creates persons anew and resurrects them from spiritual

---

[37] John 6:44
[38] Titus 3:5

death.[39] He does this only through the gospel.[40] He does it according to the good pleasure of his will.[41] If this work were left up to lost sinners, no one would ever come to know God. Thus, all the glory belongs to God alone. All God's elect chosen from eternity come to know him in spite of their moral inability.[42] Thus Jesus says, "all that which the Father gives me shall come to me" (John 6:37). God stands committed to bring each of his elect to saving knowledge.[43] He is not knowable in vain. He sees to it that a great multitude that no man can number actually does know him.[44] He personally draws each and all of them to his Son: "blessed is the man whom you choose, and cause to approach unto you" (Ps. 65:4). Therefore the saving knowledge of God will never be universal, but rather is evangelical, restricted to those in Christ.

C. The Substance of the Evangelical Knowledge of God

Introduction: the general idea of knowledge

What is saving knowledge of God? I introduce our answer with a survey of the teaching of Scripture about knowing. Knowledge in Scripture can have four distinct senses. To know something (or someone) can be to have information about it, or comprehension of it, or perception of it, or involvement with it.

First, to know is to have information about something. Thus, in Acts 5:7 Sapphira came in "not knowing what was done." She did not *know* [have information about] what had happened. Similarly, in John 7:28 Jesus says: "You both know me, and know whence I am." He means, you *have biographical information abou*t me and *have factual information about* where I'm from. In these instances men could acquire factual knowledge by research or by observation. Sometimes, however, men can only acquire factual knowledge by disclosure: "who among men knows the things of a man, save the spirit of a man, which is in him" (1 Cor. 2:11). Other men can only obtain information about secrets in a man's heart from the man himself, when he discloses them.

Second, to know can signify to have intellectual comprehension of something or someone, with various nuances. It can mean to grasp its

---

[39] Eph. 2:1-3, 4:24
[40] Matt. 11:27-28
[41] James 1:18
[42] Eph. 1:3-5
[43] Rom. 8:29-30
[44] Rev. 7:9, 10

significance (meaning or importance), or its substance (components or distinctive features). It can mean to comprehend its operation (how it works), or its functions (what role it plays), or its capabilities (what it can do), or its implications (what results from it). Thus, in Matthew 22:29 Jesus says: "You do err, not knowing the scriptures, nor the power of God." He means you do not *understand the significance* of the Scriptures or *comprehend the capabilities* of the power of God. Men acquire intellectual knowledge by study and meditation, which often involves instruction. Thus, the religious leaders wondered: "How does this man know letters, having never learned?" (John 7:15)

Third, to know can also mean to perceive or recognize, to "see" with the mind's eye. Thus, Pilate "knew that for envy they had delivered him up" (Matthew 27:18). Pilate knew [perceived] that envy was their real motive. Perceptual knowledge comes from discernment of present reality. Thus, the Lord said to Abraham: "now I know [perceive] that you fear God, seeing you have not withheld your . . . only son from me" (Gen. 22:12). Evidently the Lord cannot mean to say: now I *am finally informed*, or now I *finally understand* that you fear God. Rather, he means, "now I *discern the present reality* that you fear God." Discernment of present reality involves a process of recognition. To recognize something is to perceive its presence by noticing identifying marks previously placed on it, or by observing its distinguishing features. In this way Pilate recognized envy and the Lord recognized the fear of God.

Fourth, to know can mean to have experiential involvement or intercourse with something or someone in various relations and degrees. Thus Paul depicts Christ as: "Him who knew no sin" (2 Cor. 5:21). This cannot mean that Christ [had no information about] sin, or [had no comprehension of] sin, or [didn't discern the present reality of] sin. Clearly, Paul means that Christ [had no experiential involvement in] sin; or that Christ [had no moral intercourse with] sin. Similarly, in Luke 1:34 Mary wonders: "How shall this be, seeing I know not a man?" She means, seeing I [do not have intercourse, sexually, with] a man. Again, Lord says: "then will I profess unto them, I never knew you: depart from me" (Matt. 7:23). He can't mean I never [had any information about] you, or I [never understood] you, or I [never recognized] you. Rather, he means, I never [had loving intercourse spiritually with] you. Thus, experimental knowledge comes from personal contact, interaction, and intercourse of various kinds and degrees.

Scripture indicates that saving knowledge of God includes all these elements. It is factual, intellectual, perceptual, and experimental. It encompasses: (1) accurate information about God; (2) biblical understanding of him, especially his nature, expectations, and ways; (3) spiritual perception of him, especially his power, presence, and provisions; and (4) evangelical intercourse with him. Scripture progressively unfolds this fourfold substance. The prophets identify it in generic terms as knowing "Jehovah."[45] Immanuel Jesus reveals it personally as knowing "my Father" and "me."[46] On the eve of his passion, Christ explains it personally to his friends and disciples.[47] The Spirit of Truth reveals its substance and significance comprehensively to the apostles.[48] The apostles expound its riches in the New Testament.[49] Since we obtain this knowledge when God saves us from sin, it is knowledge of God our Redeemer and Father. Thus, in terms of its substance, we could call it *redemptive*, or *filial*, or *personal*, or *experiential*. We now unfold its fourfold substance.

1. The foundation of saving knowledge is informed awareness about God.

Saving knowledge is factual. It starts with possessing special information about God, obtainable only from the Scriptures. Saving knowledge thus involves disclosure. It is revelatory and informational. It results from exposure to the Bible and the teachings of orthodox Christianity. Exposure to this information is essential to saving knowledge of God, but not necessary evidence of saving knowledge of God. No one knows God who knows nothing about God from the Scriptures, like the Greeks of Athens (Acts 17:23). Nevertheless, some know a great deal about God from Scripture, as did many Jews, who do not know God evangelically (Rom. 2:17-20).

2. Saving knowledge involves a biblical understanding of God.

Saving knowledge is conceptual, or intellectual. It is an accurate understanding, learned from Scripture, about God himself and about his ways and glory.[50] It encompasses his eternal decree, his works in history from the creation to the consummation, and his expectations of men.[51] It focuses on his work of salvation from sin. A biblical concept of God's Word is the foundation of this knowledge. A biblical concept of God's nature and

---

[45] Jer. 9:24, 31:34
[46] Matt. 11:27-28; John 8:19
[47] John 14:8-9, 15:15
[48] John 16:13-15; 1 Cor. 2:9-10
[49] 1 Cor. 2:13; Eph. 1:17-18, 3:19; Phil. 3:10; Col. 1:9-10; 2 Pet. 1:2-3
[50] Ps. 95:10; 1 Cor. 2:9-10, 12, 14; 2 Cor. 4:6
[51] 1 Cor. 2:9-12; Eph. 1:9-11, 17-18; Heb. 10:30; Col. 1:9

works is the core of this knowledge.[52] This involves having a biblical concept of God's existence, names, and attributes. It involves understanding God's virtue and capabilities.[53] It involves conceiving biblically of his triune personality: "You know neither me nor my Father" (John 8:19). It revolves around Jesus. Its hub is to understand Christ's accomplishment of salvation.[54] It also involves a biblical grasp of the application of salvation in the Christian life and in the Christian church.[55] A biblical concept of God's expectations is the capstone of this knowledge. This involves an accurate comprehension of what he requires of us in his gospel and in his law. It means knowing his revealed will.[56] Thus, saving knowledge is theological. It is sound doctrine. No one who rejects the biblical doctrine of God and his ways has saving knowledge (1 John 4:6). Yet, some may have orthodox views of God in their heads, and yet, they do not know God (1 Cor. 8:1-3, 13:1-2).

3. Saving knowledge also involves a spiritual perception of God.

Saving knowledge is perceptual. It involves recognizing, by faith, God at work in history, manifesting his presence (John 21:12), exercising his power (Phil. 3:10), and fulfilling his purposes (1 Cor. 2:14). It involves discernment. It sees with the eye of the soul the unseen in everyday life. No one has saving knowledge of God who never perceives God working in the world. Nevertheless, some who do not know God perceive the hand of God at work in the world and recognize his special presence (Matt. 7:22-23; Heb. 6:4-5). That qualification notwithstanding, those who know God have a spiritual perception unique to themselves, unknown even the unconverted

---

[52] *Jer. 9:24*: But let him that glories glory in this, that he has understanding, and knows me, that I am Jehovah who exercises lovingkindness, justice, and righteousness, in the earth: for in these things I delight, says Jehovah.

[53] Eph. 3:19; 2 Tim. 1:12

[54] *Col. 2:2-3*: that they may know the mystery of God, even Christ, in whom are all the treasures of wisdom and knowledge hidden

[55] *Eph. 1:17-18*: that the God of our Lord Jesus Christ, The Father of glory, would give unto you a spirit of wisdom and revelation in the knowledge of him; having the eyes of your heart enlightened, that you may know what is the hope of your calling; *2 Pet. 1:2-3*: Grace to you and peace be multiplied in the knowledge of God and of Jesus our Lord; seeing that his divine power has granted unto us all things that pertain unto life and godliness, through the knowledge of him that called us through his own glory and virtue

[56] *Col. 1:9-10*: For this cause we also, since the day we heard it, do not cease to pray and make request for you, that you may be filled with the knowledge of his will in all spiritual wisdom and understanding, to walk worthily of the Lord unto all pleasing, bearing fruit in every good work, and increasing in the knowledge of God.

who profess to be Christians (1 Cor. 2:14). Only true Christians recognize the things of God through personal involvement and experience of them.

4. Saving knowledge essentially consists of an evangelical intercourse with the triune God.

Saving knowledge is experiential. It is personal and loving involvement with God the Father,[57] God the Son,[58] and God the Holy Spirit.[59] It is intimate and reciprocal: "I know mine own, and mine own know me" (John 8:19); "but now that you have come to know God, or rather to be known by God" (Gal. 4:9). It is spiritual intercourse with God in experiential religion. Thus, it is a matter of devotion. It is communion with the Lord, love for him, loyalty to him, and religious service to him. It is a knitting together of the Lord and Christians in a spiritual union of their hearts.[60] Only true believers have this evangelical intercourse with God. It is intimate, personal, reciprocal, devotional, and filial.

II. Two Distinguishing Characteristics of the Evangelical Knowledge of God

Christ commends both its sufficiency and significance when he depicts it as "*eternal* life": "And this is life eternal, that they should know you the only true God" (John 17:3). We now consider these traits.

A. The Complete Sufficiency of the Evangelical Knowledge of God

Its sufficiency stems from the fact that it is climactic and inexhaustible. We now unfold these roots.

1. Saving knowledge is completely sufficient because it is climactic and final.

Men never need to advance to a better kind of knowledge, or graduate from the school of saving knowledge. It is the institute of highest learning in the knowledge of God.[61] Saved men live and learn for all eternity in its hallowed halls. God's children need nothing more than "eternal life."

2. Saving knowledge is completely sufficient because it is inexhaustible and everlasting.

Saved men will drink for all eternity from the bottomless well of spiritual intercourse with God. They forever increase in their experiential knowledge

---

[57] Matt. 11:27
[58] John 8:19, 14:8-9, 17:3; Phil. 3:10; 2 Pet. 1:2-3
[59] John 14:17
[60] 1 Cor. 6:16-17
[61] John 10:14-15, 14:8-9, 15:15, 16:12-13

of God (John 17:26). Saving knowledge begins at conversion: "now that you have come to know God." Yet it is not static. It develops during the Christian life and even for all eternity.[62] Thus Paul depicts the experiential knowledge of Christ's love as inexhaustible: "and to know the love of Christ which passes knowledge" (Eph. 3:19). We can never know Christ's infinite love thoroughly. Rather, Christians will forever know more of it, both in understanding and experience. Its riches are unsearchable. Therefore, saving knowledge will never leave Christians empty, but will more and more fill us "unto all the fullness of God."

B. The Immense Significance of the Evangelical Knowledge of God

When Christ depicts saving knowledge of God as "eternal life," he also extols its momentous significance. Saving knowledge exerts a crucial influence over every aspect of spiritual life. It is essential to sound theology, to eternal salvation, to God-honoring churchmanship, and to acceptable worship. Now consider with me these four indications of its immense significance.

1. Saving knowledge is immensely significant because it is essential to sound theology.

Conscientious theology aims to dispense knowledge of God accurately. To the extent that theologians attain that goal, they have sound theology. Thus, if God were unknowable, there could be no sound theology. Since Scripture is the only source of saving knowledge, sound systematic theology categorizes and summarizes the knowledge of God taught in the Scriptures. If a system of theology has any other aim or focus, it can neither honor God, nor edify men. Thus John says: "We are of God: he that knows God hears us" (1 John 4:6). Here is a solemn warning to all who teach theology. We must be careful not to profane God's knowledge with vain speculations and preconceived notions. We attain sound theology only when we study Scripture with a teachable spirit, willing to have it shape the categories and substance of our thinking about God. Here is comfort for those who pursue this enormous task. God is knowable through his Word. Theology is not hopeless or futile work. Sound theology is not an impossible dream.

---

[62] *Col. 1:9-10*: For this cause we also, since the day we heard it, do not cease to pray and make request for you, that you may be filled with the knowledge of his will in all spiritual wisdom and understanding, to walk worthily of the Lord unto all pleasing, bearing fruit in every good work, and increasing in the knowledge of God

2. Saving knowledge is immensely significant because it is essential to eternal salvation.

When the Lord calls experimental knowledge "eternal life," he teaches its utmost importance for every man. The apostles confirm the saving impact of experimental knowledge.[63] Only those who know God evangelically live forever with Christ in heaven. God will damn all other human beings (2 Thess. 1:8).

3. Saving knowledge is immensely significant because it is essential to God's glory in his church.

God-honoring churchmanship pursues God's glory in the church. Saving knowledge is essential to God-honoring churchmanship because it furnishes the only proper basis for church membership. Thus, it provides the foundation for order in the church. The Lord promises that experimental knowledge of God will distinguish his people under the new covenant.[64] In this respect the people of God under the new covenant differ from what they were under the old covenant. The writer to Hebrews insists that the church, composed of Christ's disciples, is God's people under the new covenant.[65] Gentile churches observe the Lord's Supper, the token of the new covenant. Thus, new covenant Israel includes them too.[66] Thus, Paul says that those who composed the churches of Galatia had "come to know God." Every true church experiences this saving fellowship with God. Therefore, anyone who does not know the Lord has no right to be a member in a Christian church. No person should be added to the church merely on the basis of head knowledge. The promise of Jeremiah is not that, "they shall all be outwardly decent," or, "they shall all hold orthodox beliefs," but, "*they shall all know me.*" This makes Christian Israel superior to Hebrew Israel under the old covenant. Failure to implement this standard will return the church to old covenant formalism. It will eviscerate the new covenant of its blessedness and superiority. Thus the saving knowledge has immense significance for ecclesiology and churchmanship.

---

[63] *1 John* 5:20: And we know that the Son of God is come, and has given us an understanding, that we know him that is true, and we are in him that is true, even in his Son Jesus Christ. This is the true God and eternal life.

[64] *Jer. 31:34*: and they shall teach no more every man his neighbor, and every man his brother, saying, Know Jehovah; for they shall all know me, from the least of them unto the greatest of them, says Jehovah: for I will be merciful to their iniquity, and their sin will I remember no more

[65] Heb. 8:6-11, 12:23-24

[66] 1 Cor. 11:25

4. Saving knowledge is immensely significant because it is essential to acceptable worship.

In John 4:23-24 Jesus asserts that knowing God is vital for proper worship: "You worship you know not what, we worship what we know." In Acts 17:23 Paul says the same thing in essence to the men of Athens. Worship is the heart of religion. Men cannot worship an unknowable or unknown God acceptably. Worship, whether devotional or ritual, aims at religious intercourse with God. All worship, however, is not acceptable to him: "The sacrifice of the wicked is an abomination to Jehovah" (Prov. 15:8). Again the Lord says: "I desire goodness, and not sacrifice; and the knowledge of God more than burnt offerings" (Hos. 6:6). When wicked men, who do not know God, go through liturgical rituals, the Lord is not pleased but provoked to wrath. They draw near to him with their mouth, but their hearts are far from him. Without evangelical knowledge of God, all the prayers, sacrifices, fasting, burning of incense, sacraments, rituals, ceremonies, and worship services on earth are totally vain. Here is its immense significance.

III. Two Practical Applications of the Evangelical Knowledge of God

Notice with me two moral applications, its telltale signs and moral summons.

A. The Telltale Signs of the Evangelical Knowledge of God

Christ and the apostles identify its telltale signs as gospel faith and the gospel obedience that flows from it.

1. Gospel obedience is a telltale sign of saving knowledge.

The way that we live either supports or invalidates our profession of experimental communion with God. With reference to knowing God, actions speak louder than words. Thus, Christ condemns professing Christians whose sinful lives demonstrate that their claim to know God is false.[67] Similarly, Paul condemns hypocrites who by their immoral works and lifestyle deny the God that they profess to know.[68] No writer treats this theme more fully than John: "And hereby we know that we know him, if we keep his commandments. He that says, I know him, and keeps not his commandments, is a liar, and the truth is not in him" (1 John 2:3-4). Thus, a godly life displays experimental communion with God. Those who live an ungodly life and claim to know God are liars.

---

[67] *John 8:54-55*: it is my Father that glorifies me; of whom you say, that he is your God; and you have not known him

[68] *Titus 1:16*: They profess that they know God; but by their works they deny him, being abominable, and disobedient, and unto every good work reprobate.

2. Gospel faith is a telltale sign of evangelical knowledge.

John adds that gospel faith is also a telltale sign. Gospel faith regards what the apostles teach to be true: "We are of God: he that knows God hears us" (1 John 4:6). Thus, heretics who reject apostolic doctrine and claim to know God are also liars. In this lurks a great irony. Respecting universal knowledge, sinners tell an agnostic lie. They pretend not to have damning knowledge of their Creator, when in fact they do. Respecting evangelical knowledge, sinners tell a hypocritical lie. They pretend to know God as their Father, when in fact they do not.

B. The Moral Summons of the Evangelical Knowledge of God

Immanuel authorizes and designs the moral summons issued by saving knowledge. The apostles enforce his summons. Knowing God compels love for God's people and holy separation from the world.

1. Evangelical knowledge of God compels Christ-like love for God's people.

In John 17:26, the Lord says: "and I made known your name unto them, and will make it known; that the love with which you loved me may be in them, and I in them." Loving and intimate intercourse with the Father and the Son necessitates loving all those whom they love. Fellowship and communion with Christ mandates fellowship and communion with those who are in Christ, who also partake of his love. Refusal to have spiritual and fraternal intercourse with God's children is incompatible with walking in spiritual and filial intercourse with their Father. Holding fraternal and cordial fellowship with God's children is the demand and fruit of having evangelical intercourse with their Father.

2. Evangelical knowledge of God compels holy separation from the world.

Paul underscores the moral summons of saving knowledge: "Be not deceived: Evil companionships corrupt good morals. Awake to soberness righteously, and sin not; for some have no knowledge of God: I speak this to move you to shame" (1 Cor. 15:33-34). Some lack saving knowledge. Those who know God should live a holy life. Friendship with the world is enmity with God. How then can people have loving intercourse both with God and his enemies? Those who know God must separate from the evil influence and close companionship of God's enemies. They can no longer go along with their way of thinking and behaving. It is a disgrace for men who know God to act and think like a fallen world that spurns God's company. Therefore Paul says: "I speak this to move you to shame." Similarly Paul writes: "For this is the will of God, even your sanctification, that you abstain from fornication; that each one of you know how to possess himself of his own vessel in sanctification and honor, not in the passion of lust, even as the Gentiles who know not God" (1 Thess. 4:3-5). The knowledge of God mandates a radical distinction between the sexuality of God's people and the sexuality of the world. Knowing God mandates that God's people abstain from illicit sexual behavior. The conjugal intimacy of married Christians must be a pure reflection of their spiritual intimacy with the Lord (1 Cor. 6:15-19; Eph. 5:31-32). A lifestyle of fornication is incompatible with experimental knowledge of God.

Conclusion: May the Lord grant that all our efforts to unfold his knowledge will bear fruit in a closer walk with himself, that all our studies in systematic theology will be blessed seasons of *"increasing in the knowledge of God,"* for our good and his glory. Already we have gazed at the unfathomable depths of the knowledge of God. Studying what it means to know him prepares us to gaze at his incomprehensibility.

Topic 4. The Incomprehensibility of God

"Can you by searching find out God? Can you find out the Almighty unto perfection?" (Job 11:7); "his greatness is unsearchable" (Ps. 145:3); "how unsearchable are his judgments, and his ways past tracing out" (Rom. 11:33)

Section 2. The Incomprehensibility of God

Scripture presents this topic with richness and breadth. It defines the concept of God's incomprehensibility,[1] expounds its display in God's nature,[2] works,[3] and decree,[4] and commends its profound relevance to Christian experience.[5] Accordingly, we first define the *concept* of God's incomprehensibility; second, expound its *display*; and third, apply its *practical relevance*.

The Bible presents this truth experientially, not philosophically. It comes couched in devotion, not speculation. Moses trembles before God's incomprehensible wrath. David stands in awe of God's incomprehensible knowledge of his life and ways. Solomon commends incomprehensible providence. Paul marvels at the Lord's incomprehensible decisions. He preaches the incomprehensible riches of Christ. He prays for the Ephesians that the Lord would enable them to understand Christ's incomprehensible love. He blesses the God of incomprehensible power. He encourages the Philippians with God's remedy for carnal anxiety, namely, God's incomprehensible peace.

We should not wrench this truth from this biblical ethos. Our approach should be practical and devotional; our theology should be proclaimed to God's people. I underscore this because men have turned this topic into a banner day for philosophical speculation. Some wrest this truth to their own destruction. They pervert both what Scripture says and how it says it. Admirably, Reformed theologians have stood toe-to-toe with them, defending this vital truth. But sadly, even they have sometimes erred, not by denying the truth, but by wrenching it from its devotional setting. Some rely too much on reason, and speculate about the "hidden essence" of an "unknowable" God. Such quote Scripture, but don't expound or apply it. We must present this truth from the vantage point of God's Word, not of God's enemies. We must reject both their heresy and their vanity. I concede

---

[1] Job 11:7; Ps. 145:3; Rom. 11:33
[2] Pss. 90:11, 139:6; Eph. 3:19-21; Phil. 4:7
[3] Job 5:9; Eccles. 8:17; Eph. 3:8
[4] Rom. 11:33
[5] Eph. 3:8, 19-21; Phil. 4:7

that Christian polemics must interact with men's errors in order to expose their self-contradictions, lest they be wise in their own conceits (Prov. 26:4-5). Yet in systematics we expound and apply Scripture. We may say with Nehemiah: "I am doing a great work, so that I can not come down: why should the work cease, while I leave it, and come down to you?" We must say with Paul: "I came unto you . . . not with excellency of speech or of wisdom . . . my speech and my preaching were . . . in demonstration of the Spirit and of power that your faith should not stand in the wisdom of men, but in the power of God" (1 Cor. 2:1-5).

Unit 1. The Concept of God's Incomprehensibility

Our epitomizing texts[6] succinctly define God's incomprehensibility. In Job 11:7 the Hebrew word, חֵקֶר (chēqer), "searching," conveys God's incomprehensibility: "Can you by searching find out God." *Chēqer* means to discover by enumeration, examination, or investigation. It is also used in Isaiah 40:28: "The everlasting God, Jehovah, the Creator of the ends of the earth, faints not, neither is weary; there is no *searching* of his understanding." In Psalm 145:3 the Hebrew words, אֵין חֵקֶר ('ēyn chēqer), literally, "without searching," are translated "unsearchable." In Job 5:9 these words also depict God's incomprehensibility: "Who does great things and *unsearchable*, marvelous things without number." In Romans 11:33 Paul uses similar terms: "how unsearchable are his judgments, and his ways past tracing out!" The Greek word, ἀνεξερευντος (anexereuntos), is translated *"unsearchable."* It comes from ἐξερευναω (exereunao), which means to "search rigorously" (1 Pet. 1:10). Paul means that men can never completely understand God's judgments, though they examine them rigorously and diligently apply themselves to plumb their depths. A synonymous word, ἀνεξιχνιαστος (anexichniastos), is translated "past tracing out" in Romans 11:33. It also occurs in Ephesians 3:8, where it is translated "unsearchable," "to preach unto the Gentiles the *unsearchable* riches of Christ." This word comes from the Greek word, ἰχνος (ichnos), which means "steps." It can convey the notion of following in someone's footsteps.[7] Thus, Paul means that no man can "trace all the steps" either of God's ways or of Christ's riches. In sum, these texts say that God's Being (Job 11:7), greatness (Ps. 145:3), decisions (Rom. 11:33), and ways (Rom. 11:33) are all unsearchable. Accordingly, I define God's incomprehensibility as follows:

---

[6] Job 11:7; Ps. 145:3; Rom. 11:33
[7] Rom. 4:12; 2 Cor. 12:18; 1 Pet. 2:21

Although humans can and do know God personally and truly, human beings can neither comprehend him completely, nor comprehensively explain his nature, actions, or decisions.

Incomprehensibility rests on knowability. God is knowable, yet only through self-disclosure (Matt. 11:27; 1 Cor. 2:10-11). Incomprehensibility simply means that finite creatures can never completely understand their infinite God. No man, or group of men, can ever exhaustively explain who and what he is (his nature), or what he does (his works), or why he decided to do it (his decree). No one can "find out the Almighty unto perfection."

Unit 2. The Display of God's Incomprehensibility

I introduce this display with David's meditation on God's unsearchable greatness: "Great is Jehovah, and greatly to be praised; and his greatness is unsearchable" (Psalm 145:3). What is *unsearchable* greatness? At least 17 texts explicitly mention God's greatness.[8] God's greatness encompasses his capacity to love and give,[9] his capacity to design and do his works,[10] and his capacity to order and rule all things.[11] No one can ever fully comprehend these capacities. First, David extols God's regal capacity to plan and do great works (145:4-6).[12] No man can fully understand the unsearchable greatness of creation or redemption. Second, David extols the great goodness of God's character (145:7-10).[13] God's restraint of his wrath in the face of manifold provocation displays an infinite kindness that no man can

---

[8] Exod. 15:7, 16; Num. 14:17, 19; Deut. 3:24, 5:24, 9:26, 11:2, 32:3; 2 Sam. 7:21, 22; 1 Chron. 17:21, 29:11; Neh. 13:22; Pss. 66:3, 79:11, 145:6, 150:2; Isa. 40:26; Eph. 1:19.

[9] *Num. 14:17-19*: And now, I pray thee, let the power of the Lord be great, according as you have spoken, Jehovah is slow to anger, and abundant in lovingkindness . . . Pardon, I pray you, the iniquity of this people according to the greatness of your lovingkindness.

[10] *Deut. 3:24*: O Lord Jehovah, you have begun to show your servant your greatness, and your strong hand: for what god is there in heaven or in earth that can do according to your works and according to your mighty acts?; *Deut. 9:26*: O Lord Jehovah, destroy not your people and your inheritance, that you have redeemed through your greatness, that you have brought forth out of Egypt with a mighty hand.

[11] *1 Chron. 29:11*: Yours, O Jehovah, is the greatness, and the power, and the glory, and the victory, and the majesty: for all that is in the heavens and earth is yours; yours is the kingdom, O Jehovah, and you are exalted as head above all. Both riches and honor come from you, and you rule over all.

[12] One generation shall laud your works to another, and shall declare your mighty acts . . . of your wondrous works will I meditate. And men shall speak of the might of your terrible acts

[13] They shall utter the memory of your great goodness, and shall sing of your righteousness . . . Jehovah is good to all . . . your saints shall bless you

fully grasp. Next David extols the greatness of God's eternal dominion (145:11-13).[14] Even the longest human dynasty has limits. God's dominion has unlimited duration. In sum, David extols the unsearchable greatness of God's nature, works, and decree. We follow his lead.

I. God's Incomprehensible Nature: Who and What He Is

We survey five aspects of God's nature that display his incomprehensibility: his anger,[15] knowledge,[16] love,[17] power,[18] and peace.[19] If at times the biblical witness is polemical, its climate is always devotional and its thrust is ever experiential.

A. God's Incomprehensible Anger and Wrath[20]

Notice the meaning and practical application of God's incomprehensible wrath.

1. The meaning of incomprehensible wrath

God expresses his wrath, or vengeful anger, when he inflicts on sinners the punishment their sins deserve.[21] When Moses asks: "who knows the power of your anger," he implies that no man fully comprehends the extent of the power by which God punishes the wicked for sin. Moses wrote, lived, and labored among a generation that perished in the wilderness. They grieved and provoked God by their hardness of heart.[22] Death hovered all around them. They dropped like flies under divine wrath. The astounding fact that the whole generation met their death in just 40 years made them a monument to divine vengeance. God made an example of them, to warn all men everywhere about his judgment.[23] Nevertheless, their physical death in a striking manner, however monumental it may be, does not exhaust the vengeance that God inflicts on those wicked men. That awesome display of

---

[14] They shall speak of the glory of your kingdom . . . to make known . . . the glory of the majesty of his kingdom. Your kingdom is an everlasting kingdom, and your dominion throughout all generations

[15] Ps. 90:11-12

[16] Ps. 139:6; Isa. 40:28, 55:8-9

[17] Eph. 3:19

[18] Eph. 3:20-21

[19] Phil. 4:7

[20] *Ps. 90:11-12*: Who knows the power of your anger, and your wrath according to the fear that is due unto you? So teach us to number our days, that we may get us a heart of wisdom.

[21] Rom. 12:19

[22] Num. 14:26-38; Ps. 95:10-11

[23] 1 Cor. 10:5-11

God's vengeance is but a drop in the bucket of the wrath to come. Like the overthrow of Sodom,[24] it supplies a little picture of the great day of wrath. That great day of wrath and destruction of ungodly men occurs when Christ returns.[25] Then all wicked men endure all God's vengeance.[26] This involves an unfathomable display of his power. Revelation depicts this power graphically. It describes blood oozing from a wine press, and the rising smoke of eternal burning.[27] No man can fully understand what it is like to be tormented, without respite, with fire and brimstone, for all eternity. None of us can explain how men can forever be burned in the lake of fire without being consumed. None of us can conceive of the extent of the unending suffering that God will inflict on billions and billions of his enemies. God alone knows the power of his wrath. To us, it is incomprehensible.

2. Two practical applications of incomprehensible wrath

a. God's incomprehensible wrath calls us to fear God: "according to the fear that is due unto you?"

Some accuse us of using "scare tactics" because we speak of eternal punishment. If we are guilty of scare tactics, so also is Moses. Yet we are not promoting paranoia. We haven't conjured up God's wrath to incite mass hysteria. God's wrath really exists. All wicked men are really under it. Its power is incomprehensible. Therefore, the wicked have good reason to fear. Yea, we all have good reason to fear. If we who profess faith in Christ but live in hypocrisy, or fall away, God's wrath will also destroy us.[28]

b. God's incomprehensible wrath calls us to face life's brevity: "So teach us to number our days"

Moses lived constantly with premature death. He prayed that God would bring good even from the frightful judgment under which the nation groaned. He prayed that God would turn that monument of wrath into a schoolroom in which to inculcate in his people the wisdom to face realistically the brevity of life. This implies that we must learn never to take life for granted. We do not know what a day may bring forth. We too see that some die young, that few live beyond 70 or 80 years, and that none remain here on earth indefinitely. Thus, if we would be wise, we must spend our time on earth accordingly. None of us has an unlimited life span. Incomprehensible wrath calls us to make the most of our time.

---

[24] Jude 7
[25] 2 Pet. 3:4, 7-10
[26] 2 Thess. 1:7-10
[27] Rev. 14:10-11, 19-20
[28] Matt. 7:21-23; Heb. 3:12-14, 10:26-29

B. God's Incomprehensible Knowledge

Consider with me the testimony of three passages: Ps. 139:6; Isa. 40:28, 55:8-9

1. The witness of Ps. 139:6: Such knowledge is too wonderful for me; it is high, I cannot attain unto *it*.

David marvels at how much God knows about him. He calls this knowledge "unattainable." He cannot completely fathom either how much God knows about him or how he knows it. David here contemplates this incomprehensible knowledge. First, he identifies its *substance* (139:1-5). Then he enumerates its *sources* (139:7-16). Finally he considers its *summons*, its impact on religious experience (139:17-24).

a. The substance of God's incomprehensible knowledge (139:1-5)

David says that God knows all his thoughts, words, actions, and plans. David addresses God. In essence he tells God, "You know everything about me. You know every thought I think, every word I say, every place I go, every plan I make, everything I do." Surely, David is no exception. God knows everything about each of us. Scripture presents God's incomprehensibility very personally. God knows all about you and me. He knows more about us than we know about ourselves. Such knowledge is unattainable.

b. The sources of God's incomprehensible knowledge (139:7-16)

How does God know everything about us? David uncovers three roots of this knowledge. *First*, God knows us completely because he is omnipresent (139:7-12). No man can run away from God. Wherever you hide, God is there. God is even in the inaccessible places (139:8), the uninhabited places (139:9-10), the dark places (139:11-12). *Second*, God knows us completely because he created us (139:13-15). God knows everything about him because God designed and made him. The Architect/Builder of man knows exactly what he did and how he did it. David did not make himself. He could never attain the full knowledge of his own body and soul that his Creator has. This pertains equally to all of us. *Third*, God knows us completely because he decreed every event in our lives and everything we do (139:16). God knows everything about David because God ordained it. God from all eternity wrote David's every word, thought, path, and action in his book. That also pertains equally to us all. Everything about us stands written in God's book in the indelible ink of his eternal purpose. You have not read God's book about you. I have not read his book about me. God not only read the book about each of us, he wrote it.

c. *The summons issued by God's incomprehensible knowledge* (139:17-24)

It issues a threefold summons. *First*, it summons us to treasure God's knowledge and presence (139:17-18). David does not regard God as "wholly other," distant, or unapproachable. He greatly values all God's thoughts, "How precious are your thoughts unto me." He lives in the special presence of the God of unfathomable knowledge: "When I awake, I am still with you." Let us also value all God's thoughts, and walk in close communion with him. *Second*, it summons us to depart from wicked men.[29] Such despise and mock God. God is grieved with them. Deep enmity exists between them. They are in mortal combat. There can be no neutrality in this war. You stand either with God or his enemies. David says in essence: "when I contemplate God's incomprehensible knowledge, I know why I'm on God's side." Only a fool would go to war with an omniscient foe that knows everything he thinks, plans, and does. Thus, God's knowledge of us calls us to separate from the wicked and from their combat with their Maker. It calls us to sever all alliances with God's enemies, to join the Lord's camp, to be loyal to his cause, and to defend his honor. *Third*, it summons us to prayerful self-examination.[30] David ends with prayerful self-examination. He engages in soul-searching. He is concerned, not only about how he appears before men, but about what he really is in his heart. Since God knows everything about him, he pleads with God to search his heart and to show him any wicked thing to which he is blind. He examines himself in dependence on the God who knows him totally. Let us also pray: "Lord, show me my heart." This is how we should conduct self-examination. Thus, Scripture presents this truth experientially.

2. *The witness of Isa. 40:28*[31]

Isaiah introduces God's unsearchable understanding with a probing question. He asks: "have you not known, have you not heard?" Why did he probe Israel with this question? Because they felt abandoned and forgotten by God: "My way is hid from the Lord and the justice due to me is passed away from my God." They thought that they had been mistreated and denied justice. They spoke as if God didn't see what happened, because if he did,

---

[29] *Ps. 139:19-22:* Surely you will slay the wicked, O God: Depart from me therefore, you bloodthirsty men. For they speak against you wickedly: and your enemies take your name in vain. Do not I hate them, O Jehovah, that hate you? And am not I grieved with those that rise up against you? I hate them with perfect hatred: They are become mine enemies.

[30] *Ps. 139:23-24*: Search me, O God, and know my heart: Try me, and know my thoughts; And see if there be any wicked way in me, And lead me in the way everlasting.

[31] Have you not known? have you not heard? The everlasting God, Jehovah, the Creator of the ends of the earth, faints not, neither is weary; there is no searching of his understanding.

he would never have let it happen. They forgot that God views everything with insight so great that no man can plumb its depths. Isaiah reminds them that God didn't forget them. Rather, they had forgotten God's unsearchable grasp on their situation.

Isaiah applies God's unsearchable understanding with an encouraging exhortation. He calls them to trust God and wait for him to deliver them: "but they that wait for Jehovah shall renew their strength." The God who knows our needs and trials gives strength to the helpless who trust in him. Thus, we must trust God in adversity. We must not think that our "way is hid from the Lord." God never overlooks anything. He makes no mistakes. He knows exactly what he is doing. Thus, we should never be dejected or embittered in affliction. Sometimes we can't see any way out, or any way to resolve the problem, or to rectify the wrong. In those days remember: "there is no searching of his understanding."

3. *The witness of Isa. 55:8-9*[32]

Isaiah boldly asserts that God's thoughts and ways are infinitely exalted above those of humans. They are so much *"higher"* that they are beyond the range of human comprehension, somewhat like high frequency sound that is beyond the range of human hearing. Is this incomprehensible God "wholly other," utterly unapproachable? Absolutely not! Isaiah asserts the contrary. He affirms that the incomprehensibility of God's thoughts supports the free offer of the gospel.[33] Thus he exhorts wicked men to forsake their sinful ways and call upon the Lord for mercy. What arguments does he use to induce sinners to repent and believe? He employs three motivations (Isa. 55:8-13). He introduces each with the Hebrew word, כִּי (kiy), translated "for" or "because." Sinners should seek the Lord because of God's unsearchable thoughts and ways (55:8-9), because of God's efficacious Word (55:10-11), and because of God's promise to bless and deliver his people (55:12-13). Thus, God's unsearchable thoughts furnish strong incentive to forsake a godless way of living and thinking: "let the wicked forsake his way, and the unrighteous man his thoughts." Lost mankind would never conjure up gospel pardon. Sinners are too selfish and vengeful. But God thinks thoughts of incomprehensible grace.

---

[32] For my thoughts are not your thoughts, neither are your ways my ways, says Jehovah. For as the heavens are higher than the earth, so are my ways higher than your ways, and my thoughts than your thoughts.

[33] *Isa. 55:6-7*: Seek Jehovah while he may be found; call upon him while he is near: let the wicked forsake his way, and the unrighteous man his thoughts; and let him return unto Jehovah.

In sum, these three passages display God's incomprehensible knowledge, understanding, and thoughts. They present God's incomprehensible mind experientially and evangelically. His infinite mind calls saints to trust God in their adversity and perplexity. It calls saints to separate from God's enemies in gospel holiness, to conduct self-examination in dependence on God, and to treasure God's infinite understanding. God's incomprehensible knowledge furnishes strong incentive to Christians to engage in prayer, in self-examination, and in evangelism. Further, it gives sinners strong incentive to get right with God. It calls them to forsake their sinful thoughts and ways and to trust in Christ for pardon.

C. Christ's Incomprehensible Love[34]

The deity of Christ validates considering this text. This display of God's incomprehensibility gives no encouragement to agnosticism or empty speculation. To the contrary, Paul stresses that Christ's incomprehensible love is both *knowable*, "and to know the love of Christ which passes knowledge," and *profitable*, "that you may be filled unto all the fullness of God." Consider both these traits with me.

1. Christ's incomprehensible love is knowable

Paul explains both who can know Christ's infinite love and how they can know it.

a. Who can know Christ's infinite love?

All true Christians, and only true Christians, can know Christ's unfathomable love personally and experientially.[35] This knowledge belongs, not only to intellectuals or theologians, but also to every true Christian, even to babes in Christ.

b. How can Christians know Christ's infinite love?

Christians can know Christ's infinite love because the Spirit of Christ dwells in them and enables them to know it.[36] Only true Christians have the Spirit of Christ in their hearts.[37] Thus, their knowledge of Christ's love is evangelical, experiential, and personal. It consists of spiritual perception of

---

[34] *Eph. 3:19*: and to know the love of Christ that passes knowledge, that you may be filled unto all the fullness of God

[35] to the end that you . . . may be strong to apprehend with all the saints what is the breadth and length and height and depth, and to know the love of Christ which passes knowledge

[36] that you may be strengthened with power through his Spirit in the inward man; that Christ may dwell in your hearts through faith; to the end that you, being rooted and grounded in love, may be strong to apprehend with all the saints . . . the love of Christ.

[37] Rom. 8:8-9

what Christ in his redemptive work does for them and in them.[38] Persons devoid of the Spirit cannot know Christ's love. This uncovers the real reason why men devise an agnostic doctrine of God's incomprehensibility. Their agnostic view exposes their own lack of true Christian experience. Therefore, we should not let them intimidate us. Rather, we should pity them. There is more true theology in the prayers of the least true Christian, than in all the tomes of the most renowned scholars and critics who lack Christ's Spirit.

2. Christ's incomprehensible love is profitable.

Paul describes its immense profitability in grandiose terms: "and to know the love of Christ which passes knowledge, that you may be filled unto all the fullness of God." When true Christians perceive and experience Christ's love for them, it feeds and satiates their souls. Paul does not present incomprehensible love as an impenetrable wall that allows only speculation about what lies beyond it. Rather, he depicts it as an inexhaustible well of riches and glory from which thirsty saints may drink and be filled over and over, without limitation, forever. Unless we fill our souls with Christ's love, we will be hollow inside. This world is full of empty people. A man full of himself is shallow, because man is dust. Those full of the world are hollow, because the world is vain. If we fill ourselves with entertainment, or recreations, or thrills, or busyness, or romance, our souls will shrivel and wither. Thanks be to God for this inexhaustible well of love from which to fill our souls. What a wonderful provision! Let us not be empty people. Let us rather contemplate and imbibe God's love until we are filled "unto all the fullness of God." Therefore, incomprehensible love calls us not to speculate, but to pray, as Paul did, that God would grant us greater perception and understanding of "the love of Christ that passes knowledge."

D. God's Incomprehensible Power[39]

Paul refers here, not to God's power in general, but specifically to the power of true religion: "the power that works in us." This power exceeds our capacity to ask, because it surpasses *"exceeding abundantly"* the limits of our rational powers. Thus, it is incomprehensible. Paul features both its *operation*, "according to the power that works in us," and its *eventuation*, "unto him be the glory in the church and in Christ Jesus unto all generations for ever and ever."

---

[38] Eph. 5:1-2, 25-27

[39] *Eph. 3:20-21*: Now unto him that is able to do exceeding abundantly above all that we ask or think, according to the power that works in us, unto him be the glory in the church and in Christ Jesus unto all generations for ever and ever. Amen

1. Incomprehensible power operates in the heart of every Christian.

Incomprehensible power fuels true religion in our hearts. This alone explains why God's people rejoice in their afflictions. It alone explains their unshakable loyalty to Christ and their commitment "to will and to work for his good pleasure." Enabled by the Spirit, encouraged by Christ's presence, fixed on incomprehensible love, Christians trust, obey, love, hope, and endure. This affords tremendous encouragement to pray for grace to understand more of Christ's inscrutable love, to enjoy more of his special presence, and to experience more of his sanctifying power. We cannot ask more than God can do in us. We cannot even think more than God can do! Since God is incomprehensible, let us not speculate, but pray, for more of the power of true religion in our hearts. We should pray expecting great things from God. We should boldly ask all we can think, for God can do exceeding abundantly more.

2. Incomprehensible power eventuates in God's glory in his church.

What results from this power of true religion? God is glorified among his people: "unto him be the glory in the church." God alone deserves the praise for the power of true religion in the Christian life and church. Let us bless him who can do in us "exceeding abundantly above all that we ask or think."

E. God's Incomprehensible Peace[40]

As Christ's love surpasses knowledge, so God's peace surpasses understanding. God is never ruffled. Carnal anxiety never paralyzes him. Whatever happens, he is infinitely secure and tranquil in his heart. What then, is he a "wholly other" God, so far detached from our lives that he is blissfully oblivious to all that occurs here on earth? Absolutely not! To the contrary, nothing is more relevant to our sense of security than God's unfathomable peace. Paul affirms that God's peace both *shelters the hearts* of God's people: "And the peace of God, which passes all understanding, shall guard your hearts," and *attends their prayers*: "let your requests be made known unto God. And the peace of God, which passes all understanding, shall guard your hearts." Consider these two blessed fruits of God's infinite peace.

1. Incomprehensible peace shelters the hearts of God's people.

Paul says that God's peace protects our timid souls. When it *"guards our thoughts,"* it keeps our minds stayed on him in *"perfect peace"* (Isa. 26:3).

---

[40] *Phil. 4:6-7*: In nothing be anxious; but in everything by prayer and supplication with thanksgiving let your requests be made known unto God. And the peace of God, which passes all understanding, shall guard your hearts and your thoughts in Christ Jesus.

It guards our thoughts even in the midst of life's most severe storms and trials. By his Spirit, God imparts a sense of calm and security to Christians, so that we say: "yea, though I walk through the valley of the shadow of death, I will fear no evil; for you are with me" (Ps. 23:4). Thus, Christians are sometimes a mystery even to ourselves. Sometimes we can't begin to understand the sense of calm that sustains our souls under great duress.

2. *Incomprehensible peace attends the prayers of God's people.*

How we experience this peace? God uses the grateful prayers of those who trust him: "in everything by prayer and supplication with thanksgiving let your requests be made known unto God." This calls us to pour out our troubles and worries before the Lord, not with whining or self-pity, but *"with thanksgiving."* When we are afraid, we must draw near in faith, and put our trust in him. When we thus call on him, inexplicable peace pervades our souls. A well-loved hymn confirms this: "Oh what peace we often forfeit, oh what needless pain we bear, all because we do not carry everything to God in prayer." Greater peace comes through greater prayer. Incomprehensible peace is the gospel remedy for carnal anxiety.

Conclusion: God's anger, understanding, love, power, and peace are incomprehensible. These traits display the unfathomable mystery of his nature. Scripture reveals insoluble mystery in connection with God's eternal life, infinite power, unlimited faculty of mind, will, and affection, impeccable moral virtue, and triune personality. We must not think that we can fit God's infinite Being into a little package, neatly wrapped by human logic and reason. This glory of God's incomprehensible nature prepares us for the mystery we encounter in every part of the doctrine of God.

II. God's Incomprehensible Works: What He Does

We turn now from God's unsearchable nature to contemplate the infinite glory of his work. We focus on his works of conservation of his original creation, providence, and of salvation from sin in Jesus Christ.

A. God's Incomprehensible Work of Providence

Many passages could testify about the unsearchable riches of God's conservation and rule of creation in his providence. The books of Job and Ecclesiastes plead most urgently and prevail. They assert that no man can fully comprehend how God created the world, because only God was there.[41] Only the Creator of the universe fully understands everything he made and how he made it. Therefore, he alone understands how he runs and sustains everything he created. We focus on Job 5:9 and Ecclesiastes 8:17.

---

[41] Job 38:4-6

1. Job 5:9[42]

In providence God does innumerable works. The passage identifies the scope and substance of what God does in providence and applies it experientially to what we should do.

a. The scope and substance of God's unfathomable works in providence.

The Creator sustains and governs everything he made. The passage unfolds the mammoth scope of his work. He personally controls the forces of nature: "who gives rain upon the earth, and sends waters upon the fields" (Job 5:10). The larger context identifies many such works, unfathomable to us, by which he orders all creation.[43] The immediate context features how he controls the human affairs.[44] He exalts the lowly: "so that he sets up on high those that are low." He frustrates clever schemes: "he frustrates the devices of the crafty." He overthrows secret agendas: "and the counsel of the cunning is carried headlong." He protects the helpless from powerful adversaries: "he saves from the sword of their mouth, even the needy from the hand of the mighty." Thus, providence works striking irony in human affairs: "he takes the wise in their own craftiness." Thus, it gives hope to the poor and silences those who flaunt their sin: "so the poor has hope, and iniquity stops her mouth." All this is inscrutable to us. We cannot fathom how he completely controls men's sinful actions without becoming either the author or approver of sin. Nor can we fully explain how he controls the behavior of men who act of their own accord. Though we cannot explain *how* he does so, we nevertheless believe and affirm *that* he does so. We believe, since Scripture teaches it, that God works in providence with incomprehensible power and wisdom. Yet, we freely admit that we, finite creatures with tiny intellects, cannot fully explain how he does so. Yet even we perceive that he works. We see crafty Haman dangling on the gallows he prepared for helpless Mordecai. We know it is the Lord's doing, and it is marvelous in our eyes.

b. The practical application of God's unfathomable works in providence[45]

When Job's friend called Job to pray, he gave good advice in principle, even though he misapplied it to Job. Incomprehensible providence calls us to

---

[42] *Job 5:9*: Who does great things and unsearchable, marvelous things without number
[43] Job 26:14, 36:26-37:24
[44] *Job 5:11-13, 15-16*: so that he sets up on high those that are low, and those that mourn are exalted to safety. 12 He frustrates the devices of the crafty, So that their hands cannot perform their enterprise. 13 He takes the wise in their own craftiness; and the counsel of the cunning is carried headlong . . . 15 he saves from the sword of their mouth, even the needy from the hand of the mighty. 16 So the poor has hope, And iniquity stops her mouth."
[45] *Job 5:8*: But as for me, I would seek unto God, and unto God would I commit my cause

seek God and commit our cause to him. Do powerful adversaries speak evil of us or devise evil against us? Are crafty men plotting our downfall? Are snares even now being set to catch us? Do we face trials and afflictions similar Job's? Have we lost loved ones to tragedy? Have we been victims of crime? Have we lost our possessions or our livelihood? Are we suffering physical afflictions? Let us pray and commit our cause to the God of inscrutable providence.

2. *Eccles. 8:17*[46]

The text emphasizes two things: the *incomprehensible mystery* of providence, and the *invaluable lesson* that this incomprehensible mystery teaches us.

a. The incomprehensible mystery of providence

Human beings have an inquisitive nature. From our youth we repeatedly ask the simple question, "Why?" Yet, the inspired preacher says even the wisest of men cannot give a complete answer to that simple question. We wonder why some individuals suffer severe calamity, while others, living in similar circumstances, are spared.[47] We wonder why a certain person is born handicapped.[48] We wonder why one Christian is marvelously delivered from his persecutors, while another, in similar circumstances, is martyred.[49] We know that God in his providence directs and rules over all the actions and circumstances of every man.[50] Thus, we know that whatever happens to anyone is of the Lord. Yet, ultimately, the full and certain explanation of the blessing and suffering that befalls specific individuals remains hidden with God. The Lord often uses means so that some actions often give rise to predicable consequences. For example, drunkenness often gives rise to poverty.[51] Again, a violent man often himself becomes the victim of violence.[52] Again, a diligent and skillful worker often gets a promotion, while a slothful worker is often passed over or demoted.[53] Again, notorious

---

[46] *Eccles. 8:17*: Then I beheld the work of God, that man cannot find out the work that is done under the sun: because however much a man labor to seek it out, yet he shall not find it; yea moreover, though a wise man think to know it, yet shall he not be able to find it.
[47] Luke 13:1-5
[48] John 9:1-3
[49] Acts 12:1-11
[50] Eph. 1:11
[51] Prov. 23:21
[52] Matt. 26:52
[53] Prov. 12:24

evildoers often meet with striking and calamitous afflictions.[54] Scripture abounds with such general observations, especially in Proverbs.[55] However, although such blessings or sufferings are *often* consequences of men's good or evil deeds, they are not *always* so.[56] Sometimes a peaceable man becomes the victim of violent crime. Sometimes striking calamities befall good men. The life of Job furnishes the classic illustration of this enigma. Unless we embrace the mystery of providence, we will, like "Job's comforters," pummel our afflicted friends with the false accusation that great hypocrisy on their part must have caused their calamity. We will refuse to believe their protestations that they have a good conscience before God. Further, when we ponder the big picture we search for an explanation of suffering and death. Why do men suffer and die? Men suffer and die because of sin. But, why did man sin? The answer is because God ordained it. But why did God ordain sin? The ultimate reason for man's fall, with all its consequences, remains hidden with the incomprehensible God of providence.

b. The invaluable lesson that the mystery of providence teaches us

The inspired preacher delivers a message about wisdom from this mystery of providence.[57] The lesson is simply this. Wisdom consists, not in finding solutions for the enigmas of providence, but in frankly admitting that we can never fully explain them. J. I. Packer expounds this lesson.[58] He enforces it with a lucid illustration about a train switchyard.[59] Man, standing by the tracks of providence, sees what appears as inexplicable movements of trains. God, sitting high above in the signal tower, understands those movements, for he sees the intricate design and pattern of all the switches and tracks. When God imparts wisdom, he does not take us up into the signal tower with him. Rather, he enables us to realize that from where we stand we can never figure out why he moves the trains as he does. We must believe that he sees the big picture, and that he is moving all the trains of providence on the proper tracks at the proper time. Thus, we should live in the fear of God. We should learn to be content with our God-given lot in life.[60] Scripture clearly affirms that we can never fully explain either *how* or *why* God works

---

[54] Prov. 13:21

[55] Prov. 3:1-10

[56] Prov. 3:11-12, 17:26; Eccles. 8:14, 10:6

[57] *Eccles. 8:16, 17*: When I applied my heart to know wisdom, and to see the business that is done upon the earth . . . 17 then I beheld the work of God, that man can not find out the work that is done under the sun.

[58] J. I. Packer, *Knowing God* (Downers Grove, IL: Inter Varsity Press, 1974), 91-97.

[59] Ibid., 91

[60] Eccles. 3:11-14

in providence. Providence explodes in unfathomable mystery before our eyes. Our doctrine of providence is a fence around God's mystery to guard it from the hands of men.

B. God's Incomprehensible Work of Salvation in Christ[61]

Paul proclaimed both who Christ is and what he does. He preached the glory of his Person and the benefit of his work. Here he declares that the riches of Christ's Person and work are unsearchable.

1. The unsearchable riches of Christ's Person

God the Son, without relinquishing deity, became human.[62] Scripture asserts both Christ's deity, *"the Word was God,"* and his humanity, *"and the Word became flesh."* God the Son took a human body and soul, so that Jesus of Nazareth, though fully human, is also fully divine. He is the Supreme Being incarnate. He is one Person, God the Son, with a human nature and the divine nature.[63] This is the marrow of the Christian faith respecting the Person of Christ. It points us to an unfathomable mystery. This one Person has simultaneously both a limited human mind[64] and the omniscient divine mind.[65] He has both a submissive human will[66] and the sovereign divine will.[67] The mystery of Christ's Person is incomprehensible. Yet it is also practical, for Christ is Immanuel, the object of our worship (Heb. 1:6).

2. The unsearchable riches of Christ's work

The saving work of Christ also displays unsearchable riches. His life and work—his incarnation, temptation, atonement, resurrection, and second coming—lie shrouded in unsearchable mystery.

a. The unsearchable mystery of Christ's incarnation

When God the Son became human, he had a human mother, yet no human father. A virgin conceived him by the supernatural power of the Holy Spirit.

---

[61] *Eph. 3:8*: Unto me, who am less than the least of all saints, was this grace given, to preach unto the Gentiles the unsearchable riches of Christ

[62] *John 1:1, 14*: In the beginning was the Word, and the Word was with God, and the Word was God . . . 14 And the Word became flesh and dwelt among us.

[63] Col. 2:9

[64] Matt. 24:36

[65] John 2:24-25, 21:17

[66] Matt. 26:39

[67] Matt. 11:27

His conception was asexual.[68] Yet he is completely human and completely without sin.[69] Only God fully understands Christ's supernatural conception. The virgin birth of Christ is incomprehensible. Yet it is absolutely necessary for our salvation. We must believe it happened because God says it did. We must proclaim it even though we cannot fully comprehend or explain it.

b. The unsearchable mystery of Christ's temptation

God cannot be tempted.[70] Yet Christ, the God-man, though he is the Supreme Being, nevertheless was tempted.[71] Moreover, though he was tempted to sin, yet he could not sin. Christ is not two persons, a human person who could sin and a divine Person who is impeccable. Christ is one Person, an impeccable Person, God the Son. In his incarnation he never ceased to be divine. He never relinquished his divine moral virtue, his ideality. This incomprehensible mystery is also essential for our salvation. By suffering temptation he overcame the devil and became the sympathetic high priest we need to save us from sin.

c. The unsearchable mystery of Christ's atonement

When Jesus suffered the wrath of God, he endured all the punishment due to all the sins of his people.[72] Yet we deserved unending punishment in hell. Thus, he endured eternal punishment in a limited time in his suffering unto death. How can this be? We only know that this is possible because Jesus is the eternal God. God the Father forsook and punished, not a mere man, but God the Son. Only God can fully explain how he accomplished that feat. The atonement is an incomprehensible mystery. Yet nothing is more practical or suitable to be preached than the atonement of Christ.

d. The unsearchable mystery of Christ's resurrection

God raised Christ bodily from the dead by supernatural power.[73] Unfathomable mystery surrounds Christ's bodily resurrection and unending resurrection life. He has flesh and bones, yet he passed through solid walls.[74]

---

[68] Luke 1:27-35

[69] John 1:14; Heb.4:15, 7:26

[70] James 1:13

[71] Heb. 4:15

[72] Rom. 3:25-26

[73] *Eph. 1:18-19*: the exceeding greatness of his power to us-ward who believe, according to that working of the strength of his might which he wrought in Christ, when he raised him from the dead, and made him to sit at his right hand in the heavenly places.

[74] Luke 24:36-43

Only God can fully explain how he raised Christ and his resurrection mode of subsistence. It is incomprehensible. Yet it is suitable to be proclaimed. Unless we believe in our hearts that God raised him from the dead, we cannot be saved.[75]

e. The unsearchable mystery of Christ's second coming

When Christ returns he will "present the church to himself a glorious church, not having spot, or wrinkle, or any such thing" (Eph. 5:27). God will resurrect each dead Christian[76] and glorify each living Christian, body and soul.[77] Then he will burn up this world with fire. Then the entire human race will stand before Christ in judgment.[78] He will fully vindicate and avenge his people. He will forever deliver us from the presence of sin and sinners.[79] He will send the wicked away to eternal punishment. He will cast them, with the devil and demons, into the lake of fire. He will bless the righteous with eternal life. He will create new heavens and earth wherein dwells righteousness. God's children will shine forth as the sun in the kingdom of their Father.[80] For all eternity we will enjoy fellowship with him without sin, suffering, and death.[81] Only God can fully explain how he will do these things. The riches of the consummation are unsearchable. Yet they are suitable to be preached, for they are our hope.

In conclusion, what can we say to these things! Truly our great God has done great things for us in Christ, whereof we are glad. Blessed be God for the unsearchable riches of Christ's Person and work.

III. God's Incomprehensible Decree[82]

God does in history what he decided in eternity: "who works all things after the counsel of his own will" (Eph. 1:11). Note the marvelous substance, unfathomable depth, and proper response to God's decree.

---

[75] Rom. 10:9-10
[76] Rom. 8:23
[77] 1 Thess. 4:13-17
[78] Matt. 25:31-46
[79] 2 Thess. 1:7-10; Heb. 9:28
[80] Matt. 13:40-43; Rev. 20:10, 14-15
[81] 2 Pet. 3:4-13; Rev. 22:1-5
[82] *Rom. 11:33-36*: O the depth of the riches both of the wisdom and the knowledge of God! How unsearchable are his judgments, and his ways past tracing out! For who has known the mind of the Lord? Or who has been his counselor? Or who has first given to him, and it shall be recompensed unto him again? For of him, and through him, and unto him, are all things. To him be the glory for ever. Amen.

A. The Marvelous Substance of God's Incomprehensible Decree

Paul focuses on God's eternal decision respecting the response of Gentiles and Jews to the gospel of Christ. He unfolds in detail the essential content of God's gospel.[83] The heart of the gospel is that men get right with God when they receive by faith the virtue of Christ's perfect life and atoning death.[84] He explains why men need Christ's virtue,[85] how they get it,[86] and what blessings result when they have it.[87] Then, in chapters 9-11, he addresses how the Jews and Gentiles respond to that gospel. He notes that the Jewish people, by and large, rejected Christ's virtue.[88] Yet a remnant of them, elected according to God's grace, received and embraced it.[89] Those that rejected the gospel despised this remnant that received it. Wherever Paul preached the gospel he met with opposition and persecution from these kinsmen. Paul explains that they rejected the gospel because of their pride and self-righteousness. They thought that they were right with God because they were Abraham's physical descendants, received circumcision, and observed the ceremonial law. Paul also observes the irony that their disobedience to the gospel occasioned the publication of the gospel to the Gentiles. He rejoices because many Gentiles have been saved and engrafted into God's people. Paul calls this remarkable turn of events a great mystery, "For I would not, brethren, have you ignorant of this mystery" (Rom. 11:25). Then he brings this great mystery into sharp focus.[90] He marvels at the infinite wisdom of God's eternal decree to save. God decided who would be saved.[91] He decided to offer Christ sincerely to people without distinction. He even decided how each person would respond to the gospel. He decided to make Jewish disobedience the occasion to show mercy to disobedient Gentiles, so his mercy to disobedient Gentiles would occasion mercy on disobedient Jews, in order to consign every branch of humanity to disobedience, in order to show mercy indiscriminately to the whole human

---

[83] Rom. 1:16-8:39
[84] Rom. 1:16-17
[85] Rom. 1:18-3:20
[86] Rom. 3:21-31
[87] Rom. 4:1-8:39
[88] Rom. 10:1-3
[89] Rom. 11:5
[90] *Rom. 11:30-32*: For as you in time past were disobedient to God, but now have obtained mercy by their disobedience, even so have these also now been disobedient, that by the mercy shown to you they also may now obtain mercy. For God has shut up all unto disobedience, that he might have mercy upon all.
[91] Rom. 9:14-18

race. No wonder Paul exclaims, "O the depth!" Only God can plumb the depths of his unsearchable judgments that embody God's inscrutable wisdom by which he crafted his decree to save.

B. The Unfathomable Depth of God's Incomprehensible Decree

Ultimately God decides how each sinner responds to the gospel: "he has mercy on whom he will, and whom he will he hardens" (Rom. 9:18). This prompts the question: "Why does he still find fault, for who withstands his will?" (Rom. 9:19). Only God can fully explain why he decreed sin and why he decreed to offer Christ sincerely in the gospel to those very sinners whom he decreed to harden. Thus, God's decree to save explodes before us in unfathomable mystery. Some flee from the force of this mystery by denying God's indiscriminate offer of mercy. Others run from it by denying God's sovereign decision to harden reprobate sinners. Let us not run away, but stand still, and behold the glory of our incomprehensible God. The doctrine of God's inscrutable decree forms but another link in the fence around the mystery.

C. The Proper Response to God's Incomprehensible Decree

With Paul we should respond to God's decree with adoration and awe. We should humble ourselves before God and bow our minds before his Word. We should confess his greatness and that his decree is unsearchable. We should glorify God for the salvation of sinners and pray with compassion for the lost.

1. We should glorify God for the salvation of sinners.

Since God decrees salvation, he deserves all the credit, praise, and glory for the salvation of a sinner. Salvation is God centered. Thus, when Paul pondered God's decree to save, he was lost, not in resentment or in arguing, but in wonder, love, and praise: "For of him, and through him, and unto him, are all things. To him be the glory for ever. Amen" (Rom. 11:36). Let us do likewise.

2. We should pray with compassion for the conversion of lost sinners.

God's unsearchable decree did not make Paul heartless or prayerless. Rather, it moved him both to deep compassion for the lost[92] and earnest prayer for lost men.[93] We should do likewise. Since God sincerely offers Christ to people indiscriminately, this disposition should pervade our hearts. Since God decides who is saved, we should ask him to save those we love.

---

[92] Rom. 9:1-5
[93] Rom. 10:1-2

God's unsearchable decree to save offers strong encouragement, not to fatalism, but to pray and care for the lost.

Unit 3. The Practical Relevance of God's Incomprehensibility

God's incomprehensible nature, works, and decree call us to submit our minds to God's Word. His incomprehensibility urges us to believe whatever Scripture reveals about him, even though we can't fully explain it. This liberates us from trying to satisfy the demand for complete explanations. Where God is concerned, there are no complete explanations. It is futile to run ourselves ragged searching for them. I now summarize the practical applications of God's incomprehensibility we have just considered:

I. Practical Applications of God's Incomprehensible Nature

A. Unsearchable Wrath

    1. Fear God (Ps. 90:11)

    2. Face realistically the brevity of life (Ps. 90:12)

B. Unsearchable Knowledge

    1. Saints

        a. Treasure God's presence (Ps. 139:17-18)
        b. Avoid the influence of the wicked (Ps. 139:19-22)
        c. Examine ourselves prayerfully (Ps. 139:23-24)
        d. Trust God in our trials (Isa. 40:28)

    2. Sinners: Turn to the Lord (Isa. 55:6-9)

C. Unsearchable Love: Fill our souls on his love (Eph. 3:19)

D. Unsearchable Power: Pray for more of the power of true religion (Eph. 3:20-21)

E. Unsearchable Peace: Gratefully cast our care on him (Phil. 4:6-7)

II. Practical Applications God's Incomprehensible Works

A. The Unfathomable Mystery of the Conservation of Creation

    1. Commit our cause to God (Job. 5:8-9)

    2. Learn that wisdom is to realize that we can't fully explain providence (Eccles. 8:16-17)

B. The Unfathomable Mystery of Salvation in Christ

    1. Worship Christ, God incarnate (Heb. 1:6)

    2. Proclaim Christ's work, even though we can't fully explain it (Eph. 3:8)

III. Practical Applications of God's Incomprehensible Decree

A. Give God all the glory for the salvation of sinners (Rom. 11:36)

B. Care for lost sinners and pray for their conversion (Rom. 9:1-5, 10:1-2)

Finally, we must put away all our speculations, bow our heads, and worship. Unsearchable greatness demands adoration and praise. Bless God for his incomprehensible nature, works, and decree.

Topic 5. Overview of God's Nature

"Who in the skies can be compared to Jehovah?" (Ps. 89:6); "God is a Spirit" (John 4:24); "God is love" (1 John 4:16)

Part 3: The Nature of God

Introduction to Part 3: Overview of God's Nature: *Simple, Supreme, and Spiritual*

We now introduce Part 3, "The Nature of God," which is the heart of this course. God's nature embraces all his distinguishing traits: his being, form, and personality. It addresses the questions: What is God? What is God like? How does God appear? Who is God? God's attributes are the essential traits that distinguish God. They describe what he is, what he is like, and who he is. They are integral and inherent traits, not circumstantial or incidental. For example, when we study the Christian Life, we identify the experiences and blessings of every Christian. We thus formulate the essential marks of a Christian and define the Christian Life. Similarly, we address the traits essential to God's nature. This reveals the solemnity of this topic. We must proceed with caution and reverence. If we leave out any essential attribute, we misrepresent God. Thus, we do well to remember the admonition: "Be not many of you teachers, my brethren, knowing that we shall receive heavier judgment" (James 3:1).

Our texts epitomize God's nature. First, Scripture depicts how God's attributes relate to his being. It indicates in both testaments that his attributes are what he is: "God is love" (1 John 4:16); and "I am that I am" (Exod. 3:14). Accordingly, we expound the first pillar of God's nature, his *simplicity*. Second, Scripture, emphatically in the Old Testament, features that God is unique and peerless, one of a kind, "Who in the skies can be compared to Jehovah?" (Ps. 89:6); and, "To whom then will you liken me that I should be equal to him? Says the Holy One" (Isa. 40:25). Accordingly, we expound a second pillar of God's nature, his *supremacy*. Third, in the New Testament Christ words feature the most concise definition of God's nature: "God is a Spirit" (John 4:24). Accordingly, we expound God's *spirituality*.

Thus, the pillars of God's nature are his *simplicity*, *supremacy*, and *spirituality*. Our classification and presentation of God's attributes reflect their prominence. In this overview we first expound God's simplicity. Then we survey his supremacy and spirituality. We expound these in detail in topical presentations 6-22. We conclude this overview by comparing our presentation with the wide variety of classifications of God's attributes that Reformed theologians employ.

Unit 1. The Simplicity of God

I find some irony in the fact that little of what Reformed theologians say about God's nature is more complicated than what they say about God's "simplicity." This makes one wonder whether we should even include it. To resolve this I retreat to the fortress that protects us from all men's speculations. What practical relevance does it have? When John presents this subject, he intends to display the marks of true religion: "he that does not love does not know God, for God is love." John does not encourage speculations about God's hidden essence. Rather, he enables God's people to distinguish those who truly know God from those who falsely claim to know him. If we know God, we will show love, because he is love. Therefore, the quandary stands resolved. We must not neglect God's simplicity.

In this, we are in good company. Most Reformed theologians address it. Take for example: Bavinck[1], Berkhof[2], Hoeksema[3], Kersten[4], Hodge[5], Shedd[6], Boyce[7], and Strong.[8]

The Belgic Confession[9] confirms the prominent place of God's spirituality and simplicity:

> We all believe with the heart and confess with the mouth that there is one only simple and spiritual being which we call God; and that He is eternal, incomprehensible, invisible, immutable, infinite, almighty, perfectly wise, just, good and the overflowing fountain of all good.

---

[1] Herman Bavinck, *The Doctrine of God*, Translator Wiliam Hendriksen (Edinburgh: The Banner of Truth, 1977), 113-124.

[2] Louis Berkhof, *Systematic Theology* (Grand Rapids, MI: Wm. B. Eerdmans Publishing Co., 1972), 44-46.

[3] Herman Hoeksema, *Reformed Dogmatics* (Grand Rapids, MI: Reformed Free Publishing Association, 1976), 71-74.

[4] G. H. Kersten, *Reformed Dogmatics*, Translator Joel R. Beeke (2 Vols.; The Netherlands Reformed Book and Publishing Co., 1980), 1:59-60.

[5] Charles Hodge, *Systematic Theology* (3 Vols.; Grand Rapids, MI: Wm. B. Eerdmans Publishing Co., 1989), 1:370-374.

[6] W. G. T. Shedd, *Dogmatic Theology* (3 Vols.; Grand Rapids, MI: Zondervan Publishing House, n.d.), 334-339.

[7] James P. Boyce, *An Abstract of Systematic Theology*, (Christian Gospel Foundation, n.d.), 67-68.

[8] Augustus Strong, *Systematic Theology*, (Valley Forge, PA: The Judson Press, 1962), 244-246.

[9] The Belgic Confession, (as published by the Synod of the Reformed Church in the United States, 2011), Article 1

God's simplicity receives less profile in the Westminster and London Confessions. Their overview of God's nature doesn't explicitly employ, "simple."[10] But they confess it implicitly in the phrase, "without parts." This commends cross-pollination of the insights of the Reformation in England and Holland. I plan to seize every chance to commend our rich heritage from English Puritanism and Dutch Calvinism.

We consider both the *substance* and *practical relevance* of God's simplicity.

I. The Substance or Meaning of God's Simplicity

God is a "*simple Being.*" His nature is "*without parts.*" His supremacy and spirituality are not contrary to each other. They are in complete harmony. The unity of God's nature insures, grounds, and explains this harmony. Hodge and Bavinck warn us to avoid two extreme views of God's simplicity:

> In attempting to explain the relation in which the attributes of God stand to his essence and to each other, there are two extremes to be avoided. First, we must not represent God as a composite being, composed of different elements; and secondly, we must not confound the attributes, making them all mean the same thing, which is equivalent to denying them all together. The Realists of the middle ages tended to the former of these extremes, and the Nominalists to the other.[11]

> On the whole their [Christian theologians] teaching has been that God is simple, exalted above all composition, and that there is no real distinction between his being and his attributes. He *is* what he *has* . . . when we speak about God, we must maintain that each of his attributes is identical with his being . . . Whatever God is he is completely and simultaneously . . . By means of this doctrine of God's simplicity Christian theology was kept from falling into the error of regarding God's attributes as separate from and more or less independent of his essence . . . The fact, however, that we can not distinguish between God's being or essence and his attributes, inasmuch as each attribute is identical with the essence, does not imply that there is only a nominal and subjective distinction between the attributes, a distinction which has no real basis. It is necessary to emphasize this fact because many have drawn this erroneous conclusion.[12]

Heeding these warnings, I offer a twofold statement of its substance and meaning.

---

[10] The confessions present an overview of God's nature in WCF 2:1 and LCF 2:1

[11] Hodge, *Systematic Theology*, 1:369

[12] Bavinck, *Doctrine of God*, 121, 127

A. God's Nature is Unitary; His Attributes Are What He Is

Human nature is composed of two parts. Man is part material (body), and part non-material (soul). God's nature, however, is not composite, but unitary. The phrase, "*God is love*," points to how God's attributes relate to his Being. God is not part love; he is love. Yet, God is not only love. He is also holy. Yet, holiness and love are not simply different names for the same reality. Thus, God is what he is; and God is all he is. Every attribute necessarily identifies what he is. If you were to remove any attribute, then you would no longer have God. Each divine attribute is integral and essential to God's nature. Scripture both affirms and implies this aspect of God's simplicity.

1. Exod. 3:14[13]

Moses asked God his name. God replied: "I am that I am: and he said: Thus shall you say unto the children of Israel, I AM has sent me unto you." The phrase, אֶהְיֶה אֲשֶׁר אֶהְיֶה ('ehyeh 'aᵉsher 'ehyeh), signifies: "I am that I am, or, "I am what I am." God's name, "*I AM*," reveals his self-existence and eternal Being. Thus, if we take the phrase, "*I am that which I am*," in its most natural sense, it affirms his eternity, self-existence, and simplicity. Expressed in the third person, it would be, "God is what he is." Thus, God's name and attributes accurately convey his identity. If we know who and what he is, then we truly know him. Matthew Henry also sees God's simplicity here: "Do we ask what is God? Let it suffice us to know that he is what he is, what he ever was, and ever will be."[14] We cannot see behind God's attributes to some secret essence. Beyond his attributes is only incomprehensible mystery.

2. 1 John 1:5[15]

It would be wrong to say that "light is God" and wrong to say that God is *only* light. Yet "light," moral purity, defines what he really is. His character is so permeated by it that it excludes all moral impurity from his thoughts or actions. It is impossible that he should ever relinquish his moral purity, or that he would ever think or do anything incompatible with it, because it is essential to his very being.

---

[13] *Exod. 3:14*: I am that I am: and he said, thus shall you say unto the children of Israel, I AM has sent me unto you;.

[14] Matthew Henry, *Commentary on the Whole Bible* (6 Vols.; Old Tappan, NJ: Fleming H. Revell, n.d.), 1:284.

[15] *1 John 1:5*: God is light, and in him is no darkness at all;

3. 1 John 4:8, 16 [16]

To say "God *is* love" does not mean that love is God, or that God is only love. Rather, it means that love so permeates his character that it defines what he truly and essentially is. He could never relinquish a disposition to give and be kind, because love is integral to his being. Love so completely characterizes God's nature that it excludes every last gram of selfishness from his thoughts and actions. This is true of all God's attributes. Each virtue characterizes God's being so completely that it excludes every last gram of every opposing vice. Justice so pervades his nature that it excludes every drop of injustice or prejudice. Again, his faithfulness excludes all falsehood or unreliability. Similarly, every aspect of supreme spirituality so pervades his nature that he must always have, not only divine morality, but also divine incorporeality, animacy, faculty, and personality. Again, supremacy so pervades his being that it utterly excludes every gram of the traits which mark the being of creatures: incompletion or flaw, dependence, spatial limitation, origination, and mutability. In sum, God's attributes are essential characteristics of his nature. God is what he is. He can never be anything else.

B. God's Attributes are Distinct Characteristics of God's Nature.

Some have carried the first aspect of God's simplicity to an extreme. They reason that if each attribute is essential to his nature, then what we call God's "attributes," are really just different names for the same thing. In other words, omniscience, omnipotence, light, and love, are merely names that men use to describe God's one, singular nature. Yet, although God's nature is unitary, he is not unvarying. Love is not omniscience. Eternity is not faithfulness. They are not distinct in name only. Each concept defines something essential about God. They are not "parts" of God, to be disassembled. Yet, each defines a distinct quality or characteristic of God. Consider the text: "Jacob I loved, but Esau I hated."[17] Although it presents God's nature in the setting of a fallen world, it displays vital characteristics of that nature. His response to sin reveals who and what he essentially is. What then? Shall we say that love and hate are simply different names for the same reality? Shall we say that no distinction exists between God's disposition toward Jacob and his disposition toward Esau? Why then is Jacob in heaven and Esau in hell? Manifestly, such an approach to that text would be a monstrous travesty of exegesis. Or, to avoid the difficulty

---

[16] *1 John 4:8, 16*: He that does not love doesn't know God, for God is love . . . 16 And we know and have believed the love which God has in us. God is love; he that loves abides in God

[17] Mal. 1:2-3; Rom. 9:13

altogether, shall we pretend that God's wrath and detestation of sinners are not indicative of who and what he really is? If we do, we have truncated and perverted what Scripture says about his essential nature. Thus, God's love and hate are not just two different names for the same reality, even though each displays something integral to his nature.

Summary: this leads us back to God's incomprehensibility. We cannot fathom the depths of God's nature. The biblical doctrine of God's simplicity is part of the fence around that mystery. Our confession affirms this: "whose essence is comprehended only by himself" (LCF 2:1). We know that God is the Supreme Spirit. Yet, when we inquire after his substance, all we know, in positive terms, is this: (1) God's nature is not composite, but unitary and singular; his attributes are what he, the Supreme Spirit, really is; and (2) these attributes are really distinct, not simply different names for the same reality.

II. The Practical and Experimental Applications of God's Simplicity

A. God's Simplicity Comforts Believers

God's simplicity comforts his people. It implies that we can know God as he really is. God's attributes accurately display his nature. God is what he is. Therefore, this frees us from the bondage of searching for a concealed essence of God, distinct from his attributes, which would define who and what he really is. Therefore, if we know what his Word reveals about him, we really know him. His attributes truly identify his being. This affords comfort to our souls. Our God enables us to grasp all we need to know about him in order to enter and enjoy personal and saving relations with him.

B. God's Simplicity Commends Godliness and Exposes Hypocrisy

God's simplicity implies that those who know God will reflect what he really is. John did not say, "God is love," or "God is light," to foster philosophical speculation about God's essence. He said these things to press the truth that if people know God, they will reflect his love and purity in their behavior. An unselfish disposition of giving and caring displays fellowship with the God who is love. A lifestyle marked by separation from the vices of the world displays fellowship with the God whose being excludes all worldly vice. Many deceivers falsely profess to know God. John uses God's simplicity as the basis for warning God's people about them. If someone isn't a holy and loving person, then don't believe his claim that he enjoys saving fellowship with the God who is moral purity and love. Here is impact of God's simplicity. Let us take it to heart in our own lives and our efforts to deal faithfully with others.

Part 3: The Nature of God | 175

Unit 2. The Supremacy of God

God's supremacy signifies that he is unique, one of a kind, highly exalted above the limitations of creatures and above the moral failures of sinners. All Scripture extols the singularity and uniqueness of the Supreme Being. The Old Testament features it. It affirms emphatically and repeatedly that God's works display his supremacy.[18] It affirms emphatically and repeatedly that God's works are singular because God is supreme, unique, and highly exalted above every creature and so-called god.[19] He is the only true and living God.[20] No other so-called god is at all like him. Idols are nothing, and do nothing.[21] He is peerless, unequaled, God alone.[22] No angel in the skies can be compared to him.[23] He is exalted in supreme majesty above all he has made in heaven and on earth.[24]

Scripture presents God's supremacy both *existentially* and *spiritually*. In existential terms, God is supreme because he is *ideal*,[25] *self-existent*,[26] *infinite*,[27] *eternal*,[28] and *unchangeable*.[29] I call these attributes, *"existential,"* since each relates to his Being or existence. In spiritual terms, God is supreme in his incorporeal form,[30] in his life and power,[31] in his metaphysical capacities and faculties,[32] in his moral character,[33] and in his triune personality.[34] I call these attributes, *"spiritual,"* since each displays (as we

---

[18] *Ps. 86:8*: There is none like unto you among the gods, O Lord; Neither are there any works like unto your works.

[19] *Deut. 4:35, 39*: Unto you was it showed, that you might know that Jehovah he is God; there is none else beside him . . . lay it to your heart, that Jehovah he is God in heaven above and on earth beneath; there is none else;

[20] Deut. 6:4; Mark 12:29, 32

[21] Isa. 40:18-28, 46:5, 9; Jer. 10:6-16

[22] 1 Cor. 8:4

[23] Ps. 89:6; Heb. 1:13-14

[24] Ps. 113:5

[25] Exod. 15:11; 1 Sam. 2:2; Eccles. 3:14

[26] 1 Sam. 2:2; Jer. 10:16; Acts 17:25

[27] 1 Kings 8:27; Isa. 40:28

[28] Deut. 33:26; Isa. 40:28

[29] Isa. 46:5, 9; Heb. 1:10-12

[30] Phil. 4:6; 1 Tim. 6:16

[31] Ps. 89:6; Jer. 10:6, 10, 16

[32] Isa. 40:28, 46:9; Jer. 10:10

[33] 1 Sam. 2:2; 1 Kings 8:23; Micah 7:18

[34] John 5:18, 10:30-32; 1 Cor. 8:4-6; Phil. 2:6

shall presently see) a dimension of his spirituality as a spiritual Being. The Old Testament stresses that God is peerless, without equal;[35] the New stresses the equality of the Father and the Son.[36] The Son always was, and is, equal with the Father. The Son also is Jehovah, the Supreme Being. We now survey God's existential attributes, which we expound in detail in topical presentations 6-10.

I. **God Alone is Ideal**: *Inherently and Infinitely Perfect: Topic 6*

God's *ideality* is his inherent and essential completeness and flawlessness. Perfection relates to completion and to flaw. All God is and does is absolutely complete and sufficient and totally and immutably flawless.[37] God alone is infinitely perfect. He could never be improved (Eccles. 3:14). He is incapable of flaw in his capacities (Isa. 40:28) or character (Hab. 1:13). He alone is inherently impeccable and "untemptable."[38] These necessary and immutable properties of God's nature make him supreme and unique. Angelic spirits are inherently capable of improvement and flaw. This is evidenced by the fall of some of them (2 Pet. 2:4; Jude 6) and the betterment of others (1 Pet. 1:12). The fall and redemption of man demonstrate that the same is true of the human spirit. Although angels or men eventually possess perfection by God's grace (Heb. 12:23), yet, "unimprovability," "untemptability," and impeccability are not immutable properties of their nature (Mark 10:18).

II. **God Alone is Self-existent**: *Topic 7*

God's eternal self-existence is his *aseity*. There was when only God was. He alone formed everything else.[39] His being doesn't and can't depend on anything but himself.[40] He only has immortality.[41]

III. **God Alone is Infinite**: *Topic 8*

God's *infinity* means that he is limitless[42] and illimitable.[43] He only is every

---

[35] Isa. 40:18, 25, 28, 46:5, 9
[36] John 5:18, 10:30-32; Phil. 4:6
[37] Ps. 18:30; Eccles. 3:14; Matt. 5:48; Rom. 11:35, 36; Eph. 1:23; Col. 2:9
[38] Exod. 15:11; 1 Sam. 2:2; Job 4:17,18, 15:15; Mark 10:18; James 1:13
[39] Jer. 10:16
[40] John 5:26
[41] 1 Sam. 2:2; Acts 17:25; 1 Tim. 6:16
[42] Pss. 145:3, 147:5; Isa. 40:28
[43] 1 Kings 8:27

way infinite and immutably so.[44] All other spirits are finite. The devil,[45] angels, and human spirits are limited.[46]

IV. God Alone is Eternal: *Topic 9*

God's *eternity* means that only God is eternal, without origin.[47] He alone is Uncreated.[48] All other spirits originate because God created them. Angelic spirits[49] and human spirits[50] had a beginning.

V. God Alone is Unchangeable: *Topic 10*

God's *immutability* means that he alone is without alteration or change.[51] He does not develop, improve, mature, age, or decay.[52] All God is, he always was, and always will be. He is immutably perfect and infinite in his being, faculties, and character.[53] This is not true of angelic and human spirits. The fall of angelic spirits, and the fall and maturation of human spirits, confirm this divine distinctive.

Unit 3. The Spirituality of God[54]

The original reads: πνευμα ὁ θεος (pneuma ho theos), literally, "spirit the God." Clearly "the God" is the subject, and "spirit" is a predicate nominative of an implied linking verb. Thus, the correct translation is either "God is a spirit," or "God is spirit." In their commentaries on John's gospel, Hendriksen[55] and Leon Morris[56] argue that the proper translation is, "God is spirit," not "a spirit." But either translation expresses truth. The absence of the definite article in the Greek text emphasizes the quality of spirituality. Thus, Jesus stresses that God's nature is spiritual. This is the bedrock. It furnishes the irreducible foundation of a biblical concept of God. It is true,

---

[44] Isa. 40:18, 25, 28
[45] Rev. 12:12
[46] Matt. 24:36
[47] Ps. 90:2
[48] Isa. 40:25, 28; Jer. 10:6, 16
[49] Col. 1:16-17
[50] Isa. 57:16; Zech. 12:1
[51] Ps. 102:25; Heb. 1:10-12
[52] Isa. 40:25, 28
[53] Mal. 3:6; James 1:17
[54] *John 4:24*: God is a Spirit: and they that worship him must worship in spirit and truth
[55] William Hendriksen, *Exposition of the Gospel According to John* (2 Vols.; Grand Rapids: Baker Book House, 1976), 1:168
[56] Leon Morris, *The Gospel According to John* (Grand Rapids: Wm. B. Eerdmans, 1975), 271

but insufficient, simply to say that God is infinite, immutable, or perfect. If we say, "God is an immutable," or, "an infinite," or, "a perfect," the question remains, an immutable, perfect, infinite what? Jesus states exactly *what* God is, "*a spirit,*" a spiritual being. Yet he is also unique, he is the one and only supreme spiritual Being.

Here our Lord: (1) declares the existence of spiritual beings: "*a spirit*"; (2) asserts the spirituality of God's nature: "*God is a spirit*"; and (3) applies the practical relevance of God's spirituality: "*and they that worship him must worship in spirit and truth.*" Accordingly, in this survey of God's spirituality we consider: *first*, the biblical concept of a spiritual being; *second*, the singular features of God's spirituality; and *third*, the practical application of God's spirituality.

I. The Biblical Concept of a Spiritual Being

Jesus declares that spirits exist, and that we may attain a proper conception of what they are. He depicts their characteristics.[57] Scripture affirms that angels are spirits,[58] and demons,[59] and human souls separated from their body by death.[60] Thus, like other spirits, God too is a spiritual being. Our Confession expresses this with a lower case "s," "a most pure *spirit*" (LCF 2:1). Thus, we can only grasp God's spirituality when we understand the attributes of a spirit. Thus, we must examine the Scriptures to define the distinguishing characteristics of a spiritual being.

Scripture divides created spirits, in the broadest sense of the word, into two categories. These are, "*lower spirits,*" the spirits of beasts, which sustain no continued existence apart from a material body, and "*higher spirits,*" the spirits of angels and men, which can and do sustain existence apart from a material body. The preacher proclaims this fundamental distinction (Eccles. 3:21): "Who knows the spirit of man, that goes upward, and the spirit of the beast, that goes downward to the earth?" He laments the tragic degradation that death inflicts upon the sons of men. In this, he says, man is little better than an animal, for his body dies and returns to dust, just like the body of an animal (3:18-20). He observes that God orders this to prove men and humble their pride. Yet, he concludes that man is not completely identical to a beast. The enduring nature of the human spirit, in contrast with the temporary nature of an animal spirit, epitomizes human superiority. That entity which animates an animal body ceases to exist when the animal dies. It returns to

---

[57] Luke 24:37, 39
[58] Heb. 1:14
[59] Luke 4:33, 35-36; 2 Pet. 2:4
[60] Heb. 12:23

the earth. It goes downward. Thus, I call it a *"lower spirit."* The human spirit, however, does not cease to exist when its human body dies. It does not go downward to the earth. Rather: "the spirit returns unto God who gave it" (Eccles. 12:7). Thus, I call it a *"higher spirit."* Thus, higher spirits can and do exist apart from union with any material body.

We are concerned now only with the attributes of higher spirits. Based on a survey of the biblical testimony, I offer the following definition of the distinguishing traits of a spiritual being:

A spirit is a non-material and living being with metaphysical faculty, morality, and personality.

This definition pertains to all higher spirits: to disembodied human spirits, to angels and demons, and to the Supreme Spirit. It highlights the five distinguishing traits, or essential properties, which spirits possess. All spirits are non-material beings. They are living beings. They have metaphysical capacities. They have moral character. They possess personal consciousness. For this reason reformed theologians call spirituality a *"communicable"* attribute. Although God is a unique Spirit, he has created spiritual beings similar to himself. Thus, we must not carry God's uniqueness or singularity to an extreme. Now I show how Scripture ascribes these five properties to angels and devils, to the human spirit, and to God.

A. A Spirit is a Non-material Being[61]

The disciples are terrified because they think they see a spirit, a non-corporeal being. Jesus comforts them by assuring them that he is not a spirit in virtue of his resurrection body. He thus teaches that a spirit is a non-material being: *"a spirit does not have flesh and bones."* Spirits are real beings, and yet at the same time non-material beings. Spirits do not have mass or take up space. You may well ask: "how can a spirit be both real and non-material?" That is the point! There is more to reality than the material world. There is more than the mass-energy continuum. There is another dimension of reality, the realm of spirits. That realm is just as real as the material realm. A disembodied human spirit belongs to that realm, so also do the angelic spirits, and so does God.

Jesus here teaches us about the nature of spirits by negation, not by affirmation: "a spirit does *not* have flesh and bones." Much about the

---

[61] *Luke 24:36-39*: And as they spoke these things, he himself stood in the midst of them, and says unto them, Peace be unto you. But they were terrified and affrighted, and supposed that they beheld a spirit. And he said unto them: Why are you troubled? And wherefore do questionings arise in your heart? See my hands and my feet, that it is I myself: handle me, and see; for a spirit does not have flesh and bones, as you behold me having.

spiritual realm is mysterious to us. We understand the "substance" of a spirit more by negative assertion of what it is not, than by positive affirmation of what it is. As to substance or essence, we know only that a spirit is a something real, not imaginary; and yet at it is also non-material and non-corporeal. Other properties of a spirit are correlates of non-corporeality: invisibility, indivisibility, impassability, and "immortality." The 1689 London Confession closely connects these traits with God's spirituality: "a most pure spirit, invisible, without body, parts, or passions, who only hath immortality" (LCF 2:1). In virtue of its non-material nature, a spirit is non-phenomenal, or *invisible*. Bodily senses of sight, hearing, smell, taste, and touch do not perceive a spirit. Thus the incarnate Christ is: "the image of *the invisible God*" (Col. 1:15). Thus, Paul says: "*whom no man has seen, nor can see*" (1 Tim. 6:16). In virtue of its non-corporeal nature, a spirit is also *indivisible*. Unlike a body, it is not composed of parts like "*flesh and bones.*" It can't be divided or dissected. Again, a spirit, because it is non-corporeal, is *impassable*. It doesn't have bodily appetites, or the needs that generate them. It doesn't experience hunger or thirst, or the other "passions" of bodily existence. Thus, Jesus, to demonstrate that he was not a spirit, requests food and eats it before his frightened servants (Luke 24:41-43). Finally, because a spirit is non-material it is *indissoluble*, not subject to dissolution. In one sense immortality pertains only to God (1 Tim. 6:16). The human body is "mortal" because it dissolves (albeit temporarily) after death. The human spirit, however, never dissolves, but "returns unto God who gave it." All spirits possess this property of non-corporeality and its correlates, invisibility, indivisibility, impassability, and immortality. They pertain to the human spirit, angels, and God.

B. *A Spirit is a Living Being.*

The second trait of spirits is life or "*animacy.*" Spirits are not inanimate objects, but living things. They have life; they are animate. They give life; they are animating.[62] We consider biblical support for the animacy of spiritual beings, the concept of animacy, and the affirmation of divine animacy.

1. *Support for the animacy of spiritual beings*

a. *James 2:26*[63]

James illustrates the nature of saving faith. He affirms the animating influence of the spirit. Physical death is separation of a soul from its body.

---

[62] 1 Cor. 15:45

[63] *James 2:26*: For as the body apart from the spirit is dead, even so faith apart from works is dead

Without a spirit, the human body becomes a corpse. It crumbles and returns to dust, because the spirit animates the body. This relationship has its roots in the creation of man: "And Jehovah God formed man dust from the ground, and breathed into his nostrils the breath of life; and man became a living soul" (Gen. 2:7). The Creator established an intimate relation between body and soul and the animating influence of the soul on the body. Thus, man became animate, "*a living soul*," when God imparted to him a human spirit: "*breathed into his nostrils the breath of life*."

b. *Rev. 20:4*[64]

John sees the glory of heaven above, where disembodied human spirits ("souls") of Christian martyrs live and reign with the exalted Christ. Similarly, the writer of Hebrews describes heavenly Jerusalem as inhabited by the church on earth and by "the spirits of just men made perfect" (Heb. 12:23) in heaven. After death all the just continue to live. Personal subsistence is a property of their disembodied spirits, because a spirit is a living being.

c. *Luke 20:37-38*

Jesus teaches the reality of life after death. For support he appeals to God's words to Moses at the burning bush: "I am the God of your father, the God of Abraham, the God of Isaac, and the God of Jacob" (Exod. 3:6). The Lord argues from the present relationship of God to the patriarchs, expressed in the words: "*I am* the God of your father." Jesus teaches that the relevance of these words resides in the fact that: "he is not the God of the dead, but of the living." He means that God would never say to Moses: "*I am* the God of Abraham," if Abraham were not then alive. Thus, Jesus concludes that when God spoke to Moses, Abraham himself was still alive, even though his body was dead. This is true precisely because the disembodied spirit of Abraham lived then, even as now, in heaven with the Lord.

2. The concept of "animacy"

The biblical conception of *life* has two aspects, spiritual life and animacy. Spiritual life signifies experiential communion and fellowship with God.[65] Thus, sinners are dead even while they are still alive.[66] Thus, clearly, life has a dual meaning or significance. Our focus now is on animacy: "*while she*

---

[64] *Rev. 20:4*: I saw the souls of them that had been beheaded for the testimony of Jesus . . . and they lived, and reigned with Christ a thousand years.

[65] *John 17:3*: this is life eternal that they may know you the only true God, and him whom you have sent, Jesus Christ

[66] *1 Tim. 5:6*: but she that gives herself to pleasure is dead while she lives

lives." What does it mean to be animate?" This question is basic, yet very difficult to answer with precision. The Bible nowhere furnishes a formal definition of animate life. Rather, it stresses a fundamental property of living or animate beings that distinguishes them from all inanimate objects. This distinguishing trait is *self-initiated action*. Animate creatures act on their own initiative. Scripture clearly affirms an intimate and inseparable bond between *animacy* and *activity*: "the Word of God is living and active" (Heb. 4:12). Activity is the fruit of animate life, and its distinctive evidence. Dead or inanimate objects cannot act on their own initiative. They have no power or ability to do anything. The creation account displays this close connection of animacy and activity: "And God created . . . every living creature that moves" (Gen. 1:21). Again, the crucial distinctive of an animate being is that it "*moves*" spontaneously on its own initiative. It is not static, stationary, or motionless. The words translated "living creature," חַיָּה נֶפֶשׁ (nephesh chayyah), depict man in Genesis 2:7, where they are translated "*living soul.*" These words signify "animate being." Life is dynamic. The word, "soul," features personal action, subsistence. The word, "spirit," highlights a specific pattern of action, breathing. Thus, the words translated, "spirit," are also sometimes translated, "breath," or "wind." In Genesis 2:7 a synonymous expression, "*breath of life*," reveals that the rhythmic action of respiration displays human life. In sum, an animate being has *power*, which the capacity to act. And, it acts spontaneously. Thus, when a spirit animates a human body, it moves on its own initiative, and pulsates with rhythmic activity, especially displayed in breathing. Thus, power is animacy's root; and spontaneous action is its fruit. Therefore, Scripture links spirituality and power: "the spirit of the man will sustain his infirmity" (Prov. 18:14). Again, Scripture asserts the power of demons to do harm[67] and the ability of angels to serve.[68]

3. The divine animacy

Scripture frequently depicts God as "*the living God*," both in the Old Testament[69] and in the New Testament.[70] Again, the Lord asserts his life and swears by it: "*As I live, says Jehovah.*" Note these examples from the Pentateuch,[71] the prophets,[72] and the New Testament (Rom. 14:11). Again,

---

[67] Mark 9:20
[68] Heb. 1:14
[69] Deut. 5:26; Pss. 42:2, 84:2; Dan. 6:20, 26
[70] 2 Cor. 6:16; 1 Thess. 1:9; 1 Tim. 4:10; Heb. 10:31
[71] Num. 14:21, 14:28
[72] Isa. 49:18; Jer. 22:24, 46:18; Ezek. 14:16, 18, 20, 17:16, 18:3; Zeph. 2:9

men also affirm certitude by God's life, saying, *"As the Lord lives"* (1 Sam. 14:39, 45). Further, because he is the living God, he acts on his own initiative, as it pleases him, with his divine power. Numerous texts variously assert God's power, both in the Old Testament (Gen. 18:14), and in the New (Mark 10:27; Eph. 1:19, 20). One text displays clearly the intimate connection between God's life and power:

> *Dan. 6:26-27*: I make a decree, that in all the dominion of my kingdom men tremble and fear before the God of Daniel; for he is *the living God*, and steadfast forever, and his kingdom that which shall not be destroyed; and his dominion shall be even unto the end: *he delivers and rescues*, and *he works signs and wonders* in heaven and in earth, *who has delivered* Daniel from the power of the lions.

Therefore, animacy, which is marked by power and action, is a property of all spiritual beings.

C. A Spirit Has Metaphysical Faculty.

The third characteristic of a spirit is that it has metaphysical faculty or capacity. A spirit is endowed with three primary metaphysical capabilities, the faculties of mind, will, and affection. We must not think of these faculties as separate compartments of the soul, as though one part of the soul wills, another part thinks, and yet another part feels. The whole soul thinks, feels, and wills. Nor must we conceive of a spirit as thinking without willing and feeling, or as feeling without thinking and willing, or as willing without feeling and thinking. Rather, a spirit exercises each faculty simultaneously with the others, and in conjunction with the others. Still, the Bible distinguishes these various faculties. It employs distinct terminology for them and presents them in distinct relations. Thus, when we distinguish them, we neither impose man-made categories on the Bible, nor import foreign concepts.

1. A spirit has the faculty of intellect or mind

A dead body, though it has a brain, doesn't know anything, understand anything, or perceive anything. A spirit, however, thinks, understands, knows, discerns, and perceives. The Old[73] and New[74] Testaments reveal that the human spirit thinks, knows, understands, and perceives. They establish

---

[73] *Ps. 77:6*: I commune with mine own heart; and my spirit makes diligent search; *Prov. 20:27*: The spirit of man is the lamp of Jehovah, searching all his innermost parts

[74] *Mark 2:8*: Jesus, perceiving in his spirit that they so reasoned

that angelic spirits think, know, and understand.[75] They establish that God too has the faculty of mind.[76] They affirm an analogy between God's and a man's capacity to think and know. Thus, all spirits, human, angelic, and the Supreme Spirit, have a mind.

2. A spirit has the faculty of will

Scripture pictures the capacity to will with a rich variety of terms, such as, choice, desire, purpose, decision, counsel, and good pleasure. Scripture clearly affirms that the human spirit exercises the faculty of will[77] and that angelic spirits have a will.[78] It affirms repeatedly with irrefutable force that God also has a will and exercises it.[79] Thus, the spirits of men and of angels and God have the faculty of will, or "*spontaneity.*" They choose, desire, purpose, decide, and have pleasure in persons and things.

3. A spirit has the faculty of feeling or affection

Scripture describes the faculty of affection with a variety of terms and phrases. It depicts various pairs of contrasting feelings: love or delight and hate or detestation; joy or cheer and sorrow or grief; anger or wrath and being satisfied or well-pleased; being at peace and being afraid; and feeling pride and shame. I cannot now develop a theology of feeling, or expound the distinctions between human emotions and divine affections. I only aim to establish from Scripture that all spirits feel in a manner consistent with their nature. Scripture affirms that the human spirit feels affections: whether grief

---

[75] *Rev. 12:12*: the devil is gone down unto you, having great wrath, knowing that he has but a short time

[76] *1 Cor. 2:11*: For who among men knows the things of a man, save the spirit of the man, which is in him? Even so the things of God none knows, save the Spirit of God

[77] *Exod. 35:21*: every one whose heart stirred him up, and every one whom his spirit made willing; *Matt. 26:41*: the spirit indeed is willing, but the flesh is weak

[78] *Luke 4:6*: the devil said unto him, to you will I give all this authority, and the glory of them: for it has been delivered unto me; and to whomsoever I will I give it

[79] *Acts 21:14*: The will of the Lord be done; *Rom. 9:18*: So then he has mercy on whom he will, and whom he will he hardens; *1 Cor. 12:11*: all these works the one and the same Spirit, dividing to each one severally even as he will; *1 Cor. 12:18*: God has set the members each one of them in the body, even as it pleased him; *Eph. 1:5*: according to the good pleasure of his will; *Eph. 1:11*: according to the purpose of him who works all things after the counsel of his own will; *James 4:15*: you ought to say, If the Lord will, we shall both live and do this or that.

and sorrow,[80] or joy,[81] or jealousy and anger.[82] It also affirms that angelic spirits feel affections: whether joy,[83] or fear,[84] or wrath.[85] Finally, it affirms repeatedly that God feels affections: of joy[86] and grief[87]; of delight,[88] love and hate[89]; of jealousy, anger,[90] and good-pleasure[91]; and of peace.[92] Thus, all spirits feel: human spirits, angelic spirits, and the Supreme Spirit.

In conclusion, all spirits possess the faculties of mind, of will, and of affection. All spirits think and know, will and choose, and sense and feel, but dead bodies have no mind, will, or affection.

D. A Spirit has Morality.

A fourth property of spirits is that they are moral beings, or, as it is commonly put, "moral agents." Spirits, unlike inanimate objects and animals, have morality. Their morality consists of *moral capacity* and *moral character*. I cannot now develop a theology of moral capacity and character, or define the distinctions between divine and human morality. Rather, I intend only to demonstrate from Scripture that all spirits are moral beings with moral capacity and moral character.

---

[80] *Exod. 6:9*: but they hearkened not unto Moses for anguish of spirit, and for cruel bondage; *1 Sam. 1:15*: Hannah answered and said, No, my lord, I am a woman of sorrowful spirit: I have drunk neither wine or strong drink; *Prov. 18:14*: but a broken spirit who can bear; *John 11:33*: When Jesus therefore saw her weeping, and the Jews also weeping who came with her, he groaned in the spirit, and was troubled

[81] *Luke 1:47*: And my spirit has rejoiced in God my Savior

[82] *Num. 5:30*: or when the spirit of jealousy comes upon a man, and he is jealous for his wife

[83] *Job 38:7*: all the sons of God shouted for joy; *Luke 15:10*: there is joy in the presence of the angels of God over one sinner that repents

[84] *James 2:19*: the demons also believe and shudder

[85] *Rev. 12:12*: the devil is gone down unto you, having great wrath, knowing that he has but a short time

[86] *Judg. 9:13*: the vine said unto them, should I leave my new wine, which cheers God and man

[87] *Judg. 10:16*: And they put away the foreign gods from among them, and served Jehovah; and his soul was grieved for the misery of Israel; *Eph. 4:30*: Grieve not the Holy Spirit of God

[88] *Isa. 42:1*: Behold my servant whom I uphold; my chosen, in whom my soul delights

[89] *John 17:24*: for you loved me before the foundation of the world; *Rom. 9:13*: Jacob I loved, but Esau I hated

[90] *Exod. 20:5*: for I Jehovah your God am a jealous God; *Ps. 90:11*: who knows the power of your anger, and your wrath according to the fear that is due unto you?; *Rom. 1:18*: for the wrath of God is revealed from heaven

[91] *Phil. 4:18*: a sacrifice acceptable, well-pleasing to God

[92] *Phil. 4:7*: And the peace of God, which passes all understanding, shall guard your hearts

1. Moral capacity of human and angelic spirits

Moral capacity involves the capacity to discern right and wrong, the commendation and condemnation of right and wrong, and the personal consciousness of right and wrong. Scripture often calls the moral capacity of humans the "conscience."[93] Conscience is the moral capability of the human spirit, for it involves the exercise of the mind,[94] of the will,[95] and of the affections.[96] The biblical portrait of self-examination implies that moral capacity resides in the spirit: "the spirit of a man is the lamp of Jehovah, searching all his innermost parts" (Prov. 20:27). Scripture says little about the moral capacity of angels and demons. Their fall into sin and tempting others implies their moral capacity (Gen. 3:5; 2 Pet. 2:4). The devil and demons display their moral capacity when they pummel and harass God's people with false accusation,[97] and when they respond to their own condemnation with pleading, dread, and wrath.[98]

2. Moral character of human and angelic spirits

Moral character is also a trait of spirits. Spirits are never morally neutral. They are good or evil, righteous or wicked. Their character is marked either by virtue or vice. Scripture speaks of the moral character of angelic spirits: "God spared not the angels who sinned" (2 Pet. 2:4). The devil is a liar and a murderer: "You are of your father the devil, and the lusts of your father it is your will to do. He was a murderer from the beginning, and stands not in the truth, because there is no truth in him. When he speaks a lie, he speaks of his own: for he is a liar, and the father thereof" (John 8:44). Scripture also describes demons as "unclean" or "evil" spirits.[99] God's Word also predicates moral virtues and vices to human spirits. Scripture speaks of a contrite spirit,[100] a right spirit,[101] a spirit in which there is no guile,[102] a haughty spirit, and a humble spirit.[103] Paul speaks of defilement of spirit: "Let us

---

[93] Acts 24:16; Rom. 2:14, 15; 2 Cor. 1:12, 4:2; 1 Tim. 1:5; Titus 1:15; Heb. 13:18
[94] Rom. 2:14-15; Titus 1:15
[95] Heb. 13:18
[96] 1 Tim. 1:5; John 3:19; 2 Thess. 2:10, 12
[97] Rev. 12:10
[98] Matt. 8:29, 30; James 2:19; Rev. 12:12
[99] 1 Sam. 16:14, 16, 23; Matt. 3:43
[100] Ps. 34:18
[101] Ps. 51:20
[102] Ps. 32:2
[103] Prov. 16:18-19

cleanse ourselves from all defilement of flesh and spirit, perfecting holiness in the fear of God" (2 Cor. 7:1).

3. God's moral capacity and character

Having established the moral capacity and character of human and angelic spirits, we now demonstrate God's moral capacity and character. God has moral capacity. He knows the difference between good and evil, and right and wrong.[104] He defends his own integrity, when men falsely accuse him of evil.[105] God also has a moral character that is absolutely perfect (Matt. 5:48). His character displays the absence of all vice and the presence of all virtue. He is absolutely good, holy, just, and faithful.[106] God's assessment of his integrity is totally accurate and honest.[107]

Thus, morality marks all human and angelic spirits and the Supreme Spirit.

E. A Spirit has Personality.

The fifth property of spirits is personality. Spirits are personal beings. What is personality? Personality involves self-awareness. The personal pronouns: "I" (first person); "you" (second person); and "he" (third person) express self-awareness. In this way, personal beings distinguish themselves from other persons. Thus, even as action and power are the marks of life, so also personal communication and interpersonal communion are the marks of personality. I cannot now develop a theology of communion and communication, or delve into the distinctions between human and divine personality. Rather, I only design to establish from Scripture that all spirits are personal beings. Scripture clearly teaches that angels and devils are personal beings. An angel says of himself: "*I am Gabriel*" (Luke 1:19). Gabriel thus manifests self-awareness and communicates verbally. He also enters into interpersonal communion. The devils also have personality. The devil tempted Christ, saying: "All these things will I give you if you will fall down and worship me" (Matt. 4:9). Thus, the devil displays self-awareness, uses verbal communication, and enters into interpersonal relations. Thus, he is a personal being. Note also the personality of demons. They appealed to Christ (Matt. 8:29, 31): "If you cast us out, send us away into the herd of swine," and, "are you come hither to torment us before the time?" Again, these expressions demonstrate that demons have self-awareness, use verbal communication, and engage in interpersonal communion. Scripture also

---

[104] Gen. 3:5, 22
[105] Job 40:8; Ezek. 18:25, 29, 33:17
[106] Matt. 10:18; Hab. 1:13; Rom. 2:11, 3:26; Titus 2:2; James 1:13
[107] Isa. 40:25, 42:8, 45:21, 57:15; Jer. 9:24

clearly teaches that human spirits have personality. That we humans have personality is taught, I may almost say, on every page of the Bible. It is evident that human beings have self-awareness, communicate verbally, and enter interpersonal communion. The biblical description of disembodied human spirits and dead bodies makes it evident that personality is a property of the human spirit. Disembodied human spirits retain self-awareness, communicate verbally, and enter personal relations.[108] Dead bodies have no self-awareness, do not communicate verbally, and enter no interpersonal relations. Finally, Scripture clearly teaches that God is a personal Being, not an impersonal force. Again, this is so obvious that I will not weary you with many texts. The Bible itself proves it, for the whole Bible is God's verbal communication, whereby he enters personal relations with his people. Consider only one text: "Look unto me, and be ye saved, all the ends of the earth; for I am God, and there is none else" (Isa. 45:22). Therefore, all spirits are personal beings. Personality is a property of angelic spirits, of human spirits, and of the Supreme Spirit.

In summary: I have shown that spirits have five distinguishing properties: (1) spirits are non-material beings; (2) they have animate life, marked by power and action; (3) they have the metaphysical faculties of mind, will, and affection; (4) they have morality, consisting of moral capacity and character; and (5) they have personality, self-awareness, displayed in verbal communication and interpersonal communion. These five characteristics pertain to human spirits, to angelic spirits, and to the Supreme Spirit.

Conclusion: Recognition of this Biblical Concept of a Spiritual Being

This perspective on the distinctive features of spiritual beings has the imprimatur of Reformed theology.

1. Incorporeality

We have already noted that LCF affirms God's incorporeality. Bavinck features God's invisibility.[109] Most Reformed theologians in their discussions stress one or more of the correlates of incorporeality.

2. Animacy

Bavinck seems to connect spirituality with life when he classifies God's attributes,[110] but never explicitly connects them in his exposition. Augustus Strong connects them explicitly: "We come now to the positive import of

---

[108] Luke 9:30, 16:23-31; 2 Cor. 5:8; Phil. 1:23; Rev. 6:9-10
[109] Bavinck, *Doctrine of God*, 175-183
[110] Ibid., 141

the term Spirit. The spirituality of God involves the two attributes of Life and Personality."[111] John Gill also connects them explicitly:[112]

> But besides these properties, there are others still more excellent in spirits, by which they approach nearer to God, and bear a greater resemblance to him, and serve to give us clearer ideas of his nature; they are lively, active, endowed with understanding, will, and affections; they are lively, have a principle of life."

Gill connects God's life and activity: "I shall proceed now to consider such [attributes] as belong to him as an active and operative Spirit, as all spirits are, more or less; but he infinitely so . . . he is all act; and activity supposes life and operations; power, such as God performs, almighty power, or omnipotence; which are attributes next to be considered; and first his life."[113]

He then expounds God's life (pgs. 71-76) and omnipotence (pgs. 77-84).

3. Metaphysical Faculty

Gill observes that spirits are "endowed with understanding, will, and affections."[114] He then discusses how human and angelic faculties resemble God's faculties:[115]

> Spirits, angels, and the souls of men, are intelligent beings, have a faculty of understanding . . . the understanding of God is infinite . . . Spirits have the power of willing, they are voluntary agents; and God wills whatever he does, and does whatever he wills . . . Spirits have the affections of love, mercy, pity, &c. God not only loves his creatures, but is love itself.'"

He also enumerates God's affections[116]: "and the affections, to which may be reduced, the love, grace, mercy, hatred, anger, patience, and long-suffering of God." He expounds his affections, even his joy.[117]

4. Morality

Gill, also recognizes that moral character is an aspect of spirituality[118]: "under the notion of qualities and virtues, may be considered, his goodness, holiness, justice, truth, and faithfulness."

---

[111] Strong, *Systematic Theology*, 251
[112] Gill, *Body of Divinity*, 48
[113] Ibid., 71
[114] Ibid. 48
[115] Ibid.
[116] Ibid., 51
[117] Ibid., 112-148
[118] Ibid., 51

5. Personality

We have seen that Strong explicitly connects personality and spirituality. Hodge thoroughly defines the concept and implications of God's spirituality.[119] He says that we learn what a spirit is from the scriptural use of the word in the light of our consciousness of our own spirituality.[120] He then lists seven traits of a spirit:[121]

> 1. That the soul is a substance . . . Substance is that which has an objective existence . . . 2. Consciousness teaches that the soul is an individual substance . . . 3. As power of some kind belongs to every substance, the power which belongs to spirit, to the substance itself, is that of thought, feeling, and volition . . . 4. Consciousness also informs us of the unity or simplicity of the soul . . . 5. In being conscious of individual subsistence, we are conscious of personality . . . 6. We are also conscious of being moral agents, susceptible of moral character, and the subjects of moral obligation . . . 7. It need not be added that every spirit must possess self-consciousness. This is involved in all that has been said.

Hodge concludes by asserting that spirituality necessarily involves incorporeality. Incorporeality is not listed as an eighth property. It caps his entire discussion.[122] He then applies this concept of a spirit to God's spirituality[123]: "As all this is involved in our consciousness of ourselves as spirit, it must all be true of God, or God is of a lower order of being than man."

II. The Singular Features of God's Spirituality

The Lord Jesus attributes to God all the characteristics of a spirit: "*God is a spirit.*" All spiritual beings, God included, have incorporeality, animacy, faculty, morality, and personality. Thus, Reformed theologians properly call spirituality a "communicable" attribute. Yet, spirituality pertains to God in a singular manner, consonant with his supremacy. God has divine incorporeality, divine animacy, divine faculty, divine morality, and divine personality. These are incommunicable. Consider morality and personality. Other spirits have morality and personality, but they do not have divine morality or divine personality. Thus, morality and personality are

---

[119] Hodge, *Systematic Theology*, 1:376-380
[120] Ibid., 1:376-377
[121] Ibid., 1:377-378
[122] Ibid. 378-379
[123] Ibid., 379

communicable; but divine morality and personality are incommunicable. Thus, spirituality is communicable; but divine spirituality is incommunicable.

Many spirits exist, but only one God. God is a singular spiritual being. He is in a class all by himself. This uniqueness makes him the Supreme Spirit. No other spirit is "Spirit."

The London Confession affirms the prominent role of God's spirituality in its overview of God's nature:

> *LCF: 2:1*: The Lord our God *is* but one only living and true God; *whose subsistence* is in and of himself, infinite in being and perfection; *whose essence* cannot be comprehended by any but himself; *a most pure spirit*, invisible, without body, parts, or passions, who only hath immortality, dwelling in the light which no man can approach unto; *who is* immutable, immense, eternal, incomprehensible, almighty, every way infinite, *most holy*, most wise, most free, most absolute; working all things according to the counsel of his own immutable and most righteous will for his own glory; *most loving*, gracious, merciful, long-suffering, abundant in goodness and truth, forgiving iniquity, transgression, and sin; the rewarder of them that diligently seek him, *and* withal *most just* and terrible in his judgments, hating all sin, and who will by no means clear the guilty. [emphasis supplied]

I highlight transition points in the structure. When we carve the meat away, this skeleton remains:

> The Lord our *God is* but one only living and true God; whose subsistence is in and of himself . . . ; whose essence cannot be comprehended . . . *a most pure spirit* . . . ; who is immutable . . . , most holy . . .; most loving . . . , and withal most just . . .

The Confession uses "spirit" prominently: "our God is . . . a most pure spirit," that is, a spiritual being. The Shorter Catechism also gives prominence to God's spirituality. Yet it features God's uniqueness as the Supreme Spirit. Question Four asks, "What is God?" The Catechism replies:

> God is a Spirit, infinite, eternal, and unchangeable, in His being, wisdom, power, holiness, justice, goodness, and truth.

The Shorter Catechism uses a capital "S": "God is a Spirit." Therefore, the confession and the catechism both express aspects of truth. The small "s" affirms the truth that God has the characteristics of a spiritual being. The capital "S" affirms the truth that God alone is the Supreme Spirit.

Although God alone is the Supreme Spirit, we must not take his uniqueness to an extreme and allege that he is unknowable. This unscriptural and popular tenet mars much modern theology and philosophy. It leads to despair in the pit of agnosticism. We can truly grasp what God is because Scripture reveals the traits that distinguish him from all other spirits as the Supreme Spirit.

As we have already seen, the scriptural testimony to God's supremacy asserts that God is supreme in his incorporeality,[124] animacy,[125] metaphysical faculties,[126] moral character,[127] and triune personality.[128] We now survey these divine spiritual attributes, which I expound in topical presentations 11-22.

A. Divine Incorporeality: God's Majestic Form: Topic 11

God, like other spirits, does not have a body. He too is not material. Thus, he too is invisible, indivisible, impassable, and indissoluble.[129] However, his incorporeality is unique and supreme: "who only has immortality, dwelling in light unapproachable; whom no man has seen, nor can see" (1 Tim. 6:16). His singular incorporeality consists in his sole possession of *"immortality"* and in his residence in *"unapproachable light."* These define the majestic form of the Supreme Spirit.

B. Divine Animacy: God's Vivacity: Unlimited Life and Power: Topic 12

God, like other spirits, is alive, but his life is infinitely superior to their life. All the features of his supremacy define and display the superiority of his life. Only God has self-existent life: "as the Father has life in himself, even so he gave to the Son also to have life in himself" (John 5:26). Only God has unoriginated life: "we have seen, and bear witness, and declare unto you the life, the eternal life, which was with the Father, and was manifested unto us" (1 John 1:2). Only God has ideal and immutable life, *"immortality"* (1 Tim. 6:16). Further, only God has unlimited vivacity, namely, infinite ability to act on his own initiative. This is God's *omnipotence.* With God alone *"all things are possible"* (Mark 10:27). His power is eternal and

---

[124] Phil. 4:6; 1 Tim. 6:16
[125] Ps. 89:6; Jer. 10:6, 10, 16
[126] Isa. 40:28, 46:9; Jer. 10:10
[127] 1 Sam. 2:2; 1 Kings 8:23; Mic. 7:18
[128] John 5:18, 10:30-32; 1 Cor. 8:4-6; Phil. 2:6
[129] Deut. 4:15; John 1:18; Acts 17:25; Col. 1:15

unoriginated,[130] immutable,[131] and ideal, infinitely perfect and inexhaustible.[132]

C. *Divine Faculty: God's Supreme Mind, Will, and Affection: Topics 13-15*

God, like other spirits, has mind, will, and affection. Yet his faculties are infinitely superior. All the features of his supremacy, especially his ideality, infinity, and immutability, display this superiority. First, God's mind is infinite, ideal, and immutable.[133] God's knowledge and wisdom are infinitely exalted above the knowledge and wisdom of all created spirits.[134] God's singular and supreme mind is his *omniscience*. Second, God's will is unlimited, ideal and immutable.[135] God's infinite power executes his decretive will: "I know that you can do all things, and that no purpose of yours can be restrained" (Job 42:2). God's will is also unique in virtue of his aseity and independence. It is absolute and free.[136] God's supreme will is his *sovereignty*. Third, God's affection is infinite.[137] His capacity to feel is unoriginated and eternal.[138] His feelings are infinitely perfect and pure.[139] His capacity to feel is absolute (Acts 17:25) and immutable (Mal. 3:6; James 1:17). His affections are infinitely exalted above the affections of all created spirits. I am *not* predicating *human* emotion to God, but divine affection. God's faculty of feeling is singular and supreme, just like his faculties of mind and will. I call God's supreme capacity to feel his "*emotivity.*"[140]

D. *Divine Morality: God's Infinite and Impeccable Virtue: Topics 16-21*

Although God, like all spirits, has moral capacity and character, his morality is infinitely superior to the morality of all created spirits. God's supremacy

---

[130] Rom. 1:20
[131] Isa. 40:28; Heb. 1:10-12
[132] Eph. 1:19-23, 3:20
[133] Ps. 147:5; Isa. 40:28
[134] Isa. 55:8-9; Rom. 11:33-36
[135] Eph. 1:11; Isa. 14:27, 46:10-11
[136] Rom. 9:18; 1 Cor. 12:18; Eph. 1:5
[137] Ps. 90:11; Eph. 3:19
[138] John 17:24
[139] Jer. 9:24; Mt. 5:48; James 1:13
[140] I pattern this term after the word, "sovereignty," common terminology for God's unlimited will. I considered deriving a term from the Latin. The Latin for "mind" is "scientia." The term for "all" is "omni." Thus, God's unlimited, all-knowing mind is his "omniscience." Similarly, the Latin for "will" is "voluntas." Thus, God's all-controlling will could be called his "omnivolence." Similarly, the Latin for "feeling" is "sentential." Thus, God's absolute affection could be called his "omnisentence." The adjective would be "omnisentent." Thus, we could say that God is omniscient, omnivolent, and omnisentent.

marks his singular and supreme morality. Only God is morally ideal. His morality is absolutely and infinitely perfect. He could never be morally improved. He is absolutely incapable of moral flaw (Hab. 1:13). Only God is inherently and absolutely morally immutable. He alone is impeccable and intemptable.[141] Only God has infinite and absolute virtue (Eph. 3:19). He only is infinitely and absolutely good, holy, just, and faithful.[142] Thus, God's morality is singular and supreme. God's singular and supreme morality is his infinite and impeccable virtue.

E. Divine Personality: God's Triunity: Topic 22

God, like all spirits, is a personal being. Yet his personality is unique and infinitely superior to the personality of all created spirits. This remarkable uniqueness of his personality is consonant with his ideality, eternity, and aseity. Only God has eternal and self-existent personality (Ps. 90:2). He only could have interpersonal fellowship in eternity, when only he was (John 1:1). Only God has ideal, infinitely perfect personality. These remarkable truths point to the mystery of the Trinity. The Supreme Spirit is tri-personal, triune. He is three persons, the Father, the Son, and the Holy Spirit.[143] God has always experienced Trinitarian fellowship.[144] When only God was, he was never lonely. He did not create to fulfill his need for fellowship (Acts 17:25). All created spirits, human and angelic, are uni-personal. A uni-personal spirit could never have eternal, interpersonal fellowship. Uni-personal spirits can be lonely (Gen. 2:18). Thus, God's personality is unique. His supreme personality is his "triunity," or, *the Trinity*.

III. The Experimental Importance of God's Spirituality.

We return again now to our Lord's teaching in John 4:24. Christ presses the practical application of God's spirituality: *"they that worship him must worship in spirit and truth."* We will consider additional applications when we expound God's incorporeality, animacy, faculty, morality, and personality. We focus now only on how divine spirituality applies to worship. In the context, the Lord converses with a woman of Samaria. They discuss religion. Their conversation starts with his unusual request for a drink of water. His request is unusual because a Jew normally wouldn't have social dealings with a Samaritan (John 4:5-9). When the woman inquires into his unusual request, she gets an even more striking reply. The Lord says that if she knew who he was, she would be asking him for "living water."

---

[141] Exod. 15:11; 1 Sam. 2:2; Job 4:17,18, 15:15; Mark 10:18; James 1:13
[142] Matt. 10:18; Hab. 1:13; Titus 2:2; James 1:13
[143] Matt. 28:19; John 5:18, 10:32; 1 Cor. 8:4-6; Phil. 2:6; Acts 5:3, 4, 9
[144] John 1:1, 17:5

Since she could see that he had nothing with which to draw water, she is confused. Eventually, she responds to him with sarcasm: "give me this water that I thirst not, neither come all the way hither to draw" (John 4:10-15). Then Jesus says: "Go, call your husband, and come hither." That no doubt made her nervous. Rather than air the dirty laundry of her sordid life, she simply says: "I have no husband." So the Lord replies: "you have had five husbands and he whom you now have is not your husband." This opened her eyes to his identity: "Sir, I perceive that you are a prophet" (John 4:16-19). Immediately, she launches into the religious controversy that for centuries separated Samaritans and Jews:

> *John 4:20-24*: Our fathers worshipped in this mountain; and you say, that in Jerusalem is the place where men ought to worship. Jesus says to her, Woman, believe me, the hour comes, and now is, when neither in this mountain, nor in Jerusalem, shall you worship the Father. You worship that which you don't know: we worship that which we know; for salvation is from the Jews. But the hour comes, and now is, when true worshippers shall worship the Father in spirit and truth: for such does the Father seek to be his worshippers. God is a Spirit: and they that worship him must worship in spirit and truth.

This religious controversy was about worship. The Jews said worship should be in Jerusalem. The Samaritans had ordained their own feasts and priesthood. The Lord told her that the Samaritan traditions were the product of religious ignorance and that God established Jewish worship by divine revelation. Yet, the Lord said that this controversy was becoming a moot point. He said that a momentous transformation in divine worship was coming. He said that God was in the process of forming a society that would worship him acceptably. He said that God's nature as a spiritual Being determines acceptable worship, "*in spirit and in truth*." Consider the *foundations* and *features* such worship.

A. The Foundations of Worship in Spirit and Truth

Three factors support worship in spirit and truth: the proliferation of divine worship; the assemblage of true worshippers; and the institution of the new covenant and the endowment of the Holy Spirit.

1. The proliferation of divine worship: neither in this mountain, nor in Jerusalem, shall you worship the Father

Christ predicts radical transformation of divine worship on earth. Jehovah will no longer restrict his worship to his temple in Jerusalem. Acceptable worship will take place everywhere on earth.

2. The assemblage of true worshippers: the hour comes, and now is, when true worshippers shall worship

Christ predicts that God will seek and assemble "true worshippers" to worship him everywhere on earth. True worshippers worship acceptably by faith. When Christ saves his people from sin, he assembles a society of believers from every nation, *true worshippers*, to worship God everywhere on earth.

3. The institution of the new covenant and the endowment of the Holy Spirit

Christ institutes the new covenant in his blood and pours out the Holy Spirit upon this society of true worshippers. When Christ endows each society of believers with his Spirit, he consecrates them as a divine temple and proliferates divine worship. Thus, they worship by God's Spirit.[145]

B. The Features of Worship in Spirit and Truth: Christian Worship

When John says that "grace and truth" came through Jesus, he does not mean that there was no "grace" or no "truth" under the old covenant. Similarly, Jesus does not mean that there was no genuine worship before the institution of the new covenant. Abel was a true worshipper. Rather, he means under the new covenant he will for the first time assemble on earth an entire society of true worshippers. Thus, worship *in spirit and truth* denotes *Christian worship* under the new covenant. It is *spiritual* and *biblical*. True worshippers, gathered in God's special presence in spiritual temples, worship God everywhere on earth in the power of the Holy Spirit in accordance with his inspired Word recorded in the New Testament.

1. Christian Worship is spiritual.

Lenski says "*in spirit*" means from the soul or heart, that is, sincerely.[146] Leon Morris agrees.[147] Hendriksen also concurs.[148] So does Ryle.[149] Because God is a Spirit, true worshippers worship him with our spirits, from our hearts. Christian worship is with sincerity, not in empty rituals. This condemns all formalism in worship. It cuts across the grain of a Pharisaic

---

[145] *Phil. 3:3*: who worship by the Spirit of God
[146] R. C. H. Lenski, *The Interpretation of St. John's Gospel* (Minneapolis: Augsburg Publishing House, 1961), 323
[147] Leon Morris, *Commentary on John*, 270-271
[148] Hendriksen, *Commentary on John*, 1:167
[149] J. C. Ryle, *Expository Thoughts on the Gospels, St. John, Volume 1* (Camebridge: James Clarke & Co., 1975), 224-226

mentality. It isn't enough to go through the proper rituals, in the proper place, at the proper time. The Lord condemns those who go through the motions of God-ordained rituals with wicked and distant hearts: "This people draws near to me with their lips, but their hearts are far from me" (Matt. 15:9). Therefore, we must draw near with a good conscience, in fullness of faith, with sincere hearts. Thus, Christian worship is spiritual. It stems from the hearts of true worshippers in the power of the Holy Spirit.

2. Christian Worship is biblical.

Lenski says that *"in truth"* means according to the Word of God.[150] Calvin says this depicts God's Word as the rule of worship.[151] Hendriksen agrees that it refers to God's Word.[152] However, Ryle says that *"truth"* is the opposite of the types, emblems, and shadows of the ceremonial law. Thus, he says that worship *"in truth"* refers to gospel worship as distinct from Old Testament worship.[153] Both views fit the context and the meaning of "truth" elsewhere in Scripture. In John 17:17 he says: "Sanctify them in the truth. Your word is truth." This depicts "truth" as God's Word. Yet, John 1:17 says: "the law was given through Moses; grace and truth came through Jesus Christ." Grace and truth are epithets for the gospel, the divine message about salvation through Jesus Christ. We could paraphrase this as: "the law was given through Moses; the gospel came through Jesus Christ." The gospel features favor to sinners (grace) and disclosure respecting salvation in Christ (truth). Paul bridges these two uses of "truth": "when you received from us the word of the message, even the word of God, you accepted it not as the word of men, but, as it is in truth, the word of God (1 Thess. 2:13). Thus, both views have some merit. The New Testament liberates Christians from the levitical priesthood and its Jewish rituals. It defines the spiritual priesthood and sacrifices that God ordains for Christian worship.[154] Thus, Christian worship is biblical. Divine revelation, not human imagination, devices, or traditions, regulates it. This cuts across the grain of Samaritan pragmatism. They concocted their own rituals, priesthood, feasts, altar, and images. These abominations eventually caused the captivity of the northern kingdom. Therefore, Christ corrects both Samaritan and Jew. He affirms that God delivers Christians from the ills that plagued them both.

---

[150] Lenski, *Interpretation of John*, 373.
[151] John Calvin, *The Gospel According to St. John: 1-10*, Translator T. H. L. Parker, Editors David W. and Thomas F. Torrence (Grand Rapids: Wm. B. Eerdmans, 1974), 101-102
[152] Hendriksen, *Commentary on John*, 1:167
[153] Ryle, *Thoughts on John:1*, 225
[154] Heb. 7:11-12, 13:15-16; 1 Pet. 2:5, 9

Conclusion: Our Development of God's Nature in Topical Presentations 6-22

I conclude this overview with an outline of my exposition of God's attributes. My presentation primarily follows the insights of the Belgic Confession, the Shorter Catechism, the London Confession, John Gill, Charles Hodge, Augustus Strong, and Morton Smith. In this development I seek to honor God's simplicity, supremacy, and spirituality. I have already explained and applied God's simplicity. To honor it I present God's nature as a whole in 10 sections. I expound in detail God's supremacy and spirituality. Division 1 unfolds God's supremacy, existential attributes, in Sections 1-5. Division 2 unfolds his spirituality, spiritual attributes, in Sections 6-10. Reformed theologians often call existential attributes, "incommunicable," and spiritual attributes, "communicable." I summarize this arrangement below:

Division 1: EXISTENTIAL ATTRIBUTES	Division 2: SPIRITUAL ATTRIBUTES
Section 1. God's Ideality	Section 6. God's Incorporeality
Section 2. God's Aseity	Section 7. God's Animacy: Life and Power
Section 3. God's Infinity	Section 8. God's Faculty: Mind, Will, Affection
Section 4. God's Eternity	Section 9. God's Morality: moral virtues
Section 5. God's Immutability	Section 10. God's Personality: Triunity

How does this compare with other common presentations? The lists shown below, (prepared mostly by Steve Hofmaier who labors in the Philippines), present the arrangements of 14 Reformed theologians:

OTHER METHODS OF DEALING WITH GOD'S ATTRIBUTES

C. HODGE	**DABNEY**	**BOYCE**	**SMITH**
Spirituality	Unity	Unity	1. Essential
Infinity	-Spirituality	Spirituality	Spirituality
-Omnipresence	-Simplicity	INCOMMUNICABLE	-Incorporeality
-Eternity	Omnipresence	-Simplicity	-Simplicity
Immutability	Eternity	-Infinity (Eternity, Immensity)	Immutability
Knowledge	Immutability	-Immutability	Infinity (Eternity, Omnipresence)
Wisdom	Knowledge	COMMUNICABLE	2. Intellectual
Will	-Wisdom	-Power	-Omniscience
Power	Will & Power	-Knowledge	-Wisdom
Holiness	MORAL ATTRIBUTES	-Wisdom	-Freedom
Justice	-Justice	-Holiness	3. Moral
Goodness	-Goodness (Benevolence)	-Goodness	-Holiness
-Love	-Truth & Faithfulness	-Love	-Righteousness
Truth	-Holiness	-Truth	4. Emotive
	-Infinitude	-Justice	-Love, etc.

BAVINCK
INCOMMUNICABLE
-Independence
-Immutability

-Infinity

(Eternity,
Omnipresence)
-Oneness (Unity, Simplicity)
COMMUNICABLE
1. Life & Spirit

-Spirituality
(Invisibility)
2. Self-Consciousness
-Knowledge
-Wisdom
-Veracity
3. Ethical
-Goodness
-Righteousness
-Holiness

4. Sovereignty
-Will
-Freedom
-Omnipotence

5. Blessedness
-Perfection
-Blessedness

-Glory

CHARNOCK

Spirituality

Eternity
Immutability
Omnipresence

Knowledge

Wisdom
Power

Holiness
Goodness

Dominion
Patience

DAGG
Unity
Spirituality
Immensity-Omnipresence
Eternity-Immutability

Omniscience

Omnipotence

Goodness
Truth

Justice

Holiness
Wisdom

STRONG
ABSOLUTE ATTRIBUTES
1. Spirituality
Life and Personality
2. Infinity
-Self-Existence, Immutability, Unity
3. Perfection
-Truth, Love, Holiness
RELATIVE ATTRIBUTES
1. In Rel. to Time & Space
- Eternity, Immensity
2. In Relation to Creation
-Omnipresence
-Omniscience
-Omnipotence
3. In Rel. to Moral Beings
-Veracity, Mercy, Justice

PINK
Solitariness
Decrees
Knowledge

Supremacy & Sovereignty
Immutability

Holiness

Power
Faithfulness

Goodness

Patience
Grace
Mercy
Love
Wrath

A. A. HODGE
Simplicity

Unity
Spirituality
Omnipresence
Eternity

Immutability
Knowledge
-Wisdom

Power

Will

Justice

Goodness (Benevolence)
-Grace & Mercy
Truth
Sovereignty

Holiness

BERKHOF
INCOMMUNICABLE
-Self Existence (Aseity)
-Immutability

-Infinity
(Perfection,
Eternity,
Omnipresence)
-Unity (Oneness, Simplicity)
COMMUNICABLE
1. Spirituality (Invisibility)
2. Intellectual

-Knowledge
-Wisdom
-Veracity
3. Moral
-Goodness
-Holiness
-Righteousness
4. Sovereignty

-Will
-Power

GILL

Immutability
Infinity
(Omnipresence, Eternity)
Life, Omnipotence

Omniscience, Wisdom
Will and its Sovereignty
Love, Grace, Mercy

Long-suffering
Goodness
Anger and Wrath, Hatred
Joy

Holiness
Justice and Righteousness
Veracity, Faithfulness
Sufficiency and Perfection
Blessedness
Unity, plurality
Personal Relations

SHEDD	THORNWELL
INCOMMUNICABLE	Spirituality
-Self-Existence	-Self-Existence
-Simplicity	-Thought & Will
-Infinity	-Unity & Simplicity
-Omnipresence	-Communication
-Eternity	INCOMMUNICABLE
-Immutability	-Independence
COMMUNICABLE	-Eternity
-Knowledge & Wisdom	-Immensity
-Power	-All-Sufficiency
-Holiness	-Immutability
-Justice	
-Goodness	
(Benevolence Mercy & Grace)	
-Truth	

None of these arrangements is absolutely right or wrong. Scripture gives no inspired way to present God's attributes. Reformed theologians often distinguish "communicable" from "incommunicable" attributes. These correctly assert that in some ways God is analogous to man and in other ways is utterly unique. I hope the terms "existential" and "spiritual" help to clarify this distinction. Although we must beware of its dangers, we should acknowledge the truth behind this attempt at classification. Again, other Reformed theologians distinguish natural or metaphysical attributes, such as the faculties of mind, will, and affection, from moral attributes, such as the virtues of holiness, justice, goodness, and faithfulness. This distinction also displays an element of truth. It is one thing to have a mind, will, and affections, but quite another to use them righteously. This distinction is especially useful when we develop God's spiritual attributes. Other Reformed theologians distinguish between absolute and relative attributes. This also expresses an element of truth. It is especially helpful when we develop God's existential attributes. Others prefer not to classify God's attributes at all. For example, the 1689 Confession makes no such effort. However, even those who present no explicit classification, are, in the nature of the case, obliged to arrange their presentation according to some plan and principle. No one arranges God's attributes arbitrarily, or in alphabetical order. All display some topical selectivity. For example, even the non-classifiers sense correspondence between holiness, justice and goodness, and between omniscience and omnipotence. They don't try to define this correspondence, but their order of discussion betrays that they recognize it. Since Scripture does not explicitly classify God's attributes, we dare not condemn them for this. In fact, they thus express an element of truth. They extol God's unity and simplicity. Classifying only helps to the degree that it facilitates a more clear understanding of God's nature. We have sought to honor their insight by treating God's nature as a whole.

How does my presentation compare with the Shorter Catechism? They say: "God is a Spirit, infinite, eternal, and unchangeable, in his being, wisdom, power, holiness, justice, goodness, and truth." *First*, they also use God's spirituality as a foundation: "God is a Spirit." *Second,* they also group together God's existential attributes: "infinite, eternal, and unchangeable in his." With clear insight they assert that infinity, eternity, and immutability exercise a regulative influence upon God's being, wisdom, power, etc. *Third*, they also establish God's supremacy before they consider the specific elements of his spirituality: "infinite, eternal, and unchangeable in his being." *Fourth*, they feature three major dimensions of God's spirituality, his supreme faculty, animacy, and morality: "infinite, eternal, and unchangeable in his . . . wisdom [faculty], power [animacy], holiness, justice, goodness, and truth [morality]." *Fifth*, they do not identify or highlight every divine attribute. They do not explicitly mention either his perfection or self-existence. We could, however, infer that infinite, eternal being necessitates self-existence. And if he is infinitely and immutably good, then he must be ideal. Again, they only mention his metaphysical faculty of mind: "in his wisdom." They do not explicitly mention his will or affection. Nor do they feature his incorporeality, or his life, or his personality. Do not misunderstand. The Shorter Catechism contains an excellent and accurate compendium of God's nature. I am not attacking it. I merely remind you that, although it is a wonderful document, it is not inspired. We must not condemn someone simply because he accents attributes that the Shorter Catechism doesn't mention explicitly. We must not minimize God's self-existence, or perfection, or will, or affection, or life, simply because the Catechism doesn't feature them.

Finally, I sum up God's nature (Topics 5-22) as follows:

> God is a simple, supreme, and spiritual being: *Existentially*, the Supreme Being: ideal, self-existent, infinite, eternal, and unchangeable; *Spiritually*, the Supreme Spirit: unique and supreme in his incorporeality, animacy (life and power), metaphysical faculty (mind, will, and affection), morality (goodness, holiness, justice, and faithfulness), and triune personality.

May our great and glorious God grant that through these studies we may attain a more clear and complete grasp of who and what he is, and as we do, that he may draw out our hearts in ever growing measures of wonder, love, praise and devotion.

Topic 6. God's Absolute Perfection: Ideality

"God, his way is perfect" (Ps. 18:30); "him that fills all in all" (Eph. 1:23); "God cannot be tempted with evil" (James 1:13)

Division 1: God's Supreme Being: God's Existential Attributes

Introduction to Division 1:

We have seen that Scripture sets forth God's supremacy both in existential categories, drawn from the general properties of existence, and in spiritual categories, derived from the characteristics of spiritual beings. In Division 1 we focus on his existential attributes. What are existential properties and categories? Existential properties are general parameters of existence: completion, dependence, limitation, origin and duration, and alteration. The way something relates to these parameters defines its "existential" attributes. Existentially, God is without lack or flaw, without external support, without limitation, without origin or end, and without alteration or change. Thus, God is ideal, self-existent, infinite, eternal, and unchangeable. These attributes are *absolute*. They have always pertained to God, even when only God existed. They render him singular and supreme.

Yet, if we restricted our exposition of God's existential attributes to eternity past, we couldn't say much about them. Accordingly, Scripture often presents God's supremacy in relation to his creation.[1] When God created the universe and all things in it, he entered relations with all he brought into existence. The Creator displays his supremacy in relation to creation. Scripture emphasizes his self-existence in relation to his dependent creatures.[2] It emphasizes his infinity in relation to space[3] and his eternity in relation to time.[4] Now that devils and humans have brought evil, decay, and death into the world, God relates to them as sinners. Scripture emphasizes his ideality and immutability in relation to sin[5] and decay.[6]

Accordingly, we may distinguish God's *absolute* existential attributes that pertain to God in eternity from *relative* existential attributes that pertain to God in relation to creation. When we thus distinguish absolute and relative attributes, we must exercise great caution. For example, it would be imprecise to say that it is absolutely necessary for God to be omnipresent in space. This would imply that God had to create. Yet God created, not out

---

[1] 1 Kings 8:27; Isa. 40:25, 28; Jer.10:6, 16
[2] Acts 17:25
[3] 1 Kings 8:27
[4] Ps. 90:2
[5] James 1:13, 17
[6] Isa. 40:28; Heb. 1:10-12

of constraint, but freely out of the good pleasure of his sovereign will: "Of your will they are and were created" (Rev. 4:11). Nevertheless, once God created space and time, omnipresence and ever-presence are the *necessary consequence* of his infinity and eternity. Once he brings space into existence, he must be omnipresent, because he is infinite. Once he brings time into existence, he must be ever-present, because he is eternal. This is analogous to the consequent necessity of the atonement. The atonement was necessary in consequence of God's decision to save. It wasn't absolutely necessary, because he wasn't constrained to save. However, once he freely decided to save, then the atonement made by Jesus Christ was necessary, not optional. After a true likeness, omnipresence and ever-presence, in consequence of his decision to create space and time, are necessary, not optional.

The chart below displays God's supremacy in absolute terms and in relation to creation and sin.

WITH RESPECT TO	GOD IS	THIS IS GOD'S	IN RELATION TO	IT IS GOD'S
completion and flaw	ideal	Ideality	lack, need sin	Inexhaustibility Impeccability
dependence and support	self-existent	Aseity	creatures	Independence
limitation	infinite	Infinity	space	Omnipresence
origin and duration	eternal	Eternity	time	Ever-presence
alteration and change	unchangeable	Immutability	decay death	Incorruptibility Immortality

Accordingly, we expound God's existential attributes in terms of his relations to space, time, creatures, and sin. In this presentation we consider his ideality displayed in his inexhaustible fullness and absolute impeccability. In Topic 7 we consider self-existence displayed in his transcendence and immanence. In Topic 8 we consider infinity in relation to space: his immensity, omnipresence, and special presence. In Topic 9 we consider his eternity, ever-presence, and special presence in time. In Topic 10 we consider his immutability displayed in creation, fall, and redemption.

Section 1. God's Ideal Being: *Ideality*

Introduction: God's *ideality* is his inherent and infinite perfection. "*Perfect*" signifies complete and flawless. Only God is infinitely perfect.

He alone is inherently without improvement.[7] He is flawless[8] and incapable of flaw, whether metaphysical[9] or moral.[10] LCF affirms God's ideality: "infinite in being and perfection" (LCF 2:1). Thus, God's ideality has two prominent features. First, God is impeccable and "intemptable."[11] Second, God is inexhaustibly sufficient.[12] To expound God's ideality, *first*, we *survey* the scriptural testimony; and *second*, *summarize* the practical applications.

I. Survey of the Biblical Witness to God's Ideality

We first consider the testimony to God's inexhaustible sufficiency, then to his absolute impeccability.

A. The Biblical Witness to God's Inexhaustible Sufficiency

Consider the testimony of five texts: Ps. 18:30; Eccles. 3:14; Rom. 11:35, 36; Eph. 1:23; and Col. 2:9.

1. Ps. 18:30-32[13]

David emphasizes that because God is perfect, we can safely depend on him. He alone can supply all our need: strength, food, grace, everything. He is the immoveable pillar of dependability. David describes him as the "shield," "refuge," "tower," "rock," and "strength" of his people who trust in him. He makes an amazing statement: "the God that girds me with strength, and *makes my way perfect*." David could mean that God made righteousness reign in him, as he says earlier: "I also was *perfect* with him, and I kept myself from mine iniquity" (Ps. 18:23-24). David does not claim sinless perfection, but evangelical mortification. Yet, in the light of the parallel with "*God's way*" in 18:30, David probably means that God fashions his life into a complete unit, with nothing lacking. God makes his life a finished painting or tapestry, with every event perfectly woven into a beautiful design. His life, especially its conflict and trouble, is God's finished work of art. Thus he says: "for *by you* I run upon a troop, and *by my God* do I leap over a wall" (Ps. 18:29). And, "*he teaches* my hands to war" (Ps. 18:34).

---

[7] Eccles. 3:14
[8] Ps. 18:30; Matt. 5:48
[9] Isa. 40:28
[10] Hab. 1:13
[11] Exod. 15:11; 1 Sam. 2:2; Job 4:17-18, 15:15; Mark 10:18; James 1:13
[12] Ps. 18:30; Eccles. 3:14; Rom. 11:35-36; Eph. 1:23; Col. 2:9
[13] *Ps. 18:30-32*: As for God, his way is perfect: The word of Jehovah is tried: He is a shield unto all them that take refuge in Him. For who is God save Jehovah? And who is a rock, besides our God, the God that girds me with strength, and makes my way perfect.

And, "they shall fall under my feet. *For you have girded me* with strength unto the battle" (Ps. 18:38-39). And, "Jehovah lives; and blessed be my rock; and exalted be the God of my salvation, even the God that executes vengeance for me, and subdues peoples under me. He rescues me from mine enemies: yea, you lift me up above them that rise up against me, you deliver me from the violent man" (Ps. 18:46-48). Thus, David meditates on the complete sufficiency of God's provision, protection, and enablement in war. He gives David strength to see his conflicts through to completion, vindication, and victory. Thus, God orders the lives of his servants so that they reflect his own perfection: "As for God, his way is perfect . . . The God that girds me with strength, and makes my way perfect." Thus God's perfection affords much comfort in conflict. Our lives reflect a glimmer of his ideality, because we are his image.

2. *Eccles. 3:14*[14]

All God does is ideal, because God is ideal. All he does is complete and sufficient. It endures forever. None can add to it, or subtract from it. This has relevance: "and God has done it, that men should fear before Him." Since his work is ideal, we should stand in awe. His ideality should make us afraid to challenge, doubt, or find fault with him. Even our best work could improve. Yet no one could ever improve God's work. We should be afraid to second-guess our ideal God, or to murmur against him.

3. *Rom. 11:35-36*[15]

God is in debt to no creature, man or angel. No one has any claim on God. God has no need, no lack, no insufficiency. If he had need, he wouldn't ask us to supply it. He has no need of counsel, or protection, or provision from his creatures. In this way, the apostle intimates God's inexhaustible sufficiency. All things come from him. All things happen through him. All things exist for him, at his disposal, for his use, honor, and praise. God's ideality calls us to give him all the glory for all we have, and for all he does for us, especially, for our salvation from sin: "To him be the glory for ever."

4. *Eph. 1:22-23*[16]

Whatever its precise nuance, this unfathomable phrase, "him that fills all in all," displays God's complete sufficiency. God lacks nothing. He has

---

[14] *Eccles. 3:14*: And also that every man should eat and drink, and enjoy good in all his labor, is the gift of God. I know that, whatsoever God does, it shall be forever: nothing can be put to it, nor anything taken from it; and God has done it, that men should fear before Him.

[15] *Rom. 11:35-36*: who has first given to him, and it shall be recompensed unto him again? For of him, and through him, and unto him are all things

[16] *Eph. 1:22-23*: And he put all things in subjection under his feet, and gave him to be head over all things to the church, which is his body, the fullness of him that fills all in all.

provisions in abundance, more than ample to supply every material and spiritual need of every creature. Thus, Paul says: "Unto me, who am less than the least of all the saints was this grace given, to preach unto the Gentiles the unsearchable riches of Christ" (Eph. 3:8). God's sufficiency is unsearchable. He has an incomprehensible supply of gospel riches in Christ. We can know them truly, but never exhaustively. Again he says: "I have all things and abound: I am filled, having received from Epaphroditus the things that came from you, a an odor of a sweet smell, a sacrifice acceptable, well-pleasing to God. And my God shall supply every need of yours according to his riches in glory in Christ Jesus" (Phil. 4:18-19). Our ideal God supplies our "*every need*" as creatures and as Christians, from his infinite vault, his inexhaustible barn, his well that never runs dry. He reserves for us a stockpile of provision so great that all humanity could never exhaust it. An army of auditors couldn't count all his "money," or figure his "net worth." His wealth is immeasurable. What shall we say to these things? Blessed be our ideal God. Let us trust him and ask for what we need. Above all, let us thank and praise him for his abundant provision for our every need in Jesus Christ.

5. *Col. 2:8-9*[17]

Christ is ideal. The inexhaustible sufficiency and infinite perfection of the Godhead dwells bodily in him. Here is a lofty Christology. Thus, Paul warns us to beware of secular philosophy. We must beware of men's traditions and foolish speculations. Why? Everything you need for life, death, and eternity is in Christ. He is the epitome of God's ideality. Since Christ is ideal, he is all you need. Beware of anything that draws you away from Christ, that denigrates his sufficiency, or that directs you to anyone other than him for your spiritual or material needs.

B. *The Biblical Witness to God's Absolute Impeccability (Infinite Flawlessness).*

God's ideality also shines forth in his supreme holiness[18] and goodness.[19] We consider five texts that display God's impeccability: Job 4:17-18, 15:15; Hab. 1:13; Matt. 5:48; James 1:13.

---

[17] *Col. 2:8-9*: Take heed therefore, lest there be any one that makes spoil of you through his philosophy and vain deceit, after the tradition of men, after the rudiments of the world, and not after Christ: for in Him dwells all the fullness of the Godhead bodily.

[18] Exod. 15:11; 1 Sam. 2:2

[19] Mark 10:18

1, 2. Job 4:17-18[20] and *Job 15:15-16*[21]

These texts depict God's infinite perfection and flawlessness in terms that are almost shocking. Not even the angels or the heavens share God's infinite perfection. This does *not* mean that either the inanimate heavens or God's ministering angels are guilty of sin, disobedience, or rebellion. Yet, not even his glorious angels or the vast heavens can compare with him. Compared to his infinitely perfect wisdom, even the wisest angels are "foolish." Compared to infinitely perfect being, even the spotless heavens are "unclean," that is, unsuitable for contact with him. Should this prompt us to indulge in speculation? May it never be. Rather, these two texts urge mortal and sinful humans to walk humbly before an ideal God: "His angels he charges with folly: How much more them that dwell in houses of clay . . . the heavens are not clean in his sight: How much less one that is abominable and corrupt." If exalted angels can't comprehend the unfathomable depths of his wise decrees, how much less should puny humans think we can? If the spotless heavens are not suitable for intimate company with him, how much less do sinful men deserve the blessing of his nearness? This calls us, not to proud speculations, but to humble submission to his sovereign will, and to contrite admission that whatever we suffer in this life is less than our sins deserve. How can we dare to impugn his wisdom or integrity? How can we dare to challenge his decisions? What right do we have to feel sorry for ourselves, or say we don't deserve to suffer? What right do we have to blame God for our trouble? How can we dare to say he is unfair or unloving because people suffer and die for sin? These questions search out our remaining corruption and pride. They point to the tremendous importance and relevance of God's ideality.

3. Hab. 1:13[22]

Here the prophet struggles with the incomprehensible mystery of God's sovereignty over sin. Why did an ideal God decree sin? How does an ideal God control sinners? How can he use sinners to accomplish his purposes, without being the author of their sin, or without becoming an accomplice in it? In this setting, the prophet specifically ponders how the God who is so

---

[20] *Job 4:17-18*: Shall mortal man be more just than his maker? Behold he puts no trust in his servants; and his angels he charges with folly: How much more them that dwell in houses of clay.

[21] *Job 15:15-16*: Behold he puts no trust in his holy ones; Yea, the heavens are not clean in his sight: How much less one that is abominable and corrupt, A man that drinks iniquity like water

[22] *Hab. 1:13*: You that are of purer eyes than to behold evil, and that can not look on perverseness, wherefore do you look upon them that deal treacherously.

infinitely perfect that he can not even look at sin. He wonders how he can bring himself to use the wicked Chaldeans as his rod to chastise, punish, and judge Israel. For Habakkuk, as for us, trust in God resolves this tension. Faith doesn't solve the mystery, it defuses it. By faith, we trust in God's integrity and believe all his Word says about him. Faith makes us bold to embrace and proclaim God's incomprehensible ideality. Faith is not ashamed to confess an ideal God, even though reason can never fully explain him.

4. Matt. 5:48[23]

We return to this text when we expound God's moral character. For now, observe that God's perfection serves as the standard of Christian obedience. We must strive after nothing less than the sinless purity of our heavenly Father. Yes, we cannot on earth attain this standard of sinless perfection. Yes, this builds an element of frustration and failure into the Christian life and experience. Yes, for now, we pursue an impossible dream. But, in glory, we shall have what we now strive to attain. We shall join "the sprits of just men made perfect" (Heb. 12:23). When Christ comes: "we shall be like him; for we shall see him even as he is" (1 John 3:2). Therefore, we learn that God's ideality has profound implications for Christian ethics. God's flawless character, nothing less, is the immutable standard of Christian morality. We strive to put away all defilement of spirit and behavior. We strive to imitate every virtue of our ideal God and Father. Therefore, note again, that in one respect God's perfection is "communicable." Christians will one day be completely sinless and impeccable, even though we will never be infinitely perfect or ideal. Thus, sinless perfection is communicable; ideality, incommunicable. By grace, Christians will eventually obtain moral perfection, but no mere human will ever will obtain ideality.

5. James 1:13[24]

God's infinite perfection involves absolute impeccability. He is inherently incapable of sin. He cannot even be tempted to sin. Angels could be tempted, for some angels fell (2 Pet. 2:4). The human spirit is also inherently capable both of improvement and of flaw. Whatever impeccability angels or men eventually possess by God's grace, impeccability is not an inherent and immutable property of angelic or human nature. God, however, is inherently, necessarily, and immutably sinless and impeccable. He can

---

[23] *Matt. 5:48*: You therefore shall be perfect, as your heavenly Father is perfect.
[24] *James 1:13*: Let no man say when he is tempted, I am tempted of God; for God cannot be tempted with evil, and he himself tempts no man.

neither be enticed to sin, nor entice men to sin. Therefore, James says, we must learn to curb our tongues: "Let no man say when he is tempted, I am tempted of God." People know that God controls everything that happens. They know that the devil tempts them to sin. Thus, they conclude, rightly, that God completely controls the devil and his evil efforts to entice them to sin. Thus, some conclude, wrongly, that God is the one who entices and tempts them to sin. Again, we confront mystery. How can an ideal God completely control the actions of a wicked devil, without being either the author of his enticements, or without becoming an accomplice in them? Again, we flee for refuge to God's Word. By faith, without shame, we trust him. We refuse to *"charge God foolishly."* Again, we traverse a little section of the fence around the mystery.

II. Summary of the Practical Applications of God's Ideality

Scripture presents God's ideality, not as a philosophical abstraction, but as a precious truth extremely relevant to experimental religion. Now we summarize its practical implications.

A. Practical Applications of God's Inexhaustible Sufficiency

God's all sufficiency insures that his purpose for our lives is perfect. He orders our lives by his sovereign will, so that nothing can be added to it or taken from it. He brings everything infallibly to completion. God's all sufficiency certifies the ideality of all he does, so that we must revere rather than challenge his decisions and doings. Since our ideal God supplies our needs from his infinite sufficiency, we should trust, love, seek, serve, and rejoice in him. For all he gives and does, we should bless him.

I summarize these practical implications below:

1. Ideality calls us to thank and praise God for making our lives complete (Ps. 18:30).

2. Ideality calls us never to second-guess God, but rather to revere him (Eccles. 3:14).

3. Ideality calls us to thank and praise God for all we have (Rom. 11:35-36).

4. Ideality calls us to trust God to supply all our material and spiritual needs (Eph. 1:23; Phil. 4:18- 19).

5. Ideality calls us to embrace Christ, and to beware of whatever draws us away from him (Col. 2:9).

B. Practical Applications of his Absolute Impeccability

God's absolute impeccability calls us to walk humbly before him, to trust his absolute integrity, to refrain from blaming him when we are tempted, and to imitate his sinless perfection.

I summarize these practical implications below:

1. Ideality calls us to humble submission to whatever he ordains in our lives (Job 4:17-18, 15:15- 16).

2. Ideality calls us to trust in God's integrity in every situation (Hab. 1:13).

3. Ideality calls us never to blame God for sin or for temptation (James 1:13).

4. Ideality calls us to imitate our heavenly Father's flawless character (Matt. 5:48).

Topic 7. The Aseity and Independence of God

"the Father has life in himself" (John 5:26); "Neither is he served by men's hands as though he needed anything" (Acts 17:25)

Section 2. God's Self-Existent Being: *Aseity and Independence*

Introduction: Scripture presents God's self-existence both absolutely and in relation to his creatures. Christ declares God's self-existence in eternity, his "aseity": "the Father has life in himself" (John 5:26). Only the Supreme Being has self-existent life.[1] He alone has inherently immutable life, absolute "immortality."[2] His being does not and cannot depend on anything other than himself, because he made everything else.[3] In eternity God was solitary, but not lonely. He didn't form creatures because he needed anything. He was complete and self-satisfied. Pink describes this "solitariness of God":[4]

> During a past eternity God was alone: self-contained, self-sufficient, self-satisfied; in need of nothing. Had a universe, had angels, had human beings been necessary to Him in any way, they also had been called into existence from all eternity. The creating of them when He did, added nothing to God essentially. He changes not (Mal. 3:6), therefore His essential glory can be neither augmented or diminished.
> God was under no constraint, no obligation, no necessity to create. That He chose to do so was purely a sovereign act on His part . . . That he did create was simply for His manifestative glory.

Yet God's aseity is the preface of his self-existence, not the whole story. It serves as the foundation of his self-existence in history, his "independence" (Acts 17:25). God's existence is the rock on which all existence rests (1 Sam. 2:2). He brought all creatures into existence. He alone sustains their existence. They depend completely on him for everything. He ever remains self-existent. Once God creates, his independence in history is the necessary consequence of his aseity in eternity. God's independence has two prongs. *First*, God transcends all he has made. He is separate from and exalted above his creatures. This aspect of God's independence is his "transcendence." *Second*, God sustains, maintains, and oversees his creatures. They completely depend on his care and are completely under his control. This aspect of God's independence is his "immanence." In this topical presentation, I expound the inspired sermon in which Paul preached God's

---

[1] Gen. 1:1; John 1:1
[2] 1 Tim. 6:16
[3] Jer. 10:16
[4] Arthur W. Pink, *The Attributes of God* (Swengel, PA: Reiner Publications, n.d.), 1-2

independence.[5] *First*, Paul confronted men's culpable ignorance of God's independence (17:22-23). *Second*, he affirmed its dual substance, God's transcendence and immanence (17:24-28). *Third*, he pressed its practical relevance (17:29-31). Accordingly, we consider the *culpable ignorance*, *dual substance*, and *practical import* of God's independence.

I. Culpable Ignorance of God's Independence[6]

Paul launches his sermon from the platform of human ignorance. What provoked him to do so? He was in Athens waiting for Silas and Timothy. He saw the city teeming with graven images. His spirit burned with zeal for God's honor. He couldn't remain silent (17:16). He spoke out both in the synagogue among the Jews and in a public forum among the Gentiles (17:17). Thus he encountered Epicurean and Stoic philosophers (17:18). They regarded his gospel of the risen Christ as an alien doctrine with potentially dangerous implications. They wanted him to spell out its theological and moral significance (17:19-20). They brought him to "the Aereopagus," where men gathered to hear and judge "novel" ideas (17:21).

Before we examine what he preached, its helpful to consider what these Epicureans and Stoics believed about God. They desperately needed to learn God's independence. *The Epicureans* completely denied the immanence of God. They believed that the world was a big machine and that the gods, although they existed, had no influence on human affairs. They labored with ardent zeal to emancipate their fellow men from superstitious fears about the influence of the gods on human life. Thus, for them, what really mattered was ethics, how men treat each other. Thus, they were completely secular and humanistic in their approach to social norms and behavior. Accordingly, they were materialistic in their values. For them the enjoyment of tranquil pleasure and ease was the highest good, the chief end of human existence. If the gods play no part in human life, then personal peace and prosperity are all we have to live for, so "eat, drink, and be merry, for tomorrow we die." On the other hand, *the Stoics* completely denied the transcendence of God. They believed that God and the world were a composite being, that the material universe was its "body," and that "God" was its impersonal "life force." God, they said, was not a personal being separate from the universe; he did not exist prior to the universe; and he could not exist without the universe. Thus, for them, there could be no personal relationship with God

---

[5] Acts 17:22-31

[6] *Acts 17:22-23*: You men of Athens, in all things I perceive that you are very religious. For as I passed along, and observed the objects of your worship, I found also an altar with this inscription, TO AN UNKNOWN GOD. What therefore you worship in ignorance, this I set forth unto you.

or verbal communication and revelation from God. Thus, they exalted the human mind to the lofty place from which they had evicted God. For them reason was the highest good and their chief goal was to achieve mind over matter in their lives. Thus, for them sensual pleasure was worthless; appetites must be conquered. They strove totally to divorce their inner life from all external circumstances. They concocted an untouched and impersonal God, with no heart, and thought themselves virtuous when they endeavored to be like him.

Such were the men who led Paul to speak in the Aereopagus. Before him stood Epicureans, Stoics, and other Athenians. Some were skeptical, some hostile, some scoffing, some curious, drawn by an ear for novelty. All were steeped in a culture glutted with superstition and idolatry. All were ignorant of the theological roots and moral fruits of the gospel. Their philosophical speculations and idolatrous superstitions betrayed culpable ignorance of God.[7]

II. The Dual Substance of God's Independence[8]

Paul proclaims that the one true God is the Maker and Master of all mankind. God created the world. He existed before the world, separate from it. When the Creator made the world, he entered relations with the things he made. He runs preserves and rules his universe. First, Paul proclaims his transcendence, then his immanence. The philosophers wanted him to explain Christ's resurrection (17:18). Before he addresses the resurrection directly (17:31), he preaches God's independence. A child must complete grammar school before college. The doctrine of God is prerequisite to the doctrine of Christ. Thus, Paul enrolls proud philosophers in the kindergarten of theology. Scripture does not hang Christ's resurrection on a skyhook. People can only grasp its significance in its biblical setting. Thus, Paul exposes the flimsy foundation of both Stoic and Epicurean "world and life views." He overturns their theological apple cart. He proclaims the foundation of all sound philosophy: God is the Maker and Master of the universe.

---

[7] Rom. 1:19-21

[8] *Acts 17:24-28*: The God that made the world and all things therein, he, being Lord of heaven and earth, dwells not in temples made with hands; neither is he served by men's hands, as though he needed anything, seeing he himself gives to all life, and breath, and all things; and he made of one every nation of men to dwell on all the face of the earth, having determined their appointed seasons, and the bounds of their habitation . . . for in him we live, and move, and have our being.

A. God's Transcendence (17:24-25)

The transcendence of God boils down to this: the God who made the world runs and controls it. He is the Master of the universe: "he, being Lord of heaven and earth." Paul preaches God's lordship, majesty, and sovereignty. The Creator sits enthroned ruling over his creation. The true God is personal and regal, the Potentate and Sovereign of heaven and earth. Everything is under his authority, control, and care. We must not think that God is the impersonal life-force of the material world. He existed before and without it. Even now, he is separate from it, exalted above it. He is its Master. Yet, we must not think that the Lord is a celestial "King Tut," fanned, fed, fawned, flattered, and fat. The Lord doesn't spend night and day reclining on a couch eating grapes, being waited on hand and foot by a score of servants. Thus, Paul spells out the practical ramifications of God's transcendence negatively: "he dwells not in temples made with hands; neither is he served by men's hands, as though he needed anything." God does not need shelter or sustenance. He is completely self-sustaining.

B. God's Immanence (17:25-28)

We shouldn't suppose that God is indifferent to his creatures simply because he doesn't need us. God didn't wind up the world like a top, then sit back and watch it spin. Although he is exalted above creation, he also sustains creation. The continuance of the universe and the preservation of all creatures require his personal involvement. Paul presents God's immanence positively. We consider its display and essence.

1. The twofold display of God's immanence (17:25-27)

a. The immanent God provides everything humanity needs (17:25).

We depend on God. He supplies our every need: "he himself gives to all life, and breath, and all things." God is not a selfish taker, but a generous giver. He is not indifferent to human life, but personally involved with our needs and cares. What does he supply? He gives us: "life, and breath, and all things." For whom does he supply it? He "gives *to all* life." He provides for all human beings all they need and have. We wholly and continually depend on God from the cradle to the grave. Life and health, wife and children, food and gladness, shelter and clothing, convenience and comfort, possessions and talents, every good gift comes down from above (James 1:17). Modern humans need this kindergarten lesson as much as those pagans. Some claim to be "self-made" men. Such despise a "welfare mentality." They boast that they never took anything from anyone and don't owe anyone anything. Such also scoff at religion. They say: "God helps those who help themselves." They say: "I don't have heart problems because get regular exercise and watch my cholesterol. I don't have lung cancer because I don't smoke, and I don't have ulcers because I don't worry." Why don't you have leukemia? Why don't you have MS? Why don't you have a brain tumor? Why weren't you born with only one eye? Why weren't you born mentally retarded? How did you control that? Are you self-sustaining? Then prove it. Make yourself exempt from death. If you sustain your own life, then continue to live on earth forever. Where are all the so-called self-made men of the past? They're in the grave. Don't fool yourself. Men would prevent their death if they could. They can't, because they don't sustain themselves, merely deceive themselves. There is no such thing as a "self-made" man, and few things more tragic than a self-deceived man who claims to be one.

b. The immanent God governs everything humanity does (17:26-27).

Paul affirms that God also governs mankind: "and he made of one every nation of men to dwell on all the face of the earth, having determined their appointed seasons, and the bounds of their habitation." God made every nation from one man, Adam. He decides the span of their life and influence: "their appointed seasons." He determines the boundaries of their territory: "and the bounds of their habitation." He controls when and where men live and die. He orders all the affairs of men and nations with his sovereign will.[9] Proud king Nebuchadnezzar learned the hard way to acknowledge this truth.[10] Yet many resent, resist, and deny this truth. Few things evoke as much hostility as God's sovereignty over human affairs. I find this somewhat puzzling. I am glad that my life is in God's hands. It's encouraging to know that he decided what life has in store for me. It comforts my soul to know that blind and heartless chance doesn't run my life. It relieves me greatly to know that men and devils can't decide my fate. I am thankful that I don't live in an "Epicurean" world in which my heavenly Father has no influence. If you don't respond to God's immanence with gratitude, ask yourself why. Would you really rather live in a world run by chance, or sinful people, or the devil? After you have considered that for a while, thank God that you don't live in such a world. And you never will.

Further, Paul proclaims that God governs all mankind with the gracious design that men: "should seek God, if haply they might feel after him and find him." His kindness, in common grace, leads people to repentance.[11] All

---

[9] Dan. 4:35; Eph. 1:11
[10] Dan. 4:25, 34-35
[11] Rom. 2:4

God displays to people in creation,[12] and does for them in providence,[13] leaves them with no excuse for their failure to seek and find him. Nonetheless, no sinner will ever find God apart from the gospel of Christ. The fault lies not in God's common grace, but in human hearts.

2. The distilled essence of God's immanence (17:27-28)

The apostle sums up God's immanence: "though he is not far from each one of us, for in him we live, and move, and have our being; as certain even of your own poets have said, For we are his offspring." God is not distant or detached. He is intimately involved in human lives and relations: "he is not far from each one of us." He is actively involved in human affairs to such an extent that: "in him we live, and move, and have our being." Some understand the phrase, "in him," to mean, "in the sphere of his influence." Others think it signifies: "by his agency." Both senses are plausible and convey truth. In either case, Paul proclaims God's immanence. He also shows what God's immanence implies about humanity's relation to God: "*we are his offspring.*" Analogy exists between how dependent children relate to parents and how dependent humans relate to God. A parent procreates his children and provides for them. Minor children depend completely on their parents to maintain their life. So also, God originates and sustains human life. We subsist by his activity and agency. In this sense, every fallen human being is "*his offspring.*"

III. The Practical Application of God's Independence

We consider practical implications of God's independence, transcendence, and immanence.

A. General Application of God's Independence: lost sinners must repent (17:29-31)

Paul presses this application. Since human beings are God's offspring, they should not be ignorant of his transcendence and immanence (17:29). God intends to judge and punish them for their evil speculations and idolatrous superstitions, and for the whole gamut of wicked behavior that flows from them. God has furnished mankind with solid assurance of this impending judgment, the resurrection of Jesus Christ (17:31). Therefore, God, through the gospel, now calls people from every nation to repent and get right with their Maker and Master (17:30). Many today have views of God similar to those held in pagan Athens. Many think that God is "the force" behind nature. For them creation is eternal. Their own minds are the highest

---

[12] Rom. 1:19-21
[13] Matt. 5:45; Acts 14:17

authority. Many others think chance runs the world, and that humans are masters of their own fate. They think they owe God nothing, because he gives them nothing. If there is a God, they say, he has nothing to do with what happens on earth. They think that those who believe in the influence of God in human life are superstitious fools. Some call religion "the opiate of the masses." To all such, we say with Paul, repent of your evil thoughts of God. Repent of your denials of his transcendence and immanence. Repent of your evil way of living. Be assured, judgment is coming. Jesus is alive. He is the living pledge of God's solemn commitment to judge mankind for these sins.

B. Specific Applications of God's Transcendence

1. God's transcendence calls us to worship only God, not his creatures.

No creature should be the object of our adoration, veneration, and devotion.[14] God alone deserves the glory for every good thing we experience or receive. He made us. He rules us. Therefore, let us worship him alone. This doesn't mean we should take human kindnesses for granted, or fail to express appreciation to people when they do us good.

2. God's transcendence calls us humbly to recognize that God doesn't need us.

God can run the world without us. He can save sinners and build his church without us. Yet, sometimes, men lean over their pulpits and with a pitiable tone plead with young people, saying, "God needs you. He can't do the work of missions without you." Such talk is a practical denial of God's transcendence. Should we serve God because we feel sorry for him? May it never be. To the contrary, each of us is expendable. If we think we are indispensable, we're too big for our britches. When people think God needs them, they have the pressure of the whole world on their shoulders. They fret and foam as though God couldn't work in their families or churches without them. All that carnal anxiety and bluster reflects unmortified pride. God works his purposes with us or without us. We must recognize that we are expendable dust and he is the transcendent God. Again, don't misunderstand. God uses means. And he may well decide to use us to accomplish his purposes. We must bless him for whatever usefulness he gives us, and remember that God "gives the increase." I don't mean that we should be prayerless, or apathetic, or lazy. In no way, for the God who can work without our zeal, is often pleased to use our zeal, and reproves us if we loose our zeal for his name.

---

[14] Matt. 4:9-10

C. Specific Applications of God's Immanence

1. God's immanence calls us to be grateful to God for our life and possessions.

Since we depend on him from the cradle to the grave, we should thank him for all we have.

2. God's immanence calls us to acknowledge our complete dependence on God.

Since all we have comes from God, we must pray to God for everything. Since he sustains our lives, we should say: "If the Lord will, we shall both live, and do this or that" (James 4:15). Yet, we must not be haphazard. Careful plans and diligent stewardship are friends of God's immanence.

3. God's immanence calls us courageously to fear God more than we fear men.

Since God gives life, no man can take away our life until God wills us to die. Therefore, as long as God decides to keep us alive, we are invincible and invulnerable. Thus David asks: "What can man do to me?" (Ps. 56:11). Thus, the Lord exhorts his disciples courageously to face opposition, threats, and persecution.[15] Yet, we must not tempt God with presumptuous stunts.[16]

Conclusion: An evangelical leader once told me that Paul "blew it" at Athens and saw little fruit from his labor there because he philosophized rather than preach Christ. Then he said that Paul realized his error, and at Corinth he decided never to preach philosophy again, only Christ crucified (1 Cor. 2:1-5). A profound irony was lurking in his remark, for it uncovered the pride and ignorance that blind the soul of modern evangelicalism. With nonchalant smugness such evangelicals condemn Paul's inspired message. With blissful ignorance they imbibe and trivialize the grievous errors about God that Paul confronted at Athens. Many who profess to believe the gospel reject God's sovereignty over human affairs. They imagine that luck, men, or the devil rule the world. Others who profess Christian faith waver on the doctrine of creation. Some are on the verge of embracing the pagan pantheism that sees "God in every tree" and strives to unite with "the force" which animates nature. Others cower before the cocksure pretensions of men who scoff at the idea that a transcendent God made Adam and Eve literally and supernaturally. Thus, we shouldn't be shocked when people question the lost estate of all pagans. We shouldn't be surprised when they deny that to go to heaven "all men everywhere," irrespective of their being

---

[15] Matt 10:28-33
[16] Matt. 4:5-7

"very religious," must believe in the resurrected Christ and repent of their sinful thoughts of God and of their wicked way of life. It is not Paul, but his evangelical critics, who are "blowing it." Many professed evangelicals need to attend his theological kindergarten. When we graduate, we must shout from the housetops that God is the Maker and Master of all men. Our wicked and perverse generation needs few things more than it needs this simple lesson about God. May our great God in his mercy pour forth through the preaching of his Word an abundant display of his transcendence and immanence, and use it for his glory and for the eternal good of many souls.

Topic 8. God's Immensity, Omnipresence, and Special Presence in Space

"the heaven of heavens can not contain you" (1 Kings 8:27);
"Whither shall I flee from your presence" (Ps. 139:7);
"where two or three are gathered together in my name, there am I in the midst of them" (Matt. 18:20)

Section 3. God's Infinite Being: *Spatial Supremacy*

God alone is without limitation.[1] His Being is infinite in every respect (Isa. 40:18, 25, 28).[2] Nothing external to him can limit him. He is immutably infinite and illimitable. He could never become a finite God.[3] Thus, in a general sense infinity characterizes all his attributes. His eternity signifies that time does not limit him. Similarly, his ideality, or infinite perfection, signifies that completion does not limit him. Again, his aseity depicts his unlimited existence. And, his immutability affirms that alteration can never limit him. Some Reformed theologians, recognizing this fact, have treated God's infinity with respect to time and space together. We dare not condemn them. Yet, in this topical presentation I focus exclusively on God's relation to space. The next presentation addresses his relation to time. Scripture also permits this distinction.[4] I refer to God's relation to space as his "spatial supremacy." Spatial supremacy depicts God's infinity with respect to space. First, I define the concept of spatial supremacy. Second, I survey the biblical witness to his spatial supremacy. Third, I summarize its practical relevance.

I. The Concept of God's Spatial Supremacy

I follow and build on the definition that Berkhof uses.[5] Our texts epitomize God's relation to space. First, space does not limit or contain God: "the heaven of heavens can not contain you" (1 Kings 8:27). Following Berkhof, I call this God's "immensity." Second, God is present, with his whole being, at every point in space. He is everywhere: "Whither shall I flee from your presence" (Ps. 139:7); and: "do not I fill heaven and earth?" (Jer. 23:24). This is God's "omnipresence." Third, God, in a special sense, is present at some points in space. He is even especially present in more than one place at the same time: "where two or three are gathered together in my name, there am I in the midst of them" (Matt. 18:20). I call this God's "special presence." Thus, Scripture confronts us with mystery and tension. The God

---

[1] Pss. 145:3, 147:5; Isa. 40:28
[2] 1 Kings 8:27
[3] Heb. 1:10-12
[4] 1 Kings 8:27; Ps. 90:2
[5] Berkhof, *Systematic Theology*, 60-61

who is present everywhere is also especially present in some places and in more than one place at the same time. I include God's *special presence* because Scripture depicts it as crucial, not peripheral, to a biblical understanding of God's relation to space. Thus, I define God's *spatial supremacy* as follows:

> (1) God is not limited by space [immensity]; (2) God is present with his whole being at every point in space [omnipresence]; and (3) God is especially present at some points in space [special presence].

A. God's Immensity

The vast heavens cannot "contain" him. No expanse exhausts his capacity to fill. His infinite being surpasses the dimensions of the universe. My mind cannot comprehend the boundaries of the universe, or "beyond." But, if, somehow, we could traverse the vast expanse of the heavens to their very boundary, even "beyond" space, there would still be God: "the heaven of heavens can not contain you." God's immensity is incomprehensible. I can merely assert it, not explain it.

B. God's Omnipresence

He is present with his whole being at every point in space. No one can flee from his presence. Wherever we are, he is there, because he fills heaven and earth. God has no material body. He does not have mass or "take up" space. Rather, the Supreme Spirit is "in" every place. He is in the space occupied by gases, liquids, and solids. God is not outside space, looking in. He is even in the space that our bodies occupy. Two material objects cannot occupy the same space. This does not limit God, because he does not displace mass. For example, consider the space that your hand occupies. Your hand displaces the air that was in that space. If you move your hand, air again occupies that space. I assert that God is in that very space whether your hand is there or not. Other spirits are similar to God in this respect. They too can occupy the same space as a solid, liquid, or gas. Men once argued about how many angels could fit on the head of a pin. A spirit is non-material. It does not have mass. Therefore, the question is irrelevant. Yet, unlike God, space somehow limits other spirits. No other spirit can fill all space. The devil and archangels are not omnipresent. Thus, people have also wondered how fast an angel can move from one place to another. I can't answer that question either. The spirit world holds many mysteries. I don't know how space and time restrict the devil or angels. Nevertheless, created spirits are somehow limited in their relation to space. No created spirit is present, with its whole being, at every point in space. Angels and demons have a "local" presence. Nor is God partly in one place, and partly in another, like a crashed airplane strewn over the landscape. God, in his entirety, is present everywhere. Now I append a brief qualification. When I say that God is "in" every place, I do not mean that "everything" is God. Charnock appropriately warns us about this perversion of God's omnipresence.[6]

C. God's Special Presence on Earth and in Heaven.

God, according to his sovereign good pleasure is especially present, *dwells*, in diverse locations, at diverse times. Thus, such places are his "house," or "temple." There he especially communes with humans by his Word and Spirit. Thus, Jacob said of Bethel: "Surely Jehovah is in this place . . . this is none other than the house of God" (Gen. 28:17). God dwelt in the tabernacle in the wilderness, and in his temple in Jerusalem. He now dwells in every true Christian church and in every true Christian.[7] Again, all the fullness of the Godhead dwells in Jesus Christ.[8] Again, God dwells throughout history in heaven.[9] His special presence explains expressions like: "God came down to see what was happening," "God departed from him," "God was far from him," "God hid himself," and "God remained afar off."[10]

II. Survey of the Biblical Witness to God's Spatial Supremacy

I first survey the biblical testimony to God's immensity and omnipresence, then to his special presence.

A. The Biblical Witness to God's Immensity and Omnipresence

I survey five key texts: 1 Kings 8:27; Ps. 139:7-12; Prov. 15:3; Jer. 23:24; and Matt. 18:20, 28:20. Someone may wonder why I didn't include Acts 17:28: "In him we live, and move, and have our being." I hesitate to recall this text to the witness stand because it testifies more explicitly to God's immanence. Yet, one could argue with cogency that if God gives everyone life, and sustains every person's life, no matter where they are, then God must be everywhere. Thus, God's immanence implies his omnipresence.

---

[6] Charnock, *Existence and Attributes*, 166-167
[7] Matt. 18:20, 28:20; 1 Cor. 3:16, 6:19
[8] Col. 2:9
[9] 1 Kings 8:29
[10] Gen. 11:5; 1 Sam. 16:14; Ps. 10:1; Prov. 15:29

1. 1 Kings 8:27[11]

In his dedication of God's house, Solomon asserts God's immensity: "the heaven of heavens cannot contain you." Jehovah is no "local" deity. The earthly place of his special presence does not exhaust his presence. Further, his earthly temple does not even exhaust his special presence. In his prayer Solomon repeatedly mentions that God also dwells in heaven: "hear in heaven your dwelling place" (1 Kings 8:30, 32, 34, 36, 39, 43, 45, 49). The temple in Jerusalem was never the exclusive place of his special presence. Scripture confirms this: "Heaven is my throne, and the earth is my footstool: what manner of house will you build unto me? And what shall be the place of my rest?" (Isa. 66:1, quoted in Acts 7:48-49).

2. Ps. 139:7-12[12]

We have already seen how this psalm affirms God's incomprehensible knowledge of every human being (139:1-6). We have also seen that this infinite knowledge rests on God's omnipresence (139:7-12), his creative work (139:13-15), and his sovereign decree (139:16). Now we focus on David's testimony. The parallelism in verse 7 displays the intimate connection between God's Spirit and presence: "Whither shall I go from your Spirit? Or whither shall I flee from your presence?" David stresses that there is no place to escape from God's scrutiny (139:8-12). God is even in places that are inaccessible, uninhabited, and dark. God is in the *inaccessible* places (139:8). We cannot actually ascend to heaven, or tunnel into the middle of the earth. If we could, God would be there. God is in the

---

[11] *1 Kings 8:22-27*: And Solomon stood before the altar of the Lord in the presence of all the assembly of the Lord and he spread forth his hands toward heaven; and he said, O Lord, the God of Israel, there is no God like you, in heaven above, or on earth beneath; who keeps covenant and lovingkindness with your servants, that walk before you with all their heart; who has kept with your servant David my father that which you did promise him: you have fulfilled it with your hand, as it is this day. Now therefore, Lord, the God of Israel, keep with your servant David my father what you have promised him, saying: there shall not fail you a man in my sight to sit on the throne of Israel, if only your children take heed to their way, to walk before me as you have walked before me. Now therefore, O God of Israel, let your word, I pray you, be verified, which you spoke unto your servant David my father. But will God in very deed dwell on the earth? Behold, heaven and the heaven of heavens cannot contain you; how much less this house that I have built!

[12] *Ps. 139:7-12*: Whither shall I go from your Spirit? Or whither shall I flee from your presence? If I ascend up into heaven, you are there: If I make my bed in Sheol, behold, you are there. If I take the wings of the morning, And dwell in the uttermost parts of the sea; Even there shall your right hand lead me, And your right hand shall hold me. If I say, Surely the darkness shall overwhelm me, and the light about me shall be night; even the darkness does not hide from you, but the night shines as the day: the darkness and the light are both alike to you

uninhabited places (139:9-10). He is present even in "the uttermost parts of the sea." Men don't live in the middle of the ocean. It is a deserted place. Even if we sought solitude in a place completely uninhabited, God would be there. God is in the *dark* places (139:11-12). God is present even in complete darkness. He can see in places where no human can see. The absence of light makes no difference to him. Darkness does not conceal us from his presence or scrutiny. People use infrared devices to catch criminals and to defeat enemies who seek to escape detection under the cover of darkness. The omnipresent God has always possessed infinitely sophisticated "infrared technology" in his very Being: "even the darkness hides not from you." There is no such thing as a God-forsaken place. Still, people persist in futile attempts to escape from God.

Jonah is a classic example of trying to run from God's presence.[13] Although he fled to the uttermost parts of the sea, there God found him. God's fish arrested him and returned him to his post. Similarly, some today think that they can run from God. They run from the preaching of his Word on Sunday. Wherever they run, God is there. God is in the bar, on the golf course, at the football game, in the TV set. It is futile to flee from his scrutiny.

3. Prov. 15:3[14]

His eyes are "in" every place. Our eyes are the instrument of perception and discernment. God, however, has no eyes made of flesh. His "eyes" are his faculty of perception. Therefore, his faculty of discernment is in every place. This underscores that God is everywhere present "with his whole Being." Today men employ security devices to discover and record the activities of intruders. Hidden cameras serve as "eyes" in the walls. The omnipresent God has always possessed infinitely sophisticated "security technology" in his very Being. He has eyes in every place. His "cameras" are, even now, "keeping watch on the evil and the good." He is recording every sordid thing that sinners do in his world, and every good deed that his saints perform for his glory. Nothing escapes his notice because he is omnipresent. This implies that we must take to heart that God sees everything we do. There is no blind spot that his "security cameras" fail to scan. People may be able to do things that their elders don't see, or that their spouses don't see, but they

---

[13] *Jonah 1:2-3, 10*: Arise, go to Nineveh, that great city, and cry against it; for their wickedness is come up before me. But Jonah rose up to flee unto Tarshish from the presence of Jehovah . . . So he paid the fare thereof, and went down into it, to go with them unto Tarshish from the presence of Jehovah . . . 10 Then were the men exceedingly afraid, and said unto him, What is this that you have done? For the men knew that he was fleeing from the presence of Jehovah, because he had told them.

[14] *Prov. 15:3*: The eyes of the Lord are in every place, keeping watch on the evil and the good.

can never do anything that escapes God's notice. The wicked say in their hearts that God doesn't see their sin. The righteous depart from evil, saying in the fear of God: "You Lord see me." God's omnipresence implies that every person should live in the fear of God: "You shall not curse the deaf, nor put a stumblingblock before the blind; but you shall fear your God: I am Jehovah" (Lev. 19:14). Those who fear God don't curse deaf people or trip blind people. They realize that they could never get away with it because God sees whatever they do. Thus, the fear of God involves sensitivity in our hearts to God's omnipresence. Conversely, the wicked conduct their lives as though God neither hears nor sees what they do: "there is no fear of God before their eyes." Like startled criminals caught by a hidden security camera, sinners are in for a big surprise. Suddenly, God's angels will seize them red-handed in their sins and carry them off to judgment. The Judge will display the evidence. He will play "recordings" that "his eyes" have made. They will have no defense. He will find them guilty. They will hear the dread sentence. He will lead them away in eternal chains to suffer the punishment of endless suffering in hell. Further, God's omnipresence not only serves as a deterrent to hypocrisy, it also furnishes strong incentive to persist in doing good, even when people don't notice or appreciate it: "God is not unrighteous to forget" our labor of love. The Lord will recompense you at "the resurrection of the just."[15] This also furnishes incentive to avoid bitterness when we are wrongly accused. God saw what really happened. It's all on "his recording." He will vindicate you someday. We must not be bitter or impatient. We should wait on God the Judge. He will play the recording. Then, even false accusers will acknowledge the innocent.

4. Jer. 23:24[16]

This text epitomizes all we have seen. It confirms that God is present, with his whole Being, in the entire universe. This has profound practical relevance: "Can any hide himself in secret places so that I shall not see him, says Jehovah." God is on the verge of sending judgment on his people. False prophets lull them with lies into a false sense of security. They assure them, falsely, that the Chaldeans will not destroy them and that they will escape the impending doom. God sternly warns them that these Chaldeans are the instrument of his wrath and judgment. Their soldiers are coming. When they do, people will hide in caves, in closets, in all their secret places. Yet those who despise God will not escape. God's wrath will search them out. It will track down every last one of them. No one will successfully hide

---

[15] Matt. 6:4; Luke 14:14; Heb. 6:10

[16] *Jer. 23:24*: Can any hide himself in secret places that I shall not see him? says Jehovah. Do not I fill heaven and earth? says Jehovah.

from it. How much less will sinners escape from God's wrath on the last day? If searching bands of Chaldean soldiers prevailed, how much more will searching bands of angels? When they cry to the hills, "Fall on us, hide us from the wrath of the Lamb," even mountains won't be able to hide them. Nevertheless, ever since the fall, people have tried to hide from an offended God. Adam and Eve "hid themselves" among the trees in the Garden of Eden. Adam said: "I was afraid because I was naked, and I hid myself." God soon discovered and judged them. God provides the only effective shelter from the fallout of his wrath. That shelter is his Son. Only those who flee to Christ by faith will escape the wrath to come. Thus, omnipresence proclaims the gospel of Christ.

5. *Matt. 18:20*[17]

This promise links God's omnipresence and special presence. Christ's promise assumes and requires his omnipresence. How else could he be especially present, simultaneously, with disciples gathered in Europe, Asia, Africa, America, Australia, and Antarctica? God now manifests his special presence wherever his people meet in his name. He dwells, by the Holy Spirit, in every true Christian and Christian church. Under the old covenant, Scripture emphasized that God's special presence was not his exclusive presence (1 Kings 8:27). Under the new covenant, Scripture stresses that God's special presence is multiple and universal. In both cases, complete harmony exists between God's special presence and omnipresence. God is everywhere. Thus, no one can run away from him or hide from his wrath. Yet Christ's words are not a threat, but a promise, comfort, and encouragment: "And lo, I am with you always, even to the end of the age" (Matt. 28:20). Isaiah also conveys this promise: "Fear not, I am with you" (Isa. 41:10). Similar comfort flows to Joseph[18] and the liberated remnant.[19] Spiritual comfort comes from enjoying God's special presence with us, wherever we are, because he is omnipresent.

B. *The Biblical Witness to God's Special Presence*

Bavinck lists the voluminous testimony of Scripture to God's special presence.[20] I have selected a representative sample of five texts: Gen. 28:17; 1 Cor. 3:16, 6:19; 2 Cor. 6:14-18; Col. 2:9.

---

[17] *Matt. 18:20*: Again I say unto you, that if two of you shall agree on earth as touching anything that they shall ask, it shall be done for them of my Father who is in heaven. For where two or three are gathered together in my name, there am I in the midst of them.
[18] Gen. 39:21
[19] Hag. 2:3-4
[20] Bavinck, *Doctrine of God*, 157-158

1. Gen. 28:17[21]

This text inspired the hymn: "Lo God is here: let us adore, and own how dreadful is this place; let all within us feel his pow'r, and humbly bow before his face" (Trinity Hymnal, #308). We must enter his special presence reverently. Solemnity and purity, not flippancy or carnality, should mark our demeanor in God's house. Thus, God told Moses: "put off your shoes from off your feet, for the place whereon you stand is holy ground" (Exodus 3:5). Reverence for God's house should influence how we dress on the "holy ground" of his special presence. Outward appearance should express inward reverence. Yet going to church barefoot would not implement this principle properly. Culture dictates how we should dress on such occasions. For example, men show respect for the flag at a baseball game by taking off their caps. Thus, we shouldn't dress for church in any way that would clearly express disrespect in our culture.

2. 1 Cor. 3:16-17[22]

Every true church is a temple of the Holy Spirit. Therefore, if anyone tampers with or destroys a church, God will tamper with him. Some may regard that as harsh and unloving. We must not charge God foolishly. If someone ransacks a church, he desecrates God's temple, family, and home on earth. In some ways men are excessively tolerant. We tend to put up with far more disregard for God's honor than he does. We tend not to take church disruptions, splits, and scandals as seriously as we should. We should never forget that we are on holy ground when we participate in church life.

3. 1 Cor. 6:19[23]

The body of every Christian is the place of God's special presence, a temple of God. He dwells in us. This mandates sexual purity and forbids fornication: "Flee fornication. Every sin that a man does is without the body: but he that commits fornication sins against his own body" (1 Cor. 6:18).

---

[21] *Gen. 28:17*: Surely Jehovah is in this place; and I knew it not. And he was afraid, and said, How dreadful is this place! this is none other than the house of God, and this is the gate of heaven.

[22] *1 Cor. 3:16-17*: Don't you know that you are a temple of God, and that the Spirit of God dwells in you? If any man destroys the temple of God, him shall God destroy; for the temple of God is holy, and such are you.

[23] *1 Cor. 6:19*: Or don't you know that your body is a temple of the Holy Spirit which is in you, which you have from God? and you are not your own; for you are bought with a price: glorify God therefore in your body.

4. *2 Cor. 6:14-18, 7:1*[24]

Since a church is God's temple, the righteous should not join in church fellowship with the wicked. Unbelievers have no right to the responsibilities or privileges of church membership. They have no part in the "fellowship," "communion," "concord," "portion," and "agreement" of the Christian church. They threaten its unity because they violate its identity as God's temple. This has profound implications.

First, God's special presence implies that no true Christian should join or remain in an ecclesiastical society of wicked men. True Christians should sever ties with apostate churches that deny the faith. They should join churches that honor the Lord and contend for the faith once delivered to the saints.

Second, God's special presence implies that no true church should join itself to ecclesiastical societies of wicked men. Paul mandates separateness. True churches should sever formal ties with any society that denies the Christian faith or lives in flagrant immorality. For example, true churches should separate from any group of unbelievers that denies the deity or bodily resurrection of Christ. Many say we should identify with every society that professes Christianity. Yet what the world highly esteems is an abomination to God. Some may chide us for being "separatists." In response I only say: "we are a temple of the living God . . . Wherefore come out from among them, and be separate, says the Lord."

Third, God's special presence implies that no true church should receive or retain unconverted members. Thus, churches should discipline ungodly members.[25] They should depose leaders and remove members that deny any essential tenet of the Christian faith.[26] This requires vigilance, diligence, and courage. It requires that we care more for the name of God than for popularity. Love for God, and zeal for his house, must burn in our hearts,

---

[24] *2 Cor. 6:14-18, 7:1*: Do not be unequally yoked with unbelievers: For what fellowship have righteousness and iniquity? Or what communion has light with darkness? And what concord has Christ with Belial? Or what portion has a believer with an unbeliever? And what agreement has a temple of God with idols? For we are a temple of the living God; even as God has said, I will dwell in them, and walk in them; and I will be their God, and they shall be my people. Wherefore come out from among them, and be separate, says the Lord. And touch no unclean thing; and I will receive you, and will be to you a Father, and you shall be to me sons and daughters, says the Lord Almighty. 7:1 Having therefore these promises, beloved, let us cleanse ourselves from all defilement of flesh and spirit, perfecting holiness in the fear of God.

[25] 1 Cor. 5:1-13; 2 Thess. 3:6-15

[26] Rom. 16:17-18; 1 Tim. 1:19-20

as it did in Christ's when he said: "take these things hence." When God incarnate entered his temple, indignation burned in him because men polluted his house with worldly behavior. He rebuked them and drove them out forcibly. He refused to tolerate their irreverence in his house.[27] What would he say and do if he attended church in America? I fear that many would see his frown, hear his rebuke, and feel his scourge. He would drive out the clowns. He would scourge the entertainers. Let us so live and labor that he will visit us with his blessing, not with his scourge.

5. *Col. 2:9*[28]

Jesus Christ himself is the temple of God (John 2:19-21). The fullness of the Godhead dwells in him bodily. Wherever he is, God is specially present. This demonstrates Christ's complete sufficiency.

III. Summary of Practical Applications of God's Spatial Supremacy

We have seen that God's omnipresence and special presence profoundly impact personal piety and church polity. I summarize these applications below.

A. Practical Applications of God's Immensity and Omnipresence

1. It warns us to fear God and walk sincerely before him (Ps. 139:7-12; Prov. 15:3; Jer. 23:24).
2. It encourages us to wait on God for vindication (Prov. 15:3).
3. It assures us that we are never beyond the range of his protection (Matt. 18:20).

B. Practical Applications of God's Special Presence

1. It teaches us that heaven is a real place, where Christ now is (1 Kings 8:27; John 17:11,24).
2. It comforts the godly in their trials and afflictions (Matt. 18:20; Isa. 41:10).
3. It emboldens God's servants in danger and difficulty (Matt. 28:20; Hag. 2:3-4).
4. It summons Christians to keep their body free from sexual impurity (1 Cor. 6:19).
5. It summons Christians and churches not to have church fellowship with the unconverted (2 Cor. 6:14-18).
6. It moves Christians to glory in the deity and sufficiency of Jesus Christ (Col. 2:9).
7. It moves Christians to desire to be with Christ in heaven (John 17:24; Phil. 1:23).

---

[27] John 2:13-18; Matt. 21:12-13

[28] *Col. 2:9*: for in him dwells all the fullness of the Godhead bodily, and in him you are made full.

Topic 9. God's Eternity, Ever-presence, and Special Presence in Time
You have been our dwelling-place in all generations . . . Even from everlasting to everlasting, you are God (Ps. 90:1-2)

Section 4. God's Eternal Being: *Temporal Supremacy*

God is an eternal Spirit, without origin, without end.[1] He alone is the Uncreated One.[2] All other spirits, angelic and human, originate when he creates them.[3] This sets him apart as the Supreme Being.[4] This attribute is God's *eternity*. When he brought time and space into existence, he began to relate to time, even as he began to relate to space. We now focus on his relation to time, his *temporal supremacy*. First, I define the concept of his temporal supremacy; second, survey the biblical witness; and third, summarize its practical ramifications.

I. The Concept of God's Temporal Supremacy

First, our epitomizing text asserts God's *eternity*: "Before the mountains were brought forth, or ever you had formed the earth and the world, even from everlasting . . . you are God." Second, it asserts God's *ever-presence*: "Lord, you have been . . . in all generations." Third, it asserts God's *special presence* in time: "Lord, you have been *our dwelling-place* in all generations." Accordingly, I offer the following definition of God's *temporal supremacy*:

> (1) God is not limited by time [eternity]; (2) God is present with his whole being at every moment in time [ever-presence]; (3) God is specially present at some points in space at some moments in time, and somewhere in space at every moment in time [special presence].

Notice the close parallel with the biblical concept of God's relation to space. The phrase, "space-time continuum," denotes an intricate connection of space and time. Thus, I could speak comprehensively of God's relation to this "space-time continuum" as follows: (1) God is not limited by space and time [immensity and eternity]; and (2) God is present with his whole being at every point in space at every moment of time [omnipresence and ever-presence]. Simply for organizational purposes, I present the biblical testimony regarding God's relation to space and time separately.

---

[1] Ps. 90:2

[2] Isa. 40:25, 28; Jer. 10:6, 16

[3] Col. 1:16-17; Isa. 57:16; Zech. 12:1

[4] Deut. 33:26

A. God is Eternal, not Limited by Time.

At the beginning of time God already was: "In the beginning God created," "In the beginning was the Word, and the Word was with God, and the Word was God. The same was in the beginning with God." God is "from everlasting" and "to everlasting." Some things have a beginning, and yet have no ending. For example, God the Son did not have a human nature from eternity. His human nature, body and soul, originated at his incarnation. Yet it will continue to exist forever. Similarly, every human soul begins at its conception and will continue to exist forever. The eternal God, however, is both unoriginated and unending. He is completely unlimited by time.

B. God is Ever-present, Present at Every Moment of Time.

As his presence in every point in space is his "omnipresence," so also, his presence at every moment in time is his *ever-presence*. The eternal God is present in every generation throughout all time. He has an unlimited "life span." Time in no way restricts his influence on earth.

C. God is Specially Present in Time.

When I say "at some points in space at some moments in time," I refer to God's special presence on earth. When I say "somewhere in space at every moment in time," I refer his special presence in heaven. His special presence in time displays permanence, heavenly stability, and change, and earthly mobility. In history God has changed the location of his special presence on earth. First he dwelt in Eden, then at Bethel, then at Sinai, then in the tabernacle, then in the temple in Jerusalem. Then, in a new era, Scripture reveals the mystery of God's special presence in God incarnate, Jesus Christ. By his Spirit, God is especially present in every true Christian church, where and when they gather. Yet, throughout history heaven is his permanent dwelling place. God incarnate now abides there, waiting for "the day of the Lord," when he will return to earth and usher in the ultimate display of God's special presence on earth. Now God has appointed for his church on earth a day of his special presence, "the Lord's day." He calls them to gather before him on that day. Thus, Sunday is the day of assembly on which God's people all over the earth enter his special presence to commune with him by his Word and Spirit.

II. Survey of the Biblical Witness to God's Temporal Supremacy

We first survey the witness to his eternity and ever-presence, then his special presence.

Part 3: The Nature of God | 235

A. The Biblical Witness to God's Eternity and Everpresence

We consider ten texts, five in each Testament.[5]

1. Ps. 90:1-17

This passage epitomizes God's eternity. Theologians appeal to it. Ministers read or preach it at funerals. It juts out of Scripture like a great mountain. Thus, I begin with it and consider it in detail. God's temporal supremacy gives us stability, exposes our frailty, founds his wrath, and calls us to prayer.

a. God's temporal supremacy gives his people security and stability (90:1-2).[6]

The Lord is our "house," our "home." He brings stability, security, shelter, comfort, and order, all we associate with home, to our lives. God has been our home "in all generations." This intimate relationship between the Lord and his people spans the entire breadth of history. He is the God of our past because he always was,[7] of our present, because ever is,[8] and of our future because he always will be.[9]

b. God's temporal supremacy exposes human brevity and frailty (90:3-6).[10]

Unlike God humans are transitory. Our time on earth is short. Our life span is limited; our days few are and numbered. Moses reflects on just how short our life span really is. If anyone ever saw and felt the painful reality of the brevity of life, Moses did. He frequently faced the death of his contemporaries. God's eternity puts in proper perspective the brevity of human life. When compared with God's eternal being, human life span is like grass that lasts for less than a day. A millennium for God is like a moment for a human being. The events of a thousand years ago are fresher

---

[5] Ps. 90:1-17; Job 36:26, 38:1-4; Pss. 93:1-2, 102:24-28; Isa. 57:15; John 8:58, Rom. 1:20, 16:25-27; 1 Tim. 1:17; 2 Pet. 3:8-9.

[6] *Ps. 90:1-2*: Lord, you have been our dwelling-place in all generations. Before the mountains were brought forth, or ever you had formed the earth and the world, even from everlasting to everlasting, you are God.

[7] Gen. 1:1; John 1:1, 17:3, 5

[8] Exod. 3:14; John 8:58

[9] Heb. 1:10-12

[10] *Ps. 90:3-6*: You turn man to destruction, and say, Return, you children of men. For a thousand years in your sight are but as yesterday when it is past, and as a watch in the night. You carry them away as with a flood; they are as a sleep: in the morning they are like grass which grows. In the morning it flourishes, and grows up; in the evening it is cut down, and withers.

in his mind than yesterday is in ours. We remember yesterday fairly well. But what happened seven years ago on the 23rd of April? Can you tell me? Unless that date holds some special significance in your life, you can't remember. Neither can I. For God, the events of 1017 AD are as fresh as the events of 2017 AD.

c. *God's temporal supremacy founds his incomprehensible and dreadful wrath* (90:7-11).[11]

The wilderness generation died under God's curse and judgment. They went to their graves through God's wrath. Moses saw many contemporaries ushered suddenly and irrevocably into an eternity of endless torment and ruin: "we are consumed in your anger, and in your wrath we are troubled." Eternal wrath is incomprehensible: "who knows the power of your anger, and of your wrath." Eternal wrath is frightening: "according to the fear that is due unto you." As it frightened Moses it should frighten us. Unless our contemporaries repent they face the same damnation. Their condition is critical. They stand this very hour on the edge of a grand canyon filled with eternal flame. At any moment they could die and be damned. Therefore, godly fear should move us to pray earnestly for them, to warn them urgently of their danger, and to point them to their only hope of rescue. Lost sinners can't escape, defeat, or pacify divine wrath. At any moment God can take their lives, call them to account, and commence their unending punishment. This urges all fallen mankind to cling to Jesus, the only Savior from divine wrath.

d. *God's temporal supremacy calls and teaches us to pray* (90:12-17).

(1) It teaches us to pray for wisdom to grasp the brevity of life.[12]

Humans tend to act like our life will never end, as if time is cheap and we can squander it at will. This mentality is not wise. If we have a wise heart, we "number our days." When we contemplate God's eternal being and unlimited life, we discern the brevity of human life. We should live realistically. Our plans and priorities should take into account the brevity of life. The wise don't squander valuable time, effort, and resources. We have

---

[11] *Ps. 90:7-11*: For we are consumed in your anger, and in your wrath are we troubled. You have set our iniquities before you, our secret sins in the light of your countenance. For all our days are passed away in your wrath: we bring our years to an end as a sigh. The days of our years are threescore years and ten, or even by reason of strength fourscore years; yet is their pride but labor and sorrow; for it is soon gone, and we fly away. Who knows the power of your anger, and your wrath, according to the fear that is due unto you?

[12] *Ps. 90:12*: So teach us to number our days, that we may get us a heart of wisdom.

only 168 hours per week, 52 weeks per year, and as a rule, only 70 or 80 years. In that time we must do all that matters. Thus we should pray for wisdom to spend our days doing what really counts. Then we will die without the regrets of those who waste the time God gives us.

(2) It teaches us to pray that God would balance our affliction with blessing.[13]

Since our time on earth is so brief, Moses prays that God, in mercy, will send blessing and gladness into their lives. He prays that these seasons of respite and joy will offset their days of suffering, turmoil, and trouble. When we realize how short our time here really is, we appreciate the benefit of "a tranquil and quiet life" lived in godliness and gravity. We learn to pray for peace and tranquility. We learn to enjoy God and his blessings. We learn to avoid needless turmoil. We don't go looking for trouble, or try to stir it up. We pray that God would "bring us not into temptation, but deliver us from evil." We realize that life is too short to spend it consumed with needless strife, controversy, squabbling, and contention.

(3) It teaches us to pray that God would bless our children and perpetuate our work.[14]

When we go to our graves, everything we labored for all our life is out of our hands. We don't know who will run our business, or who the next three pastors of our church will be, or what will happen to our life's work. We have a last will by which we try to exercise some control over the distribution of our property. We can try to control future generations of our church with a constitution. We can try to control the future of our business. Yet we cannot guarantee that any of our plans will happen. Only God can perpetuate the blessing of our children. If our work endures, he must establish it. Thus, Moses prays that God's glory would appear on our children, and pleads: "the work of our hands, you establish it." Such prayers are not futile or absurd. We address the eternal God who influences and controls all generations.

---

[13] *Ps. 90:13-15*: Return, O Jehovah; How long? And let it repent you concerning your servants. Oh satisfy us in the morning with your lovingkindness, that we may rejoice and be glad all our days. Make us glad according to the days wherein you have afflicted us, and the years wherein we have seen evil.

[14] *Ps. 90:16-17*: Let your work appear unto your servants, and your glory upon their children. And let the favor of the Lord our God be upon us; and establish thou the work of our hands upon us; yea, the work of our hands, establish it.

2. Job 36:26, 38:1-4[15]

God's eternity displays how great he really is. We cannot fathom his "age": "the number of his years is unsearchable." As a general rule, people relate better to those their own age than to those who have lived much longer. Many things have shaped the values and perspectives of the aged, things they regard as crucial and formative, which the young have never experienced. Thus, the young have a hard time understanding the aged. How much less, therefore, can we ever hope to comprehend fully the ways and perspectives of the eternal God? Eternal experience marks his perspective on reality. In Job 38:1-4 the Lord presses the weight of this on Job. He contrasts his eternal being with Job's limited experience and knowledge. He asks Job where he was when he formed the earth. He presses him to explain how he made the world. Thus, God's eternity summons us to recognize our own smallness. It teaches us never to challenge the Lord as though we were his contemporaries or peers. It calls us to admit that he knows far more about life and reality than we do. It summons us to acknowledge that he knows what we need better than we do. It calls us to refrain from condemning him for the afflictions he sends us. Further, God's eternity rebukes those who affirm with cocksure confidence the doctrine of evolution. Where were they when the eternal God laid the foundation of the earth? How could they possibly know how he formed the world? They merely *assume* that the way the universe operates now is the way it has always operated. They build their conclusions on pure conjecture and assumptions they can never prove. Such don't have a clue what they are talking about. They have lived for a minuscule length of time, yet they claim certainty about what happened at the beginning. They thus display ignorant arrogance: "Where were you when I laid the foundations of the earth? Declare if you have understanding."

3. Ps. 93:1-2[16]

God's eternal being is the cradle of all stability and security. Since God is eternal, his "throne is established." Since God is eternal, "the world also is established, that it cannot be moved." The stability of creation and

---

[15] *Job 36:26*: Behold, God is great, and we know him not; the number of his years is unsearchable. *Job 38:1-4*: Then Jehovah answered Job out of the whirlwind, and said, who is this that darkens counsel by words without knowledge? Gird up now your loins like a man; for I will demand of you, and you declare unto me. Where were you when I laid the foundations of the earth? Declare, if you have understanding

[16] *Ps. 93:1-2*: Jehovah reigns; he is clothed with majesty; Jehovah is clothed with strength; he has girded himself therewith. The world also is established that it cannot be moved. Your throne is established of old: you are from everlasting.

providence rests on God's eternity. The universe is secure because of God's eternal power (93:1). The eternal God, by unoriginated power, made the universe. The universe did not start on its own power and does not run on its own power. Eternal power started and preserves it. Thus, the world is stable and secure. Similarly, history is secure because of God's eternal decree (93:2). God governs history according to what he decided in eternity. His unoriginated will makes history secure and stable. This has great significance. Humans are vulnerable, weak, and insecure creatures. We hunger for security. We tend to search for it in things that appear more stable than ourselves. Since a nation is more stable than a man, we look for security in national life and government. Since our environment is more stable than our lives, we search for security in the predictable and recurring cycles of nature. This psalm teaches us that we must seek security, not in created things, but in the eternal God who renders the world and history secure. No government is more stable than his government. No natural forces are more secure than his eternal power that made and preserves them. Governments rise and fall, but God's government is from everlasting to everlasting. The earth quakes and divides, rivers flood and run dry, volcanoes erupt, tidal waves and hurricanes ravage the coasts, forests burst into flame, and good land turns to desert, but his power abides fixed forever. The eternal God is more stable than any nation on earth, and more secure than any spot on earth. Therefore, let us trust and rest safely in him.

4. *Ps. 102:24-28*[17]

The writer to Hebrews reveals that this passage depicts God the Son (Heb. 1:10-12). It thus declares Christ's deity. It affirms the intimate connection of God's eternity and immutability: "But you are the same, and your years have no end." This passage features three experimental applications of God's eternal Being. *First*, the psalmist entreats the ever-present God to spare him from premature death: "take me not away in the midst of my days: your years are throughout all generations" (102:24). We all face the possibility of premature death. When we face severe affliction or danger, that specter floods into our minds (102:1-6). Then we should entreat the eternal God who holds our life and destiny in his hands. In such extremity we must fix our hope, not in doctors or any other human agency, but in the ever-present God. *Second*, the psalmist contrasts the stability of the

---

[17] *Ps. 104:24-28*: I said, O my God, take me not away in the midst of my days: your years are throughout all generations. Of old did you lay the foundation of the earth; and the heavens are the work of your hands. They shall perish, but you shall endure. Yea, all of them shall wax old like a garment; as a vesture shall you change them, and they shall be changed: but you are the same, and your years shall have no end. The children of your servants shall continue, and their seed shall be established before you.

everlasting God with the mutability and corruptibility of creation: "They shall perish but you shall endure" (102:25-27). Severe affliction makes us feel acutely how insecure we really are. Even the heavens won't last forever. Ultimate security is found only in the God who never gets old or fades away, but lives and abides forever. *Third*, the psalmist affirms the faithfulness of the eternal God to the descendants, yet unborn, of his servants: "the children of your servants shall continue" (102:28). God's eternity gives us hope for our children's future. We can buy an insurance policy to provide for our children. We can write a will that names guardians to protect them. But we cannot care for their souls or lives from the grave. Only God can establish our children and grandchildren in the way of righteousness. Our hope that they will transmit our religious heritage rests on God's eternity and faithfulness. The eternal God in covenant mercy has sworn to give his servants spiritual children. Our spiritual heirs walk in the footsteps of our faith. They are not necessarily our natural children. They include a remnant of our natural children according to the election of grace.[18] Church history displays God's faithfulness to this promise. He has fulfilled it wherever the gospel has flourished. While the heavens remain he has preserved and will preserve the church of Christ on earth. Our hope for unborn generations of our children rests, not in us, but in the eternal God, who has promised to establish, keep, and preserve his church until Jesus comes.[19]

5. Isa. 57:15[20]

The phrase: שֹׁכֵן עַד (shokēz 'ad), is translated "that inhabits eternity." The root verb, *shakēz*, means to dwell, or abide, or settle down.[21] The word in the text, its participle, *shokēz*, means "one who dwells," or "one who abides." The noun, *'ad*, means "perpetuity."[22] Thus the phrase is literally: "the one who abides in perpetuity." This means that God enjoys absolute stability and lives permanently. God has, metaphorically speaking, settled down to live in a "city" or "place" called "perpetuity." He never has to move. He never dies. Therefore, this phrase explicitly ascribes eternal

---

[18] John 8:34-44; Rom. 4:11-12, 9:6
[19] Matt. 16:18; Eph. 3:21, 5:27
[20] *Isa. 57:15*: For thus says the high and lofty One that inhabits eternity, whose name is Holy: I dwell in the high and holy place, with him also that is of a contrite and humble spirit, to revive the spirit of the humble, and to revive the heart of the contrite
[21] F. Brown, S. Driver, C. Briggs, *Hebrew and English Lexicon of the Old Testament* (Oxford: Clarendon Press, 1978), 1014, 15
[22] Ibid., 723

existence to God. E. J. Young translates it: "who dwells forever."[23] Similarly, Keil and Delitzsch offer the translation: "the eternally dwelling One."[24] What does this feature? Isaiah features two practical applications of God's eternity: his reliability and approachability. *First*, because God is eternal his Word is reliable. God's sovereignty, eternity, and integrity together insure the reliability of his Word and promises. God is sovereign: "the high and lofty One." If something could restrain his purposes, even though he had the best of intentions his promise could fail. Yet, nothing is beyond his control. Further, God has impeccable integrity. His "name is Holy." He never forgets his promises or breaks his word. He can never be unfaithful. Further, this sovereign and holy God is eternal. He is always here, a fixture permanent and perpetual. Otherwise he couldn't finish what he started. Therefore, because God is sovereign, holy, and eternal, his Word is absolutely trustworthy. *Second,* because God is eternal he is always accessible and approachable. The eternal God dwells in a "high and holy place with him that is of a humble and contrite spirit." The place where he lives is hard for men to reach. It is "high and separate." People must journey far from their pride and climb over the mountain of their self-righteousness to reach God's permanent abode. Truly, the task is beyond most. The eternal God is inaccessible to the arrogant and self-righteous. Nevertheless, he is always accessible to "him that is of a humble and contrite spirit." Such travel far from pride, worldliness, boast, pomp, and creature-confidence. They make the painful climb over the mountain of their self-righteousness. When they reach the top, broken for sin, conscious that they deserve only divine wrath, behold, God is there. He invites all such into his home. They enjoy blessed fellowship with the eternal God. He is always home when humble and broken sinners knock on his door. This affords great comfort. It furnishes much incentive to put away our pride and self-righteousness and pay him a visit.

6. *John 8:58*[25]

Jesus asserts his eternal existence. He asserts that he is Jehovah, whose name is "I AM." Thus, he claims he is the Supreme Being incarnate. His Jewish countrymen took offense at his claim to be the eternal God: "They took up stones therefore to cast at him: but Jesus hid himself, and went out

---

[23] Edward J. Young, *The Book of Isaiah* (3 Vols.; Grand Rapids: Wm. B. Eerdmans, 1976), 3:410
[24] C. Keil and F. Delitzch, *Commentary on the Old Testament* (10 Vols.; Grand Rapids: Wm. B. Eerdmans, 1973), 7:379
[25] *John 8:58*: Jesus said unto them, Verily, verily, I say unto you, Before Abraham was born, I am.

of the temple." They thought he was guilty of blasphemy and megalomania. They judged him worthy of capital punishment. They determined on the spot to execute him by stoning. We must respond to his claim, not in unbelief like they did, but rather in faith. We must not take up stones of heresy and pummel to death the mystery of God incarnate. God the Son did not cease to be the eternal God when he took to himself a human body and soul. He did not lay aside deity. Rather, he added humanity to his deity. He is one Person, God the Son, with two natures, human and divine. Thus, Scripture confronts us with the unfathomable mystery of God incarnate.[26] We must believe and confess what we cannot comprehend.

7. Rom. 1:20[27]

We considered this text when we studied God's existence. Remember that all creation displays God's eternity to all mankind. Therefore, no person has any excuse for denying God's unoriginated existence.

8. Rom. 16:25-27[28]

Paul observes progress in the revelation of the gospel. In this era, the apostolic gospel of Christ is preached universally to every nation under heaven. This takes place: "according to the commandment of the eternal God." What God commands in history he designed and determined in eternity. He eternally planned the universal spread of the gospel. Jewish unbelief didn't upset his plans, catch him by surprise, and force him hastily to devise some last minute scheme to save face. To the contrary, the eternal God commanded the apostles to preach Christ to all the nations. Thus, Scripture emphasizes that God applies salvation, both in the Christian life and church, in strict accord with what he purposed in eternity. Paul blesses God because he elected Gentile Christians for salvation in eternity.[29] He affirms that God determined in eternity to that Christ's church would unite

---

[26] John 1:1-2 17:5; Col. 1:16-17; Heb. 1:10-12

[27] *Rom. 1:20*: For the invisible things of him since the creation of the world are clearly seen, being perceived through the things that are made, even his everlasting power and divinity; that they may be without excuse.

[28] *Rom. 16:25-27*: Now to him that is able to establish you according to my gospel and the preaching of Jesus Christ, according to the revelation of the mystery which has been kept in silence through times eternal, but now is manifested, and by the scriptures of the prophets, according to the commandment of the eternal God, is made known unto all the nations unto obedience of faith: to the only wise God, through Jesus Christ, to whom be the glory for ever. Amen.

[29] *Eph. 1:4*: even as he chose us in him before the foundation of the world; and *2 Tim. 1:9*: who saved us, and called us with a holy calling, not according to our works, but according to his own purpose and grace, which was given us in Christ Jesus before times eternal.

Jews and Gentiles.[30] Thus, we should praise the eternal God who before the world began determined the universal scope of evangelism, decided the final destiny of his saints, and ordained the gospel integration of the earthly society of his people.

9. 1 Tim. 1:17[31]

In the context (1:15-16) Paul recounts how God abounded in mercy and turned the "chief of sinners" into his apostle and servant. He ascribes his marvelous transformation to the "King eternal." The King eternal decided in eternity those who would hear the gospel, be saved, and belong to his church. How should we respond? Paul shows us: "to the King eternal . . . be honor and glory forever and ever." Therefore, with him we should bless the eternal God of sovereign grace.

10. 2 Pet. 3:8-9[32]

Peter observes that some scoff at the promise of Christ's second coming: "Where is the promise of his coming." He then reminds us not to forget God's eternity. Christ's session in heaven seems to us to endure for a long period of time. Yet, for the eternal God it is just like yesterday. With him, a whole millennium is like one day. How fickle we humans can be. On the one hand, we sometimes act like we have all the time in the world to squander as we please. On the other hand, at times we act like the events we wait for will never happen. God's eternity calls us to wait patiently for him to fulfill his promises. It calls us neither to pace impatiently up and down, nor to chafe and murmur while we wait for him to work on our behalf. What can seem to us like an eternity is but a moment with God. Thus, God's eternity teaches us to keep delayed answers to our prayers in proper perspective. Beware of the "spoiled brat syndrome." Such demand immediate gratification. Unless people drop what they're doing and cater to what they want, they throw a tantrum. Some parents tolerate and encourage such behavior. Their spoiled children despise and embarrass them. Yet, they run themselves ragged trying to supply immediately their ungrateful demands. We mustn't think that temper tantrums will manipulate our eternal God. He loves his children too much to spoil us. He visits such ingratitude

---

[30] *Eph. 3:11*: according to the eternal purpose which he purposed in Christ Jesus our Lord.

[31] *1 Tim. 1:17*: the King eternal, immortal, invisible, the only God, be honor and glory forever and ever. Amen.

[32] *2 Pet. 3:8-9*: But forget not this one thing, beloved, that one day is with the Lord as a thousand years, and a thousand years as one day. The Lord is not slack concerning his promise, as some count slackness; but is longsuffering to you-ward, not wishing that any should perish, but that all should come to repentance.

with the rod. He teaches us to wait for his answers, to pray with importunity, and to value the rare jewels of Christian patience and contentment.

B. The Biblical Testimony to God's Special Presence in Time

We focus briefly on three texts in the New Testament.

1. Matt. 28:20[33]

God's special presence with his people rests on his eternity and ever-presence. In heaven God dwells with his people perpetually. When our spirits enter heaven, we dwell forever with the Lord. We remain with him perpetually in every generation until the resurrection. On earth God dwells perpetually with every true Christian and with every true church in every generation until Christ returns. Already we have seen that his special presence with us is universal (Matt. 18:20). Now we observe that his special presence with us is *perpetual*. He is with us "always." He is present in grief and joy, in sickness and health, in adversity and prosperity, in honor and reproach, in success and failure, in tranquility and turmoil—"al*ways*." He is the God of our youth, of our manhood, and of our old age. He is with us "through all the changing scenes of life." When Christ assures his people of his perpetual presence, he doesn't threaten us. Rather, he offers powerful incentive to pursue the arduous tasks of spreading the gospel and building his church. We should evangelize with courage and hope because he is "with us always." We should say with David: "I will fear no evil, for you are with me."

2. 2 Pet. 3:10-12:[34]

A day approaches that God specially claims as his own. It is a day of his visitation, a season of his special presence. It is the day when God incarnate, Jesus Christ, returns to earth (3:4, 9). Thus, Peter calls it "the day of the Lord," and the "day of God." It is the day of the *consummation*. He will consume this world in fire and bring this age to an end (3:10, 12). It is also the day of the *resurrection* both of the just and unjust.[35] It is also the day of *judgment* and reckoning for all humanity (3:7). It is the day of *re-creation*. God will usher in a new heavens and earth wherein dwells righteousness (3:13). What lessons does this coming day of his special presence teach us?

---

[33] *Matt. 28:20*: I am with you always, even to the end of the world.

[34] *2 Pet. 3:10-12*: the day of the Lord shall come as a thief; in the which the heavens shall pass away with a great noise, and the elements shall be dissolved with fervent heat, and the earth and the works that are therein shall be burned up. Seeing that these things are thus to be dissolved, what manner of persons ought you to be in all holy living and godliness, looking for and earnestly desiring the day of God.

[35] 1 Thess. 4:16, 17; Rev. 20:11-14

It calls us to live in holiness and in hope. First, it calls us to live in holiness: "Seeing that these things are thus to be dissolved, what manner of persons ought you to be in all holy living and godliness." Soon Christ will return. Then this age will end. Thus, our hearts should not be idolatrous and entangled in the things of the world. Second, it calls us to live in hope: "looking for and earnestly desiring the day of God." Our vision, ultimately, is for a utopia, not in this world, but in the world to come. We should eagerly long for that new heavens and earth, hoping for the coming day of his special presence.

3. Rev. 1:10[36]

In this age God has appointed a special time that he calls his own, in which his people congregate in his special presence. Thus, the apostle depicts this time of his special presence as *"the Lord's* day." The weekly sabbath, the day of rest and worship, is a creation ordinance.[37] Its observance is a moral duty, which rests on the fourth commandment.[38] God made the observance of the sabbath on Saturday, the seventh day, a sign of the old covenant.[39] Thus, Christians, under the new covenant, no longer stand obligated to observe Saturday.[40] Thus, the weekly sabbath is a creation ordinance and moral duty, yet Christians are no longer bound to observe Saturday. What day should Christians observe? God has appointed the first day of the week as the Christian Sabbath. On Sunday the apostolic church gathered in God's special presence for worship.[41] The apostle commanded the churches to offer the spiritual sacrifice of giving on Sunday.[42] Why did God appoint Sunday as the time of his special presence? To answer this we must ascertain why he designated Saturday in the first place. We learn that he: "blessed the seventh day, and hallowed it, because in it he rested from all his work which he created and made." Observe two things: (1) he chose that day because on it he commenced his rest from his work of creation; and (2) he demonstrated this choice when he blessed and sanctified that day. God followed this same procedure when he appointed Sunday. God the Son incarnate completed his work of redemption. He commenced his resurrection rest from that work on Sunday, the first day of the week. On

---

[36] *Rev. 1:10*: I was in the Spirit on the Lord's day

[37] Gen. 2:1-3; Mark 2:27

[38] Exod. 20:8-11; Luke 23:56

[39] Exod. 31:17

[40] Col. 2:16-17

[41] Acts 20:7

[42] 1 Cor. 16:1-2; Heb. 13:16

Pentecost Sunday, God the Spirit blessed and sanctified the first day of the week. Thus, God appointed a new day of rest and worship and openly displayed his choice to us. Thus John called Sunday, "the Lord's Day." Therefore, the church began to gather every Sunday in God's special presence. Churches have continued to gather for worship on the Lord's Day ever since, and shall continue to do so until the day of the Lord.

This calls us to remember the Christian sabbath, Sunday, to keep it holy. We should highly esteem, value, and appreciate this blessed day. We should lay aside our mundane work and recreations, so that without distraction we may hallow every hour of his special day. We should also enter with his people into his special presence every Lord's day, to offer him the spiritual sacrifices of singing and giving and to hear the reading and preaching of his Word. The Lord's day belongs, not only to the doctrine of man, as a creation ordinance, and to Christian ethics, as a moral law, but also to the doctrine of God, as the time of his special presence. Our attitude to the Lord's day reflects our attitude to the Lord, to communing with him, and to his special presence. Like a thermometer, this attitude displays men's spiritual health. When many professing Christians and Christian churches would rather enter the Super Bowl than the special presence of Christ, modern evangelicalism is grievously ill. Let us not think we stand, but watch and pray, lest we fall, lest our hearts grow weary of Christ. Let us love his sacred day and presence with all our hearts. Let us spend each Lord's day, not preoccupied with do's and don'ts, but occupied with Christ in his special presence.

III. Summary of the Practical Application of God's Temporal Supremacy

God's eternal being has a large impact on religion. It grounds our security and hope. It furnishes much fuel for humility. It calls for our praise and adoration. I summarize its practical relevance below.

A. Practical Applications of God's Eternity and Ever-presence

OLD TESTAMENT

1. It admonishes us to fear God's wrath (Ps. 90:11).
2. It teaches us to face the brevity of life (Ps. 90:12).
3. It calls us to pray:

    for seasons of gladness (Ps. 90:13-15).
    for the perpetuation of our work (Ps. 90:16-17),
    for deliverance from premature death (Ps. 103:24).
    for his blessing on our children (Pss. 90:16, 103:28).

4. It shows us how great he is and how little we know (Job 36:26, 38:1-4).
5. It encourages us to seek security in God (Pss. 93:1-2, 103:25-27).
6. It certifies the reliability of his Word (Isa. 57:15).

7. It assures us that he is always accessible to the humble and contrite (Isa. 57:15).

NEW TESTAMENT

1. It confronts us with the mystery of God incarnate (John 8:58).
2. It renders sinners inexcusable, since creation displays it to all humanity (Rom. 1:20).
3. It guarantees the fulfillment of his eternal decree to save (Rom. 16:26; Eph. 1:4, 3:11; 2 Tim. 1:9).
4. It evokes from us adoration, blessing, and praise to God (1 Tim. 1:17).
5. It teaches us to wait patiently for him to work (2 Pet. 3:8-9).

B. Practical Applications of God's Special Presence in Time

1. It encourages us in every season and in all difficult service (Matt. 28:20).
2. It summons us to a life of holiness and hope for Christ's return (2 Pet. 3:10-12).
3. It summons us to appreciate and sanctify the Lord's Day (Rev. 1:10).

Topic 10. The Immutability of God

"The counsel of Jehovah stands fast forever, the thoughts of his heart to all generations" (Ps. 33:11);
"But you are the same" (Ps. 102:27/Heb. 1:12); "I, Jehovah, change not" (Mal. 3:6)

Section 5. God's Unchangeable Being: *Immutability*

The Supreme Being asserts his immutability: "I, Jehovah, change not" (Mal. 3:6). Alteration does not limit God. He is an unchangeable Spirit. He never undergoes mutation, or ceases to be what he is. He does not and cannot age or decay.[1] His being and metaphysical faculties are immutable.[2] His infinite moral virtues are immutable.[3] All he is, he always was, and always will be. His name is "I AM" (Exod. 3:14). In this respect, he is utterly unique. He alone is absolutely unchangeable.[4] All created things, whether material or spiritual, are subject to change. The heavens and earth are mutable.[5] Angels and men are mutable. The fall of angelic spirits, and the fall and maturation of human spirits, certify this. Now I define the biblical concept, survey its biblical display, and summarize its practical applications.

I. The Biblical Concept of God's Immutability

First, I define three aspects of God's immutability: his absolute, relative, and mediatorial immutability. *Second*, I present seven qualifications of God's immutability.

A. Three Aspects of God's Immutability

1. God's absolute immutability

When only God was, he was immutable. All he ever was, he now is, and always will be: "I, Jehovah, change not." Immutability marks every distinctive of God's nature, everything he essentially is. Thus, it characterizes every divine attribute. Such breadth and interplay have occasioned considerable diversity in the presentation of this attribute. Gill begins with God's immutability, while Thornwell ends with it. My presentation follows the order of the Shorter Catechism, Boyce, Shedd, C. Hodge, and A. A. Hodge. I present it as the last existential attribute, the transition to God's spiritual attributes. Thus, God's immutability points back to his other existential attributes and forward to all his spiritual attributes.

---

[1] Ps. 102:25; Heb. 1:10-12
[2] Isa. 40:28
[3] Mal. 3:6; Heb. 6:17-18; James 1:17
[4] Isa. 40:25, 28
[5] Ps. 102:25-27

2. God's relative immutability

Scripture features God's immutability in relation to his eternal decree, the original creation, and redemption. First, the eternal decree of the immutable God is *irreversible*: "The counsel of Jehovah stands fast forever, the thoughts of his heart to all generations" (Ps. 33:11). Having decided, freely, of his own will, to fix his eternal decree, he will never or annul or revise it. I call this God's "irreversibility." Second, immutable Creator stands in sharp contrast with his mutable creation: "they shall perish, but you shall endure . . . they shall be changed: but you are the same" (Ps. 102:26-27). The heavens and earth are subject to decay and deterioration. They are *corruptible*. The Creator is "incorruptible." I call this God's "incorruptibility." Third, the Redeemer's commitment to his people is immutable: "I, Jehovah, change not; therefore you, O sons of Jacob, are not consumed" (Mal. 3:6). He swears allegiance to his people. He never violates his sworn fidelity. He is incapable of defection. I call this his "indefectibility."

3. God's mediatorial immutability

Scripture also presents God's immutability in relation to the incarnation. God the Son became human: "the Word became flesh and dwelt among us" (John 1:14). Jesus is God incarnate. The writer of Hebrews affirms that Jesus is the immutable God (Ps. 102:25-27; Heb. 1:10-12). He asserts that Jesus, the glorified God-man is: "the same, yesterday, and today, and forever" (Heb. 13:8). Jesus remains permanently the God-man, because he is the immutable God. I call this his "mediatorial permanency."

In sum, God is every way immutable. *In absolute terms*, he is immutable in his simplicity, supremacy (existential attributes) and spirituality (spiritual attributes). *In relative terms*, the immutable Sovereign is irreversible; the immutable Creator, incorruptible; the immutable Redeemer, indefectible. Once he freely decides to decree, create, and redeem, he must be irreversible, incorruptible, and indefectible, because he is immutable. *In mediatorial terms*, the immutable Mediator is permanently divine and human.

B. Seven Qualifications of God's Immutability

Many misunderstand and misrepresent God's immutability. Pits and traps surround this concept and ensnare the unwary that approach it. Thus, we must especially watch our step here. Scripture presents at least seven important distinctions or qualifications that help us to avoid these pitfalls.

1. God is immutable but not inactive or inanimate.

God's immutability does not imply his inactivity. God is not an inanimate object, but a living being. He acts and works. He created things that didn't exist before he made them. When he creates, he doesn't cease to be what he always was: "the heavens are the work of your hands. They shall perish but you shall endure . . . they shall be changed; but you are the same." After he creates the world, he relates to creation. Yet, this doesn't mean that he changed. Rather, it means that the immutable God entered necessary relations with his inanimate creation and his animate creatures.

2. God is immutable but not antisocial or impersonal.

God's immutability does not imply that he is *asocial*. Scripture insists that he is the personal and living God, who engages in personal communication and interpersonal communion: "I Jehovah, change not; therefore you, O sons of Jacob, are not consumed." He is not inert, having no interaction whatsoever with other beings. He is not autistic, reclusive, or incommunicative. Rather, he interacts personally with angels and men. He speaks things, in history, which he never said before. He progressively discloses himself and his purposes in Scripture. Verbal communication, self-disclosure, and personal interaction make him a living and personal Being, not a "mutable" being.

3. God is immutable but not apathetic or heartless.[6]

Divine immutability is not divine apathy. God not only acts, and interacts; he even reacts to historical events and individual persons. He responds to good and evil emotively, volitionally, and intellectually. This makes him, not mutable, but a spiritual being, exercising his mind, affection, and will. Our God is not the "unmoved mover" of the pagan philosophers. He is not a heartless computer, or an unconcerned machine. He responds to obedience with delight and joy, to need with compassion and mercy, to sin with anger, and to the suffering of his people with grief. He finds some events especially grievous, even to the point of feeling *regret*, which means, "a sense of loss." Some stumble at this, but Scripture affirms it repeatedly and emphatically.[7]

---

[6] For further discussion see *Divine Passibility and Impassibility in Nineteenth Century American Confessional Presbyterian Theologians* by Ligon Duncan III. It can be accessed at: http://biblicalstudies.org.uk/pdf/sbet/08-1_001.pdf

[7] *Gen. 6:5-6*: And Jehovah saw that the wickedness of man was great in the earth, and that every imagination of the thoughts of his heart was only evil continually. And it repented Jehovah that he had made man on the earth, and it grieved him at his heart. *Judg. 2:18:* then Jehovah was with the judge, and saved them out of the hand of their enemies all the days of the judge: for it repented Jehovah because of their groaning by reason of them that oppressed them and vexed them.
1 Sam. 15:11, 29, 34: "It repents me that I have set up Saul to be king; for he is turned back from following me, and has not performed my commandments . . . 29 the Strength of Israel will not lie nor repent: for he is not a man, that he should repent . . . 34 Jehovah repented that he had made Saul king over Israel.

God's immutability does not mandate heartless stoicism. God's decrees are irreversible. He will never change his decision, or alter his decree. Yet, the immutable God is grieved about Saul's inauguration. Here is the marvel. God in eternity decreed all this. He decreed to make Saul king. He decreed Saul's disobedience. He decreed to be grieved over making Saul king. He decreed to replace Saul's house with David's house. All this is irreversible because God is immutable. We must bow our heads, and say: "Oh the depth! . . . who has known the mind of the Lord." We cannot explain why God decreed to be grieved over making man or making Saul king. Yet, we must confess both his immutability and his heart.

4. God is immutable but not implacable or obdurate.

Immutability does not mean that God is incapable of relenting. He is not obstinate, or callous, or hardhearted, or intransigent. He does not always keep his anger. He will not always chide. Because he is very merciful, when men repent, he "repents" of the evil that he threatened and even pronounced against them. Again, some stumble over this. Some claim that a God who relents on his threats, even in the face of men's repentance, cannot be an immutable God. Scripture says otherwise.[8] These are the acts, not of a wishy-washy God, who vacillates in unprincipled sentiment, but of the God of immutable integrity, who acts in principled justice and kindness. Scripture sets out the principles that regulate the Lord's behavior (Jer. 18:7-10). His immutable justice cuts two ways. He invariably shows mercy to the penitent:

Jer. 18:7-8: At what instant I speak concerning a nation to . . . destroy it; if that nation, concerning which I have spoken, turn from their evil, I will repent of the evil that I thought to do unto them

Conversely, he invariably brings evil upon the presumptuous and apostate. If a nation turns from the truth, and does evil, God "repents" of the good he promised to do to them:

---

[8] *Jer. 26:3, 13, 19*: It may be that they will hearken, and turn every man from his evil way; that I may repent me of the evil that I purpose to do to them because of the evil of their doings . . . 13 Now therefore amend your ways and your doings, and obey the voice of Jehovah your God; and Jehovah will repent him of the evil that he has pronounced against you . . . 19 did he not fear Jehovah, and entreat the favor of Jehovah, and Jehovah repented him of the evil which he had pronounced against him.
Joel 2:13: turn unto Jehovah your God; for he is gracious and merciful, slow to anger, and abundant in lovingkindness and repents him of the evil. *Jonah 3:9-10*: And God saw their works, that they turned from their evil way; and God repented of the evil which he said he would do unto them; and he did it not.

Jer. 18:9-10: And at what instant I speak concerning a nation . . . to build and plant it; if they do that which is evil in my sight, that they obey not my voice, then I will repent of the good, wherewith I said I would benefit them.

The fact that God deals with people conditionally does not negate his immutability. To the contrary, it establishes his immutable justice, holiness, goodness, and faithfulness. If circumstances change, he responds accordingly. And, he decreed the conditions, people's responses, and his principled judgments.

5. God is immutable but not inexorable or unapproachable.

Immutability does not render God incapable of heeding an entreaty, request, or prayer. The immutable God truly answers prayer. He is approachable and easy to be entreated. Prayer is often the instrumental means of his actions. At times it is a preventive means that deters what otherwise would have come to pass. Thus, Moses' intercessory prayer for Israel prevailed. The Lord says to Moses: "let me alone, that my wrath may wax hot against them, and that I may consume them, and I will make of you a great nation" (Exod. 32:10). Then Moses entreats the Lord to spare them (32:11-13). Then we read: "And Jehovah repented of the evil which he said he would do unto his people" (Exod. 32:14). Some also stumble at this. They complain that effective prayer is not compatible with God's immutability. Again, we refuse to be bullied. Scripture says that prayer avails much. The God who ordained the ends, also ordained the means. He decreed in eternity that prayer would prevail with him.

6. God's immutability does not preclude augmentation, betterment, advancement, and development in his covenantal relationship with his people.

Because God is immutable, his moral law, the Decalogue, and his gospel method of salvation, the "covenant of grace," are permanent and unchanging. These constitute his immutable revealed will for all mankind. They define what he requires from and promises to all humans everywhere. Yet, he unfolds these permanent norms progressively in historical covenants with his people. He affirms development in his solemn commitments.[9] The new covenant is a "better covenant, which has been enacted on better promises" (Heb. 8:6). The ceremonial requirements, sacrificial system, and levitical priesthood of the old covenant were temporary. God imposed them only until a time of reformation.[10] Temporary requirements are not incompatible with his immutability. Rather, he employs them as the means

---

[9] Jer. 31:31-34
[10] Heb. 7:12, 9:10, 10:8-9, 18

to display his permanent revealed will. His immutable wisdom suits these externals to the moral state and spiritual immaturity of his people. When his people undergo radical reformation, moral improvement, and spiritual maturation, he rearranges their external life appropriately in perfect accord with his indefectible love and loyalty to them.

7. God incarnate has immutable deity, not immutable humanity.

When the Word became human, he did not cease to be what he always was, the Supreme Being. Yet, the immutable Son became what he never was before, human. His human nature was mutable: "Jesus advanced in wisdom and stature, and in favor with God and man (Luke 2:52). His body grew, like every little boy's body, in size, coordination, and strength. His human soul also developed. He increased "in wisdom." He gained experience. He matured in the exercise of his intellectual, volitional, and emotional faculties. He matured, in body and soul, from infancy to adulthood. Thus, his human nature is not immutable. Therefore, in God incarnate, Jesus Christ, we behold the unfathomable mystery of mutable humanity joined to immutable deity, in one Person, without confusion or composition. We must not deny this mystery simply because we can't explain it. Some falsely assert that he "laid aside" his deity, his divine nature, when he became human. This disparages his immutability. It dishonors God and obscures Christ's glory. Others, paying lip service to God's immutability, falsely claim that Christ could not be the Supreme Being. These tell us that a divine Person cannot become incarnate. They allege that the incarnation, by definition, is impossible, since God is "pure being, exalted above all becoming." These forfeit the name Christian, since they refuse to acknowledge the deity of God the Son. Let us affirm, without embarrassment, both Christ's immutable deity and mutable humanity. Let us bless and magnify God for the wonder of God incarnate.

Conclusion: God is immutable. Nevertheless, he lives, acts, interacts, reacts, responds, and feels. He judges conditionally. He answers prayer. His covenants show progression. Christ's immutable deity and mutable humanity lead us to peer over the fence around the unfathomable mystery.

II. The Biblical Display of God's Immutability

We survey Jehovah's absolute immutability as the Supreme Being, his relative immutability as Sovereign, Creator, and Redeemer, and his mediatorial immutability as the incarnate Mediator.

A. God's Absolute Immutability

God's affirmation, "I, Jehovah, change not," embraces all his attributes. Thus, this text declares his absolute immutability. His simplicity is immutable. God is always love and always light. He always remains what he is, and all he is. His supremacy is immutable. Each existential attribute permanently distinguishes his being. He can never cease to be ideal, self-existent, infinite, eternal, or unchangeable. His spirituality is immutable. Every aspect of his spirituality is unalterable. He has immutable incorporeality. He is ever non-material, and thus, ever invisible, indivisible, impassable, incorporeal, and indissoluble. He has immutable life and power. He can never loose his life or his omnipotence. He has immutable faculties of mind, will, and affection. He can never lose his mind, or freedom of will, or his capacity to feel. He can never change the manner in which he thinks, wills, or feels. He has immutable moral virtue. He can never cease to be perfectly and infinitely good, holy, just, and faithful. He has immutable personality. He can never cease to be a personal being. Nor can or will he cease to be triune. The Father is ever the Supreme Being. The Son is ever the Supreme Being. The Spirit is ever the Supreme Being. Thus, "I, Jehovah, change not," affirms the immutability of every divine attribute. His simplicity, supremacy, and spirituality have never changed, never can change, and never will change.

B. God's Immutability as Sovereign: Irreversibility

We now focus on his immutability as it relates to his eternal decree. We consider the testimony of five witnesses: Nu. 23:19; 1 Sam. 15:29; Job 23:13; Ps. 33:11; and Prov. 19:21.

1. Num. 23:19[11]

In prophecy God pulls back the veil and uncovers a little portion of his secret decree. Balaam would reverse God's decree if he could. Yet even he admits that God's decree is inviolable and irreversible. God is not a human. He doesn't change his mind about what he decrees. He doesn't revise his eternal decision. Humans change their mind about commitments because their values change, or their feelings change, or their priorities change. It is not so with God. Nor does God lie about his intentions and plans. Why do people lie about their plans? Sometimes they lie because they are ashamed of them. Sometimes they lie because they fear that if others discover what they devise, they will challenge or defeat their agenda. God is not so. He is neither ashamed of his agenda nor concerned that if people discover it they will overthrow it. No one can annul what he decrees. This text declares his

---

[11] *Num. 23:19*: God is not a man, that he should lie, neither the son of man, that he should repent. Has he said, and will he not do it? Or has he spoken, and will he not make it good? Behold, I have received commandment to bless: and he has blessed, and I can not reverse it.

decree to bless his people. Thus, men engage in great folly when they oppose, resist, and resent what God decrees. When he decrees to bless, they waste breath, time, and energy trying to undo it. It was futile for men like Balak to try to destroy Israel. Similarly, the church will never perish. Persecution will never destroy it. Temptation will never overwhelm it. Its enemies strive in vain. God has decreed its preservation and victory: "I will build my church, and the gates of hell will not prevail against it" (Matt. 16:18).

2. 1 Sam. 15:29[12]

Samuel pulled back the veil and showed Saul a piece of God's secret decree. What king Saul saw disturbed him greatly. Samuel addressed succession to the throne. He assured Saul that God had rent the kingdom from his house and had given the throne to someone better suited to lead his people. Saul, however, was determined to pick his own successor. When he perceived the one God had appointed to succeed to the throne, he became disaffected with him. He attempted to set him up for defeat and ruin. When that failed, he took more stringent measures. He falsely accused him, drove him away, and persecuted him. He made all the arrangements for another successor to sit on the throne. He did everything in his power to prevent David from becoming king. All his efforts proved futile, because God's decree is irreversible and inviolable. Let his futile controversy with God teach us to accept our limitations. Let us not resist God's Word and will. Also, when powerful adversaries seek our hurt and plot against us craftily, let us learn to trust in God, and wait for him to deliver us. We too must cling to his promises and commit our defense and vindication to him.

3. Job 23:13-14[13]

Job, in his distress and grief, confesses God's irreversibility. God performs in history exactly what he appointed for each of us in eternity. When our prayers run up against his decree, they hit a stone wall. Then they cannot turn him. Even Moses' prayers ran up against his irreversible decree. God finally told him not to pray any more about entering Canaan. He had decreed that Moses die outside Canaan, and no amount of petition would move him

---

[12] *1 Sam. 15:29*: the Strength of Israel will not lie nor repent; for he is not a man, that he should repent.

[13] *Job 23:13-14*: But he is of one mind, and who can turn him? And what his soul desires, even that he does. For he performs that which is appointed for me: and many such things are with him. Therefore am I terrified at his presence; when I consider, I am afraid of him.

to reverse, repeal, or annul it.[14] Sometimes God ordains for his people seasons of deep distress and severe affliction. Sometimes he cannot be persuaded to relent, or to give us what we request, even though we seek him repeatedly and earnestly. Then we must submit to his sovereignty. He ordains "thorns in the flesh" to teach us the sufficiency of his grace. From this we must also learn to fear him. We cannot manipulate him. We are in his hands. What he decrees is final. Do I teach fatalism? Absolutely not! What use is prayer? Prayer is of great value, in everything, even when he says, no: "my grace is sufficient." God weaves our prayers into the fabric of his decree. We must neither disparage prayer nor make "claims" on God. We should beware of presumption that makes demands on God. Such presumption soon turns to bitter cynicism. It oft leaves people disillusioned and discouraged on the brink of apostasy. I would spare you.

4. *Ps. 33:11*[15]

The counsel of Jehovah is his settled determination, design, plan, and vision for the future. In eternity he fixed his decree of creation, providence, and redemption.[16] That eternal plan "stands fast forever." It is irrevocable. It must and will happen, exactly as he planned it, because he is omnipotent and immutable. The psalmist focuses on the hope of entire nations: "Jehovah brings the counsel of the nations to naught; he makes the thoughts of the peoples to be of no effect" (33:10). Nations also have plans. They have a vision for their future, their "shining city on the hill," which they strive to attain. Sometimes this includes expansion of their territory, conquest of their neighbors or adversaries, and spread of their influence. God often frustrates them, especially their selfish dreams for conquest and control. On the other hand, he blesses the godly aspirations of his people: "Blessed is the nation whose God is Jehovah, the people whom he has chosen for his inheritance" (33:12). Under the new covenant, the Christian church is the people of God.[17] We enter into the benefit of this promise. When we fix our gaze on God's glory in his church, when we make his honor in his house our "shining city," then we can look for and expect his blessing on our designs. Thus, God's immutable decree calls us to set our hearts on those things that bring him glory through his people, to strive for those things, and to pray for them.

---

[14] Num. 20:12; Deut. 3:23-28

[15] *Ps. 33:11*: The counsel of Jehovah stands fast forever, the thoughts of his heart to all generations.

[16] Rev. 4:11; Eph. 1:3-5, 11, 3:11

[17] 1 Pet. 2:9-10

5. Prov. 19:21[18]

Here the focus is not national plans, but personal designs. Human hearts are full of plans; but what Jehovah decrees comes to pass. Again, his immutability and omnipotence combine to insure this. Therefore, we should commit our plans to Jehovah, so that our purposes may be established.[19] We should acknowledge him in all our ways.[20] We should devise our plans in his fear and guidance, and pursue our vision for his glory in complete dependence on him for wisdom, strength, and resources.

C. God's Immutability as Creator: Incorruptibility

We now focus on God's immutability as Creator. We consider two texts: Ps. 102:25-27; Isa. 40:28.

1. Ps. 102:25-27[21]

One day, the God who created heaven and earth will dismantle them: "They shall perish." Unlike them, he will never grow old or deteriorate. Our incorruptible Creator is more stable than heaven and earth. He is the fountain of stability and security. God's incorruptibility calls us to place our hope and trust in our Creator, rather than in created things. It calls us to make God our confidence for everything pertaining to this life and the life to come. Thus, God's immutability underscores every lesson and application that we derived from this text when we studied God's eternity.

2. Isa. 40:28[22]

Jehovah, the Creator, never faints. His power never deteriorates. He doesn't get tired after exertion, or become feeble with age. Nor does he become senile. His mental faculties are as sharp today as they were when he created the world. Thus, we creatures must never think that we are beyond the scope of his awareness or of his capability to help. We should never say: "My way is hid from Jehovah" (40:27). Therefore, God's incorruptibility serves as a

---

[18] *Prov. 19:21*: There are many devices in a man's heart; but the counsel of Jehovah, that shall stand.
[19] Prov. 16:3
[20] Prov. 3:6
[21] *Ps. 102:25-27*: I said, O my God, take me not away in the midst of my days. Your years are throughout all generations. Of old did you lay the foundation of the earth; and the heavens are the work of your hands. They shall perish, but you shall endure. Yea, all of them shall wax old like a garment; as a vesture shall you change them, and they shall be changed. But you are the same, and your years shall have no end
[22] *Isa. 40:28*: The everlasting God, Jehovah, the Creator of the ends of the earth, faints not, neither is weary; there is no searching of his understanding.

great encouragement to his people. It gives us security in the trials of life, in the face of death, and even at the dissolution of heaven and earth.

D. God's Immutability as Redeemer: Indefectibility

We consider three texts that reveal his immutability as Redeemer: Mal. 3:6; Heb. 6:17-18; James 1:17.

1. Mal. 3:6[23]

Already we have shown that this text affirms God's absolute immutability. Now we examine its setting. Malachi foretells the time of Christ's advent (3:1-5). He begins with the life and work of John the Baptist (3:1). He then describes Christ's work among God's people (3:2-5). That work consists of reforming and cleansing the priesthood (3:2-3). When he has cleansed them, the worship of God's purified people will be acceptable to the Lord (3:3-4). Then, the wicked among his people, who live in sin and don't fear God, will be condemned and judged (3:5). He issues a solemn call to them. They must repent from their lifestyle of disobedience that has characterized them throughout their life as a nation. He urges them pointedly to repent from their sins associated with worship (3:7-15). Thus, Jehovah asserts his immutability in conjunction with the promise of Christ's coming, the hope of the radical reformation of his people, and his solemn reproof of their sins. Remarkably, his immutability explains why he did not *consume* his stiff-necked and hard-hearted people.

God promised Abraham, Isaac and Jacob that by their seed, which is Christ, he would bless all the families of the earth.[24] God confirms his commitment to fulfill that promise, and furnishes further details about that fulfillment (3:1-5). God had also promised to reform his people through his new covenant with them. In this new covenant he promises to transform his people into a people who know him, to write his law on their hearts, to forgive their sins, to put his fear in their hearts, to preserve them in true religion, and to give them his Spirit to enable them to obey him.[25] Here the Lord also confirms this promise to reform his people (3:1-5). Jehovah God, mindful of these covenants, would never destroy his people in judgment in spite of their aggravated sin. Immutable love and faithfulness insure that he would never break his sworn promises and consume Israel. He will do everything he has sworn to do, because he is immutable. Thus, God's covenants unite him to his people in bonds of sworn fidelity and loyalty. He cannot become disaffected with his people and turn against them. He is

---

[23] *Mal. 3:6*: For I, Jehovah, change not; therefore you, O sons of Jacob, are not consumed.

[24] Gen. 22:17-18, 26:4, 28:14; Gal. 3:16-17

[25] Jer. 31:31-34, 32:40; Ezek. 36:26-27, 37:26-27

incapable of defection, of abandoning his allegiance to his people. He is incapable of breaking his oath of loyalty. He cannot even be tempted to defect, because he is immutable.

This affords great comfort. God will never renege on his gracious commitments to those who believe in Christ. He will never undergo a change of heart toward his church and her cause. Unlike a political defector, he can never change sides and work with our enemies against us. Once he sets his heart on us for good, he will never leave or forsake us. He must remain loyal to us, in spite of our remaining sin, all the days of our life, because of his covenant with us in Christ. People are not so. We can be induced or prompted to defect. We are even capable of defecting from a good cause. Jesus knew the pain of friends who proved disloyal in a crisis and through fear disowned his righteous cause. He even knew the pain of malicious betrayal. Judas, for money, defected from him and sold Christ to his enemies. Therefore, brethren, take heart. Though your former friends turn against you, your immutable Redeemer is indefectible. He remains committed to his people with an irrevocable oath of loyalty. The hymn writer says it well: "Do your friends despise, forsake you? Take it to the Lord in prayer. In his arms he'll take and shield you. You will find a solace there."

2. *Heb. 6:13, 17-18*:[26]

God made a covenant with Abraham. He solemnized his promise with an oath, because he wanted the heirs of that promise to behold his immutable commitment to them. The writer refers (6:14) to the promise of Genesis 22:16-18. This promise centers on Christ and the spiritual blessing he brings to every branch of the human race: "and in your seed shall all the nations of the earth be blessed." Thus, God certifies his commitment to bless his people through Jesus Christ, in order to assure those who inherit that promise that his affection for them is immutable. Those who inherit that promise cling by faith to Jesus Christ for refuge from sin and wrath. God solemnized that promise with an oath, because he wanted Christians to know assuredly that our Redeemer loves us immutably with indefectible loyalty. He intended, through this irrevocable commitment to bless us in Christ, to furnish our souls with an impregnable hope. Even the most severe storms

---

[26] *Heb. 6:13, 17-18*: For when God made promise to Abraham, since he could swear by none greater, he swore by himself . . . Wherein God, being minded to show more abundantly unto the heirs of the promise the immutability of his counsel, interposed with an oath; that by two immutable things, in which it is impossible for God to lie, we may have a strong encouragement who have fled for refuge to lay hold on the hope set before us, which we have as an anchor of the soul.

of affliction and the most vicious assaults of the powers of darkness cannot shake, unsettle, or destroy this hope. Thus, the immutability of our Redeemer furnishes great comfort and confidence to God's people in Christ. It calls us to trust him wholeheartedly on earth. It calls us confidently to expect him to bless and deliver us in the world to come. It assures us that he will never leave us, or forsake us, or turn against us.

3. James 1:16-18:[27]

James describes God as the "Father of lights." The commentators differ about the meaning of this phrase. Matthew Poole thinks "lights" refers to spiritual blessings.[28] Lenski says it refers to the sun, moon, and stars.[29] In any event, "lights" give off light. What role does light have? Light enables people to perceive reality. We cannot see in the dark. If we try to walk in the dark, we stumble, because we can't see where we're going. Neither can we work in the dark, because we can't see what we're doing: "the night comes when no man can work." Thus, in general terms, "lights" are "those things which give off light," "which illuminate," "which enable people to see or perceive reality." I won't quibble about whether James refers only to spiritual illumination, or includes both natural and spiritual lights. Clearly, he focuses on spiritual illumination (1:18). He asserts that God has enabled us to perceive spiritual reality. He shines the gospel light of his Word on our hearts, and opens our blinded minds with the grace of regeneration: "of his own will he brought us forth by the word of truth." The Word of God and regenerating grace are "lights." They shed light, illuminate, and enable us to see spiritual reality. The sun, moon, and stars enable people, with their physical eyes, to see created reality. Similarly, the Word of God and regenerating grace enable Christians to perceive spiritual reality with the eyes of their heart. God is the Author or Creator of illumination in general and of spiritual illumination in particular: "the Father of lights . . . of his own will he brought us forth." God sheds light by special revelation and illuminating grace: "then opened he their mind, that they might understand the scriptures" (Luke 24:45). Spiritual illumination begins in regeneration and lasts throughout the Christian life. Again, Paul pleads that "the Father

---

[27] *James 1:16-18*: Be not deceived, beloved brethren. Every good and perfect gift comes down from above, coming down from the Father of lights, with whom can be no variation, neither shadow that is cast by turning. Of his own will he brought us forth by the word of truth, that we should be a kind of firstfruits of his creatures.

[28] Matthew Poole, *Commentary on the Whole Bible* (3 Vols.; London: The Banner of Truth Trust, 1968), 3:882

[29] R. C. H. Lenski, *Interpretation of the Epistle to the Hebrews and the Epistle of James* (Minneapolis: Augsburg, 1966), 545

of glory" (a phrase very similar to "Father of lights") would continually illumine Christians with "wisdom and revelation" in the knowledge of Christ (Eph. 1:17-18). What then is James' point? Lenski, Poole, Johnstone, Calvin, and Matthew Henry agree about this. His main point is this: the Author of regeneration never turns around and authors temptation. The immutable God who gives us the spiritual light of grace and truth never engulfs us in the spiritual darkness of error, deception, delusion, and enticement to sin (1:13-16). Thus, James affirms the immutability of our Redeemer. Our indefectible Redeemer sheds spiritual light on us in conversion and the Christian life. Therefore, he will never delude us, deceive us, or entice us to sin and apostasy. He is "the Father of lights, with whom is no variation."

Therefore, we must not "be deceived." We must not entertain harsh thoughts of our Redeemer. We must never blame him when we are enticed to sin. We must not accuse him if we, in spiritual delusion, as though we walked in pitch-black darkness, call evil good, stumble, and fall into sin. Rather, we must take all the blame. We must assume full responsibility for our carnal susceptibility to temptation and for succumbing to such enticement. We must never think that our Redeemer changes his disposition toward us. He stands irrevocably disposed toward us in love and good will. Once he sets his heart on us in love, he will never turn against us or become disaffected. The God who blesses us with every spiritual blessing in Christ never takes away his good gifts, or demands them back. In this God is unlike people. For example, the multitudes that offered sacrifice and worship to the apostle soon offered him stones instead.[30] People who once loved and spoke well of you can turn into your most malicious detractors. Conversely, our chief foes can turn into our choicest friends. With our Redeemer, however, we always know exactly where we stand. He will never change his affection for Christians into disaffection, or exchange his spiritual blessings for curses. Thus, his immutability insures the preservation of the saints: "he who began a good work in you will perfect it until the day of Jesus Christ" (Phil. 1:6).

E. God Incarnate's Immutability as Mediator: Mediatorial Permanency

We consider two texts that focus on Christ's mediatorial permanency: Heb.1:10-12, and Heb.13:8.

1. Heb. 1:10-12

In Hebrews 1:10-12 the writer asserts that Psalm 102:25-27 applies to God the Son. Christ is the immutable Creator of all things visible and invisible.[31]

---

[30] Acts 14:13-20
[31] John 1:1-3; Col. 1:16

The writer stresses the superiority of Christianity. He warns us not to despise Christ's teaching or renounce our allegiance to him: "therefore we ought to give the more earnest heed to the things that were heard, lest haply we drift away from them" (2:1). If we turn away from Jesus, we turn away from the immutable Sovereign, Creator, and Redeemer.

2. Heb. 13:8:[32]

This is a remarkable assertion of the permanence of our Mediator, Jesus Christ. He always remains the same in his person and mediation. He ever abides as the God-man, one Person, with a human nature and the divine nature, immutably joined without confusion or composition. His mediation continues unabated forever. His mediation rests on an immutable basis, his perfect life and atoning death. His mediation takes place through his immutable resurrection life at God's right hand. His mediation has an immutable focus, his intercession on behalf of his people. This teaches us not to be "carried away with diverse and strange teachings" (13:9). When we hear someone propound a novel doctrine of Christ's person, or of his work, we must not be enthralled with it. No essential tenet of our Christian faith can ever change, because Christ is immutable. This calls us to hold tenaciously to the faith once delivered to the saints.

III. Practical Applications of God's Immutability

I now summarize and catalogue practical and experiential applications of God's immutability.

A. Practical Application of his Absolute Immutability

It furnishes the bedrock of all stability.

B. Practical Applications of his Immutability as Sovereign

1. It shows the futility of trying to ruin God's people (Num. 23:19).
2. It shows the futility of trying to defeat God's Word (1 Sam. 15:29).
3. It calls us to submit to his decisions about our lives (Job 23:13-14).
4. It calls us to set our hope on what he promises to do (Ps. 33:11).
5. It teaches us to commit our plans and cause to him (Prov. 19:21).

C. Practical Applications of his Immutability as Creator

1. It calls us to place our trust in our Creator, rather than in his creation (Ps. 102:27).
2. It calls never to think he has forgotten our problems (Isa. 40:28).

---

[32] *Heb. 13:8*: Jesus Christ is the same, yesterday, and today, and forever.

D. Practical Applications of his Immutability as Redeemer

1. It assures us that he will never turn against us (Mal. 3:6).
2. It encourages us confidently to expect eternal blessings (Heb. 6:17-18).
3. It certifies that he will always do us good and preserve us (James 1:16-18).

E. Practical Applications of his Immutability as Mediator

1. It warns us never to depart from Christianity (Heb. 1:10-12, 2:1).
2. It warns us to avoid novel doctrines about Christ (Heb. 13:8).

Conclusion:

What a blessed and comforting truth this is. May the Lord be pleased to write it on our hearts. We turn next to his spiritual attributes. As we do, let us remember that these too are immutable.

Topic 11. The Majestic Form of God

"who only has immortality, dwelling in light unapproachable, whom no man has seen" (1 Tim. 6:16);
"they shall see his face" (Rev. 22:4)

Division 2: God's Supreme Spirituality: God's Spiritual Attributes

Introduction to Division 2

In Division 2 I expound God's spiritual attributes: his incorporeality, animacy, faculty, morality, and personality. I cover his spiritual attributes in sections 6-10 as topics 11-22 as follows:

Section 6: Topic 11: God's Incorporeality: *The Majestic Form of God*
Section 7: Topic 12: God's Animacy: *The Vivacity and Omnipotence of God*
Section 8: Topics 13-15: God's Metaphysical Faculty
    Topic 13: God's Supreme Mind: *The Omniscience of God*
    Topic 14: God's Supreme Will: *The Sovereignty of God*
    Topic 15: God's Supreme Affection: *The Emotivity of God*
Section 9: Topics 16-21: God's Morality
    Topic 16: God's Moral Capacity and Character
    Topic 17: The Goodness of God
    Topic 18: The Holiness of God
    Topic 19: The Justice of God
    Topic 20: The Faithfulness of God
    Topic 21: God's Self-Esteem
Section 10: Topic 22: God's Personality: *The Trinity*

Section 6. God's Incorporeality: *The Majestic Form of God*

Introduction to Section 6:

Our epitomizing texts define the categories in which I present God's incorporeal form. *First*, Scripture introduces *the concept* of divine incorporeality (1 Tim. 6:16). This text depicts God's incorporeal form as *immortal*, "who only has immortality," *unapproachable*, "dwelling in light unapproachable," and *invisible*, "whom no man has seen, nor can see." Hendriksen expounds these aspects of God's incorporeality.[1] He says: "Every element stresses the incomparable greatness of God."[2] Our London Confession enlarges this concept: "a most pure spirit, invisible, without body, parts, or passions, who only hath immortality, dwelling in the light which no man can approach unto" (LCF 2:1). Accordingly, we first consider this biblical concept. *Second*, Scripture discloses *the display* of God's form:

---

[1] William Hendriksen, *New Testament Commentary: Pastoral Epistles* (Grand Rapids: Baker Book House, 1976), 205-208
[2] Ibid., 207

"they shall see his face" (Rev. 22:4). Accordingly, we survey its astounding display in divine appearances. *Third*, these texts commend the *practical application* of God's form: "to whom be honor and power eternal." Thus, we summarize its practical applications.

I. The Biblical Concept of Divine Incorporeality

We unfold the *unfathomable mystery* and *infinite majesty* of the Creator's incorporeal form.

A. The Unfathomable Mystery of Divine Incorporeality

Scripture defines God's incorporeal form by negation. Our Confession acknowledges this: "whose essence is known only to himself" (LCF 2:1). Thus, LCF defines his incorporeality negatively: invisible, immaterial ("without body"), indivisible ("without parts"), impassible ("without passions"), and immortal ("who only hath immortality"). We dare not pry further. We merely tend the fence around this mystery.

1. God is immaterial or non-material: "without body."[3]

I introduced this biblical testimony when we established the characteristics of a spiritual being. Jesus says: "a spirit has not flesh and bones, as you behold me having" (Luke 24:37-39). A spiritual being has no material body. Thus, the Supreme Spirit has no flesh or bones. Thus he is in sharp contrast with humans and animals. The Egyptians are "men and not God," and their horses are "flesh and not spirit" (Isa. 31:3). Unlike God, humans and horses have material bodies composed of flesh. Accordingly, Moses warns God's people to beware of idolatry: "for you *saw no manner of form* on the day that Jehovah spoke unto you . . . lest you corrupt yourselves and make yourselves a graven image in the form of any figure, the likeness of male or female" (Deut. 4:12, 15). The KJV renders this phrase as: "you beheld no similitude." The Hebrew word for "form" or "similitude" is תְּמֻנָה (timunah). BDB Lexicon says that it signifies "kind" or "species."[4] Sometimes it is also translated "likeness": "You shall not make unto you a graven image, nor any *likeness*" (Exod. 20:4; Deut. 5:8). An image is a concrete representation or replica. It displays the distinguishing traits of what it represents. Thus, Moses means that they saw no "concrete shape," nothing "fashioned out." They saw no *embodiment* of any kind. This emphasizes that God is non-material and without body. It also links immaterial with invisible.

---

[3] Deut. 4:12, 15; Isa. 31:3; Luke 24:37-39
[4] BDB, *Lexicon*, 568

2. *God is invisible: "whom no man has seen nor can see."*[5]

Scripture affirms this repeatedly and emphatically.[6] Bavinck cites this testimony.[7] Scripture declares that creation displays God's invisible attributes.[8] It affirms that Christ is the visible representation of the invisible God.[9] Jesus is visible because even now in glory he has a human body. In contrast, the human eye cannot see the Supreme Being because he has no body. Behold the mystery! God the Son has both a visible human nature and the invisible divine nature. Only God the Son took a human body.

3. *God is indivisible: "without parts."*

LCF adds "without parts." The Supreme Spirit does not have "*flesh and bones.*" Since he has no physical body, he does not have bodily members or parts. He cannot be divided or dissected. God's simplicity necessitates his indivisibility. Since God is all he is, his nature cannot be divided.

4. *God is impassible: "without passions."*[10]

Next LCF adds, "without passions." The word, *passion*, has various nuances.[11] In the singular, passion can depict suffering, especially Christ's suffering. Thus, it involves *vulnerability*, which is the capacity to be "acted on by external agents or forces." It can also denote ardent affection, a strong liking for something: for example: "a passion for sports." In the plural "passions" can signify capricious emotions, like blind rage: "emotions as distinguished from reason." "Passions" can also signify "intense, driving, or overmastering feelings" like bodily "appetites." Thus, God is "without passions" in at least three ways.

a. God is without "passions" because he is invulnerable to bodily suffering.

Our English word, "passion," in the singular occurs only once in the New Testament: "after his passion" (Acts 1:3). Christ's "passion" refers to his

---

[5] 1 Tim. 6:16

[6] *Exod. 33:20*: No man shall see me and live. *John 1:18*: No man has seen God at any time. *John 6:46*: Not that any man has seen the Father. *1 Tim. 1:17*: Now unto the king eternal, immortal, invisible, the only God, be honor and glory forever. *1 John 4:12, 20*: No man has beheld God at any time . . . he that loves not his brother whom he has seen, cannot love God whom he has not seen.

[7] Bavinck, *Doctrine of God*, 176

[8] *Rom. 1:20*: the invisible things of him, since the creation of the world, are clearly seen

[9] *Col.1:15*: the Son of his love . . . who is the image of the invisible God

[10] Footnote #629 cites further discussion of "without passions." I expound divine affections in Topic 15, God's Emotivity.

[11] *Webster's New Collegiate Dictionary*, editor Henry B. Woolf (Springfield, MA: G & C Merriam Company, 1980), 831

bodily suffering and vulnerability.[12] The Greek word translated "passion" is πασχω (pascho), which means, "to suffer." Scripture associates suffering with a material body: "when one member suffers all suffer with it" (1 Cor. 12:26); and, Christ "suffered being tempted" (Heb. 2:18). Again, Scripture limits Christian suffering to the bodily afflictions of this life: "after you have suffered a little while" (1 Pet. 5:10). The Supreme Spirit is invulnerable to the suffering and afflictions of bodily existence. He cannot suffer physical pain. External forces or agents cannot act upon him or hurt him. He is invulnerable to temptation. Thus, in this respect God is "without passion."

b. God is without "passions" because he is without bodily appetites.

God never experiences bodily appetites. An "appetite" is "an instinctive desire necessary for the preservation of life."[13] Since God has no body, he does not experience bodily appetites like hunger or thirst. In this respect also, he is without passion.

c. God is without "passions" because he does not have human emotions or carnal affections.

The plural, "passions," occurs twice in Scripture. Both occurrences depict human emotions: "we are men of *like passions*" (Acts 14:15), and "Elijah was a man of *like passions* with us" (James 5:17). The word translated "like passions" is ὁμοιοπαθης (homoiopathes). It means "similar feeling," or "the same quality of feeling."[14] Both passages intimate that sinful humans have "passions." Our *passions* make us unlike God, like sinners, and unfit to be an object of devotion (Acts 14:15). Our *passions* indispose us to fervent and effective prayer (James 5:17). Therefore, *passions* signify feelings tainted by sin. Therefore, God is without *passions*, because he is impeccable. His feelings are morally ideal. Further, human emotion is: "a psychic and physical reaction (as anger and fear) subjectively experienced as strong feeling and physiologically involving changes that prepare the body for immediate and vigorous action."[15] Thus, human "emotion" has both a spiritual and a physical aspect. When humans in an embodied state feel anger or fear, their body experiences physiological changes that prepare it for immediate and vigorous action. Thus, because God has no body, his feelings are not "human emotions." God feels *affections*, which are "the spiritual aspect of emotions." Thus, God is "without passions" in the sense

---

[12] Luke 22:15; 1 Pet. 2:21, 3:18

[13] *WNC Dictionary*, 54

[14] Bauer, Arndt, Gingrich; *A Greek-English Lexicon of the New Testament* (University of Chicago Press, 1957), 569

[15] *WNC Dictionary*, 369

that he does not feel either *human emotions* or *sinful affections*. Rather, he feels impeccable affections.

5. *God is immortal: "who only has immortality."*[16]

The word translated "immortality" is ἀθανασια (athanasia), literally, "without death" (1 Tim. 6:16). The word translated "immortal" is ἀφθαρτος (aphthartos), literally, "without corruption" (1 Tim. 1:17). God is both without corruption and without death.

Aphthartos depicts that which never decays. It depicts "the glory of the *incorruptible* God" (Rom. 1:23). A dead body experiences corruption, which is the process of deterioration. It decays and dissolves. The *incorruptible* God is incapable of decay or deterioration. Thus, *aphthartos* depicts the resurrection body: *"we must put on incorruption"* (1 Cor. 15:22). Thus, believers will receive a measure of immortality when God raises our bodies incorruptible. Thus, *aphthartos* also depicts our "incorruptible inheritance" reserved in heaven, which never fades away (1 Pet. 1:4). Again *aphthartos* describes God's incorruptible Word (1 Pet. 1:23). Again, it depicts the incorruptible graces of the Christian life (1 Pet. 3:4). Therefore, because God is incorruptible, his Word, his work of grace in the heart, his resurrection of the body, and his inheritance in heaven all abide forever, without decay.

Athanasia occurs in only one other passage: "this mortal must put on immortality" (1 Cor. 15:53-54). It depicts the resurrection bodies of the saints. This wonderful blessing of unending life has caused some to wonder why Paul says that *only God* has immortality. Matthew Henry says that God is the exclusive fountain and foundation of immortality so that any freedom from death and corruption that his people enjoy comes from him.[17] Thus, only God is *absolutely* immortal. He alone is immortal immutably and inherently. Only God is inherently incapable of death, decay, deterioration, and dissolution. Only God has underived life. All life comes from him.

B. *The Infinite Majesty of Divine Incorporeality: "dwelling in light unapproachable"*

When only God was, he was immaterial, invisible, indivisible, impassible, and immortal. His incorporeal being was always infinitely majestic, even

---

[16] *1 Tim. 1:17*: Now unto the king eternal, immortal [aphthartos], invisible, the only God, be honor and glory forever.
1 Tim. 6:16: who only has immortality [athanasia], dwelling in light unapproachable, whom no man has seen

[17] Matthew Henry, *Commentary*, 6:831

when there was no light to reveal it and no creatures to adore him.[18] After God says, "let there be light," he reveals his infinite majesty in creation. Paul describes the Creator's incorporeal majesty: "dwelling in light unapproachable." Now let's unpack this.

1. Dwelling

God's "dwelling" refers to his special presence with creation. God's special presence abides permanently in heaven: "heaven, your dwelling place" (1 Kings 8:30).

2. Dwelling in light

The psalmist meditates on God's greatness displayed in creation (Psalm 104). Leupold masters this psalm.[19] He notes that the psalmist structures his meditation using the order of the creation days:

> The first day: the light (104:2)
> The second day: the heavens (104:2-4)
> The third day: land and sea (104:5-12), vegetation (104:13-18)
> The fourth day: the heavenly bodies (104:19-23)
> The fifth day: sea creatures (104:24-26)
> The sixth day: all living things (104:27-30)
> The seventh day: God's refreshment (Exod. 31:17) and man's delight in creation (104:31-34)
> The conclusion: deliverance of creation from sinners (104:35)

The psalmist meditates on the work of the first day.[20] When God created light, he shrouded his special presence with it. Light is the garment under which he conceals his splendor. It covers his majestic greatness. Thus Moses humbly veiled his face, not for shame, but to conceal glory shining from it.

3. Light unapproachable

The light that emanates from God's special presence is lethal. Mortal men cannot even endure to look with open face at the sun shining in its strength. The light of the sun is so intense that staring at it causes permanent injury to our eyes. Similarly, the light of God's special presence is so bright that gazing at it is not merely blinding but lethal. Thus, God says to Moses: "You cannot see my face, for no man can see me and live" (Exod. 33:20). Thus,

---

[18] Ps. 145:3, 5

[19] H. C. Leupold, *Exposition of the Psalms*, (Grand Rapids: Baker Book House, 1974), 722-732

[20] *Ps. 104:1-2*: Bless Jehovah, O my soul; O Jehovah my God, you are very great. You are clothed with honor and majesty: Who covers yourself with light as a garment: who stretches out the heavens like a curtain.

Matthew Poole observes that God is: "continually compassed with a glory that is unspeakable . . . to which no man can in this life come nigh."[21] Again, Matthew Henry observes: "It is impossible that mortal eyes should bear the brightness of divine glory. No man can see God and live."[22] The mythical Medusa was so hideous in appearance that to see her caused insanity. The true God is so glorious in appearance that to see him would cause death. Therefore, we extol his infinite greatness as we sing the praise of our "immortal, invisible" God:[23]

> Immortal, invisible, God only wise,
> In light inaccessible hid from our eyes,
> Most blessed, most glorious, the Ancient of Days,
> Almighty, victorious, thy great Name we praise.
>
> Great Father of glory, pure Father of light,
> Thine angels adore, all veiling their sight;
> All praise we would render; O help us to see
> 'Tis only the splendor of light hideth thee!

II. The Profound Display of Divine Incorporeality: *Divine Appearances*

God's majesty is lethal to mortal men. Nevertheless, he has occasionally appeared to men and revealed some little part of his glory. Throughout history he discloses increasing measures of his majesty. He promises his people a greater display in heaven, and the most profound display when Christ returns. We now focus on divine appearances in theophanies, visions, and dreams, in the incarnation of God the Son, and in the eternal glory of heaven and the consummation.

A. Divine Appearances in Theophanies, Visions, and Dreams

The Old Testament records that God at times visibly displays his special presence to men in divine appearances, "theophanies," and in prophetic visions and dreams.

1. Divine appearances in theophanies[24]

Theophanies are visible and audible displays of God's special presence. In great condescension God allows people to see some of his glory. Scripture associates fear and mystery with these awesome experiences. God's Word records diverse visible displays of God's special presence. Jacob saw God

---

[21] Matthew Poole, *Commentary*, 3:789
[22] Matthew Henry, *Commentary*, 6:831
[23] *The Trinity Hymnal-Baptist Edition* (Suwanee, GA: Great Commission Publications, 1995), Hymn 35
[24] Gen. 32:30; Exod. 24:10-11, 33:20, 23; Num. 12:8; Judg. 13:22.

"face to face" and lived.[25] The elders of Israel "beheld God" and fellowshipped in his presence.[26] He concealed lethal aspects of his glory and allowed Moses to see his "back."[27] He spoke to him personally, "face to face."[28] Sampson's parents marvelled that they lived to declare that they had "seen God."[29]

2. Divine appearances in prophetic dreams and visions[30]

God has also revealed himself visually in visions and dreams. Mystery surrounds these revelations. God displays only a small aspect his majesty so that people survive the experience. In his sleep Jacob saw the "God of Abraham" and heard his voice.[31] In a vision God revealed his plan to judge the king of Israel.[32] When Isaiah envisioned Jehovah's glory, he was overwhelmed. He felt his own uncleanness. His vision of Christ prepared him for faithful service to the Lord.[33] Steven also saw a vision of Christ's glory. It aided him to face martyrdom with hope and grace.[34] Under the influence of God's Spirit, John saw a vision that portrayed God's sovereignty and wrath, spiritual warfare, and the hope of the saints.[35]

---

[25] *Gen. 32:30*: Jacob called the name of the place Peniel: for, he said, I have seen God face to face, and my life is preserved.

[26] *Exod. 24:10-11:* and they saw the God of Israel; and under his feet there appeared to be a pavement of sapphire, as clear as the sky itself. Yet he did not stretch forth his hand against the nobles of the sons of Israel; and they beheld God, and they ate and drank.

[27] *Exod. 33:20, 23*: You cannot see my face, for no man can see me and live . . . Then I will take my hand away and you shall see my back, but my face shall not be seen.

[28] *Num. 12:8:* With him I speak mouth to mouth, even openly and not in dark sayings; and he beholds the form of Jehovah.

[29] *Judg. 13:22:* So Manoah said to his wife, We shall surely die, for we have seen God. But his wife said to him, If Jehovah had desired to kill us, he would not have accepted a burnt offering

[30] Gen. 28:12-13, 16-17; 1 Kings 22:19; Isa. 6:1-2, 5; Acts 7:56 ; Rev. 4:2

[31] *Gen. 28:12-13, 16-17*: And he dreamed, and behold a ladder . . . the angels of God ascending and descending on it. And behold, Jehovah stood above it and said, I am the God of Abraham . . . And Jacob awaked out of his sleep, and he said, Surely Jehovah is in this place . . . And he was afraid, and said, How dreadful is this place! This is none other than the house of God.

[32] *1 Kings 22:19*: I saw Jehovah sitting on his throne, and all the host of heaven standing by him on his right hand and on his left

[33] *Isa. 6:1-2, 5*: I saw the Lord sitting upon a throne, high and lifted up; and his train filled the temple. Above him stood the seraphim . . . Then I said, Woe is me! for I am undone . . . for mine eyes have seen the king, Jehovah of hosts

[34] *Acts 7:56*: Behold, I see the heavens opened, and the son of man standing on the right hand of God

[35] *Rev. 4:2*: I was in the Spirit: and behold, there was a throne set in heaven, and one sitting

B. The Divine Appearance in the Incarnation

The most remarkable divine appearance is the incarnation. Paul describes this marvelous display: "who, existing in the form of God, counted not being on an equality with God as robbery, but emptied himself, taking the form of a servant" (Phil. 2:6-7). Prior to his incarnation, the Son was "in the form of God." He was invisible, immaterial, indivisible, impassible, and immortal. He dwelt in light unapproachable. For him, equality with the Father was not "something stolen," or "robbery." It was his rightful possession. Yet, he "emptied himself, taking the form of a servant." Remaining fully divine, he became, in addition, fully human. Thus he was "found in fashion as a man" (Phil. 2:8). He appeared as an ordinary man. Intense light did not drive people from his presence. Not even a halo of his former glory shone around him. What a marvel! God incarnate was veiled in human flesh. All the fullness of the Godhead dwells bodily in Christ (Col. 2:9). When Philip says: "Lord, show us the Father," he replies, "Have I been so long time with you, and do you not know me, Philip? He that has seen me has seen the Father" (John 14:8-9). Men conversed with him face to face. They touched and handled him.[36] Wicked men even dared to reproach, scourge, crucify, and kill him. O the depth of God's condescension! Humans often try to put our puny honor on display. He "humbles himself," veiling infinite splendor. Here we learn humility: "Have this mind in you which was also in Christ Jesus" (Phil. 2:5).

C. The Divine Appearance in Heaven and Eternity

God's people have long hoped and desired to behold God's glory in the world to come.[37] Christ teaches that all those, and only those, whose hearts God has purified with gospel grace will experience this blessed hope.[38] Christians desire to see our Lord Jesus face to face in glory. Some have called this sight of Christ's glory in heaven and eternity the "beatific vision." This vision of Christ's glory in the world to come will far surpass our present perception of his glory.[39] Only those who live in gospel holiness on earth will see Christ's glory in heaven.[40] Thus, our hope to see Christ motivates

---

on the throne.

[36] Luke 24:39; John 20:27; 1 John 1:1

[37] *Ps. 17:15*: I shall be satisfied, when I awake, with beholding your form

[38] *Matt. 5:8*: Blessed are the pure in heart: for they shall see God

[39] *1 Cor. 13:12*: now we see in a mirror, darkly; but then face to face.

[40] *Heb. 12:14*: Follow after peace with all men, and the sanctification without which no man shall see the Lord.

all genuine Christians to purify ourselves even as he is pure.[41] This hope gives comfort and strength in all our afflictions. God will abundantly fulfill our hope. All Christans will see Christ face to face and remain with him forever.[42]

III. Religious and Practical Applications of Divine Incorporeality

I conclude by summarizing five experiential applications of God's incorporeal form.

A. Repudiation of Idolatrous Worship (Deut. 4:12, 15)

God's incorporeality forbids worshiping God through statues or visible representations of any kind.

B. Appreciation of Christ's Infinite Dignity (Col. 2:9)

Christ is superior to all theophany. Christ's unique honor resides in his capacity to display all the fullness of the invisible God. Therefore, in Christ we have a vision of God's glory that far surpasses all the theophanies, visions, and dreams in the Old Testament combined. Thus we should appreciate Christ's infinite dignity. We should bless God for the privilege of seeing his glory in the face of Jesus Christ.

C. Imitation of Christ's Humility (Phil. 2:3-8)

God the Son dwelt in heaven in light unapproachable. He was invisible and invulnerable. Yet he veiled his majesty. Let us be of the same mind. As Christ humbled himself, let us also humble ourselves: "doing nothing through faction or through vainglory . . . each counting other better than himself; not looking each of you to his own things, but each of you to the things of others" (Phil. 2:3- 4).

D. Cultivation of Gospel Hope and Holiness (Heb. 12:14; 1 John 3:2-3)

Our hope to see Jesus prods us pursue gospel holiness "without which no man will see the Lord" (Heb. 12:14) because "every one who has this hope set on him purifies himself, even as he is pure" (1 John 3:3).

E. Adoration of God's Incorporeal Majesty (Ps. 104:1-2; 1 Tim. 6:16)

God dwells in light unapproachable. This incorporeal majesty elicits worship, reverence, and awe: "Bless Jehovah, O my soul; O Jehovah my God, you are very great. You are clothed with honor and majesty: Who covers yourself with light as a garment" (Ps. 104:1-2); and "whom no man

---

[41] *1 John 3:2-3*: we shall see him even as he is. Everyone that has this hope set on him purifies himself, even as he is pure.

[42] *Rev. 22:4*: they shall see his face.

has seen nor can see: to whom be honor and power eternal" (1 Tim. 6:16). Let us adore the Triune God for this splendor. Let us meditate on his glory until we say with awe: "All praise we would render; O help us to see 'Tis only the splendor of light hideth thee!" Let us contemplate Christ's glory until we exclaim: "Veiled in flesh the God-head see; Hail the incarnate Deity."[43]

---

[43] *Trinity Hymnal*, #168

Topic 12. The Vivacity and Omnipotence of God

"he is the living God . . . he delivers and rescues, and he works signs and wonders" (Dan. 6:26-27)

Section 7. God's Animacy: *The Vivacity and Omnipotence of God*

God's animacy embraces his supreme life and power. We have already established that life is an essential characteristic of spirits[1] and that Scripture explicitly connects God's life, power, and actions.[2] Gill[3] and Strong[4] recognize this connection and highlight it. Accordingly, notice how our epitomizing text categorizes divine animacy. *First*, the God of Daniel is "the living God." *Second*, God's supreme life stands closely connected to the permanent exercise and indomitable sway of his will: "the living God, and steadfast for ever, and his kingdom that which shall not be destroyed; and his dominion shall be even unto the end." *Third*, God's supreme life stands closely bound with his supernatural power and acts: "the living God . . . he delivers and rescues, and he works signs and wonders in heaven and in earth, who has delivered Daniel from the power of the lions." *In sum*, this text links God's life, purpose, and power. The living God acts on his own initiative. His supernatural actions stem from his unlimited ability to do all his holy will. Thus, we first expound God's supreme life, *vivacity*, then his supreme power, *omnipotence*.

Unit 1. The Vivacity of God

I call God's supreme life his *vivacity*. I derive this term from the Latin word, *vivax*, which means "long-lived." I unfold the concept and practical implications of God's supreme life.

I. The Concept of God's Vivacity

Note the *supremacy* of God's life and the *substance* of God's supreme life.

A. The Supremacy of God's Life[5]

God's life is ideal, self-sustained, unrestrained, unoriginated and unending. Consider three texts.

---

[1] James 2:26; Rev. 20:4

[2] *Dan. 6:26-27*: . . . for he is the living God, and steadfast for ever, and his kingdom that which shall not be destroyed; and his dominion shall be even unto the end: he delivers and rescues, and he works signs and wonders in heaven and in earth, who has delivered Daniel from the power of the lions. *Dan. 4:35*: he does according to his will . . . and none can stay his hand.
Mark 10:27: with God all things are possible

[3] Gill, *Body of Divinity*, 1:48, 71-76, 77-84

[4] Strong, *Systematic Theology*, 251-252

[5] John 5:26-27; 1 Tim. 6:16; 1 John 1:1-2

1. John 5:26-27[6]

This text depicts the Father's relationship with his incarnate Son: "because he is a son of man." The Supreme Being has self-existent life: "life in himself." It does not depend on creatures. Food sustained the life of Christ's human body. Yet the Person, God the Son, had self-sustaining life, even while he was incarnate on earth. This validates his claim to deity and leads back to the fence around the mystery.

2. 1 Tim. 6:16[7]

We just considered this text in connection with divine incorporeality. It confirms God's immutable life.

3. 1 John 1:1-2[8]

John describes God the Son as "the eternal life" who always was with the Father. Divine life is Trinitarian life. The Father, Son, and Spirit have unoriginated life. Thus God's life is utterly unique. No creature has unoriginated or triune life. Note the vast difference between the supreme life of the Creator and the derived life of animate creatures. Only the Creator's life is unoriginated, triune, independent, and inherently unchanging. Lenski affirms this unique supremacy of God's life.[9]

> in the Logos was 'life', life in the fullest, highest sense, the eternal, blessed life of God. The emphasis is on the phrase which heads the statement, 'in him' was life. This implies a contrast with all the living beings which came into existence through the creative act of the Logos. They all received life...They also are capable of death...The very attribute of the Logos is life, the life that corresponds with his being, forever inherent in his very essence, incapable of any hurt, subtraction, or deteriorating change.

---

[6] *John 5:26-27*: For as the Father has life in himself, even so he gave to the Son also to have life in himself: and he gave him authority to execute judgment, because he is a son of man.

[7] *1 Tim. 6:16*: the blessed and only Potentate, the King of kings, and Lord of lords; who only has immortality.

[8] *1 John 1:1-2:* That which was from the beginning, that which we have heard, that which we have seen with our eyes, that which we beheld, and our hands handled, concerning the Word of life (and the life was manifested, and we have seen, and bear witness, and declare unto you the life, the eternal life, which was with the Father, and was manifested unto us*).*

[9] Lenski, *Interpretation of John*, 38

B. The Substance of God's Supreme Life[10]

John intimates both the supremacy and substance of divine life. The Word is a divine Person distinct from the Father: "and the Word was with God." Yet, the Word is the Supreme Being: "and the Word was God." The phrase, "in him was life," declares the unoriginated life of the Triune God. This text identifies a twofold substance of God's supreme life. First, his life consists in his unoriginated capability to act deliberately: "all things were made through him; and without him was not anything made that has been made. In him was life." Second, his life consists in Trinitarian communion and fellowship: "the Word was with God . . . The same was in the beginning with God . . . In him was life." John underscores this connection of divine life with Trinitarian communion: "the Word of life . . . and the life was manifested, and we have seen, and bear witness, and declare unto you the life, the eternal life, which was with the Father: (1 John 1:2). Accordingly, I summarize the substance of God's vivacity as follows:

> God's vivacity, supreme life, consists both in his supreme capability to act spontaneously and deliberately and in his Trinitarian communion.

Now I focus briefly on each of these aspects of divine vivacity.

1. God's supreme life consists in his capability to act spontaneously and deliberately.

The living God acts on his own initiative. His unique ability to act purposefully and spontaneously is unoriginated, unlimited, self-sustaining, unchanging, and unending. Accordingly, Strong rightly defines God's life in conjunction with his spirituality as his purposeful "energy" and "activity":[11]

> The spirituality of God involves the two attributes of Life and Personality...Life is a simple idea and incapable of real definition...We cannot regard life in God as (a) Mere *process*, without a subject; for we cannot conceive of a divine life without a God to live it...Nor can we regard life as (b) Mere *correspondence* with outward condition and environment; for this would render impossible a life of God before the existence of the universe...Life is something more than a passive receptivity...(c) Life is rather *mental energy*, or energy of intellect, affection and

---

[10] *John 1:1-4*: In the beginning was the Word, and the Word was with God, and the Word was God. The same was in the beginning with God. All things were made through him; and without him was not anything made that has been made. In him was life; and the life was the light of men

[11] Strong, *Systematic Theology*, 251-252

> will. God is the living God, as having in his own being a source of being and activity, both for himself and others. Life means energy, activity, movement...If spirit in man implies life, spirit in God implies endless and inexhaustible life. The total life of the universe is only a faint image of that moving energy which we call the life of God.

The impact of death, the antonym of life, confirms this. A lifeless corpse is incapable of purposeful action. It can neither speak, nor move, nor act. This confirms this aspect of the substance of life.

2. God's supreme life consists in Trinitarian communion.

God's supreme life is not merely perpetual consciousness. Rather, it consists in the interpersonal communion of the Father, Son, and Spirit. This Trinitarian communion is ideal, unoriginated, self-sustaining, incorruptible, and unending. Note three ways that Scripture affirms this aspect of God's life.

a. God the Son eternally lived and subsisted in fellowship with God the Father[12]

God the Son is inherently alive: "the eternal life." He is a divine Person eternally subsisting in personal communion with the Father: "the eternal life, which was with the Father." Thus, the eternal life of the Supreme Being consists in Trinitarian fellowship.

b. The eternal life of believers consists in personal fellowship with the Triune God.[13]

Eternal life involves more than acting spontaneously. The divine life of the Son with the Father furnishes the pattern of the spiritual life of believers: "because I live, you shall live also. In that day you shall know that I am in my Father, and you in me, and I in you." Accordingly, the spiritual life of believers consists in fellowship with God. Christ explicitly identifies *eternal life* as personal fellowship with the Father and the Son: "this is life eternal, that they should know you." Matthew Henry confirms this observation.[14]

---

[12] *1 John 1:2, 5:11-13, 20*: we have seen, and bear witness, and declare unto you the life, the eternal life, which was with the Father, and was manifested unto us . . . God gave unto us eternal life, and this life is in his Son. He that has the Son has the life . . . that you may know that you have eternal life, even unto you that believe on the name of the Son of God . . . This is the true God, and eternal life.

[13] *John 14:19-20*: Yet a little while, and the world beholds me no more; but you behold me: because I live, you shall live also. In that day you shall know that I am in my Father, and you in me, and I in you. *John 17:3*: this is life eternal, that they should know you the only true God, and him whom you did send, Jesus Christ.

[14] Matthew Henry, *Commentary*, 5:1152

> *Life eternal* lies in the knowledge of God and Jesus Christ; the present principle of this life is the believing knowledge of God and Christ; the future perfection of that life will be the intuitive knowledge of God and Christ. Those that are brought into union with Christ, and live a life of communion with God in Christ, know, in some measure, by experience, what eternal life is..."

In sum: (1) the fellowship of the Father and Son is the pattern of the eternal life of believers; and (2) the eternal life of believers consists in fellowship with the Father and Son. In this way Scripture reveals that God's supreme life consists in the Trinitarian communion of the Father, Son, and Spirit.

c. The spiritual death of unbelievers consists in alienation from fellowship with the Triune God.[15]

Further confirmation comes from what Scripture teaches about spiritual death, the opposite of eternal life. Those in the state of sin act on their own initiative. Yet they are spiritually dead[16] because they are "alienated from the life of God" (Eph. 4:18). Thus, spiritual death is exclusion from the Trinitarian fellowship that constitutes God's supreme life. Again, a damned spirit retains even in hell the capability of acting on its own initiative.[17] Nevertheless, a soul in hell is not spiritually alive, but dead, because it is severed from personal communion with God (Rev. 20:4-6). Again, humans will be conscious in the lake of fire. Yet they will not be spiritually alive. They will experience "the second death."[18] This involves permanent exile from fellowship with God: "Depart from me, you cursed, into the eternal fire prepared for the devil and his angels ... And these shall go away into eternal punishment, but the righteous into eternal life" (Matt. 25:41, 46). What a horrible prospect! Thus, spiritual death in sin, hell, and the lake of fire confirm that God's supreme life consists in Trinitarian fellowship and communion.

Conclusion to the Concept of God's Veracity: historical recognition and biblical summary

Historical Recognition: commentators generally acknowledge that "*in him was life*" refers to spiritual and eternal life and that eternal life is the opposite

---

[15] *Eph. 4:18*: being darkened in their understanding, alienated from the life of God.
[16] Eph. 2:5; 1 Tim. 5:6
[17] Luke 16:23-31
[18] Rev. 20:14

of spiritual death. Two examples are Matthew Poole[19] and J. C. Ryle.[20] Further, Hendriksen defines God's life only in general terms as including all his attributes. Yet he also observes the close connection of spiritual life and personal communion with God.[21] Gill stops short of explicitly defining God's supreme life, but points in the right direction. He observes "degrees of life" and affirms that spiritual life most closely corresponds to God's life:[22]

> in order to apprehend somewhat of the life of God, for comprehend it we cannot, it may be necessary to consider life in the creatures, what that is; and by rising from the lowest degree of life, to a higher, and from that to a higher still, we may have some idea of the life of God...Life is a principle in the creature by which it moves by itself...In animals...there is the breath of life, which is common with the bodies of men...There is a higher degree of life still, which is in rational creatures, angels, and the souls of men; by which they are capable of performing acts within themselves...such as to understand, to will, to choose, and refuse; love and hate, etc. . . .But that which comes nearest to the life of God...is that which is in regenerate persons, who have a principle of spiritual life, grace, and holiness, implanted in them.

Hoeksema, explicitly identifies Trinitarian communion with God's life:[23]

> The Trinity is a perfect Threeness, a fulness of perfect divine life. In the Threeness of the Persons God lives perfectly...That divine trinitarian life is the life of the covenant...It is a life of the most perfect love, in which the three Persons of the Holy Trinity eternally find one another and are eternally united in the most perfect divine harmony in the bond of perfect union. Nowhere is there separation, nowhere disharmony in the divine life of friendship...The life of the divine Trinity is a life of the most intimate communion of friendship.

Biblical Summary: God's supreme life, *vivacity*, consists in his supreme capability to act spontaneously and intentionally and in his Trinitarian communion. Accordingly, Scripture affirms two aspects of human life: animate life, which is the capacity to move and act spontaneously; and eternal life, which is personal fellowship with the triune God. Animate life corresponds with God's supreme capacity to act spontaneously and

---

[19] Poole, *Commentary*, 3:279
[20] Ryle, *Expository Thoughts, John: Vol. 1*, 12
[21] Hendriksen, *Commentary on John*, 1:72
[22] Gill, *Body of Divinity*, 1:72-73
[23] Hoeksema, *Dogmatics*, 320-321

intentionally. Eternal or spiritual life corresponds with God's Trinitarian communion.

II. Practical Implications of God's Vivacity

Consider with me five experiential applications of God's supreme life.

A. God's Supreme Life Supports all Animate and Spiritual Life.

Since God alone has life in himself, he gives and takes life as it pleases him.[24] Our animate life totally depends on his life: "seeing he gives to all life and breath and all things . . . and in him we live and move and have our being" (Acts 17:25, 28). We should acknowledge him whenever we make or relate plans: "If the Lord will, we will both live, and do this and that" (James 4:15). Further, our spiritual life depends totally on Christ's life and our union with him by faith.[25] As our Creator supplies and sustains animate life, our Redeemer supplies and sustains spiritual life. We should thank God for animate and eternal life.

B. God's Supreme Life Grounds Stability, Reliability, and Certitude.

The Lord appeals to his life to underscore that his Word is irrevocable and inviolable: "as I live, says the Lord."[26] Men swear by the Lord's life to provide the ultimate assurance of their reliability: "*as Jehovah lives.*"[27] Thus, God's life is the foundation of all stability, reliability, and certitude.

C. God's Supreme Life Distinguishes Him from all Idols.

False gods and idols are dead. They can neither act on their own initiative nor enter into personal communion with anyone. Thus, Scripture stresses the contrast between all idols and the living God.[28] All service rendered to idols is futile and all hope in them is vain. In stark contrast, the Christian hope never fails: "you turned unto God from idols to serve the living and true God, and to wait for his Son from heaven, whom he raised from the dead, even Jesus, who delivers us from the wrath to come" (1 Thess. 1:9-10). Christian service is beneficial and hope in the living God will come to fruition.

D. God's Supreme Life Magnifies his Power.

God's supreme life is the fountain of omnipotence. Thus, it inspires dread

---

[24] John 5:26; 1 Tim. 6:16
[25] Gal. 2:20; Col. 3:3-4
[26] Num. 14:21, 28; Isa. 49:18; Jer. 22:24, 46:18; Ezek. 14:16, 18, 20, 17:16, 18:3; Zeph. 2:9; Rom. 14:11
[27] 1 Sam. 14:39, 45
[28] Ps. 115:1, 3; Isa. 44:12-20; 1 Thess. 1:9

and awe in mortals. The Israelites tremble when they hear the awesome sound of the voice of the living God and see the dreadful sights that accompany it.[29] This teaches us to revere his revealed will. Again, the writer of Hebrews warns all who profess faith in Christ never to return to the world because: "it is a fearful thing to fall into the hands of *the living God*."[30] This warns us never to provoke his wrath.

E. God's Supreme Life Spurs Communion with Him.

Although we should fear apostasy and God's wrath, we should not cower and hide from him. To the contrary, God's supreme life fosters a hearty appetite for communion with the living God. The psalmist longs to be where the living God "dwells," the place where he manifests his special presence with his people.[31] Peace, joy, comfort, and hope reside in God's special presence. Personal fellowship with the living God imparts encouragement, security, and blessing to the soul of his servants. Therefore, his saints, far from avoiding his special presence, long for that fellowship with the living God that is the very heart of spiritual life.[32] Thus, Paul exhorts the Corinthian church not to be yoked together with unbelievers. Every church, society of Christians, is a temple of "the living" God.[33] The living God dwells among his people. This obliges churches to keep the ungodly from their membership so that they may enjoy spiritual communion with him without hindrance and disruption. It also obliges Christians to mortify all defilement of outward deportment and inward disposition, with a view to uninterrupted communion with the living God through his Word and Spirit.[34]

---

[29] *Deut. 5:25-26*: for this great fire will consume us: if we hear the voice of Jehovah our God any more, then we shall die. For who is there of all flesh, that has heard the voice of the living God speaking out of the midst of the fire, as we have, and lived?

[30] *Heb. 10:30-31*: For we know him that said, Vengeance belongs unto me, I will recompense. And again, The Lord shall judge his people. It is a fearful thing to fall into the hands of the living God.

[31] *Ps. 42:1-2*: As the heart pants after the water brooks, so pants my soul after you, O God. My soul thirsts for God, for the living God: When shall I come and appear before God?

[32] *Ps. 84:1-2*: How amiable are your tabernacles, O Jehovah of hosts! My soul longs, yea even faints for the courts of Jehovah. My heart and my flesh cry out unto the living God.

[33] *2 Cor. 6:14-16*: Be not unequally yoked with unbelievers: for what fellowship does righteousness have with iniquity? or what communion has light with darkness? And what concord has Christ with Belial? Or what portion has a believer with an unbeliever? And what agreement has a temple of God with idols? For we are a temple of the living God; even as God said, I will dwell in them, and walk in them; and I will be their God, and they shall be my people

[34] 2 Cor. 7:1

Unit 2. The Omnipotence of God

Introduction: The word "*omnipotence*" comes from the Latin words, *potentia*, "power," and *omni*, "all." Thus, it describes God as the *Almighty*, the *All-Powerful*. Although God communicates power to men, his omnipotence is incommunicable. The power of creatures is derived, limited, and mutable. The Creator alone has supreme power that is ideal,[35] self-existent,[36] infinite,[37] eternal,[38] and unchangeable.[39] Scripture features the concept of omnipotence,[40] its display in creation, providence, and redemption,[41] and its relevance for experiential religion.[42] Charnock arranges his exposition accordingly.[43] His epitomizing text is: "the thunder of his power who can understand?" (Job 26:14). From this text he derives the general idea of God's power:[44]

> Infinite and incomprehensible power pertains to the nature of God, and is expressed in part in his works; or though there be a mighty expression of divine power in his works, yet an incomprehensible power pertains to his nature.

He then expounds this concept under four headings:[45]

> I. What this power is; or the nature of it: [*eight properties*] (363-379)
>
> II. Reasons to prove God to be omnipotent: [*four reasons*] (379-383)

---

[35] Gen. 18:14, 25

[36] Acts 17:25, 28

[37] Eph. 1:19-23, 3:20

[38] Rom. 1:20

[39] Isa. 40:28; Heb. 1:10-12

[40] *Dan. 4:34-35*: I blessed the Most High, and I praised and honored him that lives forever and ever . . . and he does according to his will in the army of heaven, and among the inhabitants of the earth; and none can stay his hand or say unto him, What are you doing?

[41] *Jer. 32:17-19*: Ah Lord Jehovah! Behold, you have made the heavens and the earth by your great power and by your outstretched arm; there is nothing too hard for you, who shows lovingkindness to thousands, and recompenses the iniquity of the fathers into the bosom of their children after them; the great, the mighty God, Jehovah of hosts is his name: great in counsel, and mighty in work.

[42] *Mark 10:27*: Then who can be saved? . . . With men it is impossible, but not with God: for all things are possible with God.

[43] Steven Charnock, *The Existence and Attributes of God*, 357-445

[44] Ibid., 361

[45] Ibid., 363-445

III. How his power appears: in creation, in government, in redemption (384-422)
IV. The Use (422-445): for instruction (422-437), comfort (437-440), and exhortation (440-445).

Similarly, we consider the *concept*, *display*, and *application* of omnipotence.

I. The Concept of God's Omnipotence

I begin with two misconceptions of omnipotence. Then I offer a biblical definition.

A. Two Misconceptions of Omnipotence

Bavinck[46] and Hodge[47] expose the serious errors of "*total*" and "*actual*" omnipotence.

1. The false doctrine of "total" or "absolute" omnipotence

Some falsely allege that God can do anything, even sin, or cease to exist, or make true equal false, or right equal wrong. Scripture refutes this error. It asserts plainly that his ideality, immutability, and sovereignty limit his power. He cannot do something he doesn't choose, want, and decide to do, because he is sovereign: "he does according to his will: (Dan. 4:35). He cannot lie,[48] or commit any other sin, or even be tempted to sin,[49] because he is ideal. He cannot deny himself,[50] or cease to be what he is, or change morally,[51] or make sin equal virtue, because he is immutable.

2. The false doctrine of "actual" omnipotence

We must also reject the error that claims that God can only do what he actually does. Some have dressed this old error in modern garb, and dubbed it *Process Theology*. Those who hold this error try to absolve God of blame for the evil they see in the world. They tell us that God is not responsible for evil because he can't do anything about it. They assure us that he would put an end to suffering if he could. This misguided effort to shield God disparages his credibility. It makes him a liar because his Word repeatedly

---

[46] Bavinck, *Doctrine of God*, 243
[47] Charles Hodge, *Systematic Theology*, 1:409-413
[48] *Titus 1:2*: in hope of eternal life, which God, who cannot lie, promised before times eternal. *Heb. 6:18*: by two immutable things, in which it is impossible for God to lie
[49] *James 1:13*: Let no man say when he is tempted, I am tempted of God; for God cannot be tempted with evil, and he himself tempts no man.
[50] *2 Tim. 2:13*: if we are faithless, he abides faithful; for he cannot deny himself
[51] *James 1:17*: Every good gift and every perfect gift is from above, coming down from the Father of lights, with whom can be no variation, neither shadow that is cast by turning

asserts his sovereignty over all things, even evil.[52] Jesus emphatically refutes actual omnipotence (Matt. 26:53): "Or do you think that I cannot beseech my Father, and he shall even now send me more than twelve legions of angels?" Christ could have asked his Father for an army of angels to deliver him from his enemies. He had that power, and could have used it, but he freely chose not to do so. He refrained from doing all he could have done. God's works do not exhaust his infinite potential.

B. A Biblical Definition of Omnipotence

Scripture connects God's will and power. God's sovereign will regulates the *concrete substance* of omnipotence: "he does according to his *will*," and "no *purpose* of yours can be restrained."[53] God's sovereign will is also the *supernatural instrument* of omnipotence. God needs no additional means. Sometimes he expresses this sovereign will verbally in a fiat: "he spoke and it was done."[54] Scripture also views God's power in the abstract. It thus uncovers the unlimited *fountain* or *source* of omnipotence, God's *infinite potentiality*.[55] Accordingly, I define omnipotence as follows:

> God can do anything and everything he wills to do, merely by willing it, since nothing can restrain him and nothing is too hard for him.

This definition features the *concrete substance*, the *supernatural instrument*, and the *unlimited fountain* of omnipotence. I now expound each aspect of this definition.

1. The concrete substance of omnipotence: "God can do anything and everything he wills to do"

Reformed theologians oft call this God's *ordinate* power, because it relates to what he *ordains*. For example, Berkhof, Bavinck, and Charnock affirm the close connection of God's will and power:

> The potentia ordinata can be defined as that perfection of God whereby He, through the mere exercise of His will, can realize whatsoever is present in His will or counsel[56]

> In agreement with Scripture Christian theology defines . . . God's ordinate power, as his ability to perform whatever he decrees . . . To be

---

[52] Gen. 50:20; Isa. 10:7; Eph. 1:11
[53] *Job 42:2*: I know that you can do all things, and that no purpose of yours can be restrained. *Dan. 4:34-35*: he does according to his will . . . and none can stay his hand
[54] *Ps. 33:9*: he spoke, and it was done; he commanded, and it stood fast
[55] *Gen.18:14*: Is anything too hard for Jehovah? *Mark 10:27*: all things are possible with God
[56] Berkhof, *Systematic Theology*, 80

sure, God's omnipotence consists in this, that he can do whatever he wants to do.[57]

the power of God is that ability and strength whereby he can bring to pass whatsoever he please, whatsoever his infinite wisdom can direct, and whatsoever the infinite purity of his will can resolve.[58]

What does this teach us about experiential religion? First, we should honor and praise the Almighty: "I blessed the Most High, and I praised and honored him that lives forever and ever . . . and he does according to his will" (Dan. 4:34-35). The pagan king learned this lesson the hard way. Let us learn it from Scripture, not from severe judgments by which he humbles those who despise him. Second, we should humbly face our limitations: "all the inhabitants of the earth are reputed as nothing" (Dan. 4:35). Omnipotence exposes the arrogance and fraud of secular humanism. Secular humanism boasts that humans can be anything we want to be, and do everything we want to do, if we just have confidence in ourselves. What delusion! The truth is that we depend totally on God for life and strength: "seeing he himself gives to all life, and breath, and all things," (Acts 17:25), and, "if the Lord will, we shall both live, and do this or that" (James 4:15). Third, we should not charge God foolishly, but trust him, even in severe affliction: "I know that you can do all things, and that no purpose of yours can be restrained . . . now mine eye sees you: Wherefore I abhor myself and repent in dust and ashes" (Job 42:2, 6). Dear Christian, God's purpose to work everything together for your good cannot fail. God can bestow blessing out of what you see as the tangled wreckage of your life. Remember his omnipotence.

2. *The supernatural instrument of omnipotence*: "merely by willing it"

God needs only to will whatever he pleases, and it happens. He requires no other means. He sometimes expresses his sovereign will verbally, in a fiat. Thus, he created supernaturally through his Word: "he spoke, and it was done; he commanded, and it stood fast" (Ps. 33:9). The Almighty can never lose this ability to work miraculously, either without means, or above them, or against them, at his pleasure. Thus, the omnipotent Christ often worked merely by asserting his will: "I will; be thou made clean" (Matt. 8:3). Since God's Word expresses his will, Scripture closely associates his Word and his power. His Word, like a hammer, smashes rock to pieces.[59] Like a sharp

---

[57] Bavinck, *Doctrine of God*, 243-244
[58] Charnock, *The Existence and Attributes of God*, 364
[59] Jer. 23:29

sword, it cuts apart men's inner recesses.[60] This capability is incommunicable. It proves that God's power is infinitely superior to men's. It reveals the unfathomable glory of his supreme power. Thus Hodge says:[61]

> God can do whatever he wills...With God means are unnecessary. He wills, and it is done...This simple idea of the omnipotence of God, that He can do without effort, and by a volition, whatever He wills, is the highest conceivable idea of power, and is that which is clearly presented in the Scriptures.

3. The unlimited fountain of omnipotence: "since nothing can restrain him and nothing is too hard for him"

Scripture labels God's potential in absolute and superlative terms: "all things are possible with God," and "there is nothing too hard for you," and "you can do all things, and no purpose of yours can be restrained."[62] These statements peer beyond what God ordains into the expanse of what he theoretically could do. They view his power abstractly. How much more could God do than he actually does? What limits his potential? These questions point us to the mystery of his *infinite potentiality*. Scripture presents God's infinite potential in relation to resistance, difficulty, and feasibility: in relation to *resistance*, "none can stay your hand," and "no purpose of thine can be restrained"; to *difficulty*, "nothing is too hard for you"; and to *feasibility*, "you can do all things," and "all things are possible with God." No opposition can thwart God. No problem is too complex for God. No task is too arduous for him. Infinite potential dumbfounds us (Job 26:14). Thus Paul says: "him that is able to do exceeding abundantly above all that we ask or think" (Eph. 3:20). Berkhof, Bavinck, and Charnock affirm God's infinite potential:

> the actual exercise of God's power does not represent its limits. God could do more than that, if He were so minded. In that sense we can speak of the *potentia absoluta*, or absolute power of God.[63]

> In agreement with Scripture Christian theology defines God's absolute power as his ability to do whatever is in harmony with all his perfections, i.e., with his being.[64]

> *Absolute*, is that power whereby God is able to do that which he will not do, but is possible to be done; *ordinate* is that power whereby

---

[60] Heb. 4:12
[61] Charles Hodge, *Systematic Theology*, 1:407
[62] Mark 10:27; Jer. 32:7; Job 42:2
[63] Berkhof, *Systematic Theology*, 80
[64] Bavinck, *Doctrine of God*, 243

> God does that which he has decreed to do...which are not distinct powers, but one and the same power: his ordinate power is part of his absolute; for if he had not a power to do everything that he could will, he might not have a power to do everything that he does will.[65]

Reformed theologians often call God's infinite potential his *"absolute"* power. Charnock prudently says that his ordinate power falls within its scope. To express this connection I reason from God's concrete power to his abstract potential that undergirds it: "God can do anything and everything he wills to do, merely by willing it, *since* nothing can restrain him and nothing is too hard for him." Charnock also wisely notes that God has, not two distinct powers, but one. Although Bavinck, Berkhof, and Charnock discretely distinguish *absolute* from *ordinate* power, we must use caution. Some use the term "absolute" to promote the error of total omnipotence. Berkhof and Hodge warn about this misuse of the term:

> Reformed theology rejects this distinction in the sense in which it was understood by the Scholastics, who claimed that God by virtue of his absolute power could effect contradictions, and could even sin and annihilate himself.[66]

> By absolute power, as understood by the schoolmen and some of the later philosophers, is meant power free from all the restraints of reason and morality. According to this doctrine, contradictions, absurdities, and immoralities, are all within the scope of the divine power. Nay, it is said that God can annihilate Himself.[67]

Further, Hodge defines the good sense of the term "absolute" power differently from Berkhof, Bavinck, and Charnock. He uses the term, *absolute,* to refer to the supernatural instrumentality of omnipotence:

> A distinction is commonly made between the *potentia absoluta* and the *potentia ordinata* of God. By the latter [ordinate] is meant the efficiency of God, as exercised uniformly in the ordered operation of second causes; by the former [absolute], his efficiency, as exercised without the intervention of second causes. Creation, miracles, immediate revelation, inspiration, and regeneration, are to be referred to the *potentia absoluta* of God; all his works of providence to his *potentia ordinata*. This distinction is important, as it draws the line between the natural and supernatural.[68]

---

[65] Charnock, *The Existence and Attributes of God*, 363
[66] Berkhof, *Systematic Theology*, 80
[67] Charles Hodge, *Systematic Theology*, 1:409
[68] Ibid., 1:410

Although Hodge admirably defends God's supernatural power, he does not mean by "absolute" power what Berkhof, Bavinck, and Charnock mean. Thus, men speak of "absolute" power in three different senses. For false teachers, "absolute" power means unprincipled power, divorced from virtue and wisdom. For Berkhof, Bavinck, and Charnock, "absolute" power means infinite potentiality. For Hodge, "absolute" power means supernatural power, exercised without means. I mention this with some reluctance, desiring only to dispel any confusion that your assigned reading caused.

What is the practical relevance of God's infinite potentiality? *First*, we should realize that all rebellion against him is futile.[69] Who can conquer an adversary whose power cannot be restrained? Humans dare to challenge God because they have failed to learn this simple lesson. *Second*, we should trust and believe him, even when what he says he has done, or will do, seems "scientifically" impossible. The Lord taught Sarah this lesson in his gentle rebuke.[70] God says he created the universe, out of nothing, in six days. He says he made Adam from dust, and Eve from Adam's rib. Godless science says these things are impossible. We should believe God, rather than men, for "nothing is too hard for the Lord." God says he sent supernatural plagues on Egypt. He says he supernaturally opened the Red Sea and Jordan River. Unbelieving critics say all claims of supernatural intervention are false. They allege that there must be some natural explanation. We should believe God, rather than men. God says Christ was conceived miraculously and raised bodily from the dead. He says we too shall be raised. He says that all the wicked shall be damned and that we shall dwell forever in the new heavens and earth. The wicked scoff at all this. They tell us the virgin birth is a lie, the resurrection a myth, hell a scare tactic, and heaven a pipe dream. We should believe God, rather than men. *Third*, we should remember that God can save even the most hardened sinner through the gospel: "Then who can be saved . . . With men it is impossible, but not with God: for all things are possible with God" (Mark 10:27). We live in a society where few have much interest in spiritual things. Many focus on material prosperity first and foremost. We should not loose heart. God can save multitudes from idolatrous love of money and pleasure, for the things impossible with men are possible with God.

II. The Display of God's Omnipotence

We now survey the display of God's supreme power in creation, providence, and salvation.

---

[69] Dan. 4:35
[70] Gen. 18:13-14

A. Omnipotence Displayed in Creation[71]

Jeremiah closely connects omnipotence with creation. God created the universe, ultimately from nothing, merely by the fiat of his will: "By faith we understand that the worlds have been framed by the word of God, so that what is seen has not been made out of things which appear" (Heb. 11:3). The Psalmist affirms this: "By the word of Jehovah were the heavens made, and all the host of them by the breath of his mouth . . . he spoke, and it was done; he commanded, and it stood fast" (Ps. 33:6, 9). Scripture records this awesome process.[72] It repeats six times that what he spoke happened.[73]

How should we respond? We should "stand in awe" and "fear" our Creator: "Let all the earth fear Jehovah, and all the inhabitants of the world stand in awe of him. For he spoke, and it was done" (Ps. 33:8-9). We should also rejoice in him: "Rejoice in Jehovah, O you righteous . . . Give thanks unto Jehovah . . . Sing unto him. . . For the Word of Jehovah is right; and all his work is done in faithfulness . . . By the Word of Jehovah were the heavens made" (Ps. 33:1-4, 6). To respond with joy and awe we must have faith: "*By faith* we understand that the worlds have been framed by the word of God." Thus, the false doctrine of evolution destroys both the fear of God and gratitude to him. Any society that denies creation will suffer the baneful fruits of that unbelief. When people don't stand in awe of their Creator, they give themselves with gusto to sin and perversion. When people lack gratitude to their Maker and joy in his work, they seek selfish pleasure and enjoyment any way they can. Evolution is not an innocent scientific theory. It is a doctrinal cancer with grievous moral consequences.

B. Omnipotence Displayed in Providence[74]

Jeremiah features God's providential rule over the righteous and the wicked: "who shows lovingkindness . . . and recompenses the iniquity." He shows

---

[71] *Jer. 32:17*: Behold, you have made the heavens and the earth by your great power and by your outstretched arm; there is nothing too hard for you

[72] Gen. 1:1-31

[73] *Gen. 1:3*: And God said, Let there be light: and there was light . . . *1:6-7*: And God said, Let there be a firmament . . . and it was so . . . *1:9*: And God said, Let the waters under the heavens be gathered together into one place, and let the dry land appear: and it was so . . . *1:11*: And God said, Let the earth put forth grass . . . and it was so . . . *1:14-15*: And God said, Let there be lights in the firmament of heaven . . . to give light upon the earth: and it was so . . . *1:24*: And God said, Let the earth bring forth living creatures after their kind . . . and it was so.

[74] *Jer. 32:17-19*: there is nothing too hard for you, who shows lovingkindness to thousands, and recompenses the iniquity of the fathers into the bosom of their children after them; the great, the mighty God, Jehovah of hosts is his name: great in counsel, and mighty in work; whose eyes are open upon all the ways of the sons of men, to give every one according to his ways, and according to his doings.

the mammoth scope of God's providential work: "who shows lovingkindness to thousands," and its perpetual duration: "and recompenses the iniquity of the fathers into the bosom of their children after them." Next, he uncovers the roots of divine government, omniscience and justice: "whose eyes are open upon all the ways of the sons of men, to give every one according to his ways, and according to his doings." He shows lovingkindness to the righteous and recompenses the iniquity of the wicked, because his omniscient eyes are open upon all the ways of men, and because his impeccable justice renders to each in accord with their deeds.

God's work of providential rule is incomprehensible. In this generation alone he carefully monitors the ways of about six billion people from cradle to grave. Yet this does not begin to exhaust what God does in providence. He also controls the government of all the nations,[75] their boundaries, and their duration.[76] He even personally controls every event in the realm of nature.[77] In addition, God performs the providential work of preservation. He sustains every created thing, whether visible or invisible, animate or inanimate. He gives to all life, and breath, and all things.[78] This infinite power by which God works in providence is overwhelming.

How then should we respond to this providential display of his supreme power? We should seek the Lord and trust him in all our difficulties: "But as for me, I would seek unto God, and unto God would I commit my cause; who does great things and unsearchable, marvelous things without number" (Job 5:8-9). Although Job's friend misjudged his case, his counsel was good in principle. We should also commit our just cause to the Lord who governs faithfully: "Wherefore let them also that suffer according to the will of God commit their souls in well-doing unto a faithful Creator" (1 Pet. 4:19).

C. Omnipotence Displayed in Salvation

We consider God's supreme power displayed in four aspects of salvation: (1) salvation pictured in redemption from Egypt; (2) accomplished by Christ; (3) applied to Christians; and (4) completed in glory.

---

[75] Dan. 4:25
[76] Acts 17:26
[77] Matt. 5:45
[78] Heb. 1:3; Acts 17:25

1. Omnipotence displayed in the Old Testament picture of salvation[79]

Redemption from Egypt is but a shadow of redemption from sin. God displays his power in redemption from Egypt and the conquest of Canaan. He first manifested his great power to Israel when he delivered them from slavery with outstretched arm, great terror, signs, wonders, and plagues. He sealed this awesome display when he opened the Red Sea for his people and covered their enemies in it. He displayed his supreme power many times in the wilderness. He provided manna from heaven and water from a rock. He displayed his supreme power again when he drove out the Canaanites and gave Israel their land. He opened the Jordan, toppled the walls of Jericho, and made the sun stand still in the sky. In the days of the judges he repeatedly displayed his supreme power when he delivered his people by the hand of Gideon, Samson, and others. Time would fail me to enumerate the many displays of his power to the kings of Israel and Judah. Jeremiah wonders how the immanent overthrow of Jerusalem harmonizes with God's command to buy a field.[80] God responds to his confusion by appealing to his supreme power (32:27): "is anything too hard for me?" The Lord pulls back the veil of the future. He describes the certain fall of Jerusalem,[81] the return from captivity, and the era of the new covenant.[82] Then he addresses Jeremiah's concern about the field.[83] He moves Jeremiah to trust him. The fall of Jerusalem is not the final chapter in the history of God's people. Men will buy fields again and call witnesses. Thus, we should trust God when we are perplexed about our duty. We should simply do what he says, and leave the consequences with him.

2. Omnipotence displayed in the accomplishment of salvation

We consider the display of omnipotence in Christ's birth, life, death, and resurrection.

---

[79] *Jer. 32:17, 20-22*: Ah Lord Jehovah! Behold . . . there is nothing too hard for you . . . who did set signs and wonders in the land of Egypt . . . and did bring forth your people out of the land of Egypt with signs, and with wonders, and with a strong hand, and with an outstretched arm, and with great terror, and gave them this land.
[80] Jer. 32:23-26
[81] Jer. 32:28-35
[82] Jer. 32:36-42
[83] Jer. 32:43-44

a. Omnipotence displayed in Christ's virgin conception and birth[84]

Scripture explicitly asserts that Mary was a virgin before Jesus was conceived, when he was conceived, and until he was born (Matt. 1:20, 25). His conception was the result, not of sexual activity, but of supernatural activity. The supreme power of God worked in Mary by the agency of the Holy Spirit: "the Holy Spirit shall come upon you, and *the power of the Most High* shall overshadow you."

b. Omnipotence displayed in Christ's public ministry and life

Throughout his life the Lord Jesus furnished graphic displays of his omnipotence. He repeatedly expressed his sovereign will verbally with a fiat, in a manner strikingly similar to the fiats of creation.[85]

c. Omnipotence displayed in Christ's crucifixion and death[86]

"The weakness of God" provides the most astonishing display of his omnipotence. God incarnate accomplishes his work even while he hanging on a cross in unparalleled human weakness: "for he was crucified through weakness" (2 Cor. 13:4). Christ even reveals supreme power through the cross, the epitome of helplessness, disgrace, and shame. When he accomplishes salvation, God works not simply above human power, but against it. For humans the cross epitomizes inability to protect yourself or

---

[84] *Luke 1:31, 34-35*: And behold, you shall conceive in your womb, and bring forth a son, and shall call his name Jesus . . . And Mary said to the angel, How shall this be, seeing I know not a man? And the angel answered and said unto her, The Holy Spirit shall come upon you, and the power of the Most High shall overshadow you: wherefore also the holy thing which is begotten shall be called the Son of God.

[85] *Matt. 8:2-3*: there came to him a leper and worshipped him, saying, Lord, if you will, you can make me clean. And he stretched forth his hand, and touched him, saying, I will; be thou made clean. And straightway his leprosy was cleansed.
Matt. 8:16: they brought to him many possessed with demons: and he cast out the spirits with a word
Matt. 8:26-27: Then he arose, and rebuked the winds and the sea; and there was a great calm. And the men marveled, saying, What manner of man is this, that even the winds and the sea obey him?
Matt. 9:2, 6-8: they brought to him a man sick of the palsy, lying on a bed . . . then he says to the sick of the palsy, Arise, and take up your bed, and go unto your house. And he arose, and departed to his house. But when the multitudes saw it, they were afraid, and glorified God.

[86] *1 Cor. 1:18, 22-25*: For the word of the cross is to them that perish foolishness; but unto us who are saved it is the power of God . . . Seeing that Jews ask for signs, and Greeks seek after wisdom: but we preach Christ crucified, unto the Jews a stumblingblock, and unto Gentiles foolishness; but unto them that are called, both Jews and Greeks, Christ the power of God, and wisdom of God. Because the foolishness of God is wiser than men; and the weakness of God is stronger than men.

accomplish your purposes. Thus, they taunted him: "He saved others; himself he cannot save . . . Let him come down from the cross, and we will believe on him" (Matt. 27:42). The Jews wanted a display of "power." They wanted wonders. They wanted him to conquer Rome by unfastening himself from the cross. In their minds death on a Roman cross proved his impotence. Here is the marvel. What men regard as the height of impotence, God employs as the vehicle of omnipotence! The omnipotent Christ, through his own weakness, overpowers his enemies: "the weakness of God is stronger than men." Through the cross he puts away sin, destroys death, conquers the devil, vanquishes hell, and overcomes the grave. Our God is great and greatly to be praised. Paul shows us the practical import of this display: "God chose the weak things of the world, that he might put to shame the things that are strong . . . and the base things of the world, and the things that are despised . . . that no flesh should glory before God . . . He that glories, let him glory in the Lord" (1 Cor. 1:27-29, 31). God must have preeminence in the church. Divisions arise, as in Corinth (1 Cor. 1:10-13), if we place too much stock in men's powers. If we make gifted men the center of attention and loyalty, we engender strife and rob God of glory. God holds this display of his power before us to wean us from fascination with impressive men, to prevent a party spirit in the church, and to teach us to glory in him alone for salvation.

d. Omnipotence displayed in Christ's resurrection and ascension

Jesus is no longer dead but alive, not sentimentally in the thoughts of his followers, or in legend, but in reality and history. His human soul stands forever reunited with his once dead body, which arose from its grave, and now lives again.[87] Scripture explicitly attributes Christ's resurrection to God's power.[88] Christ's bodily resurrection certifies that God can even control death. What practical relevance does this have? Belief in Christ's bodily resurrection is the essential foundation of true Christianity.[89] When people deny Christ's resurrection, they reject omnipotence, make shipwreck concerning the faith, and show themselves devoid of saving religion. We must see such for what they really are, deceivers and unbelievers. We must

---

[87] Luke 24:36-43; John 20:24-29

[88] *1 Cor. 6:14*: God both raised the Lord, and will raise us up through his power. *2 Cor. 13:4*: he was crucified through weakness, yet he lives through the power of God. *Eph. 1:19-20*: the exceeding greatness of his power to us-ward who believe, according to that working of the strength of his might which he wrought in Christ, when he raised him from the dead, and made him to sit at his right hand in the heavenly places.

[89] *Rom. 10:9*: if you shall confess with your mouth Jesus as Lord, and shall believe in your heart that God raised him from the dead, you shall be saved. *1 Cor. 15:17*: if Christ has not been raised, your faith is vain; you are yet in your sins.

cease to be impressed by their degrees, or intimidated by their pronouncements. We must be ashamed of them, as they are ashamed of Scripture. We must no longer call them "brethren," or include them on our seminary faculties, or welcome them to our pulpits.

3. Omnipotence displayed in the application of salvation

The Christian life cannot be accounted for merely in natural terms. Supernatural power fuels Christian experience. The supreme power that raised Jesus from the dead produces the Christian life: "the exceeding greatness of his power to us-ward who believe, according to that working of the strength of his might which he wrought in Christ, when he raised him from the dead" (Eph. 1:19-20). God displays this power both in the inception and in the continuation of the Christian life.

a. Omnipotence displayed in the inception of the Christian life

God confers spiritual life on dead sinners by supernatural power. Only omnipotence can turn a sinner into a Christian. If salvation were left up to sinners, no one could ever be saved: "Then who can be saved? . . . With men it is impossible, but not with God: for all things are possible with God" (Mark 10:27). The Christian life begins at conversion, when sinners repent and believe the gospel. This saving response to the gospel results from God's power, exerted according to his own eternal purpose: "knowing, brethren beloved of God, your election, how that our gospel came not unto in word only, but also in power, and in the Holy Spirit, and in much assurance" (1 Thess. 1:4-5). Thus, a Christian is God's workmanship, a new divine creation.[90] How should we respond? We must take no credit, but give God all the glory for our conversion: "not of works, that no man should glory." Further, we must pursue that life of godliness and benevolence for which he re-created us: "created in Christ Jesus for good works." This should also greatly encourage us. Take heart dear Christian. God loved you so much, even when you were dead in your sins, that his supreme power saved you. You didn't merit it: "by grace you have been saved." Therefore, if the omnipotent God delivered you from sin when you were his enemy, he will never fail or forsake you now that you are his beloved child.

b. Omnipotence displayed in the continuation of the Christian life

Peter assures us that the God who gave spiritual life to us will preserve and protect us by his supreme power until we reach heaven at last: "who *by the power of God* are guarded through faith unto a salvation ready to be revealed in the last time" (1 Pet. 1:5). God will finish the work he started at

---

[90] Eph. 2:10

conversion: "he who began a good work in you will perfect it until the day of Jesus Christ" (Phil. 1:6). His power continually produces in us the desire and effort to please him: "it is God who works in you both to will and to work, for his good pleasure (Phil. 2:13). Peter affirms the complete sufficiency of God's power in the Christian life: "his divine power has granted unto us all things that pertain unto life and godliness" (2 Pet. 1:3). How should we respond? We should strive to be obedient with holy fear: "work out your own salvation with fear and trembling, for it is God who works in you" (Phil. 2:12-13). We must put away carnal confidence. If we were left to ourselves, we would make shipwreck of our lives. We must humbly face our remaining sin and spiritual impotence: "apart from me you can do nothing" (John 15:5). Nevertheless, we should have a firm confidence that by God's power we will endure in faith and good works unto the end: "I can do all things in him that strengthens me" (Phil. 4:13). Godly confidence is Christ-centered. It grows not from self-righteousness and pride, but from faith in God's promises and power. We should also rejoice in those things that testify most emphatically that the power of the Christian life comes from God.[91] Our "thorns in the flesh" display his supreme power through our weakness. They make us depend less on ourselves and more on his power.

4. Omnipotence displayed in the completion of salvation

The completion of salvation will display omnipotence in the second coming of Christ, in the glorification of the church, in the damnation of the wicked, and in the transformation of the universe.

a. God will display omnipotence in the second coming of Christ.

The Lord's return will display God's supreme power.[92] When he appears again, he will not veil his glory or robe his power in weakness. This calls us reject the false notion that his second coming has already happened secretly (Mark 13:21-25). It also calls Christians to wait patiently for him to avenge wrongs done to us: "with the angels of his power in flaming fire, rendering vengeance" (2 Thess. 1:7-8).

---

[91] *2 Cor. 12:9-10*: he has said unto me, My grace is sufficient for you: for my power is made perfect in weakness. Most gladly therefore will I rather glory in my weaknesses, that the power of Christ may rest upon me. Wherefore I take pleasure in weaknesses, in injuries, in necessities, in persecutions, in distresses, for Christ's sake: for when I am weak, then am I strong.

[92] *Mark 13:26*: then shall they see the Son of man coming in the clouds with great power and glory. *2 Thess. 1:7*: the revelation of the Lord Jesus from heaven with the angels of his power.

b. God will display omnipotence in the glorification of the church.

God will glorify his people by the very omnipotence with which he raised Jesus.[93] He will glorify the church when Christ returns: "that he might present the church to himself a glorious church" (Eph. 5:26). The resurrection of each Christian is a vital part of this glorification.[94] How can God do it? Beasts have devoured some bodies; others have been burned and scattered; others buried in the depths of the sea. I answer simply: "Is anything too hard for Jehovah?" This teaches Christians to treat our bodies with dignity and consecration, not to degrade them by sexual perversion: "the body is not for fornication, but for the Lord; and the Lord for the body: and God both raised the Lord, and will raise us up through his power" (1 Cor. 6:13-14). It also teaches Christians to comfort each other with our hope of glory: "Wherefore, comfort one another with these words" (1 Thess. 4:18). We should remind each other, especially in sorrow, affliction, difficulty, weariness, disappointment, failure, and shame, that church history has a happy ending through the supreme power of God. It also calls us to rejoice and praise God for our hope of glory.[95]

c. God will display omnipotence in the eternal damnation of the wicked.

Scripture closely associates God's supreme power with his eternal wrath: "What if God, willing to show his wrath, and *to make his power known*, endured with much longsuffering the vessels of wrath fitted unto destruction" (Rom. 9:22); and again, "who shall suffer punishment, even eternal destruction from the face of the Lord and *from the glory of his might, when he shall come*" (2 Thess. 1:9-10); and again, "After these things I heard as it were a great voice of a great multitude in heaven, saying, Hallelujah; Salvation, and glory, *and power*, belong to our God: for true and righteous are his judgments; for he has judged the great harlot, her that corrupted the earth with her fornication, and he has avenged the blood of his servants at her hand" (Rev. 19:1-2). In this ultimate display of omnipotent wrath, he will resurrect, judge, and punish all his enemies. When he vindicates and

---

[93] *1 Cor. 6:14*: God both raised the Lord, and will raise us up through his power.

[94] *1 Cor. 15:51-52*: Behold, I tell you a mystery: We all shall not sleep, but we shall all be changed, in a moment, in the twinkling of an eye, at the last trump: for the trumpet shall sound, and the dead shall be raised incorruptible, and we shall be changed. *1 Thess. 4:16-17*: For the Lord himself shall descend from heaven with a shout, with the voice of the archangel, and with the trump of God: and the dead in Christ shall rise first; then we that are alive, that are left, shall together with them be caught up in the clouds, to meet the Lord in the air: and so we shall ever be with the Lord.

[95] *Rev. 19:6-7*: Hallelujah: for the Lord our God, the Almighty, reigns. Let us rejoice and be exceeding glad, and let us give the glory unto him: for the marriage of the Lamb has come, and his wife has made herself ready.

rewards the righteous, he will condemn and punish the wicked.[96] Christ will raise them through his verbal fiat.[97] Omnipotence will insure that they keep this appointment for judgment.[98] He will cast them, body and soul, into the lake of fire.[99] They will suffer torment and anguish without respite forever.[100] This is unfathomable. Therefore, each of us should make sure that we are right with God. We should do our best to get and keep a good conscience.[101]

d. God will display omnipotence in the final transformation of the universe.
At Christ's return, the Almighty, by his Word, will create a new cosmos.[102] As the omnipotent God made this universe by verbal fiat, in this very way he will consume it in fire. As an entire generation of sinners perished in the worldwide flood, so also, the final generation of evil humanity will perish in that cosmic fire.[103] Then the Almighty will create new heavens and a new earth as a home for his glorified church. What a dreadful display of omnipotence! Who can fathom the supreme power by which the Creator will fashion a new cosmos? Therefore, we should live holy lives in ardent hope of Christ's return.[104]

III. The Practical Relevance of God's Omnipotence

I now summarize and collate experiential applications of God's omnipotence. I follow the path marked out by Charnock. God's supreme power offers God's people instruction, comfort, and exhortation.

---

[96] Matt. 25:31-46
[97] *John 5:28-29*: Marvel not at this: for the hour comes, in which all that are in the tombs shall hear his voice, and shall come forth; they that have done good, unto a resurrection of life; and they that have done evil unto a resurrection of judgment.
[98] Rom. 14:10-12
[99] Rev. 20:11-15
[100] Rev. 14:10-11
[101] Acts 24:15-16
[102] *Isa. 65:17, 66:22*: Behold, I create new heavens and a new earth . . . the new heavens and the new earth, which I will make, shall remain before me. *Rev. 21:1, 5*: And I saw a new heaven and a new earth: for the first heaven and the first earth are passed away . . . And he that sits on the throne said, Behold, I make all things new.
[103] *2 Pet. 3:5-7, 10, 12*: there were heavens from of old, and an earth, compacted out of water . . . by the word of God, by which means the world that then was, being overflowed with water, perished: but the heavens that now are, and the earth, by the same word, have been stored up for fire, being reserved against the day of judgment and destruction of ungodly men . . . the day of the Lord shall come as a thief; in the which the heavens shall pass away with a great noise, and the elements shall be dissolved with fervent heat, and the earth and the works that are therein shall be burned up . . . the day of God, by reason of which the heavens being on fire shall be dissolved, and the elements shall melt with fervent heat.
[104] 2 Pet. 3:11-12

A. Instruction

1. Instruction regarding faith: faith confesses God's supreme power in creation and salvation (Heb. 1:3; Rom. 10:9-10).

2. Instruction regarding hypocrisy: hypocrites, devoid of saving religion, deny God's supreme power (1 Cor. 15:17).

B. Encouragement

1. We receive comfort from what supreme power has done for us in Christ (1 Cor. 1:18, 22-25).

2. We receive comfort from what supreme power did to us in conversion (Eph. 2:1-10).

3. We receive comfort from what supreme power continues to do for us in the Christian life (Phil. 1:6; 1 Pet. 1:5).

4. We receive comfort from what supreme power will do for us in glory (1 Thess. 4:16-18; 2 Pet. 3:13; Rev. 21:1-5).

C. Exhortation

1. Omnipotence exhorts us to rejoice in God and praise him (Ps. 33:1-6; Dan. 4:35; Eph. 3:20-21; Rev. 19:1-2, 6-7).

2. Omnipotence exhorts us to acknowledge God and honor him:
We must honor him by boasting, not in works, or in men's gifts, but in God alone (1 Cor. 1:10-13, 18-24, 25-31).
We must honor him by embracing our inherent weakness and impotence (John 15:5; 2 Cor. 12:9-10).
We must honor him by acknowledging his enablement in gospel obedience and service (Phil. 4:13; 1 Cor. 15:10).

3. Omnipotence exhorts us to trust God and have confidence in him.
We must trust him and not charge him foolishly in our adversity and afflictions (Job 42:6).
We must trust him and depend on him for enablement to be holy (2 Cor. 12:9; Eph. 1:19; Phil. 4:13).
We must trust him and rely on his strength to serve him (Col. 1:28-29).
We must trust him for protection and vindication from our enemies (Job 5:9; 1 Pet. 4:19).
We must trust him when we can't fathom how he can do what he says he will do (Gen. 18:13-14; Jer. 32:27).

4. Omnipotence exhorts us to fear God and reverence him (Pss. 33:9, 90:11).

5. Omnipotence exhorts us to obey God (1 Cor. 6:13-14; Eph. 2:10; Phil. 2:12-13; 2 Pet. 3:11-12).

6. Omnipotence exhorts us to hope in God and wait for him (2 Thess. 1:7-8; 2 Pet. 3:12-13).

7. Omnipotence exhorts us to pray to God with expectancy (Mark 10:27; Rom. 15:13; Eph. 3:14-21; Col. 1:9-11).

Conclusion to God's Omnipotence

I underscore the incentive that God's omnipotence gives us. Men's rebellion against their omnipotent Maker will not only prove futile, it will prove fatal. Therefore, supreme power gives sinners strong incentive to get right with God through Jesus Christ. It also gives saints strong incentive to pray for our churches and for the salvation of sinners, not with pessimism, but with optimism. We must not deflate our requests with unbelief, but boldly ask whatever we can think. Our requests cannot limit the potential of our omnipotent God. He can do: "exceeding abundantly above all that we ask or think." We should pray with boldness for our unteachable relatives and materialistic countrymen. We should pray with hope that God would send forth his Word with power and revive true religion in our churches and our land. The more God's omnipotence influences our prayer life, the more our lives and ministries will bring him honor and glory. May the Lord, with whom all things are possible, abundantly make it so.

Topic 13. The Omniscience of God

"His understanding is infinite" (Ps. 147:5); "the wisdom and knowledge of God" (Rom. 11:33); "only wise God" (Rom. 16:27)

Section 8. God's Faculty

Introduction to Section 8: In this section we consider how *metaphysical faculty*, a third essential characteristic of spiritual beings, pertains to the Supreme Spirit. Webster defines *metaphysical* as, "of or relating to the transcendent or supersensible," or as, "supernatural."[1] It defines *"faculty"* as, "an inherent capability, power, or function."[2] Thus, a *metaphysical faculty*, is "an inherent capability or power that relates to the supersensible or spiritual." What *metaphysical faculties* pertain to spiritual beings? We cannot discern spirits with our senses. Yet spirits have inherent capability to think, choose, and feel. Further, although the whole soul thinks, chooses, and feels, nonetheless, Scripture uses distinct terminology for these various spiritual capabilities. The capacity to think is "the mind," to choose is "the will," and to feel is the "affections."

In Unit 1 we consider God's infinite mind, the *omniscience* of God. In Unit 2 we expound his unlimited will, the *sovereignty* of God. In Unit 3 we unfold the biblical testimony to his absolute affections, the *emotivity* of God. In one respect, each faculty is "communicable," in another, "incommunicable." Human spirits have the capacity to think, choose, and feel. Yet, no human being has omniscience, or a sovereign will, or divine emotivity. Thus, to use that venerable distinction as my organizing principle, I would first have to consider the biblical witness to God's communicable mind, will, and affection, then to his incommunicable omniscience, sovereignty, and emotivity. This would not be very practical.

Hodge and Gill recognize that these faculties of mind, will, and affection characterize spiritual beings:

> As power of some kind belongs to every substance, *the power which belongs to spirit, to the substance itself, is that of thought, feeling, and volition.* We are not more certain that we exist, than that we think, feel, and will. We know ourselves only as thus thinking, feeling, and willing, and we therefore are sure that *these powers or faculties are the essential attributes of a spirit, and must belong to every spirit* . . . As all this is involved in our consciousness of ourselves as spirit, it must all be true of God, or, God is of a lower order of being than man . . . It need hardly be remarked that the Scriptures everywhere represent God as possessing all the above-mentioned attributes of a spirit. On

---

[1] *WNC Dictionary*, 716

[2] Ibid., 407

this foundation all religion rests; all intercourse with God, all worship, all prayer, all confidence in God as preserver, benefactor, and redeemer.[3] [emphasis supplied]

But as God is defined a Spirit in Scripture, as has been observed, I shall endeavor to sort the perfections and attributes of God in agreement with that . . . *with respect to it* [his nature] as active, and operative, the life of God, and his omnipotence: and *with respect to the faculties*, as a rational spirit, particularly *the understanding*, to which may belong his omniscience, and manifold wisdom; *and the will*, under which may be considered the acts of that, and the sovereignty of it; *and the affections*, to which may be reduced, the love, grace, mercy, hatred, anger, patience, and longsuffering of God: *and lastly, under the notions of qualities and virtues*, may be considered, his goodness, holiness, justice, truth, and faithfulness; *and, as a compliment to the whole*, his perfection or all-sufficiency, glory, and blessedness:[4] [emphasis supplied]

I proceed to consider such perfections which may be ascribed to him as an intelligent Spirit; to which rational spirits, endowed with understanding, will, and affections bear some similarity. God is said to have a mind and understanding . . . Having considered the attributes of God which belong to his understanding, as an intelligent Spirit, his knowledge and wisdom, I now proceed to consider his Will, and the sovereignty of it . . . Next to the attributes which belong to God, as an intelligent Spirit, to his understanding and will, may be considered, those which may be called Affections . . . Having considered those attributes which bear a likeness to affections in men, I proceed to consider those which in them may be called virtues; as holiness, justice, or righteousness, truth, or faithfulness[5]

Unit 1. God's Supreme Mind: *The Omniscience of God*

The term "omniscience" comes from the Latin, "scientia," "knowledge," and "omni," "all." Thus, omniscience describes God as *All-Knowing*. Scripture presents God's supreme mind with a rich variety of terms and expressions. It affirms that God's mind, knowledge, and wisdom are incomprehensible.[6] It features its *essential nature*,[7] *conspicuous display*,[8] and practical and religious *relevance*.[9] I expound omniscience accordingly.

---

[3] Charles Hodge, *Systematic Theology*, 1:378, 379, 380
[4] John Gill, *Body of Divinity*, 51
[5] Ibid., 84, 101, 112, 148
[6] Ps. 139:4,6; Isa. 40:28, 55:8-9; Rom. 11:33-34
[7] Job 37:16; Ps. 147:5; Isa. 40:28; Rom. 11:33-34, 16:27
[8] Job 37:16; Rom. 11:33-34
[9] Job 37:16; John 21:17; Rom. 16:27

I. The Essential Nature of Omniscience

In order to explain the essential nature of omniscience, I first, define the *concept* of omniscience, second, delineate its distinguishing *characteristics*, and third, discover its underlying *causes*.

A. The Concept of Omniscience

What is divine omniscience? Scripture discloses three essential features of omniscience: God's supreme mind, knowledge, and wisdom.[10] The *fountain* of omniscience is God's supreme mind, which is his faculty of comprehension and perception. The psalmist extols the *fulcrum* of omniscience, God's infinite knowledge[11] and understanding.[12] The apostle extols the *fruition* of omniscience, God's supreme wisdom.[13] Wisdom presupposes knowledge and surpasses it. It is the apex of omniscience. Thus Hodge observes: "Wisdom and knowledge are intimately related. The former [wisdom] is manifested in the selection of proper ends, and of proper means for the accomplishment of those ends."[14] Thus, I offer the following definition. God's *omniscience* is:

> God's supreme capacity to comprehend and perceive, by which he knows all things divine, possible, actual, and historical; and, by which he has supreme capability to use what he knows to devise and accomplish his plans.

1. The fountain of omniscience: God's mind: "God's supreme capacity to comprehend and perceive"

God is a rational being who thinks supremely.[15] He is also an intelligent being, who understands supremely.[16] God's understanding involves total comprehension of everything that exists[17] and universal perception of

---

[10] *Rom. 11:33-34*: O the depth of the riches both of the wisdom and the knowledge of God! How unsearchable are his judgments, and his ways past tracing out! For who has known the mind of the Lord? or who has been his counselor?

[11] *Ps. 139:4, 6*: there is not a word in my tongue, but, lo, O Jehovah, you know it altogether . . . Such knowledge is too wonderful for me; it is high, I cannot attain unto it.

[12] *Ps. 147:5*: Great is our Lord, and mighty in power; his understanding is infinite.

[13] *Rom. 16:27*: to the only wise God, through Jesus Christ, to whom be the glory for ever. Amen.

[14] Charles Hodge, *Systematic Theology*, 1:401

[15] *Isa. 55:8-9*: my thoughts are not your thoughts, neither are your ways my ways, says Jehovah. For as the heavens are higher than the earth, so are my ways higher than your ways, and my thoughts than your thoughts.

[16] *Isa. 40:28*: The everlasting God, Jehovah, the Creator of the ends of the earth, faints not, neither is weary, there is no searching of his understanding.

[17] *John 21:17*: Lord, you know all things, you know that I love you.

everything that happens.[18] God always possessed this capacity to comprehend and perceive, by which he has both knowledge and wisdom.

2. The fulcrum of omniscience: God's knowledge: "he knows all things divine, possible, actual, and historical"

God's supreme knowledge is the hub of omniscience. It cements the concept together. The name, "All-Knowing," confirms this. First, God knows "all things divine." When only God was, he had total self-comprehension and perfect self-perception.[19] Again, God knew in advance, "foreknew," everything that could exist or happen, "all things possible."[20] Again, God in his decree determined, and thus foreknew, everything that would exist and happen, "all things actual and historical."[21] He has complete comprehension of creation and perfect perception of history.[22] He knows all things past, present, and future. He remembers the past, perceives and comprehends the present, and foreknows the future.

3. The fruition of omniscience: God's wisdom: "supreme capability to use what he knows to devise and accomplish his plans"

God's knowledge culminates in his ability to use what he knows practically and beneficially. Since God devised his eternal plan by his wisdom, he displays that wisdom when he implements his plan in creation,[23] providence,[24] and redemption.[25]

B. The Distinguishing Characteristics of Omniscience

God's knowledge bears all the earmarks of his supremacy. His knowledge is ideal, self-existent, infinite, eternal, and unchangeable. These traits also characterize God's mind and his wisdom.

1. God's knowledge is infallible.

Since God is ideal, he knows all things *infallibly*. His supreme knowledge is perfect.[26] He cannot err.

---

[18] *Heb. 4:13*: And there is no creature that is not manifest in his sight: but all things are naked and laid open before the eyes of him with whom we have to do.
[19] Matt. 11:27; John 17:24,25; Rom. 8:27; 1 Cor. 2:11
[20] Matt. 11:21, 23
[21] Rom. 11:33-34; Eph. 1:11
[22] Heb. 4:13
[23] Prov. 3:19-22
[24] Eccles. 8:17
[25] 1 Cor. 1:18-24
[26] *Job 37:16*: Do you know the balancing of the clouds, the wondrous works of him who is perfect in knowledge?

2. God's knowledge is independent.

Since God is self-existent, he knows all things *independently*.[27] He does not depend on outside sources or second-hand information. He does not need a team of researchers to acquire his knowledge.

3. God's knowledge is intuitive.

Since God is infinite, he knows all things *intuitively*.[28] He does not attain supreme knowledge by a lengthy process of investigation and deduction. Rather, he knows everything inherently and completely.

4. God's knowledge is innate.

Since God is eternal, he knows all things *innately*.[29] His supreme knowledge had no beginning. It always was. He was never ignorant of anything, but always knew everything that could or would happen. Some appeal to Acts 15:18 to support this: "known unto God are all his works from the beginning of the world" (KJV). Yet the Greek text has several variant readings. And, it is also translated: "who makes these things known from of old" (ASV). Thus, we should refrain from dogmatism regarding this text.

5. God's knowledge is incessant.

Finally, since God is immutable, he knows all things *incessantly*. His mental faculty never deteriorates with time.[30] He never forgets anything. He never needs a refresher course. Everything he knows is always "at his fingertips." Although he knew all things eternally, he also perceives and comprehends all that happens while it is happening: "the eyes of Jehovah are in every place keeping watch" (Prov. 15:3). Scripture thus extols God's supreme knowledge. Only God knows infallibly, independently, intuitively, innately, and incessantly.

C. The Underlying Causes of Omniscience

Why and how does God know all things? The grounds of omniscience lie buried in mystery. Scripture doesn't explain either how God eternally and intuitively knows himself and "all things possible," or how his supreme mind functions: "his understanding is infinite." Let us not meddle with things beyond the boundaries of biblical revelation. However, God's Word addresses the underlying causes of God's supreme knowledge of creation

---

[27] Rom. 11:34
[28] Ps. 147:5; Isa. 55:8-9
[29] Isa. 40:28
[30] Ibid.

and history.[31] God's supreme knowledge of "all things actual" and "all things historical" rests on his *omnipresence*,[32] his *work of creation*,[33] and his *eternal decree*.[34]

First, God knows everything that happens in history because he is everywhere. He continually perceives every event because he is ever-present, in every place, with his whole being.

Second God knows everything that exists because God created everything. The Creator comprehends all created things. He knows their properties, capabilities, functions, and intricacies, because he designed and constructed them all: "he has established the world by his wisdom, and by his understanding he stretched out the heavens" (Jer. 10:12).

Third, God always knew everything that would exist and happen because he decreed it: "Your eyes did see my unformed substance; and in your book they were all written, even the days that were ordained for me, when as yet there were none of them" (Ps. 139:16). God knows all about us because he wrote the book on us. His decree contains an infallible and exhaustive biography of every human being. God knows exactly what is happening because he decided exactly what would happen. God's decree alone differentiates what could have been (things possible) from what is (things actual). Thus, Paul says that God "works all things after the counsel of his own will" (Eph. 1:11).

II. The Conspicuous Display of God's Omniscience: *Supreme Knowledge and Wisdom*

We first consider the biblical display of God's supreme knowledge, then of his supreme wisdom.

A. The Biblical Display of God's Supreme Knowledge

We first survey God's perfect knowledge of himself, of *all things divine*. Next, since he framed his decree in eternity, we unfold his knowledge of *all things possible*. Third, since he commenced his work with creation, we look at his knowledge of *all things actual*. We conclude with his knowledge of all that happens in history, *all things historical*.

---

[31] Ps. 139:7-16
[32] Ps. 139:7-12
[33] Ps. 139:13-15
[34] Ps. 139:16

1. God's supreme knowledge of himself, of all things divine

God the Father and God the Son know each other completely and accurately.[35] God the Holy Spirit knows all the deep things of God.[36] Thus, each Person of the Trinity knows all things divine. Humans can only know God's purposes and ways because God reveals them to us in Scripture. We depend totally on Scripture for saving knowledge of God. Thus, God's self-knowledge incites us to appreciate his Word. We should read it, study it, memorize it, revere it, believe it, obey it, and thank God for it. Further, Paul asserts that God knows "the mind of the Holy Spirit."[37] He presents this lofty truth, not to encourage philosophical speculation, but to encourage God's people in our struggles with remaining sin and affliction. He wants Christians to know that the Holy Spirit prays effectively for us, even during our deepest valleys of discouragement and weariness, when we are not even sure what we should pray.

2. God's supreme knowledge of all things possible

Scripture presents God's knowledge of things that could have happened, but never did. It sometimes traffics in the hypothetical. What would have happened, if? Even when Scripture speculates, it knows only holy speculation. It always has a devotional flavor and practical design. God's supreme knowledge of the hypothetical guides his people through life's maze of danger and difficulty. For example, consider David's experience at Keilah.[38] David hears a report that Saul plans to trap him in Keilah, a walled city. Thus, he inquires of God. He asks if the report is true. He asks if Saul will come to Keilah to destroy him. God lifts back the veil of the hypothetical. He tells David that if he remains there, Saul will come. Then David asks God if the men of Keilah would hand him over to Saul. So the Lord tells David what would happen. If Saul comes, and if David remains

---

[35] *Matt. 11:27*: All things have been delivered unto me of my Father: and no one knows the Son, save the Father; neither does any know the Father, save the Son, and he to whomsoever the Son wills to reveal him.

[36] *1 Cor. 2:10-11*: But unto us God revealed them through the Spirit: for the Spirit searches all things, yea, the deep things of God. For who among men knows the things of a man, save the spirit of the man, which is in him? even so the things of God none knows, save the Spirit of God.

[37] *Rom. 8:27*: he that searches the hearts knows what is the mind of the Spirit, because he makes intercession for the saints according to the will of God.

[38] *1 Sam. 23:11-12*: Will the men of Keilah deliver me up into his hand? Will Saul come down, as your servant has heard? O Jehovah, the God of Israel, I beseech you tell your servant. And Jehovah said, He will come down. Then said David, Will the men of Keilah deliver up me and my men into the hand of Saul? And Jehovah said, They will deliver you up. Then David and his men . . . arose and departed out of Keilah.

in Keilah for protection, then, the men of Keilah would deliver David to Saul. So David arose and fled from Keilah. Thus, what would have happened, never did happen. God decreed that David would inquire about what would happen. He decreed to show David what would happen if he remained. He decreed that David would flee from Keilah, so that what would have happened, didn't happen. I say with Paul: "O the depth of the riches both of the wisdom and knowledge of God." God knows all things possible, and uses that knowledge to guide, protect, and care for his people. Thus, we also should inquire of the Lord when we face knotty decisions with perilous alternatives. Our Heavenly Father knows every contingency. He can and will guide us by his Word in the safe way that leads to life and glory.

As our omniscient God has infinite knowledge of all things possible in the future, so our omniscient Christ has infinite knowledge of all things possible in the past. For example, Christ pulls back the veil of the past to motivate sinners to repentance.[39] He explains that if he had done his miracles in Tyre and Sidon, they would have repented. He adds that if he had preached in Sodom, it would still remain. Abraham pleaded with God for Sodom. The Lord promised to spare Sodom for the sake of only ten righteous inhabitants.[40] If Christ's mighty works had been done in Sodom, at least ten men would have been converted, the city would have been spared, and therefore, it would still remain. Yet, Sodom was not spared. Again, Tyre would have repented if they had seen Jesus' mighty works, but they never saw them, did not repent, and perished. Thus, Jesus teaches us to appreciate gospel light. It is a privilege that God sends or withholds as he sees fit. Since Christ knew what would have happened in Sodom with perfect hindsight, then assuredly, the omniscient God foresaw all this with infallible foresight. God, foreknowing all that would have happened, determined, by his sovereign will alone, what actually did happen.[41] He decided to withhold gospel light from Sodom, not because he foresaw that they would have remained impenitent, but rather, even though he foresaw that they would have repented. Thus, with these striking words, Christ proclaims God's sobering decree of reprobation.[42] Jesus speaks this way because his hearers despised their gospel privileges. He warns them that they faced more severe

---

[39] *Matt. 11:21, 23*: Woe unto you Bethsaida! for if the mighty works had been done in Tyre and Sidon which were done in you, they would have repented long ago in sackcloth and ashes ... And you, Capernaum ... you shall go down unto Hades, for if the mighty works had been done in Sodom which were done in you, it would have remained until this day.

[40] Gen. 18:22-32

[41] Rom. 9:18; Eph.1:4-5, 11

[42] 1 Pet. 2:8

punishment than the notorious sinners of Sodom. He assures them that God sovereignly dispenses saving grace. With these incentives, he motivates them to repent and calls them to himself.[43] Thus, our kind and gentle Savior incorporates reprobation into his evangelism. We must not be ashamed of Jesus or his methods. We too must deal faithfully with people's souls. As Jesus did, we must preach that salvation is of the Lord. We must love men enough to warn them plainly about the danger of despising gospel light, even while we plead with them, sincerely and graciously, to come to the Lord.

3. God's supreme knowledge of all creation and every creature, of all things actual

I survey the testimony of seven passages that display how God completely understands all creation and creatures.

a. Job 37:16[44]

Elihu asks Job to contemplate all God does and to compare God's knowledge with his own. He wants Job to embrace that God's ways are unsearchable. Then the Lord himself answers Job and "pummels" him with a barrage of questions.[45] He reminds Job how little he really knows in comparison with God. God displays his knowledge of all creation to Job to reassure him that inscrutable divine wisdom ordered his sufferings. He also displays this knowledge to reprove Job for contending with the Lord.[46] He knows that Job needs a fresh sight of his supreme power and wisdom to endure his severe trial.[47] Thus, in our seasons of perplexity and trial, we should dwell on God's supreme knowledge. We should compare our knowledge with his until we sense afresh just how little we really know. In this way, we learn to think soberly. If we contend with God during our afflictions, we manifest that we think more highly of ourselves than we ought to think. In this way God uses suffering in the path of righteousness

---

[43] Matt. 11:20-30

[44] *Job 37:16*: the wondrous works of him who is perfect in knowledge

[45] *Job 38:4-5, 18-19, 21, 33, 36-37*: Where were you when I laid the foundations of the earth? Declare if you have understanding. Who determined the measures thereof, if you know? . . . Have you comprehended the earth in its breadth? Declare if you know it all. Where is the way to the dwelling of the light? And as for darkness, where is the place thereof . . . Doubtless, you know, for you were then born, and the number of your days is great! . . . Do you know the ordinances of the heavens? . . . Who has put wisdom in the inward parts? Or who has given understanding to the mind? Who can number the clouds by wisdom?

[46] Job 40:1-2, 8

[47] Job 42:1-6

to produce in us, as he did in Job, deeper humility and greater appreciation of his grandeur (Job 42:6).

b. Ps. 139:1, 6[48]

David admits that he can never know himself as well as God knows him. In this Psalm David uncovers the three taproots of God's supreme knowledge[49] and extols its great value.[50] Then he avows his abhorrence of God's enemies[51] and seeks God's help in self-examination.[52] David thus honors God's unsearchable thoughts: "How precious also are your thoughts" (139:17-18). He appreciates constant companionship with One who understands him completely: "When I awake, I am still with you." People sometimes complain, saying, "nobody understands me." Truly, we sometimes misjudge one another. Yet, Christians always enjoy, as David did, the companionship of a Friend who never misjudges us, who always understands us and knows us better than we know ourselves. Further, David avows firm opposition to God's enemies. The wicked hate his faithful Companion. They malign his Name and use it in vain: "they speak against you wickedly, and your enemies take your name in vain" (139:20). This grieves David. For this reason he detests them with a holy abhorrence and regards them as his enemies. Thus, God's supreme knowledge teaches us to detest a world that hates and maligns our precious Companion and closest Friend. Again, David requests God to help him in the discipline of self-examination: "Search me, O God, and know my heart" (139:23-24). Accordingly, we too should examine our hearts in dependence on the God who knows everything about us.

c. Prov. 15:11[53]

Scripture states repeatedly that God fully understands every human heart.[54] Men see what is external. God perceives and comprehends what is internal and invisible to the human eye.[55] He alone knows everyone's inmost

---

[48] *Ps. 139:1, 6*: O Jehovah, you have searched me, and known me ... Such knowledge is too wonderful for me; it is high, I cannot attain unto it
[49] Ps. 139:7-16
[50] Ps. 139:17-18
[51] Ps. 139:19-22
[52] Ps. 139:23-24
[53] *Prov. 15:11*: Sheol and Abaddon are before Jehovah: how much more the hearts of the children of men!
[54] Ps. 7:9; Prov. 17:3, 21:2; Jer. 17:10; Acts 15:8; Rom. 8:27; 1 Cor. 14:25; Rev. 2:23
[55] 1 Sam. 16:7

thoughts and cherished secrets.[56] He knows every heart continually.[57] He will judge all humanity accordingly.[58] Thus, we should value heart religion, not merely its external appearance, because God will condemn those whose religion consists only in empty rituals.[59] We should put away all hypocrisy, pretense, and deceit, knowing that we can never fool the all-knowing God. Therefore, we should make his approval our primary concern; men's approval secondary.[60]

d. Matt. 10:29-30[61]

Jesus reasons from the lesser to the greater. If God pays attention to every individual bird, he will surely pay attention to his children. God even knows how many hairs each Christian has on his head. Some focus on the "big picture," but have little patience with details. Others seem to major on the trees, but have a hard time seeing the forest. The Lord, ever mindful of his overall purpose for us, also scrutinizes our lives in minute detail. What lesson does Jesus draw from this? He exhorts the disciples to serve God boldly in a hostile world: "Fear them not therefore; you are of more value than many sparrows" (Matt. 10:31). Opposition and threats should not cower us from Christ's service. We should have confidence in our Father's protection and care. Similarly, the Lord exhorts his disciples to trust their omniscient Father to provide their needs: "Be not anxious . . . *your heavenly Father knows* that you have need of all these things" (Matt. 6:31-32). Thus, God's omniscience teaches us that we should put away carnal anxiety, whether about protection from the world, or about provision for our bodily needs. Notice how Jesus enforces this lesson: "Behold the birds . . . your heavenly Father feeds them. Are you not of much more value than they? (Matt. 6:26); and, "you are of more value than many sparrows" (Matt. 10:31). God protects and provides for Christians because he considers us more valuable than "many" birds. Thus, God's omniscience teaches us that no creature is worthless or valueless. Even a bird is valuable. A Christian is far more valuable. Therefore, we only view humans and animals properly when we view God properly. Thus, when people reject the omniscient God,

---

[56] *1 Kings 8:39*: then hear in heaven your dwelling-place, and forgive, and do, and render unto every man according to all his ways, whose heart you know; for you, even you only, know the hearts of all the children of men.
[57] 1 Chron. 28:9
[58] Rom. 2:16
[59] Luke 16:15
[60] Matt. 6:4, 6, 18; 1 Cor. 4:3-5
[61] *Matt. 10:29-30*: Are not two sparrows sold for a penny? And not one of them shall fall on the ground without your Father: but the very hairs of your head are all numbered

they grope to find "self-worth." We must not overreact and say that human beings have "no value whatsoever." Rather, we must urge people to get right with our omniscient Father, who imparts to his children a wholesome sense of their value and worth.

e. John 21:17[62].

Scripture presents God's omniscience in an intensely personal way. Peter reasons from the general: "you know all things," to the particular and personal: "you know that I love you." When the Lord gently reminds Peter of his shameful denial, he appeals to Christ's omniscience. God not only knows our faults and failures, he also knows our sincere affection for him. This should comfort us. That comfort should evoke ardent service to the Lord: "Feed my sheep." Does the Lord know that you love him, Christian? Then serve him. Put your heart and soul into your service for his kingdom and people.

f. Heb. 4:13[63]

When Scripture speaks of God's "eyes," it refers to his faculty of perception. It draws analogy between man's limited perception and God's infinite perception. Men see with interruption, only in one direction, and only in one place. God sees without interruption, in all directions, and in all places. The writer uses God's omniscience to enforce his exhortation to pursue heaven with diligence: "Let us therefore give diligence to enter that rest, that no man fall after the same example of disobedience" (Heb. 4:11). He recounts the bad example of the wilderness generation. He warns professing Christians not to follow their bad example or harden their hearts in unbelief and disobedience.[64] He exhorts professing Christians that live in an orderly way to maintain their present course with diligence. Winds of persecution and temptation threaten to blow them off course, and shipwreck their souls on the rocks of apostasy. Thus, they must remember the omniscience of God. God's omniscience furnishes strong incentive to stand firm in Christian faith when tempted to vacillate or compromise with error.

---

[62] *John 21:17*: He said unto him the third time, do you love me? And he said unto him, you know all things; you know that I love you. Jesus says unto him, Feed my sheep

[63] *Heb. 4:13*: there is no creature that is not manifest in his sight; but all things are naked and laid open before the eyes of him with whom we have to do.

[64] Heb. 4:1-8

g. 1 John 3:19-21[65]

Throughout this letter, John teaches Christians how to attain assurance of salvation (1 John 5:13). When we love the brethren in word and deed, we display one vital piece of evidence that we are Christians. If we fail to discern any love for other Christians in our hearts and lives, our conscience condemns us. If our own conscience condemns us, how much more the God who "knows all things"? Thus, God's omniscience commends conscientiousness. A good conscience emboldens us before the omniscient God.

4. God's supreme knowledge of history, of all things historical, of the past, present, and future

God's knowledge of the past is his *remembrance*, of the present, his *perception*, and of the future, his *foreknowledge*.

a. God's remembrance of the past

Scripture highlights that God remembers *the vows* of his covenants,[66] *the virtues* of his people,[67] and *the vices* of his enemies.[68]

First, Scripture highlights that God remembers the vows of his covenants: "to remember his holy covenant; the oath which he swore unto Abraham our father" (Luke 1:72). Scripture repeatedly affirms that God remembers his oath-bound promises.[69] God in kindness sometimes even associates visible reminders, or tokens, with these promises. He ordains these tokens, not for his sake, but for ours. When he sees the token, he remembers his promise.[70] God's remembrance of his oaths supplies his people with effectual

---

[65] *1 John 3:19-21*: Hereby shall we know that we are of the truth, and shall assure our heart before him: because if our heart condemn us, God is greater than our heart, and knows all things. Beloved, if our heart condemn us not, we have boldness before God.

[66] *Luke 1:68-69, 72*: Blessed be the Lord, the God of Israel; for he has visited and wrought redemption for his people, and has raised up a horn of salvation for us . . . to show mercy to our fathers, and to remember his holy covenant; the oath which he swore unto Abraham our father.

[67] *Heb. 6:10*: God is not unrighteous to forget your work and the love which you showed toward his name, in that you ministered unto the saints and still do minister.

[68] *Rev. 18:4-5*: Come forth, my people, out of her, that you have no fellowship with her sins, and that you receive not of her plagues: for her sins have reached even unto heaven, and God has remembered her iniquities.

[69] Gen. 9:15-16; Exod. 2:24, 6:5; Lev. 26:42; Pss. 105:8, 42, 106:45

[70] Gen. 9:15-16; Num. 10:9

arguments to plead before him in prayer. It also provides us with great encouragement and strong hope. It also moves us to bless his name.[71]

Second, Scripture highlights that God remembers his people's works of love. He never forgets our faithful service or good works.[72] This prods us to abound in benevolent deeds by which we minister to needy Christians. Even if people forget our kindness, despise our service, or take us for granted, God is never "unrighteous to forget." This astonishing truth motivates us to continue diligently in well-doing.[73] It encourages us to plead with God that he would remember us for good, in the light of our faithful service to him.[74] Finally, since God never forgets either our good works or his sworn promises to bless us, we should never feel sorry for ourselves or despair.[75] Dear Christian, Christ's hands supply a sufficient reminder of his love for you. The omniscient God can never forget those for whom Christ died.

Third, Scripture highlights God's remembrance of the sinful words and actions of his enemies. God remembers the ways of the wicked and will punish them for their iniquity.[76] Therefore, we should have no fellowship with them in their sins. Therefore, we have strong incentive to plead with God to thwart and judge evil efforts to undermine the work of the Lord.[77] This displays the folly of those that think they can sin and get away with it. Although God suffers long with sinners, and delays implementing his judgment, he never forgets. Sooner or later his reckoning will come. He remembers their sin and will punish them eternally. Thus, all everyone should get right with the omniscient God who never forgets.

b. God's perception of the present

Scripture underscores that God's omnipresence supports his perception of everything that happens in history, while it is happening: "the eyes of Jehovah are in every place, keeping watch upon the evil and the good" (Prov. 15:3). God never sleeps. He never even blinks. He knows everything that happens because he is always present, with his entire Being, everywhere.

---

[71] Exod. 32:13; Heb. 6:13-20; Luke 1:68
[72] Matt. 25:36-40; Acts 10:3
[73] Heb. 6:11
[74] Ps. 20:3; Neh. 13:22, 31
[75] *Isa. 49:14-16*: But Zion said, Jehovah has forsaken me, and the Lord has forgotten me. Can a woman forget her suckling child, that she should not have compassion on the son of her womb? Yes, these may forget, yet will I not forget you. Behold, I have graven you on the palms of my hands.
[76] Ezek. 21:23-24; Amos 8:7; Rev. 16:19
[77] Neh. 13:29

c. God's foreknowledge of the future

God alone has infallible and complete knowledge of the past and future. This knowledge proves that he is the only true God.[78] Accordingly, he challenges false gods to display what they know about the future: "that we may know that you are gods." Thus, divine prophecy protects us from idolatry.[79] He publishes his foreknowledge to shut the mouth of unbelief: "lest you should say, My idol has done it." Thus, the prophets have great value for us. When they publish the Lord's foreknowledge, they confirm that he alone is God, and that the Bible alone is his Word. This reproves our doubts and strengthens our resolve to trust and believe God in a generation of skeptics.

B. *The Display of God's Supreme Wisdom*

I survey the display of his wisdom in creation, providence, and salvation.

1. God's wisdom displayed in creation

We survey the testimony of three texts that feature this display: Ps. 104:24; Prov. 3:19-20; Jer. 10:11-12.

a. Ps. 104:24[80]

As we have seen, this psalm unfolds the wonders of creation. This text affirms that every aspect of creation displays God's supreme wisdom. The display of God's glory in creation evokes thanksgiving and praise: "Bless Jehovah, O my soul. O Jehovah my God, you are very great; you are clothed with honor and majesty . . . I will sing unto Jehovah as long as I live: I will sing praise to my God while I have any being" (Ps. 104:1, 33). We too should contemplate creation until praise to our Creator bursts from our hearts. True religion should foster a scientific effort to discern God's handiwork in the world. Good science accurately analyzes creation with a devotional heart that pleases the Creator: "Let my meditation be sweet unto him" (Ps. 104:34). Thus, science should study the world with an eye to behold the wisdom of its Designer, not with an evil mind, bent on denying

---

[78] *Isa. 41:22-24*: Let them bring forth, and declare unto us what shall happen: declare ye the former things, what they are, that we may consider them, and know the latter end of them; or show us things to come. Declare the things that are to come hereafter, that we may know that you are gods: yes, do good, or do evil, that we may be dismayed, and behold it together. Behold, you are of nothing, and your work is of naught; an abomination is he that chooses you.

[79] *Isa. 48:5*: therefore I have declared it to you from of old; before it came to pass I showed it to you; lest you should say, My idol has done it

[80] *Ps. 104:24*: O Jehovah, how manifold are your works! In wisdom you have made them all: the earth is full of your riches.

his workmanship. Therefore, evolutionary science can never be good science. It can never please God or analyze creation accurately. It must fail because it operates with a pre-formed commitment to prove, contrary to fact, that the world exists by chance, not intelligent design. Finally, God's wisdom displayed in creation moves us to hope for the day when the world will be free from sin: "Let sinners be consumed out of the earth, and let the wicked be no more" (Ps. 104:35). The wicked obscure our view of God's glory in creation. This moves us to long for new heavens and earth, and to pray, "Lord Jesus, come quickly."

b. *Prov. 3:19-20*[81]

The wise man urges his son to get and retain wisdom.[82] God's wisdom displayed in creation bolsters his appeal. Thus, this display underscores the tremendous value of biblical wisdom. Therefore, we should contemplate God's wisdom in creation until it stirs godly longings to pursue biblical wisdom. This commends using the biblical means of getting wisdom: studying God's Word,[83] walking in his fear,[84] following godly parental guidance,[85] avoiding wicked company,[86] and praying for wisdom.[87]

c. *Jer. 10:11-12*[88]

Jeremiah contrasts the Creator's wisdom and power with the ignorance and impotence of idols. The demise of false gods shows the disgrace of idolatry. Thus, God's people should not imitate such evil behavior: "Learn not the way of the nations, and be not dismayed at the signs of heaven; for the nations are dismayed at them. For the customs of the peoples are vanity" (Jer. 10:2-3). God's wisdom displayed in creation teaches us never to tremble at superstitions that stem from idolatry.

---

[81] *Prov. 3:19-20*: Jehovah by wisdom founded the earth; by understanding he established the heavens. By his knowledge the depths were broken up, and the skies drop down the dew.

[82] *Prov. 3:13, 21-22*: Happy is the man that finds wisdom, and the man that gets understanding . . . My son, let them not depart from your eyes; Keep sound wisdom and discretion: so shall they be life unto your soul, and grace to your neck.

[83] Prov. 1:1-6

[84] Prov. 1:7, 9:10

[85] Prov. 1:8-9, 3:1, 4:1-5

[86] Prov. 1:10-16

[87] Prov. 2:4-6; James 1:5

[88] *Jer. 10:11-12*: Thus shall you say unto them, The gods that have not made the heavens and the earth, these shall perish from the earth, and from under the heavens. He has made the earth by his power, he has established the world by his wisdom, and by his understanding has he stretched out the heavens.

2. God's wisdom displayed in providence[89]

As God robes his wisdom in creation in majesty, so he robes his wisdom in providence in mystery. The inspired preacher finds such wisdom inscrutable. Even a wise man cannot uncover the rationale for what transpires in history. We can't explain why one good man dies at young age of cancer, while another experiences an extraordinary cure that adds twenty years to his life. We only know that God orders all in incomprehensible wisdom. This mystery of providence teaches us to embrace our limits. Some events may seem random, even haphazard, as though the All-Wise God left the helm. We must judge, not by appearance, but by Scripture. We must believe that God runs the world wisely. Packer affirms this:[90]

> Now, the mistake that is commonly made is to suppose that . . . the gift of wisdom consists in a deepened insight into the providential meaning and purpose of events going on around us, an ability to see why God has done what He has done in a particular case, and what He is going to do next. People feel that if they were really walking close to God, so that He could impart wisdom to them freely, then they would, so to speak, find themselves in the signal box; they would discern the real purpose of everything that happened to them, and it would be clear to them every moment how God was making all things work together for good . . . So far from the gift of wisdom consisting in the power to do this, the gift actually presupposes our conscious inability to do it.

For us wisdom does not involve entering God's control tower and seeing all the intricacies of providence. Rather, it involves the realization that, as long as we live, we behold our lives moving in what seems sometimes as a maze of confusion. It also involves the conviction that God is always operating the signal tower of providence, and, that he operates it competently, carefully, justly, and wisely.

3. God's wisdom displayed in salvation

I survey the testimony of five texts: Luke 11:49; Rom. 11:33; 1 Cor. 1:20-25; Eph. 3:8-11; Col. 2:3.

---

[89] *Eccles. 8:16-17, 9:1*: When I applied my heart to know wisdom, and to see the business that is done upon the earth, (for also there is that neither day nor night sees sleep with his eyes), then I beheld all the work of God, that man cannot find out the work that is done under the sun: because however much a man labor to seek it out, yet he shall not find it; yea moreover, though a wise man think to know it, yet shall he not be able to find it. For all this I laid to my heart, even to explore all this: that the righteous, and the wise, and their works, are in the hand of God; whether it be love or hatred, man knows it not; all is before them.

[90] James I. Packer, *Knowing God*, 92

a. Luke 11:49[91]

Jesus describes the frightening judgment that God pronounced on the final generation of Hebrew Israel. When they killed Jehovah Jesus, their rebellion reached its zenith and brought ruin on their society.[92] Then his wisdom took his kingdom from them and gave it to the Christian church, a spiritual nation "bringing forth the fruits thereof."[93] God bears long with disobedience. When his forbearance reaches its limit, with wisdom he judges swiftly, severely, and irrevocably. Thus, we should not try his patience. We should value the servants that he sends in his name. Our attitude to them reflects our attitude to him.

b. Rom. 11:33[94]

God in his wisdom makes the rebellion of Hebrew Israel the means of showing mercy to all the nations. Then in wisdom he makes that mercy the means of showing mercy to his rebellious people: "For God has shut up all unto disobedience, that he might have mercy upon all" (Rom. 11:32). God's plan of salvation leaves him on center stage. It shines the spotlight on his mercy. This extols his supreme wisdom.

c. 1 Cor. 1:20-25[95]

God robes his wisdom in providence in mystery. He robes his wisdom in salvation in the appearance of folly. The "foolishness of God" paradoxically displays the grandeur of supreme wisdom. His wisdom in salvation opposes, not merely surpasses, the wisdom of worldly men. He decided that the world would never attain fellowship with him through its philosophical quest. He decided to save sinners from his wrath only through the preaching of Christ crucified, a message that worldly philosophers regard as absurd. Christ is the divine wisdom that solved mankind's greatest problem. Thus God

---

[91] *Luke 11:49*: Therefore also said the wisdom of God, I will send unto them prophets and apostles; and some of them they shall kill and persecute; that the blood of all the prophets, which was shed from the foundation of the world, may be required of this generation

[92] 1 Thess. 2:15-16

[93] Matt. 21:43; 1 Pet. 2:9-10

[94] *Rom. 11:33*: O the depth of the riches both of the wisdom and the knowledge of God. How unsearchable are his judgments, and his ways past tracing out!

[95] *1 Cor. 1:20-25*: Has not God made foolish the wisdom of the world? For seeing that in the wisdom of God the world through its wisdom knew not God, it was God's good pleasure through the foolishness of the preaching to save them that believe. Seeing that . . . the Greeks seek after wisdom: but we preach Christ crucified . . . unto the Gentiles foolishness; but unto them that are called . . . Christ . . . the power of God, and the wisdom of God. Because the foolishness of God is wiser than men; and the weakness of God is stronger than men

renders men's insights useless for salvation. Paul explains why: "But God chose the foolish things of the world, that he might put to shame them that are wise . . . that no flesh should glory before God" (1 Cor. 1:27, 29). God aims to receive all the glory for salvation, both for its accomplishment and application. He accomplishes salvation through the cross. He applies salvation to "not many wise after the flesh, not many mighty, not many noble," to humble us all, and bring himself all credit. He leaves no room for anyone to steal his glory, not philosophers, nor preachers, nor penitents. God's wisdom in salvation teaches us this ultimate lesson: "him that glories, let him glory in the Lord" (1 Cor. 1:31).

d. Eph. 3:8, 10-11[96]

The church displays God's "manifold" wisdom. God ordered this display, not after he failed to work out a plan for a Jewish kingdom, but "according to his eternal purpose." Angels, not merely men, see this profound display: "unto the principalities and powers in the heavenly places." Paul conducts his ministry to Gentiles with the noble vision that churches planted through his labor would display God's supreme wisdom. The church gathers those that believe in Christ from every ethnic background into one spiritual nation, society, and family. Thus, in God's wise design, the church displays publicly that sinners get right with God through Christ alone, by grace alone, through faith alone. Further, since God designs the Christian ministry to foster this display of his wisdom, we should realize its great value. Those who labor in gospel ministry should keep this noble aim in view.

e. Col. 2:3[97]

Paul pulls back the veil and shows us what he prays for God's people. He prays that they may know greater comfort and love. He prays that "they may know the mystery of God, even Christ." He prays this way because he stands convinced of Christ's sufficiency. Jesus Christ is an infinite treasure chest of wisdom, the unique display of God's supreme wisdom. Thus, Paul warns the Colossians about growing dissatisfied with Christ. He warns them not to look for the answers to their problems in the world: "This I say that no one may delude you with persuasiveness of speech . . . Take heed lest there shall be anyone who makes spoil of you through his philosophy and vain deceit, after the tradition of men, after the rudiments of the world, and not

---

[96] *Eph. 3:8, 10-11*: Unto me . . . was this grace given, to preach unto the Gentiles the unsearchable riches of Christ . . . to the intent that now unto the principalities and powers in the heavenly places might be made known through the church the manifold wisdom of God, according to the eternal purpose which he purposed in Christ Jesus our Lord.

[97] *Col. 2:3*: the mystery of God, even Christ, in whom are hid all the treasures of wisdom and knowledge.

after Christ" (Col. 2:4, 8). We must greatly beware this tendency to look to the teaching of the world, rather than to the Word of Christ, for guidance and insight in raising our children, in tackling emotional problems, and in restoring troubled marriages. We must remember that all wisdom and knowledge reside in Christ, not in worldly philosophy and psychology.

III. The Practical Relevance of God's Omniscience

Omniscience is useful for instruction, consolation, confirmation, provision, and exhortation.

A. Instruction from God's Omniscience

1. It teaches us the excellency of wisdom (Prov. 3:19-20).
2. It teaches us the value of all creatures, the Christian gospel, church, and ministry (Matt. 6:26, 10:31, 11:21, 23; Eph. 3:8, 10-11).
3. It teaches us the inscrutability of divine providence (Eccles. 8:16-17, 9:1).
4. It teaches us the sufficiency of Jesus Christ (Col. 3:5-8).
5. It teaches us the absurdity of thinking anyone can get away with sin (Rev. 18:5).

B. Comfort from God's Omniscience

1. It comforts us because God ever watches over us (Isa. 40:28).
2. It comforts us because God never forgets us (Isa. 49:14-16).
3. It comforts us because God always keeps his sworn promises to us (Luke 1:72).
4. It comforts us because God always remembers our faithful service to him (Heb. 6:10).
5. It comforts because the Holy Spirit prays for us, even when we don't know what to pray (Rom. 8:27).

C. Confirmation from God's Omniscience

Divine foreknowledge strengthens our faith that Jehovah is the one true God (Isa. 41:21-24, 48:5).

D. Provision from God's Omniscience

1. It supplies a stockpile of wisdom and knowledge (Col. 3:5; James 1:5).
2. It supplies effectual argument to plead before God (Neh. 13:22, 29, 31; Luke 1:72).

E. Exhortation from God's Omniscience

It exhorts about fellowship with God, cultivation of grace, and contemplation of his work.

1. God's omniscience exhorts us about fellowship with the Lord.

a. Omniscience calls us to seek God for guidance and counsel (1 Sam. 23:11-12; Prov. 3:13, 21-22; Col. 3:5).
b. Omniscience calls us to praise God (Pss. 104:1, 33, 147:5; Rom. 11:33-36, 16:27).
c. Omniscience calls us to appreciate God's special presence (Ps. 139:17,18).

d. Omniscience calls us to cleave to God alone (Jer. 10:10-12).

e. Omniscience calls us to trust God for protection and provision (Matt. 6:31-32, 10:29-31).

f. Omniscience calls us to serve God (John 21:17).

g. Omniscience calls us to honor God (Rom. 11:33-36; 1 Cor. 1:17-31).

2. God's omniscience exhorts us about diligent cultivation of grace.

a. Omniscience urges us to cultivate humility (Job 1:21, 37:16, 38:1-39:30; Gen. 18:25).

b. Omniscience urges us to cultivate expectancy for eternal glory (Ps. 104:35; Heb. 6:10).

c. Omniscience urges us to cultivate sanctity (Ps. 139:19-22).

d. Omniscience urges us to cultivate sincerity (Ps. 139:23-24; Prov. 15:11; Ezek. 11:5; 1 John 3:19-21).

e. Omniscience urges us to cultivate sagacity (Prov. 3:13-15, 21-22).

f. Omniscience urges us to cultivate honesty (Matt. 11:21, 23).

g. Omniscience urges us to cultivate tenacity (Heb. 4:11-13).

3. God's omniscience exhorts us about biblical contemplation of his works.

a. We should study and analyze creation until praise and gratitude flow from our lips (Ps. 104:24).

b. We should meditate on the mystery of providence until we stand lost in wonder (Eccles. 8:16-17, 9:1).

c. We should contemplate salvation until we give God all the glory (Rom. 11:33-36; 1 Cor. 1:17-25).

In Conclusion, omniscience graciously invites all sinners to forsake their sinful ways and thoughts and seek the Lord, while there is still time (Isa. 55:6-9). May the Lord be pleased to write these many lessons of his supreme mind, knowledge, and wisdom on our hearts.

Topic 14. The Sovereignty of God

the good pleasure of his will . . . the counsel of his own will" (Eph. 1:5, 11); "Your will be done, as in heaven, so on earth" (Matt. 6:10)

Unit 2. God's Supreme Will: *The Sovereignty of God*

Introduction to Unit 2: I highly commend *The Sovereignty of God* by A. W. Pink.[1] This book greatly helped me as a new Christian. It unfolds God's sovereignty masterfully. It has probably done more to rekindle interest in and love for this truth than any other piece of literature circulated in the Reformed movement. We could call God's supreme will his "omnivolence," from the Latin, "voluntas," "will," and "omni," "all." I prefer "sovereignty," because it has more substance and wider acceptance. Webster defines sovereignty as "freedom from external control, autonomy," or as, "controlling influence."[2] These ideas, taken together, convey precisely the distinctive features of God's supreme will. God's supreme will is completely autonomous and free from all external control and constraint. And God's supreme will has controlling influence both over all reality and over all morality. Our texts epitomize this dual influence. Paul unfolds the "decretive" function of God's supreme will, by which it exercises controlling influence over all reality: "him that works all things after the counsel of his own will" (Eph. 1:11). In that passage he clusters all the major terms and concepts associated with God's decretive will. Jesus introduces the "preceptive" function of God's supreme will, by which it exercises controlling influence over all morality. God's will defines, desires, and demands what is good and right, both in heaven and on earth: "your will be done, as in heaven, so on earth" (Matt. 6:10). Hoeksema affirms this:[3]

> absolute sovereignty is not merely supreme, or highest, lordship; it is that virtue according to which God is sovereign in Himself. His is the only sovereignty; and there is no sovereignty anywhere but it is derived from His Lordship. His is the sole prerogative to establish the law for all the universe, to judge the creature, and to execute his will. There is no criterion above or next to God, whereby He can be measured and judged, to which He must conform Himself. There is no law to which He is subject, no tribunal to which He is responsible. He alone is the standard for all law and righteousness. He is the sole High One.

So, God has one supreme faculty of will with two closely related functions. Further, these two aspects at times appear contradictory. What he decrees oft seems at odds with what he demands. Paul commends the religious

---

[1] Arthur W. Pink, *The Sovereignty of God* (London: The Banner of Truth Trust, 1968)
[2] *WNC Dictionary*, 1104
[3] Hoeksema, *Reformed Dogmatics*, 69

importance of God's decretive will; Jesus of his preceptive will. Accordingly, I first summarize the *biblical teaching* on God's supreme will; second, survey the *biblical testimony* to its two functions; third, examine its *seeming contradiction*, and fourth, summarize its *practical applications*. Bavinck lists the major New Testament terms for God's will.[4] He clearly displays the rich variety of terms. Scripture presents God's will with five major word groups, clustered around the words: "will," "pleasure," "purpose," "choose," and "ordain." Words like "mind" and "thought" sometimes also depict divine volition (Rev. 17:17). I have appended to this topical presentation a summary of the major biblical terminology.

I. The Biblical Teaching on God's Supreme Will

Scripture presents God's will in relation to three major issues. First, Scripture presents the *concept* of God's will: "of his own will" (Eph. 1:11). Second, it portrays the *characteristics* of God's will: "the good and acceptable and perfect will of God" (Rom. 12:2). Third, it unfolds the *content* of God's will: "in everything give thanks: for this is the will of God in Christ Jesus to you-ward" (1 Thess. 5:18).

A. The Concept of God's Supreme Will

I present this topic deductively. Otherwise my definition would not appear until the end. Yet, I derived this definition inductively, from the survey and exposition of the biblical testimony that follow it. Based on this survey, I offer the following definition of God's sovereign will:

> God's sovereign will is his faculty of self-determination, his supreme capacity to act intentionally (on purpose) and preferentially (as he pleases), to form desires and to make and fix decisions: by which, in its preceptive function, he comprehensively defines morality and propriety, openly demands the same from his moral creatures, and sincerely desires their compliance; and by which, in its decretive function, he designed and determined in eternity everything that happens in history.

This definition has two sections. Everything prior to the colon defines the *unity* of God's faculty of will; after the colon, its *duality* of function.

1. The unity of God's will: one faculty: "his faculty of self-determination . . . his supreme capacity . . . to make and fix decisions"

God himself, with his entire Being, wills. The will of the Triune God is not an independent entity, totally separate from his mind and heart, but a capability of the Supreme Being.

---

[4] Bavinck, *Doctrine of God*, 342

First, notice the general endowment of God's will. In generic terms, God's supreme will is "his faculty of *self-determination.*" All God's actions and responses are voluntary. Webster defines *voluntary* as, "proceeding from one's own consent," "unconstrained," "intentional."[5] Thus, men sometimes aptly call this faculty God's "spontaneity." Webster defines *spontaneous* as "controlled and directed internally," "self-acting," "proceeding from native tendency, without external constraint."[6] God's self-determination involves: "his supreme capacity to act intentionally (on purpose) and preferentially (as he pleases)." God acts *intentionally.* His actions are not accidental or inadvertent, but deliberate. He thinks before he acts. His thoughts regulate his actions. He does nothing aimlessly, by chance. He does all by design. He also acts *preferentially.* His own sovereign prerogative governs his actions in accord with his impeccable virtue and infinite wisdom. God does, not what circumstances force on him, but whatsoever he pleases.

Second, observe the specific capabilities of God's will. Specifically, God's will involves: "his ability to form *desires* and to make and fix *decisions.*" The Greek word *thelo* stresses his power of inclination or desire, the word, *boulomai,* his power of resolution or decision. Desires are conscious inclinations toward what gratifies or pleases. Webster defines a desire as: "a conscious impulse toward an object or experience which promises satisfaction."[7] Making a decision requires the capacity to choose or select. Thus, Webster defines to decide as: "to arrive at a solution which ends uncertainty."[8] God's selections display his resolve and determination. His will differentiates between things possible and actual. His desires coalesce with his selections and decisions. The general endowment of his will supports all this. His desires and his decisions move in the orbit of intention. They precede his actions and regulate his works. Further, God's desires and decisions also move in the orbit of preference and good pleasure. He freely desires and decides whatever seems good to him.

2. The duality of God's will: *two functions*: "in its preceptive function . . . in its decretive function"

I speak of two *functions* of God's will to avoid the false notion that God has two completely different, separate, and distinct wills. Rather, God's one will carries out two distinct but integrally related functions. Theologians call its preceptive function his preceptive, declarative, or revealed will. They call

---

[5] *WNC Dictionary*, 1303
[6] Ibid., 1116
[7] Ibid., 305
[8] Ibid., 291

its decretive function his decretive or secret will. We shouldn't balk at these, as long as we realize that they define, not two separate faculties of will, but two distinct functions of God's will.

In its preceptive function God's will performs threefold service. First, it "comprehensively defines morality and propriety." God's preceptive will formulates what seems morally good to him, what, in his estimation, should and ought to be done.[9] Second, it "openly demands the same from his moral creatures." Because it pleases him when men do his will, he commands and urges them to obey it.[10] Third, it "sincerely desires their compliance." His will expresses his disposition toward his creatures and his desires for them. When men do his will, he is gratified and pleased.[11] He wants men to do his will.[12] Therefore, he works in his people the desire to do it.[13] Nonetheless, sinners despise, disobey, and frustrate his preceptive will.[14]

In its decretive function God's will performs one basic and vital task. It "designed and determined in eternity everything that happens in history." Thus, it is the determinative, certain, and ultimate cause of whatsoever comes to pass.[15] In its decretive function humans can never restrain, frustrate, or reverse it.[16]

In sum, in its decretive function, God's will has controlling influence over all reality and history; in its preceptive function, over all morality and propriety. Just as its basic role, in its decretive function, is formulating purpose, even so, its basic role, in its preceptive function, is formulating propriety. Scripture reveals all God's preceptive will; providence all his decretive will. Sometimes a verbal fiat attends its display in providence, or prophecy precedes it. Finally, God's good pleasure regulates his will, whether it functions decretively or preceptively. Whether it formulates his purposes[17] or precepts,[18] his sovereign prerogative is its inscrutable fountain. A. W. Pink unfolds this duality of function masterfully:[19]

---

[9] Ezra 10:11; Ps. 5:4
[10] Ezek. 18:32, 33:11
[11] Ezek. 18:23, 33:11; Heb. 13:21
[12] Ps. 51:6
[13] Ps. 40:8; Jer. 31:34; Phil. 2:13; Heb. 13:21
[14] Matt. 6:10, 23:37; Rom. 2:4
[15] 1 Sam. 2:25; Acts 2:23, 4:27-28; Eph. 1:11; James 4:15; 1 Pet. 2:8-9
[16] Job 23:13; Pss. 115:3, 135:6; Isa. 14:24; Dan. 4:35; Rom. 9:18-20, 22
[17] Eph. 1:5, 9, 11
[18] Gen. 2:16-17; Mark 7:19; 1 Tim. 4:3-4; Heb. 9:10
[19] Pink, *The Sovereignty of God*, Appendix 1, 297-298

In treating the will of God, some theologians have differentiated between his *decretive* will and his *permissive* will, insisting that there are certain things that God has positively fore-ordained, but other things which He merely suffers to exist or happen. But such a distinction is really no distinction at all, inasmuch as God only permits that which is according to His will. No such distinction would have been invented had these theologians discerned that God could have *decreed* the existence and activities of sin *without* Himself being the *Author* of sin. Personally, we much prefer to adopt the distinction made by the older Calvinists between God's secret and revealed will, or, to state it in another way, His disposing and his preceptive will.

God's revealed will is made known in His Word, but His secret will is His own hidden counsels. God's revealed will is the definer of our duty and the standard of our responsibility. The primary and basic reason why I should follow a certain course or do a certain thing is because it is *God's will* that I should, His will being clearly defined for me in His Word. That I should not follow a certain course, that I must refrain from doing certain things, is because they are *contrary* to God's revealed will. But suppose I *disobey* God's Word, then do I not *cross* his will? And if so, how can it still be true that God's will is *always* done and His counsel accomplished at all times? Such questions should make evident the necessity for the distinction here advocated. God's *revealed* will is frequently crost, but His secret will is *never* thwarted. That it is legitimate for us to make such a distinction concerning God's will is clear from Scripture. Take these two passages: "For this is the will of God, even your sanctification" (1 Thess.4:3); "For who has resisted his will?" (Rom.9:19). Would any thoughtful reader declare that God's "will" has precisely the same meaning in both of these passages? We surely hope not. The first passage refers to God's revealed will, the latter to his secret will. The first passage concerns our duty, the latter declares that God's secret purpose is immutable and must come to pass notwithstanding the creature's insubordination. God's revealed will is never done perfectly or fully by any of us, but His secret will never fails of accomplishment even in the minutest particular. His secret will mainly concerns *future* events; His revealed will, our *present* duty: the one has to do with His irresistible purpose, the other with His manifested pleasure: the one is wrought upon us and accomplished through us, the other is to be done by us.

B. The Characteristics of God's Supreme Will: supremacy, liberty, and secrecy

1. The supremacy of God's will

God's supreme being characterizes his faculty of will. It is illimitable,[20] eternal,[21] unchangeable,[22] independent,[23] and ideal.[24] It is the will of the Father,[25] of the Son,[26] and of the Holy Spirit.[27]

2. The liberty of God's will

In general, God is free to will whatever is consistent with his impeccable moral virtue and infinite wisdom, without limitation by his creatures. Consider its moral and magesterial freedom.

a. The moral freedom

Note the similarity and distinction between the freedom of God's will and of the human will. Our 1689 LCF properly defines the moral freedom of man's will: "God hath endued the will of man with that natural liberty and power of acting upon choice, that it is neither forced, nor by any necessity of nature determined to do good or evil" (LCF 9:1).

Observe how God's moral freedom is similar to man's. The human will is not: "forced . . . to do good or evil." The devil or circumstances do not force humans to sin. The human will, not external constraint, determines whether people do good or evil (Gen. 50:20). The same is true of God. He freely chooses and requires what is morally good, not because of external constraint, but because he wants to. He never desires to do evil or requires his creatures to do it, because he has no pleasure in it (Ps. 5:4).

Observe how God's moral freedom is different from man's. The human will is not: "by any necessity of nature determined to do good or evil." To determine means "to fix," or, "to settle conclusively." This phrase depicts, not external compulsion of the will, but its "moral fixation," or, "*habitus.*" The 1689 LCF confirms this: "renewing their wills and by his almighty power determining them to that which is good" (LCF 10:1). In regeneration God resets the moral fixation of the will. All humans in the state of sin have

---

[20] Isa. 14:27; Dan. 4:35
[21] Rom. 8:29-30; Eph. 1:3-11; 2 Tim. 1:9
[22] Heb. 6:17
[23] Job 23:13; Ps. 115:3; Eph. 1:5, 9
[24] Rom. 12:2
[25] James 1:18
[26] Matt. 11:27; John 5:21
[27] 1 Cor. 12:11

their will set on doing evil (LCF 9:3), in the states of grace and glory, on doing good (LCF 9:4, 5). Thus, the moral liberty of the human will also consists in the fact that its moral habitus is not inherently immutable. However, the moral habitus of God's will is inherently immutable, forever "determined to" good. He is inherently impeccable. Man is not, though saints will become impeccable in the world to come. God can only will what is consistent with his impeccable holiness, goodness, justice, and faithfulness. He can never even be tempted to sin. This is not bondage, but divine moral freedom. Berkhof explains this divine moral freedom clearly.[28]

b. The magisterial freedom

God is free to will whatever he pleases in accord with his character and wisdom.[29] In some small way a king pictures this magisterial freedom.[30] Yet, in this respect, God is unique. No man, not even a king, has unrivaled sovereignty.[31] No human can completely control the free moral actions of others.[32] No human can make anything happen, let alone everything, simply by exercising his will (Eph. 1:11). God's magisterial freedom introduces one of the great and insoluble mysteries of the Bible. Only God fully understands his decrees. We know only that he does whatever he wills and wills whatever he thinks best.

3. The secrecy of God's will

Paul speaks of "the mystery of his will" (Eph. 1:9). God's will is inherently secret. He unveils his preceptive will in Scripture. He reveals his decretive will when he implements it in providence, or pre-discloses it in prophecy. At times he implements his decrees in providence with a verbal fiat.[33] His fiats call us to fear him (Ps. 33:8-9). Even if he unveils the future in prophecy, his preceptive will still defines our duty (Deut. 29:29).

C. The Content of God's Supreme Will

We consider the content of God's preceptive will, then of his decretive will.

1. The content of God's preceptive will

Respecting its preceptive function, we consider the *identity, disclosure,* and *implementation* of what God wills.

---

[28] Berkhof, *Systematic Theology*, 78
[29] 1 Sam. 2:25; Pss. 115:3, 135:3; Prov. 21:1; Jonah 1:14; Acts 2:23, 4:27-28
[30] Eccles. 8:3
[31] Rom. 9:18-19
[32] Gen. 50:20; Isa. 10:7; Dan. 4:35
[33] Gen. 1:3; Matt. 8:3; Mark 4:39-41; John 11:43-44

a. The identity of God's preceptive will

His moral law[34] and his gospel[35] define the content of his preceptive will for all mankind. The book of mosaic law defines its additional content for his people under the old covenant.[36] Christ and his apostles define its additional content for his people under the new covenant.[37] God exercises magisterial prerogative even when he defines his preceptive will. He even grants some prerogative to parents in the home, to elders in the church, and to rulers in the state. If he grants discretionary power to those with delegated authority, shall anyone dare say that he has reserved none for himself? He does indeed posit some precepts simply because they seem good to him. For example, in Eden he commands Adam not to eat from the tree of the knowledge of good and evil, though it was good for food (Gen. 2:16, 17, 3:6). Again, he first appoints Saturday as his sabbath, then, upon accomplishing redemption, changes it to Sunday. Again, under the old covenant, he imposes dietary codes on his people. If the forbidden foods are poisonous, why does he "bless" Noah with permission to eat them (Gen. 9:1-7)? If these dietary rules are abiding moral absolutes, why are his people now free from them (Heb. 9:10)? Why does Jesus make all meats clean (Mark 7:19)? Why does Paul say that all meats are good (1 Tim. 4:3-4)? The idea that he uses no prerogative when he forms precepts leads to legalism, crippling scruples, and a judgmental spirit.

b. The disclosure of God's preceptive will

Regarding how we know God's preceptive will, Scripture comprehensively reveals God's preceptive will for all mankind and for his people (2 Tim. 3:15-16).

c. The implementation of God's preceptive will

Regarding its jurisdiction, observance, and rejection, God's will defines the duty of all men.[38] Disobedience to his will is sin.[39] His will is obeyed by

---

[34] Ps. 40:8; Rom. 3:19-20
[35] Acts 20:21, 27
[36] Rom. 2:18; Gal. 3:10
[37] 1 Cor. 14:37; Eph. 5:17, 6:6
[38] Matt. 6:10; 1 Pet. 4:2
[39] Ezra 10:10; 1 John 3:4

Christ,[40] by Christians,[41] by the church,[42] and by the holy angels.[43] The wicked disobey his will.[44] Gospel obedience to his will is necessary for eternal salvation[45] and brings his blessing and gracious reward.[46] We should diligently study the content of his will for us[47] and pray that he would aid and bless our efforts to discern and do it.[48]

2. The content of God's decretive will

God's works of creation, providence, and salvation display the content of his decretive will.

a. Creation displays the content of God's decretive will.

God created all things simply because he willed to do so.[49] He was under no constraint. He created, not out of personal need, but because it pleased him, in the magisterial liberty of his will. He thus deserves all the glory and honor.

b. Providence displays the content of God's decretive will.

Did God create with an act of will, then become indecisive? Absolutely not! He wills whatever comes to pass. All history displays his will (Eph. 1:11). His will controls everything in the inanimate and animal realms, the affairs of men and angels, even what appears to be chance events, in minute detail.[50] He even controls men's sinful actions.[51] He even decrees the murder of God incarnate, the worst crime ever perpetrated by human hands.[52] His sovereign control over sin neither makes him an accomplice in sin, nor relieves sinners of their guilt for sin (Rom. 9:18-20). Scripture refuses to water down his sovereignty. It does not say that he "permitted" or "allowed" men to sin, but

---

[40] Matt. 26:39, 42
[41] Ps. 40:8; Matt. 12:50; Heb. 10:36
[42] Eph. 5:22-24
[43] Matt. 6:10
[44] Rom. 8:7; 1 Pet. 4:2
[45] Matt. 7:21; 1 John 2:17
[46] Heb. 10:36
[47] Rom. 12:1-2; Eph. 5:17
[48] Ps. 143:10
[49] *Rev. 4:11*: You are worthy, our Lord and our God, to receive the glory and the honor and the power: for you did create all things, and because of your will they were, and were created.
[50] 1 Sam. 2:25; Pss. 115:3, 135:6; Prov. 21:1; Dan. 4:35, Jonah 1:14; James 5:14
[51] Gen. 50:20; Isa. 10:5-7
[52] Acts 2:22-23, 4:26-28

that he meant (Gen. 50:20), determined (Acts 2:23, 4:28), and willed (Rom. 9:19) their sin.

c. Salvation displays the content of God's decretive will.

God saves sinners simply because it pleases him to do so, because it seems good in his sight. Picture God, in eternity, faced with a decision. He has decided to create and that man will fall into sin. Now what? Shall he damn every sinner and create a totally new humanity? Rather, God decided to save some, in Christ. What determined his decision? Scripture answers: "the good pleasure of his will" (Eph. 1:3-5). As he chose freely to create, so also he chose to save in Christ a remnant of fallen humanity. His decretive will is displayed: first, in his eternal plan salvation[53]; second, in his sworn promises of salvation[54]; third, in Christ's accomplishment of salvation[55]; fourth, in the application of salvation[56]; and fifth, in the completion of salvation.[57] This manifests unity. He plans, promises, accomplishes, applies, and completes the salvation of his elect, whom he chose for himself in his good pleasure.[58] Some, trying to absolve God, express this very mildly. They speak of God "passing over some," and "allowing others to harden themselves." God's Word is not as fastidious. It says bluntly that he: "hides these things from the wise and prudent," and "hardens whom he will" (Matt. 11:25-26; Rom. 9:18). This leads to great mystery. It is mystery enough that the triune God who always enjoyed complete happiness and satisfaction should select to create. Is it even greater mystery that the impeccable God should decree the fall. It is the zenith of mystery that he should select in Christ a remnant of sinful humanity and send him to suffer his wrath for them. We know only that God wills it because it pleased him.

II. The Biblical Testimony to God's Supreme Will

Having outlined the concept, characteristics, and content of God's will, I now survey biblical testimony both to support this teaching and to show how I derived it. I restrict this survey to select witnesses, first, to the decretive function of God's will, then, to its preceptive function. I then collate this testimony.

---

[53] Rom. 8:29-30; Eph. 1:3-5; 2 Tim. 1:9; 1 Pet. 2:8-9
[54] Heb. 6:17
[55] Ps. 40:7; Isa. 53:10-11; Matt. 26:39; Acts 2:23, 4:28
[56] Matt. 11:27; John 1:13, 5:21; Rom. 9:16, 18; James 1:18
[57] Eph. 1:3, 9
[58] Rom. 8:29-30, 32-34

A. Biblical Testimony to the Decretive Function of God's Supreme Will

Scripture views specific works that display his decretive will: creation[59]; providence[60]; and salvation.[61] Some texts view the whole landscape of his decretive will.[62] Some texts disclose the general pattern of his decretive will to save sinners.[63] One key passage, Ephesians 1:3-11, probes the nature and eternal activity of God's decretive will. We examine twelve texts, five in the Old Testament, seven in the New.

1. Job 23:13-14[64]

Job moves from general principle: "what his soul desires, even that he does," to specific application: "he performs that which is appointed for me," to experimental implication: "Therefore I am terrified." He begins with the sweeping assertion that God's will controls everything that happens. He describes the decretive function of his will with the verb אָוָה ('avah). This word sometimes describes the holy inclinations of righteous men toward what gratifies them.[65] Sometimes it depicts sinful lusts.[66] Sometimes it depicts the inclinations of men, as creatures, toward what gratifies their appetite for food and beauty.[67] It also describes God's inclination toward what he finds gratifying.[68] After Job states plainly that the Lord's desires control all reality, he applies this general principle to his own life. He depicts God as the great Sovereign and Potentate of history, who personally appointed his afflictions. He uses the word, חֹק (choq). This word usually describes an official or legal enactment, a "statute," or "decree."[69] It's root means "to engrave," since laws in ancient times, like the ten commandments, were oft engraved in stone. When Job faces this, he feels vulnerable, helpless, and afraid of God: "I am afraid of him." God's sovereignty over

---

[59] Rev. 4:11

[60] 1 Sam. 2:25; Prov. 21:1; Isa. 44:28; Dan. 4:17, 25, 32, 5:21; Jonah 1:14; Acts 18:21, 21:14; Rom. 15:32; 1 Cor. 4:19, 15:38

[61] Matt. 11:25-26; Acts 2:23, 4:27-28, 13:48; 1 Pet. 2:8-9

[62] Job 23:13; Pss. 115:3, 135:6; Isa. 14:24, 46:9-10; Dan. 4:35; James 4:15

[63] Isa. 55:11; Matt. 11:27; John 5:21; Rom. 9:18-20, 22; 1 Cor. 12:11, 18; James 1:18

[64] *Job 23:13-14*: But he is of one mind, and who can turn him? And what his soul desires, even that he does. For he performs that which is appointed for me: and many such things are with him. Therefore I am terrified at his presence; when I consider, I am afraid of him.

[65] Isa. 26:9

[66] Deut. 5:21; Prov. 21:10

[67] Deut. 14:26; Ps. 45:11

[68] Ps. 132:13-14

[69] Deut. 4:1, 5:1; Ps. 2:7; Jer. 5:22

affliction calls us to tremble before him. It calls us to face soberly and to confess humbly how helpless and vulnerable we really are.

2. Ps. 115:3[70]

The psalmist asserts that God's sovereignty distinguishes him from all idols. It sets him apart as the one and only true and living God. The word, חָפֵץ (chaphēts), is translated, "pleased." It also depicts God's decretive will in the following passages where it is translated similarly:

Ps. 135:6: Whatsoever Jehovah pleased, that has he done.
Isa. 44:28: that says of Cyrus, He . . . shall perform all my pleasure, even saying of Jerusalem, She shall be built.
Isa. 46:10: My counsel shall stand, and I will do all my pleasure.
Isa. 55:11: my word . . . shall accomplish that which I please.
Jonah 1:14: you, O Jehovah, have done as it pleased you.

Again, *chaphēts* depicts God's decretive will when it is translated, "minded": "notwithstanding, they hearkened not unto the voice of their father, because Jehovah *was minded* to slay them (1 Sam. 2:25), and "will": "the king's heart is in the hand of Jehovah as the watercourses: he turns it whithersoever *he will*" (Prov. 21:1). Further, *chaphēts* also describes human desire, such as wanting to live[71] or a willing mind.[72] It always conveys inclination toward what gratifies, self-determination, freedom from external constraint, spontaneity, and sovereign prerogative. Scripture thus asserts, in the plainest possible language, that God brings to pass whatever pleases him, not from compulsion, but from the sovereign prerogative of his will.

3. Isa. 14:24, 27[73]

Through Isaiah the Lord himself asserts that his will controls all reality: "as I have purposed, so shall it stand." God's will forms purposes, plans, and designs. Isaiah describes God formulating his purposes with the word, יָעַץ (ya'ets), which means to "counsel." It often refers to human collaboration to devise a plan of action.[74] When the Lord devises a plan of action, it must succeed. No man, or society of men, or any other array of creatures, can overthrow or annul the plan of action that the living God devises.

---

[70] *Ps. 115:3*: But our God is in the heavens: he has done whatsoever he pleased.
[71] Ps. 34:12
[72] 1 Chron. 28:9
[73] *Isa. 14:24, 27*: Jehovah of hosts has sworn saying, Surely, as I have thought, so shall it come to pass; and as I have purposed, so shall it stand . . . For Jehovah of hosts has purposed, and who shall annul it?
[74] 2 Sam. 17:15; 1 Kings 12:13; Prov. 11:14

4. Isa. 46:9-10[75]

Again, the Lord asserts that his designs control all reality: "my counsel shall stand." The word translated "counsel" is עֵצָה (ētsah). This noun signifies a "plan of action." It comes from the verb, *ya'ets*, used in Isaiah 14:27. The Lord pulls back the veil and shows us how he devises his plan of action: "I will do all my pleasure." The sovereign prerogative of God's will regulates his eternal plan for reality.

5. Dan. 4:35[76]

The proud king articulates clearly and eloquently what he learned in "the school of hard knocks" about God's absolute sovereignty. He asserts that God's will has controlling influence over all that happens in heaven and on earth. The word translated "*will*," צְבָא (tsᵉba'), signifies leaning or being inclined toward something.[77] Thus, God's will formulates, not only his purposes, but also his desires.

6. Eph. 1:3-5, 9, 11[78]

This passage clusters the major New Testament terms for God's decretive will. The word, θελημα (thelema), is translated, "will" (1:5, 9, 11). This term depicts God's capacity for inclination, intention, and selection. Paul also uses the word, ευδοκια (eudokia), "good-pleasure," to uncover the fountain of God's decretive will (1:5, 9). He also describes its basic endowment, the capacity to form intentions, with the verb προεθετο (proetheto), translated "purposed" (1:9). He further describes this basic capacity with two nouns, προθεσις (prothesis), translated "purpose," and βουλη (boule), translated "counsel" (1:11). Further, Paul describes the eternal act of God's will that formed and fixed his plan for reality (1:4, 5, 11). The word, ἐξελεξατο (exelexato), "chose," depicts its formulation (1:4). The word, προοριζω (proorizo), "predestinated" (KJV), "foreordained" (ASV), depicts its fixation (1:5, 11). Thus, this text paints a

---

[75] *Isa. 46:9-10*: I am God, and there is none like me; declaring the end from the beginning, and from ancient times things that are not yet done; saying, My counsel shall stand, and I will do all my pleasure

[76] *Dan. 4:35*: and he does according to his will in the army of heaven, and among the inhabitants of the earth; and none can stay his hand, or say unto him, What are you doing?

[77] BDB, *Lexicon*, 839

[78] *Eph. 1:3-5, 9, 11*: Blessed be the God and Father of our Lord Jesus Christ . . . even as he chose us in him before the foundation of the world . . . having foreordained us unto adoption as sons . . . according to the good pleasure of his will . . . making known unto us the mystery of his will, according to his good pleasure which he purposed in him . . . in whom we were made a heritage, having been foreordained according to the purpose of him that works all things after the counsel of his own will.

comprehensive picture of God's decretive will. It defines its essential nature and features: its fountain, "good pleasure" (1:5, 9); its prominent trait, "mystery" (1:9); and its preeminent role, "counsel" (1:11). It also defines its eternal activity. Before the foundation of the world, God's will formed (1:4) and fixed (1:5, 11) his eternal plan. We now unfold these essential features and eternal acts of his decretive will.

a. The inscrutable fountain of his will: God's good pleasure (Eph. 1:5, 9)

The Greek word, εὐδοκια (eudokia), "good pleasure," occurs twice in this passage: "the good pleasure of his will" (1:5), and "his good pleasure which he purposed" (1:9). This word is a compound, formed by joining a prefix, "eu," "good," to the stem "dokeo," "to seem" or "to appear." Similarly, the English word, "euphonic," "good-sounding," adds the prefix, "eu," to the stem, "phonic," "relating to sound." Thus, in general, God's "good-pleasure" is "that which seems good in his sight." Accordingly, Jesus says: "for so it was well-pleasing in your sight" (Matt. 11:26). This reads, literally, "for so it was [eudokia] before you," that is, "seemed good" to you. Christ thus sets before us divine prerogative. God's impeccable virtue and infinite wisdom regulate his prerogative, since they form his estimation of what is good. In Scripture "good" sometimes depicts moral right, as opposed to "evil," moral wrong.[79] Sometimes it depicts beneficial and useful, as opposed to harmful or unprofitable.[80] Sometimes it depicts what God prefers and desires, as opposed to things that he simply does not prefer to do.[81] Thus, within the domain of what his infinite virtue and wisdom deem "good," remains the vast expanse of what "seems good" to his sovereign prerogative, what he prefers. God exercises this prerogative in creation, providence, and redemption.[82]

In Romans 10:1 Paul speaks of the "good-pleasure" (eudokia) of his heart. The ASV renders it: "the *desire* of my heart." Israel's conversion was his heart's "eudokia." Paul would be most gratified and well-pleased if God would save them. Thus, the heart's "good-pleasure," is that which, if realized, would most gratify and bring a sense of satisfaction. Similarly he says: "for it is God who works in you both to will and to work, for his good-pleasure" (Phil. 2:13). The word translated "for" is ὑπερ (huper), which means, "on behalf of." This could mean that God works in us, or that

---

[79] Gen. 3:22
[80] Gen. 1:31; Luke 6:43-44
[81] 1 Sam. 3:18
[82] 1 Cor. 15:38; Jonah 1:14; Matt. 11:26; 1 Cor. 2:11.

Christians work, "on behalf of his good pleasure." In either case, God's "good-pleasure" refers to that which gratifies and pleases him.

Possibly Paul employs an additional nuance of *eudokia*," in which it signifies, "good will," or "kind intention": "Some indeed preach Christ of envy and strife; and some also of *good will*" (Phil. 1:15). Arndt and Gingrich[83] and the ASV take it in this sense in this verse. The KJV also sometimes translates *eudokia* this way: "glory to God in the highest, and on earth peace, *good will* toward men" (Luke 2:14). Since "good" sometimes refers to what is "beneficial," eudokia could possibly mean, "what seems beneficial." Thus, Paul may intend to say that some preach Christ because it "seems beneficial," because they have "good will." However, he could also mean that some preach Christ because it gratifies and pleases them, from their "unfeigned desire," unlike those who proclaim him from envy, insincerely.

What then is the significance of the "good pleasure" of God's will in in Ephesians 1:5? Does it signify "sovereign prerogative" (Matt. 11:26), or "desire," "what pleases" (Rom. 10:1; Phil. 2:13), or "benevolence" (Phil. 1:15)? Commentators differ. Hodge offers several reasons why Paul must refer to God's "sovereign" will, rather than to his "benevolent" will.[84] Eadie with equal conviction favors God's "benevolent purpose."[85] The NASV adopts Eadie's view and interprets the phrase: "according to the *kind intention* of his will." Matthew Poole says that Paul refers to: "his sovereign grace and good will, as the only spring from which predestination issued, God being moved to it by nothing out of himself."[86] Poole shows us the safest road. On the one hand, any attempt to excise God's "sovereign prerogative" from "good pleasure" runs roughshod both over the basic idea of the word and the context. This entire passage bristles with God's self-determination and sovereignty. What seems good to God surely "would please" him. Thus, "*good pleasure*" signifies "what seems good," "what would please." On the other hand, any attempt to excise the nuance of unmerited kindness from this phrase would not honor its immediate context: "having foreordained us unto adoption as sons . . . *according to* the good pleasure of his will." Since Paul has our adoption in mind, what seems good to God and would please him, in this instance, coalesces with his

---

[83] BAG, *Lexicon*, 319-320

[84] Charles Hodge, *Commentary on the Epistle to th Ephesians* (Grand Rapids: Wm. B. Eerdmans, 1966), 37

[85] John Eadie, *Commentary on the Epistle to the Ephesians* (Grand Rapids: Zondervan Publishing House, 1977), 33-35

[86] Matthew Poole, *Commentary*, 3:663

"benevolent purpose" toward us. Further, Paul places "will" in the genitive case: "good pleasure *of* his will." Thus, God's sovereign prerogative and benevolent intent are self-determined and voluntary. When he exercises his will, he expresses his sovereign prerogative and inclination toward what pleases him. In this instance, his will, expressing his sovereign prerogative, fashions his kind disposition toward us into specific purposes of salvation and sonship.

What then is the significance of the "*good pleasure* which he purposes" in Ephesians 1:9? Paul here discloses what God wills for our future. Where is history going? The destiny of the universe focuses on Christ: "the mystery of his will, according to his good pleasure, which he purposed in him, unto a dispensation of the fullness of the times, to sum up all things in Christ, the things in the heavens, and the things upon the earth; in him." God resolutely intends to consummate everything in heaven and earth in Christ. God's "good pleasure" is the decisive factor in his plan. Again, "what seems good" to God, his sovereign prerogative, regulates his purpose and constitutes the fountain of his decretive will. Yet God's sovereign prerogative does not primarily connote or always imply "good will" to men (Matt. 11:26). Here Paul dwells on Christ's second coming, which consummates both God's kindness to his people and his severity to his enemies (2 Thess. 1:7-10). In this consummation punishment also "seems good" to God and "will please" him. Thus, the NASV goes way out on a limb when it offers the interpretation, "according to his *kind intention* which he purposed in him." Though I am uncomfortable with their rendering of verse 5, I am aghast at their "rending" of verse 9. The ASV, KJV, NKJV, and NIV rightly translate it, "good pleasure." Yet, the NASV, to its credit, offers the proper translation in a marginal note, "literally, good pleasure." Still, it would be better to put the right translation in the text, and reserve interpretive comments for the margin.

How does Paul unfold God's good pleasure in this verse? First, he affirms its resolution: "which he purposed in him." God's good pleasure stands clearly defined and firmly fixed. God will bring it to pass. Paul expresses this with προεθετο (proetheto), from προτιθημι (protithemi), "to place before." It occurs in only two other texts in the New Testament: Rom. 1:13, 3:25. In Romans 3:25 it apparently signifies a public display: "whom God *set forth* a propitiation." Yet in Romans 1:13 it means, "to put in place beforehand," to "predetermine," or "purpose": "oftentimes *I purposed* to come unto you and I was hindered hitherto." Here context strongly suggests that *proetheto* depicts God's eternal purpose for Christ, rather than the public display of his good pleasure in his incarnation. Further, the KJV renders the phrase: "which he *purposed in himself.*" Paul could mean either that God's eternal purpose is associated with Christ, "*in him,*" or was formulated unilaterally, "*in himself.*" Both things are true, and asserted elsewhere in this passage. Second, he specifies its implementation: "*unto a dispensation of the fullness of the times.*" God will implement this good pleasure at the consummation of all things. Third, he defines its content or substance: "to sum up all things in Christ." Christ's preeminence and centrality in the age to come seem good to God and please him.

In sum, both uses of *eudokia* in this passage affirm that God's sovereign prerogative is the inscrutable fountain of his decretive will. Whether Paul views eternity past, when God in his kindness decided to save and adopt sinners; or eternity future, when God sums up everything in Christ, condemns his enemies, and glorifies his people, he sees the whole river of history flowing from God's good pleasure. Why does God decree what he does? Because it seems good to him. Why does it seem good to him? Because it seems good to him. Scripture takes us no further than God's "good pleasure." Our place is not to explain the imperial decision of his decretive will, but to behold it, marvel at it, and bless him for it.

b. The prominent trait of his will: inherent secrecy (Eph. 1:9): "the mystery of his will"

God's plan for salvation and the future are inherently secret. Paul depicts this secrecy with μυστηριον (musterion). Our English word "mystery" transliterates this Greek word. What is a divine mystery? In the New Testament *musterion* occurs 27 times. It always refers to a divine secret, an aspect of his eternal decree, which men can understand only by special revelation. Thus, Arndt and Gingrich offer as translations: "secret," "secret rite," or, "secret teaching."[87] *Musterion* describes God's secrets associated with: his kingdom (Matt. 13:11), the gospel (Eph. 6:19), the Christian faith (1 Tim. 3:9), the person of Christ (Col. 4:3), the rise of a false and worldly "Christendom" (2 Thess. 2:7), and the world's hatred to Christ (Rev. 17:5, 7). Especially, *musterion* describes God's plan to transform his people. It depicts the partial hardening of the Jewish nation, the excision of unbelieving Jews,[88] the inclusion of Gentile Christians,[89] their spiritual union with Christ,[90] and their glorious consummation when he returns.[91]

---

[87] BAG, *Lexicon*, 531-532
[88] Rom. 11:25
[89] Rom. 11:25, 16:25; Eph. 3:3; Col. 1:26
[90] Eph. 5:32
[91] 1 Cor. 15:51

Further, "will" is again in the genitive: "the mystery *of* his will." This means that his will is "inherently secret," not that his secret is "inherently voluntary." Similarly, "the blasphemy *of* the Spirit" means that the Spirit is blasphemed, not the blasphemer. Thus, Paul tells us that we necessarily encounter mystery "with reference to God's will." Unaided human investigation and insight can never discover or explain any divine mystery. God must disclose it. Although we learn his decrees, in retrospect and in part, as he implements them in history, yet without special revelation we cannot fully understand them, even when they unfold before our very eyes.[92] God uncovers this mystery for the apostles: *"making known to us* the mystery of his will." Their inspired writings display his plan for salvation and the consummation.[93] This shows the inestimable value of Scripture, which alone discloses God's decretive will about salvation and the future.

c. *The preeminent role of his will: planning* (Eph. 1:11) "the counsel of his own will"

The Greek word, βουλη (boule), "counsel," refers to a purposed course of action formulated by deliberation. Arndt and Gingrich affirm this significance. They also observe that in other literature it can refer to "a council meeting," since this group, as a body, deliberates, reaches decisions, and formulates plans of action.[94] In the New Testament *boule* occurs twelve times. It refers seven times to God. Twice it depicts his sovereign decree concerning the death of Christ (Acts 2:23, 4:28). Once it depicts his immutable purpose of grace in his sworn promise to Abraham (Heb. 6:17). Acts 13:36 says that David "served *the counsel* of God." This probably refers to David's special role in God's plan to save. The other two uses, Luke 7:30 and Acts 20:27, refer to God's preceptive will. In both texts *boule* depicts God's plan to save, fully proclaimed by Paul (Acts 20:27) and openly rejected by Jewish leaders (Luke 7:30). The other five uses of *boule* relate to men forming plans, purposes, and decisions. In Luke 23:51, we learn that Joseph "had not consented to their *counsel* and deed." Their *counsel* is to their plan to put Christ to death (John 11:47-53). In Acts 5:38 *boule* refers to the apostles' resolve openly to proclaim the resurrection of Jesus. This passage makes clear that a plan of action can originate either with men or God. Both God and men formulate plans. Only God's plan is invincible (Acts 5:39). In Acts 27:12 *boule* depicts the majority plan about where to winter: literally, "the plan of action put forth" and urged by most who were

---

[92] 1 Cor. 2:7-8
[93] Rom. 16:25; 1 Cor. 2:7, 15:51; Eph. 3:3, 5:32, 6:19; Col. 4:3
[94] BAG, *Lexicon*, 145

traveling with Paul. In Acts 27:42 *boule* depicts the soldiers' plan to prevent escape, which was to kill the prisoners. Luke calls this plan *"their purpose"* (Acts 27:43), using a word from the same family, βουλημα (boulema), which signifies "settled intention." In 1 Corinthians 4:5 *boule* refers to the hidden *"counsels* of the hearts," which the Lord uncovers on judgment day, primarily the noble aims with which God's servants purpose to honor him.

Thus, in light of this use in Scripture, in Ephesians 1:11 *boule*, "counsel," clearly signifies the "settled purpose," or "plan of action," which the Triune God formed before the world began. Paul again uses the genitive case, "the counsel *of* his will." This indicates that God formulates his plan voluntarily and freely, without external constraint. His purpose is "self-determined." It also indicates that his will devises his plans and forms his purposes. His will decides his ends and devises ways and means by which to attain them. In virtue of his will, God acts intentionally and deliberately, on purpose.

Paul features both the universal efficacy and redemptive focus of God's plan. First, consider the universal efficacy of God's eternal plan: *"who works all things after* the counsel of his own will." God's plan has controlling influence over all reality. It has "sovereignty" in the most profound and complete sense of that word. When Paul says that "all things" conform to God's eternal purpose, he means that God himself, by his will alone, predetermined everything that exists and happens. History, from beginning to end, constitutes the unfolding of his eternal plan. History is neither aimless, nor circular, nor meaningless, since God gives it meaning, direction, and destiny. Some may scoff at this, others may find it offensive, but to us, it is the Lord's doing, and it is marvelous in our eyes.

Second, notice the redemptive focus of God's eternal plan: *"in whom we were made a heritage, having been foreordained according to the purpose of him* who works all things after the counsel of his own will." God's plan to save is the core and zenith of his overall plan for reality and history. To describe this redemptive purpose, Paul uses προθεσις (prothesis), from the same family as προεθετο (proetheto). This word *prosthesis* literally means, "something placed before." It occurs twelve times in the New Testament. On four occasions it refers to the "showbread."[95] In this respect it signifies "something put forth," or a "presentation."[96] On eight occasions it refers to a purpose, possibly as "put in place beforehand," or as something customarily "put forth," "proposed," or "presented." It refers three times to

---

[95] Matt. 12:4; Mark 2:26; Luke 6:4; Heb. 9:2
[96] BAG, *Lexicon*, 713

human purposes.[97] In four texts in addition to Ephesians 1:11 it refers to divine purposes of grace.[98] Paul says that God purposed our calling as Christians (Rom. 8:28), Jacob's selection as Abraham's heir (Rom. 9:11), the display of divine glory through the church (Eph. 3:11), and the conveyance of grace in Christ (2 Tim. 1:9). Paul stresses that God formed his saving purposes before the world began.[99] He also stresses that salvation flows from God's unmerited and unconstrained kindness, not from human merit.[100] In Ephesians 1:11 he says that God purposed our destiny as God's heirs. He stresses that God's will decided our blessed destiny and made it absolutely certain. This underscores that the ultimate cause of salvation from sin is not man's will, or merit, or response, or cooperation, or action of any kind. It also underscores that God stands committed, with inviolable resolution, to save to the uttermost everyone whom he chose before the foundation of the world for sonship and glory.

d. The formation of God's eternal plan: election (Eph. 1:4) "he chose us"[101]

Paul affirms that God's will formed his eternal purpose, selecting goals and the means to attain them. He uses ἐκλέγομαι (eklegomai), which means, "to choose, to pick, to select by preference." The word occurs twenty times in the New Testament. Five times it refers to men's choices and preferences.[102] Six times it refers to Christ's selection of the apostles.[103] The other nine uses refer to various choices that God made. God chose a successor for Judas (Acts 1:24), Israel as his people (Acts 13:17), and Peter as the first conveyor of gospel light to Gentiles (Acts 15:7). God personally selects those whom he saves (Mark 13:20; Ephes. 1:4). He selects persons and methods designed to deflate carnal human pride.[104] We should not assume that choices are purely arbitrary simply because they are acts of the will. For example, when the Pharisees chose the most honorable seats for themselves (Luke 14:7), clearly their selection was anything but arbitrary. Jesus affirms that sinful pride determined their preference. Similarly, when God selects methods that the world deems ineffective and inane; and when

---

[97] Acts 11:23, 27:13; 2 Tim. 3:10
[98] Rom. 8:28, 9:11; Eph. 3:11; 2 Tim. 1:9
[99] Rom. 8:29; Eph. 3:11; 2 Tim. 1:9
[100] Rom. 9:11; 2 Tim. 1:9
[101] *Eph. 1:4*: even as *he chose us* in him before the foundation of the world, that we should be holy and without blemish before him
[102] Luke 10:42, 14:7; Acts 6:5, 15:22, 25
[103] Luke 6:13; John 6:70, 13:18, 15:16, 19; Acts 1:2
[104] 1 Cor. 1:27-28; James 2:5

most of his heirs are ordinary folks, the nobodies of the world, whom he chooses from the ranks of the unheralded and obscure, his choice is not arbitrary. Rather, Paul says that God's design to humble men's sinful pride determined his preference (1 Cor. 1:27-31). Although we must say that a principled commitment to his own glory regulates his selections, we must also remember that he formed his eternal plan in his inexplicable prerogative.

e. *The finalization of God's eternal plan: foreordination* (Eph. 1:5, 11) "foreordained"[105]

Though I explain *formation* and *finalization* in turn, you must not think that God first formed then "afterward" fixed his eternal purpose. Rather, God's plan is at once a finished product, fixed and formed eternally by the activity of his will. God's will made his eternal purpose certain. He determined and resolved to bring his chosen ends and means to pass. Paul expresses this with προοριζω (proorizo), which means, "to fix, set, ordain, or determine beforehand." This word occurs only four other times in the New Testament.[106] It always portrays some aspect of God's eternal decision by which he fixed his eternal plan. It portrays how God fixed the destiny of his Son, by ordaining that he would accomplish salvation on the cross (Acts 4:28). It portrays how God fixed the destiny of his people, by deciding that they would experience conformity to Christ through the application and completion of salvation (Rom. 8:29-30). It portrays how God fixed the destiny of gospel wisdom. He decided that inspired apostles would proclaim it to enlightened people amid a blind and skeptical world (1 Cor. 2:7). *Proorizo* comes from ὁριζω (horizo), "to ordain, decide, or determine." *Horizo* appears eight times in the New Testament. Once, in Acts 11:29, it refers to a decision of the church in which they resolved to send benevolence to needy brethren. In every other instance it depicts divine determination. In Acts 2:23 it depicts the "determinate counsel" of God, which is his "fixed and resolute" purpose respecting Christ's death. In Acts 10:42 and 17:31 it depicts God's "irrevocable appointment" of Jesus Christ as Judge of mankind. In Acts 17:26 it refers to God "setting" the stakes along every nation's boundary and "fixing" the span of every nation's history. In Romans 1:4 it describes God "irrevocably appointing" Christ at his coronation as king of God's people and David's heir. In Hebrews 4:7 it refers to "fixing and setting" a day of mercy, space for repentance. Finally, in Luke 22:22 it refers to the "fixed and settled" manner of Christ's death,

---

[105] *Eph. 1:5, 11*: in love *having foreordained us* unto adoption as sons unto himself, according to the good pleasure of his will . . . *having been foreordained* according to the purpose.
[106] Acts 4:28; Rom. 8:29, 30; 1 Cor. 2:7

through betrayal. The text does not say, explicitly, who fixed and settled the matter. We know that it was the Lord because he revealed his decision in his Word before he implemented it (Matt. 26:24). Thus, we learn that God's will forms his eternal purpose and stands resolved to bring to pass its every detail.

What does God's decretive will call us to do? It calls us not to complain or squabble, but to praise God. Paul blesses the Lord for the spiritual blessings we receive by virtue of his supreme will.[107] Thus, Paul underscores that God's decretive will has great practical and religious relevance.

7. Rom. 9:18-19[108]

God's sovereignty in salvation evokes our praise to God. Yet it also provokes some to challenge God's goodness and justice. Paul anticipates the objection that people commonly raise to God's sovereign will. He describes God's sovereign prerogative with θελω (thelo): "whom he will" (9:18). Arndt and Gingrich say it means: "to desire," "want," "resolve," or "wish for."[109] It occurs just over 200 times in the New Testament. It usually depicts human volition, whether as desire, resolution, or preference. These seven texts furnish especially graphic examples.[110] It depicts divine volition at least these ten other times.[111] Further, *thelo* refers to Christ's exercise of divine volition in at least five texts.[112] At least three of these fifteen texts depict God's preceptive will;[113] eleven depict his decretive will; one is debatable (1 Tim. 2:4).

In Romans 9:18 *thelo* clearly describes God's resolve. Paul asserts plainly that God's will alone determines whether he hardens people in sin or shows

---

[107] *Eph. 1:3-5*: Blessed be the God and Father of our Lord Jesus Christ, who has blessed us with every spiritual blessing in the heavenly places in Christ: even as he chose us in him . . . having foreordained us . . . according to the good pleasure of his will.

[108] *Rom. 9:18-19*: So then he has mercy on whom he will, and whom he will he hardens. You will then say unto me, Why does he yet find fault? For who withstands his will? Nay but, O man, who are you that replies against God?

[109] BAG, *Lexicon*, 355-356

[110] *Matt. 1:19*: Joseph . . . *not willing* to make her a public example. *Matt. 16:25*: whosoever *would* save his life shall loose it. *Luke 15:28*: But he was angry, and *would not* go in. *John 21:18*: another shall gird you, and carry you whither you *would not*. *1 Cor. 7:39*: she is free to be married to whom *she will*; only in the Lord. *Phil. 2:13*: God . . . works in you both *to will* and to work for his good pleasure. *2 Thess. 3:10*: If any *will not* work, neither let him eat.

[111] Matt. 9:13, 26:39; Acts 18:21; Rom. 9:22; 1 Cor. 4:19, 12:18, 15:38; Col. 1:27; 1 Tim. 2:4; James 4:15

[112] Matt. 8:3, 23:37; Mark 1:40, 41; John 5:21

[113] Matt. 9:13, 23:37, 26:39

them mercy. Further, God's will, which acted in eternity, remains active in history: "whom he will." His will does not cease to function when history begins. Rather, the living God acts in history by resolving to perform exactly what he planned in eternity.

In Romans 9:19 Paul refers to God's faculty of will: "who withstands *his will*." He describes God's volitional faculty with the word, βουλημα (boulema), which signifies settled intention or purpose. This word only occurs in two other texts in the New Testament.[114] In Acts 27:43 it refers to a human plan of action. In 1 Peter 4:3 it describes evil human designs. This underscores that the preeminent endowment of God's will in its decretive function is the capacity to form settled intentions and plans. Finally, Paul underscores the seeming contradiction and difficulty associated with God's sovereign will. He raises the question: "How can God's sovereignty over sin be compatible with human responsibility for sin?" He teaches us to expect opposition to God's sovereign will. He also teaches us how to respond to it.

8. *1 Cor. 12:11, 18*[115]

The word, βουλομαι (boulomai) describes the exercise of divine volition: "even as he will" (12:11). Arndt and Gingrich offer two senses: (1) to wish, want, or desire; and (2) to reach resolution after deliberation.[116] *Boulomai* occurs 34 times in the New Testament. It emphasizes settled intention. One could make a good case that in the New Testament it always implies an element of resolve, even in those texts that Arndt and Gingrich cite as examples for the first use, "to desire."[117] Five texts furnish a clear picture of its meaning in reference to human volition.[118] *Boulomai* explicitly describes divine volition in five additional texts. It invariably describes God's resolute intention to save. In Hebrews 6:17 it refers to God's resolve to encourage to his people: "God, *being minded* to show more abundantly unto the heirs of the promise the immutability of his counsel, interposed with an oath." In

---

[114] Acts 27:43; 1 Pet. 4:3

[115] *1 Cor. 12:11, 18*: all these works the one and the same Spirit, dividing to each one severally, even as he will . . . But now God has set the members each one of them in the body, even as it has pleased him.

[116] BAG, *Lexicon*, 145-146

[117] Acts 25:22; Philem. 13; 1 Tim. 6:9; James 4:4

[118] *Matt. 1:19*: Joseph . . . not willing to make her a public example, *was minded* to put her away privily. *Acts 12:4*: Herod . . . put him in prison . . . *intending* after the Passover to bring him forth. *Acts 18:15*: I am *not minded* to be a judge of these matters. *Acts 27:43*: the centurion, *desiring* to save Paul, stayed them from their purpose. *2 Cor. 1:15*: In this confidence I *was minded* to come to you

Luke 22:42 it refers to the Father's resolve to accomplish salvation by Christ's death: "Father, if you *are willing*, remove this cup from me." In Matthew 11:27 it describes the sovereign resolve of the Son to apply salvation: "neither does any know the Father, save the Son, and he to whomsoever the Son *wills* to reveal him." In James 1:18 it describes the Father's resolve to regenerate his elect through the gospel: "*of his own will* he brought us forth by the word of truth.*"* In 2 Peter 3:9, it describes God's resolve to apply salvation to his all his elect: "the Lord . . . is longsuffering to you-ward, *not willing* that any should perish, but that all should come to repentance." In 1 Corinthians 12:11 *boulomai* describes the resolve of the Holy Spirit by which he dispenses spiritual gifts to Christians. Thus, each Person of the Trinity exercises the divine faculty of will: the Father (James 1:18), the Son (Matt. 11:27), and the Holy Spirit (1 Cor. 12:11).

In 1 Corinthians 12:18 Paul describes God's sovereign prerogative in the church with the word θελω (thelo), "as it has pleased him." God's desire to unite individuals with his church (12:18) coalesces with his resolve to dispense spiritual gifts (12:11). Similarly, Scripture associates Joseph's resolve with his desire: "Joseph . . . not willing [thelo] to make her a public example, was minded [boulomai] to put her away privily" (Matt. 1:19). Joseph resolved to do what would achieve his desire. He resolved private divorce because he desired to spare her public humiliation.

9. *1 Cor. 15:38*[119]

Again *thelo* describes God's sovereign prerogative. The Creator dispenses a unique form and appearance to every grain and seed. God in the work of creation exercises prerogative and discretion. The Creator designs and makes whatever pleases him in accord with his aesthetic sense of order and proportion.

10. *James 4:15*[120]

When we announce plans we should acknowledge that God's will has sovereignty over reality. Scripture stresses this truth and provides good models for us to emulate.[121]

---

[119] *1 Cor. 15:38*: but God gives it a body even as *it pleased him*, and to each seed a body of its own.

[120] *James 4:15*: For that you ought to say, If *the Lord will*, we shall both live, and do this or that.

[121] Acts 18:21, 21:14; Rom. 15:32; 1 Cor. 4:19

11. 1 Pet. 2:8-9[122]

Peter teaches that God's will alone fixed his eternal plan for all reality, even for men's rejection of Christ. He uses τιθημι (tithemi), "to ordain," "appoint," "put in place." Paul uses it this way in 1 Thessalonians 5:9. Similarly, Luke uses τασσω (tasso), "to ordain," in Acts 13:48.

12. Rev. 4:11[123]

God's will (thelema) is the ultimate cause of creation. God creates, not out of constraint, but freely and voluntarily. This calls us to bless him: "You are worthy . . . to receive the glory . . . for you did create."

B. Biblical Testimony to the Preceptive Function of God's Supreme Will

In contrast with the decretive function of God's will, no passge epitomizes this testimony. Though no text is a great champion, each is a faithful soldier. Together they form a mighty army, able to dispel all the wiles of error. I survey twenty texts, five in the Old Testament, fifteen in the New.

1. Ezra 10:10-11[124]

Ezra commands the men of Israel to do God's "pleasure," that is, to obey his will. He uses the word, רָצוֹן (ratsôn). It signifies either God's favor,[125] or his acceptance,[126] or his will, desire, or pleasure.[127] Brown, Driver, and Briggs confirm this threefold use.[128] It can also refer to men's favor[129] or will and desire.[130] It comes from the root *ratsah*, which means, "to be well pleased with," "to have pleasure in." In the realm of morality, *ratsah* depicts the mixture of approbation and delight that characterize God when he perceives what is good, right, just, and true.[131] When men obey God's will,

---

[122] *1 Pet. 2:8-9*: for they stumble at the word, being disobedient; whereunto they were also appointed.
[123] *Rev. 4:11*: you did create all things, and because of *your will* they were, and were created.
[124] *Ezra 10:10-11*: You have trespassed, and have married foreign women, to increase the guilt of Israel. Now therefore make confession unto Jehovah, the God of your fathers, and do his pleasure; and separate yourselves from the peoples of the land, and from the foreign women.
[125] Ps. 5:12; Prov. 18:22
[126] Exod. 28:38
[127] Pss. 40:8, 103:21, 143:10
[128] BDB, *Lexicon*, 953
[129] Prov. 14:35
[130] Gen. 49:6; Lev. 1:3; Ps. 145:16, 19; Dan. 11:3, 16, 36
[131] Ps. 147:11; Prov. 16:7

he has delight and approbation. Conversely, he has disapproval and disgust when he perceives what is morally wrong. Thus, when men disobey God's will, he responds in anger: "shall we again break your commandments, and join in affinity with the peoples that do these abominations? Would you not be angry with us till you had consumed us" (Ezra 9:14). God's will formulates his concept of propriety into general moral principles and specific magisterial precepts. His will not only develops and drafts the decalogue, his code of behavior for all men, it also enacts additional legislation for his people. This text views one aspect of that special legislation, his requirement that his people remain separate from the nations.

2. Ps. 5:4[132]

Here David uses חָפֵץ (chaphēts), from the same word family that repeatedly describes God's decretive will (Ps. 115:3, etc.). This word depicts the heart's inclination toward what would gratify and please it. Thus, God has no immoral inclination of any kind. He never has been inclined toward evil, and never can be. He never would or could find any pleasure in something immoral. Rather, he stands immutably inclined towards what is holy, just, righteous and good. His will is immutably fixed on good. He ever desires to do good[133] and always wants his creatures to do good.[134]

3. Ps. 40:8[135]

The word translated *"will"* is *ratsôn*. God expresses his will in his law. God's moral law, the ten commandments, displays God's *"pleasure,"* what he deems morally right. This links the Old and New Testaments. In Hebrews 10:6 the writer uses θελημα (thelema) to translate *ratsôn*. This text describes Christ's disposition. Christ does God's will because God's law is within his heart. God produces this very disposition in sinners when he converts them (Jer. 31:34; Phil. 2:13). Since only true Christians share Christ's attitude towards God's will and law, this distinguishes them from hypocrites.

4. Ps. 51:6[136]

David employs *chaphēts*, which depicts God's decretive will in Psalm 115:3, to describe his preceptive will. Thus, "truth in the inward parts" pleases

---

[132] *Ps. 5:4*: For you are not a God that *has pleasure* in wickedness: evil shall not sojourn with you. The arrogant shall not stand in your sight

[133] Ps. 35:27; Micah 7:18

[134] Ps. 51:6; Ezek. 18:23, 32, 33:11; Hos. 6:6

[135] *Ps. 40:8*: I delight to do *your will*, O my God; yea, your law is within my heart

[136] *Ps. 51:6*: Behold, you *desire* truth in the inward parts.

God. It seems morally good to him. Conversely, he has no pleasure in hypocrisy and insincerity. Thus, God always wants men to be inwardly pure and sincere.

5. *Ezek. 18:23, 32, 33:11*[137]

Ezekiel also uses *chaphēts* to depict God's preceptive will. Again, this very word, in this very form, often depicts God's decretive will. Perhaps you grow weary of these studies. Why this detailed examination? The answer is simple. The false doctrines on this topic usually arise from outright denial or truncation of some aspect of this testimony. Unwillingness to study carefully *all* that Scripture says about God's will has led some to disparage his preceptive will, and others to dilute his decretive will. We must not conduct such study with laziness or prejudice. God has pleasure, not in men's impenitence and ruin, but in their repentance unto life: "I have no pleasure in the death of the wicked; but that the wicked turn from his way and live." Repentance is morally right to God, impenitence morally wrong. When the wicked repent, he experiences gratification and delight. He wants sinners to repent and live, not to remain in their sins and die: "turn you, turn you from your evil ways; for why will you die, O house of Israel."

6. *Matt. 6:10*[138]

The Lord describes God's preceptive will with θελημα (thelema), the very word that depicts his decretive will (Eph. 1:5, 9, 11, etc.). Christ associates God's will and kingdom. God's kingdom is the realm in which his will is done. A king legislates within his realm and jurisdiction. So God legislates throughout the universe, for he is king of heaven and earth. In heaven the holy angels honor God's right to make the rules. His will is done. On earth, however, sinners reject his authority. They refuse to submit to his will and violate his law. Although they challenge his right to regulate their lives, they cannot dethrone him. His will still defines morality and propriety. Sinners can pretend to redefine it. They can *call* evil good until they are blue in the face, but they can never *make* evil good. Christ underscores the religious relevance of God's sovereignty over morality. He teaches us to long and pray for that glorious day when everyone on earth will submit to God's preceptive will.

---

[137] *Ezek. 18:23, 32, 33:11*: Have I any pleasure in the death of the wicked? says the Lord Jehovah; and not rather that he should return from his way, and live? . . . For I have no pleasure in the death of him that dies, says the Lord Jehovah: wherefore turn yourselves, and live . . . Say unto them, As I live, says the Lord Jehovah, I have no pleasure in the death of the wicked; but that the wicked turn from his way and live: turn ye, turn ye from your evil ways; for why will you die, O house of Israel?

[138] *Matt. 6:10*: Your kingdom come. *Your will* be done, as in heaven, so on earth.

7. Matt. 7:21[139]

Jesus describes the preceptive function of God's will with *thelema*. He asserts that everyone who lives and dies in moral rebellion against God will be damned, irrespective of religious privilege and professed belief. Evangelical obedience to God's will furnishes the only certain evidence of saving religion. He warns that if religion consists *only* in doctrine, in ceremonies, and in ministerial gifts, it is false religion.

8. Matt. 12:50[140]

Again, the Lord uses *thelema*. He asserts that God's family is a spiritual family, composed of all who obey the will of God. Gospel obedience to God's preceptive will defines spiritual kinship. Thus, it demarcates Christ's spiritual family. Thus, God's preceptive will plays the decisive role in defining his household under the new covenant.

9. Matt. 23:37[141]

The Lord describes God's preceptive will with the verb, θελω (thelo), which depicts God's decretive will in Romans 9:18-19. He asserts his desire and inclination to bless Jerusalem with his favor and peace. If Jerusalem were to experience conciliation with her Maker and enjoy his blessing, it would gratify and please the Lord. The Lord has long been disposed with a conciliatory demeanor toward the Jewish nation and leaders. Yet, they want none of it: "and you would not." Their wills are set against God and his Son. They have a longstanding pattern of stubborn resistance to his overtures of mercy and peace. For many centuries they have killed the prophets and stoned the messengers he sends in his name. Some, trying to avoid conflict with God's decree, offer the explanation that Christ speaks merely as a man, in reference to his human will. Sometimes Christ does so speak, as in our next text. However, the Lord here views far more than his incarnation and public ministry. When he says: *"how often* would I have gathered your children together," he refers to the entire era in which they killed God's messengers. He speaks as God and for God. He expresses the preceptive function of God's supreme will, not merely his human will.

---

[139] *Matt. 7:21*: Not every one that says unto me, Lord, Lord, shall enter into the kingdom of heaven; but he who does *the will* of my Father who is in heaven.

[140] *Matt. 12:50*: For whosoever shall do *the will of my Father* who is in heaven, he is my brother, and sister, and mother.

[141] *Matt. 23:37*: O Jerusalem . . . that kills the prophets . . . how often would I have gathered your children together . . . and you would not!

Part 3: The Nature of God | 353

10. Matt. 26:39, 42[142]

We behold here a great mystery. God incarnate, Jesus Christ, has both the divine will and also a human will. Christ, in virtue of his human soul, submits his godly human will to his Father's divine will. Christ wants, not something inherently evil, for he could never sin, but something inherently good. He desires to live and avoid the horrors of the cross. His will to live was not in itself morally wrong, but it was contrary to God's will for him. Thus, rather than engage his Father in a battle of wills, or challenge him, he submitted to his will. These words express his submission: "not my will, but yours, be done." Thus, godliness consists, not in cancellation of our human will, but in its submission to God's will.

11. Luke 7:30[143]

Luke records that wicked men reject God's *counsel*. We have seen that *boule* describes God's plan or purpose. When Luke says that they *"rejected"* it, he means that they refused to admit that God sent John the Baptist. John's mission constitutes an integral part of God's plan of redemption. Their rejection reaches its zenith when they refuse to submit to John's baptism. This shows us the connection between God's plan of redemption and his preceptive will. God requires men to embrace his plan of salvation and to submit to its moral and religious demands.

12. Acts 20:27[144]

Again Luke describes God's plan of salvation with *boule*. Paul can't possibly mean that he declared God's entire secret decree. Rather, he means that he taught them, comprehensively, God's plan of salvation. He stresses that he proclaimed repentance toward God and faith in Jesus Christ (Acts 20:21). Again, note the connection between God's plan to save and his preceptive will. The gospel declares God's preceptive will for all men.[145] God commands all men everywhere to repent and believe. Jesus confirmed this when he evangelized indiscriminately (Mark 1:15).

13. Rom. 2:4[146]

This does not explicitly mention God's will. It presents divine intention *implicitly*. This intention is preceptive, rather than decretive, since some

---

[142] *Matt. 26:39, 42*: My Father, if it be possible, let this cup pass away from me: nevertheless, not as I will, but as you will . . . if this cannot pass away, except I drink it, your will be done.
[143] *Luke 7:30*: But the Pharisees and the lawyers rejected for themselves the counsel of God, being not baptized of him.
[144] *Acts 20:27*: I shrank not from declaring unto you the whole *counsel* of God.
[145] Acts 20:21, 24, 27
[146] *Rom. 2:4*: the goodness of God leads you to repentance

despise and resist it to their own ruin.[147] Paul pictures God's goodness as a guide, or shepherd, leading and pointing sinners toward repentance. God is longsuffering in his forbearance with sinners. His kindness to them intends to nudge them to get right with him. Paul uses similar language in his gospel message in Athens: "having determined their appointed seasons, and the bounds of their habitation; *that they should seek God*, if haply they might feel after him and find him" (Acts 17:27). The phrase, "that they should seek God," is an infinitive of purpose. It discloses that God determined the territories and times of the nations with the intent that they seek him. Again, this divine purpose is preceptive, rather than decretive, since many despise and frustrate God's benevolent design in providence. Again, Christ used similar language in his appeal to his countrymen: "howbeit I say these things *that you might* be saved" (John 5:34). Jesus uses the subjunctive of purpose with ἵνα (hina). Literally, he says: "in order that you be saved." He spoke these words indiscriminately to lost sinners who hated and despised him. Again, some reply that he spoke merely as a man, expressing his human purpose and intent. Possibly this is so, but it is not very likely. The context bristles with his claim to be the Supreme Being, God the Son (5:18-46). He speaks to persuade them that his claim to deity is valid. How strange that men plead that he here speaks only as a man, when in this entire discourse he labors to prove that he is God! Thus, these three texts present God's benevolent intent to sinners implicitly. God displays this benevolent intent in his forbearance, providence, and general gospel call. People often despise and frustrate his kind intent and perish in spite of it. Thus, humanity should appreciate God's forbearance, put away presumption, and get right with God.

14. Rom. 2:18[148]

Paul associates God's will (thelema) with his law and its disclosure with his Word. God comprehensively reveals his preceptive will in Scripture. Paul uncovers the general principle that has always regulated how God reveals his will. From the dawn of history God has revealed man's duty with his Word (Gen. 2:16-17). God with an audible voice from Sinai uttered the decalogue, the sum of moral obligation.[149] As providence displays all God's

---

[147] *Rom. 2:4-5*: you despise the riches of his goodness and forbearance and longsuffering, not knowing that the goodness of God leads you to repentance. But after your hardness and impenitent heart you treasure up for yourself wrath in the day of wrath.

[148] *Rom. 2:18*: you bear the name of a Jew, and rest upon the law, and glory in God, and *know his will*, and approve the things that are excellent, being instructed out of the law.

[149] Rom. 3:19-20; 1 John 3:4

secret decrees, even so Scripture, the completed Word of God, reveals God's moral laws for all mankind and his royal precepts for his people.

15. Rom. 12:2[150]

Paul calls upon God's people to give diligence to understand what God wants them to do. He delineates three attributes of God's preceptive will. *First*, whatever God expects of us is *"good."* This could mean that God never requires evil from us. Or, it could mean that what God wills is beneficial for us. We live more happily and productively when we obey God rather than despise his preceptive will. *Second*, God's preceptive will is *"acceptable."* He uses, εὐάρεστος (euarestos), which usually depicts what God finds well-pleasing.[151] It possibly refers once to what pleases an earthly master (Titus 2:9). Thus, Paul asserts that if we obey God's preceptive will, he responds with approbation, approval, and commendation. *Third*, God's preceptive will is *"perfect."* This could mean either complete, lacking nothing, or without flaw, impeccably right. Both things are true. Everything God requires is absolutely good. And, his preceptive will sets out the complete code of behavior for Christians. It is totally sufficient for us. God's will, revealed in the Bible, propounds everything we need to know in order to please him.

16. Eph. 5:17[152]

Paul tells us that wisdom consists in understanding what God wants us to do. Here *thelema* refers to the content of God's preceptive will. The context indicates that God wants Christians to live under the influence, not of alcohol, but of the Holy Spirit: "be not drunken with wine, wherein is riot, but be filled with the Spirit" (5:18). Similarly, God wants us to pursue holiness by abstaining from fornication[153] and to be grateful at all times.[154] In these texts God's will in its preceptive function defines the substance of Christian duty. This teaches us to pray: "teach me to do your will; for you are my God" (Ps. 143:10).

17. Eph. 6:6[155]

Paul exhorts Christian servants to do God's preceptive will from the heart. They should obey their earthly masters conscientiously because their

---

[150] *Rom. 12:2*: the good and acceptable and perfect will of God
[151] Rom. 12:1, 14:18; 2 Cor. 5:9; Eph. 5:10; Phil. 4:18; Col. 3:20; Heb. 13:21
[152] *Eph. 5:17*: Wherefore be ye not foolish, but understand what the will of the Lord is.
[153] 1 Thess. 4:3
[154] 1 Thess. 5:18
[155] *Eph. 6:6*: Servants, be obedient . . . not in the way of eyeservice, as men-pleasers; but as servants of Christ, *doing the will* of God from the heart.

heavenly Master is always watching. Christ is Lord of their conscience. God delegates authority to parents in the home (Eph. 6:1, 2), to elders in the church (Titus 1:7; Heb. 13:17), and to rulers in the state (Rom. 13:1-4). When we submit to their polity (as long as they do not overstep their jurisdiction or violate God's law) we submit to God's will, for he has given them authority. Men derive all legitimate authority from God. He alone has the right to set the bounds of human jurisdiction. His preceptive will disclosed in Scripture defines the limits of human authority.

18. Heb. 10:36[156]

These lines furnish great comfort to God's people. The writer motivates Christians to press on by appealing to their lifestyle of gospel obedience to God's will: *"having done* the will of God." What a remarkable statement! Even though those Christians never kept God's will flawlessly, since sinless perfection is impossible on earth, yet, they *did God's will* truly and evangelically. Let us do likewise.

19. Heb. 13:20-21[157]

God enables Christians to do his will. He works in us by his grace a willingness to please him (Phil. 2:13). The God who makes the rules also gives us strength to keep them. When we have done his will, we must give him all the credit and glory, for he worked in us to do it. Thus Paul has great confidence: "I can do all things in him that strengthens me" (Phil. 4:13).

20. 1 John 2:17[158]

Only those who live in gospel obedience to God's will enter heaven and enjoy eternal life. Some openly hate God and despise his will (Rom. 8:7). Others pay lip service to God. John solemnly warns all whose religion is only in their mouths.

Conclusion: *Collation of this Survey:* I now collate biblical support for my definition and exposition.

> *1. Biblical support for the concept of God's supreme will*
>
> God's will is his faculty of self-determination, his supreme capacity to act intentionally[1] (on purpose) and preferentially[2] (as he pleases), to form desires[3] and to make[4] and fix[5] decisions[6]: by which, in its

---

[156] *Heb. 10:36*: For you have need of patience, that, having done the *will of God*, you may receive the promise.

[157] *Heb. 13:20-21*: Now the God of peace . . . make you perfect in every good thing to do *his will*, working in us that which is pleasing in his sight, through Jesus Christ.

[158] *1 John 2:17*: the world passes away, and the lust thereof; but he that does *the will* of God abides forever

preceptive function, he comprehensively defines morality[7] and propriety[8], openly demands the same from his moral creatures[9], and sincerely desires their compliance[10]; and by which, in its decretive function, he designed[11] and determined[12] in eternity everything that happens in history.[13]

1. Isa. 14:27; Eph. 1:9, 11
2. Pss. 115:3, 135:6; Matt. 11:25, 26; 1 Cor. 15:38; Eph. 1:5, 9
3. Job. 23:13; Ps. 40:8; Acts 13:22; Matt. 6:10; Eph. 1:5, 9, 11
4. Eph. 1:4
5. Eph. 1:5, 11
6. Matt. 11:27; 1 Cor. 12:11; James 1:18
7. Ezra 10:11; Ps. 5:4
8. Gen. 2:16, 17; Ps. 40:7; Ezra 10:11; Heb. 9:10
9. Ps. 35:27; Ezek. 18:32, 33:11; Hos. 6:6; Micah 7:18
10. Ps. 51:6; Ezek. 18:23, 33:11; Heb. 13:21
11. Isa. 14:24, 27, 46:9, 10; Eph. 1:4, 11
12. Acts 2:23, 4:28; Rom. 8:29, 30; Eph. 1:5, 11; 2 Tim. 1:9
13. Job 23:13; Ps. 115:3; Dan. 4:35; Eph. 1:11; James 4:15

2. Biblical support for the characteristics of God's supreme will

God's will is distinguished by supremacy[1], liberty[2], and secrecy[3].

1. Isa. 14:27; Rom. 12:2; 2 Tim. 1:9; Heb. 6:17; Eph. 1:5, 9, 11
2. Ps. 5:4; James 1:13; Job 23:13; Ps. 115:3; Dan. 4:35
3. Eph. 1:9

3. Biblical support for the content of God's supreme will

God's works in creation[1], providence[2], and salvation[3] display the content of God's decretive will. God's law[4] and gospel[5] define the content of his preceptive will for all men, the old[6] and new[7] covenants its additional content for his people. Scripture reveals all its content[8], all the righteous sincerely implement it[9], sinners wickedly spurn it.[10]

1. Rev. 4:11
2. 1 Sam. 2:25; Job 23:13; Prov. 21:1; Isa. 44:28; Dan. 4:17, 25, 32, 35, 5:21; Jonah 1:14; Acts 18:21, 21:14; Rom. 15:32; 1 Cor. 4:19, 15:38
3. Isa. 55:11; Matt. 11:25-27; John 5:21; Acts 2:23, 4:27, 28, 13:48; Rom. 9:18-20,22; 1 Cor. 12:11, 18; Eph. 1:3-11; James 1:18; 1 Pet. 2:8, 9
4. Ps. 40:8; Rom. 3:19, 20
5. Acts 20:21, 27
6. Rom. 2:18; Gal. 3:10; Heb. 9:10
7. 1 Cor. 14:37; Eph. 5:17, 6:6
8. 2 Tim. 3:15, 16
9. Ps. 40:8; Matt. 6:10, 12:50, 26:39, 42; Eph. 5:22-24; Heb. 10:36
10. Ezra 10:10; Matt. 7:21; Rom. 8:7; 1 Pet. 4:2; 1 John 2:17

III. The Seeming Contradiction Associated with God's Supreme Will

I have summarized the biblical teaching and surveyed the biblical testimony. I now bring a word of confirmation due to a seeming contradiction between the decretive and preceptive functions of God's supreme will. The apostle declares both *the tension* and *the resolution* of this seeming contradiction.[159]

A. The Tension of this Seeming Contradiction

God's sovereignty over sin and over salvation highlights this tension.

1. God's Sovereignty over Sin

With reference to God's sovereignty over sin, Paul asserts, not that God permitted or allowed human sin, but that he willed it: "who withstands his will?" Scripture also declares that God meant it,[160] planned it,[161] and ordained it.[162] Then, "Why does he yet find fault?" Why does he find fault with Joseph's brothers, or with the Assyrian,[163] or with Pharaoh,[164] or with the wicked men who crucified Christ? Didn't they all do his will? Yes, but only in one sense, for they violate his preceptive will which forbids their sin. He does not want or desire them to sin.[165] He has no pleasure in their sin, but hates it. He holds them responsible and guilty for their sin.[166] God both decrees and forbids sin. In its decretive function God's will says: "man shall certainly sin." In its preceptive function God's will says to man: "you shall not sin. I do not want you to sin or perish. I deem you guilty for your sin. I intend to punish you for your sin. Why do you sin to your own hurt? Turn from your sin, before it's too late!"[167] God neither authors nor approves sin, although he decreed it.

---

[159] *Rom. 9:18-22*: So then he has mercy on whom he will, and whom he will he hardens. You will then say unto me, Why does he yet find fault? For who withstands his will? Nay but, O man, who are you that replies against God? Shall the thing formed say to him that formed it, Why did you make me thus? Or has not the potter the right over the clay, from the same lump to make one part a vessel unto honor, and another unto dishonor? What if God, willing to show his wrath, and to make his power known, endured with much longsuffering vessels of wrath fitted unto destruction

[160] Gen. 50:20

[161] Acts 2:23

[162] Acts 4:28

[163] Isa. 10:7

[164] Rom. 9:14-18

[165] Pss. 40:7, 51:6

[166] Ps. 5:4; Isa. 10:7; Matt. 7:21

[167] Ps. 51:6; Ezek. 33:11

2. God's sovereign grace and the free offer of the gospel

Further, Paul intimates that God's will respecting salvation displays this same tension: "he has mercy on whom he will, and whom he will he hardens." God's decretive will to save to his elect, often called "sovereign grace," appears incompatible with his preceptive will sincerely to call sinners indiscriminately to Christ, oft termed "the free offer of the gospel." Respecting his preceptive will, Scripture plainly asserts, not merely that he "commands" and "requires" sinners without distinction to repent, but that he has pleasure in, desires, and intends their repentance unto life.[168] It even asserts that he purposes that sinners would seek him and be saved.[169] Nevertheless, in its decretive function, his will appoints some sinners, the reprobate, to disobey the gospel and to suffer his wrath for their sin.[170] Accordingly, he decrees not to appoint Christ to make atonement and intercession for the reprobate[171] and not to draw them, with regenerating grace, to repentance.[172] Scripture is very bold, and says that he decrees to hide gospel light from their eyes,[173] to harden them in their sin,[174] and, because they spurn gospel privileges, even to increase the measure of their suffering in hell.[175] Thus, God's decretive will says concerning the reprobate: "they shall not repent and shall suffer my wrath for their sins. I will not enable them to repent. Christ will not atone for their sins. I will hide the gospel from them, harden them in their sins, and increase their punishment for spurning my gospel." Yet, God's preceptive will says, even to the reprobate: "I command, desire, have pleasure in, and design your repentance unto life. I do not want you to die in your sins and perish. Don't remain in your sins to your own ruin." If he has no pleasure in their eternal ruin, why did he appoint them to wrath? Why didn't he design the atonement for them? Why doesn't he enable their hearts to repent? Why does he harden them in their sins? Why does he hide gospel light from them?

B. The Resolution of this Seeming Contradiction

If we accurately state the teaching of Scripture on God's will, then we must anticipate such questions. We must expect heated objections to our teaching.

---

[168] Ezek. 18:23, 32, 33:11; Rom. 2:4
[169] John 5:34; Acts 17:27
[170] 1 Thess. 5:9; 1 Pet. 2:8, 9
[171] Rom. 8:32; John 17:9
[172] Rom. 8:7; John 6:44
[173] Matt. 11:25-26
[174] Rom. 9:18
[175] Matt. 11:20-24

Like Paul, we must not shrink, in the fear of man, from teaching this truth. To the contrary, we must teach the whole truth about God's will so plainly that men cannot avoid this seeming contradiction. Sadly, some have erroneously devised whole theological systems simply to evade facing the pressure of such tensions. These false systems, because they exalt human logic above God's Word, cannot possibly succeed in honoring the Lord. They are doomed to failure, since the human mind cannot reconcile God's sovereignty over sin with man's responsibility for sin, or sovereign grace with the free offer of the gospel. Human logic, unaided by Scripture, would always draw the wrong conclusion. It would conclude that if God is sovereign over sin, then man couldn't possibly be responsible for his sin. Or, if grace is sovereign, then God's offer of mercy couldn't possibly be indiscriminate and well-intentioned. Paul here puts human logic in its place. Logic has a place, to be sure, but that place is not the lofty perch of supreme authority. Proud logic must with shame take a lower seat, for that lofty place belongs to God's Word alone. Thus, we must not think that our province consists in explaining everything the Bible says, or in reconciling what appears contradictory. Rather, we must labor, without embarrassment, to state biblical tensions clearly, and to embrace them humbly. We can never resolve these seeming contradictions, or fully explain how these two functions of God's will mesh. Only God understands how to reconcile everything the Bible declares. He alone fully grasps how his decretive and preceptive will harmonize. We must embrace all Scripture says by faith, and leave the rest with him.

Further, we must remember that no contradiction exists in fact, only in appearance. Let me illustrate. Picture a little boy standing on the railroad tracks next to his father. The tracks stretch out straight before them for many miles, all the way to the horizon. Suddenly the little boy becomes greatly concerned. "Daddy, daddy," he says, "the tracks come together way down at the end, the train won't have room, it will fall off." "No son," says the dad, "the tracks don't really come together, it only seems like they do." Dad doesn't worry because he understands that things are not always what they appear to be. From one very limited perspective, parallel lines appear to converge. They create an optical illusion. Similarly, from man's very limited perspective, God's decretive and preceptive will appear to contradict each other. They create a "logical illusion." We must not be children in mind or in the things of God. We must believe what our Heavenly Father in his Word tells us about this seeming contradiction.

How then does Paul answer those who object to his doctrine of God's sovereignty over sin and grace? He has no sympathy for their objection.[176] Paul says that even raising such an objection is wicked. He doesn't enter into a sympathetic and sensitive dialogue. Rather, he says, in essence: "God made you, you didn't make God. You're accountable to God, not vice versa. Don't talk like God owes you an explanation. You're not the judge, sitting on the throne, judging God. God is the judge, sitting on the throne, judging you. You've got things all confused and twisted around." The answer is simple, brethren. God does not owe an account of himself to man. Man owes an account of himself to God. Therefore, we must simply embrace this biblical tension. It boils down to our willingness to take our place as a creature and to submit to our Maker, Lord, and Judge. Suffer a word of caution. Remember that the servant of the Lord must not strive, but be gentle. Paul reproves proud rebels, not confused but tenderhearted Christians. Let us learn to distinguish the godly questions of perplexed Christians from the arrogant objections of men who challenge God. Finally brethren, never be ashamed of any tenet of God's Word. Declare plainly and boldly all Scripture says about God's decretive will. Openly confess his sovereignty over sin and grace. Declare with equal clarity and boldness all Scripture says about God's preceptive will. Openly display God's sincere desire that sinners turn from sin and get right with him through Christ.

IV. Practical and Religious Applications of God's Supreme Will

I first summarize experiential applications of God's decretive will, then of his preceptive will. I collate *warnings, comforts,* and *gospel duties* associated with these two functions of God's supreme will.

A. Applications of God's Decretive will

1. Warnings

a. Beware using his decretive will as an excuse to disobey his preceptive will (Rom. 9:19-20).

b. Beware using his decretive will as an excuse to blame God for sin, suffering, and eternal ruin (Rom. 9:19-20).

2. Comforts

a. *For all:* God's decretive will orders the affairs of all governments and rulers for his glory (Dan. 4:35).

---

[176] Nay but, O man, who are you that replies against God? Shall the thing formed say to him that formed it, Why did you make me thus? Or has not the potter the right over the clay, from the same lump to make one part a vessel unto honor, and another unto dishonor?

b. *For Christians:* God's decretive will orders every event in your life for your good and his glory (Rom. 8:28): even your afflictions (1 Pet. 4:19), sins and faults (Rom. 5:20-6:2; 1 John 2:1), and persecutions (Gen. 50:20).

c. *For Ministers:* God's decretive will orders rejection of faithful ministry for your good and his glory.[177]

3. Gospel Duties

a. Bless God for the blessings his decretive will gives (Matt. 11:25-26; 1 Cor. 12:11; Eph. 1:3; Rev. 4:11).

b. Fear God, since his decretive will controls everything that happens to us (Job 23:13, 14; Ps. 33:8-9).

c. Submit, without bitterness and murmuring, to whatever his decretive will ordains in our lives (1 Pet. 4:19).

d. Acknowledge his decretive will when we announce plans (Acts 18:21; Rom. 15:32; 1 Cor. 4:19; James 4:15).

e. Appreciate biblical prophecy because it discloses God's decretive will for the future (Isa. 46:9-10; Eph. 1:9).

B. Applications of God's Preceptive Will

1. Warnings

a. *Beware self-deception and hypocrisy*: religious hypocrites live in rebellion to God's preceptive will.[178]

b. *Beware the error of legalism*: which alleges that God has no prerogative when with his preceptive will he forms his magisterial precepts (Gen. 2:17; Heb. 9:10).

c. *Beware the error of formalism*: which alleges that God's people under the new covenant are marked out by bloodlines and religious rituals, rather than by obedience to God's preceptive will.[179]

2. Comforts

a. God enables Christians by grace to obey his preceptive will and rewards our obedience.[180]

---

[177] Matt. 11:25-26
[178] Matt. 7:21; 1 John 3:20
[179] Ps. 40:8; Jer. 31:34; Matt. 12:50; Phil. 2:13
[180] Heb. 10:36, 13:21

b. God discloses in Scripture all his preceptive will requires from us (2 Tim. 3:15-16).

3. Gospel Duties

a. Obey whatever God's preceptive will requires us to do (Matt. 6:10, 26:39, 42).

b. Pray about God's preceptive will: for guidance to know it, grace to do it, and that all on earth will do it.[181]

c. Study Scripture to learn the content of God's preceptive will (1 Thess. 4:3, 5:18; 2 Tim. 3:15-16).

d. Honor God's preceptive will as the final arbiter of gospel duty (Matt. 6:10).

e. Imitate the gracious disposition expressed in God's preceptive will.[182]

In closing: note well that we must embrace by faith the biblical tension surrounding God's will. We must never shrink from declaring the "whole counsel of God." May the Lord be pleased, for his people's good and for his glory, to grant us, in abundant measure, the faith to believe and confess all Scripture says about his supreme will.

---

[181] Ps. 143:10; Rom. 12:2; Eph. 5:17; Matt. 6:10
[182] Ezek. 18:23, 32, 33:11; Rom. 9:1-5, 10:1, 2; 1 Cor. 11:1

APPENDIX: BIBLICAL TERMINOLOGY FOR GOD'S FACULTY OF WILL
NEW TESTAMENT TERMS

1. Will, desire (Eph. 1:5, 9, 11)

θελημα (thelema): will, desire: at least these 45 times: Matt. 6:10, 7:21, 12:50, 18:14, 26:42; John 4:34, 5:30, 6:38, 39, 40, 7:17, 9:31; Acts 13:22 (plural), 21:14, 22:14; Rom. 1:10, 2:18, 12:2, 15:32; 1 Cor. 1:1; 2 Cor. 1:1, 8:5; Gal. 1:4; Eph. 1:1, 5, 9, 11, 5:17, 6:6; Col. 1:1, 9, 4:12; 1 Thess. 4:3, 5:18; 2 Tim. 1:1; Heb. 10:7, 9, 10, 36, 13:21; 1 Pet. 2:15, 3:17, 4:2,19; 1 John 2:17, 5:14; Rev. 4:11.

θελω (thelo): will, desire: at least these 16 times: Matt. 8:3, 9:13, 23:37, 26:39; Mark 1:40, 41; John 5:21; Acts 18:21; Rom. 9:18, 22; 1 Cor. 4:19, 12:18, 15:38; Col. 1:27; 1 Tim. 2:4; James 4:15

θελεσις (thelesis): will: Heb. 2:4

βουλομαι (boulomai): will, resolve: Matt. 11:27; Luke 22:42; 1 Cor. 12:11; Heb. 6:17; James 1:18; 2 Pet. 3:9

βουλημα (boulema): will, intention: Rom. 9:19

2. Good pleasure, be pleased, desire (Eph. 1:5, 9)

ευδοκια (eudokia): good pleasure: Matt. 11:26; Luke 10:21; Eph. 1:5, 9; Phil. 2:13
ευδοκεω (eudokeo): be pleased: Luke 12:32; 1 Cor. 1:21; Gal. 1:15; Col. 1:19
ζητεω (zeteo): seek, desire: John 4:23
επιθυμεω (epithumeo): desire: Gal. 5:17

3. Purpose, plan of action (Eph. 1:9, 11)

βουλη (boule): counsel, plan: Luke 7:30; Acts 2:23, 4:28, 5:38, 13:36, 20:27; Eph. 1:11; Heb. 6:17
προτιθημι (protithemi): purpose: Eph. 1:9
προθεσις (prothesis): purpose: Rom. 8:28, 9:11; Eph. 1:11, 3:11; 2 Tim. 1:9
μελλω (mello): would, intend: John 6:6
ινα (hina): in order that: for example: John 5:34

4. Choose, select, prefer (Eph. 1:4)

ελογη (ekloge): election: Rom. 9:11, 11:5, 7, 28; 1 Thess. 1:4; 2 Pet. 1:10
ελεκτος (eklektos): elect: Mark 13:20; Luke 18:7; Rom. 8:33, 16:13; Col. 3:12; Tit. 1:1; 1 Pet. 1:2, 2:4, 9
εκλεγομαι (eklegomai): choose: Mark 13:20, 15:7; 1 Cor. 1:27(2), 28; Eph. 1:4; James 2:5
αιρεομαι (aireomai): choose: 2 Thess. 2:13
αιρετιζω (airetizo): choose: Matt. 12:12
προχειριζομαι (procheipizomai): choose, appoint: Acts 22:14, 26:16
προχειροτονεομαι (procheirotoneomai): choose before: Acts 10:41

5. Ordain, foreordain, appoint (Eph. 1:5, 11)

προοριζω (proorizo): foreordain: Acts 4:28; Rom. 8:29, 30; 1 Cor. 2:7; Eph. 1:5, 11
οριζω (horizo): ordain: Acts 2:23, 10:42, 17:26, 31; Heb. 4:7

τιθημι (tithemi): appoint: John 15:16; 1 Thess. 5:9; 1 Pet. 2:8
προθεσμια (prothesmia): appoint: Gal. 4:2
τασσω (tasso): ordain: Acts 13:48; Rom. 13:1
διατασσω (diatasso): command, appoint: 1 Cor. 9:14
προτασσομαι (protassomai): fore-ordain, predestine: Acts 17:26

OLD TESTAMENT TERMS

1. Will, desire

צְבָא (ts^{e}ba') will: Dan. 4:17, 25, 32, 35, 5:21

אָוָה ('avah) desire: Job 23:13; Ps. 132:13, 14

אַוָּה ('avvah) desire: Hos. 10:10

רָצוֹן (ratsôn) (will): Pss. 40:8, 103:21, 143:10

רְעוּת (r^e'ûth): will: Ezra 7:18

אָבָה ('abah) would not: Deut. 10:10, 23:5, 29:20; 2 Kings 8:19, 24:4; 2 Chron. 21:7

נָדִיב (nadîb) (willing): Ps. 51:12

2. Pleasure, be pleased

חָפֵץ (chaphēts): verb: to be pleased, be minded, desire, delight: occurs 75 times in the Old Testamemt: features God's will at least these 18 times: Judges 13:23; 1 Sam. 2:25; Pss. 40:6, 51:6, 16, 115:3, 135:6; Prov. 21:1; Eccles. 8:3; Isa. 53:10, 55:11, 58:2; Hos. 6:6; Ezek. 18:23, 32, 33:11; Hos. 6:6; Jonah 1:14

חָפֵץ (chaphēts): adjective: desiring, wanting, willing, delighting in: derived from the verb *chaphēts*: Occurs 11 times: Features God's will twice: Pss. 5:4, 35:27.

חֵפֶץ (chēphets): noun: derived from verb chaphēts: pleasure, desire, delight, longing, purpose: occurs 39 times: Features God's will at least these 8 times: 1 Sam. 15:22; Job 22:3; Eccles. 5:4, 12:10; Isa. 44:28, 46:10, 48:14, 53:10.

רָצָה (ratsah): be pleased: Ps. 40:13

3. Purpose

חָשַׁב (chashab): mean, purpose, devise: Gen. 50:20; Jer. 26:3, 36:3; Lam. 2:8; Mic. 2:3

עֵצָה ('ētsah): plan, counsel: Ps. 33:11; Prov. 19:21; Isa. 46:10; Mic. 4:12

יָעַץ (ya'ets): purpose: Isa. 14:24, 26, 27, 19:12, 23:9

מַחֲשֶׁבֶת (machashebeth): purpose, thought, device, plan: Ps. 33:11; Jer. 18:11, 51:29; Mic. 4:12

מְזִמָּה (m^{e}zimmah): device, purpose, intent: Jer. 30:24; possibly also Job 42:2.

מֵאֵת יְהוָה (mē'ēth y^{e}hovah): it was of, or, from, Jehovah: for example: Josh. 11:20

4. Choose

בָּחַר (bachar): choose, select: Occurs at least these **86** times: Deut. 7:6, 12:5, 11, 14, 18, 21, 26, 14:2, 23, 24, 25, 15:20, 16:2, 6, 7, 11, 15, 16, 17:8, 10, 15, 18:5, 6, 21:5, 23:16, 26:2, 31:11; 1 Sam. 2:28, 10:24, 16:8, 9, 10; 2 Sam. 6:21; 1 Kings 3:8, 8:16, 44:48, 11:13, 32, 34, 36, 14:21; 2 Kings 21:7, 23:27; 1 Chron. 15:2, 28:4, 5, 6, 10, 29:1; 2 Chron. 6:5, 6, 34, 38, 7:12, 16, 12:13, 29:11, 33:7; Neh. 1:9, 9:7; Pss. 33:12, 47:4, 65:4, 78:67, 68, 70, 105:26, 132:13, 135:4; Isa. 14:1, 41:8, 9, 43:10, 44:1, 2, 48:10, 49:7, 58:5, 6, 66:4; Jer. 33:24; Hag. 2:23; Zech. 1:17, 2:12, 3:2.

5. Ordain, appoint

חֹק (choq): appoint, decree: Job 23:14, 28:26; Pss. 2:7, 148:6; Prov. 8:29; Jer. 5:22

יָכַח (yacach): appoint: Gen. 24:14, 44

מָנָה (manah): appoint, prepare: Jonah 1:17, 4:6, 7, 8

צָוָה (tsavah): appoint, command: Ps. 33:9

קוּם (qûm): appoint: Dan. 2:21, 44, 5:21

שִׁית (shîth): appoint, set, fix: Gen. 4:25; Exod. 23:31

Topic 15. The Emotivity of God

"I Jehovah love justice, I hate robbery with iniquity" (Isa. 61:8); "that cheers God and man" (Judg. 9:13); "Grieve not the Holy Spirit" (Eph. 4:30); "well-pleasing to God" (Phil. 4:18); "the wrath of God" (Rom. 1:18); "the peace of God" (Phil. 4:7)

Unit 3. God's Supreme Affection: *The Emotivity of God*

Introduction: We now consider God's supreme capacity to feel, his "*emotivity.*" Our texts epitomize God's supreme affections. God feels both anger and gratification: "for the wrath of God is revealed from heaven against all ungodliness and unrighteousness of men" (Rom. 1:18), "a sacrifice acceptable, well-pleasing to God" (Phil. 4:18). He feels delight and love, as well as hate and detestation: "I Jehovah love justice, I hate robbery with iniquity" (Isa. 61:8). He senses both joy and grief: "Grieve not the Holy Spirit" (Eph. 4:30), "that cheers God and man" (Judg. 9:13). He has incomprehensible peace: "the peace of God, which passes all understanding" (Phil. 4:7). I present the *concept* of God's emotivity, exhibit its biblical and theological *support*, survey its manifold *display*, and summarize its practical *application*.

I. The Concept of God's Emotivity

When I define God's supreme capacity to feel, I am in uncharted water. Although Reformed theologians acknowledge that God feels, they do not pay as much attention to this faculty as to his mind or will. Thus, defining God's emotivity precisely involves greater difficulty. Thus, I offer my definition with fear and trembling. Yet, based on my survey of the biblical witness, I define God's emotivity as follows:

> God's emotivity is his supreme capacity to act responsively and sensationally; to feel pure and principled affections of love and hate, joy and grief, pleasure and anger, and peace; in accord with his supreme, spiritual, and simple Being and impeccable virtue.

This definition features the *general nature, specific expressions,* and *distinguishing traits* of his emotivity.

A. The General Nature of God's Emotivity

In its *general nature* God's emotivity is "his supreme capacity to act responsively and sensationally." God feels spiritual sensation. He is not the "unmoved mover" of Greek philosophy. He reacts and interacts with genuine concern. In eternity God relates emotively to Trinitarian reality; upon creation, to created reality; upon the advent of sin, to immorality and its baneful fruits; upon the exercise of grace, to redemptive reality. He lives a life, not of apathy, but of concern. He responds to persons and things, not merely with his mind and will, but with his heart. In his heart he feels "pure and principled affections." I call God's feelings "affections," rather than "emotions," to avoid misconception. Webster defines an emotion as: "a psychic and physiological reaction (as anger or fear), subjectively experienced as strong feeling and physiologically involving changes that prepare the body for immediate action."[1] Divine affections, like human emotions, are "reactions" and "sensations." Yet human emotions involve the body (physiological) as well as the soul (psychic). We see a face "blanched with fear," or "flushed with anger." Since God has no body, he does not experience the physiological aspects of an emotion. Thus, I don't explicitly define his emotivity with the word, "emotions." Further, Webster defines affection as "the feeling aspect of consciousness," or as "a mild feeling."[2] Since "affection" describes only the psychic (spiritual) aspect of an emotion, not its physiological (material) aspect, it is a far superior term for God's feelings. It probably also refers to a mild human emotion because a mild feeling, unlike a strong feeling, does not involve a noticeable degree of bodily change. Yet, by using the term I do not mean to imply that God only has mild feelings. Further, divine affections are "pure and principled affections." "Pure" distinguishes divine feeling from carnal impulsiveness and evil passions, such as a fit of "blind" rage. "Principled" distinguishes divine affection from sentimentality. Webster defines sentimental as "marked or governed by feeling," or, "resulting from feeling rather than reason or thought."[3] God's affections are not unprincipled sentiments.

B. *The Specific Expressions of God's Emotivity*

The *specific expressions* of his emotivity are: "love and hate, joy and grief, pleasure and anger, and peace." God responds emotively to beauty and disarray, to beneficiality and harm, to propriety and moral wrong, and to personal security. Beauty and beneficiality evoke his delight and joy. Conversely, disarray and harm arouse his detestation and grief. Moral propriety evokes delight, joy, and pleasure. Conversely, moral wrong provokes anger, hate, and grief in his heart. Absolute security and invulnerability evoke absolute peace. One of my students once observed that Scripture predicates an aspect of fear to God, in the sense that God perceived a threat to his reputation and responded out of concern to surmount it. Yet, God is never in danger. He is invulnerable. He can't be startled, overthrown, or assaulted. No calamity can ever touch or hurt him. Nor does

---

[1] *WNC Dictionary*, 369
[2] Ibid., 19
[3] Ibid., 1048

he feel anxiety about unfulfilled need. He has no need of creatures or support. Further, he calms our fears by assuring us that he is with us. What comfort is that if he too is vulnerable and afraid? Thus, God does not feel anything akin to the fear that vulnerable creatures feel. Rather, he feels uninterrupted and absolute peace.

C. The Distinguishing Traits of God's Emotivity

Its *distinguishing traits* spring from the fact that his being and virtue regulate it. First, God feels "in accord with his supreme, spiritual, and simple Being." God's spirituality insures that his affections, unlike human emotions, lack a physiological aspect. His simplicity demands that he feels with his whole being. His supremacy (infinity, eternity, immutability, ideality and aseity) guarantees that his affections do not render him dependent or vulnerable, or mar his infinite perfection, or make him mutable. Again, immutability and aseity imply that God's emotive capacity is independent of his creatures and unalterable. Nevertheless, the immutable God responds differently to saints and sinners (Ps. 5:5). When man sins, God's relation and response to him change accordingly. The immutable God is not an untouchable and apathetic "absolute" that enters no relations. Though Greek philosophy venerates such a "god," Scripture does not know him. Berkhof corrects this false notion of immutability:[4]

> The divine immutability should not be understood as implying *immobility*; as if there were no movement in God . . . The Bible teaches us that God enters into manifold relations with man, and as it were, lives their life with them. There is change round about Him, change in the relations of men to Him, but there is no change in His Being, His attributes, His purpose, His motives of action, or His promises."

Second, God feels in accord with his "impeccable virtue." Every divine affection is holy, good, just, and faithful. Thus, there is similarity between human emotion and divine affection, because man is the image of God. Yet, there is also a profound difference. God does not feel human emotion. He is the exalted, impeccable Creator; man is but a lowly, flawed creature.

II. Support for God's Emotivity

I exhibit how Scripture and Reformed theology support God's emotivity.

A. Biblical Support for God's Emotivity

We have already seen that the capacity to feel is an essential property of every spirit and that God's emotive faculty is supreme and spiritual.

---

[4] Berkhof, *Systematic Theology*, 59

Scripture depicts God's capacity to feel as his *heart*[5] and his *soul*.[6] Sometimes it combines these terms.[7] These terms primarily describe the non-material aspect of a human being, the human spirit, or soul, or heart. For this reason in the Doctrine of Man course, when we expound man's constitution, I present comprehensively the biblical terms for heart[8] and soul.[9] Now consider with me how each aspect of this testimony supports God's emotivity.

1. The biblical testimony to God's heart supports God's emotivity.

In his heart God thinks.[10] In his heart God purposes, intends, and plans.[11] God's heart thus depicts his supreme mind and will, his capacity to think and plan. Further, in his heart God communes personally and communicates verbally.[12] Further, in his heart God feels spiritual sensations of

---

[5] Two Hebrew terms, *lēb* and *lēbab*, and one Greek term, *kardia*, depict God's heart. I present the comprehensive use of these terms in the Doctrine of Man, Topic 5, when I expound man's pyschosomatic constitution.

[6] The Hebrew term, *nephesh*, and the Greek term, *psyche*, depict God's soul. I also present their use comprehensively when I expound man's constitution in the Doctrine of Man, Topic 5.

[7] *Jer. 32:41*: Yes, I will rejoice over them to do them good, and I will plant them in this land assuredly with my whole heart (lēb) and with my whole soul (nephesh).

[8] The Hebrew term לֵב (lēb): "heart," depicts the human heart some 513 times. It depicts God's heart at least these 19 times: Gen. 6:6, 8:21; 2 Sam. 7:21; 1 Kings 9:3; 1 Chron. 17:19; 2 Chron. 7:16; Job 7:17, 34:14, 36:5; Ps. 33:11; Jer. 3:15, 7:31, 19:5, 23:20, 30:24, 32:35, 41; Ezek. 28:2; Hos. 11:8. The cognate term, לֵבָב (lēbab): "heart," depicts the human heart at least 242 times. It depicts God's heart at least these 3 times: 1 Sam. 2:35, 13:14; 2 Kings 10:30. The Greek term, καρδια (kardia), "heart," refers to the human heart 154 times. Once it depicts the heart of the Supreme Being: Acts 13:22.

[9] The Hebrew term נֶפֶשׁ (nephesh): "soul," "life," "self," "person," "being," depicts the human soul some 347 times. It refers to God's personal subsistence at least these 20 times: Lev. 26:11, 30; Judg. 10:16; 1 Sam. 2:35 ["mind"]; Job 23:13; Ps. 11:5; Isa. 1:14, 42:1; Jer. 5:9, 29, 6:8, 9:9, 12:7, 14:19, 15:1 ["mind"], 32:41, 51:14 ["himself"]; Ezek. 23:18(2); Amos 6:8 ["himself"]. The Greek term, ψυχη (psyche): "soul," "life," "self," "person," "being," occurs 104 times with a variety of nuances. On two occasions it depicts the personal subsistence or self-awareness of the Supreme Being: Matt. 12:18; Heb. 10:38.

[10] *Ps. 33:11*: The counsel of Jehovah stand forever, the *thoughts of his heart* (lēb) to all generations. *Jer. 23:20*: The anger of Jehovah shall not return, until he has executed, and until he has performed *the thoughts of his heart* (lēb): in the latter days you shall consider it perfectly.

[11] *Jer. 30:24*: The fierce anger of Jehovah shall not return, until he has done *it*, and until he has performed *the intents of his heart* (lēb): in the latter days you shall consider it

[12] *Gen. 8:21*: And Jehovah smelled the sweet savor; and *Jehovah said in his heart* (lēb), *I will not* again curse the ground any more for man's sake, for that the imagination of man's heart

compassion.[13] In his heart he feels grief[14] over sin. With his whole heart he feels joy over his people.[15] Therefore, God's heart is the living God himself, thinking, willing, and feeling as a personal being. Thus, when God says that "his heart will be there," he means that he himself, personally, will be especially present at his temple.[16] Scripture thus cements God's capacity to feel to his capacity to think and intend as a personal being. Therefore, God really thinks, intends, feels, and communes personally and verbally.

God created man in his image. Scripture explicitly affirms this analogy.[17] The human heart thinks, intends, and feels personally. Thus, the human heart pictures, albeit dimly, the heart of God. Thus, Scripture depicts David as a man whose heart reflected God's heart.[18] Thus, God promised to give his people spiritual leaders who would reflect his heart toward them.[19] God's thoughts, intents, and feelings are higher than man's, because they have all the traits of his supreme Being. Nevertheless, even as he really and truly thinks and plans, even so he really and truly feels. Therefore, God's capacity to feel is just as real as his capacity to think, intend, and commune personally.

(lēb) is evil from his youth; neither will I again smite any more everything living, as I have done.

[13] *Hos. 11:8*: How shall I give you up, Ephraim? *how* shall I cast you off, Israel? how shall I make you as Admah? *how* shall I set you as Zeboiim? *my heart (lēb) is turned (haphak) within me,* my compassions (nichûm) are kindled together

[14] *Gen. 6:6*: And it repented Jehovah that he had made man on the earth, and *it grieved him at his heart* (lēb).

[15] *Jer. 32:41*: Yes, *I will rejoice over them* to do them good, and I will plant them in this land assuredly *with my whole heart* (lēb) and with my whole soul (nephesh).

[16] *1 Kings 9:3*: And Jehovah said unto him, I have heard your prayer and your supplication, that you have made before me: I have hallowed this house, which you have built, to put my name there for ever; and my eyes [capacity to perceive] and *my heart* (lēb) [capacity to feel, purpose, and think personally] *shall be there* perpetually.

[17] *Ezek. 28:2*: Son of man, say unto the prince of Tyrus, Thus says the Lord Jehovah; Because your heart (lēb) *is* lifted up, and you have said, I *am* a god, I sit *in* the seat of God, in the midst of the seas; yet you *are* a man, and not God, though you set your heart (lēb) as the heart (lēb) of God:

[18] *1 Sam. 13:14*: But now your kingdom shall not continue: Jehovah has sought him a man after his own heart (lēbab), and Jehovah has commanded him *to be* captain over his people, because you have not kept *that* which Jehovah commanded you. *Acts 13:22*: And when he had removed him, he raised up unto them David to be their king; to whom also he gave testimony, and said, I have found David the *son* of Jesse, a man after my own heart (kardia), which shall fulfil all my will.

[19] *Jer. 3:15*: And I will give you shepherds according to my heart (lēb), which shall feed you with knowledge and understanding

2. The Biblical testimony to God's personal subsistence and self-awareness supports God's emotivity.

Scripture depicts God's personal subsistence and consciousness, his *soul*, with the terms *nephesh*[20] and *psyche*.[21] Scripture connects God's capacity to will with his personal consciousness.[22] Scripture also connects God's capacity to feel with his personal subsistence. Subsisting personally, the living God feels disgust and abhorrence over idolatry.[23] In his personal consciousness he feels grief over the misery of his people,[24] hatred for those that love violence and for false religion,[25] and anger for his rebellious nation.[26] In his capacity for self-awareness, the living God also feels love for and delight in his people.[27] He also feels delight and good pleasure, the opposite of anger, in his Son incarnate, Jesus Christ.[28] Therefore, just as surely as God truly lives personally, so just that surely God actually feels.

---

[20] *Jer. 51:14*: Jehovah of hosts has sworn by himself (nephesh), *saying*, Surely I will fill you with men, as with the canker-worm; and they shall lift up a shout against you. *Ezek. 23:18*: So she uncovered her whoredoms, and uncovered her nakedness: then my soul (nephesh) was alienated from her, like as my soul (nephesh) was alienated from her sister. *Amos 6:8*: The Lord Jehovah has sworn by himself (nephesh), says Jehovah, the God of hosts: I abhor the excellency of Jacob, and hate his palaces; therefore will I deliver up the city with all that is therein.

[21] *Heb. 10:38*: But my righteous one shall live by faith: And if he shrink back, my soul (psyche) has no pleasure in him

[22] *Job 23:13*: But he is in one *mind*, and who can turn him? And what *his soul (nephesh) desires*, even that he does.

[23] *Lev. 26:30*: And I will destroy your high places, and cut down your sun-images, and cast your dead bodies upon the bodies of your idols; and my *soul (nephesh) shall abhor* you.

[24] *Judg. 10:16*: And they put away the foreign gods from among them, and served Jehovah; and his *soul (nephesh) was grieved* for the misery of Israel.

[25] *Ps. 11:5*: Jehovah tries the righteous; but the wicked and him that loves violence *his soul (nephesh) hates*. *Isa. 1:14*: Your new moons and your appointed feasts *my soul (nephesh) hates*; they are a trouble unto me; I am weary of bearing them. *Jer. 14:19*: Have you utterly rejected Judah? has *your soul (nephesh) loathed* Zion? why have you smitten us, and there is no healing for us? We looked for peace, but no good came; and for a time of healing, and, behold, dismay!

[26] *Jer. 5:9*: Shall I not visit for these things? says Jehovah; and shall not *my soul (nephesh) be avenged* on such a nation as this?

[27] *Lev. 26:11-12*: And I will set my tabernacle among you: and *my soul (nephesh) shall not abhor you*. 12 And I will walk among you, and will be your God, and ye shall be my people. *Jer. 12:7*: I have forsaken my house, I have cast off my heritage; I have given *the dearly beloved of my soul* (nephesh) into the hand of her enemies.

[28] *Isa. 42:1*: Behold, my servant, whom I uphold; my chosen, in whom *my soul (nephesh) delights*: I have put my Spirit upon him; he will bring forth justice to the Gentiles. *Matt. 12:18*: Behold, my servant whom I have chosen; My beloved in whom my *soul (psyche) is well pleased*: I will put my Spirit upon him, and he shall declare judgment to the Gentiles

Part 3: The Nature of God

Conclusion: collation of the biblical support

I now collate biblical support for God's emotivity in accord with my definition:

> God's emotivity is his supreme capacity to act responsively and sensationally[1]; to feel pure and principled affections of love[2] and hate[3], joy[4] and grief[5], pleasure[6] and anger[7], and peace[8]; in accord with his supreme[9], spiritual[10], and simple[11] Being and impeccable virtue.[12]

1. Gen. 6:6; Judg. 10:16; Isa. 1:14; Hos. 11:8
2. Deut. 7:13, 10:15; Ps. 18:19, Prov. 11:1, 12:22, 15:8; Isa. 42:1, 61:8; Jer. 9:24; John 17:24
3. Pss. 5:5, 11:5; Prov. 6:16; Isa. 1:14, 61:8
4. Deut. 28:63, 30:9; Judg. 9:13; Neh. 8:10; Pss. 16:11, 60:6, 104:31; Isa. 62:5, 65:19; Jer. 32:41; Zeph. 3:17; Luke 15:7, 10; John 15:11, 17:13
5. Gen. 6:6; Judg. 10:16; Pss. 78:40, 95:10; Isa. 63:10; Eph. 4:30; Heb. 3:10, 17
6. Num. 23:27, 24:1; 1 Kings 3:10; Pss. 69:3, 149:4; Prov. 16:7, Eccles. 7:26; Ezra 10:11; Rom. 8:8; Phil. 4:18; Col. 3:20; 1 Thess. 4:1; Heb. 11:5, 6, 13:16, 21
7. Num. 11:10, 22:22; Deut. 4:25, 6:15, 7:4, 9:18, 19, 13:17, 29:20; Josh. 7:1; Judg. 2:12, 14, 20, 3:8, 10:7; Pss. 2:12, 7:11, 78:49, 85:3, 90:11, 103:8, 145:8; Jer. 4:8; Rom. 1:18, 2:5, 9, 9:22, 12:19; Eph. 2:3, 5:6; Col. 3:6; 1 Thess. 1:10, 2:16, 5:9; Heb. 3:11; Rev. 6:16, 17, 14:10, 19, 15:1, 7, 16:1, 19, 19:15
8. Ps. 23:4; John 14:27; Rom. 15:33; Phil. 4:7, 9; 1 Thess. 5:23; 2 Thess. 3:16; Heb. 13:20
9. Ps. 90:11; John 17:24; Eph. 3:19
10. Isa. 31:3; Luke 24:37-39; John 4:24; Col. 1:15
11. 1 John 4:8, 16
12. Jer. 9:24; James 1:13

B. Theological Support for God's Emotivity

Some may think that this teaching smacks of theological novelty. Since Scripture is so plain on this topic, even if it were novel, the fault would not lie with me. Yet other teachers of systematic theology do not completely miss or deny what Scripture so clearly teaches. Rather, they repudiate the erroneous idea that God is unfeeling, heartless, and apathetic. Consider the testimony of five witnesses.

1. Charles Hodge

> As power of some kind belongs to every substance, the power which belongs to spirit, to the substance itself, is that of thought, feeling and volition...We are not more certain than we exist, than that we think, feel and will. We know ourselves only as thus thinking, feeling, and willing, and we therefore are sure that these powers or faculties are the essential attributes of a spirit, and must belong to every spirit...As all this is involved in our consciousness of

> ourselves as spirit, it must all be true of God, or God is of a lower order of being than man.[29]
>
> If this be understood to mean that the divine perfections are really what the Bible declares them to be; that God truly thinks, feels, and acts; that He is truly wise, just, and good; that He is truly omnipotent, and voluntary, acting or not acting, as He sees fit; that He can hear and answer prayer; then it may be admitted.[30]
>
> The schoolmen, and often the philosophical theologians, tell us that there is no feeling in God. This, they say, would imply passivity, or susceptibility of impression from without, which it is assumed is incompatible with the nature of God...Here again we have to choose between a mere philosophical speculation and the clear teaching of the Bible, and of our own moral and religious nature. Love of necessity involves feeling, and if there be no feeling in God, there can be no love.[31]

Although Hodge doesn't expound God's emotivity, he affirms and defends it in the plainest possible terms. He says that God "truly feels," and opposes unbiblical speculation of "philosophical theologians."

2. Morton Smith

Smith expounds God's attributes.[32] He considers first, "the essential attributes," God's spirituality, immutability, and infinity.[33] Second, he considers "attributes that are chiefly intellectual," God's omniscience, wisdom and freedom.[34] Third, he considers "attributes that are chiefly moral," God's holiness and righteousness.[35] Fourth, he considers "attributes that are chiefly emotive." He begins with God's love, then considers God as "gracious, merciful, and long-suffering," and concludes his consideration of God's emotive attributes with "the wrath of God."[36] Of love he says: "It should be observed that love is emotive in character." He then cites part of the passage in Warfield's sermon on John 3:16 that I am about to cite.[37]

---

[29] Hodge, *Systematic Theology*, 1:378-379
[30] Ibid., 373-374
[31] Ibid., 428-429
[32] Morton H. Smith, *Systematic Theology* (2 Vols.; Greenville: Greenville Seminary Press, 1994), 1:126-146
[33] Ibid., 1:130-137
[34] Ibid., 1:137-139
[35] Ibid., 1:139-141
[36] Ibid., 1:141-146
[37] Ibid., 1:143

Clearly, Smith does not deny God's emotivity or proclaim a heartless and unfeeling God.

3. B. B. Warfield

In a sermon on John 3:16, which he titles, "God's Immeasurable Love," Warfield explicitly denounces the false doctrine that God is the unmoved absolute with no emotional life. He says bluntly that such a "god" would be "no God at all":

> now the text tells us of . . . God . . . that He loves. In itself, before we proceed a step further, this is a marvelous declaration. The metaphysicians have not yet plumbed it and still protest inability to construe the Absolute in terms of love. We shall not stop to dwell upon this somewhat abstract discussion. Enough for us that a God without an emotional life would be a God without all that lends its highest dignity to personal spirit whose very being is movement; and that is as much as to say no God at all.[38]

Further, in his article, "The Emotional Life of our Lord," he says:[39]

> The moral sense is not a mere faculty of discrimination between the qualities which we call right and wrong, which exhausts itself in their perception as different. The judgments it passes are not merely intellectual but what we call moral judgments; that is to say, they involve approval and disapproval according to the qualities perceived. It would be impossible, therefore, for a moral being to stand in the presence of perceived wrong indifferent and unmoved . . . The emotions of indignation and anger belong therefore to the very self-expression of a moral being as such and cannot be lacking to him in the presence of wrong.

Warfield uncovers precisely why God's emotivity is so crucial. If God really were an "unmoved mover," he would at best be "amoral," totally oblivious to moral good and evil. Yet God does know good and evil (Gen. 3:5, 22). When a being who knows good and evil stands apathetic in the presence of evil, he behaves wretchedly. An unmoved "god," who doesn't feel, wouldn't be holy or just, but "ungodly." Such indifference would make him immoral! Divine emotivity doesn't contradict immutability. Rather, divine apathy in the presence of evil would contradict impeccability. When a righteous moral being responds to moral wrong with anger, and to moral

---

[38] Benjamin B. Warfield, *The Savior of the World*, (Edinburgh: The Banner of Truth Trust, 1991), 117. Also found in *Biblical and Theological Studies*, editor Samuel G. Craig (Philadelphia: The Presbyterian and Reformed Publishing Co., 1968), 513-514.

[39] B. B. Warfield, *The Person and Work of Christ*, editor Samuel G. Craig (The Presbyterian and Reformed Publishing Co., 1970), 107

right with good pleasure, he doesn't change his essential nature. Rather, his essential nature causes him to react appropriately to right and wrong. Therefore, any who oppose God's emotivity oppose, albeit unwittingly, his impeccability.

Finally, in his article, "God," Warfield refers to God's capacity to feel as "sensibility":[40]

> Thus we come to know God as a personal Spirit, infinite, eternal and illimitable, alike in his being, and in the intelligence, sensibility and will which belong to him as personal spirit.

Webster defines "sensibility" as, "the ability to receive sensations," and "sensation" as "excited interest or feeling."[41] Thus Warfield explicitly asserts that God experiences spiritual sensations, or in other words, he says that God "feels."

4. Leon Morris

When Leon Morris explains propitiation, he expounds the display of God's wrath in the Old and New Testaments.[42] He says that God "reacts" to evil and that his reaction involves "hostility." Yet, he affirms that God has sinless anger, not blind rage, or "capricious passion":

> There is a consistency about the wrath of God in the Old Testament. It is no capricious passion, but the stern *reaction* of the divine nature to evil in man. It is aroused only and inevitably by sin.[43] [emphasis supplied]
>
> Where the term 'wrath' does not occur, we find strong expressions for the divine *hostility* to all that is evil.[44] [emphasis supplied]

5. John Gill

We have already seen that John Gill uses God's faculties as his organizing principle. Among Reformed theologians he presents the most detailed

---

[40] B. B. Warfield, *The Selected Shorter Writings of Benjamin B. Warfield—1*, editor John E. Meeter (Nutley, NJ: Presbyterian and Reformed Publishing Co., 1970), 71. Also found in *The Works of Benjamin B. Warfield* (10 Vols.; Grand Rapids: Baker Book House, 1981), 9:111.
[41] *WNC Dictionary*, 1047
[42] Leon Morris, *The Apostolic Preaching of the Cross* (Grand Rapids: Wm. B. Eerdmans, 1976), 129-136, 161-166
[43] Ibid., 131
[44] Ibid., 163

exposition of God's affections.[45] He expounds God's love,[46] grace,[47] mercy,[48] long-suffering,[49] goodness[50] anger and wrath,[51] hatred,[52] and joy.[53] He introduces and concludes this exposition as follows:

> Next to the attributes which belong to God, as an intelligent Spirit, to his understanding and will, may be considered those which may be called Affections; for though, properly speaking, there are none in God, he being a most pure and simple act, free from all commotion and perturbation, yet there being some things said and done by him, which are similar to affections in intelligent beings, they are ascribed to him; as love, pity, hatred, anger, &c., from which must be removed everything that is carnal, sensual, or has any degree of imperfection in it.[54]

> Having considered those attributes of God which bear a likeness to affections in men, I proceed to consider those which in them may be called virtues; as holiness, justice, or righteousness, truth, or faithfulness.[55]

Gill duly qualifies divine emotivity. Human emotions are *like* divine affections. Yet, God, does not feel human emotions or sinful affections. Thus, Gill depicts God's affections as: "those attributes of God which bear a likeness to affections in men." He denies that God feels human emotions: "for though, properly speaking, there are none in God." He explains why God cannot feel human emotion: "he being a most pure and simple act, free from all commotion and perturbation." Webster says that "perturb" means "to throw into confusion."[56] Similarly, Webster defines "commotion" as "noisy confusion," or "mental confusion."[57] Thus, Gill affirms that God does not feel unprincipled sentiment, or become confused. God never "looses it" or "goes nuts." Again, Gill correctly guards against attributing sinful

---

[45] Gill, *Body of Divinity*, 1:112-148
[46] Ibid., 1:112-117
[47] Ibid., 1:117-122
[48] Ibid., 1:122-128
[49] Ibid., 1:128-131
[50] Ibid., 1:131-136
[51] Ibid., 1:136-143
[52] Ibid., 1:143-146
[53] Ibid., 1:146-148
[54] Ibid., 1:112
[55] Ibid., 1:148
[56] *WNC Dictionary*, 849
[57] Ibid., 225

passions or the bodily aspects of human emotion to God: "similar to affections in intelligent beings . . . from which must be removed everything that is carnal, sensual, or has any degree of imperfection in it." Divine affections never involve anything bodily or sinful. Again, while expounding God's longsuffering, he says: "the very nature and essence of God, which is free from all passion and perturbation, from all suffering, grief, and pain."[58] Finally, Gill defends the idea that God feels anger:[59]

> anger belongs to God, or may be predicated of him. This is denied by some philosophers of the Cynic and Stoic sects, because it is a passion; they allow grace, good-will, and beneficence in God toward men, but not anger; this they suppose to be a weakness, and even a sort of madness . . . The Epicureans deny that either is in God; neither favour and good-will, nor anger and wrath; for they imagine he has no concern in the affairs of men . . . and so is neither pleased or displeased with them; and is neither kind and favorable to them, nor is angry with them, nor resents what is done by them. But the Scriptures everywhere ascribe anger to God.

III. The Display of God's Emotivity

Introduction: I now build on the solid foundation laid by our fathers in the Reformed faith. I unfold how Scripture displays God's seven primary affections: love, hate, joy, grief, pleasure, anger, and peace. I introduce this display with two general observations. First, Scripture displays distinct and contrasting pairs of divine affections: "I Jehovah *love* justice, I *hate* robbery with iniquity" (Isa. 61:8). It also contrasts joy with grief, and anger with gratification or pleasure. Only Divine peace stands alone, since its counterpart would be fear. Second, Scripture displays divine affections absolutely and relatively. We could distinguish "absolute affections," experienced when only God was, from "relative affections," experienced in relation to creation, fall, and redemption. This would parallel the distinction between infinity and omnipresence. Like infinity, emotivity is an absolute attribute. God did not need to create or save in order to feel spiritual sensation. This distinction helps us to think clearly about affections such as God's hate. Hate is an attribute of God in a similar way as omnipresence. Hate is not an *absolute* divine affection, but a *relative* divine affection. Although God never changes, he did not feel hate in eternity, before there was moral evil. Nor did God feel grief before there was suffering. Nevertheless, hate is necessary in consequence of sin. God could no more cease to respond to sin with revulsion and detestation than he could cease to

---
[58] Gill, *Body of Divinity*, 1:128
[59] Ibid., 1:137

be omnipresent in space. Thus, before the world was, God felt only delight, joy, pleasure, and peace in Trinitarian fellowship. The Father, Son, and Spirit, perceiving divine beauty, felt pure delight; perceiving divine beneficiality and blessedness, felt unmingled joy; perceiving divine virtue, felt perfect gratification or pleasure; and perceiving divine security and stability, felt absolute peace. Upon the occurrence of sin, God felt spiritual sensations of anger, grief, and detestation in relation to fallen creatures. Scripture thus places priority on the affections of delight, joy, pleasure, and peace. Thus, I first survey these, then their negative counterparts. I conclude with God's peace.

A. God's Delight and Love

Love often denotes a sensation of delight, felt for someone or something that the soul regards as beautiful, pleasant, or attractive. In this emotive sense, it describes Isaac's delight in savory meat[60] and Amnon's delight in Tamar.[61] Sometimes, love depicts voluntary attachment and loyalty, as opposed to rejection. Thus, Leah, hoping Jacob would dwell with her, said: "now will my husband love me" (Gen. 29:32-34). Thus the Lord calls voluntary cleaving to a master, love: "No man can serve two masters: for either he will hate the one, and love the other; or else he will hold to the one, and despise the other" (Matt. 6:24). Sometimes, love has a moral connotation. It refers to the virtue of goodwill and unselfishness, in contrast to malice, selfishness, and evil doing. In this sense Scripture commands us to love the Lord,[62] our neighbor,[63] and even our enemies.[64] Our duty to love our enemies discloses that having goodwill does not always coalesce with feeling delight. Nor is feeling delight necessarily joined to having goodwill, as Amnon's mistreatment of Tamar confirms. In some relations love is emotional, volitional, and moral. In godly, conjugal love, a husband and wife feel delight in each other, voluntarily cleave to each other, and display goodwill for each other. Similarly, God delights in his people, cleaves to them, and has goodwill to them. Therefore, God's love illustrates an inherent weakness in my arrangement of God's attributes. In one respect God's love for his saints is a feeling; in another sense, it is a virtue. Gill also sensed the difficulty this poses for our arrangement. He lists goodness as a divine virtue, but never distinctly expounds it as such. He blends it with his

---

[60] Gen. 27:4
[61] 2 Sam. 13:4, 15
[62] Deut. 6:5
[63] Lev. 19:18
[64] Luke 6:27

exposition of God's affections.[65] How do I proceed? I focus now on God's feeling of delight and survey texts that feature it. Under Topic 17 I expound God's goodness to his saints in whom he delights and even to the wicked that he detests. Since God's love bridges his feeling of delight and his virtue of goodness, I suffer some overlap. I collate this testimony to God's delight around five primary objects: Christ, God's creative genius, his justice and mercy, the moral virtue of righteous men, and the society of his people.

1. God's delight in Christ

Christ's enemies use sarcasm.[66] In arrogant blindness, they dare to presume that God finds Jesus Christ as detestable as they do. The word translated "delights in" is חָפֵץ (chaphēts). This word often depicts God's faculty of will.[67] This shows the close connection between the good pleasure of God's will and his feelings of delight. Further, the Father explicitly affirms his delight in the incarnate Christ.[68] Here he employs the word רָצָה (ratsah), which means to be pleased with, or satisfy. This word also displays the connection of God's heart and will, since *ratsôn*, translated "*will*" in Psalm 40:8, comes from it. *Ratsah* also displays the close connection between God's feelings of delight (the opposite of hate) and pleasure (the opposite of anger). Thus, when the Father beholds Jesus, he feels a sensation composed of intense delight and gratification. He finds in Jesus nothing repulsive or morally wrong. Accordingly, Jesus traces God's love for him to its eternal source.[69] The Father *loved* the Son before the world was. This love embraces divine feeling, volition, and virtue. God's eternal love has a moral aspect. The Father has only goodwill toward the Son. This eternal love also has a volitional aspect. The Father stands eternally committed to the Son in bonds of Trinitarian loyalty. Yet, even from eternity, this love has an emotive aspect. The Father before the foundation of the world feels a spiritual sensation of delight in the Son. Jesus appeals to the Father's eternal love when he intercedes for his people. John Flavel captures this wonderful truth in his sermon on Christ's primeval glory:[70]

> these delights of the Father and the Son in one another knew not a moment's interruption, or diminution: thus did these great and

---

[65] Gill, *Body of Divinity*, 1:51, 136

[66] *Ps. 22:8*: Let him rescue him, seeing he delights in him

[67] Ps. 51:6, etc. See the Appendix to Topic 14 where I catalogue this use.

[68] *Isa. 42:1*: Behold my servant, whom I uphold; my chosen in whom my soul delights

[69] *John 17:24*: for you loved me before the foundation of the world

[70] John Flavel, *The Works of John Flavel* (6 Vols.; London: The Banner of Truth Trust, 1968), 1:43-44

glorious persons mutually let forth their fullest pleasure and delight, each into the heart of the other; they lay as it were embosomed in one another, entertaining themselves with delights and pleasures ineffable, and unconceivable. Hence we observe, Doct. *That the condition and state of Jesus Christ before his incarnation, was a state of the highest and most unspeakable delight and pleasure, in the enjoyment of his Father*

Clearly Flavel proclaims a God that truly feels. Christ's eternal delight commends his unfathomable love. He lays aside his glory for a while and endures human hatred, bodily suffering, and divine abandonment.

2. God's delight in his creative genius and wisdom

Scripture affirms that God delights in his wisdom.[71] The word translated "*delight*" is שַׁעֲשֻׁעַ (sha'ashu'a), which means "enjoyment," "pleasure," or "delight." It comes from the verb שָׁעַע (sha'a'), which means, "to look upon with complacency," "to dandle," or "to delight in." This displays the close connection between God's feelings of delight and joy. Here wisdom personified speaks as the subject in the first person. Here wisdom is God's creative genius that designed, formed, and established the universe. Thus, when the Supreme Being contemplates his wisdom in creation, he feels a sensation of joyful delight. Some take this text to refer to God the Son prior to his incarnation.[72] Clearly, God the Father creates through God the Son.[73] And, Paul calls God the Son, "*the wisdom of God.*"[74] Therefore, even if this text in Proverbs does not depict Christ explicitly, it at least implies that God rejoices in God the Word, as "the wisdom of God" through whom he created everything that he made.

3. God's delight in his justice and mercy

When God exercises justice and kindness toward men, he experiences delight.[75] Again, when he shows mercy to sinners, pardons their iniquity, and puts away his anger, he feels a sensation of delight.[76] These texts both translate *chaphēts* as "delight." Thus, Scripture underscores that God's

---

[71] *Prov. 8:30*: Then I was by him, as a master workman; and I was daily his delight, rejoicing always before him
[72] For example: Flavel, *Works*, 1:42-43
[73] John 1:3-4
[74] 1 Cor. 1:24, 30
[75] *Jer. 9:24*: I am Jehovah who exercises lovingkindness, justice, and righteousness in the earth: for in these things I delight, says Jehovah
[76] *Mic. 7:18*: Who is a God like unto you, that pardons iniquity . . . he retains not his anger for ever, because he delights in lovingkindness

feelings of delight in his justice and redemptive mercy stand closely bound to the unconstrained good pleasure of his will. Further, these feelings of delight coalesce. God redeems from sin justly. He punishes sin when he pardons sin. When he sees the sins of believers punished and pardoned, he experiences delight. No sin goes unpunished, not even the sins of Christians, but some sins, the sins of the damned, go unpardoned. In their case, God delights in the justness of retribution. Yet, he does not have sadistic feelings of delight or pleasure in their death (Ezek. 18:23, 32, 33:11).

4. God's delight in the righteous and their moral virtue

Scripture highlights God's delight in righteousness[77] and justice.[78] It stresses his delight in gospel obedience[79] and godly devotion.[80] It features his delight in the righteous[81] and their ways.[82] Scripture depicts this delight with *chaphēts*,[83] *ratsôn*,[84] and אהב ('ahab) translated, *"love."*[85] Thus, with delight in his heart God delivers and protects the righteous, hears their prayers, and rewards their obedience. This should encourage Christians. Dear Christian, beset with much trouble, consider what delight God feels when you pour out your heart in prayer and walk before him in gospel obedience. This calls us so to abound in gospel virtue that his soul will "reverberate" with spiritual sensations of delight.

5. God's delight in the society of his people: in their obedience, their fathers, and their capital, Zion

In the midst of the fear and unbelief, Joshua and Caleb express their hope in God's favor toward his people. They appeal to God's delight in his people to motivate cynical countrymen to have confidence that the Lord will lead

---

[77] *Ps. 11:7*: Jehovah is righteous; he loves righteousness. *Ps. 33:5*: He loves righteousness and justice

[78] *Ps. 37:28*: Jehovah loves justice, and forsakes not his saints. *Prov. 11:1*: A false balance is an abomination to Jehovah; but a just weight is his delight. *Isa. 61:8*: I Jehovah love justice, I hate robbery with iniquity.

[79] *1 Sam. 15:22*: Has Jehovah as great delight in burnt-offerings and sacrifices, as in obeying the voice of Jehovah?

[80] *Prov. 15:8*: The sacrifice of the wicked is an abomination to Jehovah; but the prayer of the upright is his delight.

[81] *Ps. 18:19*: He delivered me, because he delighted in me. *Prov. 12:22*: Lying lips are an abomination to Jehovah; but they that deal truly are his delight

[82] *Ps. 37:23-4*: A man's goings are established of Jehovah; And he delights in his way. Though he fall, he shall not be utterly cast down.

[83] 1 Sam. 15:22; Pss. 18:19, 37:23-24

[84] Prov. 11:1, 12:22, 15:8

[85] Pss. 11:7, 33:5, 37:28; Isa. 61:8

the Hebrew nation safely to Canaan.[86] Similarly, Moses motivates the Israelites to obey God by telling them that obedience evokes delight in his heart.[87] When his people obey him evangelically, God feels delight in them. When God thus loves and delights in them, he blesses and multiplies them. Some theologians call God's delight in those who obey him, his "complacent" love. Again, Moses explains to the Israelites that the Lord's delight in the patriarchs moved him to select them as his people.[88] Further, the sons of Korah extol the Lord's special delight in Zion, the city in which he chose to dwell.[89] The Lord promises that he will someday restore Zion to her special place as the object of his delight.[90] He fulfills this promise wondrously under the new covenant through the ministry of his Son and Spirit. Scripture depicts this delight with *chaphēts*,[91] with חָשַׁק (chashaq),[92] which means "to cling to," "to join," or, "to love, and with *'ahab*, "love."[93]

B. *God's Detestation and Hate*

As love has volitional, emotive, and moral aspects, so also does hate. Morally, hate is the vice of malice and ill will, as opposed to the virtue of unselfishness and goodwill. Volitionally, hate is rejection as opposed to attachment and loyalty. Emotively, hate is detestation as opposed to delight. Thus, we now focus on God's feeling of hate.

The Bible displays God's feelings of detestation, loathing, disgust, and abhorrence with a variety of terms and expressions. It sometimes contrasts his detestation with his delight and love.[94] Scripture also displays divine detestation merely by negating his delight.[95] Scripture depicts whatever the

---

[86] *Num. 14:8*: If Jehovah delight in us, then he will bring us into this land, and give it unto us.

[87] *Deut. 7:12-13*: because you hearken to these ordinances, and keep and do them, that Jehovah your God will . . . love you, and bless you, and multiply you.

[88] *Deut. 10:15*: Only Jehovah had a delight in your fathers to love them, and he chose their seed after them

[89] *Ps. 87:2*: Jehovah loves the gates of Zion more than all the dwellings of Jacob.

[90] *Isa. 62:4*: You shall no more be termed Forsaken . . . but you shall be called Hephzibah . . . for Jehovah delights in you.

[91] Num. 14:8; Isa. 62:4

[92] Deut. 10:15

[93] Deut. 7:13; Ps. 87:2

[94] *Isa. 61:8*: I Jehovah love justice, I hate robbery with iniquity. *Amos 5:21*: I hate, I despise your feasts, and I will take no delight in your solemn assemblies.

[95] *Isa. 65:12*: you did that which was evil in mine eyes, and chose that wherein I delighted not.

Lord hates and loathes as *an abomination* to him.[96] Sometimes, Scripture asserts that God rejects and detests specific persons or things.[97] The Greek term, μισεω (miseo), "hate," depicts God's detestation.[98] Its Hebrew counterpart, שָׂנֵא (śanē'), translated "hate," or, "odious," depicts divine disgust or revulsion.[99] The Greek, βδελυγμα (bdelugma), depicts what is *abomination* to God.[100] Its Hebrew counterpart, תּוֹעֵבָה (to'ēbah), "something disgusting," "abomination," depicts divine revulsion.[101] It comes from תָּעַב (ta'ab), "to loathe," "to detest," sometimes translated "abhors" (Ps. 5:6). Three other terms also depict divine abhorrence: גָּעַל (ga'el), "to detest" (Lev. 26:30); נָאַץ (na'ats), "to scorn" (Deut. 32:19); and מָאַס (ma'as), "to spurn" (Ps. 78:59).

Scripture features two special objects of divine hatred: false religion and the wicked with their deeds

1. God's hatred of false religion

When God beholds false religion and idolatry, he feels a sensation of intense revulsion and disgust. He abominates and hates idolatry.[102] Thus it provokes his vengeful anger.[103] This displays the close connection between his revulsion and anger. Further, he responds to the occult with a feeling of loathing,[104] not with indifference, as though it were a harmless novelty.

---

[96] *Deut. 12:31*: for every abomination to Jehovah, which he hates, have they done unto their gods.

[97] *Amos 6:8*: I abhor the excellency of Jacob, and hate his palaces; therefore will I deliver up the city with all that is therein.

[98] Rom. 9:13

[99] Deut. 12:31, 16:22; Ps. 11:5; Prov. 6:16; Isa. 1:14, 61:8; Jer. 44:4; Amos 5:21; Zech. 8:17; Mal. 2:16.

[100] Luke 16:15

[101] Deut. 7:25, 12:31, 17:1, 18:10-12 (2), 23:18, 24:4, 32:16; Prov. 6:16, 11:1, 20, 12:22, 15:8, 9, 26, 16:5, 17:15, 20:10; Isa. 1:13; Jer. 44:4.

[102] *Jer. 44:4-5*: Oh, do not this abominable thing that I hate. But they hearkened not, nor inclined their ear to turn from their wickedness, to burn no incense unto other gods.

[103] *Lev. 26:30*: And I will destroy your high places, an cut down your sun-images, and cast your dead bodies upon the bodies of your idols; and my soul shall abhor you. *Deut. 32:16, 19*: they moved him to jealousy with strange gods; with abominations they provoked him to anger . . . Jehovah saw it, and abhorred them. *Ps. 78:58-59*: and moved him to jealousy with their graven images. When God heard this he was wroth, and greatly abhorred Israel

[104] *Deut. 18:10-12*: There shall not be found with you any one that makes his son or his daughter to pass through the fire, one that uses divination, one that practices augury, or an enchanter, or a sorcerer, or a charmer, or a consulter with a familiar spirit, or a wizard, or a necromancer. For whosoever does these things is an abomination unto Jehovah: and because of these abominations Jehovah your God drives them out from before you.

Further, God hates hypocrisy in religion.[105] He detests worldly innovations in his worship.[106] Let us take this to heart. Let us worship him sincerely with pure hearts and good consciences. Let us worship him biblically according to his Word. Let us worship him in such a way that he feels delight, rather than disgust and revulsion.

2. God's hatred of moral wickedness and its perpetrators

Some say that God "hates wickedness, but loves the wicked." This saying contains an element of truth. God in common grace shows goodwill and kindness to "the unthankful and evil." Yet, Scripture features a far less popular dimension of the truth. God feels detestation both for wickedness and the wicked. He hates "all the workers of iniquity."[107] His soul loathes wicked, violent, and dishonest people.[108] He hates, not merely haughtiness, but "haughty eyes." He abhors lies and the "lying tongue" that tells them. He hates shedding innocent blood and the "hands that shed" it. He abhors wicked purposes and the "heart that devises" them. He hates running to mischief and the "*feet*" swift to do it. He abhors false testimony and the "false witness" who utters it. He hates discord among brethren and those "that sow" it.[109] Thus, he detests the wicked and delights in the righteous. He doesn't feel the same thing for everyone.[110]

---

[105] *Prov. 15:8*: The sacrifice of the wicked is an abomination to Jehovah; but the prayer of the upright is his delight. *Isa. 1:13-14*: Bring no more vain oblations; incense is an abomination unto me . . . Your new moons and your appointed feasts my soul hates; they are a trouble unto me; I am weary of bearing them. *Amos 5:21*: I hate, I despise your feasts, and I will take no delight in your solemn assemblies. *Luke 16:15*: You are they that justify yourselves in the sight of men; but God knows your hearts: for that which is exalted among men is an abomination in the sight of God.

[106] *Deut. 12:31*: for every abomination to Jehovah, which he hates, have they done unto their gods.

[107] *Ps. 5:5*: The arrogant shall not stand in your sight: you hate all the workers of iniquity.

[108] *Ps. 11:5-6*: the wicked and him that loves violence his soul hates . . . Jehovah abhors the bloodthirsty and deceitful man

[109] *Prov. 6:16:* There are six things which Jehovah hates; yea, seven which are an abomination unto him: haughty eyes, a lying tongue, and hands that shed innocent blood; a heart that devises wicked purposes, feet that are swift in running to mischief, a false witness that utters lies, and he that sows discord among brethren.

[110] *Prov. 11:20*: They that are perverse in heart are an abomination to Jehovah; but such as are perfect are his delight. *Prov. 12:22*: Lying lips are an abomination to Jehovah; but they that deal truly are his delight.

Further, Scripture emphasizes that God detests every form of moral evil. He emphatically loathes, arrogance,[111] swindling[112] and stealing,[113] marital treachery,[114] civil injustice,[115] perjury,[116] and sexual perversions.[117] This calls us to put away from our lives everything that God hates.

C. God's Joy

"Sadly," among the renowned reformed teachers of systematics, John Gill alone expounds God's joy.[118] Scripture uses a rich variety of expressions that paint a remarkable picture of God's sensation of joy. The Hebrew language in its graphic beauty relates light with gladness and darkness with gloominess. Similarly, in the vernacular we say, "lighten up." Accordingly, the Hebrew word שׂוּשׂ (śûś), "to make mirth, "to be bright," depicts God's rejoicing.[119] Also, the word שָׂמַח (śamach), "to brighten up," "to make merry," "to rejoice," depicts God feeling joy.[120] Further, the word עָלַז ('alaz), "to leap," "to jump for joy," translated *"exult,"* depicts God's joy.[121] Again, the word מָשׂוֹשׂ (maśôś), "joy" or "mirth," depicts divine joy.[122] Again, the word גּוּל (gûl), literally "to spin," which pictures someone "reeling with delight," depicts God rejoicing.[123] Again, the word שִׂמְחָה (śimchah), "blithesomeness," or "glee," describes God's joy.[124] In the New

---

[111] *Prov. 16:5*: Every one that is proud in heart is an abomination to Jehovah.

[112] *Prov. 11:1*: A false balance is an abomination to Jehovah; but a just weight is his delight. *Prov. 15:26*: Evil devices are an abomination to Jehovah. *Prov. 20:10*: Diverse weights, and diverse measures, both of them alike are an abomination to Jehovah.

[113] *Isa. 61:8*: I Jehovah love justice, I hate robbery with iniquity

[114] *Mal. 2:16*: I hate putting away, says Jehovah, the God of Israel, and him that covers his garment with violence, says Jehovah of hosts: therefore take heed to your spirit, that you deal not treacherously

[115] *Prov. 17:15*: He that justifies the wicked, and he that condemns the righteous, both of them alike are an abomination to Jehovah.

[116] *Zech. 8:17*: let none of you devise evil in your hearts against your neighbor; and love no false oath: for all these are things that I hate, says Jehovah.

[117] *Lev. 20:23*: And you shall not walk in the customs of the nation, which I cast out before you: for they did all these things, and therefore I abhorred them. (Lev. 20:10-21 catalogues many sexual perversions of the Canaanites)

[118] Gill, *Body of Divinity*, 1:146-148

[119] Deut. 28:63, 30:9-10; Isa. 65:19; Jer. 32:41; Zeph. 3:17

[120] Judg. 9:13; Ps. 104:31

[121] Ps. 60:6

[122] Isa. 62:5

[123] Isa. 65:19; Zeph. 3:17

[124] Zeph. 3:17

Testament, the word χαρα (chara), "cheerfulness," depicts heavenly[125] and human joy.[126]

Scripture stresses that God feels joy in his creation and creatures, in his people and their redemption, and when sinners turn from sin and get right with him. We consider these and conclude with his eternal joy.

1. God's joy in his creation

God feels joy in his creative works.[127] God's joy in his creation is like the sensation of satisfaction, exuberance, and fulfillment that men feel when they do a job well: "Wherefore I saw that there is nothing better, than that a man should *rejoice in his works*; for that is his portion" (Eccles. 3:22). Again, the Creator feels joy when his creatures enjoy his benefits.[128] When Scripture asserts that wine "*cheers*" both the creature and the Creator, it evidently doesn't mean that the Lord occasionally takes a drink of alcohol. Rather, the point is that the Creator rejoices when his creatures enjoy the good gifts that he has richly bestowed on them. Though drunkenness grieves the Lord (Eph. 4:17-18), he rejoices when people enjoy alcohol in moderation. We must not think that God is a "spoil sport," or ascetic, or caustic, or grim, or oppressive. He does not frown even at men's most meager enjoyment. To the contrary, he experiences a sensation of joy when he sees people enjoy creation to the full. Could it be that in this respect some of us need to become more like our God, and less like monks and Pharisees? Are some of you, even as you read, becoming angry with me for writing these things? Put away your judgmental anger, and submit your mind to God's Word: Should I leave my new wine, which "*cheers* God and man."

2. God's joy in his people

Under the old covenant this rejoicing cuts two ways. When his people walk in obedience to his law, he rejoices in blessing them. If as a society they break his covenant and serve other gods, then he rejoices, but not sadistically, in their punishment.[129] God experiences joy in being faithful to sworn commitments, even if his faithfulness must inflict the curses of his

---

[125] Luke 15:7, 10

[126] Matt. 2:10, 13:44, 28:8; Luke 24:52

[127] *Ps. 104:31*: Let the glory of Jehovah endure forever; Let Jehovah rejoice (śamach) in his works.

[128] *Judg. 9:13*: And the vine said to them, Should I leave my new wine, which cheers (śamach) God and man, and go to wave to and fro over the trees?

[129] *Deut. 28:63*: And it shall come to pass, that, as Jehovah rejoiced (śûś) over you to do you good, and to multiply you, so Jehovah will rejoice (śûś) over you to cause you to perish, and to destroy you, and you shall be plucked from the land whither you go in to possess it.

covenant. Yet this joy is not unmingled, because he has no delight in the suffering or death of the wicked. Thus, he promises his people a better day in which he will transform them morally. He promises to rejoice over them to do them good exclusively and permanently.[130] Scripture likens this unmingled divine joy to the intense sensation of exuberance, exhilaration, and satisfaction that a groom feels: "as the bridegroom rejoices (maśôś) over the bride, so shall your God rejoice (maśôś) over you" (Isa. 62:5). Scripture uses God's joy to encourage God's people and motivate us to diligence: "Fear not; O Zion, let not your hands be slack. Jehovah your God is in the midst of you, a mighty one who will save; and he will rejoice (gûl) over you with joy (śimchah); he will rest in his love; he will joy (gûl) over you with singing" (Zeph. 3:17). It also gives us hope to enter his joyful presence in heaven: "You will show me the path of life: in your presence is fullness of joy; in your right hand there are pleasures for evermore" (Ps. 16:11). There God will rejoice over his people and eradicate all our sorrow.[131]

Under the new covenant, God incarnate conveys his own joy, in some measure, to his people even here on earth.[132] For this Christ intercedes to his Father: "that they may have my joy made full in themselves" (John 17:13). He associates his joy with Trinitarian fellowship.[133] Thus, the joy of Christians on earth stems from the presence and grace of the Holy Spirit: "righteousness and peace and joy in the Holy Spirit" (Rom. 14:17). Therefore, by the Spirit's power and presence, God enables believers to experience some measure of that spiritual sensation of blessedness that God, the Father, Son, and Holy Spirit, has always felt and enjoyed.

3. God's joy over penitent sinners

The Lord affirms that when a sinner repents joy is felt "in heaven."[134] Christ does not explicitly identify its source. Possibly, he means to say that the

---

[130] *Deut. 30:9-10*: And Jehovah your God will make you plenteous in all the work of your hand, in the fruit of your body, and in the fruit of your cattle, and in the fruit of your ground, for good: for Jehovah will again rejoice (śûś) over you for good, as he rejoiced (śûś) over your fathers; if you shall obey the voice of Jehovah. *Jer. 32:40-41*: I will make an everlasting covenant with them, that I will not turn away from following them, to do them good; and I will put my fear in their hearts, that they may not depart from me. Yea, I will rejoice (śûś) over them to do them good.

[131] *Isa. 65:19*: I will rejoice (gûl) in Jerusalem, and joy (śûś) in my people; and there shall be heard in her no more the voice of weeping and the voice of crying.

[132] *John 15:11*: These things have I spoken unto you, that my joy may be in you, and that your joy may be full.

[133] John 17:23, 24, 26

[134] *Luke 15:7, 10*: I say to you, that even so there shall be joy (chara) in heaven over one sinner that repents, more than over ninety and nine righteous persons, who need no repentance

angels themselves rejoice when a sinner repents. Let us assume, for the sake of argument, that this is so. What then? Shall we conceive of angels brimming with a sensation of exuberance over God's redemptive work while the Redeemer himself, who performed the work, who gave that sinner repentance unto life, sits on his throne unmoved, feeling nothing, devoid of exhilaration or satisfaction? Preposterous! Yes, rather, outrageous! To the contrary, God's joy over one penitent sinner surpasses the exuberance that he feels when he beholds a hundred righteous people.

Conclusion: the eternal joy of the Trinity

Finally, Scripture, at least implicitly, points to the eternal joy of the Trinity: "I was daily his delight, rejoicing always before him" (Prov. 8:30). This text personifies divine wisdom and describes his eternal experience. Even if this is a literary device, it is an inspired one, which points implicitly to Christ. Christ is a Person, called God's Wisdom and Word, who always existed. He was the object of God's eternal delight, the very delight of which wisdom, speaking as a person, claims to be the object. Therefore, it is not careless exegesis to see implicit correspondence between the eternal joy that Christ actually felt and the eternal joy that wisdom, speaking here as a person, claims to have felt. Therefore, this text is relevant.

In this text the word שָׂחַק (śachaq), "to laugh," depicts this eternal joy. This word denotes the combination of delight and exuberance. It is elsewhere translated "to rejoice," or "to sport." It pictures a child playing in front of its parent, while the parent watches with intense delight. If you have children, you probably remember happy times when they frolicked around you and you watched with joy. Thus, Scripture uses domestic bliss to picture the intense exhilaration and satisfaction that God has always felt. What a privilege that we, in Christ, should to some degree enter into that eternal joy.

D. *God's Grief or Sorrow*

Scripture contrasts joy with grief: "No chastening for the present seems joyous but grievous," and, "that they may do this with joy, not with grief" (Heb. 12:11, 13:17). Other passages in both testaments confirm and underscore this contrast.[135] Before the foundation of the world, the triune God felt only joy. When he created, the Creator felt only joy. However, upon the advent of sin, suffering, and death, God now also feels the sensation of sorrow or grief.

... Even so, I say, there is joy (chara) in the presence of the angels of God over one sinner that repents.

[135] Esth. 9:22; John 16:20; 2 Cor. 6:10

Scripture uses several terms for God's grief. It depicts divine grief with the Hebrew word, עָצַב ('atsab), literally "to carve," translated "grieve," "vex," "hurt," or "make sorry."[136] This word paints a graphic picture of a heart cut by a sense of wrong and harm. It also denotes God's grief with the word, קָצַר (qatsar), literally to "curtail" or "to harvest," translated "cut down," "discourage," "shorten," or "grieve."[137] This word graphically pictures a heart "cut short," like harvested grain, by dire circumstances. Scripture also employs the word, קוּט (qût), "cut off," translated "detest," or "grieve."[138] In the New Testament the Greek word λυπεω (lupeo), "to distress," translated, "grieve," or "cause sorrow," depicts God's grief.[139] So does the word προσοχθιζω (prosochthizo), "to be vexed with something irksome," or, "to be indignant at," translated, "grieved" or "displeased."[140]

However, Scripture also speaks of a kind of grief that only humans feel. This human grief accompanies bodily pain and suffering. The word, מַכְאֹב (mak'ob), often depicts this human grief. Scripture never uses this word to depict divine grief. Therefore, Scripture never ascribes to God either bodily suffering or the inward grief that accompanies it. Nevertheless, God expresses sympathetic understanding for his people when they suffer this kind of grief and sorrow: "I know their sorrows [mak'ob]" (Exod. 3:7).

Thus, God's grief is a sensation of sorrow that he feels when he perceives harm[141] and moral wrong.[142] Thus, Scripture closely associates God's grief with his anger and displeasure.[143] Among men too, anger often accompanies the sensation of being grieved. For example, Christ responds to the cruel legalism of the Pharisees with a mingled sensation of sorrow and indignation: "And when he had looked round about on them with anger, being grieved at the hardening of their heart, he says to the man, Stretch forth your hand" (Mark 3:5).

Scripture features four occasions of God's grief: (1) incessant human wickedness; (2) the suffering of his people; (3) the rebellion of the wilderness generation; and (4) carnality in a temple of the Holy Spirit.

---

[136] Gen. 6:6; Ps. 78:40; Isa. 63:10
[137] Judg. 10:16
[138] Ps. 95:10
[139] Eph. 4:30
[140] Heb. 3:10, 17
[141] Judg. 10:16
[142] Isa. 63:10
[143] Ps. 95:10; Heb. 3:10

1. God's grief over incessant human wickedness

This grief is so intense that before the flood God actually felt sorry that he made man.[144] When God watched sin spread like cancer through the human race, he felt intense sorrow over incessant human wickedness: "And Jehovah saw that the wickedness of man was great in the earth, and that every imagination of the thoughts of his heart was only evil continually" (Gen. 6:5). In God's holy sight everything that fallen people think, feel, purpose, say, and do is evil. Day after day, month after month, and year after year, he sustains and provides for people who cause him to feel incessant moral revulsion. Thus, after centuries of provocation, he says in the days of Noah: "I will destroy man whom I have created from the face of the ground" (Gen. 6:7). He determines to redress his constant sorrow. Yet, in mercy he shows favor to Noah and his family. We owe our existence to that favor. Scripture closely connects God's feeling of grief with his virtue of longsuffering. God in his goodness with longsuffering endures grief while Noah prepares the ark. Again, after the flood, he covenants that he will never again destroy the earth with water. Even now he waits. Now he endures "with much longsuffering the vessels of wrath" (Rom. 9:22). He endures them because he is not willing that any of his people "should perish" (2 Pet. 3:9). While he forestalls the final conflagration and judgment, we behold his great goodness as he endures his sensation of grief over incessant human sin.

2. God's grief over the suffering of his people

When God beheld his people suffering, he felt a sensation of sorrow over their misery.[145] This grief moved him to deliver them from their misery. On account of their sin, God himself sent this affliction on his people. When they provoked him to anger by serving other gods, he punished them. When they sincerely humbled themselves, put away their false gods, and pleaded with the Lord for help, then his heart felt grief for them. He granted their request and rescued them from their enemies.

3. God's grief over the rebellion of the wilderness generation

The wilderness generation stands as the chief biblical monument to God's grief over rebellion among his people.[146] Their notorious behavior was

---

[144] *Gen. 6:5-6*: And Jehovah saw that the wickedness of man was great in the earth, and that every imagination of the thoughts of his heart was only evil continually. And it repented Jehovah that he had made man on the earth, and it grieved him at his heart.

[145] *Judg. 10:16*: And they put away the foreign gods from among them, and served Jehovah; and his soul was grieved for the misery of Israel

[146] *Ps. 78:40*: How oft did they rebel against him in the wilderness, and grieve him in the desert! *Ps. 95:10*: Forty years long was I grieved with that generation. *Isa. 63:10*: But they rebelled, and grieved his Holy Spirit: therefore he was turned to be their enemy, and himself

aggravated. They rebelled against God repeatedly: "these ten times" (Num. 14:22). They rebelled in the face of numerous and stupendous miracles, both in Egypt and in the wilderness: "How long will this people despise me? and how long will they not believe in me, for all the signs which I have wrought among them?" (Num. 14:11). Scripture posts their unbelief and its punishment as a warning for us: "Now these things happened unto them by way of example; and they were written for our admonition, upon whom the ends of the ages are come" (1 Cor. 10:11). The writer to Hebrews also presses this admonition on our consciences.[147] We should learn from the wilderness generation. We should keep a tender conscience. We should not reject light from God's Word.

4. God's grief over carnality in a temple of the Holy Spirit

Scripture says plainly: "And grieve not the Holy Spirit of God, in whom you were sealed unto the day of redemption" (Eph. 4:30). Paul exhorts the church to mortify carnal vices that grieve the Holy Spirit and to cultivate the opposite virtues. He calls them to put away dishonesty and cultivate transparency (4:25). He calls them to resolve grievances quickly (4:26). He calls them to put away thievery and cultivate considerateness (4:27). He calls them to put away unprofitable talk and cultivate edifying speech (4:29). He calls them to put away malice and bitterness and cultivate goodwill and kindness (4:31-32). He then calls the church to fellowship in holy love, not in sexual lust (5:1-14). We must take this to heart. If we grieve the Spirit, we will know less of his presence and power as Comforter, Sanctifier, Spirit of Truth, and Spirit of Adoption. If we grieve him, our prayer will turn feeble, our Bible will grows dim, and our peace and joy will shrivel. Brethren, let us not grieve God's Spirit.

In closing, some may think that the idea of God feeling grief is incompatible with his immutability. Yet we must not deny either the joy or grief of our immutable God. Some may allege that these texts contain nothing more than a figure of speech, since God can't really feel sensations of grief. Yet Scripture ascribes this feeling of sorrow to God's heart: "it grieved him *at his heart*." God is not a heartless being. He created the human heart. He that created the heart, shall he not feel? Does God have an *unfeeling heart*? Such a notion would be nonsense, a contradiction in terms. Remember that God is incomprehensible. We can never fully understand him. We must get

---

fought against them. *Heb. 3:10*: I was displeased with that generation, and said, They do always err in their heart. *Heb. 3:17*: And with whom was he displeased forty years? Was it not with them that sinned, whose bodies fell in the wilderness?

[147] Heb. 3:7-4:1

our view of God from Scripture. We must not impose on Scripture a view of God that we derive from philosophy.

E. *God's Gratification or Pleasure*

God's pleasure is the spiritual sensation of gratification and satisfaction that he feels when he sees what is morally good and acceptable in his sight. Scripture presents God's feeling of gratification with a variety of terms and expressions. In the Old Testament the phrase יָטַב בְּעֵינֵי (yatab bᵉ‘êynēy), translated "*pleased*," depicts God's pleasure.[148] Literally, it means "to be right, sound, or beautiful in the eyes of." Thus, God feels pleasure over whatever seems morally proper in his eyes. Also, the Hebrew word, *yatab*, translated "*please*," depicts God's pleasure, literally, "it will be right, or beautiful to Jehovah."[149] Scripture also depicts God's pleasure with *ratsah*, translated "*pleases*." This term shows the close association of God's sensation of moral satisfaction with his preceptive will. When men obey his preceptive will, he feels pleased.[150] Again, the expression טוֹב לִפְנֵי (tôb lipᵉnēy), translated "*pleases*," depicts God's gratification.[151] This phrase literally means, "the one good before the face of."

In the New Testament two major word families describe God's feeling of moral gratification. First, it depicts God's pleasure with the Greek verb εὐαρεστεω (euaresteo), "to gratify entirely," translated "please," or "be well-pleasing,"[152] its cognate adjective εὐαρεστος (euarestos), "fully agreeable," translated "acceptable" or "well-pleasing,"[153] and its adverb εὐαρεστως (euarestos), "acceptably."[154] Second, it depicts God's pleasure with the Greek verb ἀρεσκω (aresko), "to be agreeable," translated "please,"[155] its cognate noun ἀρεσκεια (areskeia), "complaisance," "that which pleases," translated "pleasing,"[156] and the adjective ἀρεστος (arestos), "agreeable," translated "things that please" or "are pleasing."[157] In addition, the New Testament occasionally uses the verb εὐδοκεω (eudokeo), to "seem

---

[148] 1 Kings 3:10
[149] Ps. 69:31
[150] Prov. 16:7
[151] Eccles. 7:26
[152] Heb. 11:5-6, 13:16
[153] Rom. 12:1, 14:18; 2 Cor. 5:9; Eph. 5:10; Phil. 4:18; Col. 3:20; Heb. 13:21
[154] Heb. 12:28
[155] Rom. 8:8; 1 Thess. 2:4, 4:1
[156] Col. 1:10
[157] John 8:29; 1 John 3:22

good," to describe his feeling of gratification. In this connection, it is translated "be well-pleased."[158] This underscores the connection between the good-pleasure of God's will and his sensation of gratification with moral good.

This testimony highlights the fact that no wicked person can ever please God.[159] Even their benevolent deeds or acts of devotion don't please him because: "without faith it is impossible to be well-pleasing unto him" (Heb. 13:6). This testimony features the fact that God is pleased with the impeccable virtue of his incarnate Son, Jesus Christ, and with the gospel virtue of those who believe in him.

1. God's gratification over the impeccable virtue of his Son

The Old Testament God foretells God's pleasure with Christ.[160] After the incarnation, at Christ's baptism[161] and transfiguration[162] the Father declares with an audible voice from heaven that he feels pleasure in his Son. Jesus, aware of his sinless perfection, asserts that he always pleases God.[163] Paul calls Christ's impeccable virtue in God's eyes "the righteousness of God."[164] Christ's virtue stems from his impeccable obedience to God's revealed will expressed in his moral law[165] and in his messianic commandment about the cross.[166]

2. God's gratification over the gospel virtue of Christians

No Christian can ever attain sinless perfection in this life, or ever perform even one completely sinless act. Nevertheless, Scripture boldly declares that all Christians please God when they obey God's commandments evangelically.[167] Think of it! When God sees our sincere and Spirit-wrought efforts to obey him, even though our remaining corruption clings like leaches to them, he feels gratification, not revulsion or anger. Our evangelical obedience moves him, not to chide and avenge, but to commend and reward

---

[158] Matt. 3:17, 12:18, 17:5; Luke 3:22
[159] *Rom. 8:8*: and they that are in the flesh cannot please God. But you are not in the flesh, but in the Spirit, if so be that the Spirit of God dwells in you.
[160] Matt. 12:18
[161] *Luke 3:22*: You are my beloved Son; in you I am well-pleased.
[162] Matt. 17:5
[163] John 8:29
[164] Rom. 1:17, 3:21, 22, 5:18, 19, 10:3; 2 Cor. 5:21
[165] Ps. 40:7-8
[166] Matt. 26:39, 42; Heb. 10:7-10
[167] Phil. 4:18; Heb. 13:16, 21; 1 Thess. 4:1; 1 John 3:22

Christians. God himself enables his people to obey and please him.[168] Thus he deserves all the glory and credit. When we please God, he makes enemies to be at peace with us,[169] protects us,[170] and grants us the desires of our hearts.[171] God feels revulsion when he beholds the worship of the wicked. Yet he is gratified with the sincere and godly worship of believers. Their spiritual sacrifices of giving[172] and singing praise[173] truly please him. Christian ministry falls short of the whole-hearted devotion and loyalty he deserves. Yet God feels satisfaction, not revulsion and anger, over faithful ministry.[174] When little children who believe in Christ obey their parents with gospel obedience, God feels gratification and pleasure.[175] Therefore take heart. Pleasing God here on earth is not impossible.[176] In whatever we do, let us make it our aim to be well-pleasing unto him (2 Cor. 5:9). Let us abound more and more in doing those things that please him.[177]

F. God's Anger, Wrath, and Displeasure

In this fallen world God responds emotively with anger to moral evil. Webster defines "anger" as: "a strong feeling of displeasure and usu. of antagonism."[178] Thus, God's anger is the sensation of dissatisfaction and

---

[168] *Heb. 13:20, 21*: That now the God of peace . . . make you perfect in every good thing to do his will, working in us that which is well-pleasing in his sight, through Jesus Christ.

[169] *Prov. 16:7*: When a man's ways please Jehovah, he makes even his enemies to be at peace with him.

[170] *Eccles. 7:26*: And I find more bitter than death the woman whose heart is snares and nets, and whose hands are bands: whoso pleases God shall escape from her.

[171] *1 John 3:22*: and whatsoever we ask we receive of him, because we keep his commandments and do the things that are pleasing in his sight.

[172] *Phil. 4:18*: But I have all things and abound: I am filled, having received from Epaphroditus the things that came from you, an odor of a sweet smell, a sacrifice acceptable, well-pleasing to God. *Heb. 13:16*: to do good and to communicate forget not: for with such sacrifices God is well-pleased.

[173] *Ps. 51:19*: then you will delight in the sacrifices of righteousness. *Ps. 69:30, 31*: I will praise the name of God with a song, and will magnify him with thanksgiving. And it will please Jehovah better than an ox.

[174] *1 Thess. 2:4*: so we speak; not as pleasing men, but God who proves our hearts.

[175] *Col. 3:20*: Children, obey your parents in all things, for this is well-pleasing in the Lord.

[176] *Heb. 11:5, 6*: By faith Enoch was translated that he should not see death; and he was not found, because God translated him: for he has had witness born to him that before his translation he had been well-pleasing to God, and without faith it is impossible to be well-pleasing unto him.

[177] *1 Thess. 4:1*: Finally then, brethren, we beseech and exhort you in the Lord, that, as you received of us how you ought to walk and to please God, even as you do walk,-that you abound more and more.

[178] *WNC Dictionary*, 43

indignity, or affront, which he experiences when he beholds moral wrong. Scripture closely associates God's *anger* and *wrath*.[179] Accordingly, Webster defines *wrath* as "strong vengeful anger or indignation."[180] While enlarging the concept of anger they observe: "WRATH may imply either rage or indignation but is likely to suggest a desire or intent to revenge or punish."[181] Thus, God's wrath is his vengeful anger. God's *wrath*, his settled intention to avenge and punish sin, accompanies his *anger*, his intense displeasure and affront at sin.

In an appendix to this topic, I list major biblical terms for God's anger and wrath. I catalogue 433 references to God's anger and wrath in the Old Testament, 37 in the New, a total of 470. I did not include secondary terms associated with his anger, such as his "jealousy," or "vengeance." Nor have I listed idiomatic expressions like, a "consuming fire" (Heb. 12:29). Morris confirms this mammoth scope:[182]

> There are more than 20 words used to express the wrath conception as it applies to Yahweh (in addition to a number of other words which occur with only reference to human anger). These are used so frequently that there are over 580 occurrences to be taken into consideration. Now, this constitutes such a formidable body of evidence that we cannot hope to deal with it fully, and can only indicate in general terms the result of a detailed examination.

As he notes, time precludes conducting an exhaustive survey in this lecture. The biblical witness to no other divine affection even begins to approach a testimony this massive. Why such emphasis? At very least, God assures us that he takes sin very personally and stands resolutely determined to punish it. Sin not only grieves and repulses him, he regards it as a personal affront that he must and will avenge.[183]

The Old Testament graphically pictures God's anger using physiological changes associated with human anger. These depictions are "anthropopathisms." They portray his spiritual sensation of anger in terms of the physical aspects of human anger. For example, Scripture pictures an

---

[179] *Rom. 2:8*: But unto them that are contentious, and do not obey the truth . . . indignation (thumos) and wrath (orge).

[180] Ibid., 1343

[181] Ibid., 43

[182] Leon Morris, *The Apostolic Preaching of the Cross*, 131. [I assume that his "580 occurrences" also include texts where these terms depict human anger.]

[183] *Rom. 12:19*: vengeance is mine, says the Lord, I will repay.

angry God as "breathing rapidly,"[184] as "heated,"[185] as "agitated,"[186] and even as "frothing at the mouth."[187] These expressions all convey the intensity of God's feelings of anger and wrath.

Scripture features God's anger toward the society of his people, toward notorious sinners among his people, toward true saints in Christ, and toward fallen humanity in Adam.

1. God's anger toward the society of his people

Scripture highlights the provocation, infliction, and cessation of his anger on the society of his people.

a. The provocation of God's anger toward the society his people

False religion and flagrant immorality especially provoke divine anger. When God's people serve other gods[188] and profane his appointed worship,[189] they provoke the Lord to anger. Again, when his people flagrantly disregard his moral law and oppress the weak, they provoke his wrath.[190]

b. The infliction of God's anger on the society of his people

When Hebrew Israel provokes his anger, he responds accordingly. He threatens to withdraw his special presence and power from them unless they

---

[184] 168 times, Exod. 4:14, etc.
[185] 85 times, Lev. 26:28, etc.
[186] 43 times, Deut. 4:25, etc.
[187] 21 times, Pss. 7:11, 38:3, etc.
[188] *Deut. 7:2-4*: When Jehovah your God shall deliver them [the Canaanites] up before you . . . you shall make no covenant with them, nor show mercy unto them; neither shall you make marriages with them . . . For he will turn away your son from following me, that they may serve other gods: so will the anger of Jehovah be kindled against you, and he will destroy you quickly
[189] *1 Kings 14:7-10*: Go tell Jeroboam . . . you . . . have done evil above all that were before you, and have gone and made you other gods, and molten images, to provoke me to anger, and have cast me behind your back: therefore, behold, I will bring evil upon the house of Jeroboam, and will cut off from Jeroboam every man-child. *2 Kings 17:17, 18*: And they caused their sons and their daughters to pass through the fire, and used divination and enchantments, and sold themselves to do that which was evil in the sight of Jehovah, to provoke him to anger. Therefore Jehovah was very angry with Israel, and removed them out of his sight.
[190] *Exod. 22:22-24*: You shall not afflict any widow, or fatherless child. If you afflict them at all, and they cry at all unto me, I will surely hear their cry; and my wrath shall wax hot, and I will kill you with the sword; and your wives shall be widows, and your children fatherless.

remove the provocation.[191] He humbles them with defeat and subjugation before their enemies.[192] In his anger he inflicts on his people escalating judgments. These include: plagues in the wilderness,[193] forty years of wandering,[194] servitude to their enemies,[195] eviction from Canaan,[196] scattering among the nations,[197] and ultimately rejection as his people. He inflicted this ultimate judgment on Hebrew Israel when they rejected and killed God incarnate.[198] He took his theocracy from them and gave it "to a nation bringing forth its fruits" (Matt. 21:43). He did this to provoke them to jealousy,[199] so they would appreciate the privileges they lost and get right with him.

---

[191] *Josh 7:1, 12*: But the children of Israel committed a trespass in the devoted thing . . . and the anger of Jehovah was kindled against the children of Israel . . . Therefore the children of Israel can not stand before their enemies . . . because they are become accursed: I will not be with you any more, except you destroy the devoted thing from among you.

[192] *Judg. 3:7, 8*: And the children of Israel did that which was evil in the sight of Jehovah, and forgat Jehovah their God, and served Baalim and the Asheroth. Therefore the anger of Jehovah was kindled against Israel, and he sold them into the hand of Cushanrishathaim king of Mesopotamia.

[193] *Num. 11:33*: While the flesh was yet between their teeth, ere it was chewed, the anger of Jehovah was kindled against the people, and Jehovah smote the people with a very great plague.

[194] *Num. 32:10, 13*: And Jehovah's anger was kindled in that day, and he swore, saying, Surely none of the men that came out of Egypt, from twenty years old and upward, shall see the land which I swore to Abraham . . . And Jehovah's anger was kindled against Israel, and he made them wander to and fro in the wilderness forty years.

[195] *Ps. 106:39, 40*: Thus were they defiled with their works, and played the harlot in their doings. Therefore was the wrath of Jehovah kindled against his people, and he abhorred his inheritance. And he gave them into the hand of the nations.

[196] *Deut. 29:25-28*: they forsook the covenant of Jehovah . . . and served other gods and worshipped them . . . therefore the anger of Jehovah was kindled against this land, to bring upon it all the curse that is written in this book; and Jehovah rooted them out of their land in anger, and in wrath, and in great indignation, and cast them into another land, as at this day.

[197] *1 Kings 14:15*: Jehovah will smite Israel . . . and he will root up Israel out of this good land which he gave to their fathers, and will scatter them beyond the River, because they have made their Asherim, provoking Jehovah to anger. And he will give Israel up because of the sins of Jeroboam, which he sinned, and wherewith he made Israel to sin.

[198] *1 Thess. 2:14-16*: the Jews; who both killed the Lord Jesus and the prophets, and drove us out, and please not God, and are contrary to all men; forbidding us to speak to the Gentiles that they may be saved; to fill up their sins always: but the wrath is come upon them to the uttermost.

[199] *Deut. 32:16, 21, 22*: They moved him to jealousy with strange gods; with abominations they provoked him to anger . . . They have moved me to jealousy with that which is not God; they have provoked me to anger with their vanities: and I will move them to jealousy with those that are not a people; I will provoke them to anger with a foolish nation. For a fire is kindled in mine anger, and burns unto the lowest Sheol.

c. The cessation of God's anger toward the society of his people

Scripture testifies plainly and repeatedly that sin *occasions* God's anger: "And Jehovah's anger was kindled *in that day*, and he swore, saying, Surely none of the men that came out of Egypt, from twenty years old and upward, shall see the land which I swore to Abraham (Num. 32:10). His anger was not kindled "before the foundation of the world." He decreed it in eternity, but it was kindled, "in that day," when their sin provoked him. Thus, the living God responds to sin in history by feeling anger in history in his heart. As God feels anger in history, even so, God in history "puts away" his anger and "turns from" it.[200] As sin occasions the kindling of God's anger, so God has appointed means of stilling and pacifying his anger. When God's people commit criminal offenses, civil punishment is his appointed means to pacify his temporal vengeance toward the society of his people.[201] Further, God establishes covenantal relations with his people through his chosen mediator. Accordingly, he appointed the intercessory prayer of his mediator, Moses, as the means of placating his vengeful anger and turning it away from his people.[202] Ultimately, Christ, the mediator of the new covenant, turns God's vengeful anger away from his people.[203] Christ pacifies God's anger toward his people by making atonement for their sins[204] and by morally transforming them.[205] In the new covenant he writes his law on their hearts and puts his fear in their hearts.[206] The society of his people under the new covenant, Christian Israel, by means of faith experiences Christ's propitiation of God's anger through his blood.[207]

---

[200] *Ps. 85:3*: You have brought back the captivity of Jacob. You have forgiven the iniquity of your people; you have covered all their sin. You have taken away all your wrath; you have turned from the fierceness of your anger.

[201] *Num. 25:3-4*: And Israel joined himself unto Baal-peor: and the anger of Jehovah was kindled against Israel. And Jehovah said unto Moses, Take all the chiefs of the people, and hang them up unto Jehovah before the sun, that the fierce anger of Jehovah may turn away from Israel.

[202] *Deut. 9:18-19*: I fell down before Jehovah . . . because of all your sin which you sinned, in doing evil in the sight of Jehovah, to provoke him to anger. For I was afraid of the anger and hot displeasure, wherewith Jehovah was wroth against you to destroy you. But Jehovah hearkened unto me that time also.

[203] *Isa. 54:8*: In overflowing wrath I hid my face from you for a moment; but with everlasting lovingkindness will I have mercy on you, says Jehovah your Redeemer.

[204] Isa. 53:10-13

[205] Isa. 54:10, 13, 14

[206] Jer. 31:31-34, 32:40

[207] Rom. 3:25

2. God's anger toward notorious sinners among his people

Under the old covenant those who sinned with a high hand became special objects of God's anger.[208] Their ruin was so striking that they became monuments and warnings to us all. Similarly, under the new covenant the Lord warns his people about flagrant sinning. Scandalous sinners in the society of Christian Israel, the church, experience divine discipline, anger, and temporal vengeance.[209] Those who renounce their profession of faith in Christ become special objects of his vengeful anger.[210]

3. God's anger toward true saints in Christ

When through fear his faithful servants repeatedly doubt his ability to keep his promises, we provoke his parental anger.[211] When his beloved children do not mortify our remaining sin, we grieve his Holy Spirit and provoke his parental rebuke and chastening.[212] Yet his anger toward the righteous is always parental anger from a loving Father. It is never judicial wrath from the Supreme Judge. He chastens his beloved children "for our profit," to make us holy.[213] He at times chastens his children, not with bodily afflictions, but by dwindling our spiritual comforts. When he renews our hearts unto repentance, he restores our sense of his favor and nearness.[214] Sometimes his chastening of his children for remaining sin involves temporal suffering and even physical death.[215] Yet it never involves suffering punishment of any kind or duration after death.[216]

---

[208] *Deut. 29:18-20*: lest there should be among you a man . . . saying, I shall have peace, though I walk in the stubbornness of my heart . . . Jehovah will not pardon him, but the anger of Jehovah and his jealousy will smoke against that man, and all the curse that is written in this book shall lie upon him, and Jehovah will blot out his name from under heaven.

[209] 2 Cor. 2:6; 1 Thess. 4:6

[210] Heb. 10:26-31

[211] *Exod. 4:14*: And the anger of the Lord was kindled against Moses

[212] *Ps. 38:1-3*: Jehovah, rebuke me not in your wrath; neither chasten me in your hot displeasure. For your arrows stick fast in me . . . There is no soundness in my flesh because of your indignation; neither is there any health in my bones because of my sin.

[213] Heb. 12:10-11

[214] Job 42:6; Psalm 51; Rev. 3:19-20

[215] *2 Sam. 6:6, 7*: Uzzah put forth his hand to the ark of God, and took hold of it; for the oxen stumbled. And the anger of Jehovah was kindled against Uzzah; and God smote him there for his error; and there he died by the ark of God.

[216] *1 Cor. 11:30-32*: For this cause many among you are weak and sickly, and not a few sleep But if we discerned ourselves, we should not be judged. But when we are judged, we are chastened of the Lord, that we may not be condemned with the world.

4. God's anger toward fallen humanity in Adam

Scripture, especially in the New Testament, features the provocation, infliction, and confirmation of God's wrath on fallen humanity in Adam.

a. The provocation of God's wrath on fallen humanity in Adam

Fallen humanity in Adam provokes God's anger and wrath when they suppress what they know from creation and conscience to be true about him.[217] They provoke him to wrath when they condemn others hypocritically for what they themselves do and harden their hearts in a life of rebellion.[218] They provoke him to wrath when they live in flagrant violation of his moral law[219] and open rejection of his gospel.[220]

b. The infliction of God's wrath on fallen humanity in Adam

In this life he inflicts his wrath on fallen humanity with temporal judgments. He made Sodom[221] and Egypt[222] monuments of this vengeful anger. Throughout this age, when a society of fallen humans refuses to acknowledge their Creator, he inflicts his vengeful anger on that society. He withdraws the restraining influences of his common grace and abandons that society to promiscuity, perversion, and a lack of common decency.[223] After death, he inflicts on the spirits of fallen humanity in Adam suffering and punishment in hell. In the age to come, however, when Christ returns in glory, he will pour out all his wrath on fallen humanity in Adam.[224] They

---

[217] *Rom. 1:18*: for the wrath of God is revealed from heaven against all ungodliness and unrighteousness of men, who suppress the truth in righteousness

[218] *Rom. 2:5-6, 8*: after your hardness and impenitent heart you treasure up for yourself wrath in the day of wrath and revelation of the righteous judgment of God; who will render to every man according to his works . . . unto them that are factious, and obey not the truth, but obey unrighteousness, shall be wrath and indignation, tribulation and anguish

[219] *Eph. 5:5-6*: no fornicator, nor unclean person, nor covetous man, who is an idolater, has any inheritance in the kingdom of God and Christ. Let no man deceive you with empty words: for because of these things the wrath of God comes upon the sons of disobedience

[220] *John 3:36*: He that believes on the Son has eternal life; but he that obeys not the Son shall not see life, but the wrath of God abides on him.

[221] *Deut. 29:23*: like the overthrow of Sodom and Gommorah . . . which Jehovah overthrew in his anger, and in his wrath

[222] *Ps. 78:49-51*: He cast upon them the fierceness of his anger, wrath, and indignation, and trouble, a band of angels of evil. He made a path for his anger; he spared not their soul from death, but gave their life over to the pestilence, and smote all the first-born in Egypt.

[223] Rom. 1:24-31

[224] Matt. 25:31-46

will not escape his eternal damnation.[225] They will endure unending torment of body and soul, in the eternal fire prepared for the devil and his angels.[226]

c. The confirmation of God's wrath on fallen humanity in Adam

As long as sinners in Adam live on earth apart from Christ they abide under God's wrath. Yet, while they live, there is hope that they will turn from sin and escape the wrath to come.[227] Yet if fallen humans in Adam die in their sins, they are beyond hope. Then their damnation is confirmed and sealed. God will punish them forever.[228] People either repent from sin and believe in Christ while they live on earth, or they will suffer divine wrath forever.[229]

Conclusion: Practical lessons from God's anger

Scripture warns all mankind to face the reality of God's anger before it's too late: "who knows the power of your anger ('aph), and of your wrath ('eb^{e}rah) according to the fear that is due unto you?" (Ps. 90:11). Ironically, what Scripture features most about God's affections, many seem to value least. Yet, few things would do the people of America as much good as paying careful attention to God's anger and wrath. All humanity should face God's wrath against sin and flee from it to Christ before it's too late.

Sadly, even in some evangelical churches God's anger receives little attention. Possibly some avoid this topic because people don't want to hear about God's wrath. Yet, this unpopular divine affection teaches Christians invaluable lessons essential to God's glory and their peace. *First*, Christians should praise God with gratitude for refuge from his wrath in Christ.[230] To the degree that we downplay God's wrath, to that degree we minimize the value of Christ's atonement, grace, and redeeming love. *Second*, Christians

---

[225] *Rev. 6:16-17*: hide us from the face of him that sits on the throne, and from the wrath of the Lamb: for the great day of their wrath is come; and who is able to stand?

[226] *Rev. 14:9-11*: If any man worships the beast . . . he also shall drink of the wine of the wrath of God, which is prepared unmixed in the cup of his anger; and he shall be tormented with fire and brimstone in the presence of the holy angels, and in the presence of the Lamb: and the smoke of their torment goes up for ever and ever; and they have no rest day and night

[227] *Ps. 2:12*: kiss the Son, lest he be angry, and you perish in the way, for his wrath will soon be kindled. Blessed are all they that take refuge in him *Matt. 3:7*: But when he saw many of the Pharisees and Saducees coming to his baptism, he said unto them, You offspring of vipers, who warned you to flee from the wrath to come

[228] *Jer. 23:19*: Behold, the tempest of Jehovah, even his wrath, is gone forth, yea, a whirling tempest: it shall burst upon the head of the wicked.

[229] *Ps. 7:11-12*: God is a righteous judge, yea, a God that has indignation every day. If a man turn not, he will whet his sword.

[230] Ps. 2:12; Rom. 3:25; 1 John 4:9-10

should defer to God's vengeful anger.[231] We should never avenge ourselves. We should not live our lives in bitterness over the wrongs fellow humans have done to us. Yet, if God has no wrath, how can we defer to it? Therefore, note well. The false doctrine of a wrathless God will not promote godliness. Rather, it will produce people full of vengeful anger and bitterness, because no one can defer to the vengeance of a God that has no vengeful anger. *Third*, accordingly, Christians should pray about God's anger and wrath both with intercessions[232] and, when appropriate, with imprecations.[233]

G. *God's Peace*

Sharp disparity exists between the massive testimony of Scripture to God's anger and wrath and the rather spartan testimony to his supreme peace.[234] Scripture often contrasts peace with war.[235] War connotes both *conflict* and *danger*. When there is conflict, humans feel anger, alienation, enmity, and hostility. When there is danger, humans feel fear and anxiety. Thus, we should not be surprised that Scripture contrasts peace at times with hostility and alienation[236] and at other times with fear and anxiety.[237]

The Hebrew word for peace is שָׁלוֹם (shalôm), which means "safe." It comes from the verb שָׁלַם (shalam), "to be safe," or "make complete." The Greek word for peace is ειρηνη (eirene). It signifies "rest" or "quietness." This word, *eirene*, belongs to a family of cognate words: ειρενευω (eireneuo), "to live in peace";[238] ειρηνικος (eirenikos), "peaceable";[239] ειρηνοποιεω (eirenopoieo), "to make peace";[240] and ειρηνοποιος (eirenopoios), "peacemaker."[241] The general use of these terms shows that peace involves both cessation of hostility and a sense of security from danger. We focus

---

[231] Rom. 12:19-21

[232] Deut. 9:18-19; Acts 7:60

[233] Ps. 69:21, 24, 26; 2 Tim. 4:14-16

[234] Jer. 16:5; Ps. 23:4; Isa. 43:5; John 14:27; Rom. 15:33, 16:20; Phil. 4:6-7, 9; 2 Thess. 3:16; Heb. 13:20-21

[235] Josh. 9:15, 10:1; 1 Kings 2:5; Ps.120:6,7; Prov. 16:7; Eccles. 3:8; Matt. 10:34; 1 Thess. 5:3

[236] *Rom. 5:1*: being therefore justified by faith, we have peace with God

[237] *Isa. 26:3*: you will keep him in perfect peace whose mind is stayed on you, because he trusts in you

[238] Mark 9:50; Rom. 12:18; 2 Cor. 13:11; 1 Thess. 5:13

[239] Heb. 12:11; James 3:17

[240] Col. 1:20

[241] Matt. 5:9

now on God's sensation of tranquility. God always experiences an incomprehensible sensation of total calmness. This infinite divine peace stems from his absolute security, immutability, and invulnerability, from his infinite foresight and insight, and from his irresistible sovereignty. His supreme tranquility is an absolute calm. It stands completely unmingled with anxiety, alarm, disquiet, or commotion. Nothing ever startles or terrifies God. He never frets about unfulfilled need. Yet, as one of my students observed long ago, God with invulnerable calm anticipates and thwarts all potential threats to his reputation.[242]

The dual significance of peace in Scripture makes it difficult to identify and isolate texts that refer uniquely to God's supreme tranquility. For example, the expression, "the God of peace," sometimes features his conciliatory influence upon his people. Thus, "the God of peace be with you" (Rom. 15:33) highlights the hope that God's conciliatory presence will check division and controversy in the church. Again, "the God of peace shall bruise Satan under your feet shortly" (Rom. 16:20) emphasizes that God will soon end spiritual conflict by vanquishing our enemy, Satan. Thus, "the God of peace," sometimes stresses, "the God who ends hostility," more than, "the God who feels absolute tranquility." Nevertheless, even in these texts, God's tranquility is implicitly in view. This is because war involves danger, and danger in turn gives rise to fear. In other contexts, such phrases "my peace," "the God of peace," and "the peace of God," feature God's tranquility. Now let's briefly survey this testimony.

Under the old covenant, God shelters the godly among his people, so that his tranquil presence calms the fears of those believe in him even in their darkest trials: "I will fear no evil, for you are with me" (Ps. 23:4). Accordingly, he encourages those who love and trust him: "Fear not, I am with you" (Isa. 43:5). Nevertheless, due to aggravated provocation and idolatry, Lord removed the calming influence of his tranquility from the society of his people.[243] When he thus removed his peace from Judah and Jerusalem, he severely judged them for their sins. Thus, a close connection exists between the departure of divine tranquility from his people and his infliction of wrath on them.

Under the new covenant, however, he restores his peace to his people. He incessantly imparts in some measure his own sensation of tranquility and

---

[242] *Deut. 32:27*: Were it not that I feared the provocation of the enemy, Lest their adversaries should judge amiss, Lest they should say, Our hand is exalted, and Jehovah has not done all this.

[243] *Jer. 16:5*: have taken away my peace from this people says Jehovah, even lovingkindness and tender mercies

calm to the society of his people. For this reason Christ exhorts his disciples not to fearful or troubled, even in the midst of danger.[244] God's people in Christ experience his blessed tranquility in the path of prayer. When with gratitude we cast all our worries on him, then his incomprehensible tranquility guards our hearts and thoughts.[245] We also experience his tranquility in the path of holiness. When by grace we do his will in gospel obedience, then the God of peace conveys his blessed tranquility to us.[246] Therefore, our hope and prayer is that the "Lord of peace" would impart to us ever increasing measures of his tranquility.[247] God conveys to his people his spiritual sensation of calmness through the special presence and powerful influence of the Holy Spirit that dwells in every Christian heart and church.[248] The God of hope conveys his peace to us in conjunction with our hope of eternal blessing when Jesus returns.[249]

Conclusion to the Display of God's Emotivity: Before the world was, God felt only Trinitarian joy, delight, pleasure, and peace in contemplation of his own infinite beauty, virtue, blessedness, and security. When he created all things and creatures, both material and spiritual, he felt delight, joy, and pleasure in his work. When creatures sinned, he felt detestation, grief, and vengeful anger. The miseries that their sin brought upon them also grieve him. In conjunction with redemption, the Lord feels affections that are something like what men call, "mixed emotions." His soul is grieved for the affliction of his people. Yet he rejoices over them. He delights in his people and is well-pleased with their evangelical obedience. Yet he detests their remaining corruption and is displeased with it. In the consummation, when his people no longer have any sin, his anger at their remaining sin will pass

---

[244] *John 14:27*: Peace I leave with you; my peace I give unto you: not as the world gives, give I unto you. Let not your heart be troubled, neither let it be fearful

[245] *Phil. 4:6-7, 9*: In nothing be anxious; but in everything by prayer and supplication with thanksgiving let your requests be made known unto God. And the peace of God, which passes all understanding, shall guard your hearts and your thoughts in Christ Jesus . . . the things which you both learned and received and heard and saw in me, these things do: and the God of peace shall be with you.

[246] *Heb. 13:20-21*: Now the God of peace, who brought again from the dead the great shepherd of the sheep with the blood of an eternal covenant, even our Lord Jesus, make you perfect in every good thing to do his will, working in us that which is well-pleasing in his sight through Jesus Christ.

[247] *2 Thess. 3:16*: The Lord of peace himself give you peace at all times in all ways. The Lord be with you all.

[248] *Rom. 14:17*: the kingdom of God is . . . righteousness and peace and joy in the Holy Spirit..

[249] *Rom. 15:13*: the God of hope fill you with all joy and peace in believing, that you may abound in hope, in the power of the Holy Spirit

away. When their suffering ends, then his grief over their present affliction will also pass away. Throughout eternity, in the new heavens and earth, he will feel unmingled delight, joy and pleasure in his people. Yet throughout eternity he will incessantly detest the wicked and pacify his vengeful anger with their unending punishment. Finally, from eternity to eternity, he feels uninterrupted and absolute tranquility.

IV. Practical Application of God's Emotivity

God's affections inspire heartfelt worship, incite filial imitation, and instill gospel obligation.

A. God's Affections Inspire Heartfelt Worship.

The display of God's heart and affections inspires heartfelt worship. With clear consciences we should bless God for his delight in justice and the righteous. With hatred for sin we should praise him for his detestation of wickedness and the wicked. With gravity we should stand in awe of his anger over sin. With gladness we should praise him for his pleasure in Christ's impeccable virtue and our gospel virtue. With appreciation we should bless him for his compassionate heart that grieves over our afflictions. With exuberance should praise him for imparting to us a measure of his incomprehensible peace and joy.

B. God's Affections Incite Filial Imitation.

God himself furnishes a flawless example of wholesome emotive life. His spiritual children should make God's spotless affections the pattern of our own feelings. We should love what he loves and hate what he hates. We too should detest sinners and their sin.[250] We should never delight in wickedness or in the company of the world.[251] We too should delight in the righteous and their godly ways. We should never detest those in whom the Lord delights. We too should grieve over the sufferings of God's people and rejoice with them in their blessings.[252] We too should rejoice with the Lord over sinners that repent. We too should be displeased with sin and pleased with the gospel obedience of his saints. When we are afraid, we should trust in the Lord. We should cast all our anxiety on him, in order to experience ever greater measures of his incomprehensible peace.

---

[250] *Ps. 139:21*: Do not I hate them, O Jehovah, that hate you? And am not I grieved with those that rise up against you?
[251] *1 John 2:15*: Love not the world, neither the things that are in the world. If any man love the world, the love of the Father is not in him.
[252] *Rom. 12:15*: Rejoice with them that rejoice; weep with them that weep.

C. God's Affections Instill Gospel Obligation.

God's affections oblige Christians to apply his emotivity conscientiously and evangelically to every aspect of our lives. We should live in such a way that God feels delight, joy, and pleasure in us. We must never do what he detests, or grieve him, or provoke him to jealousy. We should fear his wrath and flee from whatever provokes it. We should never take our own revenge, but always defer to his vengeful anger (Rom. 12:19). We should plead with him to fill our hearts with his incomprehensible peace. In sum, we should embrace God's emotivity wholeheartedly and live conscientiously in its light.

Conclusion: *Confession of God's Emotivity*

Finally, must confess with faithfulness and courage what Scripture so plainly declares about God's emotivity. We must not succumb to pressure to deny or even to neglect God's emotivity. Some of those who deny God's emotivity say that the capacity to feel is incompatible with God's immutability, self-existence, and sovereignty. In the estimation of such, a God that is self-existent, immutable, and sovereign can have an intellect and will, but he cannot have a heart. He cannot actually feel. These dismiss the massive biblical witness to God's heart and feelings as nothing more than figurative language, mere "anthropopathisms." They liken all the passages we have considered to *anthropomorphisms* that ascribe to God parts of a material body. For example, Scripture depicts "the arm of the Lord" (Isa. 53:1) and "the eyes of the Lord" (Prov. 15:3). *Arms* and *eyes* are members of the human body. God has no body. Clearly then, "the arm of the Lord" is a figure of speech designed to picture an important truth about God. However, the capacity to feel is not an aspect or function of the human body. Dead bodies have no capacity to feel. Corpses do not feel anything. Rather, the capacity to feel spiritual sensations is a faculty of all spiritual beings, even of devils. Jesus speaks factually, not figuratively, when he says: "God is a Spirit." He means that God in fact has all the distinguishing traits of a spiritual being. Therefore, there are no exegetical grounds to deny the emotivity of the Supreme Spirit. Therefore, those who deny God's capacity to feel do not honor God or his Word.

Consider the roots of rejecting God's emotivity. If the allegation that God can't feel doesn't stem from careful exegesis, where does it come from? Some think that it comes from a philosophical tradition in the church. But what drives some theologians to adopt such philosophy? Possibly the denial that God truly feels stems from an unwillingness submit to incomprehensible mystery. Truly the emotivity of an immutable and self-existent God leads us back to the fence around the mystery. We must simply embrace by faith all the Bible declares about God. Possibly also more is involved. In some instances the rejection of divine emotivity could stem from a jaundiced attitude toward human emotion. Possibly, a crippled emotional life that typifies many men in western and northern European culture fuels this erroneous rejection. Possibly some have recreated in their own image a heartless God that can't feel, rather than conform their theology and emotional experience to God's Word.

Consider the baneful fruits of rejecting God's emotivity. If we say that God has no feelings, we encourage the tendency to regard all expression of feeling as effeminate. We promote the tendency to think that the suppression of all emotion is a masculine virtue that we should cultivate. Yet a stoic or "Vulcan" suppression of all feeling is not in fact a virtue. It is an "ungodlike" vice. Similarly, Scripture presents feminine compassion as the living picture of God's compassionate heart. Therefore, denial of God's emotivity will tend to demean the value of godly femininity. Further, the denial of God's emotivity pushes us toward thinking that the expression of emotion is unsuitable for communion with an unfeeling God. This will tend toward the suppression of feeling in praying, in preaching, and even in singing. Thus, this denial will tend to produce worship that is cerebral and devoid of exuberance and the joy of the Lord. Further, because man, male and female, is the image of God, the denial of God's emotivity will tend to undermine the dignity of human emotion. This in turn will tend to minimize the value of cultivating godly feelings. Similarly, consider the fruits of neglecting God's emotivity. If we minimize God's heart and feelings, this will tend toward neglecting what Scripture teaches about human feelings. This in turn will leave the church vulnerable to look to the world for instruction regarding feelings. When we neglect truth, error will fill the void. If God's servants forfeit the field by silence about feelings, the world will whisper a secular doctrine of feeling to God's people that will lead them astray. Therefore, we must neither neglect nor deny God's emotivity. Rather, we must confess, expound, and apply God's heart and affections for his glory and for the good of our fellow human beings.

APPENDIX: MAJOR BIBLICAL TESTIMONY TO GOD'S ANGER AND WRATH

OLD TESTAMENT TERMS

אָנַף ('anaph): literally, "to breathe hard," "be enraged,": from the rapid breathing associated with anger: translated, "be angry," "displeased": depicts God's anger **14** times: Deut. 1:37, 4:21, 9:8,20; 1 Kings 8:46, 11:9; 2 Kings 17:18; 2 Chron. 6:36; Ezra 9:14; Pss. 2:12, 60:1, 79:5, 85:5; Isa. 12:1.

אַף ('aph): the term most frequently translated *"anger"* in the OT: In Exod. 34:6, Num. 14:18, Ps. 86:15, Jer. 15:15, translated "longsuffering": derived from *'anaph*: literally "nose," "nostril" (Gen. 2:7): used of God's anger at least these **168** times: Exod. 4:14, 22:24, 32:10, 11, 12; Num. 11:1, 10, 33, 12:9, 22:22, 25:3, 4, 32:10, 13, 14; Deut. 6:15, 7:4, 9:19, 11:17, 13:17, 29:20, 23, 24, 27, 28, 31:17, 32:22; Josh. 7:1, 26, 23:16; Judg. 2:14, 20, 3:8, 6:39, 10:7; 1 Sam. 28:18; 2 Sam. 6:7, 24:1; 2 Kings 13:3, 23:26, 24:20; 1 Chron. 13:10; 2 Chron. 12:12, 25:15, 28:11, 13, 29:10, 30:8; Ezra 8:22, 10:14; Neh. 9:17; Job 9:13, 14:13, 16:9, 19:11, 20:23, 28, 21:17, 35:15, 42:7; Pss. 2:5, 12, 6:1, 7:6, 21:9, 27:9, 30:5, 56:7, 69:24, 74:1, 76:7, 77:9, 78:21, 31, 38, 49, 50, 85:3, 5, 90:7, 11, 95:11, 103:8, 106:40, 110:5, 145:8; Prov. 24:18; Isa. 5:25(2), 9:12, 17, 21, 10:4, 5, 25, 12:1, 13:3, 9, 13, 30:27, 30, 42:25, 48:9, 63:3, 6, 66:15; Jer. 2:35, 4:8, 26, 7:20, 10:24, 12:13, 15:14, 17:4, 18:23, 21:5, 23:20, 25:37, 38, 30:24, 32:31, 37, 33:5, 36:7, 42:18, 44:6, 49:37, 51:45, 52:3; Lam. 1:12, 2:1(2), 3, 6, 21, 22, 3:43, 66, 4:11; Ezek. 5:13, 15, 7:3, 8, 13:13, 20:8, 21, 22:20, 25:14, 43:8; Dan. 9:16; Hos. 8:5, 11:9, 13:11, 14:4; Joel 2:13; Jonah 3:9, 4:2; Micah 5:15, 7:18; Nah. 1:3, 6; Hab. 3:8, 12; Zeph. 2:2(2), 3, 3:8; Zech. 10:3.

זָעַם (za'am) (verb): "to foam at the mouth": translated "be angry," "have indignation": in Num. 23:8, translated "denounce": used of God's anger **5** times: Ps. 7:11; Prov. 22:14; Isa. 66:14; Zech. 1:12; Mal. 1:4.

זַעַם (za'am) (noun): "froth": translated, "anger," "indignation," "rage": used of God's anger at least these **16** times: Pss. 38:3, 69:24, 78:49, 102:10; Isa. 10:5, 25, 13:5, 30:27; Jer. 10:10, 50:25; Lam. 2:6; Ezek. 21:31, 22:31; Nah. 1:6; Hab. 3:12; Zeph. 3:8.

זָעַף (za'aph) (verb): "to boil up": translated, "be wroth": used only of men's anger; 2 Chron. 26:19.

זָעֵף (za'eph) (adj), translated "displeased": used only of men's anger: 1 Kings 20:43, 21:4.

זַעַף (za'aph) (noun): "anger": translated, "indignation," "rage," "wrath": derived from the verb *za'aph*; used **2** times of God's anger: Isa. 30:30; Micah 7:9.

חֵמָה (chemah): "heat": translated, "hot displeasure," "fury," "rage," "wrath": used of God's anger at least these **85** times: Lev. 26:28; Num. 25:11; Deut. 9:19, 29:23, 28; 2 Kings 22:13,17; 2 Chron. 12:7, 28:9, 34:21,25, 36:16; Job 21:20; Pss. 6:1, 38:1, 59:13, 78:38, 79:6, 88:7, 89:46, 90:7, 106:23, Isa. 27:4, 34:2, 42:25, 51:17, 20, 22, 59:18, 63:3,5, 6, 66:15; Jer. 4:4, 6:11, 7:20, 10:25, 18:20, 21:5,12, 23:19, 25:15, 30:23, 32:31,37, 33:5, 36:7, 42:18(2), 44:6; Lam. 2:4, 4:11; Ezek. 5:13(2), 15, 6:12, 7:8, 8:18, 9:8, 13:13(2), 15, 14:19, 16:38, 42, 20:8, 13, 21, 33, 34, 21:17, 22:20, 22, 24:8, 13, 25:14, 17, 30:15, 36:6, 18, 38:18; Dan. 9:16; Micah 5:15; Nah. 1:2, 6; Zech. 8:2.

חָרָה (charah): "to glow, blaze": translated, "be angry," "be incensed," "be wroth": often used with a word for God's anger and translated "be kindled" or "wax hot": "my wrath shall *wax hot*" (Exod. 22:24), "so will the anger of Jehovah *be kindled*" (Deut. 7:4), etc.: used by itself of God's anger **5** times: Gen. 18:30, 32; 2 Sam. 22:8; Ps. 18:7; Hab. 3:8.

חָרוֹן (charôn): "a burning": derived from *charah*: translated "displeasure," "fury," "wrath": oft used with a word for God's anger and translated "fierce," or "fierceness": "the *fierce* anger of Jehovah" (Num. 25:3), "the *fierceness* of his anger" (Deut. 13:17), etc.; used by itself of God's anger at least these **6** times: Exod. 15:7; Neh. 13:18; Pss. 2:5, 88:16; Ezek. 7:12, 14.

חָרַר (charar): "to glow": translated "be angry," "burn": only depicts human anger: Song of Sol. 1:6

כָּעַס (ka'as) (verb): "to trouble": translated, "provoke to anger," "be angry," "grieve," "enrage," "vex," "have indignation": used of God's anger **43** times: Deut. 4:25, 9:18, 31:29, 32:16, 21; Judg. 2:12; 1 Kings 14:9, 15, 15:30, 16:2, 7,13, 26, 33, 21:22, 22:53; 2 Kings 17:11, 17, 21:6, 15, 22:17, 23:19, 26; 2 Chron. 28:25, 33:6, 34:25; Pss. 78:58, 106:29; Isa. 65:3; Jer. 7:18, 19, 8:19, 11:17, 25:6, 7, 32:29, 30, 32, 44:3, 8; Ezek. 8:17, 16:26; Hos. 12:14.

כַּעַס (ka'as) (noun): "vexation": derived from the verb *ka'as*: translated "anger," "provocation," "wrath": used of God's anger **6** times: Deut. 32:19; 1 Kings 15:30, 21:22; 2 Kings 23:26; Ps. 85:4; Ezek. 20:28.

כַּעַשׂ (ka'aś) (noun), "vexation"; also derived from the verb *ka'as*: form used only in Job: translated "wrath," "indignation": used **1** time of God's anger: Job 10:17.

עָבַר ('abar): "to cross over": used of a transition; in the Hithpael theme translated: "provoke to anger," "rage," "be wroth": used of God's anger **5** times: Deut. 3:26; Pss. 78:21, 59, 62, 89:38.

עֶבְרָה ('eb^erah): "outburst": derived from *'abar*: translated, "anger," "rage," "wrath": used of God's anger at least these **25** times: Job 21:30, (40:11, by implication); Pss. 78:49, 85:3, 90:9, 11; Prov. 11:4, 23 (at least implicitly); Isa. 9:19, 10:6, 13:9,13; Jer. 7:29; Lam. 2:2, 3:1; Ezek. 7:19, 21:31, 22:21, 31, 38:19; Hos. 5:10, 13:11; Hab. 3:8; Zeph. 1:15, 18.

עָשַׁן ('ashan): "to smoke": translated, "be angry": twice used with a word for God's anger and translated "smoke": "his jealousy *shall smoke* against that man" (Deut. 29:20), "why does your anger *smoke*" (Ps. 74:1); used by itself of God's anger **1** time: Ps. 80:4

קָצַף (qatsaph): "to break off," "to burst forth": translated, "be angry," "be displeased," "be wroth": used of God's anger **22** times: Lev. 10:6; Nu. 16:22; Deut. 9:7, 8, 19, 22; Josh. 22:18; Pss. 38:1, 106:32; Eccles. 5:6; Isa. 47:6, 54:9, 57:16,17(2), 64:5,9; Lam. 5:22; Zech. 1:2,15(2), 8:14

קֶצֶף (qetseph): "a splinter," as broken off: derived from *qatsaph*: translated "wrath," "indignation": used with a word for God's displeasure and translated "sore," or "very sore," "Jehovah has been *sore* displeased" (Zech. 1:2), "I am *very sore* displeased" (Zech. 1:15); used by itself of God's anger **23** times: Num. 1:53, 16:46, 18:5; Deut. 29:28; Josh. 9:20, 22:20; 1 Chron. 27:24; 2 Chron. 19:2, 10, 24:18, 29:8, 32:25, 26, Pss. 38:1, 102:10; Isa. 34:2, 54:8, 60:10; Jer. 10:10, 21:5, 32:37, 50:13; Zech. 7:12.

קְצַף (q^etsaph) (verb): Aramaic: corresponds to Heb., *qatsaph*: translated "be furious": used only of man's anger: Dan. 2:12.

קְצָף (qᵉtsaph) (noun): Aramaic: derived from verb qᵉtsaph;: translated "*wrath*": used **1** time of God's anger: Ezra 7:23.

רָגַז (ragaz): "to quiver": translated "be wroth," "rage": used **3** times of God's anger: Job 12:6; Isa. 28:21; Ezek. 16:43.

רֹגֶז (rogez), "restlessness": derived from *ragaz*: translated, "rage," "wrath": used of thunder in Job 37:2: used **1** time of God's anger: Hab. 3:2.

רְגַז (rᵉgaz) (verb): Aramaic: corresponds to *ragaz*: translated "provoked to wrath": depicts God's anger **1** time: Ezra 5:12.

NEW TESTAMENT TERMS

ὀργή (orge):"excitement": translated, "anger," "indignation," "vengeance," "wrath": used **29** times of God's anger: Matt. 3:7; Mark 3:5; Luke 3:7, 21:23; John 3:36; Rom. 1:18, 2:5, 8, 3:5, 4:15, 5:9, 9:22, 12:19, 13:4, 5; Eph. 2:3, 5:6; Col. 3:6; 1 Thess. 1:10, 2:16, 5:9; Heb. 3:11, 4:3; Rev. 6:16, 17, 11:18, 14:10, 16:19, 19:15.

θυμός (thumos): "breathing hard": translated "fierceness," "indignation," "wrath": can depict sinful anger of humans and the devil: used **8** times of God's anger: Rom. 2:8; Rev. 14:10, 19, 15:1, 7, 16:1, 19, 19:15.

COLLATION AND SUMMARY

Word	Uses	Word	Uses
Old Testament		New Testament	
'anaph	14	orge	29
'aph	168	thumos	8
za'am (verb)	5		
za'am (noun)	16		
za'aph (noun)	2		
chēmah	85		
charah	5		
charôn	6		
ka'as (verb)	43		
ka'as (noun)	6		
ka'aś (noun)	1		
'abar	5		
'ebᵉrah	25		
'ashan	1		
qatsaph	22		
qetseph	23		
qᵉtsaph	1		
ragaz	3		
rogez	1		
rᵉgaz	1		
OT TOTAL	433	NT TOTAL	37
		BIBLE TOTAL	**470**

Part 3: The Nature of God | 415

Topic 16. God's Moral Capacity and Character
"you shall be as God, knowing good and evil" (Gen. 3:5);
"you shall therefore be perfect, as your heavenly Father is perfect" (Matt. 5:48)

Section 9. God's Morality: The Supreme Virtue of God

Introduction: God's Moral Capacity and Character: *Overview of God's Supreme Virtue*

We now consider how morality, a fourth essential property of spiritual beings, pertains to the Supreme Spirit. I outline Section 9, in which I cover Topics 16-21, as follows:

Topic 16: Introduction: God's Moral Capacity and Character: *Overview of God's Supreme Virtue*
Topic 17: Unit 1. God's Goodness
Topic 18: Unit 2. God's Holiness
Topic 19: Unit 3. God's Justice
Topic 20: Unit 4. God's Faithfulness
Topic 21: Conclusion: God's Self Esteem: God's Consciousness of his Supreme Virtue

Now I introduce Section 9, in which I expound God's supreme virtue, with an overview. God's supreme virtue embraces his *moral capacity*, "knowing good and evil" (Gen. 3:5), and *moral character*, "your heavenly Father is perfect" (Matt. 5:48). God's supremacy regulates his supreme virtue. Thus, his moral capacity and character are infinite, eternal, unchangeable, ideal, and self-existent. In this overview I unfold God's supreme *moral capacity*, summarize his supreme *moral character*, which I expound in topics 17-20, and conclude with practical applications.

I. *God's Supreme Moral Capacity*

God's moral capacity is similar to human moral capacity: "the man *is become as* one of us to know good and evil" (Gen. 3:22). Yet, human moral capacity as originally created was not fully developed, unlike God's ideal moral capacity: "you *shall be* as God" (Gen. 3:5). Accordingly, I now unfold both the general concept of moral capacity and the supremacy of God's moral capacity.

A. The General Concept of Moral Capacity

Moral capacity is "the knowledge of good and evil." Precise definition presents a formidable challenge. When I expounded God's knowability, Topic 3, I observed a fourfold significance of knowing: "to know something (or someone) can be to have *information* about it, or *comprehension* of it, or *perception* of it, or *involvement* with it." Thus, moral consciousness is multi-faceted. Moral knowledge has factual, intellectual, perceptual, and experiential aspects. Thus, the knowledge of good and evil involves an *informed awareness* about morality, an *accurate comprehension* of morality, a *spiritual perception* of morality, and *personal intercourse* with morality. Accordingly, I define moral capacity as follows:

> *Moral capacity* is the ability to act as a moral being: to have personal consciousness of morality; to possess information about, understand, discern, and have experiential involvement with right and wrong.

Before the fall, Adam had ability to act morally and personal consciousness of morality: "and they were both naked, the man and his wife, and were not ashamed" (Gen. 2:25). Even infants have moral capacity in seed form. They have potential to act as moral beings and to develop moral consciousness. Thus, human moral capacity develops[1] even as the human mind develops.[2] Scripture reveals how Adam gained the knowledge of good and evil. He gained, at least in one sense, the knowledge of right and wrong when he sinned. Prior to the fall, Adam was had informed awareness of right and wrong. He knew that it was wrong to disobey God.[3] He also had an accurate comprehension of right and wrong. He understood the destructive nature of evil: "in the day that you eat thereof, *you shall surely die.*" The Bible doesn't disclose explicitly whether Adam perceived the presence of evil before his fall. However, based on Paul's observation that "Adam was *not beguiled*" (1 Tim. 2:14), one could argue that Adam had a spiritual perception right and wrong *before* he ate the forbidden fruit. This all creates a strong presumption that when Adam sinned he primarily gained experiential knowledge of good and evil. Evil confronted him, tempted him, and overcame him.[4] Thus, he came to *"know sin."* He experienced *personal intercourse* with evil. Thus, he knew that he was "naked." He felt exposed and ashamed. Thus, fallen Adam and God both have experiential knowledge

---

[1] *Deut. 1:39*: Moreover your little ones, that you said should be a prey, and your children, that this day have no knowledge of good or evil, they shall go in thither, and unto them will I give it, and they shall possess it.

[2] Luke 2:52

[3] Gen. 2:16-17

[4] *Gen. 3:4-7*: And the serpent said unto the woman, You shall not surely die: for God does know that in the day you eat thereof, then your eyes shall be opened, and you shall be as God, knowing good and evil. And when the woman saw that the tree was good for food, and that it was a delight to the eyes, and that the tree was to be desired to make one wise, she took of the fruit thereof, and did eat; and she gave also unto her husband with her, and he did eat. And the eyes of them both were opened and they knew that they were naked

of good and evil.⁵ Yet they do not have it in the same way. God has it by doing good. Adam has it by spurning good and doing evil. Therefore, God has the experiential moral knowledge of a righteous moral being. Adam came to have the experiential moral knowledge of a wicked moral being. George Bush, commenting on Genesis 3:5, concurs:

> By 'opening the eyes', she understood a further and higher degree of wisdom, such as the phrase imports, Acts 26:18, Eph. 1:18, but he meant it of perceiving their own misery, and feeling remorse of conscience. By 'being as gods' (Elohim), she probably understood being elevated almost to an equality with the Deity himself in point of knowledge and dignity; but he probably meant it of their being brought to the condition of the angels that fell, as angels are sometimes styled *Elohim*, Ps. 8:6. By 'knowing good and evil' she doubtless understood a kind of divine omniscience, whereas his meaning was that they should have a *woeful experience* of the difference between good and evil, or between happiness and misery, such as he, himself, had.⁶

Again, commenting on Genesis 3:7, Bush affirms:

> That is, the eyes of their minds. They had a mental perception of their guilt and misery. They had a sense, a discovery, of the consequences of their sin which they never had nor could have before. A similar effect always follows the commission of known sin. A terrible light is let in on the soul to which, during the process of the temptation, it was a comparative stranger. It is in fact the *experimental* knowledge of the difference between good and evil. The result in the case of our first parents was, that they saw themselves *naked*; by which is meant, not so much that they were sensible that their bodies were destitute of clothing, for of this they were doubtless aware before, but they now recognized their nakedness with shame and confusion, and were at the same time conscious of a sad privation of innocence, which had before covered them as with a robe. They felt themselves *bereaved* of the comfortable presence and favor of their Maker, and thus were made *naked* through exposure to his wrath.⁷

Thus it follows that if Adam had resisted the temptation he would have attained the experiential moral knowledge of a righteous moral being. Keil & Delitzsch concur:

---

⁵ *Gen. 3:22*: Jehovah God said, Behold, the man is become as one of us to know good and evil

⁶ George Bush, *Notes on Genesis*, (2 Vols.; Minneapolis, MN: Klock & Klock Christian Publishers, 1981), 1:76

⁷ Ibid., 1:78-79

That is to say, it is not because the fruit of the tree will injure you that God has forbidden you to eat it, but from ill-will and envy, because He does not wish you to be like Himself. 'A truly satanic *double entendre,* in which a certain agreement between truth and untruth is secured!' By eating the fruit man did obtain the knowledge of good and evil, and in this respect became like God (vers.7 and 22). This was the truth which covered the falsehood 'you shall not die', and turned the whole statement into a lie, exhibiting its author as the father of lies, who abides not in the truth (John 8:44). For the knowledge of good and evil, which man obtains by going into evil, is as far removed from the true likeness of God, *which he would have attained by avoiding it,* as the imaginary liberty of a sinner, which leads into bondage to sin and ends in death, is from the true liberty of a life of fellowship with God.[8] [emphasis supplied]

B. The Supremacy of God's Moral Capacity

God alone possesses supreme ability to act as a moral being. He has omniscient information about, comprehension of, and perception of right and wrong. He has ideal experiential involvement with good and evil. Consider three important implications of God's supreme moral capacity.

1. God does not and cannot have any personal intercourse with sin.

God has ideal knowledge of good and evil. Therefore, experientially, he can never "*know*" sin: "him who *knew no sin* he made to be sin for us" (2 Cor. 5:21). Paul does not mean that Christ was uninformed respecting sin, or that he lacked comprehension of it, or that he was oblivious to it. He means that the impeccable Christ never had any personal intercourse with sin. It is impossible for God to commit sin. He cannot even be tempted with evil.[9] In this sense, God does not and can never "*know*" sin.[10] He didn't attain experiential knowledge of good by enduring temptation. He knows good experientially because he alone is good eternally and permanently. When only God was, there was only good.

2. God himself is the final Judge of morality.

God's personal consciousness of morality is eternal, independent, and ideal. Thus, God himself is the final Arbiter of morality. Knowledge of right and wrong presupposes a standard of right and wrong. God himself is the

---

[8] Keil & Delitzsch, *OT Commentary,* 1: 95

[9] *James 1:13*: God cannot be tempted with evil

[10] *Hab. 1:13*: you that are of purer eyes than to behold evil, and that can not look on perverseness.

ultimate Judge of what ought to be. To some this may sound like God is somewhat self-serving. To me it sounds like anyone who doesn't want God as his Judge is somewhat self-serving. This is a kindergarten lesson in the school of moral discernment. It is the lesson of the forbidden fruit. Why was it wrong to eat tasty fruit from a tree good for food? It was morally wrong only because God said it was wrong. Who is God to define morality? He is God. He owes no creature an account of himself. Good is what he says it is. If humans disobey him, they do evil. Creatures can only change this if they ascend into heaven, overthrow God, and make themselves the arbiters of morality. The devil tried and miserably failed. No creature, or army of creatures, can ever dethrone the Supreme Being. Moral creatures can't even erase from their consciences their sense of obligation to obey him (Rom. 1:32).

3. God himself is the living Exemplar of moral good.

God's moral capacity is infinite, unchangeable, and ideal. Thus, God himself is the living Standard of moral good. He is the Righteous One, because he is God. Good is what he is. He stands consciously and irrevocably committed to be what morally good. He cannot be evil, become evil, or do evil. He immutably assesses himself, and his judgment is final, to be right and good.[11]

II. *God's Supreme Moral Character*

I present an overview of the *general concept* and *constituent elements* of God's supreme moral character.

A. The General Concept of God's Supreme Moral Character

I define the general idea of God's supreme moral character as follows:

> God possesses infinitely perfect (ideal) moral integrity and virtue, which is completely free of all vice, and which can never become worse, by moral lapse, or better, by moral improvement.

Infinitely perfect virtue has, and can have, no mixture of vice. It can never be diminished or improved. Thus, God alone is the epitome of moral good. If he could be morally other, or have a moral peer, he wouldn't be God. Scripture affirms repeatedly God's unique moral supremacy. When God created the world, everything was good, even flawless. Yet God alone is necessarily and impeccably good: "none is good save one, even God" (Mark 10:18). Again, God alone is ideally holy: "Who is like unto you, O Jehovah, among the gods? Who is like unto you, glorious in holiness, fearful in

---

[11] Ezek. 18:25, 29, 33:17

praises, doing wonders?" (Exod. 15:11); and: "there is none holy as Jehovah; for there is none besides you" (1 Sam. 2:2).

Consider the biblical depictions of God's supreme virtue. The New Testament depicts God's virtue with ἀρετη (arete), "virtue"[12] or "excellency."[13] It depicts moral "strength" or "manliness," the opposite of moral weakness. Again, it uses δικαιοσυνη (dikaiosune), "righteousness,"[14] and its cognate δικαιος (dikaios), "righteous."[15] This word family depicts "equity" or "propriety." The Old Testament depicts God's virtue with יָשָׁר (yashar), "upright."[16] It means morally "straight" as opposed to morally crooked, or perverse. Again, it uses צְדָקָה (tseᵉdaqah), "righteousness,"[17] and its cognates צֶדֶק (tsedeq), "righteousness," or "righteously,"[18] and צַדִּיק (tsaddîq), "righteous."[19] This word family conveys the idea of moral "rectitude" or "rightness."

This leads us to the basic meaning of "rectitude" or "rightness" and "integrity" or "virtue." Webster defines "right" as: "qualities .. that together constitute the ideal of moral propriety or merit moral approval."[20] Again, it defines "virtue" as: "a particular moral excellence," or, "a conformity to a standard of right."[21] Thus, right depends on someone's approval. Someone's standards, values, and ideals define morality. Someone must arbitrate or assess virtue.

This leads to the crucial issue. Who arbitrates morality? Scripture teaches, not that "might makes right," or that "the majority makes right," but that God makes right. His approval defines virtue.[22] Proud humans attempt to

---

[12] Phil. 4:8; 2 Pet. 1:3
[13] 1 Pet. 2:9
[14] Eph. 4:24; Rev. 19:11
[15] John 17:25; 2 Tim. 4:8; Rev. 16:5
[16] Pss. 25:8, 92:15
[17] Pss. 143:1, 145:7
[18] Pss. 97:6, 98:9, 119:142; Jer. 11:20
[19] Ezra 9:15; Neh. 9:8; Pss. 11:7, 116:5, 119:137, 129:4, 145:17
[20] *WNC Dictionary*, 989
[21] Ibid., 1298
[22] *Deut. 12:25, 28*: you shall do that which is right in the eyes of Jehovah . . . Observe and hear that which I command you, that it may go well with you, and with your children after you for ever, when you do that which is good and right in the eyes of Jehovah your God. *Deut. 13:18*: you shall hearken to the voice of Jehovah your God, to keep all his commandments which I command you this day, to do that which is right in the eyes of Jehovah your God.

redefine moral propriety.[23] The wicked view virtue differently than God.[24] God's definition of virtue must prevail, because he is God. Thus, God's virtue consists in his self-approval, in his doing and being what is right in his own eyes.

How does the Lord make this moral self-assessment? Does he behold an abstract standard of virtue and conform himself to it? Or, does he behold his own character and appoint himself as the standard of virtue? If we adopt the former approach, we run the risk of positing a God less than ideal, who could sin if he violated an abstract law to which he and his creatures are subject. If we take the latter approach, we run the risk of positing a capricious God, who would be right in his own eyes no matter what he did. Scripture does not explain how God reaches this moral self-assessment. It simply leads us to the brink of this mystery. We know only that God himself is both the Arbiter and Exemplar of moral virtue. He judges himself supremely virtuous in a way that neither denies his ideality nor renders him capricious.

B. The Constituent Elements of God's Supreme Moral Character

Scripture associates God's integrity or uprightness with four distinct and closely related moral virtues. It associates God's uprightness with his goodness,[25] with his holiness, or separateness from sin,[26] with his justice,[27] and with his faithfulness, or reliability.[28] Thus, God's supreme moral rightness displays these four primary virtues. Reformed theology faithfully and accurately distinguishes and expounds these four divine virtues. I may almost say that "every" treatment of God's attributes somehow expounds them.

Conclusion: Practical applications of God's moral capacity and character

As we close, consider with me three practical applications of God's supreme moral virtue.

---

[23] *Prov. 12:15*: The way of a fool is right in his own eyes. *Prov. 21:1*: every way of man is right in his own eyes, but Jehovah weighs the spirits

[24] *Luke 16:15*: you are they that justify yourselves in the sight of men; but God knows your hearts.

[25] *Ps. 25:8*: Good and upright is the Lord. *Ps. 116:5*: gracious is Jehovah, and righteous; yea, our God is merciful. *Ps.145:7*: they shall utter the memory of your great goodness, and shall sing of your righteousness.

[26] *Deut. 32:4*: The Rock, his work is perfect; all his ways are justice: a God of faithfulness and without iniquity, just and right is he

[27] *Ps. 98:9*: he will judge the world with righteousness, and the peoples with equity.

[28] *Neh. 9:8*: and have performed your words; for you are righteous

A. Imitation of God's Supreme Virtue[29]

Christ says that Christians should be "perfect," like our heavenly Father. In some contexts this word, τελειος (teleios), signifies completion[30] or maturity.[31] However, clearly in this context *teleios* depicts moral flawlessness.[32] Thus he means, as your Father is *morally flawless*, so you too should be *morally flawless*. Thus, Christ declares the gospel obligation of Christians to imitate the moral perfection of our heavenly Father. Christians, as God's spiritual children, must strive in all things to be like our heavenly Father. Sinless perfection is our present duty, not merely our future hope. We are responsible to conform to God's spotless character. Christ is the living exemplar of this standard. All progress in holiness occurs in union with him, by his strength, through the power of his Spirit that dwells in us. We must in union with Christ strive to be good, holy, just, and faithful in all our ways. Even as our Father lives without sin, so must we strive by Christ's Spirit that lives in us to eradicate every vestige of sin from our lives. We must by Christ's enablement put away sin from our thoughts, feelings, decisions, words, and actions. No sin is ever excusable. Therefore, remember that we study God's virtues, not as disinterested scientists, but as his beloved children obliged to emulate him. He himself is our standard of right and wrong. We must not devise our own notion of virtue and pursue it. Rather, we must identify his virtue and imitate it. Thus, for now, we pursue an impossible dream. No Christian can attain sinless perfection in this life. But, in glory our frustration will end. We will have what we now by his grace strive to attain. We will join "the spirits of just men made perfect" (Heb. 12:23). When Christ returns: "we shall be like him; for we shall see him even as he is" (1 John 3:2).

Therefore, God's flawless character, nothing less, is the immutable standard of Christian morality. We must in union with Christ put away all defilement of spirit and behavior (2 Cor. 7:1). We must imitate every virtue of our ideal God and Father. Observe that our Christian pursuit of sinless perfection is evangelical, not legalistic. Christ speaks here of progressive sanctification, not of justification. He does not tell sinners to get right with God by striving for perfection. Rather, he exhorts those who are already right with God, his spiritual children: "as *your heavenly Father* is perfect." God's children have Christ's perfect virtue imputed to them by means of faith alone, when they believe in Christ. Observe further, that Christians do not pursue sinless

---

[29] *Matt. 5:48*: You shall therefore be perfect, even as your heavenly Father is perfect

[30] James 1:4

[31] 1 Cor. 2:6, 14:20; Eph. 4:13; Phil. 3:15; Heb. 5:14

[32] Heb. 12:23

perfection by our own strength. We pursue sinlessness by the power of the Holy Spirit who dwells in us: "I will put my Spirit within you, and cause you to walk in my statutes (Ezek 36:27); and "If by the Spirit you are putting to death the deeds of the body, you will live" (Rom. 8:13). Again, our motive is not to earn heaven, but to honor and please our heavenly Father, because we love him, because he first loved us in Christ. Again, all takes place in union with Christ, by his enablement.

B. Reflection of God's Supreme Virtue[33]

It is our privilege as God's people to display his moral excellencies. Here is a lofty view of the Christian church. Peter sets forth the tremendous privilege of God's people under the new covenant. God calls out of darkness those who formerly were no people in order that his church would show forth his virtues. Thus, as we study his supreme moral virtues, let us remember that he has formed his church to display them. Let us conduct all our church affairs with this solemn privilege clearly in view. The church must draw near to God and relate to humanity in a manner marked by holiness, goodness, justice, and faithfulness. This vision should regulate who belongs to our churches, who gives leadership to our churches, and how our churches conduct their worship, benevolence, discipline, evangelism, and prayer.

C. Cultivation of Conformity to God's Supreme Virtue[34]

God's power and grace in Christ enables Christians to cultivate conformity to God's virtues: "*his divine power has granted* unto us all things that pertain unto life and godliness." In what sense are Christians "partakers of the divine nature"? In the sense that when we imitate his holiness, justice, goodness and faithfulness, we display through our lives, albeit dimly, God's moral excellencies. Thus, in a limited way God's moral virtues are communicable. This does not mean that Christians possess ideal virtue: "for there's none good but one, even God." Nevertheless, God communicates true virtue to his people. What a privilege it is to reflect, even in a small way, his moral excellencies. Therefore, as we study his moral virtues, let us

---

[33] *1 Pet. 2:9-10*: But you are an elect race, a royal priesthood, a holy nation, a people for God's own possession, that you may show forth the excellencies of him who called you out of darkness into his marvelous light: who in time past were no people, but now are the people of God

[34] *2 Pet. 1:3-4*: seeing that his divine power has granted unto us all things that pertain unto life and godliness, through the knowledge of him that called us by his own glory and virtue; whereby he has granted unto us his precious and exceeding great promises; that through these you may become partakers of the divine nature, having escaped from the corruption that is in the world by lust

pray that he will to enable us, by his grace, to cultivate and display his moral excellencies in our lives. Let us plead "his precious and exceeding great promises," with longing and hope that he will work ever growing measures of goodness, holiness, justice, and faithfulness in our hearts.

Topic 17. The Goodness of God

"I will make all my goodness pass before you" (Exod. 33:19); "Behold then the goodness and severity of God" (Rom. 11:22)

Unit 1. The Goodness of God

Introduction: *the tremendous importance of God's goodness*

I begin with the tremendous importance of studying God's goodness. Isn't it obvious that God is good? Why spend a whole lecture on something so obvious? Indeed, I would like to spend my whole life studying it. Christians will spend all eternity enthralled with it. Why is it so important? For one thing, nothing more satisfies the reverent hunger of God's children for experiential knowledge of God than feeding our souls on his goodness. When Moses pleaded: "Show me, I pray you, *your glory*," the Lord replied: "I will make all *my goodness* pass before you, and will proclaim the name of Jehovah before you." Evidently, the Lord himself regards his goodness as of utmost importance when he displays his glory to his saints to satisfy their spiritual hunger. Again, faith in God's goodness is the foundation of a right relationship with God: "he that comes to God must believe that he is, and that he is a rewarder of them that seek after him" (Heb. 11:6). People only come to God when they believe that in his goodness he graciously rewards those who seek him. Again, Peter appeals to God's goodness to motivate Christians to pray: "casting all your anxiety upon him, because he cares for you" (1 Pet. 5:7). Believers pour out their hearts and troubles to God because they believe that in his goodness he cares for them. Thus, the devil tells lies and casts aspersions on God's motives to sow seeds of doubt in people's minds about God's goodness. Since the beginning he has used this tactic (Gen. 3:4-5). If he managed to attack God's goodness in an unfallen world when he had only one prohibition to pervert for his evil ends, how much more will he use the many restrictions, disappointments, sufferings, afflictions, and needs of this fallen world to cast aspersions on God's goodness? Thus, if we would avoid his influence in the midst of our afflictions and disappointments, we must keep our hearts steeped in God's goodness. Therefore, let us diligently study his goodness with reverent hunger, biblical faith, and sober watchfulness against the wiles of the devil.

Our epitomizing texts frame the biblical testimony to his supreme goodness. First, they introduce the *general concept*: "I will make all my goodness pass before you; and, "The goodness and severity of God." Second, context specifies its *major features*: "a God merciful and gracious, slow to anger, and abundant in lovingkindness." Third, their contexts describe its *manifold display*: "Jehovah, Jehovah, a God . . . forgiving iniquity and transgression and sin . . . visiting the iniquity of the fathers upon the children, and upon the children's children, upon the third and upon the fourth generation"; and, "Behold then the goodness and severity of God: toward them that fell, severity; but toward you, God's goodness." Finally, their contexts also commend its *practical relevance*: "And Moses made haste, and bowed his head toward the earth, and worshipped"; and, "Be not high-minded, but fear: for if God spared not the natural branches, neither will he spare you." Accordingly, I unfold the *general concept, major features*, and *manifold display* of God's goodness. Then I conclude with its *practical relevance*.

I. The General Concept of God's Goodness

In general terms, Scripture defines "goodness," or "being good," as a disposition and commitment to do good: "the good man out of the good treasure of his heart brings forth that which is good; and the evil man, out of the evil treasure, brings forth that which is evil" (Luke 6:45), and, "You are good, and do good" (Ps. 119:68). Thus, to understand God's goodness, we must first grasp the biblical meaning of "*good*." The two primary words translated "good" are טוֹב (tôb) in the Old Testament and ἀγαθος (agathos) in the New Testament. These terms have two basic meanings. First, these terms refer to moral *propriety*. When something is "good" in this sense, it is morally as it should be. In this sense good is the opposite of moral wrong or evil: "you shall be as God, knowing good and evil" (Gen. 3:5), and, "Depart from evil, and do good; and dwell for evermore" (Ps. 37:27). Second, these terms refer to *beneficiality*. When something is "good" in this sense, it is useful and beneficial, conducive to health, well-being, or happiness. In this sense, good is the opposite of harm, of what is unpleasant, destructive, or unprofitable. Scripture often uses both *tôb*[1] and *agathos*[2] to depict beneficiality.

Thus, in the broadest sense, God's goodness refers to his disposition to do what is morally right. In the narrower sense it depicts his gracious disposition to do what is beneficial and kind. Scripture thus features God's

---

[1] *Job 2:10*: shall we receive good at the hand of God, and shall we not receive evil? *Isa. 41:23, 45:7*: yea, do good, or do evil, that we may be dismayed, and behold it together . . . I make peace, and create evil; I am Jehovah that does all these things. *Jer. 44:27*: Behold, I watch over them for evil, and not for good; and all the men of Judah that are in the land of Egypt shall be consumed by the sword and by the famine.

[2] *Matt. 13:47-48*: like unto a net, that was cast into the sea, and gathered of every kind: which when it was filled, they drew up on the beach; and they sat down, and gathered the good into vessels, but the bad they cast away. *Luke 6:43-44*: There is no good tree that brings forth corrupt fruit; nor again a corrupt tree that brings forth good fruit. For each tree is known by its own fruit. For of thorns men do not gather figs, nor of a bramble bush gather they grapes. *Luke 8:8*: And other fell into the good ground, and grew, and brought forth fruit.

benevolence as the core of his goodness. I catalogue the biblical testimony below:

MAJOR BIBLICAL TERMS FOR GOD'S GOODNESS
OLD TESTAMENT TERMS

טוֹב (tôb) (verb): "to be, do, or make good": translated: "be good," "do good," "do well," "cheer," "please": used explicitly of God's goodness 3 times: Pss. 119:68, 125:4; Jer. 32:41.

טוֹב (tôb) (noun, adj.): "good": derived from the verb: basic word for good in the Old Testament: sometimes depicts what seems best or wisest to someone (2 Sam. 10:12, 15:26, 1 Chron. 19:13): usually depicts what is morally proper or beneficial: translated "good," "goodness," "kindness," "fine," "prosperity," "bountiful," "welfare," with a variety of other nuances: used of God's goodness at least these 84 times: Gen. 50:20; Num. 10:29, 32; Deut. 30:9; Josh. 23:14, 15; 1 Sam. 24:19, 25:30; 2 Sam. 7:28, 16:12; 1 Kings 8:56, 66; 1 Chron. 16:34, 17:26; 2 Chron. 5:13, 6:41 [implicit], 7:3, 10, 30:18; Ezra 3:11, 8:18, 22; Neh. 2:8, 18, 5:19, 9:20, 13:31; Job 2:10; Pss. 21:3, 23:6 [implicit], 25:8, 34:8, 10 [implicit], 12 [implicit], 54:6, 65:11, 68:10, 73:1, 84:11, 85:12, 86:5, 17, 100:5, 103:5, 104:28, 106:1, 107:1, 9, 118:1, 29, 119:65, 68, 122, 128:2 [implicit], 135:3, 136:1, 143:10, 145:9; Eccles. 3:13, 5:18, 7:14, 8:12 [implicit]; Isa. 3:10 [implicit]; Jer. 5:25 [implicit], 14:11 [implicit], 15:11, 17:6 [implicit], 21:10, 29:10, 32, 32:39, 42, 33:9 (2), 11, 14, 39:16, 42:6 [implicit], 44:27; Lam. 3:25, 38; Amos 9:4; Nah. 1:7; Zech. 1:17.

טוּב (tûb): "goodness, gladness, welfare, beauty": derived from the verb tôb: translated "goodness," "good," "go well with": used of God's goodness at least these 17 times: Exod. 33:19; Deut. 6:11; Neh. 9:25, 35, 36; Pss. 25:7, 27:13, 31:19, 65:4 [implicit], 145:7; Isa. 1:19 [implicit], 63:7; Jer. 2:7, 31:12, 14; Hos. 3:5; Zech. 9:17.

יָטַב (yatab): "to make well, sound, right"; translated "make better," "benefit," "go well with," "do good," "make good," "goodness," "deal well with," with a wide variety of nuances: used of God's goodness at least these 19 times: Gen. 32:9, 12(2); Exod. 1:20; Num. 10:32; Deut. 8:16, 28:63, 30:5; Josh. 24:20; Judg. 17:13; 1 Sam. 2:32, 25:31; 1 Kings 1:47; Ps. 51:18; Jer. 18:10, 32:40; Mic. 2:7; Zeph. 1:12; Zech. 8:15.

NEW TESTAMENT TERMS

ἀγαθος (agathos): "good": the general word for good: depicts what is morally proper and what is beneficial: translated "good," "benefit," "well": depicts God's goodness at least these 10 times: Matt. 19:17; Mark 10:18; Luke 18:19; Luke 1:53, 11:13 [implicit]; Phil. 1:6; Heb. 9:11 [implicit], 10:1 [implicit]; James 1:17; 1 Pet. 3:10 [implicit].

ἀγαθοποιεω (agathopoieo): "to be a well-doer": translated "do good," "do well": used **once** of God's goodness: Acts 14:17

χρηστος (chrestos): "useful": translated "good," "goodness," "kind": depicts Christian grace that pictures God's goodness (Eph. 4:32): used of God's goodness 3 times: Luke 6:35; Rom. 2:4; 1 Pet. 2:3.

χρηστοτης (chrestotes): "usefulness," "moral excellence": translated "goodness," "gentleness," "kindness": used of Christian goodness produced by the Holy Spirit (Gal. 5:22): used of God's goodness **6** times: Rom. 2:4, 11:22(3); Eph. 2:7; Titus 3:4.

χρηστευομαι (chresteuomai): "show oneself useful," "act benevolently": translated "be kind": used only once in the New Testament: depicts the nature of love: 1 Cor. 13:4.

TABULATION

OLD TESTAMENT		NEW TESTAMENT	
WORD	USES	WORD	USES
tôb (vb)	3	agathos	10
tôb (n)	84	agathopoieo	1
tûb	17	chrestos	3
yatab	19	chrestotes	6
TOTAL in OT	123	TOTAL in NT	20
		TOTAL in SCRIPTURE	**143**

Based on a detailed survey of this testimony, I offer the following definition of God's goodness:

> *God's goodness* is: God's unalloyed disposition and irrevocable commitment to do good, his impeccable moral propriety[1]: consisting predominately in his abundant kindness or beneficiality[2], composed of his dependable lovingkindness and mercy[3], his unconstrained goodwill and grace[4], his generous philanthropy and love[5], his keen compassion[6], and his conciliatory long-suffering[7]; yet also consisting indispensably in his impeccable severity[8].
>
> 1. Ps. 119:68; Mark 10:18
> 2. Rom. 11:22; Ps. 106:1
> 3. Exod. 34:6; Titus 3:4, 5
> 4. Exod. 34:6; Titus 3:4, 7
> 5. Jer. 31:3; Titus 3:4; Eph. 2:4
> 6. Exod. 34:6; Luke 6:35, 36
> 7. Exod. 34:6; Rom. 2:4
> 8. Exod. 34:6, 7; Rom. 11:22

This definition begins with God's goodness in its broader sense, his *absolute propriety*. It dwells on the primary focus of God's goodness, his *abundant beneficiality*. It enumerates five essential aspects of God's beneficiality. It concludes with its indispensable complement, his *impeccable severity*. I now enlarge this definition. I use God's beneficiality, the core of divine goodness, as my organizing principle. I unfold: first, its *broad foundation*, his absolute propriety; second, its *distilled essence*, his commitment to do what is kind; third, its *essential aspects*, his lovingkindness, grace, love, compassion, and long-suffering; and fourth, its *indispensable complement*, his impeccable severity.

A. The Broad Foundation of God's Beneficiality: God's absolute propriety

In its broadest sense God's goodness is his "unalloyed disposition and irrevocable commitment to do good, his impeccable moral propriety." God stands irrevocably committed to do what is morally right. God alone is good infinitely, eternally, immutably, independently, and ideally: "none is good save one, even God" (Mark 10:18). When I speak of God's "disposition to do good," I mean that the impetus to do what is right characterizes his being. Webster defines "disposition" as "prevailing inclination, temperamental makeup, the tendency of something to act in a certain manner."[3] Thus, God does what he does, because God is who he is: "You are good, and do good" (Ps. 119:68). When I assert that his disposition to do good is "unalloyed," I mean that God is 100% free from any tendency, inclination, or temptation to do moral evil. Again, when I say that God has an "irrevocable commitment" to do good, I mean that his will stands fixed immutably to do good. God does good because he wills to do it. Thus, God's absolute propriety is the foundation of his abundant beneficiality. The diagram below illustrates this:

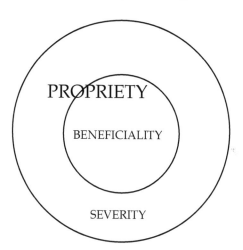

Thus, in its broadest sense, God's goodness, his moral propriety, includes both his beneficiality and his righteous severity: "all my goodness . . . that will by no means clear the guilty." In its narrower sense, his goodness, his beneficiality, excludes his severity and stands in sharp contrast to it: "the goodness and severity of God."

---

[3] *WNC Dictionary*, 327

B. The Distilled Essence of God's Beneficiality

We come now to the primary focus of God's goodness: "predominately in his abundant kindness or beneficiality." When Scripture extols God's goodness, it features his beneficiality.[4] A survey of all of the 143 texts listed above confirms this emphasis. Again, when God shows Moses all his goodness, this emphasis is evident. I derive *beneficiality* from the use of "good" to mean "what is beneficial." Thus, God's "beneficiality" is his commitment to do what is useful, kind, and conducive to health, well-being and happiness. Packer confirms this when he defines God's goodness:[5]

> When the biblical writers call God 'good', they are thinking in general of all those moral qualities which prompt His people to call Him 'perfect', and in particular of the generosity which moves them to call Him 'merciful' and 'gracious', and to speak of His 'love'...Within the cluster of God's moral perfections there is one in particular to which the term 'goodness' points...This is the quality of generosity. Generosity means a disposition to give to others in a way which has no mercenary motive and is not limited by what the recipients deserve, but consistently goes beyond it. Generosity expresses the simple wish that others should have what they need to make them happy.

Dr. Packer uses "generosity" as the equivalent of "abundant beneficiality." When he speaks of a non-mercenary disposition, he pictures the unselfish attitude that Jesus commends: "do good, and lend, hoping for nothing again" (Luke 6:35). Thus, Dr. Packer confirms that God's goodness consists primarily in his unselfish disposition to do what is conducive to health and happiness.

C. The Essential Aspects of God's Beneficiality

Scripture reveals that God's beneficiality is "composed of his dependable lovingkindness and mercy, his unconstrained goodwill and grace, his generous philanthropy and love, his keen compassion, and his conciliatory long-suffering." Each of these virtues has its own nuance, yet they are intertwined as inseparable aspects of his beneficiality. Scripture associates each with God's goodness. When the Lord shows Moses his goodness, he explicitly connects his goodness with his compassion (*rachûm*), grace (*channûn*), longsuffering (*'erek 'aph*), and lovingkindness (*chesed*).[6] That

---

[4] *Rom. 11:22*: behold then the goodness and severity of God. *Ps. 106.1*: he is good; for his lovingkindness endures forever

[5] J. I. Packer, *Knowing God*, 145-146

[6] *Exod. 33:19, 34:6*: And he said, I will make all my goodness [tôb] pass before you, and will proclaim the name of Jehovah before you; and I will be gracious to whom I will be gracious,

text does not explicitly link his goodness and love. However, another text explicitly binds his love and lovingkindness: "I have *loved* (*'ahab*) you with an everlasting *love* (*'ahabah*): therefore with *lovingkindness* (*chesed*) have I drawn you" (Jer. 31:3). The New Testament underscores these connections. Paul closely binds God's goodness with his "love toward man," "mercy," and "grace."[7] In the Septuagint (LXX) ἔλεος (eleos), "mercy," most frequently translates חֶסֶד (chesed), "lovingkindness. Again, he connects his mercy (eleos) with his love (agape).[8] In the LXX *agape* often translates *'ahabah*, "love." Paul also connects his goodness with his longsuffering.[9] In the LXX *makrothumia*, "long-suffering" translates *'erek 'aph*, "slow to anger." Again, Christ connects God's goodness and mercy.[10] In the LXX, *oiktirmos*, "mercy," a cognate of *oiktirmon*, most frequently translates *rachûm*, "merciful." Gill confirms these close associations:[11]

> Having treated of the love, grace, mercy, and long-suffering of God, it will be proper to take some notice of *his goodness, from which they all proceed*; for that God loves any of his creatures, in the manner he does, bestows favors upon them, shows mercy to them, and bears much with them, *is owing to the goodness of his nature*. [emphasis supplied]

Gill lists four aspects of God's goodness. I add his *lovingkindness*. I could expound lovingkindness as a species either of love or of compassion. I expound it separately because, with faithfulness, it has special significance in reference to his covenant promises. The biblical testimony to these five

---

and will show mercy on whom I will show mercy . . . And Jehovah passed by before him, and proclaimed, Jehovah, Jehovah, a God merciful [rachûm] and gracious [channûn], slow to anger ['erek 'aph], and abundant in lovingkindness [chesed] and faithfulness ['emeth]. I consider God's faithfulness as a separate topic, although in virtue of its close association with his lovingkindness, this text also links it with God's goodness.

[7] *Titus 3:4, 5, 7*: But when the kindness [chrestotes] of God our Savior, and his love toward man [philanthropia], appeared, not by works done in righteousness, which we did ourselves, but according to his mercy [eleos] he saved us, through the washing of regeneration and renewing of the Holy Spirit . . that, being justified by his grace [charis], we might be made heirs according to the hope of eternal life.

[8] *Eph. 2:4*: but God being rich in mercy [eleos], for his great love [agape] wherewith he loved us.

[9] *Rom. 2:4*: Or do you despise the riches of his goodness [chrestotes] and forbearance [anoche] and long-suffering [makrothumia], not knowing that the goodness [chrestos] of God leads you to repentance?

[10] *Luke 6:35-36*: you shall be sons of the Most High: for he is kind [chrestos] to the unthankful and evil. You be merciful, even as your Father is merciful [oiktirmon]

[11] Gill, *Body of Divinity*, 1:131-132

aspects of divine goodness is massive. I catalogue this witness in detail as an appendix to this topic. I tabulate it below.

Loving-kindness	Grace, Favor	Long-Suffering	Compassion	Love		TOTALS
OLD TESTAMENT TERMS						
chasad 2	chanan 42	'erek 'aph 10	racham 36	'ahab	22	
chesed 184	channûn 12	'arak 1	rachamîm 27	'ahabah	10	
chasîd 1	chēn 16		rachûm 12	chasaq	3	
			chamal 17	dôd	1	
			chem^{e}lah 2	chasab	1	
			chûs 12			
Total OT 187	Total OT 70	Total OT 11	Total OT 106	Total OT	37	All OT 411
NEW TESTAMENT TERMS						
eleos 20	charis 118	anoche 2	oiktirmos 2	agape	23	
eleeo 13	charizomai 10	makrothumia 5	oiktirmon 2	agapao	39	
	charitoo 2	makrothumeo 2	oiktireo 1	agapetos	13	
	charisma 13		splagchna 1	philanthropia	1	
			polusplagchnos 1	phileo	3	
Total NT 33	Total NT 143	Total NT 9	Total NT 7	Total NT	79	All NT 271
TOTAL 220	TOTAL 213	TOTAL 20	TOTAL 113	TOTAL	116	**BIBLE 682**

D. The Indispensable Complement to God's Beneficiality: God's impeccable severity

The core of God's goodness is his beneficiality. God's severity stands in stark contrast with his beneficiality. Yet, if God were not severe, he would not be good. Thus, his severity is "indispensable." Scripture describes God's severity with a variety of terms and expressions. In the New Testament, the word translated "severity," ἀποτομια (apotomia), occurs only in Romans 11:22. This word belongs to a family that includes ἀποτόμως (apotomos), translated "sharply,"[12] and τομώτερος (tomoteros), translated "sharper."[13] According to the lexicon in Strong's Concordance, this word family is from a verb that depicts a decisive cut or severance, as if by a single stroke, rather than by repeated hacking. The Old Testament expresses God's severity with the phrase: "will by no means clear the guilty" (Exod. 34:6). This phrase, literally: "clearing will never clear," twice employs the verb נָקָה (naqah), which means "to hold guiltless," "to leave unpunished," or "to acquit." It depicts Abraham's servant being released from the liability incurred by taking an oath to seek a wife for Isaac.[14] The Old Testament also uses graphic expressions for his severity, like, "set my face against them for evil," and "watch over them for evil."[15]

God's severity stems from his irrevocable commitment to hold all the wicked accountable: "that will by no means clear the guilty." He will call to account all that insult his Name.[16] No aggregate of human force will prevent divine punishment.[17] His longsuffering does not mean that sinners will get away with sin.[18] He displays severity when he judges with startling decisiveness.[19] With severity he will inflict eternal punishment suddenly and irremediably on all the wicked at Christ's return.[20]

Under the old covenant he displays his severity by his irrevocable commitment to punish all the wicked in the society of his people. In his severity he inflicts the curses of the old covenant on all the profane and

---

[12] *2 Cor. 13:10*: that I may not when present deal *sharply*, according to the authority which the Lord gave me for building up, and not for casting down. *Titus 1:13*: for which cause reprove them *sharply*, that they may be sound in the faith.

[13] *Heb. 4:12*: the word of God is living, and active, *sharper* than any two-edged sword, and piercing even to the dividing of soul and spirit.

[14] *Gen. 24:8*: if the woman be not willing to follow you, then *you shall be clear* from this my oath

[15] Jer. 44:11, 27

[16] *Deut. 5:11*: Jehovah will not hold him guiltless that takes his name in vain

[17] *Prov. 16:5*: Every one that is proud in heart is an abomination to Jehovah: though hand join in hand, he shall not be unpunished

[18] *Nah. 1:2-3*: Jehovah is a jealous God and avenges; Jehovah avenges and is full of wrath; Jehovah takes vengeance on his adversaries, and he reserves wrath for his enemies. Jehovah is slow to anger, and great in power, and will by no means clear the guilty

[19] *Ps. 73:3, 17, 19*: I was envious at the arrogant, when I saw the prosperity of the wicked . . . Until I went into the sanctuary of God, and considered their latter end . . . they are become a desolation in a moment!

[20] *1 Thess. 5:3*: the day of the Lord so comes as a thief in the night. When they are saying, Peace and safety, then sudden destruction comes upon them

rebellious in Israel.[21] With a frightening, swift, and sudden stroke, he severs the wicked, either from his land, or from the land of the living,[22] or from the enjoyment of his favor, generosity, and goodwill.[23] When Christ's institutes the new covenant, God judicially severs all the unconverted from his people.[24] Due to God's severity, no unbeliever has any right to be included in his church on earth. And, in his severity he will suddenly cut off every hypocrite from Christ's church at his return.

Finally, consider the tremendous importance of God's severity. Some today obscure or reject his severity. Such view God's goodness as unlimited sentiment or unqualified indulgence. Scripture affirms that God's goodness mainly consists in his compassion, grace, long-suffering, lovingkindness, and love. Yet, it insists that his goodness is not unlimited forbearance. Rather, precisely because God is good, he visits the iniquity of the wicked upon their children that imitate their sins to the third and fourth generations. God's beneficiality has a limit. People abuse it when they use it to foster a false sense of security. Such reason that because God is good, there is no hell. These comfort themselves with the delusion that a good God would never punish eternally. Rather, we should confess plainly both his kindness and his severity.

---

[21] *Deut. 29:18, 20, 21*: lest there should be among you a man, or woman, or family, or tribe, whose heart turns away this day from Jehovah our God, to go serve the gods of those nations, lest there should be among you a root that bears gall and wormwood . . . Jehovah shall not pardon him, but the anger of Jehovah and his jealousy will smoke against that man, and all the curse that is written in this book shall lie upon him, and Jehovah shall blot out his name from under heaven. And Jehovah will set him apart unto evil out of all the tribes of Israel, according to all the curses of the covenant that is written in this book of the law.

[22] *Jer. 16:5, 6, 10, 12, 13*: I have taken away my peace from this people, says Jehovah, even lovingkindness and tender mercies. Both great and small shall die in this land . . . Wherefore has Jehovah pronounced all this great evil against us? . . . you have done evil more than your fathers . . . therefore will I cast you forth out of this land . . . for I will show you no favor.

[23] *Jer. 44:11, 12, 22, 27*: Behold I will set my face against you for evil, even to cut off all Judah. And I will take the remnant of Judah, that have set their faces to go into the land of Egypt to sojourn there; and they shall all be consumed . . . Jehovah could no longer bear, because of the evil of your doings, and because of the abominations which you have committed; therefore is your land become a desolation . . . I watch over them for evil and not for good; and all the men of Judah that are in the land of Egypt shall be consumed by the sword.

[24] *Rom. 11:20-22*: by their unbelief they were broken off, and you stand by your faith. Be not high-minded, but fear: for if God spared not the natural branches, neither will he spare you. Behold then the goodness and severity of God: toward them that fell, severity; but toward you, God's goodness, if you continue in his goodness: otherwise you also shall be cut off.

II. The Major Features of God's Goodness

The major features of God's goodness are the essential aspects of God's beneficiality: his lovingkindness, grace, love, compassion, and longsuffering. I now summarize the extensive biblical witness.

A. God's Faithful Lovingkindness and Mercy

The Old Testament most frequently connects his goodness with his lovingkindness, *chesed*. Psalm 136 epitomizes this connection. *Chesed* occurs 26 times, once in each verse. This psalm is a meditation on the manifold display of God's lovingkindness in his works. It embraces all the lovingkindness by which God does good in creation, redemption, and providence. It contemplates his lovingkindness as Creator (136:5-9), as Redeemer (136:10-24), and as the Lord of providence, who gives food to all (136:25). It features his redeeming goodness that emancipated his people from slavery in Egypt (136:9-15), gave them their land (136:16-22), and delivered them from their enemies (136:23-24). Thus, creation is the foundation of God's lovingkindness, redemption is its core, and his providential care is its framework.

In the Old Testament *chesed* emphasizes the covenantal favor by which Jehovah binds himself by oath to do good.[25] Scripture explicitly associates God's lovingkindness with his covenant promises to his servants Abraham[26] and David,[27] and with his old[28] and new[29] covenants with his people. The New Testament reinforces this. Luke uses, *eleos*, "mercy," which translates *chesed* in the LXX, to depict God's fulfillment through Jesus Christ of his covenantal lovingkindness to Abraham and his children.[30] This explains the

---

[25] *Deut. 7:9*: the faithful God, who keeps covenant and lovingkindness with them that love him and keep his commandments to a thousand generations

[26] *Deut. 7:12*: Jehovah your God will keep with you the covenant and the lovingkindness which he swore to your fathers

[27] *Ps. 89:28*: my lovingkindness will I keep for him for evermore; and my covenant shall stand fast with him

[28] *Ps. 106:44, 45*: he regarded their distress, when he heard their cry: for he remembered for them his covenant, and repented according to the multitude of his lovingkindnesses

[29] *Isa. 54:8,9, 10*: with everlasting lovingkindness will I have mercy on you, says Jehovah your Redeemer . . . for as I have sworn that the waters of Noah shall no more go over the earth, so have I sworn that I will not be wroth with you . . . my lovingkindness shall not depart from you, neither shall my covenant of peace be removed, says Jehovah that has mercy on you

[30] *Luke 1:54, 55, 72, 73, 78*: He has given help to Israel his servant, that he might remember mercy (as he spake unto our fathers) toward Abraham and his seed forever . . . to show mercy towards our fathers, and to remember his holy covenant; the oath which he swore to Abraham

frequent combination of his lovingkindness and faithfulness.[31] God in covenantal mercy promises with an oath to bless his people. When he fulfills these commitments, all his mercy is done in faithfulness. Therefore, I call it his *faithful* mercy. All God's redemptive goodness to his people rests on his solemn promises to bless Abraham and his posterity. This blessing is voluntary and sovereign. Only because it pleased him, he promises with an oath to perpetuate David's throne and to bless Abraham and his children. God's covenant promises to Abraham supply his Christian heirs with confidence, encouragement, and hope.[32] Thus, Scripture repeatedly calls us to praise our Redeemer for his covenant mercy. Accordingly, Psalm 136 begins and ends with this exhortation: "Oh give thanks unto Jehovah for he is good; for his lovingkindness endures forever."

B. *God's Unconstrained Goodwill and Grace*

The general idea of grace is *unearned benefit or unmerited favor*. The Old Testament affirms this.[33] The New Testament confirms it: "to him that works, the reward is not reckoned as of grace, but as of debt" (Rom. 4:4). Thus, God's grace is his unmerited favor by which he blesses his creatures and his people. The Old Testament closely associates divine favor with the material benefits that all mankind living today enjoy through Noah.[34] We are all Noah's children, and because we are, God in grace blesses us with life, food, families, and the strength and skill to harness the earth. In gracious goodwill, he promises us, with an oath, that no flood will ever again destroy all mankind. Further, his people under the old covenant enjoy

---

our father . . . because of the tender mercy of our God, whereby the dayspring from on high shall visit us.

[31] Exod. 34:6; Num. 14:18; Deut. 7:9; 2 Sam. 2:6; Pss. 25:7, 10, 26:3, 36:5, 40:10, 11, 57:3, 10, 61:7, 85:10, 88:11, 89:1, 100:5, 108:4, 115:1, 117:2, 138:2

[32] Heb. 6:17-18

[33] *Gen. 18:3, 5*: If now I have found favor in your sight, pass not away, I pray you, from your servant . . . and they said, So do, as you have said. *Judg. 6:17-18*: If now I have found favor in your sight, then show me a sign that it is you that talk with me. Depart not hence . . . And he said, I will tarry until you come again

[34] *Gen. 6:8, 17-19, 9:1-3, 8-11*: but Noah found favor (chēn) in the eyes of the Lord . . . And I behold, I do bring the flood of waters upon the earth, to destroy all flesh wherein is the breath of life, from under heaven; everything that is in the earth shall die. But I will establish my covenant with you; and you shall come into the ark, you, and your sons, and your wife, and your son's wives with you. And of every living thing of all flesh, two of every sort shall you bring into the ark, to keep them alive with you . . . And God blessed Noah and his sons, and said unto them, Be fruitful, and multiply, and replenish the earth . . . Every moving thing that lives shall be food for you; as the green herb have I given you all . . . I establish my covenant with you, and with your seed after you; and with every living creature . . . neither shall all flesh be cut off any more by the waters of the flood.

enhanced measures of this favor. Although Hebrew Israel merits only wrath, his gracious heart is disposed to grant them requests and favors when they cry to him out of their sense of need.[35] This underscores that his graciousness involves approachability, his willingness to be entreated.[36]

As the Old Testament most often connects God's goodness with his lovingkindness, *chesed*, so the New Testament most frequently associates his goodness with his grace, *charis*. Grace, *charis*, occurs 118 times in the New Testament.[37] It always depicts some aspect of the unearned gospel favor with which he blesses his people in and through Jesus Christ.[38] As lovingkindness stresses *covenantal* kindness, grace stresses *evangelical* favor. The New Testament highlights many facets of this gospel favor. God shows gospel favor to sinners in their gospel calling,[39] conversion,[40] and justification.[41] Gospel favor shines brightly against the backdrop of human sin.[42] Thus, the hallmark of saving grace is that God bestows it, not merely on the "undeserving," but on the "ill-deserving." He shows favor to sinners that merit damnation. He bestows saving grace to sinners freely, without constraint, solely upon the sovereign prerogative of his will. The apostle explicitly affirms the sovereignty of divine favor.[43] He quotes the Old Testament display of God's goodness.[44] Thus, I call his grace, "unconstrained." Further, God continues to lavish this gospel grace upon his saints throughout the Christian life. He stands disposed in grace to the society of the saints, the Christian church.[45] His grace strengthens his saints

---

[35] *2 Chron. 30:9*: for Jehovah your God is gracious and merciful, and will not turn away his face from you, if you return to him

[36] *Exod. 22:26-27*: if you at all take your neighbor's garment to pledge, you shall restore it unto him before the sun goes down . . . it shall come to pass, when he cries unto me, that I will hear; for I am gracious

[37] See the use of *charis* in the appendix to this presentation

[38] *John 1:17*: the law was given through Moses, grace and truth came through Jesus Christ. *Heb. 2:9*: that by the grace of God he should taste of death for every man

[39] *Gal. 1:6*: I marvel that you are so quickly removing from him that called you in the grace of Christ unto a different gospel

[40] *Eph. 2:8-9*: for by grace you have been saved through faith; and that not of yourselves, it is the gift of God; not of works, that no man should glory

[41] *Rom. 3:24*: being justified freely by his grace through the redemption which is in Christ Jesus

[42] *Rom. 5:20*: where sin abounded, grace did abound more exceedingly

[43] Rom. 9:14-18

[44] *Exod. 33:19*: I will be gracious to whom I will be gracious, and I will show mercy on whom I will show mercy.

[45] *2 Thess. 1:2*: grace to you and peace, from God the Father and the Lord Jesus Christ

in their weakness.[46] His grace empowers his saints that walk in humility before him.[47] His grace enables his saints to serve him effectively and faithfully in gospel ministry.[48]

In sum, Scripture emphasizes that God conveys unmerited favor through creative blessing in Noah, "common grace," and through gospel blessing in Christ, "saving grace."

C. God's Generous Philanthropy and Love

We consider the testimony of each testament and then summarize the whole.

1. The New Testament testimony to God's love

In the New Testament three primary terms depict God's love.[49] We now consider their significance.

a. Philanthropia: love for mankind

Scripture explicitly identifies God's goodness with his love for mankind: "But when *the kindness* of God our Savior, and *his love toward man* (philanthropia) appeared, not by works done in righteousness, which we did ourselves, but according to his mercy he saved us" (Titus 3:4-5). This word, *philanthropia*, from which we derive our English word, *philanthropy*, occurs only one other time in the New Testament, where it refers to human kindness and goodwill.[50] The barbarians sensed the need of those shipwrecked and did what they could to supply it. Motivated by goodwill, they kindled a fire, because it was cold and rainy, and the shipwrecked were probably drenched and shivering. Thus, generally, *philanthropia* describes a disposition of goodwill that senses and supplies human need. Specifically, it describes God's remedial goodwill to sinners, which, with a view to their eternal happiness, supplies their deepest spiritual need and rescues them from their sins.

b. The agape word family: love

The agape family depicts God's love at least 75 times.[51] In general *agape*

---

[46] *2 Cor. 12:9*: My grace is sufficient for you: for my power is made perfect in weakness. Most gladly therefore will I rather glory in my weaknesses, that the power of Christ may rest upon me

[47] *James 4:6*: God resists the proud, but gives grace to the humble

[48] *Rom. 15:15-16*: the grace that was given me of God, that I should be a minister of Christ

[49] See the appendix for the uses of *philanthropia,* the *agape* family, and *phileo.*

[50] *Acts 28:2*: and the barbarians showed us no common kindness (philanthropia): for they kindled a fire, and received us all, because of the present rain and the cold

[51] See the appendix for details: *agape* (23 times), *agapao* (39 times), *agapetos* (13 times).

signifies commitment to treat others righteously and benevolently. It couples goodwill, unselfishness, generosity, and sensitivity.[52] Love so characterizes God that it excludes from his being and character all selfishness and malice.[53]

Generically, God's love is his unselfish, generous, and benevolent disposition to all his creatures, even to sinners, by which he supplies their material and temporal needs as their Creator. Thus, Christ calls on Christians to love their enemies in order to reflect the love[54] and goodness[55] of their heavenly Father. When Christians show goodwill to those who hate them, they reflect their Creator's kind and loving heart.

Preeminently, God's love is his disposition of unselfishness, generosity, and goodwill by which he supplies the spiritual and eternal needs of his children as their Redeemer. In redeeming love he commits to deliver to his people at great personal cost from sin and wrath. Accordingly, an inseparable bond joins God's redemptive love and saving grace.[56] God's love for his people is unearned and shown to those that merit damnation. In love and grace he accomplishes salvation by Christ[57] and applies it to hell-deserving sinners that are spiritually dead in sin and children of wrath.[58] In the epitome of redeeming love God sent his own Son to endure his wrath for the sins of his people.[59] God the Son incarnate gave himself for them.[60] He shed his blood to appease divine wrath, satisfy divine justice, and emancipate them from

---

[52] *Rom. 13:10*: love works no ill to his neighbor. *1 Cor. 13:4, 5*: love suffers long and is kind . . . love seeks not its own. *1 John 3:16*: hereby we know love, because he laid down his life for us
[53] *1 John 4:8, 16*: God is love
[54] *Matt. 5:45*: love your enemies . . . that you may be sons of your Father who is in heaven: for he makes his sun to rise on the evil and on the good, and sends rain upon the just and the unjust
[55] *Luke 6:36*: love your enemies, and do good, and lend never despairing; and your reward shall be great, and you shall be sons of the Most High: for he is kind to the unthankful and evil.
[56] *2 Thess. 2:16*: God our Father who loved us and gave us eternal comfort and good hope through grace
[57] *Rom. 5:8*: God commends his own love for us, in that, while we were yet sinners, Christ died for us
[58] *Eph. 2:4*: God, being rich in mercy, for his great love wherewith he loved us, even when we were dead through our trespasses, made us alive together with Christ
[59] *1 John 4:8-10*: God is love . . . Herein is love, not that we loved God, but that he loved us, and sent his Son to be the propitiation for our sins
[60] *Gal. 2:20*: the Son of God, who loved me, and gave himself up for me

their sins.[61] Christ's sacrificial love calls every Christian to imitate his conciliatory heart and be kind, generous, and forgiving.[62] Christ's sacrificial love calls every Christian husband to reflect his generous and gentle heart and treat our wives with sensitivity and unselfishness.[63] Christ's sacrificial love gives every Christian certain expectation of future blessing[64] and confidence that God in this life will withhold nothing we need for our eternal welfare.[65] Finally, God's redeeming love in Christ is the foundation of gospel hope for sinners from every branch of fallen humanity.[66]

c. Phileo: intimate personal affection

Phileo also depicts God's love. This word signifies personal and special affection for someone. It relates this personal affection to the intimacy of friendship and family. Thus, it describes the Father's Trinitarian affection for the Son that engenders total transparency with him.[67] It also depicts God's personal affection for his spiritual children who love and believe in his Son.[68] Again, it signifies the familial personal affection that moves the Lord to chasten and reprove his beloved spiritual children.[69] Accordingly, Peter calls Christians to pour out all our needs and fears before the Lord: "casting all your anxiety upon him, because he cares for you" (1 Pet. 5:7). Peter appeals to the fact that God takes a personal interest in us, has genuine concern for us, and thus, pays careful attention to us.

2. The Old Testament testimony to God's love

In the Old Testament several key terms depict God's love.[70] The Old Testament emphasizes God's affection, goodwill, and care for his people. It

---

[61] *Rev. 1:5*: Unto him that loves us, and loosed us from our sins by his blood.
[62] *Eph. 5:2*: walk in love, even as Christ also loved you, and gave himself up for us, an offering and a sacrifice to God
[63] *Eph. 5:25*: Husbands, love your wives, even as Christ also loved the church, and gave himself up for it
[64] *Rom. 8:35, 39*: who shall separate us from the love of Christ . . . nor any other creature, shall be able to separate us from the love of God, which is in Christ Jesus our Lord
[65] *Rom. 8:32*: he that spared not his own Son, but delivered him up for us all, how shall he not also with him freely give us all things?
[66] *John 3:16*: for God so loved the world, that he gave his only begotten Son, that whosoever believes on him should not perish, but have eternal life
[67] *John 5:20*: the Father loves the Son, and shows him all things that himself does
[68] *John 16:27*: for the Father himself loves you, because you have loved me, and have believed that I came forth from the Father.
[69] *Rev. 3:19*: as many as I love, I reprove and chasten: be zealous therefore, and repent
[70] Key terms are: *'ahab* (22 times), *'ahabah* (10 times), *chasaq* (3 times), *dôd* (1 time), *chasab* (1 time). See the appendix to this topic for further details.

repeatedly depicts God's love as his affection for his people, as his unique attachment to them, and as his irrevocable commitment to benefit them with fatherly provision and protection. This love has its roots in God's eternal decree[71] and in his special affection for their fathers, Abraham, Isaac, and Jacob.[72] For their sake, he selected Israel as his unique possession,[73] redeemed them from Egypt,[74] entered the old covenant with them, and gave them their inheritance in Canaan.[75] In love he identified compassionately with their suffering and endured with longsuffering their provocations.[76] In love he provided for them and protected them in Canaan, endured their ingratitude, rebellion, and treachery, delivered them from captivity, and restored a remnant of them to their land. Finally, in the fullness of time, in love he sent his Son to them, saved a select remnant of them, and established with them his new covenant.[77]

Summary: Generically, God's love consists in his unselfish disposition of goodwill and generosity. Scripture features three specific aspects of God's love. First, God's love consists in his unselfish goodwill and generosity as Creator for all his creatures, even for his enemies. Second, it consists in his unselfish goodwill and generosity as Redeemer for his people under the old covenant, Hebrew Israel, composed of Abraham's physical descendants. This *typical redemptive* love consists of his special affection for them, his unique attachment to them, and his irrevocable commitment to benefit them in accordance with his conditional covenant with them.[78] This species of redemptive love is a special expression of common grace. It uniquely

---

[71] *Jer. 31:3*: I have loved you with an everlasting love: therefore with lovingkindness have I drawn you

[72] *Deut. 4:37*: because he loved your fathers, therefore he chose their seed after them, and brought you out with his presence, with his great power

[73] *Deut. 10:15*: Only Jehovah had a delight in [lit., set love upon] your fathers to love them, and he chose their seed after them, even you above all peoples, as at this day

[74] *Deut. 7:7-8*: Jehovah did not set his love upon you, nor choose you, because you were more in number than any people; for you were the fewest of all peoples; but because Jehovah loves you, and because he would keep the oath which he sware to your fathers, has Jehovah brought you out with a mighty hand

[75] *2 Chron. 20:7*: Did not you, O our God, drive out the inhabitants of this land before your people Israel, and give it to the seed of Abraham your friend [lit., beloved] for ever?

[76] *Isa. 63:9*: In all their affliction he was afflicted, and the angel of his presence saved them: in his love and in his pity he redeemed them; and bare them, and carried them all the days of old

[77] *Zeph. 3:17*: Jehovah your God is in the midst of you, a mighty one who will save; he will rejoice over you with joy; he will rest in his love; he will joy over you with singing.

[78] I refer to the Mosaic or old covenant with Hebrew Israel, which was conditional (Exod. 19:3-6)

typifies saving grace and fosters it. Therefore, I call it "typical redemptive" love. Third, God's love consists in his unselfish disposition of goodwill and generosity as Redeemer for his people under the new covenant, Christian Israel, composed of Abraham's spiritual children.[79] This redemptive love consists of his special affection for them, his unique attachment to them, and his irrevocable commitment to benefit them in accordance with his unconditional covenant with them.[80] Thus, his redemptive affection under the new covenant consists in his disposition and sworn commitment to bless his people in Christ with every spiritual benefit. This redemptive affection in Christ embraces every individual Christian and the entire Christian church, the society of the saved.

D. God's Keen Compassion

Both Testaments testify to God's deep concern for the needy. Some say that "God helps those who help themselves." The Bible commends the compassionate God who helps those who "cannot help themselves" (Ps. 72:12-13). Compassion is sympathy for those with unfulfilled needs, especially for those who suffer. The Hebrew with graphic imagery uses the female womb to symbolize compassion.[81] The responsiveness of a nursing mother to her baby's needs pictures the Lord's tender care and mercy. Again, the tender care of a father for a needy child pictures God's compassion for his spiritual children.[82] Yet, God's compassion infinitely surpasses even the greatest human sympathy. Thus, I call it his "keen" compassion. Generally, God's compassion is the sympathy, empathy, and sensitivity with which he supplies the needs of all his creatures.[83] Emphatically, his compassion is the sympathy, empathy, and sensitivity with

---

[79] Rom. 9:5-6

[80] I refer to the new covenant with Christian Israel, which has *unconditional* promises as its essential substance (Jer. 31:31-34)

[81] *Isa. 49:15*: can a woman forget her suckling child, that she should not have compassion on the son of her womb? Yes, these may forget, yet will I not forget you

[82] *Ps. 103:13*: Like as a father pities his children, so Jehovah pities them that fear him. For he knows our frame; he remembers that we are dust

[83] *Luke 6:36*: You be merciful, even as your Father is merciful

which he succors the afflicted,[84] limits the degree and duration of affliction,[85] and alleviates suffering.[86]

He focuses his compassion on his people. In compassion he remains loyal to Hebrew Israel[87] in spite of their many provocations.[88] In compassion he tempers their chastisement.[89] In compassion, when they put away idolatry, he fulfills his covenant commitment to bless them with fecundity.[90] In compassion he gathers a remnant from captivity that he scattered among the nations for their sin.[91] The pinnacle of his compassion for his people is the sympathy, empathy, and sensitivity with which he delivers his spiritual children from the eternal anguish, misery, and suffering that their sin deserves.[92] He delivers them through Christ's work[93] by means of his gospel.[94] God shows this redemptive compassion to lost sinners according to the good pleasure of his will.[95] Accordingly, Scripture closely binds

---

[84] *2 Cor. 1:3-4*: Blessed be the God and Father of our Lord Jesus Christ, the Father of mercies, and God of all comfort; who comforts us in all our affliction

[85] *Lam. 3:22, 32*: It is of Jehovah's lovingkindnesses that we are not consumed, because his compassions fail not. They are new every morning; great is your faithfulness . . . though he cause grief, yet will he have compassion according to the multitude of his lovingkindnesses. For he does not afflict willingly

[86] *James 5:11*: you have heard of the patience of Job, and have seen the end of the Lord, how that the Lord is full of pity and merciful

[87] *Deut. 4:30-31*: When you are in tribulation, and all these things are come upon you, in the latter days you shall return to Jehovah your God, and hearken unto his voice: for Jehovah your God is a merciful God; he will not fail you, neither destroy you, nor forget the covenant of your fathers which he swore unto them

[88] *Neh. 9:18-19*: they . . . had wrought great provocations, yet you in your manifold mercies forsook them not in the wilderness: the pillar of cloud departed not from over them by day, to lead them in the way; neither the pillar of fire by night, to show them light

[89] *2 Sam. 24:14*: let us fall now into the hand of Jehovah; for his mercies are great; and let me not fall into the hand of man

[90] *Deut. 13:17*: there shall cleave none of the devoted thing to your hand; that Jehovah may turn from the fierceness of his anger, and show you mercy, and have compassion upon you, and multiply you as he has sworn to your fathers

[91] *Deut. 30:3*: Jehovah your God will turn your captivity, and have compassion on you, and will return and gather you from all the peoples whither Jehovah your God has scattered you

[92] *Ps. 51:1-2*: according to the multitude of your tender mercies blot out my transgressions. Wash me thoroughly from mine iniquity, and cleanse me from my sin

[93] *Luke 1:78*: because of the tender [lit., bowels of] mercy of our God, whereby the dayspring from on high shall visit us

[94] *Prov. 28:13*: He that covers his transgressions shall not prosper; but whoso confesses and forsakes them shall obtain mercy

[95] *Exod. 33:19*: I will be gracious to whom I will be gracious, and I will show mercy to whom I will show mercy. [Rom. 9:18]

God's compassion to his covenant love and faithfulness[96] and to his grace.[97] When his needy children cry to God for relief, his response simultaneously involves both grace, by which he grants their request, and compassion, by which he rescues and comforts the sufferer. This redemptive compassion calls every Christian out of gratitude for his gospel blessings to serve God with our entire being, body and soul.[98]

E. God's Conciliatory Long-suffering

Eight of the twenty texts that explicitly disclose God's long-suffering combine it with one or more of the other aspects of his goodness.[99] This indicates its vital connection with his lovingkindness, grace, compassion, and love. In general long-suffering signifies the peaceable demeanor by which someone endures prolonged provocation without responding with hostility. Thus, a man who "is slow to anger appeases strife" (Prov. 15:18). God is infinitely more "slow to anger" than any human. His long-suffering is the gentle demeanor by which he patiently endures prolonged provocation before, finally, at length, he responds in vengeful anger. The root of his long-suffering is his readiness to forgive and pardon.[100] For this reason I call it "conciliatory." Thus, his long-suffering has a redemptive design and motive. It provides space for his saving work in order to fulfill his eternal plan to bring all his elect in every generation to repentance[101] through his gospel. Scripture features his long-suffering with the wicked, with his people, Hebrew Israel, and over his spiritual children.

1. God's long-suffering with the wicked

Scripture features his conciliatory demeanor toward the wicked. With kindness that prompts them to repent he endures much provocation from

---

[96] Deut. 4:30-31; Lam. 3:22
[97] Exod. 33:19, 34:6; 2 Chron. 30:9; Ps. 116:5
[98] *Rom. 12:1*: I beseech you therefore, brethren, by the mercies of God, to present your bodies a living sacrifice
[99] Exod. 34:6; Num. 14:18; Neh. 9:17; Pss. 86:15, 103:8, 145:8; Joel 2:13; Jonah 4:2
[100] Num. 14:18; Neh. 9:19; Joel 2:13; Jonah 4:2; Rom. 2:4
[101] *2 Pet. 3:9, 15*: the Lord is not slack concerning his promise . . . but is longsuffering to you-ward, not wishing that any should perish, but that all should come to repentance . . . And account that the longsuffering of our Lord is salvation.

his enemies.[102] If they turn from their sins in repentance[103] and faith,[104] then he forgives them and does not inflict his wrath on them. Yet his longsuffering is not everlasting. Eventually he inflicts vengeance on his enemies:[105] both with temporal punishment, such as the flood,[106] and ultimately with eternal punishment.[107]

2. God's long-suffering with his people, Hebrew Israel

Scripture also features his conciliatory demeanor toward Hebrew Israel. With covenantal love and loyalty,[108] he patiently endured much provocation.[109] Finally, at length, when they persisted in breaking his covenant through idolatry and gross immorality, he inflicted on them all the vengeance of the old covenant.

3. God's long-suffering over his spiritual children

Scripture also features his conciliatory demeanor regarding the righteous. For thousands of years, from Abel to Christ, he patiently endured the appearance of injustice, because he pardoned and received into heaven all the Old Testament saints before he fully punished their sins on the cross.[110]

---

[102] *Rom. 2:4*: Or do you despise the riches of his goodness and forbearance and longsuffering, not knowing that the goodness of God leads you to repentance?

[103] *Jonah 4:2*: Therefore I hasted to flee unto Tarshish; for I knew that you are a gracious God, and merciful, slow to anger, and abundant in lovingkindness, and repentest thee of the evil

[104] *Joel 2:13*: rend your heart, and not your garments, and turn unto Jehovah your God; for he is gracious and merciful, slow to anger, and abundant in lovingkindness, and repents him of the evil

[105] *Nah. 1:2-3*: Jehovah is a jealous God and avenges; Jehovah avenges and is full of wrath; Jehovah takes vengeance on his adversaries, and he reserves wrath for his enemies. Jehovah is slow to anger, and great in power, and will by no means clear the guilty

[106] *1 Pet. 3:19-20*: he went and preached unto the spirits in prison, that aforetime were disobedient, when the longsuffering of God waited in the days of Noah, while the ark was a preparing

[107] *Rom. 9:22*: What if God, willing to show his wrath, and to make his power known, endured with much longsuffering vessels of wrath fitted unto destruction

[108] *Neh. 9:17*: in their rebellion appointed a captain to return to their bondage. But you are a God ready to pardon, gracious and merciful, slow to anger, and abundant in lovingkindness, and forsook them not

[109] *Num. 14:18*: Jehovah is slow to anger, and abundant in lovingkindness, forgiving iniquity and transgression; and that will by no means clear the guilty . . . Pardon, I pray thee, the iniquity of this people according unto the greatness of your lovingkindness, and according as you have forgiven this people, from Egypt even until now

[110] *Rom. 3:25*: to show his righteousness because of the passing over of the sins done aforetime, in the forbearance of God

Again, in his long-suffering he patiently endures the persecution of his saints throughout this age. Yet the day is coming when he will avenge fully at the final judgment the wrongs his people have suffered on earth.[111]

Now we take up the manifold display of God's goodness.

III. The Manifold Display of God's Goodness

We have uncovered the distinct nuance of God's lovingkindness, grace, love, compassion, and long-suffering. Yet it would be highly impractical to consider their display separately. He often displays them simultaneously. He displays them together when he forgives sin,[112] remains committed to an unfaithful people,[113] shows his faithful servants tokens of his favor,[114] removes his vengeance from those that repent,[115] and imparts spiritual life to dead sinners in Christ.[116] I organize this display following the categories suggested in Psalm 136. We consider the display of God's goodness in creation, providence, and redemption.

---

[111] *Luke 18:7*: And shall not God avenge his elect, that cry to him day and night, and *yet* he is longsuffering over them?

[112] *Exod. 34:6, 7*: Jehovah, Jehovah, a God merciful and gracious, slow to anger, and abundant in lovingkindness and truth; keeping lovingkindness for thousands, forgiving iniquity and transgression and sin. *Num. 14:18*: Jehovah is slow to anger, and abundant in lovingkindness, forgiving iniquity and transgression . . . Pardon, I pray thee, the iniquity of this people according unto the greatness of your lovingkindness, and according as you have forgiven this people, from Egypt even until now.

[113] *Neh. 9:17*: in their rebellion appointed a captain to return to their bondage. But you are a God ready to pardon, gracious and merciful, slow to anger, and abundant in lovingkindness, and forsook them not

[114] *Ps. 86:14-17*: O God, the proud are risen against me, and a company of violent men have sought after my soul, and have not set you before them. But you, O Lord, are a God merciful and gracious, slow to anger, and abundant in lovingkindness and truth. Oh turn unto me, and have mercy upon me; give strength unto your servant, and save the son of your handmaid. Show me a token for good, that they who hate me may see it, and be put to shame.

[115] *Joel 2:13*: rend your heart, and not your garments, and turn unto Jehovah your God; for he is gracious and merciful, slow to anger, and abundant in lovingkindness, and repents him of the evil. *Jonah 4:2*: Therefore I hasted to flee unto Tarshish; for I knew that you are a gracious God, and merciful, slow to anger, and abundant in lovingkindness, and repentest thee of the evil

[116] *Eph. 2:4-6*: but God, being rich in mercy, for his great love wherewith he loved us, even when we were dead through our trespasses, made us alive together with Christ (by grace have you been saved). *Titus 3:4, 5, 7*: But when the kindness of God our Savior, and his love toward man, appeared, not by works done in righteousness, which we did ourselves, but according to his mercy he saved us, through the washing of regeneration and renewing of the Holy Spirit . . . that, being justified by his grace, we might be made heirs according to the hope of eternal life

A. God's Goodness Displayed in Creation

The psalmist meditates on God's goodness in the heavens, the earth, and the heavenly bodies:

> *Ps. 136:5-9*: To him that by understanding made the heavens; for his lovingkindness endures forever: To him that spread forth the earth above the waters; for his lovingkindness endures forever: To him that made great lights; for his lovingkindness endures forever: The sun to rule by day; for his lovingkindness endures forever: The moon and stars to rule by night; for his lovingkindness endures forever

The Creator with a sensitive hand fashioned and furnished a home for all his creatures, especially man. Everything reflects his goodness: "and God saw everything that he had made, and, behold, it was very good" (Gen. 1:31). The atmosphere provides air for man to breathe. The earth supplies home and food. The sun, moon, and stars provide light and heat to sustain life. Their recurring cycles order life.[117] All this comes from our kind and generous Creator. Charnock expounds God's goodness in detail.[118] While expounding his goodness in creation,[119] he says:[120]

> The goodness of God appears in the conveniences he provided for and gave to man. As God gave him a moral being perfect in regard of righteousness, so he gave him a being naturally perfect in regard of delightful conveniences, which was the fruit of excellent goodness; since there was no quality in man to invite God to provide him so rich a world, nor to bestow on him so comely a being. [1.] The world was made for man. God crowned the earth with his goodness to gratify man..[2.] God richly furnished the world for man. He did not only erect a stately palace for his habitation, but provided all kind of furniture as a mark of his goodness for the entertainment of his creature man. He arched over his habitation with a bespangled heaven, and floored it with a solid earth, and spread a curious wrought tapestry upon the ground where he was to tread.

Charnock captures the wonder of creation. The Creator is not only wise and powerful but also abundantly kind. Creation drips with his goodness, kindness, generosity, and love.

---

[117] Gen. 1:14, 17
[118] Charnock, *Existence and Attributes*, 533-657
[119] Ibid., 564-575
[120] Ibid., 568-569

B. God's Goodness Displayed in Providence

The psalmist concludes his meditation with God's goodness displayed in providence to all his creatures: "Who gives food to all flesh; for his lovingkindness endures forever" (Ps. 136:25). Providence is an ongoing work: "who *gives* food to all flesh." "All flesh" includes all living creatures. God does not simply wind up the world like a top and leave its care to impersonal forces of nature. To the contrary, in his great goodness the Creator remains personally concerned with the welfare of each of his billions of creatures. He provides food generously for man and animal alike. This is only one tiny part of the good things that the Master of the universe does for his creatures. The display of God's goodness in providence is massive and overwhelming. Scripture highlights its covenantal framework, major facets, indiscriminate scope, remedial design, temporary duration, redemptive focus, and sovereign limitation.

1. The covenantal framework of this display: the Noahic covenant economy

The display of God's goodness in providence has a covenantal framework. In this "now" world, between the cataclysmic flood and fire, all God's goodness in providence flows from divine grace in the Noahic covenantal economy. This economy includes his covenant with Noah before the flood[121] and his covenant after the flood with all creatures that emerged from the ark and their posterity for as long as the world remains.[122] We consider this in greater detail when we study common grace and God's covenants.

2. The major facets of this display: the renewed creation blessing

God's renewed creation blessing defines four major facets of this display of divine goodness in providence.[123] God displays his goodness in family

---

[121] *Gen. 6:8, 17-19*: but Noah found favor (chēn) in the eyes of the Lord . . . And I behold, I do bring the flood of waters upon the earth, to destroy all flesh wherein is the breath of life, from under heaven; everything that is in the earth shall die. But I will establish my covenant with you; and you shall come into the ark, you, and your sons, and your wife, and your son's wives with you. And of every living thing of all flesh, two of every sort shall you bring into the ark, to keep them alive with you

[122] *Gen. 9:8-11*: And God spoke unto Noah and to his sons with him, saying, And I behold, I establish my covenant with you, and with your seed after you; and with every living creature . . . neither shall all flesh be cut off any more by the waters of the flood.

[123] Gen. 9:1-7

living,[124] in dominion over animals,[125] in provision for life,[126] and government.[127]

a. Family living displays God's goodness in providence.

In goodness God perpetuates marriage and procreation. Love, marriage, parental nurture, and the countless benefits of family life flow to us from his goodness. The renewed creation blessing begins and ends with this blessing to underscore its importance. The "nuclear family" is the foundation of a happy life and of a healthy society.

b. Dominion over animals displays God's goodness in providence.

In his goodness he tempers the curse. He graciously puts in animals the fear of man. This protects both human life and the life of animals. Similarly, every convenience, invention, comfort, and tool that lessens human hardship in this world displays the goodness of God.

c. Provision for life displays God's goodness in providence.

In his goodness God provides food to sustain life. In addition to herbs and vegetables he gives humanity all meats for food. Similarly he provides water, clothing, and shelter. Again, he bestows medical knowledge and medicine to check the spread of disease. In many other ways he provides generously what humanity needs to sustain life.

d. Government displays God's goodness in providence.

In his goodness God restrains sin in society. He institutes capital punishment for murder to deter violence and engender respect for the dignity of human life: "for in the image of God made he man." He uses civil government to provide stability and safety in society. Similarly, he graciously uses conscience, parental training, and other means to restrain man's inhumanity to man.

In sum, Paul summarizes these facets when he says that God gives to all "life, and breath, and all things" (Acts 17:25). Again, James sums them when he says that "every good and perfect gift" comes from God (James

---

[124] *Gen. 9:1, 7*: And God blessed Noah and his sons, and said unto them, Be fruitful, and multiply, and replenish the earth. . . And you, be fruitful, and multiply; bring forth abundantly in the earth, and multiply therein

[125] *Gen. 9:2*: and the fear of you and the dread of you shall be upon every beast of the earth . . . into your hand they are delivered

[126] *Gen. 9:3-4*: Every moving thing that lives shall be food for you; as the green herb have I given you all . . .

[127] *Gen. 9:5-6*: . . . Whoso sheds man's blood, by man shall his blood be shed: for in the image of God made he man

1:17). In his goodness God supplies all humanity with life and the ability to enjoy it: "he did good and gave you from heaven rain and fruitful seasons, filling your hearts with food and gladness" (Acts 14:17). In this generous display of his goodness, he gives life, health, food and drink, property, liberty, prosperity, happiness, tranquility, beauty, skill, family, marriage, children, and friendship: indeed, every good thing.

3. The indiscriminate scope of this display: all creatures

God lavishes his goodness in providence on all his creatures. Scripture depicts its recipients with indiscriminate language and inclusive terms.[128] Although Scripture affirms the universal scope of God's goodness, it features his compassion for widows and orphans, strangers and sojourners, and the poor and oppressed.[129] Further, it stresses that this display of divine goodness extends to evil and ungrateful people. In a display of his love for the unjust, as well as the just, God blesses them with sunshine and needful rain.[130] God even displays his kindness, mercy, and love to the "unthankful and evil," who take his goodness for granted. He blesses them with every facet of his renewed creation blessing.[131] The living God does good even to those who serve false gods and idols, when he sends them "rain and fruitful seasons" and fills them with "food and gladness."[132] Accordingly, Paul entreats them to turn from their idols to serve the true God.

4. The remedial design of this display: leads to repentance[133]

Paul reflects on God's remedial intention in showing his goodness to those who are "treasuring up for themselves wrath." God's kindness to evil

---

[128] *Ps. 145:8-9, 15-17*: Jehovah is gracious, and merciful; slow to anger, and of great lovingkindness. Jehovah is good to all; and his tender mercies are over all his works . . . The eyes of all wait for you; and you give them their food in due season. You open your hand, and satisfy the desire of every living thing. Jehovah is righteous in all his ways, and gracious in all his works

[129] Exod. 22:22, 27; Deut. 24:17-22; Pss. 103:2, 6, 107:23-31

[130] *Matt. 5:45*: love your enemies . . . that you may be sons of your Father who is in heaven: for he makes his sun to rise on the evil and on the good, and sends rain upon the just and the unjust

[131] *Luke 6:35-36*: But love your enemies, and do them good, and lend, never despairing; and your reward shall be great, and you shall be sons of the Most High: for he is kind to the unthankful and evil. You be merciful, even as your Father is merciful

[132] *Acts 14:15, 17*: you should turn from these vain things unto a living God, who made the heaven and the earth and the sea, and all that in them is . . . he left not himself without witness, in that he did good and gave you from heaven rain and fruitful seasons, filling your hearts with food and gladness

[133] *Rom. 2:4*: Or do you despise the riches of his goodness and forbearance and long-suffering, not knowing that the goodness of God leads you to repentance?

persons has a remedial motive: "the goodness of God leads you to repentance." Why doesn't he execute judgment against an evil work immediately? He gives his enemies room to repent. During that time, he feeds them, clothes them, and showers on them rain, sunshine, and gladness. How do the wicked respond? Far too often, they lightly esteem the riches of God's goodness and forbearance. Their hearts are fully set in them to do evil. Sadly, most wrest his goodness to their own destruction. Therefore, this remedial purpose, though sincere, is often ineffectual. Though his goodness leads all his enemies to repentance, it does not effectually draw them all. In many instances its stated intention to benefit their souls remains unfulfilled. Many of wicked through the hardness of their hearts despise God's goodness and perish in their sins. Yet, there is more to the story. In such cases, in addition to his stated purpose, which is remedial, God has a secret purpose, which is damning. The Lord himself ordains in his eternal decree that some will harden their hearts, despise his goodness, and frustrate its remedial design: "he has mercy on whom he will, and whom he will he hardens" (Rom. 9:18). He even ordains that this hardness of heart will increase their punishment in hell: "it shall be more tolerable for the land of Sodom in the day of judgment, than for you" (Matt. 11:24). This decretive purpose of God can never be frustrated: "him that works all things after the counsel of his own will" (Eph. 1:11). Thus, God's goodness in providence, in the case of those who perish in sin, has both a stated remedial purpose and a secret reprobating purpose. Though this truth does not fit neatly into some systems of theology, it forms a crucial section of the fence around the mystery.

5. The temporary duration of this display: in this life, while the world remains

In the Noahic community covenant God promises with an oath that no flood will ever again destroy all flesh.[134] In his goodness he stands committed to bestow his renewed creation blessings throughout this age: "while the world remains" (Gen. 8:22). Thus, he grants ample time for many to come to repentance. Yet, suddenly, at death, this display of his goodness ends.[135] Then those that despise his goodness immediately suffer his wrath in hell. Further, his kindness and forbearance toward fallen humanity in Adam ends on "the day of wrath and revelation of the righteous judgment of God" (Rom. 2:5). The display of his goodness in providence terminates on "the day of judgment and destruction ungodly men" at the second coming of Christ.[136]

---

[134] Gen. 9:8-11; Isa. 54:9
[135] Ps. 73:3, 12, 16-20
[136] 2 Pet. 3:7

6. The redemptive focus of this display: his people and spiritual children

Although the display of God's goodness in providence reaches the ungrateful and evil, even in this age it has a redemptive focus. As a loving Father, God especially displays his goodness in providence to his spiritual children: "Like as a father pities his children, so Jehovah pities them that fear him" (Ps. 103:13). He protects and provides for his spiritual children even when society goes through difficult times.[137] He preserves them, hears their prayer, and grants the desire of their hearts.[138] He promises them that when they fear him and depart from evil they will abound in the blessings of his providential goodness.[139] He withholds no good thing from them.[140] In this he clearly and dramatically distinguishes his spiritual children that love and fear him from the wicked that despise him and live in sin.[141] Accordingly, Abraham pleads with God to preserve the righteous when he judges the wicked for their sins.[142] Christ stresses this to encourage his disciples to trust God to provide for them and protect them.[143] He uses God's

---

[137] *Ps. 37:18, 19, 20, 25*: Jehovah knows the days of the perfect . . . they shall not be put to shame in the time of evil; and in the days of famine they shall be satisfied. But the wicked shall perish . . . I have been young, and now am old; yet have I not seen the righteous forsaken, nor his seed begging bread

[138] *Ps. 145:8, 9, 15, 17, 19, 20*: Jehovah is gracious, and merciful; slow to anger, and of great lovingkindness. Jehovah is good to all; and his tender mercies are over all his works . . . Jehovah is righteous in all his ways, and gracious in all his works . . . He will fulfill the desire of them that fear him; he will hear their cry, and will save them. Jehovah preserves all them that love him; but all the wicked he will destroy

[139] *Prov. 3:3, 5, 7-10*: Let not kindness and truth forsake you . . . so shall you find favor and good understanding in the sight of God and man . . . Fear Jehovah, and depart from evil: It will be health to your navel, and marrow to your bones. Honor Jehovah with your substance . . . So shall your barns be filled with plenty, and your vats shall overflow with new wine

[140] *Ps. 84:11*: For Jehovah God is a sun and a shield: Jehovah will give grace and glory; No good thing will he withhold from them that walk uprightly.

[141] *Eccles. 8:12-13*: Though a sinner do evil a hundred times, and prolong his days, yet surely I know that it shall be well with them that fear God, that fear before him: but it shall not be well with the wicked, neither shall he prolong his days, which are as a shadow; because he fears not before God

[142] *Gen. 18:25*: That be far from you to do after this manner, to slay the righteous with the wicked, that so the righteous should be as the wicked; that be far from you: shall not the Judge of all the earth do right?

[143] *Matt. 6:31-33, 7:11*: Be not therefore anxious, saying, What shall we eat? or, What shall we drink? or, Wherewithal shall we be clothed? For after all these things do the Gentiles seek; for your heavenly Father knows that you have need of all these things. But seek ye first his kingdom, and his righteousness; and all these things shall be added unto you . . . If you then, being evil, know how to give good gifts unto your children, how much more shall your Father who is in heaven give good things to those that ask him?

goodness in providence to motivate them to pray with expectation of divine blessing. Accordingly, Peter encourages Christians to cast all their cares on their heavenly Father: "casting all your anxiety upon him, because he cares for you" (1 Pet. 5:7).

In sum, God focuses the display of his providential goodness on his spiritual children. He pays careful attention to their needs. He delights to grant their requests. He withholds no good thing from them, protects them, and delivers them from every foe.

7. The sovereign limitation of this display: temporal affliction and suffering

God in providence sends not only blessing but also affliction and suffering. In this way he limits the blessing by which he displays his goodness in providence. He sends affliction in this life, not only on the wicked, but also on the righteous. He sometimes sends affliction for specific sins. Yet at other times no specific sin is the cause of affliction. Rather, he afflicts as seems good in his sight, simply according to the free choice of his will. Thus, I call this limitation, "sovereign." Yet, nevertheless, he never afflicts anyone *unjustly*. All Adam's fallen descendants are liable in this life to suffering and death due to sin. He displays his justice even when he displays his wrath.[144] Again, when he afflicts the wicked, he never afflicts *sadistically*. Thus he says: "I have no pleasure in the death of the wicked; but that the wicked turn from his way and live" (Ezek. 33:11). Again, when he afflicts his people, he never afflicts *harshly*. Rather, he shows great kindness. His goodness determines the manner and duration of affliction. Thus David says: "let us fall now into the hand of Jehovah; for his mercies are great; and let me not fall into the hand of man" (2 Sam. 24:14). Again, when he afflicts his spiritual children, he never does so *malevolently*. Rather, he corrects us "for our profit." He chastens us to develop our moral character and to correct specific sins.[145] Thus, ironically, God displays his goodness even when he limits with affliction the blessings by which he displays his providential goodness!

How then should we respond to afflictions? Righteous Job exemplifies a godly response.[146] He recognizes that God sometimes limits with affliction

---

[144] Rom. 3:5
[145] 1 Cor. 11:30-32; Heb. 12:10-11; Rev. 3:19
[146] *Job 1:20-22, 2:10*: Job arose, and rent his robe, and shaved his head, and fell down upon the ground, and worshipped; and he said, Naked came I out of my mother's womb, and naked shall I return thither: Jehovah gave, and Jehovah has taken away; blessed be the name of Jehovah. In all this Job sinned not, nor charged God foolishly . . . shall we receive good at the hand of God, and shall we not receive evil? In all this did not Job sin with his lips

the creation blessings that display his goodness in providence: "shall we receive good at the hand of God, and shall we not receive evil?" (Job 2:10). Unlike Job, many "charge God foolishly." Such complain that a God that sends affliction cannot be good. Others, believing that lie, claim that God cannot be sovereign over suffering because a good God would prevent affliction if he could. We must avoid both of these extremes. We should neither blame God for affliction nor deny his sovereignty over suffering.

When God's spiritual children suffer affliction, we should neither despise God's chastening, nor faint under it.[147] With Job we should rend our robes, fall on our faces, and worship. Yet, we should never, like Job's friends, wrongly condemn the righteous when they suffer. We should not think that all afflictions come as the direct result of great sin.[148] Sometimes God afflicts the righteous to bring about great good, as in the life of Joseph.[149] Sometimes, he severely afflicts the righteous and their families to display his power to heal and deliver, as in the life of the man born blind.[150] Sometimes God's gracious design in affliction eventually becomes clear. Sometimes only eternity will unveil it. Without special divine revelation we can never explain accurately or fully why God brings any specific affliction on some and not on others.[151] Thus, when God in his goodness sends affliction in providence, he leads us back to the fence around the mystery.

C. God's Goodness Displayed in Redemption

God displays his redemptive goodness by blessing his people through his covenants with them. His covenantal blessing of his people has its inception

---

[147] *Prov. 3:11-12*: My son, despise not the chastening of Jehovah; neither be weary of his reproof: for whom Jehovah loves he reproves; even as a father the son in whom he delights

[148] *Luke 13:2-3*: he answered and said unto them, Think ye that these Galilaeans were sinners above all the Galilaeans, because they have suffered these things? I tell you, Nay, but, except you repent, you shall all in like manner perish

[149] *Gen. 50:20*: as for you, you meant evil against me; but God meant it for good, to bring to pass, as it is this day, to save much people alive.

[150] *John 9:1-3*: he saw a man blind from his birth. And his disciples asked him, saying, Rabbi, who sinned, this man or his parents, that he should be born blind? Jesus answered, Neither did this man sin, nor his parents: but that the works of God should be made manifest in him.

[151] *Eccles. 8:13-14, 17, 9:2, 11*: it shall not be well with the wicked, neither shall he prolong his days, which are as a shadow; because he fears not before God. There is a vanity which is done upon the earth, that there are righteous men to whom it happens according to the work of the wicked; again, there are wicked men to whom it happens according to the work of the righteous . . . man cannot find out the work that is done under the sun . . . All things come alike to all: there is one event to the righteous and to the wicked . . . the race is not to the swift, nor the battle to the strong, neither yet bread to the wise, nor riches to men of understanding, nor yet favor to men of skill; but time and chance happens to them all.

in the covenant of grace.[152] Through this promise to accomplish and apply redemption he blesses his spiritual children in Christ. In his sovereign good-pleasure he entered covenant with Abraham and constituted him the father of his people. In fulfillment of his sworn promises to the Patriarchs[153] he successively entered two covenants, old and new, with his people, Israel.[154] Accordingly, I unfold his goodness to Hebrew Israel under the old covenant, his goodness to Christian Israel under the new covenant, and his goodness to his spiritual children in Christ through the covenant of grace in every generation from Abel until the second coming.

1. God's goodness to Hebrew Israel under the old covenant

Under the old covenant God blessed his people in conjunction with redemption from Egypt and inheritance of Canaan. All God's redemptive goodness to Hebrew Israel flowed from his faithfulness to his promises to the Patriarchs.[155] In his great goodness he fulfilled his oath to them, selected their descendants as the special objects of his favor,[156] and constituted them as his people.[157] Thus, in his goodness and love he emancipated Hebrew Israel from slavery in Egypt.[158] In his goodness he continued his special relation with them in spite of their great provocations in the wilderness.[159] In

---

[152] Gen. 3:15

[153] *Deut. 7:9, 12*: the faithful God, who keeps covenant and lovingkindness with them that love him and keep his commandments to a thousand generations . . . Jehovah your God will keep with you the covenant and the lovingkindness which he sware to your fathers

[154] Jer. 31:31-34

[155] *Deut. 7:7, 8, 12*: Jehovah did not set his love upon you, nor choose you, because you were more in number than any people; for you were the fewest of all peoples; but because Jehovah loves you, and because he would keep the oath which he sware to your fathers, has Jehovah brought you out with a mighty hand . . . Jehovah your God will keep with you the covenant and the lovingkindness which he sware to your fathers

[156] *Deut. 10:15*: Only Jehovah had a delight in [lit., set love upon] your fathers to love them, and he chose their seed after them, even you above all peoples, as at this day

[157] Deut. 29:12-13

[158] *Deut. 4:37*: because he loved your fathers, therefore he chose their seed after them, and brought you out with his presence, with his great power   *Isa. 63:9*: In all their affliction he was afflicted, and the angel of his presence saved them: in his love and in his pity he redeemed them; and bare them, and carried them all the days of old.   *Hos. 11:1*: When Israel was a child then I loved him, and called my son out of Egypt.

[159] *Num. 14:18*: Jehovah is slow to anger, and abundant in lovingkindness, forgiving iniquity and transgression; and that will by no means clear the guilty . . . Pardon, I pray thee, the iniquity of this people according unto the greatness of your lovingkindness, and according as you have forgiven this people, from Egypt even until now.   *Neh. 9:17-19*: in their rebellion appointed a captain to return to their bondage. But you are a God ready to pardon, gracious and merciful, slow to anger, and abundant in lovingkindness, and forsook them not . . . they

his goodness he gave them Canaan as their inheritance.[160] In Canaan he blessed them according to the conditions of the old covenant.[161] If and when the society of his people obeyed and served him alone, then he lavished on them material blessing. When they turned to other gods and served them, he withheld these blessings, and inflicted on them the curses of the covenant.[162] Yet, even when he afflicted for sin, he had compassion[163] and preserved a remnant of his people.[164] He liberated that remnant from captivity and brought them back to their land.[165] In the fullness of time, he sent his Son to that remnant, morally transformed them, and entered a new and better covenant with them.[166]

Therefore, throughout their history Hebrew Israel experienced God's parental care.[167] As a good Father, he preserved, protected, and provided for his people. He communed with them and guided them. He chastened and

---

... had wrought great provocations, yet you in your manifold mercies forsook them not in the wilderness: the pillar of cloud departed not from over them by day, to lead them in the way; neither the pillar of fire by night, to show them light.

[160] *Neh. 9:25*: they took fortified cities, and a fat land, and possessed houses full of good things . . . and delighted themselves in your great goodness

[161] Deut. 28:2, 15

[162] *Deut. 28:2-6, 15*: all these blessings shall come upon you, and overtake you, if you hearken unto the voice of Jehovah your God. Blessed shall you be in the city, and blessed shall you be in the field. Blessed shall be the fruit of your body, and the fruit of your ground, and the fruit of your beasts . . . Blessed shall be your kneading-trough. Blessed shall you be when you come in, and blessed shall you be when you go out . . . But it shall come to pass, if you will not hearken unto the voice of Jehovah your God . . . that all these curses shall come upon you and overtake you. {*Covenant blessings*: 28:2-14; *Covenant curses*: 28:15-68}

[163] *2 Sam. 24:14*: let us fall now into the hand of Jehovah; for his mercies are great; and let me not fall into the hand of man

[164] *Lam. 3:22, 32*: It is of Jehovah's lovingkindnesses that we are not consumed, because his compassions fail not. They are new every morning; great is your faithfulness . . . though he cause grief, yet will he have compassion according to the multitude of his lovingkindnesses. For he does not afflict willingly

[165] *Deut. 4:30-31*: When you are in tribulation, and all these things are come upon you, in the latter days you shall return to Jehovah your God, and hearken unto his voice: for Jehovah your God is a merciful God; he will not fail you, neither destroy you, nor forget the covenant of your fathers which he swore unto them. *2 Chron. 30:9*: for Jehovah your God is gracious and merciful, and will not turn away his face from you, if you return to him.

[166] *Deut. 30:3, 5, 6*: Jehovah your God will turn your captivity, and have compassion on you, and will return and gather you from all the peoples whither Jehovah your God has scattered you . . . Jehovah your God will bring you into the land which your fathers possessed, and you shall possess it; and he will do you good, and multiply you above your fathers. And Jehovah your God will circumcise your heart, and the heart of your seed, to love Jehovah your God with all your heart, and with all your soul, that you may live

[167] Exod. 4:22-23; Hos. 11:1

pardoned them. In his love he determined and stabilized their civil government.[168] He loved them and continued faithful to them in spite of all their sins.[169] Finally, in his redemptive goodness God furnished Hebrew Israel with spiritual privileges and special advantages.[170] Through these provisions of the old covenant economy they came into the orbit of gospel light. They beheld God's ways in and through the types and shadows of the sacrificial system. They heard gospel promises unfolded in his Word with increasing clarity and fullness.[171] They had an abiding opportunity, afforded to no other nation,[172] to hear his Word about salvation from sin.[173] The Lord himself appealed to them to turn from sin and get right with him.[174]

2. God's goodness to Christian Israel under the new covenant, the Christian church

God's redemptive goodness to the church of Christ, which is Christian Israel under the new covenant, also rests on his faithfulness to his promises to the patriarchs.[175] In lovingkindness God fulfills his oath to Abraham, blesses all the nations with gospel blessing in Christ, and pours out his Spirit on Abraham's spiritual children, who walk in the footsteps of his faith.[176] He removes unbelieving Jews from the society of his people and grafts in believing Gentiles.[177] In this way he fulfills his promise[178] that his people *as a society* would have heart circumcision as a distinguishing trait.[179] Thus in his goodness he constitutes Abraham's spiritual children as his people,

---

[168] *1 Kings 10:9*: because Jehovah loved Israel forever, therefore he made you king, to do justice and righteousness.

[169] *Isa. 43:4, 5*: Since you have been precious in my sight, and honorable, and I have loved you; therefore will I give men in your stead, and peoples instead of your life. Fear not; for I am with you. *Hos. 3:1:* even as Jehovah loves the children of Israel, though they turn unto other gods

[170] Rom. 2:18, 3:2, 9:4-5

[171] Isa. 45:22, 55:1-3

[172] Amos 3:2

[173] Pss. 32:1-2, 73:24-26

[174] Isa. 1:18; Ezek. 33:11

[175] Gen. 22:18; Luke 1:77-78; Acts 3:25; Gal. 3:8, 16, 19

[176] John 8:39-40; Rom. 4:11-12, 16; Gal. 3:7, 14, 29

[177] Rom. 11:20-22; 1 Pet. 2:9-10

[178] Col. 2:11, 13; 1 Pet. 1:3-4

[179] *Deut. 30:5-6*: Jehovah your God will bring you into the land which your fathers possessed, and you shall possess it; and he will do you good, and multiply you above your fathers. And Jehovah your God will circumcise your heart, and the heart of your seed, to love Jehovah your God with all your heart, and with all your soul, that you may live

Christian Israel. As he fulfilled his promise to Abraham when he redeemed Hebrew Israel from Egypt, even so in tender mercy he fulfills his pledge to the patriarchs when he accomplishes the redemption of Christian Israel,[180] ratifies with them the new covenant in Jesus' blood,[181] and gives them his Holy Spirit as the down payment of their heavenly inheritance.[182] He liberates them from the yoke of the ceremonial law, dismantles the sacrificial system, and grants them unrestricted access through Jesus to the holy place of his special presence.[183]

Thus under the new covenant he lavishes spiritual blessing on Christian Israel through the gospel.[184] As a society they possess every spiritual blessing in Christ. In his great mercy[185] he blesses them morally, taking out their heart of stone, giving them a heart of flesh, writing his law on their hearts, and enabling them to keep it.[186] He blesses them legally, pardoning all their sins and accepting them as righteous on the basis of Christ's virtue.[187] He blesses them experientially, placing his Spirit within them, putting his fear in their hearts, and bringing them into filial fellowship with himself.[188] He also blesses them with every spiritual grace. He grants them evangelical repentance and saving faith in Christ.[189] He gives them the adorning graces of hope and love, and the manifold fruit of the Spirit.[190] In his mercy he preserves them by his power so that they persevere in the faith and in holiness until the return of Jesus.[191] As their loving Father he protects them, provides for them, pardons them, chastens them, nurtures them, communes with them, and guides them from grace to glory. Then he presents them to himself a glorious church, in resurrection glory, free from sin and its

---

[180] *Luke 1:78*: because of the tender [lit., bowels of] mercy of our God, whereby the dayspring from on high shall visit us
[181] 1 Cor. 11:25
[182] Eph. 1:13-14; Acts 2:33, 10:45-47, 11:15-18
[183] Heb. 7:12, 9:8-10, 10:18-22
[184] Gal. 3:7-8, 14; Eph. 1:3
[185] *1 Pet. 1:3-4*: Blessed be the God and Father of our Lord Jesus Christ, who according to his great mercy begat us again unto a living hope by the resurrection of Jesus Christ from the dead, unto an inheritance incorruptible, and undefiled, and that fades not away, reserved in heaven for you.
[186] Jer. 31:33; Ezek. 36:26
[187] Jer. 31:34
[188] Jer. 31:34, 32:40; Ezek. 36:27; Gal. 4:6
[189] Acts 11:18; Phil. 1:29
[190] Rom. 15:13; Gal. 5:22
[191] Isa. 54:9, 17; Jer. 32:39-40; Matt. 16:18; Phil. 1:6; 1 Pet. 1:3-5

consequences.[192] In the new heavens and earth he will lavish goodness on them in ways scarcely imaginable by mortals on earth.[193]

Thus in faithfulness he fulfills his promise that in the latter days the society of his people will seek him, embrace his goodness,[194] and be satisfied with it.[195] Thus he fulfills his promise to manifest his great goodness and love, save his people as his flock,[196] dwell with them, and rejoice over them.[197]

Yet, even under the new covenant, his redemptive goodness has limits.[198] God's kindness does not guarantee the salvation of every church member: "if you continue in his goodness." By their unbelief some Jews were broken off from God's people. Gentiles stand grafted into Christian Israel by faith. Thus, we must not be high-minded. Gentile Christians should walk humbly in gospel fear. If God cut Abraham's physical descendants out of his people for their rejection of Jesus, how much more will he excise Gentile church members that live in unbelief? God shows goodness to those who have faith and shows severity to apostates who repudiate faith and return to a wicked life and to hypocrites who profess faith while they live a wicked life. Under the new covenant he grants to all the nations indiscriminately the spiritual privilege hearing his gospel offer of mercy in Christ.[199] Thus, children brought up in Christian homes and unbelievers married to Christians have even greater spiritual privilege.[200]

3. God's goodness to his spiritual children in Christ in the covenant of grace

In every generation God displays redemptive goodness to his spiritual children in the covenant of grace. He plans their redemption in eternity, accomplishes it through Jesus Christ, applies it to them at their conversion, continues to apply it to them throughout their lives, and completes it in glory.

---

[192] Eph. 5:25-26
[193] 1 John 3:2
[194] Hos. 3:5: afterward the children of Israel shall return, and seek Jehovah their God, and David their king, and shall come with fear unto Jehovah and to his goodness in the latter days
[195] Jer. 31:12, 14: And they shall come and sing in the height of Zion, and shall flow into the goodness of Jehovah . . . and my people shall be satisfied with my goodness, says Jehovah
[196] Zech. 9:16-17: Jehovah their God will save them in that day as the flock of his people . . . For how great is his goodness, and how great is his beauty
[197] Zeph. 3:17: Jehovah your God is in the midst of you, a mighty one who will save; he will rejoice over you with joy; he will rest in his love; he will joy over you with singing
[198] Rom. 11:22: Behold then the goodness and severity of God: toward them that fell, severity; but toward you, God's goodness, if you continue in his goodness: otherwise you also shall be cut off
[199] Isa. 45:22; Acts 17:30-31
[200] 1 Cor. 7:14

a. The display of God's goodness in the plan of redemption in eternity

God's eternal plan of redemption displays his goodness and grace in Christ.[201] Therefore, God designs that his eternal plan should eventuate in "the praise of his glorious grace."[202]

b. The display of God's goodness in the accomplishment of redemption by Christ

Christ epitomizes God's goodness to his people. Divine generosity sends Christ from heaven on a rescue mission to accomplish redemption by his perfect life and atoning death. This divine love is completely unmerited by Christians: "while we yet were sinners, Christ died for us" (Rom. 5:8). Even the most profound human generosity fades into insignificance when compared to God's redeeming love.[203] He gives the greatest gift, at the greatest personal cost, for the most unworthy objects. In order to rescue his enemies from sin, he inflicts his wrath on his only Son. In love Christ gives himself up to suffer the worst punishment, divine wrath, on behalf of the most unworthy.[204] Thus, Christ's remedial mission epitomizes unmerited divine favor.[205] The atonement highlights the grace of God[206] and Christ.[207] Therefore, let us praise him for his unfathomable love, grace, and goodness. Let every Christian imitate Christ's conciliatory love.[208] Let every Christian husband reflect Christ's unselfish love.[209] Let us with grace and hope

---

[201] *2 Tim. 1:8-9*: Be not ashamed therefore of the testimony of our Lord, nor of me his prisoner: but suffer hardship with the gospel according to the power of God; who saved us, and called us with a holy calling, not according to our works, but according to his own purpose and grace, which was given us in Christ Jesus before times eternal.

[202] *Eph. 1:3-6*: Blessed be the God and Father of our Lord Jesus Christ, who has blessed us with every spiritual blessing in the heavenly places in Christ: even as he chose us in him before the foundation of the world, that we should be holy and without blemish before him: in love having foreordained us unto adoption of sons through Jesus Christ unto himself, according to the good pleasure of his will, to the praise of the glory of his grace

[203] *1 John 4:8-10*: God is love ... Herein is love, not that we loved God, but that he loved us, and sent his Son to be the propitiation for our sins.

[204] *Gal. 2:20*: the Son of God, who loved me, and gave himself up for me

[205] *John 1:17*: the law was given through Moses, grace and truth came through Jesus Christ

[206] *Heb. 2:9*: that by the grace of God he should taste of death for every man

[207] *2 Cor. 8:9*: For you know the grace of our Lord Jesus Christ, that, though he was rich, yet for your sakes he became poor, that you through his poverty might become rich

[208] *Eph. 5:2*: walk in love, even as Christ also loved you, and gave himself up for us, an offering and a sacrifice to God

[209] *Eph. 5:25*: Husbands, love your wives, even as Christ also loved the church, and gave himself up for it

proclaim to fallen mankind indiscriminately God's redeeming love that sent Christ to accomplish redemption for sinners from every branch of the human race.[210]

c. *The display of God's goodness in the application of redemption at conversion*

The conversion of a sinner displays all God's goodness.[211] Conversion highlights divine lovingkindness or mercy (eleos),[212] his longsuffering (makrothumia),[213] his compassion (eusplagchnos),[214] his grace (charis),[215] and his love (agape[216] and philanthropia[217]). Paul's letter to Titus epitomizes this display.[218] Prior to their conversion God's spiritual children also were foolish, disobedient, deceived, and serving different lusts and pleasures (3:3). The goodness of God, not our works of righteousness, changed us. In love he transformed every Christian morally, legally, and experientially. In mercy he morally renewed our sinful hearts: "the washing of regeneration and the renewing of the Holy Spirit" (3:5). With generosity he gave us his

---

[210] *John 3:16*: for God so loved the world, that he gave his only begotten Son, that whosoever believes on him should not perish, but have eternal life

[211] *Ps. 25:8*: good and upright is Jehovah: therefore will he instruct sinners in the way. *Joel 2:13*: rend your heart, and not your garments, and turn unto Jehovah your God; for he is gracious and merciful, slow to anger, and abundant in lovingkindness, and repents him of the evil

[212] *1 Pet. 1:3*: Blessed be the God and Father of our Lord Jesus Christ, who according to his great mercy [eleos] begat us again unto a living hope

[213] *1 Tim. 1:16*: Christ Jesus came into the world to save sinners; of whom I am chief: howbeit for this cause I obtained mercy, that in me as chief might Christ Jesus show forth all his longsuffering [makrothumia]

[214] *Eph. 4:32*: And you be kind one to another, tenderhearted [eusplagchnos], forgiving each other, even as God also in Christ forgave you

[215] *Rom. 3:24*: being justified freely by his grace [charis] through the redemption which is in Christ Jesus. *Eph. 2:8-9*: for by grace [charis] you have been saved through faith; and that not of yourselves, it is the gift of God; not of works, that no man should glory. *Phil. 1:29*: to you it has been granted [charizomai] on behalf of Christ, not only to believe on him, but also to suffer in his behalf

[216] *Eph. 2:4-6*: but God, being rich in mercy [eleos], for his great love [agape] wherewith he loved [agapao] us, even when we were dead through our trespasses, made us alive together with Christ—by grace [charis] have you been saved

[217] Titus 3:4

[218] *Titus 3:4-7*: But when the kindness of God our Savior, and his love toward man [philanthropia], appeared, not by works done in righteousness, which we did ourselves, but according to his mercy [eleos] he saved us, through the washing of regeneration and renewing of the Holy Spirit, which he poured out on us richly through Jesus Christ our Savior; that, being justified by his grace [charis], we might be made heirs according to the hope of eternal life

Spirit: "the Holy Spirit, which he poured out on us richly" (3:6). By grace he cleared our guilty record ("justified by his grace") and gave us the rights of his sons ("made heirs") (3:7). This calls us to remember our past wickedness, to give God all the credit for our salvation, and to walk softly at all times with meekness toward everyone: "put them in mind to be" (3:1-2).

d. The display of God's goodness in the application of redemption in the Christian life

After God brings forth spiritual children, he continues to care for us throughout our lives. He is no "deadbeat dad." He never shirks the parental care of his children. Rather, our Father provides generously for his children everything that we need.[219] In his goodness he teaches us his Word[220] and watches over us all the days of our lives.[221] In his goodness he protects us and communes with us in troublous times.[222] With every aspect of his goodness he rescues us from godless and violent foes.[223] With grace and mercy he delivers us from mortal danger.[224] With great compassion he preserves us in faith and holiness through every trial[225] so that nothing can sever us from his love.[226] In his goodness he never forgets us or holds our wicked past against us.[227] In his tender mercy he pardons our remaining

---

[219] *Rom. 8:32*: He that spared not his own Son, but delivered him up for us all, how shall he not also with him freely give us all things?

[220] *Ps. 119:68*: You are good, and do good; teach me your statutes

[221] *Ps. 23:6*: Surely goodness [tôb] and lovingkindness [chesed] shall follow me all the days of my life; and I shall dwell in the house of Jehovah for ever

[222] *Nah. 1:7*: Jehovah is good, a stronghold in the day of trouble; and he knows them that take refuge in him

[223] *Ps. 86:14-17*: O God, the proud are risen against me, and a company of violent men have sought after my soul, and have not set you before them. But you, O Lord, are a God merciful and gracious, slow to anger, and abundant in lovingkindness and truth. Oh turn unto me, and have mercy upon me; give strength unto your servant, and save the son of your handmaid. Show me a token for good, that they who hate me may see it, and be put to shame

[224] *Ps. 116:3-7*: The cords of death compassed me ... Then I called upon the name of Jehovah: O Jehovah I beseech you, deliver my soul. Gracious is Jehovah and righteous; yea, our God is merciful. Jehovah preserves the simple: I was brought low, and he saved me

[225] *James 5:11*: you have heard of the patience of Job, and have seen the end of the Lord, how that the Lord is full of pity and merciful

[226] *Rom. 8:35, 39*: who shall separate us from the love of Christ ... nor any other creature, shall be able to separate us from the love of God, which is in Christ Jesus our Lord

[227] *Ps. 25:7*: Remember not the sins of my youth, nor my transgressions: according to your lovingkindness remember me, for your goodness' sake, O Jehovah:

sins[228] and grievous falls.[229] In his love he nurtures us, reproves our faults,[230] and chastens us for our spiritual growth.[231] With grace he enables us to serve and honor him.[232] In graciousness,[233] longsuffering,[234] and mercy[235] he hears our petitions. As the "Father of mercies," with compassion he comforts us in all our afflictions[236] and with love he fills us with hope.[237] He continues his good work in us so that each of his children makes it to heaven[238] and dwells in his heavenly house forever. Even after we go to heaven, by grace he establishes our labor for his name that we wrought faithfully on earth.[239]

Scripture repeatedly stresses that God works and stores up this great goodness only for those whose hearts he has purified[240] so that they that fear him and cling to him,[241] wait for him and seek him,[242] and walk humbly with him.[243] This is his children's bread. It is for them alone. This gives sinners much incentive to get right with God and join his spiritual family. It also gives all those that profess to be his spiritual children much incentive to put away all hypocrisy.

---

[228] Pss. 25:7, 86:5

[229] *Ps. 51:1, 2*: according to the multitude of your tender mercies blot out my transgressions. Wash me thoroughly from mine iniquity, and cleanse me from my sin

[230] *Prov. 3:12*: whom Jehovah loves he reproves; even as a father the son in whom he delights

[231] Heb. 12:10-11

[232] *2 Cor. 12:9*: My grace is sufficient for you: for my power is made perfect in weakness. Most gladly therefore will I rather glory in my weaknesses, that the power of Christ may rest upon me

[233] *Exod. 22:27*: And it shall come to pass, when he cries unto me, that I will hear; for I am gracious.

[234] *Luke 18:7*: shall not God avenge his elect, that cry to him day and night, and yet he is longsuffering over them?

[235] *Heb. 4:16*: Let us therefore draw near with boldness unto the throne of grace, that we may receive mercy, and may find grace to help us in time of need

[236] *2 Cor. 1:3, 4*: Blessed be the God and Father of our Lord Jesus Christ, the Father of mercies, and God of all comfort; who comforts us in all our affliction

[237] *2 Thess. 2:16*: Now our Lord Jesus Christ himself, and God our Father who loved us and gave us eternal comfort and good hope through grace

[238] *Phil. 1:6*: he who began a good work in you will perfect it until the day of Jesus Christ

[239] *Ps. 90:17*: And let the favor of the Lord our God be upon us; and establish the work of our hands upon us; yes, the work of our hands establish it

[240] *Ps. 73:1*: Surely God is good to Israel, *even* to such as are pure in heart

[241] *Ps. 31:19*: O how great is your goodness, which you have laid up for them that fear you, which you have wrought for them that take refuge in you

[242] *Lam. 3:25*: Jehovah is good unto them that wait for him, to the soul that seeks him

[243] *James 4:6*: God resists the proud, but gives grace to the humble

Accordingly, Scripture highlights the tremendous import of his redemptive goodness to his spiritual children on earth. Without confidence that we will see his goodness in this life, we shrivel spiritually and emotionally.[244] Thus, his goodness calls us to trust him, to bring our concerns and burdens to him,[245] and to ask him to supply all our needs.[246] We should so appreciate his gospel mercies that we consecrate ourselves to him.[247] We should praise him at all times for his great goodness to us throughout our lives.

e. The display of God's goodness in the completion of redemption in glory

God continues to display his goodness to his saints even after we die.[248] He will endlessly display ineffable goodness to his children. None can grasp fully what these "exceeding riches" of his goodness and grace in Christ will be.[249] He reveals that after death he removes all sin from the spirits of believers[250] and they enter heaven and fellowship personally with Jesus.[251] There they remain and reign with Christ in honor, joy, and glory until his return.[252] When Christ returns to judge the world in righteousness, then God consummates his goodness to his children on earth and in heaven. He gives each and all of them a resurrection body like Christ's body.[253] Then in new heavens and earth we will glorify and enjoy God forever. We cannot fully fathom this everlasting display of his goodness and love. We know only that we shall see him as he is and be like him.[254] Every child of God that has this hope is purifying himself even as Christ is pure.[255] This calls every child of God to continue in his love, to encourage each other in our faith, to pray

---

[244] *Ps. 27:13*: I had fainted unless I had believed to see the goodness of Jehovah in the land of the living

[245] 1 Pet. 5:7

[246] Matt. 7:11; Luke 11:13

[247] Rom. 12:1-2

[248] *Ps. 23:6*: and I shall dwell in the house of Jehovah forever

[249] *Eph. 2:7*: that in the ages to come he might show the exceeding riches of his grace in kindness toward us in Christ Jesus

[250] Heb. 12:23

[251] 2 Cor. 5:8; Phil. 1:23

[252] Rev. 3:21, 20:4

[253] Phil. 3:21

[254] *1 John 3:1, 2*: Behold what manner of love the Father has bestowed upon us, that we should be called the children of God . . . now are we the children of God, and it is not yet made manifest what we shall be. We know that, if he shall be manifested, we shall be like him; for we shall see him even as he is

[255] 1 John 3:3

fervently by his Spirit, and to eagerly await for his goodness and mercy at the second coming of Christ.[256] Even so, come Lord Jesus.

Conclusion: *Practical Application of God's Goodness: seven religious implications*

1. God's children should contemplate his goodness.

We should consider carefully God's creative and redemptive goodness. Such meditation brings consolation, encouragement, peace, and joy to God's spiritual children. It fosters gratitude, godliness, love, zeal, and hope. It confirms and commends true religion. Thus, we should study God's goodness and consider it in every season of our lives.[257]

2. God's children should articulate his goodness.

We should tell the story of our experiences of God's goodness in conversion and in our Christian lives.[258] We should declare his goodness especially to other Christians.[259] This fosters true religion in them and strengthens it in us.

3. God's children should reciprocate his goodness.

God initiates the Christian life. This uncovers the genius of Christian motivation. God's children reciprocate his love. We love, obey, and serve him because he first loved us and did so much for us.[260] The greater our sense of forgiveness, the greater our love and appreciation for Christ.[261]

4. God's children should imitate his goodness.

Christians should imitate God's goodness. We should also be kind and conciliatory even to evil men, because our Father is kind and merciful to them.[262] We should be tenderhearted and forgiving to our brethren, just as

---

[256] *Jude 20, 21*: you, beloved, building up yourselves on your most holy faith, praying in the Holy Spirit, keep yourselves in the love of God, looking for the mercy of our Lord Jesus Christ unto eternal life.

[257] *Ps. 107:43*: Whoso is wise will give heed to these things; and they will consider the lovingkindness of Jehovah.

[258] *Ps. 145:7*: They shall utter the memory of your great goodness.

[259] *Ps. 66:16*: Come, and hear, all you that fear God, and I will declare what he has done for my soul

[260] *1 John 4:19*: we love, because he first loved us.

[261] *Luke 7:47*: her sins, which are many, are forgiven; for she loved much: but to whom little is forgiven, the same loves little

[262] Matt. 5:45; Luke 6:35-36

our heavenly Father in his goodness in Christ forgave us.[263] We should love all God's spiritual children because he loves them all.[264]

5. *God's children should anticipate his goodness.*[265]

When Moses sees all God's goodness, he pleads that the Lord would go up in their midst, pardon them, and take them for his inheritance (Exod. 34:9). Without this, we would be of all men most miserable.[266] Accordingly, Christ underscores God's great goodness to motivate his disciples to pray.[267]

6. *God's children should appreciate his goodness.*[268]

God dispenses saving goodness graciously, not meritoriously. Thus, we should be thankful. Again, since he dispenses his goodness incessantly, singing and thanksgiving should characterize our lives.

7. *God's children should venerate and worship God for his goodness.*[269]

When God showed Moses his goodness, Moses responds with worship. All holy contemplation of God's goodness produces what it produced in him. God's goodness should move us, not to flippancy or frivolity, but to worship. Therefore, let us make haste, and bow our heads, and worship.

---

[263] *Eph. 4:32*: And be ye kind one to another, tenderhearted, forgiving each other, even as God also in Christ forgave you

[264] *1 John 4:10-11*: Herein is love, not that we loved God, but that he loved us, and sent his Son to be the propitiation for our sins. Beloved, if God so loved us, we also ought to love one another

[265] *Ps. 31:19*: O how great is your goodness, which you have laid up for them that fear you, which you have wrought for them that take refuge in you

[266] *Ps. 27:13*: I had fainted unless I had believed to see the goodness of Jehovah in the land of the living

[267] *Matt. 7:11*: if you then, being evil, know how to give good gifts unto your children, how much more shall your Father who is in heaven give good things to them that ask him?

[268] *Ezra 3:11*: And they sang one to another in praising and giving thanks unto Jehovah, saying, for he is good, for his lovingkindness endures for ever toward Israel. *Ps. 106:1*: Oh give thanks unto Jehovah; for he is good; for his lovingkindness endures for ever.

[269] *Exod. 34:8*: And Moses made haste, and bowed his head toward the earth, and worshipped.

APPENDIX: BIBLICAL TERMS FOR THE FIVE MAJOR FEATURES OF GOD'S GOODNESS

OLD TESTAMENT TERMS

1. Lovingkindness, mercy

חָסַד (chasad): "to bow in kindness and courtesy": translated "show yourself merciful": used twice of God's mercy: 2 Sam. 22:26; Ps. 18:25.

חֶסֶד (chesed): translated "lovingkindness", "mercy", "goodness"; the word most frequently coupled with God's goodness in the Old Testament: derived from *chasad*: commonly also combined with God's faithfulness, especially to his solemn covenantal promises: "abundant in lovingkindness and truth" (Exod. 34:6); "Jehovah is good; his lovingkindness endures forever, and his faithfulness to all generations" (Ps. 100:5): used of God's lovingkindness at least these 184 times (124 times in Psalms): Gen. 24:12, 27, 32:10, 39:21; Exod. 15:13, 20:6, 34:6, 7; Num. 14:18, 19; Deut. 5:10, 7:9, 12; Ruth 1:8; 1 Sam. 20:14; 2 Sam. 2:6, 7:15, 9:3, 22:51; 1 Kings 3:6(2), 8:23; 1 Chron. 16:34, 41, 17:13; 2 Chron. 5:13, 6:14, 42, 7:3, 6, 20:21; Ezra 3:11, 7:28, 9:9; Neh. 1:5, 9:17, 32, 13:22; Job 10:12, 37:13; Pss. 5:7, 6:4, 13:5, 17:7, 18:50, 21:7, 23:6, 25:6, 25:7, 10, 26:3, 31:7, 16, 21, 32:10, 33:5,18,22, 36:5, 7, 10, 40:10, 11, 42:8, 44:26, 48:9, 51:1, 52:1, 8, 57:3, 10, 59:10, 16, 17, 61:7, 62:12, 63:3, 66:20, 69:13, 16, 77:8, 85:7, 10, 86:5, 13, 15, 88:11, 89:1, 2, 14, 24, 28, 33, 49, 90:14, 92:2, 94:18, 98:3, 100:5, 101:1, 103:4, 8, 11, 17, 106:1, 7, 45, 107:1, 8, 15, 21, 31, 43, 108:4, 109:21, 26, 115:1, 117:2, 118:1, 2, 3, 4, 29, 119:41, 64, 76, 88, 124, 149, 159, 130:7, 136:1-26 (26 times), 138:2, 8, 143:8, 12, 144:2, 145:8, 147:11; Prov. 14:22 [implicit], 16:6 [implicit]; Isa. 16:5, 54:8, 10, 55:3, 63:7(2); Jer. 9:24, 16:5, 31:3, 32:18, 33:11; Lam. 3:22, 32; Dan. 9:4; Hos. 2:19; Joel 2:13; Jonah 4:2; Micah 7:18.

חָסִיד (chasîd): literally "kind": derived from the verb, *chasad*: usually translated "saints," or "holy," or "godly": depicts those religiously kind or pious: Ps. 4:3, 12:1, 37:28: sometimes translated "merciful," 2 Sam. 22:26: refers **once** to God's merciful disposition: Jer. 3:12.

2. Grace, favor

חָנַן (chanan): "to bend," "to stoop in kindness to an inferior," "to favor": translated "be gracious," "deal graciously," "grant graciously," "show mercy," "favor," "have pity": used of God's graciousness at least these 42 times: Gen. 33:5, 11, 43:29; Exod. 33:19(2); Num. 6:25; 2 Sam. 12:22; 2 Kings 13:23; Job 33:24; Pss. 4:1, 6:2, 9:13, 25:16, 26:11, 27:7, 30:10, 31:9, 41:4, 10, 51:1, 56:1, 57:1(2), 59:5, 67:1, 77:9, 86:3,16, 102:13, 119:29, 58, 132, 123:2, 3(2); Isa. 27:11, 30:18,19(2), 33:2; Amos 5:15; Mal. 1:9.

חַנּוּן (channûn): "gracious": derived from *chanan*: used only once of human graciousness (Ps. 112:4): every other use depicts God's graciousness: always translated "gracious": depicts God's grace these **12** times: Exod. 22:27, 34:6; 2 Chron. 30:9; Neh. 9:17, 31; Pss. 86:15, 103:8, 111:4, 116:5, 145:8; Joel 2:13; Jonah 4:2.

חֵן (chēn): "favor": derived from *chanan*: translated "grace," "favor": used of God's grace, or finding favor in his eyes, at least these 16 times: Gen. 6:8, 18:3; Exod. 33:12, 13(2), 16, 17, 34:9; Num. 11:11; Judg. 6:17; 2 Sam. 15:25; Ps. 84:11; Prov. 3:4, 34; Jer. 31:2 [implicit]; Zech. 12:10 [implicit].

3. Long-suffering

אֶרֶךְ אַפַּיִם ('erek 'apphayim): "slow of anger": combination of אֶרֶךְ ('erek), "slow, prolonged, drawn out, long, patient" and אַף ('aph), the most common word for anger: translated "slow to anger," "longsuffering": depicts God's longsuffering these 10 times: Exod. 34:6; Num. 14:18; Neh. 9:17; Ps. 86:15, 103:8, 145:8; Jer. 15:15; Joel 2:13; Jonah 4:2; Nah. 1:3.

אָרַךְ ('arak): "to be or make long, draw out, lengthen"; translated "prolong," "lengthen," "defer": *'erek* is derived from it; refers **once** to God deferring his anger: Isa. 48:9

4. Compassion

רָחַם (racham): "to fondle," "to caress gently," "to be compassionate": translated, "have compassion," "show mercy," "love," "have pity on": a mother's love pictures divine compassion (Isa. 49:15): used of God's compassion at least these 36 times: Exod. 33:19(2); Deut. 13:17, 30:3; 2 Kings 13:23; Pss. 102:13, 103:13, 116:5; Prov. 28:13; Isa. 9:17, 14:1, 27:11, 30:18, 49:10, 13, 54:8, 10, 55:7, 60:10; Jer. 12:15, 13:14, 30:18, 31:20(2), 33:26; Lam. 3:32; Ezek. 39:25; Hos. 1:6, 7, 2:4, 23, 14:3; Mic. 7:19; Hab. 3:2; Zech. 1:12, 10:6.

רַחֲמִים (rachamîm); "compassions, mercies": derived from *racham*: plural of the noun רֶחֶם (*racham*), "the womb" Gen. 49:25: translated "mercy," "tender love," "tender mercies," "bowels," "compassions": used of God's compassion at least these 27 times: Deut. 13:17; 2 Sam. 24:14; 1 Chron. 21:13; Neh. 9:19, 27, 28, 31; Pss. 25:6, 40:11, 51:1, 69:16, 77:9, 79:8, 103:4, 119:77, 156, 145:9; Isa. 54:7, 63:7, 15; Jer. 16:5, 42:12; Lam. 3:22; Dan. 9:9, 18; Hos. 2:19; Zech. 1:16.

רַחוּם (rachûm): "merciful": derived from *racham*: used only once of human mercy (Ps. 112:4): every other time of divine mercy: translated "merciful," "full of compassion": depicts God's compassionate disposition these **12** times: Exod. 34:6; Deut. 4:31; 2 Chron. 30:9; Neh. 9:17, 31; Pss. 78:38, 86:15, 103:8, 111:4, 145:8; Joel 2:13; Jonah 4:2.

חָמַל (chamal); "to commiserate," "to spare": translated "spare," "have pity," "have compassion": depicts God's compassion at least these 17 times: 2 Chron. 36:15; Job 16:13, 27:22; Jer. 13:14; Lam. 2:2, 17, 21, 3:43; Ezek. 5:11, 7:4, 9, 8:18, 9:10, 36:21; Joel 2:18; Zech. 11:6; Mal. 3:17.

חֶמְלָה (chemᵉlah): derived from the verb *chamal*: translated "being merciful to," "pity": used only twice in the Old Testament, both times of God's compassion: Gen. 19:16, Isa. 63:9.

חוּס (chûs): "to cover," "to be compassionate": translated "pity," "regard," "spare": depicts God's compassion at least these 12 times: Neh. 13:22; Ps. 72:13 [implicit]; Jer. 13:14; Ezek. 5:11, 7:4, 9, 8:18, 9:10, 20:17, 24:14; Joel 2:17; Jonah 4:11.

5. Love

אָהַב ('ahab) [or 'ahēb]: "to have affection for": the most common word for love in the Old Testament: depicts feeling delight, becoming attached, being disposed to give and do good: translated "like," "friend," "love": used of God's love at least 22 times: Deut. 4:37, 10:15, 18, 23:5; 2 Sam. 12:24; 2 Chron. 20:7; Neh. 13:26; Pss. 47:4, 78:68, 87:2, 146:8; Prov. 3:12, 15:9; Isa. 41:8, 43:4, 48:14; Jer. 31:3; Hos. 11:1, 14:4; Mal. 1:2(3).

אַהֲבָה ('ahabah); "affection": derived from the verb 'ahab: depicts the affection of delight, heart attachment, and the virtuous disposition to give and do good: translated "love": depicts God's love for his people at least these 10 times: Deut. 7:8; 1 Kings 10:9; 2 Chron. 2:11, 9:8; Isa. 63:9; Jer. 31:3; Hos. 3:1, 9:15, 11:4; Zeph. 3:17.

חָשַׁק (chashaq): "to cling, join, attach to": depicts becoming attached, feeling delight, being disposed to give and do good: translated, "long," "desire," "delight," "set love upon": depicts God's love 3 times: Deut. 7:7, 10:15; Isa. 38:17.

דּוֹד (dôd): "warm affection," "lover," "friend," "uncle": translated "well-beloved," "uncle," "love": used once, in a metaphor, of the love that moved God to "marry" his people: Ezek. 16:8.

חָבַב (chabab): "to hide, as in the bosom," "to cherish," "be endeared to": translated "love": used once of God's love to his people: Deut. 33:3

NEW TESTAMENT TERMS

1. Mercy, lovingkindness

ἔλεος (eleos): translated "mercy": primary word in LXX that translates Hebrew, *chesed*, lovingkindness: used of God's mercy 20 times: Luke 1:50, 54, 58, 72, 78; Rom. 9:23, 11:31, 15:9; Gal. 6:16; Eph. 2:4; 1 Tim. 1:2; 2 Tim. 1:2, 16, 18; Titus 1:4 [BYZ], 3:5; Heb. 4:16; 1 Pet. 1:3; 2 John 3; Jude 2.

ἐλεεω (eleeo): translated "have mercy": pictures divine mercy in a parable, Matt. 18:33: used of God's mercy 13 times: Matt. 5:7; Rom. 9:15, 16, 18, 11:30, 31, 32; 1 Cor. 7:25; 2 Cor. 4:1; Phil. 2:27; 1 Tim. 1:13, 16; 1 Pet. 2:10.

ἐλεημων (eleemon): translated "merciful": used of only righteous men (Matt. 5:7) and of Christ (Heb. 2:17).

2. Grace, favor

χαρις (charis): "grace," "favor," "thank," "pleasure," "liberality": illustrates divine grace, Rom. 4:4: used of God's grace at least these 118 times: Luke 1:30, 2:40,52; John 1:14, 16(2), 17; Acts 7:46, 11:23, 13:43, 14:3, 26, 15:11, 40, 18:27, 20:24, 32; Rom. 1:5, 7, 3:24, 4:16, 5:2, 15, 17, 20, 21, 6:1, 14, 15; 11:5, 6(4), 12:3, 6, 15:15, 16:20, 24; 1 Cor. 1:3, 4, 3:10, 15:10(3), 16:23; 2 Cor. 1:2, 12, 6:1, 8:1, 9, 9:8, 14, 12:9, 13:14; Gal. 1:3, 6, 15, 2:9, 21, 5:4, 6:18; Eph. 1:2, 6, 7, 2:5, 7, 8, 3:2, 7, 8, 6:24;

Phil. 1:2, 7, 4:23; Col. 1:2, 6, 4:18; 1 Thess. 1:1, 5:28; 2 Thess. 1:2, 12, 2:16, 3:18; 1 Tim. 1:2, 14, 6:21; 2 Tim. 1:2, 9, 2:1, 4:22; Titus 1:4, 2:11, 3:7,15; Philem. 3, 25; Heb. 2:9, 4:16(2), 10:29, 12:15, 13:25; James 4:6(2); 1 Pet. 1:2, 10, 13, 4:10, 5:5, 10, 12; 2 Pet. 1:2, 3:18; 2 John 3; Jude 4; Rev. 1:4, 22:21.

χαριζομαι (charizomai): translated, "freely give," "grant," "forgive": illustrates divine grace in a parable, Luke 7:42-43: used of God's graciousness at least these 10 times: Acts 27:24; Rom. 8:32; 1 Cor. 2:12; Gal. 3:18; Eph. 4:32; Phil. 1:29, 2:9; Col. 2:13, 3:13; Philem. 22.

χαριτοω (charitoo): translated "highly favor," "make accepted": used only twice in the New Testament, both times of God's favor: Luke 1:28; Eph. 1:6.

χαρυσμα (charisma): translated "gift," "free gift": refers to God's gracious bestowal of spiritual benefits at least these 13 times: Rom. 5:15, 16, 6:23, 11:29, 1 Cor. 1:7, 12:4, 9, 28, 30, 31; 1 Tim. 4:14; 2 Tim. 1:6; 1 Pet. 4:10.

3. Long-suffering

ἀνοχη (anoche); translated "forbearance": used only twice, both times of God's forbearance: Rom. 2:4, 3:25

μακροθυμια (makrothumia); translated "longsuffering": in LXX often translates the Hebrew, *'erek 'apphayim*: used of God's and Christ's long-suffering 5 times: Rom. 2:4, 9:22; 1 Tim. 1:16; 1 Pet. 3:20; 2 Pet. 3:15.

μακροθυμεω (makrothumeo); translated "suffer long over," "have patience with": used twice of God's long-suffering: Luke 18:7; 2 Pet. 3:9.

4. Compassion

οἰκτιρμος (oiktirmos): translated "compassion," "mercy": in LXX often translates *rachûm*: used five times in the New Testament: twice of God's compassion: Rom. 12:1; 2 Cor. 1:3.

οἰκτιρμων (oiktirmon): translated "merciful": used only twice in the New Testament, both refer to God's compassion: Luke 6:36; James 5:11.

οἰκτιρεω (oiktireo): translated "have compassion": in LXX often translates *racham*: used once in NT: depicts God's mercy: Rom. 9:15.

σπλαγχνα (splagchna): literally, "bowels" (Acts 1:18): translated "bowels," "tender mercy": used once of God's compassion: Luke 1:78.

σπλαγχνιζομαι (splagchnizomai): translated "be moved with compassion": pictures divine compassion in two parables: Matt. 18:27; Luke 15:20: used once of men's compassion: Luke 10:33: nine times of Christ's compassion: Matt. 9:36, 14:14, 15:32, 20:34; Mark 1:41, 6:34, 8:2, 9:22; Luke 7:13.

εὐσπλαγχνος (eusplagchnos); literally "good-gutted"; translated "tender-hearted," "pitiful": used only twice in the New Testament: Eph. 4:32, 1 Pet. 3:8: refers to Christian compassion which reflects God's gracious disposition.

πολυσπλαγχνος (polusplagchnos): translated "full of pity": once depicts God's great compassion: James 5:11.

5. Love

αγαπη (agape); translated "love," "charity," "dear": implies God's love: Rom. 5:5, 2 Thess. 3:5, 1 John 4:12: in LXX usually translates the Hebrew, *'ahabah*: depicts divine love, of the Father, Son, or Spirit, at least these 23 times: John 15:9, 10(2), 17:26; Rom. 5:8, 8:35, 39, 15:30; 2 Cor. 13:11, 14; Eph. 1:4, 2:4, 3:19; Col. 1:13; 1 John 3:1, 16, 4:8, 9, 10, 16(2); 2 John 3; Jude 2.

αγαπαω (agapao): translated, "to love," "beloved": in LXX usually translates the Hebrew, *'ahab*: used of God's love, whether of the Father or of the Son, at least these 39 times: John 3:16, 35, 10:17, 11:5, 13:1(2), 23, 34, 14:21, 23, 31, 15:9(2), 12, 17:23(2), 24, 26, 19:26, 21:7; Rom. 8:37, 9:13; 2 Cor. 9:7; Gal. 2:20; Eph. 1:6, 2:4, 5:2, 25; Col. 3:12; 1 Thess. 1:4; 2 Thess. 2:13, 16; Heb. 12:6; 1 John 4:10, 11, 19; Rev. 1:5, 3:9, 20:9.

αγαπητος (agapetos): translated "beloved": depicts God's love for Christ in a parable: Luke 20:13: in LXX usually translates *yachîd*, "only son": used of God's love, especially of the Father for the Son, at least these 13 times: Matt. 3:17, 12:18, 17:5; Mark 1:11, 9:7, 12:6; Luke 3:22, 9:35; Rom. 1:7, 11:28, 16:8; Eph. 5:1; 2 Pet. 1:17.

φιλανθρωπια (philanthropia): translated "love toward man," "kindness": used only twice in the New Testament: once of men's common courtesy (Acts 28:2): once of God's kindness: Titus 3:4.

φιλεω (phileo): translated "kiss" (Matt. 26:48), "love": commonly refers to human love: refers once to Christ's chastening love (Rev. 3:19): once to God the Father's love for Christ (John 5:20): once to his love for Christians (John 16:27).

TABULATION

Lovingkindness	Grace, Favor	Long-Suffering	Compassion	Love	TOTAL
OLD TESTAMENT TERMS					
chasad 2 chesed 184 chasîd 1	chanan 42 channûn 12 chēn 16	'erek 'aph 10 'arak 1	racham 36 rachamîm 27 rachûm 12 chamal 17 chemᵉlah 2 chûs 12	'ahab 22 'ahabah 10 chasaq 3 dôd 1 chasab 1	
Total OT 187	Total OT 70	Total OT 11	Total OT 106	Total OT 37	All OT 411
NEW TESTAMENT TERMS					
eleos 20 eleeo 13	charis 118 charizomai 10 charitoo 2 charisma 13	anoche 2 makrothumia 5 makrothumeo 2	oiktirmos 2 oiktirmon 2 oiktireo 1 splagchna 1 polusplagchnos 1	agape 23 agapao 39 agapetos 13 philanthropia 1 phileo 3	
Total NT 33	Total NT 143	Total NT 9	Total NT 7	Total NT 79	All NT 271
TOTAL 220	TOTAL 213	TOTAL 20	TOTAL 113	TOTAL 116	BIBLE **682**

Summary: the general terms for divine goodness occur 143 times, these more specific terms 682 times, a total of **825** references to God's goodness. Thus, Scripture features and highlights this divine virtue.

Epitomizing Texts in Context

Exod. 33:19, 34:6-8: And he said, I will make all my goodness pass before you, and will proclaim the name of Jehovah before you; and I will be gracious to whom I will be gracious, and will show mercy on whom I will show mercy . . . and Jehovah passed by before him, and proclaimed, Jehovah, Jehovah, a God merciful and gracious, slow to anger, and abundant in lovingkindness and truth; keeping lovingkindness for thousands, forgiving iniquity and transgression and sin; and that will by no means clear the guilty, visiting the iniquity of the fathers upon the children, and upon the children's children, upon the third and upon the fourth generation. And Moses made haste, and bowed his head toward the earth, and worshipped

Rom. 11:20-22: by their unbelief they were broken off, and you stand by your faith. Be not high-minded, but fear: for if God spared not the natural branches, neither will he spare you. Behold then the goodness and severity of God: toward them that fell, severity; but toward you, God's goodness, if you continue in his goodness: otherwise you also shall be cut off.

Topic 18. The Holiness of God

"Holy, holy, holy is Jehovah of hosts" (Isa. 6:3); "You only are holy" (Rev. 15:4)

Unit 2. The Holiness of God

Introduction: The biblical testimony to God's holiness[1] commends the following categories of thought: First, Scripture defines *the concept* of God's holiness.[2] Second, it unfolds *its display* in creation, special revelation, redemption, and damnation.[3] Third, it overtly faces the *seeming contradictions* associated with it.[4] Fourth, it commends its *practical application* to experiential religion.[5] Charnock expounds holiness similarly.[6] He frames his exposition with an epitomizing text.[7] In his introduction he stresses its preeminence.[8] Then he expounds its "nature." He identifies six distinguishing properties.[9] Next he unfolds its "demonstration"[10] and explains its "relations" to sin: "the purity of his nature in all his acts about sin."[11] Finally, he applies its practical "uses."[12]

I. *The Concept of God's Holiness*

Introduction: definition of God's holiness

From my study of the biblical testimony I offer the following definition of God's holiness:

> God's holiness is: from eternity, his eternal moral purity, which is his supreme separateness and immaculateness; upon creation, his moral supremacy, which separates him from and exalts him above all creatures and so-called gods; and upon sin, his absolute

---

[1] I catalogue the use of the major biblical terms for God's holiness in an appendix to this topic.

[2] Exod. 15:11; Josh. 24:19; 1 Sam. 2:2; Job 4:17; Pss. 5:4, 111:9; Isa. 40:25; Hab. 1:13; 2 Cor. 6:16-7:1; Heb. 7:26; James 1:13; Rev. 15:4

[3] Lev. 20:26; 2 Kings 19:22; Pss. 5:4-6, 12:6, 19:8, 89:35, 111:9; Isa. 6:3; Hab. 1:13; Luke 1:49; Rom. 7:12; Eph. 4:24; Heb. 12:10; Rev. 6:10

[4] Ezek. 36:20-22, 39:7; Hab. 1:13

[5] Lev. 19:2; Josh. 24:19; 1 Sam. 6:20; Pss. 33:21, 99:3, 5, 9, 106:47; Isa. 6:3, 57:15; Eph. 4:24; James 1:13; 1 Pet. 1:15-16; 1 John 3:3; Rev. 6:10, 15:4

[6] Charnock, *Existence and Attributes of God*, 446-532

[7] *Exod. 15:11*: Who is like unto you, O Jehovah, among the gods? Who is like unto you, glorious in holiness, fearful in praises, doing wonders?

[8] Charnock, *Existence and Attributes of God*, 446-452

[9] Ibid., 452-461

[10] Ibid., 461-473

[11] Ibid., 473-500

[12] Ibid., 501-532

impeccability, which separates him from and sets him vehemently against all sin.

This definition specifies God's *absolute* holiness in eternity and two *relational* aspects of his holiness, his moral supremacy in relation to creation and absolute impeccability in relation to sin. Although Berkhof defines majesty holiness more generally, he confirms these two relational aspects of divine holiness:[13]

> The Scriptural idea of holiness then is twofold. In its original sense it denotes that He is absolutely distinct from all His creatures, and is exalted above them in infinite majesty. So understood, the holiness of God is one of His transcendental attributes, and is sometimes spoken of as His central or supreme perfection . . . It may be called the majesty-holiness of God, and is referred to in such passages as Ex.15:11; 1 Sam.2:2; Isa.57:15; Hos.11:9.
>
> But the holiness of God also has a specific ethical or moral aspect in Scripture, and it is with this aspect of it that we are more directly concerned. The ethical idea of the divine holiness may not be disassociated from the idea of God's majesty-holiness . . . The fundamental idea of the ethical holiness of God is also that of separation, but in this case, it is separation from moral evil or sin. In virtue of His holiness, God can have no communion with sin, Job 34:10; Hab. 1:13 . . . But the idea of ethical holiness is not merely negative (separation from sin); it also has a positive content, namely, that of moral excellence or ethical perfection. If man reacts to God's majestic holiness with a feeling of utter insignificance and awe, his reaction to the ethical holiness reveals itself in a sense of impurity, a consciousness of sin, Isa. 6:5 . . . The ethical holiness of God may be defined as *that perfection of God, in virtue of which He eternally wills and maintains His own moral excellence, abhors sin, and demands purity in His moral creatures*."

I now expound and support God's *eternal holiness, moral supremacy* and *absolute impeccability*.

A. *God's Eternal Holiness: his supreme separateness and immaculateness*

God's holiness exists before the creation of the universe or the advent of sin. God's *eternal moral purity* is his "*supreme separateness and immaculateness*." Divine holiness is an absolute attribute, essential to God's very being. If God were not holy, he would not be God. God always was

---

[13] Berkhof, *Systematic Theology*, 73-74

supremely separate and immaculate. Charnock confirms that God's supreme moral purity is eternal:[14]

> The holiness of God *negatively* is a perfect . . . freedom from all evil. As we call gold pure that is not imbased by any dross, and that garment clean that is free from any spot, so the nature of God is estranged from all shadow of evil, all imaginable contagion. *Positively*, it is the rectitude or integrity of the divine nature . . . He is essentially and necessarily holy. It is the essential glory of his nature. His holiness is as necessary as his being, as necessary as his omniscience. As he cannot but know what is right, so he cannot but do what is just . . . He is as necessarily holy as he is necessarily God; as necessarily without sin as without change. As he was God from eternity, so he was holy from eternity.

God's *supreme separateness* is the reality behind ceremonial rituals that sanctify various persons and inanimate objects. When something is ceremonially "sanctified," it is separated from similar things and common use and consecrated especially to God. It is dedicated to a solely religious use and especially devoted to God's honor and glory. Similarly, his "supreme separateness" is his total dedication to his own glory, his complete devotion to his own sovereign designs. God's *eternal immaculateness* is his unalloyed moral purity, the total absence of moral contamination. Thus, it summarily embraces all his virtues. Separateness from all moral contamination is separateness from malice, injustice, and dishonesty. In positive terms, separateness from malice is goodness or love; separateness from injustice is justice; and separateness from dishonesty is faithfulness. Scripture affirms this by closely associating God's holiness with his justice[15] and faithfulness.[16] Boyce confirms this feature of God's holiness:[17]

> Holiness is, however, not a distinctive attribute, but rather the combination of all these [moral] attributes. We may suppose a being in whom there may be love without justice, or truth, or any one of these to the exclusion of the other two; but no being can be holy, who does not combine in himself all of these, and all other moral perfections . . . It is evident, therefore, that holiness is the sum of all excellence and the combination of all the attributes which constitute perfection of character.

---

[14] Charnock, *Existence and Attributes*, 452
[15] Acts 3:14
[16] Rev. 6:10
[17] Boyce, *Abstract of Systematic Theology*, 92-93

Thus, in eternity God's holiness consisted in his complete dedication to his own glory and in his infinite moral perfection. Now consider biblical support for God's eternal holiness.

1. Isa. 57:15[18]

This text explicitly connects God's holiness with his eternal existence. We considered this text when we expounded God's eternity. It literally asserts that God "abides in perpetuity." God ever was, now is, and always will be. "*Holy*" is the name of the God who now is and always was. Therefore, God now is holy and always was holy. He did not become holy only after he created. Rather he was eternally holy. Before he created the world he was morally immaculate and supremely dedicated to his own glory.

2. Rev. 16:5[19]

Similarly, this text asserts that God always was holy: "who are and *who was, you Holy One*." Further, this text identifies God's holiness with all his moral virtue: "*You are righteous*, who are and who was, *you Holy One*." The text also discloses how God displays, in history, the holiness that characterized him from eternity: "You are righteous, who are and who was, you Holy One, *because you did thus judge:* for they poured out the blood of saints and prophets, and you have given them blood to drink: they are worthy." God's just punishment of sinners springs from and displays his eternal immaculateness (freedom from moral contamination) and his eternal separateness (dedication to his own purpose and glory).

B. God's Moral Supremacy

God's moral supremacy "separates and exalts him above all creatures and so-called gods." God's moral supremacy exalts him infinitely above his creatures. God always was supremely holy. After he creates a myriad of beings that are finite, temporal, mutable, dependent, and lapsable, his holiness necessarily consists in his infinite moral exaltation above all creatures. This especially pertains to every created being or thing that people worship as their god. In reference to morality God alone is inherently and infinitely immaculate. Even if there were no sin, with respect to morality God would still be infinitely separate from and exalted above his creatures. God alone has ideal moral purity that can never be improved, for it already is infinitely perfect. God alone has unoriginated moral purity. God alone has inherently immutable moral purity. His moral purity is not only

---

[18] *Isa. 57:15*: For thus says the high and lofty One that inhabits eternity, whose name is Holy

[19] *Rev. 16:5*: You are righteous, who are and who was, you Holy One

impeccable but also untemptable. God alone has self-existent holiness that does not need any standard or arbiter outside himself. God alone is both its norm and its judge. In these ways only God is "holy," morally supreme. His supreme holiness is infinite, eternal, immutable, ideal, and independent. Charnock confirms God's moral supremacy:[20]

> God is only absolutely holy: 'There is none holy as the Lord,' 1 Sam. 2:2. It is the peculiar glory of his nature. As there is none good but God, so none holy but God. No creature can be essentially holy, because mutable; holiness is the substance of God, but a quality and accident in a creature. God is infinitely holy, creatures finitely holy . . . As all the wisdom, excellency, and power of the creatures, if compared with the wisdom, excellency, and power of God, is but folly, vileness, and weakness, so the highest created purity, if set in parallel with God, is but impurity and uncleanness . . . Job 25:15; 'the heavens are not pure in his sight, and his angels he charged with folly,' Job 4:18.

Consider with me five biblical witnesses that testify of God's moral supremacy in relation to creation.

1. Exod. 15:11[21]

This text contrasts the living God with false gods: "who is like unto you, O Jehovah, among the gods?" God's uniqueness consists in his immaculate virtue, "glorious in holiness," and supernatural power, "fearful in praises, doing wonders." God displays his holiness and power when he overthrows the Egyptian army. When God thus displays supreme moral purity, the sea covers his enemies (15:10) and the earth swallows them (15:12). In contrast, when he displays lovingkindness, he guides Israel to their inheritance (15:13). This powerful display of his holiness elicits praise and adoration from his people (15:11) and dread from their enemies (15:14-15). His moral opposition to sin is bound to omnipotence. What holiness demands, omnipotence supplies. Thus, sinners should fear the God of singular holiness.

2. 1 Sam. 2:2[22]

This text closely connects God's supreme holiness with his Supreme Being: "There is none holy as the Jehovah, *for there is none besides you*, neither is

---

[20] Charnock, *Existence and Attributes of God*, 453-454

[21] *Exod. 15:11*: Who is like unto you, O Jehovah, among the gods? Who is like you, glorious in holiness, fearful in praises, doing wonders?

[22] *1 Sam. 2:2*: There is none holy as Jehovah; for there is none besides you, neither is there any rock like our God

there any rock like our God." God's unique holiness rests on his identity as the bedrock of all existence. There is none as morally immaculate as the Lord, because God's moral purity is infinite, eternal, unchangeable, self-existent, and ideal. Thus, God's infinite moral perfection separates him from all created beings. This text reveals that omniscience undergirds his infinite moral purity: "Talk no more exceeding proudly, let not arrogancy come out of your mouth, for the Lord is a God of knowledge, and by Him actions are weighed" (2:3). In infinite moral purity he humbles and condemns the wicked, but blesses and comforts his saints: "he will keep the feet of his holy ones; but the wicked shall be put to silence in darkness" (2:9). This display of his moral supremacy does not evoke from God's children a desire to run in dread from an unapproachable God. Rather, it produces a disposition to draw near to him with joy: "Hannah prayed, and said: My heart exults in Jehovah; my horn is exalted in Jehovah; my mouth is enlarged over my enemies; because I rejoice in your salvation. There is none holy as Jehovah" (2:1-2).

3. *Job 4:18, 15:15, 25:5*[23]

Scripture affirms that God's moral purity is infinite: "his angels he charges with folly"; "the heavens are not clean in his sight"; and, "the stars are not pure in his sight." These passages present God's absolute immaculateness in almost shocking terms. When I expounded God's ideality I observed: "This does *not* mean that either the inanimate heavens or God's ministering angels are guilty of sin, disobedience, or rebellion. Yet, not even his glorious angels or the vast heavens can compare with him. Compared to his infinitely perfect wisdom, even the wisest angels are 'foolish.' Compared to infinitely perfect being, even the spotless heavens are 'unclean,' that is, unsuitable for contact with him." Thus, these texts affirm that in relation to creation God's holiness is his supreme immaculateness.

4. *Isa. 40:25*[24]

Scripture again contrasts the Almighty with his creatures: "to whom then will you liken me, that I should be equal to him? Says the Holy One." In this passage, Scripture reproves men who turn created things into false gods: "To whom then will you liken God? Or what likeness will you compare unto him? The image, a workman has cast it" (40:18-19). It then describes God's supremacy as Master of the universe (40:21-22). Isaiah affirms that

---

[23] *Job 4:18*: his angels he charges with folly; *15:15*: the heavens are not clean in his sight; *25:5*: the stars are not pure in his sight

[24] *Isa. 40:25*: To whom then will you liken me, that I should be equal to him? says the Holy One

his sovereign rule renders human rulers insignificant: "that brings princes to nothing, that makes the judges of the earth as vanity" (40:23-24). This exalted Sovereign describes himself as, "the Holy One." The unequaled Holy One hates idolatry and makes human rulers into nobodies because: "all the nations are as nothing before him; they are accounted as less than nothing and vanity" (40:17). This Holy Ruler ever remains supremely devoted to his own honor and glory: "I am Jehovah, that is my name, and my glory will I not give to another, neither my praise to graven images" (42:8). Thus, this text underscores that God's supreme holiness, in relation to creation, consists in his supreme devotion to his own infinite glory as the Creator and Ruler of the universe.

5. *Rev. 15:3-4* [25]

As God alone is supremely good, even so God's holiness is supreme and unique: "only you are holy." This passage depicts the ultimate infliction of God's wrath and vengeance on sin (15:1-16:21). His vengeance stems from his supreme holiness. Thus, this passage highlights the fact that his holiness consists in his supreme opposition to sin and his resolve to avenge it. Further, God's supreme holiness elicits both fear and respect: "Who shall not fear, O Lord, and glorify your name, *for* only you are holy." Thus, his holiness produces in creatures a sense of utmost helplessness and dependence. In sinners, it produces a sense of their wretchedness and decadence. Supreme holiness deflates human pride and self-righteousness. Nevertheless, God's holiness draws the righteous from every nation to bow before him in adoration and worship: "for only you are holy; *for* all the nations shall come and worship before you."

In sum, these passages affirm clearly that God in reference to creatures is uniquely holy. He alone is supremely dedicated to his own glory. He alone is morally immaculate immutably and independently. Yet, nevertheless, God's moral creatures truly reflect his singular holiness and moral purity.[26]

Conclusion: a modern view of "majesty holiness"

I conclude with a modern view of God's holiness. Some claim that his holiness in relation to creation is not a moral attribute, but rather is his transcendence, or essential deity. For example, Berkhof, says: "holiness in

---

[25] *Rev. 15:3-4*: they sing the song of Moses the servant of God, and the song of the Lamb, saying, Great and marvelous are your works, O Lord God, the Almighty; righteous and true are your ways, O thou King of the ages. Who shall not fear, O Lord, and glorify your name? for you only are holy; for all the nations shall come and worship before you; for your righteous acts have been made manifest

[26] Heb. 12:10; 1 Pet. 1:15-16

this sense of the word is not really a *moral* attribute . . . but is rather something which is co-extensive with, and applicable to everything that can be predicated of God."[27] It is true that God's supreme moral purity exalts him infinitely above his creatures. Yet Berkhof defines "majesty holiness" so generically that he eliminates its moral significance. Yet Scripture does not support severing holiness from morality. Bavinck outlines the historical development of this modern notion:

> Very closely related to God's goodness is his holiness. Formerly it was defined as 'purity, free from every stain, wholly perfect and immaculate in every detail.' . . . Protestant theologians defined God's holiness in terms similar to the definition just quoted; it was said to consist in 'moral perfection, purity,' and was discussed now in connection with God's justice, then in connection with his goodness or with his veracity or wisdom. The study of the Biblical concept of holiness has gradually brought about a different view concerning the character of this attribute. At present all acknowledge the fact that the concept of 'holiness' in Old and New Testament indicates a relation of God to the world. But opinions are divided with respect to the exact character of that relation . . . Menken thought of God's condescending goodness or grace. Baudissin, however, was of the opinion that God's holiness was expressive rather of his absolute transcendence above and power over all creatures . . . Schultz . . . defines God's holiness as his consuming majesty, his unapproachability and inviolability, the infinite distance which separates him from every creature.[28]
>
> Now the idea of holiness becomes clear when we consider what it signifies when it is ascribed to God . . . holiness is not primarily a relation of the creature to the Creator, but vice versa . . . it pertains to God in the first place, and to the creature in a secondary sense . . . Now when the word holy is ascribed to Jehovah, it doesn't signify one definite attribute. On the contrary, God is called holy in a very general sense: in connection with every revelation which impresses man with God's exalted majesty. Holiness is synonymous with divinity, Amos 4:2.[29]

It is true that God's holiness embraces all his moral virtues. But Amos 4:2: "the Lord Jehovah has sworn by his holiness," does not prove that holiness means "deity" rather than "moral purity." Surely we are not twisting Scripture if we take the text to mean, "the Lord Jehovah has sworn by his [moral purity]." We skate on thin ice if we read it: "has sworn by his

---

[27] Berkhof, *Systematic Theology*, 73
[28] Bavinck, *Doctrine of God*, 209-210
[29] Ibid., 213

[transcendence]." An imaginative mind could read almost any attribute into this text. Yet that is not how to conduct biblical studies. Again, some cite Hosea 11:9:[30] "for I am God, and not man; the Holy One in the midst of you." Yet, the fact that God identifies himself as the "Holy One" does not affirm or even imply that holiness equals deity. What it actually affirms is that the Supreme Being is unlike sinful humanity because he is *holy*, "totally dedicated to his own glory and averse to all sin." Here is the marvel. This holy God dwells in the midst of his people, not in wrath, but in compassion. In sum, I have found no compelling evidence that clearly supports, let alone demands, that God's holiness is his *deity* or *transcendence*.

Finally, it seems impossible to reconcile this new idea with these texts: "as he who called you is holy, you yourselves also be holy" (1 Pet. 1:15), or, "For they indeed for a few days chastened us as seemed good to them; but he for our profit, that we may be partakers of his holiness" (Heb. 12:10). These texts cannot possibly mean: "that we may be partakers of his [deity]" or, "as he who called you is [transcendent], you yourselves also be [transcendent]." Thus, *holiness* is *communicable*. Christians are devoted to God's glory and separate from sinners. The glorified spirits in heaven are totally devoted to God's glory and impeccably separate from all sin. Yet even the glorified spirits are not *transcendent*. Again, Christ says, "there is none good but one, even God." Clearly he doesn't mean "there is none [transcendent] but one." Rather, he means that God alone has supreme goodness that is ideal, independent, infinite, eternal, and unchangeable. Similarly, "you alone are holy," means that God alone has supreme holiness that is ideal, independent, infinite, eternal and unchangeable. Thus, *supreme* holiness is *incommunicable*. Our definition of divine holiness must fit the *total witness* of Scripture.

C. God's Absolute Impeccability

In relation to sin God's holiness signifies his *absolute impeccability*: "which separates him from and sets him vehemently against all sin." Both Charnock and Berkhof confirm this aspect of divine holiness and stress its importance. God's infinite moral purity and supreme devotion to his own glory mandate his absolute separateness from all sin and vehement opposition to it. His holiness stands in sharp contrast with the pollution of fallen men and angels. As space emphatically displays God's infinity, and as time emphatically

---

[30] *Hos. 11:8-9*: How shall I give thee up, Ephraim? *How* shall I cast you off, Israel? How shall I make you as Admah? *How* shall I set you as Zeboiim? My heart is turned within me, my compassions are kindled together. 9 I will not execute the fierceness of my anger, I will not return to destroy Ephraim: for I am God, and not man; the Holy One in the midst of you; and I will not come in wrath

displays his eternity, so also, sin emphatically displays his holiness. Consider with me the testimony of ten passages that highlight God's absolute impeccability.

1. Josh. 24:19[31]

Joshua warns that because God is holy he stands so resolved to punish sin that sinners cannot serve him acceptably. Jehovah is devoted to his own honor and infinitely pure. Therefore, he stands vehemently opposed to sin. Their treacherous idolatry provokes his jealousy and evokes his vengeance. Therefore they "cannot serve Jehovah." Thus, Joshua urges them to put away their foreign gods and incline their hearts to the Lord (24:23). Clearly God's holiness consists in his separation from sin. This separation involves his indignation toward sin, his detestation of sin, and his resolve to avenge sin.

2. Job 4:17[32]

This text compares men's moral character with God's. The ASV margin translates it: "can a mortal man be pure before his Maker." No matter which reading we adopt, the text presents divine virtue as infinitely superior to human purity. Human purity involves purging sin from the heart: "Who can say, I have made my heart clean, I am pure from my sin?" (Prov. 20:9). Thus, divine moral purity consists in his total freedom from any tendency to sin and even from the capacity to be tempted to sin.

3. Ps. 5:4-6[33]

This text presents God's holiness by negation: "you *are not* a God that has pleasure in wickedness. Evil *shall not* sojourn with you. The arrogant *shall not stand* in your sight." God separates from sin by banishing the wicked from his special presence. He will not fellowship with the arrogant. Because God is holy, he dwells only with humble and contrite souls (Isa. 57:15). This passage also depicts the import of God's holiness: "You hate all the workers of iniquity. You will destroy them that speak lies. The Lord abhors the blood-thirsty and the deceitful man." God separates from sinners because he detests them. In holiness he will punish them and "destroy" them forever in hell.

---

[31] *Josh. 24:19*: And Joshua said unto the people, you cannot serve Jehovah; for he is a holy God; he is a jealous God; he will not forgive your transgression nor your sins

[32] *Job 4:17*: Shall mortal man be more just than God? Shall a man be more pure than his Maker?

[33] *Ps. 5:4-6*: For you are not a God that has pleasure in wickedness: Evil shall not sojourn with you. The arrogant shall not stand in your sight: You hate all workers of iniquity. You will destroy them that speak lies: Jehovah abhors the bloodthirsty and deceitful man

4. Hab. 1:13[34]

This text pictures God's holiness in human terms: "purer eyes." As holy men turn their eyes away from things they know they shouldn't see, so also the holy God repudiates sin. He can't stand the sight of sin. He never looks with delight or desire at sin. He has no experiential fellowship with sin.

5. 2 Cor. 7:1[35]

This text relates holiness to sin. Paul exhorts Christians to strive to complete holiness. This involves cleansing ourselves from all sin, both inwardly in our souls and outwardly in our words and actions. This text does not mention divine holiness explicitly. Yet it affirms plainly that Christian holiness, which reflects divine holiness, consists in separation from all sin.

6. Eph. 4:24[36]

This text affirms explicitly that Christian holiness reflects divine holiness. God re-created the Christian morally in his image: "the new man, that *after God has been created in righteousness and holiness* of truth." Even as Christian holiness consists in separation from sin, so also does divine holiness. Scripture explicitly confirms this: "For they indeed for a few days chastened us as seemed good to them; but he for our profit, that we may be partakers of his holiness" (Heb. 12:10). When he conforms us to his holiness, we partake in his moral virtue. This virtue consists in his dedication to his own glory and separateness from sin. In glory God will conform every Christian to his holiness impeccably and permanently.

7. Heb. 7:26[37]

This text declares that Christ's suitability as high priest stems from his holiness and his exaltation. The writer amplifies the features of divine holiness: "guileless," "undefiled," and "separated from sinners." Holiness

---

[34] *Hab. 1:13*: You that are of purer eyes than to behold evil, and that can not look on perverseness, why do you look upon them that deal treacherously, and hold your peace when the wicked swallows up the man that is more righteous than he?

[35] *2 Cor. 6:16-7:1*: And what agreement has a temple of God with idols? for we are a temple of the living God; even as God said, I will dwell in them, and walk in them; and I will be their God, and they shall be my people. Wherefore Come ye out from among them, and be ye separate, says the Lord, and touch no unclean thing; and I will receive you, and will be to you a Father, and you shall be to me sons and daughters, says the Lord Almighty. Having therefore these promises, beloved, let us cleanse ourselves from all defilement of flesh and spirit, perfecting holiness in the fear of God

[36] *Eph. 4:24*: and put on the new man, that after God has been created in righteousness and holiness of truth

[37] *Heb. 7:26*: For such a high priest became us, holy, guileless, undefiled, separated from sinners, and made higher than the heavens

is the absence of guile and defilement. It is separation from sinners. Thus, in relation to sin, holiness is freedom from sin's pollution and separation from those who live in sin and delight in it.

8. *James 1:13*[38]

This text addresses divine holiness implicitly. God's separation from sin is so complete he cannot even be tempted or induced to sin. Thus, God's supreme holiness involves total detachment from moral evil.

9. *1 Pet. 1:15-16*[39]

This text presents God's holiness as the pattern for Christian holiness. Clearly, God's holiness is his moral purity. God stands devoted to his own glory in a world that despises him. So also, Christians should be devoted to live for God's glory. God is morally separate from this wicked world. So also, his spiritual children must avoid the corrupting influence of sinners.

10. *1 John 3:3*[40]

This text also stresses the correspondence of Christian moral purity with God's. Those that hope to see Christ and be like him purify themselves from every stain of remaining sin. Our immaculate Savior is the pattern of our holiness. When we see him, we too will be impeccably dedicated to God's honor and absolutely free of all moral contamination.

Conclusion: God's holiness is eternal moral purity, moral supremacy, and absolute impeccability. God always was supremely devoted to his own glory and infinitely immaculate. In relation to creatures God alone has moral purity and devotion to his glory that are infinite, eternal, unchangeable, self-existent, and ideal. In relation to sinners God's moral purity and devotion to his glory separate from and oppose all sin. Now I collate biblical support:

> God's holiness is: from eternity, his eternal moral purity, which is his supreme separateness and immaculateness;[1] upon creation, his moral supremacy, which separates him from and exalts him above all creatures and so-called gods;[2] and upon sin, his absolute impeccability, which separates him from and sets him vehemently against all sin.[3]

1. Isa. 57:15; Hab. 1:9; Rev. 16:5
2. Exod. 15:11; 1 Sam. 2:2; Job 4:18, 15:15, 25:5; Isa. 40:25; Rev. 15:4
3. Josh. 24:19; Job 4:17; Ps. 5:4-6; Hab. 1:13; 2 Cor. 6:16-7:1; Eph. 4:24; Heb. 7:26, 12:10; James 1:13; 1 Pet. 1:15, 16; 1 John 3:3

---

[38] *James 1:13*: Let no man say when he is tempted, I am tempted of God; for God can not be tempted with evil, and he himself tempts no man

[39] *1 Pet. 1:15-16*: but like as he who called you is holy, be ye yourselves also holy in all manner of living; because it is written, You shall be holy; for I am holy

[40] *1 John 3:3*: And every one that has this hope set on him purifies himself, even as he is pure

II. The Manifold Display of God's Holiness

Concerning this display I recommend Charnock and Gill. Charnock unfolds God's holiness as Creator, Lawgiver, and Redeemer.[41] Gill shows how each Person of the Trinity displays God's holiness.[42] All God's works display his moral purity and virtue.[43] I develop its display in *creation*, in *special revelation*, in *redemption* from Egypt and from sin, and in *damnation*.

A. The Display of God's Holiness in Creation

When God created the universe and all things in it, he displayed his moral purity in his creative work. Scripture features this display in his entire creation, in his angels, and in man.

1. All creation displays God's holiness.[44]

God creates everything for his own glory: "for of him, and through him, and *unto him* are all things" (Rom. 11:36). Therefore, the purpose of all creation displays divine holiness. It displays his ultimate devotion to his own glory. This calls on every moral being to praise their holy Creator.[45]

2. The creation of angels displays God's holiness.

The creation of angels displays God's moral purity.[46] Originally every angel was morally pure. Even the devil once reflected God's moral purity. Angels that did not sin reflect the spotless moral purity of God.[47] The good angels ever remain totally dedicated to God's glory and totally free from all sin.

3. The creation of man displays God's holiness.

The creation of man, God's image, preeminently displays God's holiness. Angels have no material body. They are invisible. God created man as his living visible representation: "in the image of God made he him" (Gen. 1:27). Adam heart was preeminently devoted to God's glory and morally immaculate. Further, man is visible. Thus, Adam and Eve displayed God's

---

[41] Charnock, *Existence and Attributes*, 461-473

[42] Gill, *Body of Divinity*, 1:151-153

[43] *Ps. 145:17*: Jehovah *is* righteous in all his ways, and holy in all his works.

[44] *Isa. 6:3*: And one cried unto another, and said, Holy, holy, holy, is Jehovah of hosts: the whole earth is full of his glory

[45] *Rev. 4:8-10*: . . . Holy, holy, holy is the Lord God the almighty, who was and who is and who is to come . . . the four and twenty elders . . . shall worship . . . saying, You are worthy, our Lord and our God, to receive the glory and the honor and the power, for you did create all things, and because of your will they were and were created

[46] *Mark 8:38*: he comes in the glory of his Father with the holy angels (also: Acts 10:22; Rev. 14:10)

[47] 2 Pet. 2:4; Jude 6

holiness visibly. Further, as God patterned the original humanity after himself, so also his new creation of man restores what sin defaced. Christians, as God's new creation, reflect God's commitment to his own glory and separateness from sin.[48]

B. The Display of God's Holiness in Special Revelation

Special revelation especially displays God's holiness in Scripture, in God's law, and in his gospel.

1. Scripture displays God's holiness.

Scripture is preeminently dedicated to God's glory and totally free from moral contamination.[49] The authors of Old[50] and New[51] Testaments are set apart for God's glory. Every word of Scripture is pure truth.[52] Every word is absolutely reliable, completely without error, and incapable of falsehood. Holy Scripture enlightens about living by faith for God's honor and glory.[53]

2. God's law, the Decalogue, displays God's holiness

God's moral law, the Decalogue, defines the duty all mankind. It displays his supreme purity. It is totally dedicated his glory and absolutely opposed to all sin.[54] It gives light in a world darkened by sin.[55]

3. God's gospel displays God's holiness.

Similarly, God's gospel defines God's revealed will concerning salvation from sin. Peter warns about those who turn from its "holy" requirement.[56]

---

[48] *Eph. 4:24*: and put on the new man, that after God has been created in righteousness and holiness of truth

[49] *Rom. 1:2*: the holy scriptures

[50] *Luke 1:70*: As he spoke by the mouth of his holy prophets, which have been since the world began (also: Acts 3:21; 2 Pet. 1:21; Rev. 18:20, 22:6)

[51] *Eph. 3:5*: Which in other ages was not made known unto the sons of men, as it is now revealed unto his holy apostles and prophets by the Spirit

[52] *Ps. 12:6*: The words of Jehovah are pure words; as silver tried in a furnace on the earth, purified seven times

[53] *2 Tim. 3:15*: And that from a child you have known the holy scriptures, which are able to make you wise unto salvation through faith which is in Christ Jesus.

[54] *Rom. 7:12*: the law is holy, and the commandment holy, righteous, and good.

[55] *Ps. 19:8*: the commandment of Jehovah is pure, enlightening the eyes

[56] *2 Pet. 2:20-21*: For if, after they have escaped the defilements of the world through the knowledge of the Lord and Saviour Jesus Christ, they are again entangled therein and overcome, the last state is become worse with them than the first. 21 For it were better for them not to have known the way of righteousness, than, after knowing it, to turn back from the holy commandment delivered unto them

The gospel is holy because it is completely devoted to God's glory and opposed to all sin.

C. The Display of God's Holiness in Redemption from Egypt

Scripture highlights five ways that the redemption of Hebrew Israel displays his holiness: his covenant commitment to them, their separation from the nations, his special presence with them, his jealousy over their idolatry, and their restoration from captivity.

1. God's covenant commitment to Hebrew Israel displays his holiness.

God's sworn commitment to Abraham and his posterity is holy.[57] It is wholly dedicated to God's glory. When he redeemed Israel from Egypt and brought them to the land of Canaan, he fulfilled this holy promise.[58] He revealed his holy name.[59] Thus, his covenant promises to Abraham and his posterity, framed in love and fulfilled in faithfulness, display God's supreme dedication to his own glory.

2. God's separation of Hebrew Israel from the nations displays his holiness.

God displays his holiness in his unique relationship with his people. The holy God is separate from the world of sinners. He sets his people apart from sinful nations and dedicates Israel supremely to his own glory as his special possession.[60] Thus he makes them "holy" unto himself. He joins himself in covenant loyalty to them alone. Therefore, he calls them to serve him alone. He calls them to a lifestyle separate from the ways of wicked nations.[61] He even calls them to be separate from sinners in their dress and diet.[62] Thus, he displays his separateness from sinners and dedication to his own glory.

---

[57] *Luke 1:72-73*: To perform the mercy *promised* to our fathers, and to remember his holy covenant; the oath that he swore to Abraham our father

[58] *Ps. 105:42*: For he remembered his holy promise, *and* Abraham his servant.

[59] *Ps. 111:9*: He has sent redemption unto his people; he has commanded his covenant for ever: holy and reverend is his name

[60] *Lev. 20:26*: And you shall be holy unto me: for I, Jehovah, am holy, and have set you apart from the peoples, that you should be mine

[61] *Lev. 19:2*: Speak unto all the congregation of the children of Israel, and say unto them, You shall be holy: for I Jehovah your God *am* holy

[62] *Lev. 11:44-45*: For I am Jehovah your God: sanctify yourselves therefore, and you be holy; for I am holy: neither shall you defile yourselves with any manner of creeping thing that moves upon the earth. For I am Jehovah that brought you up out of the land of Egypt, to be your God: you shall therefore be holy, for I am holy

3. God's special presence with Hebrew Israel displays his holiness.

In grace, mercy, and forbearance the holy God manifests his special presence with his people.[63] The place of his special presence is his temple, Zion. His temple is holy. It excludes the wicked nations.[64] Those that walk uprightly abide there.[65] It is dedicated to his glory. There his people bless and worship him.[66] Thus, his holy temple displays his holiness.[67] It is a tremendous blessing to witness this profound display.[68] It satisfies his people spiritually and brings them great joy.[69]

4. God's jealousy over idolatry in Hebrew Israel displays his holiness.

God displays his holiness by his opposition to the idolatry and immorality of his people.[70] Idolatry provokes the jealousy of the holy God who stands vehemently opposed to all sin. His people cannot serve both Jehovah and other gods because the Lord is wholly dedicated to his own glory. In the wilderness he dwells outside the camp so that he will not consume them for rebellion and unbelief. When they profane his worship, in his jealousy he consumes them in their sin.[71] This elicits fear and awe. Therefore, God's holiness calls his people to worship him alone, only in the manner he prescribes in his Word.

---

[63] *Ps. 5:7*: But as for me, I will come *into* your house in the multitude of your mercy: *and* in your fear will I worship toward your holy temple

[64] *Ps. 24:3*: Who shall ascend into the hill of Jehovah? or who shall stand in his holy place? 4 He that has clean hands, and a pure heart; who has not lifted up his soul unto falsehood, and has not sworn deceitfully.

[65] *Ps. 15:1-2*: A Psalm of David. Jehovah, who shall abide in your tabernacle? Who shall dwell in your holy hill? 2 He that walks uprightly, and works righteousness, and speaks truth in his heart

[66] *Ps. 138:2*: I will worship toward your holy temple, and praise your name for your lovingkindness and for your truth: for you have magnified your word above all your name

[67] *Ps. 99:9*: Exalt Jehovah our God, and worship at his holy hill; for Jehovah our God *is* holy.

[68] *Ps. 65:4*: Blessed *is the man whom* you choose, and cause to approach *unto you, that* he may dwell in your courts: we shall be satisfied with the goodness of your house, *even* of your holy temple

[69] *Ps. 46:4*: *There is* a river, the streams whereof shall make glad the city of God, the holy *place* of the tabernacles of the most High.

[70] *Josh. 24:19*: And Joshua said unto the people, you cannot serve Jehovah; for he is a holy God; he is a jealous God; he will not forgive your transgression nor your sins

[71] *1 Sam. 6:19-20*: And he smote of the men of Beth-shemesh, because they had looked into the ark of Jehovah, he smote of the people seventy men, *and* fifty thousand men; and the people mourned, because Jehovah had smitten the people with a great slaughter. 20 And the men of Beth-shemesh said, Who is able to stand before Jehovah, this holy God?

5. God's restoration of Hebrew Israel from captivity displays his holiness.

God displays his holiness when delivers a remnant of his people from captivity.[72] Their restoration displays "his jealousy for his holy name." He frees them from the oppression of the wicked. This displays his strong opposition to sin. Further, he brings his people back to Canaan in fulfillment of his promise to David to perpetuate his throne.[73] When he keeps his word, he displays his dedication to his own purposes and glory. He displays his moral purity and virtue: "once I have sworn *by my holiness*: I will not lie unto David." This text confirms that when God swears by his holiness, he swears by his moral purity, in virtue of which he cannot and will not lie. This affords great comfort and hope to his people. It elicits joyful adoration and praise (Ps. 106:47).[74]

D. *The Display of God's Holiness in Redemption from Sin*

We consider this display in the accomplishment, application, and completion of redemption.

1. The accomplishment of redemption from sin displays God's holiness.

The immaculate incarnation of the Son displays God's moral purity and devotion to his own honor and glory.[75] The sinless life of Christ displays divine holiness.[76] When God pours out his wrath upon Christ on the cross to atone for sin, Christ enters the "holy place."[77] This displays, to the uttermost, God's absolute devotion to his own honor and glory and his vehement opposition to sin.

2. The application of redemption from sin displays God's holiness.

God applies redemption from sin both individually in the Christian life and corporately in the Christian church. He displays his holiness when he renews, fellowships with, and preserves his people in Christ.

---

[72] *Ezek. 39:25*: Therefore, thus says the Lord Jehovah: Now I will bring back the captivity of Jacob, and have mercy on the whole house of Israel; and I will be jealous for my holy name.

[73] *Ps. 89:34-6*: My covenant I will not break, nor alter the thing that is gone out of my lips. Once I have sworn by my holiness: I will not lie unto David. His seed shall endure forever, and his throne as the sun before me

[74] *Ps. 106:47*: Save us, O Jehovah our God, and gather us from among the nations, to give thanks unto your holy name, and to triumph in your praise

[75] *Luke 1:49*: For he that is mighty has done to me great things; and holy is his name

[76] *Heb. 7:26*: For such a high priest became us, holy, guileless, undefiled, separated from sinners, and made higher than the heavens.

[77] *Heb. 9:12*: Neither by the blood of goats and calves, but by his own blood he *entered in once into the holy place*, having obtained eternal redemption *for us*

a. God's moral renewal of his people in Christ displays his holiness.

The Christian life is a "holy calling." It is a life of dedication to God's glory and separateness from sin.[78] Thus, God displays his holiness in the moral renewal of Christians at conversion[79] and throughout the Christian life.[80] This calls us to imitate God's moral purity.[81] It calls us to strive for nothing less than the sinless perfection of Christ.[82] It calls us to a life of wholehearted consecration to God.[83] In this way Christians display God's dedication to his own glory and his aversion to all sin. Further, God morally renews the entire society of his people so that they are a holy priesthood[84] and spiritual nation.[85] In virtue of this corporate renewal Christian churches also display God's holiness. They "show forth the excellences of him who called" them "out of darkness into his marvelous light."

b. God's fellowship with his people in Christ displays his holiness.

God displays his holiness in communion with his people in Christ. At Pentecost by his Spirit he dwells with his people, after he has purged them of the wicked and washed them in the blood of Christ. Thus, he makes his people his temple[86] and walks among them by his Holy Spirit.[87] Thus, all his people are priests, called to draw near to him in the holy place of his special

---

[78] *2 Tim. 1:9*: Who saved us, and called *us* with an holy calling, not according to our works, but according to his own purpose and grace, which was given us in Christ Jesus before the world began

[79] *Eph. 4:24*: and put on the new man, that after God has been created in righteousness and holiness of truth

[80] *Heb. 12:10*: For they indeed for a few days chastened us as seemed good to them; but he for our profit, that we may be partakers of his holiness

[81] *1 Pet. 1:15-16*: but like as he who called you is holy, yourselves also be holy in all manner of living; because it is written, You shall be holy; for I am holy

[82] *1 John 3:3*: And every one that has this hope set on him purifies himself, even as he is pure.

[83] *Rom. 12:1*: I beseech you therefore, brethren, by the mercies of God, that ye present your bodies a living sacrifice, holy, acceptable unto God, *which is* your reasonable service.

[84] *1 Pet. 2:5*: Ye also, as lively stones, are built up a spiritual house, an holy priesthood, to offer up spiritual sacrifices, acceptable to God by Jesus Christ.

[85] *1 Pet. 2:9*: But ye *are* a chosen generation, a royal priesthood, an holy nation, a peculiar people; that ye should shew forth the praises of him who hath called you out of darkness into his marvellous light:

[86] *1 Cor. 3:17*: If any man defile the temple of God, him shall God destroy; for the temple of God is holy, which *temple* you are

[87] *Eph. 2:21-22*: In whom all the building fitly framed together groweth unto an holy temple in the Lord: 22 in whom ye also are builded together for a habitation of God in the Spirit

presence to offer spiritual sacrifices.[88] Thus, the reverence and exuberance of Christian worship display God's holiness. Acceptable worship is God-centered, devoted to God's glory. Thus it displays humility and contrition.[89] Thus, it is profoundly reverent.[90] When men lose sight of God's holiness, their worship deteriorates into a circus. They center on their own entertainment rather than on God. They address the High and Holy One as if they were speaking to a common and lowly man. Yet, God-centered worship is also joyful and exuberant, because divine holiness makes his saints glad.[91] Thus, God's holiness calls the churches remain pure. It calls them never to receive unbelievers into membership, and, if they discover any in membership, to remove them.[92] God's holiness also calls his disciples to seek his face together in peace, hearts devoted to God's glory and hands unstained with sin.[93] God's holiness also calls Christians to engage in fellowship marked by separateness from worldly lusts.[94]

c. God's preservation of his people in Christ displays his holiness.

God also displays his holiness in the certain preservation of his saints. As their rock, their place of security, the Holy One protects and preserves his people.[95] He keeps us in spite of our weakness and waywardness, in the face of foes we could never defeat. He stands committed to preserve his church in every generation. He stands committed to preserve every Christian through every trial unto glory. Complete redemption of Christ's church and every Christian is as secure as his devotion to his own glory.

---

[88] 1 Pet. 2:5, 9

[89] *Isa. 57:15*: For thus says the high and lofty One that inhabits eternity, whose name is Holy: I dwell in the high and holy place, with him also that is of a contrite and humble spirit, to revive the spirit of the humble, and to revive the heart of the contrite

[90] *Heb. 12:28-29*: let us have grace, whereby we may render service well-pleasing to God with reverence and awe: for our God is a consuming fire

[91] *Ps. 33:21*: For our heart shall rejoice in him, because we have trusted in his holy name. *Ps. 105:3*: Glory in his holy name; let the heart of them rejoice that seek Jehovah.

[92] *2 Cor. 6:14-16:14*: Be not unequally yoked with unbelievers: for what fellowship have righteousness and iniquity? or what communion has light with darkness? 15 And what concord hath Christ with Belial? or what portion hath a believer with an unbeliever? 16 And what agreement has a temple of God with idols? For we are a temple of the living God; even as God said, I will dwell in them, and walk in them; and I will be their God, and they shall be my people.

[93] *1 Tim. 2:8*: I will therefore that men pray every where, lifting up holy hands, without wrath and doubting

[94] *1 Cor. 16:20*: All the brethren greet you. Greet one another with an holy kiss.

[95] *1 Sam. 2:2*: There is none holy as Jehovah; for there is none besides you, neither is there any rock like our God

3. The completion of redemption from sin displays God's holiness.

At death Christians attain the sinless perfection toward which they pressed throughout life.[96] When Jesus comes again, God will display his holiness climactically in the total eradication of sin from his people individually[97] and corporately.[98] Then his people will be completely dedicated to his glory and totally free from sin forever. This calls us to remain steadfast in a life of faith and godliness.[99]

E. The Display of God's Holiness in Damnation

God stands committed to punish the wicked.[100] When he redeems his people from Egypt, he displays his holiness in the judgment of the Egyptians.[101] When Jesus comes, God furnishes the ultimate display of his holiness by damnation of the wicked in the lake of fire.[102] Ironically, even God's enemies display his opposition to all sin and devotion to his own honor and glory. That awful display will last forever.

III. Seeming Contradictions Associated with God's Holiness

Scripture frankly acknowledges two seeming contradictions associated with the concept and display of God's holiness. The first difficulty stems from the tension between God's holiness and his relation to sin. The second difficulty arises from the tension between God's holiness and his union with his sinful people. Men have not imposed these tensions on the Bible. Rather, Scripture presses them on us.

A. The Seeming Contradiction Between God's Holiness and his Control over Sin

How can a holy God, completely separate from sin, decree sin in eternity and be sovereign over it in history? I commend Charnock's treatment of the

---

[96] Heb. 12:23

[97] *Eph. 1:4*: that we should be holy and without blemish before him

[98] *Eph. 5:27*: that he might present the church himself a glorious church, not having spot or wrinkle or any such thing; but that it should be holy and without blemish

[99] *Col. 1:22-23*: to present you holy and without blemish and unreprovable before him. 23 if so be that ye continue in the faith, grounded and stedfast, and not moved away from the hope of the gospel

[100] *Ps. 5:4-6*: For you are not a God that has pleasure in wickedness: Evil shall not sojourn with you. The arrogant shall not stand in your sight: You hate all workers of iniquity. You will destroy them that speak lies: Jehovah abhors the bloodthirsty and deceitful man

[101] Exod. 15:11

[102] Rev. 6:10, 15:4, 16:5

tension.[103] The prophet Habakkuk agonizes over this.[104] It troubles him greatly. He pours out his deep consternation before God. Wicked men swallow up those more righteous than they. How can a holy God ordain that? How can he watch that happen and hold his peace? How can he use sin to achieve his purposes without being contaminated by it? Why did he decree? Consider with me biblical testimony that states and resolves this tension.

1. The tension stated: Scripture declares both God's holiness and his sovereignty over sin.

Habakkuk unashamedly confesses God's holiness: "O Jehovah my God, my Holy One? . . . You that are of purer eyes than to behold evil, and that cannot look on perverseness." Yet, he also confesses his sovereignty over sin: "O Jehovah, you have ordained him for judgment; and you, O rock, have established him for correction." We must do likewise. We must not deny either his moral purity or his sovereignty.

2. The tension resolved

Consider with me three aspects of the biblical testimony to the resolution of this tension.

a. God holds the wicked fully accountable for their sin and fully avenges it.

In part resolution lies in the fact that a holy God holds wicked men fully accountable for their sin and thoroughly avenges it.[105] In the final analysis people don't get away with mistreatment of their fellow humans. The stone they roll on others eventually returns on their own heads, because God is holy.

b. God ordains wickedness to fulfill his own righteous purposes.

In part resolution lies in the fact that God has no fellowship with their evil designs. Rather, he ordains their wickedness to fulfill his own righteous purposes: "O Jehovah, you have ordained him for judgment; and you, O rock, have established him for correction." God ordains to use Chaldean ambition as a rod to correct his people for their idolatry and rebellion. The Chaldeans have evil designs, but God intends their conquest of Israel for good. Much mystery cleaves to God's method. We can't understand how

---

[103] Charnock, *Existence and Attributes of God*, 473-500
[104] Hab. 1:12-13: Are you not from everlasting, O Jehovah my God, my Holy One? we shall not die. O Jehovah, you have ordained him for judgment; and you, O rock, have established him for correction. You that are of purer eyes than to behold evil, and that cannot look on perverseness, wherefore do you look upon them that deal treacherously, and hold your peace when the wicked swallows up the man that is more righteous than he?
[105] Hab. 2:1-17

the Almighty, without contaminating his own infinite purity, uses sinful actions to achieve his good and holy purposes. Nonetheless, Scripture affirms explicitly and repeatedly that he does so.[106]

c. We must embrace by faith all Scripture teaches, even if we can't explain it.

Ultimately, resolution lies in our faith in God. We must believe whatever he tells us in his Word: "the righteous shall live by his faith" (Hab. 2:4). This emphasizes that the righteous, by trusting in God, believing his Word, and obeying it, will escape from God's wrath inflicted by means of the Chaldeans. Accordingly, we must trust God and believe whatever his Word says, even though we cannot explain logically how it can all be true. In the final analysis we cannot fully explain this seeming contradiction. We must believe that God is both holy and sovereign over sin because Scripture declares it. Thus, Scripture leads us back to the fence around the mystery.

B. The Seeming Contradiction Between God's Holiness and his Union with Sinners

How can a holy God join himself to a sinful people? Consider biblical testimony regarding this tension.

1. The tension stated: Scripture declares that his union with Israel causes profaning of his holy name

When God's people behave wickedly, they profane the holy name of their God among the nations.[107] God's enemies blaspheme his holy name because of his union with sinful people in covenantal loyalty.[108] How can a holy God join himself to a sinful nation without being sullied by their sin?

2. The tension resolved

Consider with me two aspects of the biblical testimony to the resolution of this tension.

---

[106] Gen. 50:20; Isa.10:5-7; Acts 2:23, 4:27-28

[107] *Ezek. 36:20-22*: And when they came unto the nations, whither they went, they profaned my holy name; in that men said of them, These are the people of Jehovah, and are gone forth out of his land. But I had regard for my holy name, which the house of Israel had profaned among the nations, whither they went. Therefore say unto the house of Israel, Thus says the Lord Jehovah: I do not this for your sake, O house of Israel, but for my holy name, which you have profaned among the nations

[108] *Rom. 2:24*: The name of God is blasphemed among the Gentiles because of you, even as it is written

a. God judges and punishes the sins of his people.

The resolution lies in the fact that God chastises his people and punishes their sins. When he sends judgments on them for their sin, he distances himself from complicity in its pollution. Thus, the child conceived from David's adultery dies in infancy,[109] and Israel and Judah go into captivity.[110] Ultimately, God vindicates his holy name when God the Son himself comes to earth and dwells with his people.[111] The cross displays God's vehement opposition to the sins of his people. Christ pacifies in his blood all God's wrath against our sin. God thus displays his purity in his forbearance and forgiveness of our sin.[112]

b. God eradicates the sin of his people.

The resolution also lies in the fact that God completely removes sin from his people. He removes our sin corporately and individually, not all at once, but through the process of progressive moral renewal. In each Christian this process begins at conversion, continues throughout life, and consummates at death or at the return of Christ. For the community of God's people this process begins with removal of unbelievers from the society of the saved under the new covenant, continues throughout the heavenly reign of Christ, and consummates when Jesus returns in glory.[113] This underscores the importance of gospel holiness for each Christian and each Christian church. If we live wickedly, God's enemies blaspheme his holy name and Word.[114] We should thus take to heart the solemn stewardship of union with God's holy name before the eyes of men and angels.[115]

---

[109] 2 Sam. 12:14

[110] Isa. 10:5; Hab. 1:12

[111] *Ezek. 39:7*: And my holy name I make known in the midst of my people Israel; neither will I suffer my holy name to be profaned any more: and the nations shall know that I am Jehovah, the Holy One in Israel

[112] *Rom. 3:25-26*: whom God set forth a propitiation, through faith, in his blood, to show his righteousness because of the passing over of the sins done aforetime, in the forbearance of God; for the showing, I say, of his righteousness at this present season: that he might himself be just, and the justifier of him that has faith in Jesus.

[113] Eph. 5:25-27

[114] Titus 2:5

[115] *1 Tim. 6:1*: Let as many as are servants under the yoke count their masters worthy of all honor, that the name of God and the doctrine be not blasphemed.

Conclusion: *Practical Application of God's Holiness*

I commend Charnock's treatment of what he calls "uses" for information, comfort, and exhortation.[116] We consider the practical application of God's holiness to sinners and saints.

A. *Practical Application of God's Holiness to Lost Sinners*

God's holiness calls sinners to face the fact that they can't serve God acceptably while they live in sin.[117] It calls them to face the certainty of his punishment.[118] It calls them to face the finality and propriety of his punishment.[119] It presses them to get right with God through Christ now, while they still have a chance to do so.[120] Death is coming. Christ is coming. When they come, it will be too late.

B. *Practical Application of God's Holiness to Christians*

1. *God's holiness calls Christians to humility and contrition before God.*

God's holiness uncovers our remaining corruption. The more we behold his purity and devotion to his honor, the more we see our uncleanness and self-centeredness. The more we dwell in his presence, the more we feel helpless and wretched.[121] Thus Job[122] and Isaiah[123] came to feel their remaining sin.

---

[116] Charnock, *Existence and Attributes of God*, 500-532: information (500-514), comfort (514-517), exhortation (517-532)

[117] *Josh. 24:19*: And Joshua said unto the people, you cannot serve Jehovah; for he is a holy God; he is a jealous God; he will not forgive your transgression nor your sins

[118] *Ps. 5:4-6*: For you are not a God that has pleasure in wickedness: Evil shall not sojourn with you. The arrogant shall not stand in your sight: You hate all workers of iniquity. You will destroy them that speak lies: Jehovah abhors the bloodthirsty and deceitful man

[119] *Rev. 16:5*: You are righteous . . . you Holy One, because you did thus judge: for they poured out the blood of saints and prophets, and you have given them blood to drink: they are worthy.

[120] *Rev. 6:10*: and they cried with a great voice, saying, How long, O Master, the holy and true, do you not judge and avenge our blood on them that dwell on the earth?

[121] *Isa. 57:15*: For thus says the high and lofty One that inhabits eternity, whose name is Holy: I dwell in the high and holy place, with him also that is of a contrite and humble spirit, to revive the spirit of the humble, and to revive the heart of the contrite

[122] *Job 4:17*: Shall mortal man be more just than God? Shall a man be more pure than his Maker?

[123] *Isa. 6:3, 5*: And one cried unto another, and said, Holy, holy, holy, is Jehovah of hosts: the whole earth is full of his glory . . . Then said I, Woe is me! for I am undone; because I am a man of unclean lips, and I dwell in the midst of a people of unclean lips: for my eyes have seen the King, Jehovah of hosts

2. God's holiness calls Christians to filial fear of God.

God's unequivocal devotion to his own glory elicits dread. We have meaning, purpose, and value only in relation to him and his design for us. He holds our life in his hands, to do with as he pleases, when he pleases, for his glory. Thus we should walk softly with him in filial fear.[124]

3. God's holiness calls Christians to reverent and joyous worship.

Divine holiness demands both reverence[125] and joy[126] in our worship. The display of his holiness in creation[127] and redemption[128] calls for songs of adoration and praise. Our infinitely holy God stands worthy of incessant praise from his creatures in heaven and on earth.[129]

4. God's holiness calls Christians to imitate to his holy character.

God's holiness mandates putting away sin. Imitating his holy character is essential evidence of true religion.[130] To this end he re-created us in his image[131] and chastens us in love.[132] We should imitate our Father because we love him and want to be like him[133] and in order to defend his good name.[134]

---

[124] *Rev. 15:4*: Who shall not fear, O Lord, and glorify your name? for you only are holy.
[125] *Heb. 12:28-29*: let us have grace, whereby we may render service well-pleasing to God with reverence and awe: for our God is a consuming fire
[126] *1 Chron. 16:10*: Glory in his holy name: Let the heart of them rejoice that seek Jehovah
[127] *Rev. 4:8-10*: ... Holy, holy, holy is the Lord God the almighty, who was and who is and who is to come ... You are worthy, our Lord and our God, to receive the glory and the honor and the power, for you did create all things, and because of your will they were and were created.
[128] *Ps. 106:47*: Save us, O Jehovah our God, and gather us from among the nations, to give thanks unto your holy name, and to triumph in your praise
[129] *Ps. 99:3, 5, 9*: Let them praise your great and terrible name: Holy is he ... Exalt ye Jehovah our God, and worship at his footstool: Holy is he ... Exalt ye Jehovah our God, and worship at his holy hill; for Jehovah our God is holy
[130] *1 John 3:3*: And every one that has this hope set on him purifies himself, even as he is pure.
[131] *Eph. 4:24*: and put on the new man, that after God has been created in righteousness and holiness of truth
[132] *Heb. 12:10*: For they indeed for a few days chastened us as seemed good to them; but he for our profit, that we may be partakers of his holiness
[133] *1 Pet. 1:15-16*: but like as he who called you is holy, be ye yourselves also holy in all manner of living; because it is written, You shall be holy; for I am holy
[134] 1 Tim. 6:1

5. God's holiness calls Christians to trust him and rely on him.

God is our Rock.[135] He has sworn to bless us in Christ. His honor stands bound to our welfare. Holiness moves him to protect and preserve us. Thus, we must trust him to fulfill his sworn commitments to us.[136] We must rely on our Holy One for help, security, and provision of all our needs in Christ.[137]

In conclusion, we should never forget the great importance of God's holiness. Let us dwell on it until we live every day devoted to his glory and longing to see him as he is and be like him.

---

[135] *1 Sam. 2:2*: There is none holy as Jehovah; for there is none besides you, neither is there any rock like our God
[136] *Ps. 89:35*: Once have I sworn by my holiness: I will not lie unto David.
[137] *Ps. 33:21*: For our heart shall rejoice in him, because we have trusted in his holy name

Part 3: The Nature of God | **501**

APPENDIX: PRIMARY BIBLICAL TERMS FOR GOD'S HOLINESS
OLD TESTAMENT TERMS

First, the primary word family for God's holiness includes three words and a phrase: (1) the noun, קֹדֶשׁ (qodesh), "holiness," or "holy"; (2) the adjective קָדוֹשׁ (qadôsh), translated, "holy," or "the Holy One"; (3) the phrase קְדוֹשׁ בְּיִשְׂרָאֵל (qadôsh bᵉyiśra'ēl), translated, "the Holy One of Israel"; and (4) the verb, קָדַשׁ (qadash), "to consecrate," "to honor as sacred." In general this word family conveys the notion of "separateness" or "apartness." These words most frequently refer to persons and things set apart for God, consecrated to him, or wholly devoted to a sacred purpose. They depict divine separateness some 110 times. *First*, the noun, *qodesh* depicts divine separateness at least these 31 times: Exod. 15:11; Lev. 20:3, 22:2, 32; 1 Chron. 16:10, 35, 29:16; Pss. 30:4, 33:21, 60:6, 89:35, 97:12, 98:1, 103:1, 105:3, 106:47, 108:7, 145:21; Jer. 23:9; Ezek. 20:39, 36:20, 21, 22, 39:7(2), 25, 43:7, 8; Amos 2:7, 4:2; Mal. 2:11. Scripture closely associates his holiness with the place of his special presence (Deut. 26:11, Isa. 63:15, and Zech. 2:13) with various phrases: "the habitation of your holiness"; Pss. 2:6: "the hill of my holiness," 5:7: "the temple of your holiness," 20:6: "heaven of his holiness," 47:8: "the throne of his holiness," 48:1: "the mountain of his holiness." *Second*, the adjective, *qadôsh*, "holy," "the Holy," or "the Holy One": depicts divine separateness at least these 27 times: Lev. 11:44, 45, 19:2(2), 20:26, 21:8; Josh. 24:19; 1 Sam. 2:2, 6:20; Job 6:10; Pss. 22:3, 99:3, 5, 9, 111:9; Prov. 9:10, 30:3; Isa. 5:16, 6:3(3), 10:17, 40:25, 57:15; Hos. 11:9; Hab. 1:12, 3:3. *Third*, the phrase, *qadôsh bᵉyiśra'ēl*, "the Holy One of Israel," or similar expression, depicts divine separateness at least these 35 times: 2 Kings 19:22; Pss. 71:22, 78:41, 89:18; Isa. 1:4, 5:19, 24, 10:20, 12:6, 17:7, 29:19,23, 30:11, 12, 15, 31:1, 37:23, 41:14, 16, 20, 43:3, 14, 15, 45:11, 47:4, 48:17, 49:7(2), 54:5, 55:5, 60:9, 14; Jer. 50:29, 51:5; Ezek. 39:7. *Fourth*, the verb, *qadash*, in the Niphal and Piel themes, depicts honoring God and his Name as sacred at least these 17 times: Lev. 10:3, 22:32; Num. 20:12, 13, 27:14; Deut. 32:51; Isa. 5:16, 8:13, 29:23(2); Ezek. 20:41, 28:22, 25, 36:23, 38:16, 23, 39:27.

A second word family for God's holiness includes the noun טָהוֹר (tahôr), translated "pure," "clean"; and the verb טָהֵר (tahēr), translated "cleanse," "make pure." This word family signifies to be clear, unalloyed, unadulterated, uncontaminated. These words usually refer to ceremonial cleanness or chemical purity. Occasionally, they depict moral purity (Ps. 51:7, 10; Prov. 15:26, 20:9, 22:11; Ezek. 36:25). The noun, *tahôr*, depicts God's moral purity 2 times: Ps. 12:6, "The words of Jehovah are *pure* words"; and Hab. 1:13: "you are of *purer* eyes than to behold evil." The verb, tahēr, depicts it once: Job 4:17, "Shall a man *be* more *pure* than his Maker?"

A third word family for God's holiness includes the verb בָּרַר (barar), translated, "purify," "polish," "make shining," the adjective בַּר (bar), "pure," "clear," and the noun בֹּר (bor), "cleanness," "pureness." These words often refer to physical purging, polishing, and purifying. They also depict moral purity among men (2 Sam. 22:21, 27; Pss. 18:26, 24:4, 73:1). The verb, *barar*, in the Hithpael theme, depicts God's moral purity 2 times: "with the pure you will *show yourself pure*" (2

Sam. 22:27; Ps. 18:26). The adjective, *bar*, refers to the purity of God's law once: "the commandment of Jehovah is *pure*, enlightening the eyes" (Ps. 19:8).

Fourth, the Old Testament also presents God's holiness by affirming his impeccability at least 2 times: Ps. 5:4: "evil shall not sojourn with you"; and Hab. 1:13: "that can not look on perverseness."

Fifth, general assertions of God's infinite perfection imply his holiness. At least 3 occasions of this are: Job 4:18, "his angels he charges with folly," 15:15, "the heavens are not clean in his sight," and 25:5, "the stars are not pure in his sight."

NEW TESTAMENT TERMS

The first word family for God's holiness includes the adjective ἅγιος (hagios), translated, "holy," the nouns ἁγιοτης (hagiotes) and ἁγιοσυνη (hagiosune), both translated "holiness," and the verb ἁγιαζω (hagiazo), "to set apart as sacred," "to honor as sacred." Much like the *qadôsh* family in the Old Testament, these words signify "separateness," "apartness." Peter's quotation of Lev. 19:2 (1 Pet. 1:15, 16) confirms the close connection of these two word families. These words often describe persons and things consecrated to God, devoted wholly to his service. They sometimes depict the moral purity of Christians, that is, their separateness from this sinful world and its wicked ways (2 Cor. 7:1). They depict divine separateness some 15 times. The adjective, *hagios*, translated "holy," depicts divine holiness at least these 8 times: Luke 1:49; John 17:11; 1 Pet. 1:15, 16; Rev. 4:8(3), 6:10. On several occasions it refers to Christ as "the Holy One" (Mark 1:24; Luke 4:34; Acts 3:14) and as God's "holy child" (Acts 4:27, 30). It most frequently (92 times) serves as a proper name for the Third Person of the Trinity, "the Holy Spirit." It also depicts the purity of God's revealed will (Rom. 7:12). The noun, *hagiotes*, "holiness," occurs only once, Heb. 12:10, where it depicts divine holiness. The noun, *hagiosune*, also translated "holiness," occurs 3 times. Twice it depicts the moral purity of God's people (2 Cor. 7:1, 1 Thess. 3:13). Once, it designates the Spirit of God (Rom. 1:4). The verb *hagiazo*, to sanctify, depicts the consecration God the Son for his redemptive mission 2 times: John 10:36, 17:19. It depicts honoring God and his Name as sacred **3** times: Matt. 6:9; Luke 11:2; 1 Pet. 3:15

A second word family for God's holiness includes the adjective ὅσιος (hosios), translated "*holy*", and the noun ὁσιοτης (hosiotes), translated "holiness." They signify what is intrinsically right, moral purity (Strong's Lexicon, p. 53). They depict God's holiness 3 times. The adjective, *hosios*, depicts God's holiness at least these 2 times: Rev. 15:4, 16:5. It twice depicts Christ as God's "Holy One" (Acts 2:27, 3:25). It also describes Christ's holiness as High Priest (Heb. 7:26). The noun, *hosiotes*, occurs only twice. In Luke 1:75 it depicts the holiness of God's people. Once, in Eph. 4:24, it depicts the new man, created in holiness after the image of God, and thus, at least implicitly, denotes God's moral purity.

Third, the adjective ἁγνος (hagnos), "*pure*", depicts divine moral purity once: 1 John 3:3.

Fourth, the New Testament also affirms God's impeccability at least **2** times: Titus 1:2; James 1:13.

Fifth, the New Testament presents God's holiness graphically: Heb. 12:29, "our God is a consuming fire."

Summary: These terms and idioms account for at least 121 references to God's holiness in the Old Testament, 22 in the New. Thus, in total, the Bible contains at least 143 references to divine holiness. If we add the 94 references to the "Holy Spirit" (2 OT + 92 NT), and the 8 to Christ's holiness, the total becomes 245. This emphasis, though significant, falls far short of that placed on God's goodness (825 references). Thus, we should present God's character biblically, and not as if there were four times as many references to his holiness in the Bible than to his goodness.

Topic 19. The Justice of God
"there is no respect of persons with God" (Rom. 2:11); "that he might himself be just" (Rom. 3:26)

Unit 3. The Justice of God

Introduction: Scripture testifies to the salient features of God's justice.[1] Accordingly, first, I expound a biblical *definition* of divine justice.[2] Second, I unfold its biblical *display* in creation, providence, redemption, and judgment.[3] Third, I present its biblical *defense*.[4] Finally, I conclude with its *practical application* to experiential religion.[5]

I. A Biblical Definition of God's Justice

Based on a survey of the biblical testimony, I offer the following definition of divine justice:

> *God's* justice is: God's supreme equitableness and conscientiousness: consisting in his executive justice, in which as Sovereign he diligently orders and administers every aspect of his kingdom; in his legislative justice, in which as Lawgiver he prescribes and requires only what is right and equal; and in his judicial justice, in which as Judge he gives equitable remuneration and retribution without prejudice or partiality.

This definition begins with God's absolute justice from before the foundation of the world: "God's supreme equitableness and conscientiousness." It also specifies three relative aspects of God's justice: his "executive justice," "legislative justice," and "judicial justice." I now enlarge and support this definition.

A. *God's Absolute Justice: supreme equitableness and conscientiousness*

God's justice is an absolute attribute, essential to his very being. If God were not just, he would not be God. When only God was, he was supremely equitable and conscientious. Supreme equitableness signifies God's absolute commitment to be what he deems right and to do what he deems right, equal, and impartial. Supreme conscientiousness signifies God's absolute commitment to be principled, rather than whimsical or capricious,

---

[1] I have appended to this topic a catalogue that summarizes my survey of this biblical testimony to God's justice.

[2] Deut. 32:4; Job 34:10, 12; Ps. 96:12, 13; Rom. 2:5, 6, 11, 3:26, 7:12; Col. 4:1; 2 Tim. 4:8

[3] Gen. 18:25; Ps. 96:12, 13; Eccles. 7:29; Rom. 2:5, 6, 3:25

[4] Job 8:3; Eccles. 3:16-18; Ezek. 18:29; Rom. 3:25, 6, 9:14, 19

[5] Gen. 18:25; Exod. 23:6, 7; Ps. 37:28; Isa. 30:18; Dan. 4:37; Rom. 2:1-16, 12:19, 13:1-5; Col. 4:1; 2 Tim. 4:8; 1 Pet. 2:23, 4:19; Rev. 16:5-7, 19:1, 2

and to act scrupulously, not underhandedly or heedlessly. Berkhof affirms God's absolute justice:[6]

> A distinction is generally made between the absolute and the relative justice of God. The former is *that rectitude of his nature, in virtue of which God is infinitely righteous in Himself,* while the latter is *that perfection of God by which He maintains Himself over against every violation of His holiness, and shows in every respect that he is the Holy One* . . . Justice manifests itself especially in giving every man his due, in treating him according to his just deserts. The inherent righteousness of God is naturally basic to the righteousness which He reveals in dealing with His creatures . . .

Scripture affirms that justice involves both equitableness and conscientiousness and attributes justice to God supremely.

1. Justice involves both equitableness and conscientiousness.

Justice necessarily involves conscientious impartiality. It involves judgment according to truth, whether the persons concerned are powerful or weak,[7] great or ordinary,[8] or rich or poor.[9] Thus, men wrest justice when they respect persons[10] and take bribes.[11] Justice treats citizens or alien residents equitably, delivers the oppressed, and never condemns or oppresses the innocent.[12] Justice also necessarily consists in equitableness regarding

---

[6] Berkhof, *Systematic Theology*, 74, 75

[7] *Lev. 19:15*: You shall do no unrighteousness in judgment: you shall not respect the person of the poor, nor honor the person of the mighty; but in righteousness shall you judge your neighbor

[8] *Deut. 1:17*: you shall not respect persons in judgment; you shall hear the small and the great alike; you shall not be afraid of the face of man; for the judgment is God's

[9] *Exod. 23:6-7*: You shall not wrest the justice due to your poor in his cause. Keep thee far from a false matter; and the innocent and righteous slay thou not: for I will not justify the wicked

[10] *Deut. 16:19*: You shall not wrest justice: you shall not respect persons; neither shall you take a bribe

[11] *Prov. 17:23*: A wicked man receives a bribe out of the bosom, to pervert the ways of justice

[12] *Jer. 22:2-3*: Hear the word of Jehovah, O king of Judah, that sits upon the throne of David, you, and your servants, and your people that enter in by these gates. Thus says Jehovah, Execute ye justice and righteousness, and deliver him that is robbed out of the hand of the oppressor: and do no wrong, do no violence, to the sojourner, the fatherless, nor the widow; neither shed innocent blood in this place

goods[13] and services[14] Thus, people wrest justice when they commit robbery[15] or use other people's services without compensation.[16]

2. God alone is just supremely.

Scripture declares that God is conscientiousness and equitable in all his ways.[17] He never judges with prejudice.[18] His balance and scales are always equitable.[19] He loves justice[20] and never perverts it.[21] Further, Scripture asserts that God never learned justice from anyone else, but rather, is essentially and eternally just.[22] Therefore, he alone is supremely just. Thus, his justice is the source of human justice.[23]

B. God's Relative Justice: executive, legislative, and judicial

My definition distinguishes three relative aspects of divine justice: executive, legislative, and judicial (or distributive) justice. Upon divine creation the world and all things in it, these facets of justice correspond to the branches of his government of the universe: "Jehovah is our judge, Jehovah is our lawgiver, Jehovah is our king" (Isa. 33:22). Unlike the separation of powers in America, divine government unifies all legislative, executive, and judicial power in the Supreme Lord of heaven and earth. Further, the Lord of the universe has no constitution outside of himself that defines and limits his power and authority. He himself is the living "constitution" by which he governs every aspect of his realm. Accordingly, God's relative justice is his

---

[13] *Lev. 19:35-36*: You shall do no unrighteousness in judgment in matters of length, of weight, or of quantity. Just balances, just weights, a just ephah, and a just hin, shall you have

[14] *Col. 4:1*: Masters, render unto your servants that which is just and equal

[15] *Isa. 61:8*: For I, Jehovah, love justice, I hate robbery with iniquity

[16] *Jer. 22:13*: Woe unto him that builds his house by unrighteousness, and his chambers by injustice; that uses his neighbor's service without wages, and gives him not his hire

[17] *Deut. 32:3-4*: For I will proclaim the name of Jehovah: ascribe ye greatness unto our God. The Rock, his work is perfect; for all his ways are justice: a God of faithfulness and without iniquity, just and right is he

[18] *Rom. 2:11*: for there is no respect of persons with God

[19] *Prov. 16:11*: a just balance and scales are Jehovah's

[20] Isa. 61:8

[21] *Job 34:10-12*: Therefore hearken unto me, you men of understanding: far be it from God, that he should do wickedness, and from the Almighty, that he should commit iniquity. For the work of a man will he render unto him, and cause every man to find according to his ways. Yea, of a surety, God will not do wickedly, neither will the Almighty pervert justice

[22] *Isa. 40:14:* With whom took he counsel, and who instructed him, and taught him in the path of justice, and taught him knowledge, and showed him the way of understanding?

[23] *1 Kings 3:28*: And all Israel heard of the judgment which the king had judged; and they feared the king: for they saw that the wisdom of God was in him, to do justice

supreme equitableness and conscientiousness as Sovereign, Lawgiver, and Judge.

Reformed theologians confess God's relative justice. Berkhof distinguishes two aspects of relative justice. He affirms what he calls, "rectoral justice":[24]

> There is first of all a *rectoral justice* of God. This justice, as the very name implies, is the rectitude which God manifests as the Ruler of both the good and the evil. In virtue of it He has instituted moral government in the world, and imposed a just law upon man.

He also affirms what he calls God's "distributive justice":[25]

> Closely connected with the rectoral is the *distributive justice* of God. This term usually serves to designate God's rectitude in the execution of the law, and relates to the distribution of rewards and punishments . . . It is of two kinds: (1) *Remunerative justice*, which manifests itself in the distribution of rewards to both men and angels . . . (2) *Retributive justice*, which relates to the infliction of penalties."

Similarly, Bavinck, distinguishes between God's legislative and judicial justice:[26]

> God is indeed the supreme Lawgiver, and the entire judicial order with respect to every sphere is rooted in him . . . Furthermore God also *maintains* that judicial order in every sphere of life. He who is justice in person and the source of all rights is also the 'arbiter and vindicator of justice.' His 'legislative justice' implies 'judicial justice.' . . . by reason of its very nature God's 'justice or righteousness' must needs be 'judicial justice'; hence, on the one hand, 'remunerative,' on the other hand, 'retributive.'"

Similarly, John Gill, after establishing God's eternal and absolute justice, treats what he calls God's "retributive justice," which he divides into "remunerative" and "punitive":[27]

> without this attribute, he would not be fit to be the governor of the world, and judge of the whole earth; his government would be tyranny . . . it is originally and essentially in God; it is in and of himself, and not of another; it is his nature and essence . . . God has no law without himself, he is a law to himself; his nature and will are the law and rule of righteousness to him . . . Retributive justice is a distribution either of rewards or punishments; the one

---

[24] Berkhof, *Systematic Theology*, 75
[25] Ibid., 75
[26] Bavinck, *Doctrine of God*, 222-223
[27] Gill, *Body of Divinity*, 153, 154

may be called remunerative justice, the other punitive justice; and both may be observed in God"

These Reformed theologians, athough they use some terms differently, clearly declare God's executive justice as Sovereign, legislative justice as Lawgiver, and judicial justice as Judge.

1. God's executive justice as Sovereign

In his executive justice "as Sovereign he diligently orders and administers every aspect of his kingdom." This depicts God's equitable and conscientious rule over his "providential" kingdom, which is the entire universe,[28] and over his "covenantal" kingdom, which is the society of his people.[29] Christ epitomizes his just rule over his people.[30] God's executive justice is the foundation of his throne.[31] It stems from his love of justice.[32]

2. God's legislative justice as Lawgiver

In his legislative justice "as Lawgiver he prescribes and requires only what is right and equal." Legislative justice includes the equitable rules and regulations by which he regulates conscientiously and impartially all his moral creatures. God's moral law, the decalogue, defines the moral duty of all mankind.[33] This law is just, holy, and good.[34] Legislative justice superlatively consists in the just laws, ordinances, and statutes that he enacts for his people as their Lawgiver.[35] All his civil statutes and ceremonial ordinances are just and right.[36] As a body of legislation, his law is singularly just.[37]

---

[28] *Dan. 4:37*: Now I, Nebuchadnezzar, praise and extol and honor the King of heaven; for all his works are truth, and his ways justice; and those that walk in pride he is able to abase

[29] *Ps. 37:28*: For Jehovah loves justice, and forsakes not his saints; they are preserved for ever: but the seed of the wicked shall be cut off.

[30] *Isa. 9:6-7*: his name shall be called Wonderful, Counsellor, Mighty God, Everlasting Father, Prince of Peace. Of the increase of his government and of peace there shall be no end, upon the throne of David, and upon his kingdom, to establish it, and to uphold it with justice and with righteousness from henceforth even forever

[31] *Ps. 97:1, 2*: Jehovah reigns . . . righteousness and justice are the foundation of his throne

[32] *Ps. 33:5*: For the word of Jehovah is right; all his work is done in faithfulness. He loves righteousness and justice: the earth is full of the lovingkindness of Jehovah

[33] Rom. 3:19, 20, 31

[34] *Rom. 7:12*: so that the law is holy, and the commandment holy, and righteous, and good

[35] *Neh. 9:13*: You came down also upon mount Sinai, and spoke with them from heaven, and gave them right ordinances and true laws

[36] Pss. 19:8, 9, 119:137, 138

[37] *Deut. 4:8*: O what great nation is there that has statutes and ordinances as righteous as this whole law which I am setting before you today?

3. God's judicial justice as Judge

In his judicial justice "as Judge he gives equitable remuneration and retribution without prejudice or partiality." Judicial justice involves his conscientious distribution of rewards and punishments to every individual and nation. It also refers to his conscientious distribution of reward and punishment to his people individually and corporately.[38] Accordingly, God is just in all his judgments in history.[39] His historical judgments of all the nations and peoples of the earth are just and right.[40] Further, on the last day, he is just in his judgment of all mankind.[41] Then in justice he will render to every person according to his work.[42] He will vindicate[43] and bless[44] the righteous in accord with their gospel integrity on earth. He will condemn and punish the wicked in accord with their sins on earth.[45]

Conclusion: collation of biblical support for this definition

I now collate this biblical support for my definition. God's justice is:

> God's supreme[1] equitableness and conscientiousness[2]: consisting in his executive justice, in which as Sovereign he diligently orders and administers every aspect of his kingdom[3]; in his legislative justice, in which as Lawgiver he prescribes and requires only what is right and equal[4]; and in his judicial justice, in which as Judge he gives equitable

---

[38] *Ps. 99:4*: You execute justice and righteousness in Jacob

[39] *Gen. 18:25*: That be far from you to do after this manner, to slay the righteous with the wicked, that so the righteous should be as the wicked; that be far from you. Shall not the Judge of all the earth do right?

[40] *Ps. 96:13*: before Jehovah; for he comes, for he comes to judge the earth: he will judge the world with righteousness, and the peoples with his truth

[41] *Ps. 9:7-8*: But Jehovah sits as king for ever: he has prepared his throne for judgment; and he will judge the world in righteousness, he will minister judgment to the peoples in uprightness

[42] *Rom. 2:5, 6, 11*: the righteous judgment of God; who will render to every man according to his works . . . for there is no respect of persons with God

[43] *1 Pet. 2:23*: when he suffered, threatened not, but committed himself to him that judges righteously

[44] *2 Tim. 4:8*: henceforth there is laid up for me the crown of righteousness, which the Lord, the righteous judge, shall give to me at that day; and not to me only, but also to all them that have loved his appearing

[45] *Rev. 16:5-7*: And I heard the angel of the waters saying, You are righteous, who are and who was, you Holy One, because you did thus judge: for they poured out the blood of the saints and the prophets, and blood have you given them to drink: they are worthy. And I heard the altar saying, Yea, O Lord God, the Almighty, true and righteous are your judgments.

remuneration and retribution without prejudice or partiality[5].

1. Deut. 32:4; Isa. 40:14; Rom. 2:11
2. Exod. 23:6, 7; Lev. 19:15, 35, 36; Deut. 1:17, 16:19; Prov. 16:11, 17:23; Isa. 61:8; Jer. 22:2, 3, 22:13; Col. 4:1
3. Pss. 33:5, 37:28, 97:2; Isa. 9:7, 33:22; Dan. 4:37
4. Deut. 4:8; Neh. 9:13; Ps. 19:8,9, 119:137, 138; Rom. 7:12.
5. Gen. 18:25; Ps. 9:7, 8, 96:13, 99:4; Rom. 2:5, 6, 11; 2 Tim. 4:8; 1 Pet. 2:23; Rev. 16:5-7

II. The Manifold Display of God's Justice

Gill unfolds the display of God's justice in providence and grace.[46] Similarly, I unfold its display in creation, providence, redemption, and the final judgment.

A. The Display of God's Justice in Creation

We consider how creation displays God's executive, legislative, and judicial justice.

1. Creation displays God's executive justice.

God as Sovereign creates man as his image. In justice he delegates to mankind authority to rule over the creatures: "let them have dominion over the fish of the sea" (Gen. 1:26, 28). In justice he appoints Adam as representative head of the human race[47] and as the head of his wife.[48] In justice he delegates domestic authority to parents.[49] Further, in justice he holds all human beings personally accountable for their own moral behavior.[50] Thus, in creation God displays his executive justice in the corresponding principles of individual accountability and representative solidarity.

2. Creation displays God's legislative justice.

In his justice as Lawgiver he obliges mankind to keep his law inscribed on the human heart.[51] In justice he commands Adam not to eat from the tree of the knowledge and attaches a just penalty to his legislation: "in the day that you eat thereof you shall surely die" (Gen. 2:16-17).

---

[46] Gill, *Body of Divinity*, 157-158
[47] Rom. 5:12-21
[48] Gen. 2:18, 23; 3:20; 1 Cor.11:3, 9; 1 Tim. 2:13
[49] Gen. 1:28
[50] Gen. 3:2, 3, 13
[51] Rom. 2:14-15

3. Creation displays God's judicial justice.

As Judge he assesses Adam and Eve. In justice he finds them "very good" (Gen. 1:31), and pronounces his blessing upon them (Gen. 1:28-30).

B. The Display of God's Justice in Providence

We consider how providence displays God's executive, legislative, and judicial justice.

1. Providence displays God's executive justice.

As Sovereign over this fallen world, prior to the flood in justice he appoints Cherubim as guardians of the garden of Eden and himself alone as avenger of blood.[52] After the flood, in justice he ordains the Noahic covenantal economy to structure life while the earth remains.[53] Within that framework, in justice he appoints man as avenger of blood: "Whoso sheds man's blood, by man shall his blood be shed" (Gen. 9:6). Upon the growth of the Noah's posterity, in justice he establishes the times and influence of every nation: "and he made of one every nation of men to dwell on all the face of the earth, having determined their appointed seasons, and the bounds of their habitation" (Acts 17:26). Upon the spread of nations, in justice he ordains civil government as his instrument to enact justice among men.[54]

2. Providence displays God's legislative justice.

After the fall, God as Lawgiver calls men to get right with himself through the gospel. In justice he requires for salvation repentance from sin and faith in himself as Savior.[55] Further, after the flood in justice he requires all Noah's posterity to obey his prescription for capital punishment and his restriction on eating flesh with the blood.[56]

3. Providence displays God's judicial justice.

As Judge of all the earth, he righteously judges all mankind, every nation, and every individual man. Immediately after the fall, he displays his righteous judgment when he inflicts his curse on Adam and Eve and their posterity.[57] When mankind corrupts the earth with violence, he displays his righteous judgment when he destroys all flesh with the flood and spares a

---

[52] Gen. 3:24, 4:15
[53] Gen. 8:22, 9:1-17
[54] Rom. 13:1-5
[55] Gen. 3:15, 4: 7, 26; Rom. 10:13; Heb. 11:4
[56] Gen. 9:4, 6
[57] Gen. 3:16-19, 24

remnant through Noah.[58] After that remnant of humanity in pride begins to build the tower of Babel, he displays his righteous judgment when he confounds their language and scatters them over the entire earth.[59] Further, consider how providence displays his righteous judgment of every nation. Upon the proliferation of the nations, he judges each society and kingdom in accord with their deeds.[60] Through Jeremiah he articulates the principle by which he displays his justice in his righteous judgment of the nations throughout history.[61] Finally, consider how providence displays God's righteous judgment of each man. The Judge of all the earth distinguishes the righteous from the wicked. Thus, Abraham successfully appeals to God's justice when he pleads that the Lord would spare the righteous in his dealings with Sodom.[62]

C. The Display of God's Justice in Redemption

God displays his justice when he redeems his people from Egypt, when he accomplishes redemption from sin, and when he applies redemption from sin the society of his people and to every believer in Christ.

1. The Redemption of Hebrew Israel from Egypt displays God's justice.

Under the old covenant he displays his justice in the society he redeemed from Egypt. He displays his executive justice when as Sovereign he selects Moses as his mediator and appoints judges to execute justice for his people.[63] He also displays it when he appoints a king after his heart, who establishes justice in his land.[64] He displays his legislative justice when as Lawgiver he personally declares the decalogue to his people and gives them a whole body of just statutes and ordinances to observe in the land.[65] He displays his

---

[58] Gen. 6:5-8

[59] Gen. 11:1-9

[60] Pss. 9:7, 8, 96:13

[61] *Jer. 18:7-10*: At what instant I shall speak concerning a nation to . . . destroy it; if that nation, concerning which I have spoken, turn from their evil, I will repent of the evil that I thought to do unto them. And at what instant I shall speak concerning a nation . . . to build and plant it; if they do that which is evil in my sight, that they obey not my voice, then I will repent of the good, wherewith I said I would benefit them

[62] *Gen. 18:23-25*: And Abraham drew near, and said, Will you consume the righteous with the wicked? Peradventure there are fifty righteous within the city: Will you consume and not spare the place for the fifty righteous that are therein? That be far from you to do after this manner, to slay the righteous with the wicked, that so the righteous should be as the wicked; That be far from you: Shall not the Judge of all the earth do right?

[63] Exod. 18:13-27

[64] 2 Sam. 8:15; 1 Kings 3:28

[65] Deut. 4:8; Neh. 9:13

judicial justice when as Judge he commends and blesses his people when they walk in his ways[66] and condemns and punishes them when they forsake him and rebel against him.[67]

2. The accomplishment of redemption from sin by Christ displays God's justice.[68]

Redemption from sin involves Christ's penal, substitutionary atonement and justification by faith: "whom he set forth to be a propitiation . . . that he might himself be just, and the justifier of him that has faith in Jesus." When God justifies believing sinners on the grounds of Christ's propitiation, he displays every aspect of his justice. He displays his executive justice when he appoints Christ as the Redeemer and representative Head of his redeemed, so that, in solidarity with them he acts for them and as them (Rom. 5:14,18, 19). He displays legislative justice when for atonement he requires from the Redeemer exactly what sin deserves, infliction of its total penalty, God's awful wrath; and when for pardon, he requires from the redeemed faith in their Redeemer: "propitiation, through faith, in his blood . . . that he might himself be just." He displays judicial justice when he imputes all the liability and sin of the redeemed to Christ and inflicts upon him all the penalty and wrath due to their sin. He also displays it when he imputes all the merit and satisfaction of the Redeemer to those who believe in him, pardons them, and declares them righteous: "him who knew no sin he made be sin on our behalf; that we might become the righteousness of God in him" (2 Cor. 5:21). Oh blessed justice! Our pardon from sin is just pardon. It abides the scrutiny of our conscientious God. As one fittingly said: "the opposite of justice is not mercy; the opposite of justice is injustice." In the Canons of Dort the Reformed fathers confirm this display of divine justice:[69]

> *Head 2: Art. 1*: God is not only supremely merciful, but also supremely just. And His justice requires . . . that our sins committed against His infinite majesty should be punished, not only with temporal but with eternal punishments, both in body

---

[66] Deut. 28:1-13

[67] Deut. 28:14-68

[68] *Rom. 3:23-26*: for all have sinned, and fall short of the glory of God; being justified freely by his grace through the redemption that is in Christ Jesus: whom God set forth to be a propitiation, through faith, in his blood, to show his righteousness because of the passing over of the sins done aforetime, in the forbearance of God; for the showing, I say, of his righteousness at this present season: that he might himself be just, and the justifier of him that has faith in Jesus.

[69] The Canons of the Synod of Dort: Head 2 "Of the death of Christ and the Redemption of men thereby": Articles 1, 2.

and soul; which we can not escape, unless satisfaction be made to the justice of God.

Head 2: Art. 2: Since, therefore, we are unable to make that satisfaction in our own persons, or to deliver ourselves from the wrath of God, He has been pleased of His infinite mercy to give His only begotten Son for our Surety, who was made sin, and became a curse for us and in our stead, that He might make satisfaction to divine justice on our behalf.

Warfield also makes an astute observation about this display of God's justice:[70]

> It is the distinguishing characteristic of Christianity, after all, not that it preaches a God of love, but that it preaches a God of conscience.
>
> A somewhat flippant critic, contemplating the religion of Israel, has told us, as expressive of his admiration for what he found there, that, 'an honest God is the noblest work of man.' There is a profound truth lurking in the remark. Only it appears that the work were too noble for man; and probably man has never compassed it. A benevolent God, yes: men have framed a benevolent God for themselves. But a thoroughly honest God, perhaps never. That has been left for the revelation of God Himself to give us. And this is the really distinguishing characteristic of the God of revelation: He is a thoroughly conscientious God—a God who deals honestly with Himself and us. And a thoroughly conscientious God, we may be sure, is not a God who can deal with sinners as if they were not sinners. In this fact lies, perhaps, the deepest ground of the necessity of an expiatory atonement.
>
> And it is in this fact also that there lies the deepest ground of the increasing failure of the modern world to appreciate the necessity of an expiatory atonement. Conscientiousness commends itself only to an awakened conscience; and in much of recent theologizing conscience does not seem especially active.

3. The application of redemption from sin to Christ's saved society displays God's justice.

God displays his executive justice when as Sovereign he appoints his Son as Head of his church,[71] apostles to rule his church universal,[72] and elders to rule

---

[70] Benjamin B. Warfield, *The Person and Work of Christ*, (The Presbyterian and Reformed Publishing Co., 1970), 386

[71] Isa. 9:6, 7; Eph. 1:22, 23

[72] Acts 16:4; 1 Cor. 7:17

the church local.[73] He also displays executive justice when he appoints all his redeemed as his spiritual priesthood,[74] and when he invests each local church with authority to exercise church discipline in accord with his word.[75] He displays his legislative justice as Lawgiver when God incarnate personally declares his just requirements for his church and when he inspires the New Testament.[76] He displays judicial justice as Judge when he commends and blesses churches that keep his word, and reproves and chastens those that rebel.[77]

4. The application of redemption from sin to every believer displays God's justice.

God displays executive justice as Sovereign when he ordains the preservation of every believer in Christ through the furnace of affliction and persecution.[78] He displays legislative justice as Lawgiver when he requires his redeemed to love each other and keep his commandments.[79] He also displays it when he requires Christians to confess our remaining sin throughout our lives.[80] He displays judicial justice as Judge when he commends and honors his redeemed for true religion.[81] He also displays it when he reproves and chastens believers for our remaining sin.[82] Thus, he vindicates and honors Abraham.[83] Thus, he chastens Eli[84] and David.[85]

D. The Display of God's Justice in the Final Judgment

Judgment day displays God's executive justice. As Sovereign he appoints his Son as the Judge of the universe,[86] and his redeemed as judges.[87] Judgment day also displays his legislative justice. As Lawgiver, he requires

---

[73] Acts 14:23, 20:28; Heb. 13:17
[74] 1 Pet. 2:5, 9
[75] 1 Cor. 5:12, 13; 2 Cor. 2:6
[76] Matt. 18:15-20; 1 Cor. 14:37
[77] Rev. 2:1-3:22
[78] Ps. 37:28; Rom. 8:33-39; 2 Thess. 1:5, 6; 2 Tim. 3:12; 1 Pet. 2:20-23, 4:16-19
[79] John 13:34; 1 John 2:4-10
[80] 1 John 1:9
[81] Ps. 18:19-24; James 2:21-25
[82] 1 Cor. 11:30; Rev. 3:19
[83] Gen. 22:15-18
[84] 1 Sam. 3:13, 14, 18
[85] 2 Sam. 12:11-14
[86] Acts 17:30-31
[87] Matt. 19:28; 1 Cor. 6:3

all moral beings to bow to his Son and to confess his rightful authority over them.[88] Judgment day also displays his judicial justice. As Judge, he judges each man according to his works.[89] When Christ returns[90] he gathers all humanity before him for judgment.[91] Then with justice he condemns the wicked and punishes them with just retribution in eternal damnation.[92] Then with justice he comforts and commends the righteous and rewards them with the crown of glory that fades not away.[93] Even so come, Lord Jesus.

III. Biblical Defense of God's Justice

Scripture defends God's justice from charges that people level against it. We consider challenges to God's justice in creation, providence, and redemption that Scripture records and addresses.

A. Biblical Defense of God's Justice in Creation: The Solidarity and Individuality Challenge

Scripture affirms that God incorporates into his flawless system of justice both representative solidarity and individual accountability.[94] Some on this ground charge God with injustice:

> Ezek. 18:25, 29: Yet you say, The way of the Lord is not equal. Hear now, O house of Israel: Is not my way equal? are not your ways unequal? ... 29 Yet says the house of Israel, The way of the Lord is not equal. O house of Israel: are not my ways equal? are not your ways unequal? Therefore I will judge you, O house of Israel, every one according to his ways

God defends his justice. He asserts that anyone who uses solidarity to deny individual responsibility is unjust: "are not your ways unequal?" Today some also pit solidarity against individual responsibility. They take the other

---

[88] Rom. 14:10-12; Phil. 2:9-11

[89] *Rom. 2:5, 6, 11*: the righteous judgment of God; who will render to every man according to his works ... for there is no respect of persons with God

[90] *2 Thess. 1:6-9*: if so be that it is righteous thing with God to recompense affliction to them that afflict you, and to you that are afflicted rest with us, at the revelation of the Lord Jesus from heaven with the angels of his power in flaming fire, rendering vengeance to them that know not God, and to them that obey not the gospel of our Lord Jesus 9 who shall suffer punishment, *even* eternal destruction from the face of the Lord and from the glory of his might

[91] Matt. 12:36, 37, 25:31-46

[92] *Rev. 19:1-2*: After these things I heard as it were a great voice of a great multitude in heaven, saying, Hallelujah; Salvation, and glory, and power, belong to our God: for true and righteous are his judgments; for he has judged the great harlot, her that corrupted the earth with her fornication, and he has avenged the blood of his servants at her hand

[93] 2 Tim. 4:8; 1 Pet. 2:23

[94] Rom. 2:1-16, 5:12-21

extreme. They affirm individual accountability and disparage representative solidarity as unjust. These allege that since God holds each person responsible for his or her actions, everyone is his own Adam. They say it would be unjust for God to appoint Adam to act for us and as us, since we had no say in the matter. Yet, if representative solidarity in Adam is unjust, then representative solidarity in Christ is equally unjust. Then also justification by faith is unjust, and sinners have no hope.

B. Biblical Defense of God's Justice in Providence: The Blessing and Affliction Challenge

Scripture affirms that God in his just providence sometimes blesses the wicked with prosperity and ease and afflicts the righteous with suffering and persecution.[95] On this ground some struggle with God's justice.[96] We consider God's justice in the prosperity of the wicked and in the affliction of the righteous.

1. God's justice in the prosperity of the wicked

The psalmist agonizes over the prosperity of the wicked. He finds resolution when he meditates on their future: "until I went into the sanctuary of God, and considered their latter end. Surely you set them in slippery places: you cast them down to destruction. How they are become a desolation in a moment. They are utterly consumed with terrors" (Ps. 73:17-19). Don't be deceived by appearances. The prosperity of wicked people is short lived. After their few years of peace and ease on earth, suddenly, unexpectedly, God in justice casts them into an endless eternity of horrible torment in hell. We should not misjudge God and regard his longsuffering with the wicked as injustice.

2. God's justice in the affliction of the righteous

Job is a monument to divine justice in the affliction of his saints. His friends rightly resolved to defend God's justice in his affliction.[97] Yet they thought wrongly that Job's severe affliction proved that he was a hypocrite.[98] God sometimes afflicts believers very grievously to demonstrate, not their

---

[95] *Eccles. 3:16-18*: And moreover I saw under the sun, in the place of justice, that wickedness was there; and in the place of righteousness, that wickedness was there. I said in my heart, God will judge the righteous and the wicked; for there is a time there for every purpose and for every work. I said in my heart, It is because of the sons of men, that God may prove them, that they may see that they themselves are but as beasts

[96] Job 8:3, 34:10-12; Ps. 73:1-9, 13, 16-22; Eccles. 3:16-18, 8:11

[97] *Job 8.3*: Does God pervert justice? Or does the Almighty pervert righteousness?

[98] Job 8:4-7

hypocrisy, but their deep sincerity and integrity.[99] Thus, Scripture defends God's justice in the affliction of godly Job.[100] He appoints affliction for the godly to conform them to Christ and to increase their glory, honor, and reward in heaven.[101] Surely we should not misjudge God. We should never regard as injustice his bestowal, through affliction, of great spiritual honor on the righteous.

C. Biblical Defense of God's Justice in Redemption: The Sovereignty over Grace and Sin Challenge

Scripture affirms God's sovereignty over sin and grace. God is sovereign over sin. Yet, he holds sinners responsible for the sin that he decreed they would commit.[102] God is also sovereign over saving grace. He discriminates in the application of salvation. He does not dispense saving grace equally to every human being. Scripture records that on these grounds some charge God with injustice. Paul epitomizes the biblical testimony and response:

> *Rom. 9:14-20*: What shall we say then? Is there unrighteousness with God? God forbid. 15 For he says to Moses, I will have mercy on whom I have mercy, and I will have compassion on whom I have compassion. 16 So then it is not of him that wills, nor of him that runs, but of God that has mercy. 17 For the scripture says unto Pharaoh, For this very purpose did I raise you up, that I might show in you my power, and that my name might be published abroad in all the earth. 18 So then he has mercy on whom he will, and whom he will be hardens. 19 You will say then unto me, Why does he still find fault? For who withstands his will? 20 Nay but, O man, who are you that replies against God? Shall the thing formed say to him that formed it, Why did you make me thus?

Scripture responds with two simple truths. First, regarding sovereign grace, Paul says that no sinner deserves salvation: "he has mercy on whom he will, and whom he will he hardens." Second, regarding God's sovereignty over sin, Paul simply says that God is not accountable to men: "nay but, O man, who are you that replies against God?" Whenever people charge God with injustice regarding their sin, they forget that he is God, and they only fallen human beings.

---

[99] Job 1:22, 2:3, 10

[100] *Job 34:10-12*: far be it from God, that he should do wickedness, and from the Almighty, that he should commit iniquity. For the work of a man will he render unto him, and cause every man to find according to his ways. Yea, of a surety, God will not do wickedly, neither will the Almighty pervert justice

[101] Matt. 5:11, 12; Acts 5:41; 1 Pet. 2:20-21, 4:13-16

[102] Acts 2:23, 4:27-28

Conclusion: *Practical Application of God's Justice*

I conclude by applying God's justice practically to sinners and saints.

A. *Practical Application of God's Justice to Lost Sinners*

God's justice calls all lost sinners everywhere to repentance.[103] No sinner can escape God's just judgment.[104] Thus, people should not misread his forbearance or despise it.[105] Lost sinners should not count on receiving special treatment from God based on their heritage, or religious privileges, or parental training. God judges everyone, without respect of persons, by gospel standards, according to their deeds. Therefore, every sinner should get right with him, immediately, by repentance from sin and faith in Jesus.

B. *Practical Application of God's Justice to Christians*

I now briefly summarize seven ways that God's justice applies to Christians.

1. *Christians should reflect God's justice.*

We should reflect God's justice in our personal relations and financial dealings. We should put away partiality and prejudice. We should put away robbery and oppression.[106] We should put on equitableness and conscientiousness in all our ways.[107]

2. *Christians should revere God's justice.*

God's justice should move us to fear the Lord and depart from all evil.[108] We should live conscientiously always, knowing that we will give account to a conscientious and impartial Father.[109]

---

[103] *Acts 17:30-31*: now he commands men that they should all everywhere repent: inasmuch as he has appointed a day in which he will judge the world in righteousness by the man whom he has ordained

[104] *Rom. 2:3*: And do you reckon this, O man, who judges them that practice such things, and does the same, that you will escape the judgment of God?

[105] Eccles. 8:11; Rom. 2:4

[106] *Exod. 23:6-7*: You shall not wrest the justice due to your poor in his cause. Keep you far from a false matter; and the innocent and righteous slay not: for I will not justify the wicked

[107] *Col. 4:1*: Masters, render unto your servants that which is just and equal; knowing that you also have a Master in heaven.

[108] *Ps. 37:28*: Depart from evil, and do good; and dwell for evermore. For Jehovah loves justice, and forsakes not his saints; they are preserved for ever: but the seed of the wicked shall be cut off

[109] *1 Pet. 1:17-19*: if you call on him as Father, who without respect of persons judges according to each man's work, pass the time of your sojourning in fear: knowing that you were redeemed . . . with precious blood.

3. Christians should hope in God's justice for remuneration.

We should look to God for remuneration for our conscientious service to him.[110] We should never lose heart, or think our labor vain, or our service unappreciated. When we suffer in his service in the path of godliness, we should hope for his just reward, and wait patiently for it.[111] We should imitate Christ's hope in God's justice.[112] Surely, even if people malign us, despise our ministry, and take us for granted, the Lord is not unjust to forget our sincere labor for his name.[113]

4. Christians should defer to God's justice for retribution.

We should put away a vigilante spirit. When people wrong us, we should never take justice into our own hands.[114] Rather, we should defer to the just retribution of God.[115]

5. Christians should use God's appointed means for exercising his justice on earth.

Yet, as occasion requires, we should utilize the means that God has appointed as the vehicles for his justice, both in the church[116] and in the state.[117]

6. Christians should appeal to God's justice in our intercessory prayers.

Even as Abraham pleads God's justice when he intercedes for Sodom,[118] so also, we should appeal to divine justice as we intercede for our family, our city, our country, and all our fellow human beings.

---

[110] *Isa. 30:18*: And therefore will Jehovah wait, that he may be gracious unto you; and therefore will he be exalted, that he may have mercy upon you: for Jehovah is a God of justice; blessed are all they that wait for him

[111] *2 Thess. 1:6-7*: if so be that it is righteous thing with God to recompense affliction to them that afflict you, 7 and to you that are afflicted rest with us, at the revelation of the Lord Jesus from heaven with the angels of his power in flaming fire

[112] *1 Pet. 2:23*: when he suffered, threatened not, but committed himself to him that judges righteously.

[113] 2 Tim. 4:8; Heb, 6:10

[114] *Rom. 12:19*: Avenge not yourselves, beloved, but give place unto the wrath of God: for it is written, Vengeance belongs unto me, I will recompense, says the Lord

[115] *Rev. 6:10*: How long, O Master, the holy and true, do you not judge and avenge our blood on them that dwell on the earth?

[116] Matt. 18:15-20

[117] *Rom. 13:2-5*: he that resists the power, withstands the ordinance of God . . . he is a minister of God to you for good . . . he is a minister of God, an avenger of wrath to him that does evil

[118] *Gen. 18:23-25*: And Abraham drew near, and said, Will you consume the righteous with the wicked? Peradventure there are fifty righteous within the city: Will you consume and not

7. Christians should bless and praise God for his justice.

Finally, we should ever praise God for his glorious justice. We should praise him for the display of his supreme justice in creation,[119] in providence,[120] in redemption,[121] and in the final judgment of mankind,[122] both in his vindication of the righteous[123] and in his condemnation of the wicked.[124]

---

spare the place for the fifty righteous that are therein? That be far from you to do after this manner, to slay the righteous with the wicked, that so the righteous should be as the wicked; That be far from you: Shall not the Judge of all the earth do right?

[119] *Ps. 33:3-5*: Sing unto him a new song; play skillfully with a loud noise. For the word of Jehovah is right; and all his work is done in faithfulness. He loves righteousness and justice: the earth is full of the lovingkindness of Jehovah

[120] *Dan. 4:37*: Now I, Nebuchadnezzar, praise and extol and honor the King of heaven; for all his works are truth, and his ways justice; and those that walk in pride he is able to abase

[121] *Rev. 1:5-6*: ... Unto him that loves us, and loosed us from our sins by his blood; 6 and he made us *to be* a kingdom, *to be* priests unto his God and Father; to him *be* the glory and the dominion for ever and ever. Amen

[122] *Ps. 6:12-13*: Let the field exult, and all that is therein; then shall all the trees of the wood sing for joy before Jehovah; for he comes, for he comes to judge the earth: he will judge the world with righteousness, and the peoples with his truth

[123] *Rev. 19:1-2*: After these things I heard as it were a great voice of a great multitude in heaven, saying, Hallelujah; Salvation, and glory, and power, belong to our God: for true and righteous are his judgments; for he has judged the great harlot, her that corrupted the earth with her fornication, and he has avenged the blood of his servants at her hand

[124] *Rev. 16:5-7*: And I heard the angel of the waters saying, You are righteous, who are and who was, you Holy One, because you did thus judge: for they poured out the blood of the saints and the prophets, and blood have you given them to drink: they are worthy. And I heard the altar saying, Yea, O Lord God, the Almighty, true and righteous are your judgments

APPENDIX: BIBLICAL TERMINOLOGY FOR GOD'S JUSTICE
OLD TESTAMENT TERMS

First, a key word for divine justice is מִשְׁפָּט (mishphat), which comes from the verb, שָׁפַט (shaphat), "to judge." Thus, *mishphat* describes the result or act of judging: a verdict, sentence, decree, or ordinance: or, in the abstract, justice. Accordingly, *mishphat* is translated with a variety of terms such as, "justice," "judgment," "ordinances," "right." It often refers to justice generically. This reflects on God's justice, since he is the root and ground of all justice. The following 25 texts clearly illustrate this general idea of justice: Gen. 18:19; Exod. 23:6; Deut. 16:18, 19, 24:17; 1 Kings 3:11, 28; Prov. 1:3, 2:8, 9, 12:5, 13:23, 16:8, 11, 17:23, 19:28, 21:3, 7, 15, 28:5, 29:4; Jer. 22:3, 13; Ezek. 18:5, 8, 9; Micah 6:8. Further, *mishphat* often refers to God's ordinances or "judgments" (Ps. 19:9), and to his acts of judging (Hab. 1:12). These also reflect on God's justice, since all his ordinances and acts of judging are just and right. *Mishphat* explicitly depicts God's virtue of justice at least these 46 times: Gen. 18:25; Deut. 1:17, 32:4; Job 8:3, 34:5,12, 37:23, 40:8; Pss. 9:7, 25:9, 33:5, 37:28, 89:14, 97:2, 99:4(2), 101:1, 103:6, 111:7, 119:84, 146:7; Isa. 1:27, 4:4, 5:16, 9:7, 28:6, 17, 30:18, 33:5, 40:14, 27, 42:1, 3, 4, 49:4, 51:4, 61:8; Jer. 9:24, 23:5, 3:15; Ezek. 34:16, 39:21; Hos. 2:19; Mic. 7:9; Zeph. 3:5; Mal. 2:17.

Second, the צָדַק (tsadaq) word family often conveys the broader significance of "righteousness." It sometimes especially depicts God's justice. This special bond stems from the fact that God alone is both the Supreme Standard and Arbiter of virtue and morality. The verb *tsadaq* stresses God's justice at least these 3 times: Exod. 23:7; Job 4:17; Ps. 19:9. The adjective, often substantive, צַדִּיק (tsaddîq), translated "justice," or "just," or, "righteous," features divine justice at least these 10 times: Deut. 32:4; Neh. 9:13; Pss. 119:137, 129:4; Isa. 45:21; Jer. 12:1; Lam. 1:18; Dan. 9:14; Zeph. 3:5; Zech. 9:9. The noun, צֶדֶק (tsedeq), translated, "righteousness," depicts justice generically in Lev. 19:15, 36; Deut. 1:16, 16:18, 20, 25:15; Prov. 1:3; Eccles. 3:16, 5:8; Jer. 22:13; Ezek. 45:10. It emphasizes divine justice at least these 15 times: Pss. 89:14, 96:13, 97:2, 98:9, 119:7, 62, 75, 106, 138, 144, 160, 164, 172; Isa. 11:4; Jer. 11:20. The noun, צְדָקָה (ts^{e}daqah), translated "righteousness," "justice," depicts justice generically: Gen. 18:19; Deut. 33:21; 2 Sam. 8:15; 1 Kings 10:9; Prov. 21:3; Isa. 56:1; Ezek. 18:27, 45:9. It features God's justice 8 times: Pss. 11:7, 33:5, 99:4, 103:6; Isa. 9:7, 28:17; Jer. 23:5, 33:15.

Third, the verb יָשַׁר (yashar): "to be straight," "even": most often depicts moral virtue generally: usually translated "upright": depicts God's justice at least these 4 times: Deut. 32:4; Pss. 19:8, 119:137; Neh. 9:13. The plural noun מֵישָׁרִים (mēsharîm), derived from *yashar*, is translated, "equity," or "justice." It at times depicts justice generically (Prov. 1:3, 2:9). It depicts God's justice at least 7 times: Pss. 9:8, 17:2, 75:2, 96:10, 98:9, 99:4; Isa. 45:19.

Fourth, the verb תָּכַן (takan), "to balance," or "equalize," translated, "to weigh," "mete out," "equal," depicts divine justice 9 times: Ezek. 18:25 (3), 29 (3), 33:17 (2), 20.

Fifth, the Old Testament presents justice in general with the idiom, *"respect of persons"* (Lev. 19:15; Deut. 1:17, 16:19; Prov. 24:23, 28:21). This idiom describes God's justice at least 2 times: 2 Sam. 14:14; 2 Chron. 19:7.

NEW TESTAMENT TERMS

First, the δικαιος (dikaios) word family often conveys the broader significance of "righteousness." The adjective *dikaios*, translated both "righteous" and "just," sometimes describes justice generically: Luke 12:57; John 7:24; Eph. 6:1; Col. 4:1; Phil. 4:8. It stresses God's justice at least these 10 times: John 5:30; Rom. 3:26; 2 Thess. 1:5, 6; 2 Tim. 4:8; 1 John 1:9; Rev. 15:3, 16:5, 7, 19:2. The adverb, δικαιως (dikaios), "righteously," describes God's justice once: 1 Pet. 2:23. Four nouns feature various facets of God's justice: δικη (dike), "vengeance," "judgment," twice: 2 Thess. 1:9; Jude 7; δικαιοσυνη (dikaiosune), "righteousness," once: Rev. 19:11; δικαιοκρισια (dikaiokrisia), "righteous judgment," once: Rom. 2:5; δικαιωμα (dikaioma), "judgment," once: Rom. 1:32.

Second, the word ισοτης (isotes), "equality," "equity," once defines justice generically: Col. 4:1. By implication, this text reveals the nature of divine justice. It draws an analogy between the heavenly Master and earthly masters: "Masters, render unto your servants that which is just and *equal;* knowing that you also have a Master in heaven."

Third, the New Testament also presents justice with the idiom, "respect of persons" (James 2:1, 9). This idiom describes God's justice 5 times: Acts 10:34; Rom. 2:11; Eph. 6:9; Col. 3:25; 1 Pet. 1:17.

In sum, Scripture uses these primary terms for God's justice 104 times in the Old Testament, 22 times in the New, a total of 126. If we take into account ancillary terms like ordinances, statutes, and judgment, and the broader use of righteousness, it places more emphasis on God's justice. This too falls short of the emphasis on divine goodness (825 references). It reminds us that we should present God's moral character in biblical categories and proportions.

Topic 20. The Faithfulness of God
"Great is your faithfulness" (Lam. 3:23)

Unit 4. The Faithfulness of God

Introduction: Scripture testifies to the salient features of God's faithfulness.[1] Accordingly, first, I offer a *biblical definition* of God's faithfulness.[2] Second, I unfold its *manifold display* in his works and Word.[3] Finally, I conclude with its *practical application* to experiential religion.[4]

I. A Biblical Definition of God's Faithfulness

The Old Testament highlights the close association of God's faithfulness and goodness.[5] The New Testament features its close association with his justice and holiness.[6] John Gill distinguishes God's truth, or veracity, from his faithfulness and expounds them separately.[7] We must not condemn this. Yet the biblical usage closely binds God's *veracity* to his *reliability*: "shall their want of faith make of none effect *the faithfulness* of God? God forbid: yea, let God be found *true*, but every man a liar" (Rom. 3:3-4). Accordingly, I expound his veracity and reliability together as aspects of his faithfulness. Based on a survey of the biblical terminology, I offer the following definition:

> *God's faithfulness* is God's supreme fidelity: consisting in his infallible veracity and truthfulness, whereby every word he speaks is truth; and in his unfailing reliability and trustworthiness, whereby he always keeps his word, whether promise, or threat, or prediction, and whereby he steadfastly maintains his work as Creator and as Redeemer.

This definition identifies God's absolute faithfulness, his "supreme fidelity," and two relative aspects of his faithfulness, his "infallible veracity" and his "unfailing reliability." I now expound and support God's *supreme fidelity*, *infallible veracity*, and *unfailing reliability*.

---

[1] I have appended to this topic a catalogue that summarizes my survey of this biblical testimony to God's faithfulness.

[2] Num. 23:19; Deut. 7:9; 2 Sam. 7:28; Ps. 33:4; Rom. 3:3-4; 2 Tim. 2:13; Titus 1:2; Heb. 6:18, 11:11; Rev. 19:11

[3] Deut. 7:9; Pss. 33:4, 89:1-5, 33-36, 96:13, 111:7, 119:90, 142, 151, 160; John 17:17; 1 Thess. 5:23-24; Rev. 15:3

[4] Deut. 7:9-11; Pss. 40:10, 89:1, 96:13, 143:1; Lam. 3:22-25; 1 Cor. 10:13; 2 Thess. 3:3; Heb. 6:17-18, 10:23, 11:11; 1 Pet. 4:19; 1 John 1:9; Rev. 15:3

[5] Deut. 7:9; Ps. 100:5

[6] Rev. 6:10, 15:3, 16:7, 19:2

[7] Gill, *Body of Divinity*, 1:159-162, 163-170

A. God's Supreme Fidelity

God's faithfulness is essential to his very being. If he were not faithful, he would not be God. When only God was, he was supremely truthful and trustworthy. Gill affirms God's eternal faithfulness:[8]

> It is essential to him, and without which he would not be God; to be unfaithful, would be to act contrary to his nature, to deny himself, 2 Tim. 2:13; an unfaithful God would be no God at all.

Gill cites the biblical affirmation God's eternal fidelity. Paul says that God "abides faithful" always.[9] In eternity, when only God was, he could never "deny himself." His faithfulness is independent of his creatures: "if we are faithless, he abides faithful." Paul also says that God "cannot lie."[10] He always perceives himself as he is in fact. He always relates to himself in perfect accord with what he knows he really is. First and foremost, God is true to himself. He can never deny that he is the only true God. He can never deny anything that he essentially is. He can never deny that he is infinite, eternal, unchangeable, self-existent, or ideal. He can never deny his supreme incorporeality, animacy, faculty, morality, or personality. Thus, God's promise, formed "before times eternal," is absolutely reliable. Thus, God's eternal faithfulness consists in his supreme fidelity to himself.

B. God's Infallible Veracity

In history God's supreme fidelity is his "infallible veracity and truthfulness whereby every word he speaks is truth."[11] From the dawn of history God spoke to mankind with special revelation. Now he speaks to all mankind in Scripture. When Christ returns, God will speak to all mankind in the final judgment. Thus, the biblical testimony to God's infallible veracity focuses on his verbal utterance, his written Word, and his Word spoken in judgment.

1. All God's verbal utterance is truth.

God's veracity means that his verbal utterance, spoken or written, is truth.[12] God has spoken at various times through various means.[13] The Word he

---

[8] Ibid., 1:163

[9] *2 Tim. 2:13*: if we are faithless, he abides faithful; for he cannot deny himself

[10] *Titus 1:1-2*: Paul, a servant of God, and an apostle of Jesus Christ, according to the faith of God's elect, and the knowledge of the truth which is according to godliness, in hope of eternal life, which God, who cannot lie, promised before times eternal

[11] Rom. 3:3-4

[12] *John 17:17*: sanctify them in the truth: your word is truth

[13] *Heb. 1:1*: God, having of old time spoken unto the fathers in the prophets by divers portions and in divers manners, 2 has at the end of these days spoken unto us in *his* Son

spoke to Adam was truth: "in the day you eat thereof you shall surely die." It proved to be true, even though the devil claimed it was false: "you shall not surely die." His covenant promises to Noah, Abraham, and David are truth.[14] The law he spoke from heaven to Israel is truth.[15] The gospel he spoke through his Son is truth.[16] It is God's Word[17] essential for salvation from sin.[18] All Christ's words are God's Word, because he is God the Word incarnate.[19]

Truth is in complete accord with fact and reality.[20] God cannot err because he perceives reality with infinite accuracy and precision. He can never be wrong or mistaken. Further, God cannot lie. He always communicates his perception of reality with absolute fidelity. He never deliberately misrepresents what he knows is true. Therefore, every word of God is true, and all his verbal utterance, collectively, is truth.

2. God's written word, Scripture, is truth.

Scripture embodies God's infallible veracity to us. It is the written Word of God. He breathed it from his mouth.[21] It can never become obsolete.[22] It can never be proved wrong.[23] The Old Testament is the embodiment of

---

[14] *2 Sam. 7:28*: And now, O Lord Jehovah, you are God, and your words are truth, and you have promised this good thing unto your servant

[15] *Ps. 119:142, 151, 160*: your law is truth . . . all your commandments are truth . . . the sum of your word is truth

[16] *Eph. 1:13*: having heard the word of truth, the gospel of your salvation

[17] *1 Thess. 2:13*: And for this cause we also thank God without ceasing, that, when you received from us the word of the message, *even the word* of God, you accepted *it* not *as* the word of men, but, as it is in truth, the word of God, which also works in you that believe.

[18] *2 Thess. 2:10, 12, 13*: they received not the love of the truth, that they might be saved . . . who believed not the truth, but had pleasure in unrighteousness . . . God chose you from the beginning unto salvation in sanctification of the Spirit and belief of the truth

[19] John 1:1, 14

[20] *Deut. 13:14*: then you shall inquire, and make search, and ask diligently; and, behold, if it be truth, and the thing certain, that such abomination is wrought in the midst of you *Deut. 22:20*: But if this thing be true, that the tokens of virginity were not found in the damsel

[21] *2 Tim. 3:16*: All scripture *is* given by inspiration of God, and *is* profitable for doctrine, for reproof, for correction, for instruction in righteousness:

[22] *Matt. 5:17-18*: Think not that I came to destroy the law or the prophets: I came not to destroy, but to fulfil. 18 For verily I say unto you, Till heaven and earth pass away, one jot or one tittle shall in no wise pass away from the law, till all things be accomplished.

[23] *John 10:35*: If he called them gods, unto whom the word of God came, and the scripture cannot be broken

truth.[24] Everything it says is true[25] and certain.[26] The New Testament is also Scripture.[27] It is the Word of Christ.[28] Thus, the Bible is God's Word, the written embodiment of God's veracity. When Gill expounds his veracity, he affirms this:[29]

> God is true in his written word; The Scriptures are the Scriptures of truth, even the whole of them, Dan. 10:21, they are given by inspiration from God, are the breath of God, who is the God of truth, and therefore are to be received, *not as the word of man, but as it is in truth the word of God*, 1 Thess. 2:13

3. *God spoken word on Judgment Day is truth.*

Christ will declare the truth about every human being when he judges every person according to his works.[30] His words will reflect reality accurately and comprehensively.

C. *God's Unfailing Reliability*

In history God's supreme fidelity also consists in his "unfailing reliability and trustworthiness, whereby he always keeps his word, whether promise, or threat, or prediction, and whereby he steadfastly maintains his work as Creator and as Redeemer." God's reliability especially relates to his Word and his works.[31] First, God always keeps his Word. His Word frames his reliability. He always does what he says he will do. He fulfills his Word exactly. Second, God always maintains and preserves his work. God displays his reliability in all his works.[32] He shows unfailing fidelity as Creator and Redeemer.[33]

---

[24] *Rom. 2:20*: having in the law the form of knowledge and of the truth

[25] *Ps. 19:9*: the ordinances of Jehovah are true, and righteous altogether

[26] *Ps. 111:7*: all his precepts are sure

[27] *2 Pet. 3:16*: as also in all *his* epistles, speaking in them of these things; wherein are some things hard to be understood, which the ignorant and unstedfast wrest, as *they do* also the other scriptures, unto their own destruction.

[28] *1 Cor. 14:36-37*: What? was it from you that the word of God went forth? or came it unto you alone? 37 If any man thinks himself to be a prophet, or spiritual, let him take knowledge of the things which I write unto you, that they are the commandment of the Lord.

[29] Gill, *Body of Divinity*, 1:162

[30] *Rev. 19:11, 13*: I saw the heaven opened; and behold, a white horse, and he that sat thereon called Faithful and True; and in righteousness does he judge and make war . . . and his name is called The Word of God

[31] *Ps. 33:4*: For the word of Jehovah is right; and all his work is done in faithfulness

[32] *Ps. 111:7*: The works of his hands are truth and justice

[33] Ps. 119:90; 1 Thess. 5:23-24

Gill affirms God's reliability in his Word and works:[34]

> he is the faithful Creator, and covenant-God and Father of his people; to whom they may safely commit themselves, and depend upon him for all mercies promised, both temporal and spiritual, 1 Pet. 4:19, 1 Thess. 5:23, 24; for the faithfulness of God chiefly lies in the performance of his word, which is certain, with respect to all that is spoken by him: for *hath he said, and shall he not do it? or hath he spoken, and shall he not make it good?* Verily he will, Num. 23:19, Luke 1:45

Conclusion: collation of biblical support

> *God's faithfulness* is: God's supreme fidelity:[1] consisting in his infallible veracity and truthfulness,[2] whereby every word he speaks is truth;[3] and in his unfailing reliability and trustworthiness,[4] whereby he always keeps his word,[5] whether promise,[6] or threat,[7] or prediction,[8] and whereby he steadfastly maintains his work as Creator[9] and as Redeemer.[10]

1. 2 Tim. 2:13; Titus 1:1-2
2. Rom. 3:3-4
3. 2 Sam. 7:28; Pss. 19:9, 119:142, 151, 160; John 10:35, 17:17
4. Deut. 32:3-4
5. Deut. 7:9; Ps. 89:33-36
6. Deut. 7:9; Heb. 11:11
7. Deut. 7:10
8. Num. 23:19
9. Ps. 119:90; 1 Pet. 4:19
10. 1 Thess. 5:23-24; Rev. 15:3

II. The Manifold Display of God's Faithfulness

I unfold this display in Scripture, creation, redemption, and the judgment.

A. Scripture Displays God's Faithfulness.

Scripture displays God's veracity and reliability. When God fulfills his promises, it demonstrates that his Word is true. Accordingly, we consider the infallible testimony and unfailing fulfillment of Scripture.

1. The infallible testimony of Scripture displays God's faithfulness.

Scripture is the testimony of the Triune God. In it the Father bears witness,[35] the Son bears witness,[36] and the Spirit bears witness.[37] Scripture is the word

---

[34] Gill, *Body of Divinity*, 1:163
[35] *1 John 5:10*: he that believes not God has made him a liar; because he has not believed in the witness that he has borne concerning his Son
[36] *Rev. 3:14*: And to the angel of the church in Laodicea write: These things says the Amen, the faithful and true witness.
[37] *John 15:26*: the Spirit of truth, which proceeds from the Father, he shall bear witness of me

of God the Father, Son, and Spirit.[38] God the Son is the "faithful and true witness." God the Spirit is "the Spirit of truth." God's words are wholly true and totally reliable in whatever they affirm. Thus, the Bible can never err, whether it addresses religious doctrine, or created reality, or human history. Thus, when we believe the Bible, we affirm God's veracity and reliability.[39] Conversely, when people reject any aspect of its testimony, they reject, not the words of men, but the witness of God. They call him a liar and impugn his character.

2. The unfailing fulfillment of Scripture displays God's faithfulness.

Scripture displays God's faithfulness when God fulfills his promises, threats, and predictions.

a. Scripture displays God's fidelity when he fulfills his promises and covenants.

God's displays his veracity and reliability when he keeps his promises, especially his oath-bound promises, or *covenants*: "the faithful God, who keeps covenant" (Deut. 7:9). He keeps his sworn promise of the Noahic covenant when he refrains from destroying the whole world with another flood.[40] He keeps the sworn promises of the Abrahamic covenant when he makes all his physical posterity, even Ishmael and Esau, into nations, when he redeems Israel from slavery in Egypt and gives them the land of Canaan,[41] and when he blesses all the nations, in Christ, with spiritual blessing.[42] He fulfills the sworn promises of the old covenant when he sends prosperity upon Israel, if they serve him only and obey him sincerely, and curses them when they forsake him and serve other gods.[43] He fulfills his sworn promises of the Davidic covenant[44] when he maintains his dynasty until the captivity and raises Christ from the dead to sit forever at his right hand on David's

---

[38] John 3:34, 17:17; 1 Cor. 2:13

[39] *John 3:33-34*: He that has received his witness has set his seal to this, that God is true 34 For he whom God hath sent speaks the words of God: for he giveth not the Spirit by measure

[40] Isa. 54:9-10

[41] *Neh. 9:8*: and made a covenant with him to give him the land of the Canaanite . . . to give it unto his seed, and you have performed your words; for you are righteous

[42] Gen. 21:13; Josh. 23:14; Neh. 9:8; Acts 3:25; Gal. 3:14, 16, 29

[43] *Josh. 23:14*: you know in all your hearts and in all your souls, that not one good thing failed of all the good things which Jehovah your God spoke concerning you; all are come to pass unto you, not one thing has failed thereof

[44] *Ps. 89:33-36*: But my lovingkindness will I not utterly take from him, nor suffer my faithfulness to fail. My covenant will I not break, nor alter the thing that is gone out of my lips. Once have I sworn by my holiness: I will not lie unto David: his seed shall endure for ever, and his throne as the sun before me

throne.⁴⁵ He fulfills his oath-bound promise to Jesus Christ when he makes him royal high priest forever, and grants royal priesthood to his spiritual seed.⁴⁶ He fulfills the new covenant when he morally transforms his people, so that, as a society they possess every spiritual blessing as their distinguishing trait.⁴⁷ Finally, he fulfills his sworn promises to Abraham, David, Jesus, and his people, when he gives his redeemed eternal life in glory.⁴⁸

b. Scripture displays God's fidelity when he fulfills his threats and curses.

Just as God always keeps his promises, even so he always keeps his threats.⁴⁹ If he made idle threats, he would not be faithful. When he swears in wrath that no rebel will see the promised land, they all die in the wilderness. When he assures Jeroboam, Baasha, and Ahab that he will exterminate their posterity, they all die under his curse. When he assures Israel and Judah that for their idolatry he will evict them from his land, they go into captivity. When the Lord threatens to damn all that reject his Son, people should take that threat seriously. No one should never test the Lord, or dare him to damn us.

c. Scripture displays God's fidelity when he fulfills all his predictions and prophecies.

All his predictions come true.⁵⁰ Scripture describes this fulfillment in sweeping terms.⁵¹ The faithful God fulfills his every prediction for the future in minute detail. I could cite numerous instances. Let it suffice us to scan the forest of this display, rather than examine each tree.

---

⁴⁵ *Acts 13:32-33*: the promise made unto the fathers, that God has fulfilled the same unto our children, in that he raised up Jesus.

⁴⁶ Heb. 7:21, 27-28; 1 Pet. 2:5, 9

⁴⁷ Jer. 31:31-34; Gal. 4:9; Col. 2:11-13; 1 Pet. 2:9-10

⁴⁸ Titus 1:2; 2 Pet. 3:13

⁴⁹ *Deut. 7:9-11*: Jehovah your God, he is God, the faithful God, who keeps covenant and lovingkindness with them that love him and keep his commandments to a thousand generations, and repays them that hate him to their face, to destroy them: he will not be slack to him that hates him, he will repay him to his face. You shall therefore keep the commandment, and the statutes, and the ordinances, which I command you this day, to do them

⁵⁰ *Num. 23:19*: God is not a man, that he should lie, neither the son of man, that he should repent: has he said, and will he not do it? Or has he spoken, and will he not make it good?

⁵¹ *Matt. 5:17-18*: Think not that I came to destroy the law or the prophets: I came not to destroy, but fulfill. For verily I say unto you, Till heaven and earth pass away, one jot or one tittle shall in no wise pass away from the law, till all things be accomplished

In conclusion, the display of God's faithfulness in Scripture provides strong encouragement[52] and engenders hope.[53] Confidence in his faithfulness to his promises strengthens our faith.[54]

B. *Creation Displays God's Faithfulness.*

God's fidelity as Creator embodies all the richness and fullness of the Hebrew, *'aman*. God displays his fidelity when he establishes, supports, nourishes, preserves, and sustains creation.[55] Respecting this display of divine faithfulness in creation John Gill observes:[56]

> and whereas God has given reason to expect that his creatures should be preserved in their being, and provided for by him, with the necessaries of life; he hath not left himself without witness to his faithfulness, in all ages and nations, giving rain from heaven and fruitful seasons; and so filling the hearts of his creatures with food and gladness; whose eyes all of them wait upon him, and he gives them their meat in due season, Acts 14:17; Pss. 36:5, 6, 145:15, 16.

If the faithful Creator feeds his birds and clothes his flowers, he surely will sustain, nourish, and support his own children.[57] Peter appeals to God's faithfulness as Creator to motivate Christians to trust him in their seasons of privation and suffering encountered in the path of gospel obedience.[58]

C. *Redemption from Sin Displays God's Faithfulness.*

God displays his faithfulness when he accomplishes, applies, and completes redemption from sin.

1. *The accomplishment of redemption displays God's faithfulness.*

In Christ God displays his faithfulness to all his promises and prophecies about the redemption of his people from their sins.[59] God the Son displayed God's faithfulness when he humbled himself, took human nature, and

---

[52] Heb. 6:17-18

[53] *Heb.10:23*: let us hold fast the confession of our hope that it waver not; for he is faithful that promised

[54] *Heb. 11:11*: By faith even Sarah herself received power to conceive . . . since she counted him faithful who had promised

[55] *Ps. 119:90*: Your faithfulness is unto all generations: you have established the earth, and it abides

[56] Gill, *Body of Divinity*, 1:163-164

[57] Matt. 6:25-34

[58] *1 Pet. 4:19*: Wherefore let them also that suffer according to the will of God commit their souls in well-doing unto a faithful Creator.

[59] Matt. 5:17-18; 2 Cor. 1:18-20

became obedient unto death.[60] He displayed God's faithfulness when he became high priest and made propitiation for the sins of his people.[61]

2. The application of redemption displays his faithfulness.

We consider five texts that attest to God's faithfulness in the application of salvation from sin.

a. Ps. 119:75[62]

When God afflicts his spiritual children for our good and his glory, he displays his faithfulness. He chastens us "for our profit," to deliver our souls from remaining sin and to make us more like himself.[63] Our afflictions flow, not from his malice, but from his love for us.[64] With David we can look back over our lives and say, "before I was afflicted I went astray; but now I observe your word," and, "it is good for me that I have been afflicted; that I may learn your statutes" (Ps. 119:67, 71). Thus, when he afflicts us, we should not despair. We should trust God and search our hearts. Where needful, we should amend our ways and observe his word.

b. Lam. 3:22-25[65]

God displays his faithfulness when he comforts and supports his spiritual children in our afflictions: "his compassions fail not. They are new every morning; great is your faithfulness." Even when he removes earthly comforts, he enables us to say: "Jehovah is my portion, says my soul; therefore will I hope in him. Jehovah is good unto them that wait for him, to the soul that seeks him." By his Spirit he manifests his special presence with our souls. He fills our hearts with hope, peace, and joy. In this way our faithful Redeemer supports Christians in all our sorrows, sufferings, and persecutions.

---

[60] *Heb. 3:1-2, 5-6*: consider the Apostle and High Priest of our confession, Jesus; who was faithful to him that appointed him . . . Moses indeed was faithful in all his house as a servant . . . but Christ as Son over his house, whose house we are.

[61] *Heb. 2:17*: it behooved him in all things to be made like his brethren, that he might become a merciful and faithful high priest in things pertaining to God, to make propitiation for the sins of the people

[62] *Ps. 119:75*: I know, O Jehovah, that your judgments are righteous, and that in faithfulness you have afflicted me

[63] Heb. 12:10

[64] Rev. 3:19

[65] *Lam. 3:22-25*: It is of Jehovah's lovingkindnesses that we are not consumed, because his compassions fail not. They are new every morning; great is your faithfulness. Jehovah is my portion, says my soul; therefore will I hope in him. Jehovah is good unto them that wait for him, to the soul that seeks him

c. 1 Cor. 10:13[66]

God displays his faithfulness when limits our temptations and provides for us a way to escape from them. He records his punishment of the wilderness generation for our benefit.[67] That generation warns us about the danger of idolatry,[68] fornication,[69] skepticism,[70] and murmuring.[71] This limiting of our temptations should not make us careless (10:12). Rather, we should be ever watchful. We should flee from the things that ruined the wilderness generation of Israel (10:14).

d. 2 Thess. 3:3-5[72]

God displays his faithfulness when protects us in the midst of spiritual foes. He establishes and nourishes us in the faith. In faithfulness he protects us from the devil's influence. Little do we know how many times our faithful Redeemer has ordered our lives to keep us from his evil designs and plots. Only eternity will uncover these great riches of his faithfulness toward us in the spiritual war against sin.

e. 1 John 1:9[73]

God displays his faithfulness when he continually grants parental forgiveness to his children. If we refuse to admit our remaining sin, we make him a liar (1:8, 10). If we live with a bad conscience laden with unconfessed sin, it disrupts our fellowship with our Father. When we confess our remaining sins, our heavenly Father forgives us, because he is faithful. If our Father would not forgive penitent children, he would deny his fidelity as our Redeemer. This affords us great comfort. It calls us to be swift to maintain a conscience void of offense to God and men in all things.

---

[66] *1 Cor. 10:13*: There has no temptation taken you but such as man can bear: but God is faithful, who will not suffer you to be tempted above that you are able; but will with the temptation make also the way of escape, that you may be able to endure it

[67] 1 Cor. 10:5-11

[68] Exod. 32:19

[69] Num. 25:9

[70] Num. 21:5

[71] Num. 16:41, 17:5, 10

[72] *2 Thess. 3:3*: But the Lord is faithful, who shall establish you, and guard you from the evil one

[73] *1 John 1:9*: If we confess our sins, he is faithful and righteous to forgive us our sins, and to cleanse us from all unrighteousness.

3. The completion of redemption displays God's faithfulness.[74]

God displays his fidelity when he completes the redemption of every Christian that he calls to Christ through the gospel. God's faithfulness insures the preservation and perseverance of all his saints. Every true believer will persevere in faith because God is faithful. The church of Christ will persevere in the faith because God is faithful. Our security rests, not in us, but in his unfailing faithfulness.

D. The Final Judgment Displays God's Faithfulness.

God will display his veracity and his reliability when he judges the world. He will display his reliability when he fulfills his Word and brings every moral creature to his throne for judgment. When God speaks to mankind in judgment, he will judge every nation and person with truth, according to fact and reality.[75] Thus he will display his veracity. On judgment day, no innocent person will be wrongly convicted sent to eternal punishment. No guilty person will be acquitted and rewarded with eternal life. The faithful Judge will mete out remuneration and retribution in strict accord with gospel truth. Thus he will prevail.[76] Accordingly, we should praise God for his fidelity in judgment.[77] We should wait patiently for it. We should anticipate it and plead with God to unveil is display.[78]

Conclusion: *Practical Application of God's Faithfulness*

I focus on its application to Christians. I conclude with its application to lost sinners. God's faithfulness establishes Christians in our faith, encourages us in our hope, and exhorts us in our gospel duty.

---

[74] *1 Thess. 5:23-24*: And the God of peace himself sanctify you wholly; and may your spirit and soul and body be preserved entire, without blame at the coming of our Lord Jesus Christ. Faithful is he that calls you, who will also do it.
[75] *Ps. 96:13*: he will judge the world with righteousness, and the peoples with his truth
[76] *Rom. 3:3-4*: shall their want of faith make of none effect the faithfulness of God? God forbid: yea, let God be found true, but every man a liar; as it is written, That you might be justified in your words and might prevail when you come into judgment.
[77] *Rev. 16:7*: And I heard the altar saying, Yea, O Lord God, the Almighty, true and righteous are your judgments *Rev. 19:2*: for true and righteous are his judgments; for he has judged the great harlot, her that corrupted the earth with her fornication, and he has avenged the blood of his servants at her hand.
[78] *Rev. 6:10*: and they cried with a great voice, saying, How long, O Master, the holy and true, do you not judge and avenge our blood on them that dwell on the earth?

A. God's Faithfulness Establishes Christians in our Faith.

God's faithfulness supports and establishes our faith.[79] We believe his entire testimony because he is completely truthful, the faithful witness who cannot lie.[80] Therefore, the more we stand convinced of God's fidelity, veracity, and reliability, the more we believe whatsoever he says in his Word.[81] Christians should be ashamed of ourselves if we give more credence to the words of fallible scientists than to the Word of our infallible God. Therefore, let us have more confidence in his faithfulness, so that we may increase in our faith and in our confidence in his Word.

B. God's Faithfulness Encourages Christians in our Hope.

God's faithfulness also establishes our hope for his future blessing.[82] It furnishes strong encouragement[83] that he will keep his promise to preserve us from evil[84] and give us unending life.[85] Heaven and eternal glory are as sure and certain as his faithfulness.[86] Therefore, let us grow in our confidence in his faithfulness, so that we may abound in hope, peace, and joy in believing.[87]

C. God's Faithfulness Exhorts Christians in our Gospel Duty.

We consider ten ways in which God's faithfulness exhorts Christians.

---

[79] *Heb. 11:11*: By faith even Sarah herself received power to conceive seed when she was past age, since she counted him faithful who had promised.

[80] *John 3:33*: He that has received his witness has set his seal to this, that God is true

[81] *Ps. 119:142, 151, 160*: your law is truth . . . all your commandments are truth . . . the sum of your word is truth

[82] *Lam. 3:22-25*: It is of Jehovah's lovingkindnesses that we are not consumed, because his compassions fail not. They are new every morning; great is your faithfulness. Jehovah is my portion, says my soul; therefore will I hope in him. Jehovah is good unto them that wait for him, to the soul that seeks him

[83] *Heb. 6:17-18*: Wherein God, being minded to show more abundantly unto the heirs of the promise the immutability of his counsel, interposed with an oath; that by two immutable things, in which it is impossible for God to lie, we may have a strong encouragement

[84] *2 Thess. 3:3*: But the Lord is faithful, who shall establish you, and guard you from the evil one

[85] *Titus 1:1-2*: in hope of eternal life, which God, who cannot lie, promised before times eternal

[86] *1 Thess. 5:23-24*: And the God of peace himself sanctify you wholly; and may your spirit and soul and body be preserved entire, without blame at the coming of our Lord Jesus Christ. Faithful is he that calls you, who will also do it

[87] *Heb. 10:23*: let us hold fast the confession of our hope that it waver not; for he is faithful that promised.

1. God's fidelity calls us to serve and obey him.[88]

We should live in gospel obedience to the Decalogue because our faithful God blesses those who obey him and repays those that hate him to their face.

2. God's fidelity calls us to plead with him in prayer.

God's faithfulness furnishes great incentive and fuel for our prayers.[89] As David does, we should appeal to his faithfulness to his promises when we present our requests, desires, and needs before him.[90] We learn also that we should pray specifically for those blessings and graces, such as the fear of God, which he has promised to give us in Christ.[91]

3. God's fidelity calls us to proclaim the glorious display of his faithfulness.

We should testify openly of God's faithfulness.[92] We should proclaim the many ways that he has displayed his fidelity to us personally and to all his people.[93]

4. God's fidelity calls us to worship, praise, and adore him.

All generations should praise God for his faithfulness displayed in his works and Word. Yet, each generation of Christians should make his faithful dealings into fuel for new songs of praise.[94] We should praise him for his faithfulness to his promises.[95] We should praise him for his faithfulness to

---

[88] *Deut. 7:9-11*: Jehovah your God, he is God, the faithful God, who keeps covenant and lovingkindness with them that love him and keep his commandments to a thousand generations, and repays them that hate him to their face, to destroy them: he will not be slack to him that hates him, he will repay him to his face. You shall therefore keep the commandment, and the statutes, and the ordinances, which I command you this day, to do them.

[89] *Ps. 143:1*: Hear my prayer, O Jehovah; give ear to my supplications: in your faithfulness answer me, and in your righteousness.

[90] *2 Sam. 7:28*: And now, O Lord Jehovah, you are God, and your words are truth, and you have promised this good thing unto your servant

[91] Jer. 32:40

[92] *Deut. 32:3-4*: For I will proclaim the name of Jehovah: ascribe greatness unto our God. The Rock, his work is perfect; for all his ways are justice: a God of faithfulness and without iniquity, just and right is he

[93] *Ps. 40:10*: I have not hid your righteousness within my heart; I have declared your faithfulness and your salvation; I have not concealed your lovingkindness and your truth from the great assembly.

[94] *Ps. 33:3-4*: Sing unto him a new song; play skillfully with a loud noise. For the word of Jehovah is right; and all his work is done in faithfulness

[95] *Ps. 89:1*: I will sing of the lovingkindness of Jehovah for ever: with my mouth will I make known your faithfulness to all generations

his people in all ages.[96] We should praise him in corporate worship for his faithfulness in as Creator and Redeemer.[97] We should praise him for his faithfulness in the judgment of all mankind.[98]

5. God's fidelity calls us to trust him in all our afflictions.

When God afflicts us, we should not charge him foolishly. We should trust him[99] because we know that in faithfulness he has afflicted us.[100]

6. God's fidelity calls us to discover and use his means of escaping every temptation.[101]

We should earnestly resist every temptation to sin, knowing that our God has provided some means of escape because he is faithful.

7. God's fidelity calls us to be reliable and truthful in all our ways.

As God is faithful, so also fidelity should mark all our words and works, because we are his children. To be faithful in our words, we must keep confidences,[102] deliver accurate messages,[103] give truthful testimony,[104] administer biblical reproof,[105] and keep our promises.[106] To be faithful in our works, we must embrace our stewardships, keep right priorities, and implement responsibilities conscientiously.[107]

---

[96] *Rev. 15:3*: And they sing the song of Moses the servant of God, and the song of the Lamb, saying, Great and marvelous are your works, O Lord God, the Almighty; righteous and true are your ways, you King of the ages.

[97] *Ps. 92:1-2*: It is a good thing to give thanks unto Jehovah, and to sing praises unto your name, O Most High; to show forth your lovingkindness in the morning, and your faithfulness every night

[98] *Ps. 96:12-13*: Let the field exult, and all that is therein; then shall all the trees of the wood sing for joy before Jehovah; for he comes to judge the earth: he will judge the world with righteousness, and the peoples with his truth

[99] *Ps. 31:5-6*: Into your hand I commend my spirit: you have redeemed me, O Jehovah, you God of truth. I hate them that regard lying vanities; but I trust in Jehovah

[100] *Ps. 119:75*: I know, O Jehovah, that your judgments are righteous, and that in faithfulness you have afflicted me.

[101] *1 Cor. 10:13*: There has no temptation taken you but such as man can bear: but God is faithful, who will not suffer you to be tempted above that you are able; but will with the temptation make also the way of escape, that you may be able to endure it.

[102] Prov. 11:13

[103] Prov. 13:17

[104] Prov. 14:5

[105] Prov. 27:6

[106] *2 Cor. 1:18*: But as God is faithful, our word toward you is not yea and nay.

[107] 1 Cor. 4:1-2; Heb. 3:2

8. God's fidelity calls us to remain loyal to his name and cause.[108]

God's faithfulness does not depend on ours. If we forsake and deny him, he will certainly deny us access to heaven. Thus, his fidelity demands that we persevere in gospel faith, hope, and obedience to the end.

9. God's fidelity calls us rely on him to provide all our needs.[109]

Because our Creator is faithful, we should trust him to nourish, sustain, and support us even while we suffer persecution and privation in the path of righteousness.

10. God's fidelity calls us to confess our remaining sins to him.[110]

Because our heavenly Father is faithful, he always grants parental forgiveness to his children when we confess and forsake our remaining sin. This furnishes us with strong motivation and incentive to keep a good conscience before him always.

In conclusion, consider how God's faithfulness applies to lost sinners. Unbelief and skepticism call God a liar.[111] When sinners reject his testimony, they insult his truthfulness. When they attack his credibility, they manifest enmity toward him. Surely, such behavior is outrageous. It will catch up with sinners sooner or later. Therefore, I entreat such. Take to heart that God is faithful. His word is true. His threats are reliable. While there is still time, turn from your futile controversy with God. Get right with God through Christ.

Finally, May God be pleased to enable each of us to behold and embrace his great faithfulness.

---

[108] *2 Tim. 2:13*: if we are faithless, he abides faithful; for he cannot deny himself.
[109] *1 Pet. 4:19*: Wherefore let them also that suffer according to the will of God commit their souls in well-doing unto a faithful Creator.
[110] *1 John 1:9*: If we confess our sins, he is faithful and righteous to forgive us our sins, and to cleanse us from all unrighteousness.
[111] *1 John 5:10*: He that believes on the Son of God has the witness in him: he that believes not God has made him a liar; because he has not believed in the witness that God has borne concerning his Son.

APPENDIX: MAJOR BIBLICAL TERMS FOR GOD'S FAITHFULNESS
OLD TESTAMENT TERMS

First, the primary word family for divine faithfulness comes from the verb אָמַן ('aman): to confirm, to support, or to nourish, to establish, to verify, to be reliable, faithful, trusty: with a broad variety of nuances and applications. For example: it is translated, "nursing father" (Num. 11:12), "steadfast" (Ps. 78:8), "established" (2 Sam. 7:16), "sure" (1 Sam. 2:35), and "be verified" (Gen. 42:20). It sometimes refers to human reliability (Num. 12:7; 2 Sam. 20:19; Ps. 12:1; Prov. 11:3, 25:13, 27:6). It describes God's faithfulness at least these 9 times: Deut. 7:9; Pss. 19:7, 89:28, 93:5, 111:7; Isa. 49:7, 55:3; Jer. 42:5; Hos. 5:9. The word, אֱמוּנָה ('emûnah), "faithfulness," "truth," derived from *'aman*, signifies firmness, steadfastness, or fidelity (BDB, *Lexicon*, p. 53). It describes Moses' "steady" arms (Exod. 17:12) and civil "stability" (Isa. 33:6). It sometimes describes human faithfulness (1 Sam. 26:23; 2 Chron. 19:9; Prov. 12:22, 28:20). It refers to God's fidelity at least these 25 times: Deut. 32:4; Pss. 33:4, 36:5, 40:10, 88:11, 89:1, 2, 5, 8, 24, 33, 49; 92:2, 96:13, 98:3, 100:5, 119:75, 86, 90, 138, 143:1; Isa. 11:5, 25:1; Lam. 3:23; Hos. 2:20. The word, אֱמֶת ('emeth): "truth," "true," "truly," "sure,": also comes from *'aman*. It signifies firmness, faithfulness, truth (BDB *Lexicon*, p. 54). It sometimes refers to truth in a general sense (Deut. 13:14, 22:20; 1 Kings 10:6; Ps. 85:10, 11): sometimes refers to the true or genuine, as opposed to the false or counterfeit: "the true God" (2 Chron. 15:3; Jer. 10:10). It often depicts human truthfulness (Exod. 18:21; Prov. 3:3, 12:19, 14:25, 29:14, etc.). It refers to divine fidelity and truthfulness at least these 50 times: Gen. 24:27, 32:10; Exod. 34:6; 2 Sam. 7:28, 15:20; 1 Kings 17:24; Neh. 9:13, 33; Pss. 19:9, 25:5, 10, 26:3, 30:9, 31:5, 40:10, 11, 43:3, 54:5, 57:3, 10, 61:7, 69:13, 71:22, 86:11, 15, 89:14, 91:4, 108:4, 111:7, 115:1, 117:2, 119:43, 142, 151, 160, 132:11, 138:2, 146:6; Prov. 22:21; Isa. 38:18, 19, 42:3; Jer. 42:5; Dan. 8:26, 9:13, 10:1, 21; Micah 7:20; Zech. 8:8; Mal. 2:6. The word, אָמֵן ('amēn), usually simply transliterated as, "Amen" (Deut. 27:15, etc.), also comes from *'aman*. It twice refers to God's fidelity as the "God of truth": Isa. 65:16 (2). The word, אֹמֶן ('omen), "truth," is also from *'aman*: it refers once to God's fidelity: Isa. 25:1 in combination with *'emûnah*. The word, אֵמוּן ('ēmûn), "faithful," also comes from *'aman*. This word depicts human fidelity (Prov. 13:17, 14:5, 20:6), but never explicitly describes divine faithfulness.

Second, the word קְשׁוֹט (qᵉshôt), "truth," describes divine fidelity **once**: Dan. 4:37. Similarly, קֹשֶׁט (qoshᵉt), "certainty," **once** describes the veracity of God's Word: Prov. 22:21; and קֹשֶׁט (qoshet), "truth," **once** refers to divine veracity generically: Ps. 60:4.

Third, the Old Testament also presents God's fidelity negatively, when it affirms that God will never lie at least twice: Num. 23:19; 1 Sam. 15:29.

Fourth, the Old Testament also presents God's fidelity implicitly with general expressions at least these **4** times: Josh. 23:14 (2); Neh. 9:8; Zeph. 3:5.

NEW TESTAMENT TERMS

First, πιστος (pistos), "faithful," "true," signifies fidelity, reliability. It sometimes depicts human faithfulness: Matt. 24:45, 25:21(2), 1 Cor. 4:2; 2 Tim. 2:2; Heb. 3:5; 1 Pet. 5:12; Rev. 2:10, 13, etc. It refers to divine fidelity and reliability at least these 15 times: 1 Cor. 1:9, 10:13; 2 Cor. 1:18; 1 Thess. 5:24; 2 Thess. 3:3; 2 Tim. 2:13; Heb. 2:17, 3:2, 10:23, 11:11; 1 Pet. 4:19; 1 John 1:9; Rev. 1:5, 3:14, 19:11.

Second, the ἀληθεια (aletheia) family depicts divine fidelity. The noun, *aletheia*, "truth," refers to various aspects of divine fidelity, in all, at least 26 times: The fidelity of "the Spirit of truth," 5 times: John 14:17, 15:26, 16:13, 1 John 4:6, 5:6; The fidelity of God the Son, 2 times: John 1:14, 14:6; The fidelity of the Word of God, viewed in various ways, at least 19 times: John 17:17, 19; Rom. 2:2, 8, 20, 3:7, 15:8; 2 Cor. 6:7; Gal. 2:5, 14, 3:1 (KJV/BYZ), 5:7; Eph. 1:13; Col. 1:5; 2 Thess. 2:10, 12, 13; 2 Tim. 2:15; James 1:18. The adjective ἀληθινος (alethinos), "true," sometimes refers to truth in a general sense (John 19:35), sometimes to the literal or real, as opposed to the merely symbolic (Heb. 8:2), sometimes to the true and genuine, as opposed to the false and counterfeit (John 17:3, 1 Thess. 1:9, 1 John 5:20). It describes divine fidelity and truthfulness at least 10 times: John 7:28; 1 John 5:20(2); Rev. 3:7, 14, 6:10, 15:3, 16:7, 19:2, 19:11. The adjective, ἀληθης (alethes), "true," sometimes refers to truth in a general sense (Matt. 22:16; John 5:31, 32, 8:13, 14, 16, 17), sometimes to the literal or real as opposed to the symbolic (Acts 12:9). It describes divine fidelity at least **twice**: John 3:33; Rom. 3:4.

Third, the New Testament presents God's fidelity negatively twice: God "cannot lie": Titus 1:2; Heb. 6:18.

In sum, Scripture refers to God's faithfulness at least these 96 times in the Old Testament, 55 in the New, a total of **151**: the same magnitude as holiness and justice: lesser emphasis than on God's goodness (825 references). The Old Testament especially stresses the close association of God's faithfulness with his goodness (Deut. 7:9; Ps. 100:5); the New Testament, its close association with his justice and holiness (Rev. 6:10, 15:3, 16:7, 19:2).

Topic 21. God's Self-Esteem

"To whom then will you liken me, that I should be equal to him? (Isa. 40:25); "my glory will I not give to another" (Isa. 42:8)

Conclusion: God's Self-Esteem: *God's Consciousness of his Supreme Virtue*

We hear a lot today about self-esteem. We hear that people need greater esteem for themselves. In truth we need greater esteem for God and his moral virtues. First, in Topic 16 we took a broad look at God's supreme moral capacity and character. Then we expounded his four primary virtues: his goodness (Topic 17), holiness (Topic 18), justice (Topic 19), and faithfulness (Topic 20). Now we conclude our study of God's morality. Does God know that he is supremely good, holy, just, and faithful? Does he want his creatures to adore and glorify him for his virtues? Scripture answers with a resounding, "Yes." God is deeply concerned that no creature would steal his glory. Although Scripture never explicitly asserts that God has a "conscience," it affirms his high esteem of his own virtue. A good conscience in humans reflects God's moral self-awareness, his flawless self-esteem. Accordingly, I offer the following definition of God's assessment of his own virtue:

> God's *self-esteem* is his moral self-awareness, his infallible perception and infinite esteem of his own supreme virtue.

God's self-esteem implies his moral capacity, since it involves his ability to perceive his own virtues. Yet his self-esteem is itself a virtue. God's children reflect this divine virtue in the graces of reverence and humility. Now I *summarize* and *apply* the biblical testimony to God's self-esteem.

I. Summary of the Biblical Testimony to God's Self Esteem

Scripture attests God's self-esteem in both testaments. It reveals the Lord's *declaration* of his supreme virtue, *dedication* to it, and *defense* of it.

A. God's Declaration of His Supreme Virtue

God personally declares his goodness, holiness, justice, and faithfulness.

1. God declares his goodness.[1]

He shows Moses his glory. He proclaims all his goodness to him. He affirms that he is merciful, gracious, slow to anger, and abundant in lovingkindness and faithfulness. Thus, God perceives his own goodness accurately and thoroughly. He is not ashamed of it. He wants his people to perceive it too.

---

[1] *Exod. 33:19, 34:6*: I will make all my goodness pass before you . . . and Jehovah passed by before him, and proclaimed, Jehovah, Jehovah, a God merciful and gracious, slow to anger, and abundant in lovingkindness and truth

2. God declares his holiness.[2]

Through Isaiah the Lord declares his supreme holiness: "To whom then will you liken me that I shall be equal to him? Says the Holy One." He is aware that he is morally peerless. He knows that he alone has eternal, unchangeable, ideal, and self-existent holiness.

3. God declares his justice.

Through Isaiah the Lord also declares his supreme justice.[3] He says that no one taught him justice. He perceives that his justice is self-existent, eternal, and unchangeable. Through Jeremiah he declares that he "exercises justice" in the earth.[4] He perceives accurately the display of his justice in providence and redemption. He declares emphatically[5] and repeatedly that through Christ his King he will establish justice in the earth.[6]

4. God declares his faithfulness.

Through the psalmist he declares his faithfulness to his covenant promise to David.[7] He closely associates his faithfulness with is dedication to his own glory, "once I have sworn by my holiness." God the Son incarnate, from his throne in glory, declares his veracity and reliability.[8] Thus, God is aware of his supreme fidelity and affirms it to strengthen the faith of his people.

---

[2] *Isa. 40:25*: To whom then will you liken me, that I should be equal to him? says the Holy One

[3] *Isa. 40:13-14*: Who has directed the Spirit of Jehovah, or being his counselor has taught him? 14 With whom took he counsel, and who instructed him, and taught him in the path of justice, and taught him knowledge, and showed to him the way of understanding?

[4] *Jer. 9: 23-24*: Thus says Jehovah, Let not the wise man glory in his wisdom, neither let the mighty man glory in his might, let not the rich man glory in his riches; 24 but let him that glories glory in this, that he has understanding, and knows me, that I am Jehovah who exercises lovingkindness, justice, and righteousness, in the earth: for in these things I delight, says Jehovah

[5] *Isa 51:4*: Attend unto me, O my people; and give ear unto me, O my nation: for a law shall go forth from me, and I will establish my justice for a light of the peoples.

[6] *Jer. 23:5*: Behold, the days come, saith Jehovah, that I will raise unto David a righteous Branch, and he shall reign as king and deal wisely, and shall execute justice and righteousness in the land.

[7] *Ps. 89:33-35*: But my lovingkindness will I not utterly take from him, Nor suffer my faithfulness to fail. 34 My covenant will I not break, Nor alter the thing that is gone out of my lips. 35 Once have I sworn by my holiness: I will not lie unto David:

[8] *Rev. 3:14*: And to the angel of the church in Laodicea write: These things says the Amen, the faithful and true witness.

B. God's Dedication to His Supreme Virtue[9]

God is aware of his supreme virtue and highly esteems it. He stands determined never to relinquish his honor. God's supreme virtue gives him the sole right to the devotion of his moral creatures. He will never share his glory with any angel, human being, or idol. He is supremely dedicated to declare and display the glory of his moral character.

C. God's Defense of His Supreme Virtue

In the first temptation the devil called God a liar and cast aspersions on his goodness. In a fallen world God faces numerous assaults on his moral virtue. At times God stoops in kindness and personally defends his integrity. Scripture features his response to the doubts of saints, to the accusations of sinners, and to the insults of God the Son incarnate.

1. Doubts of godly saints[10]

Even the godly sometimes struggle with God's integrity in a fallen world. When righteous Job experienced severe affliction, he did not charge God foolishly. Yet he struggled to discern God's justice and goodness in his afflictions. Therefore, God defends his integrity to Job: "will you even condemn me?" God is not unjust. He intended Job's affliction, not to punish him for hypocrisy, but to display his genuine faith and eminent godliness. When Job perceives God's righteous intention, he humbles himself and acknowledges God's wisdom and justice in his affliction: "but now my eye sees you, wherefore I abhor myself, and repent in dust and ashes."

2. Accusations from sinners among his people[11]

Sinners among God's people charge him with gross injustice: "the way of the Lord is not equal." They oppose God's gospel goodness and severity. They charge God with injustice because of his severity with apostates and hypocrites and because of his mercy to sinners that repent. The Lord answers their false charges. He does not come under conviction of sin. Guilt does not cripple him. He doesn't cower in self-doubt before their bony finger of blame. To the contrary, he defends his integrity: "are not my ways equal." Further, he brings counter-charges against his adversaries: "are not your ways unequal." He declares his commitment to continue to judge them

---

[9] Isa. 42:8: I am Jehovah, that is my name; and my glory will I not give to another, neither my praise unto graven images.

[10] Job 40:8: Will you even annul my judgment? Will you condemn me, that you may be justified?

[11] Ezek. 18:29: Yet says the house of Israel, The way of the Lord is not equal. O house of Israel: are not my ways equal? are not your ways unequal.

with gospel mercy and severity: "Therefore I will judge you, O house of Israel, every one according to his ways." Human disapproval doesn't pressure God to abandon his principles of judgment. He stands boldly entrenched in his gospel justice in the face of his detractors and adversaries.

3. Personal insults to God the Son incarnate[12]

The assault on God's integrity reaches its zenith when God incarnate dwells with his sinful people. Then they insulted God personally, face to face, with many grievous and false charges. They accused the Son of breaking God's law by healing on the sabbath. They charged Christ with blasphemy because he asserted his deity and equality with God the Father. They even alleged that he was demon possessed and performed his miracles by the power of the devil. Jesus doesn't break under the pressure of their repeated insults. He doesn't become paralyzed with false guilt. To the contrary, he defends his spotless integrity: "I do always the things that are pleasing to him . . . Which of you convicts me of sin? . . . I have not a demon; but I honor my Father." He says plainly that they have no grounds for the disdain with which they treat him. He insists that he deserves their respect: "I honor my Father, and you dishonor me." Further, he counters their slanderous attacks and exposes their hypocrisy: "it is my Father that glorifies me; of whom you say that he is your God; and you have not known him: but I know him; and if I should say, I know him not, I shall be like unto you, a liar: but I know him, and keep his word." Christ could never withstand these detractors without clear perception of his own integrity. Thus, in Christ we see the most profound display of God's self-esteem.

II. Practical Application of the Biblical Testimony to God's Self-Esteem

We consider the application of God's self-esteem to Christians and to lost sinners.

A. Application of God's Self-Esteem to Christians

God's self-esteem applies both to our esteem of God's moral character and of our own moral character.

1. We should reflect God's esteem of his ideal moral character.

We must reflect in our hearts God's disposition toward his virtue and exhibit it in our lives. God's honor and glory must be our top priority. If people

---

[12] *John 8:29, 46, 49, 54, 55*: I do always the things that are pleasing to him . . . Which of you convicts me of sin? . . . I have not a demon; but I honor my Father, and you dishonor me . . . it is my Father that glorifies me; of whom you say that he is your God; and you have not known him: but I know him; and if I should say, I know him not, I shall be like unto you, a liar: but I know him, and keep his word

were more enthralled with God's grandeur and virtue, and less focused on ourselves, we wouldn't be preoccupied with our own self-esteem. Therefore, we should meditate on his moral perfections, esteem them highly, and labor to reflect them in our own character. The more we contemplate and revere his supreme virtue, the more we will show forth his moral excellences in our lives. The Lord calls us for this very purpose.[13] He creates us in Christ Jesus for good works.[14] He does this, not for our own glory, but so that men would see our good works and glorify our Father in heaven.[15] Thus, when we reflect his goodness, holiness, justice, and faithfulness, we must give all credit to his grace, and all praise and honor to his name. Let us be jealous for his honor. Let our great burden be to defend and display of his moral virtue.

2. We should reflect God's esteem of our Christian moral character.

The poet says, "Oh that some power the gift would give us, to see ourselves as others see us." If we change it to, "to see ourselves as God sees us," we grasp this application of God's self-esteem. We should see our moral character as God sees it. We should assess our own character, not by the fickle dictates of the world, but by the unchanging norms of God's holy Word. We should think of ourselves soberly, according to truth, exactly as God thinks of us. This means that all Christians should be aware both of our reigning righteousness and of our remaining sin. We do not esteem ourselves soberly, according to truth, if we deny our remaining sin.[16] Nor do we esteem ourselves soberly, according to truth, if we deny our reigning righteousness.[17] In this life every Christian struggles with the tension between the gospel integrity that reigns in us and the iniquity that remains in us.[18] We must, therefore, maintain a biblical consciousness of both aspects of our moral character. We must remain ever ashamed of our remaining sin and wretchedness, so that we walk softly in humility, so that we don't become brazen in self-righteousness and pride.[19] Yet, we must always maintain a good conscience, a biblical sense of our evangelical integrity before God, so that we may stand for the truth and withstand false

---

[13] 1 Pet. 2:9-10
[14] Eph. 2:10
[15] Matt. 5:16
[16] Pss. 51:3, 143:2; 1 John 1:8, 10
[17] Ps. 18:20-24; 1 John 3:9
[18] Rom. 7:14-25
[19] Ezek. 16:63

accusations.[20] Christ teaches us the proper attitude toward our reigning righteousness: "when you shall have done all the things that are commanded you, say, We are unprofitable servants; we have done that which it was our duty to do" (Luke 17:10). Christ doesn't urge us to say, "we are *unprofitable* servants, we never did anything right, we have no evangelical obedience." Nor does he tell us to say: "we are *profitable* servants, we've done our duty." Christ directs us to say, when we have done our duty, "we are unprofitable servants." True godliness takes no credit for itself. It gives God all the glory. He alone is worthy, because his grace in us produces our gospel obedience. Therefore, when we walk in gospel obedience, let us do so with humility and gratitude to God.

B. Application of God's Self-Esteem to Lost Sinners

God's self-esteem also has application to those in the state of sin. It calls them to realize that they cannot please God.[21] As long as they live in sin, everything they do is an abomination in his sight. If the wicked esteem themselves in this way, they do not suffer from *bad self-esteem*. To the contrary, this would be proper self-esteem, for it is exactly how God esteems them. If lost sinners want to improve their self-assessment, they must get right with God through the gospel of Christ. If sinners manage by some other means to improve their estimate of where they stand with God, they suffer from self-delusion. Ironically, they end up with a worse self-esteem than they had in the first place.

Finally, may the Lord write on all our hearts a deep appreciation for his esteem of his moral character and of ours.

---

[20] Acts 23:1; 1 Tim. 1:19, 3:3; 1 Pet. 3:16
[21] Rom. 8:7-9

Topic 22. The Trinity

"into the name of the Father and of the Son and of the Holy Spirit" (Matt. 28:19)

Section 10. God's Personality: The Trinity

Introduction to Section 10

We established in Topic 5 that all spirits are personal beings and that personality involves self-awareness, or personal consciousness, expressed in personal communication and interpersonal communion. We also established that the Supreme Spirit has supreme personality. His personality is infinite, eternal, unchangeable, self-existent, and ideal. Infinite personality means that God remains ever aware of his infinite Being, and that can nothing can ever limit his self-awareness. Eternal personality signifies that God always has experienced interpersonal communion, now does experience it, and always will. Unchangeable personality means that his self-awareness and interpersonal communication abide forever the same. Self-existent personality means that his interpersonal communication depends on God alone. Ideal personality means that his personality is infinitely perfect and never improves or deteriorates.

These remarkable traits of God's personality point us to a great mystery. Supreme personality cannot possibly be *uni-personal*. How could a uni-personal God have interpersonal communion eternally and independently? Although we can thus discern that God's personality must involve plurality, we cannot define this plurality further without additional divine revelation. Yet, he does not leave us in suspense. He unveils in Scripture the nature of this plurality. Scripture reveals that God is tri-personal, triune. Three distinct Persons, the Father, the Son, and the Holy Spirit, are the one Supreme Being: "the name of the Father and of the Son and of the Holy Spirit." Thus, God's personality is unique and essential. It is unique, since God alone is tri-personal. All other spirits, angelic and human, are uni-personal. It is essential, since God cannot cease to be tri-personal and remain God. Berkhof affirms this:[1]

> man is uni-personal, while God is tri-personal. And this tri-personal existence is a necessity in the divine being . . . He could not exist in any other than the tri-personal form . . . Personality does not develop or exist in isolation, but only in association with other persons. Hence, it is not possible to conceive of personality in God apart from an association of *equal* persons in Him.

Further the one divine nature, in its entirety, pertains to each divine Person, for all have one "name." This shows us that God's personality is

---

[1] Berkhof, *Systematic Theology*, 84, 85

incomprehensible. We can never fully grasp, explain, or illustrate this profound mystery. The Trinity is part of the fence that guards God's mystery from the hands of men. First, we study the *biblical disclosure* of God's personality. Second, based on this study, I expound the *biblical doctrine* of God's personality.

Unit 1. The Biblical Disclosure of God's Personality

Regarding this disclosure, I highly commend B. B. Warfield's article, *"The Biblical Doctrine of the Trinity."*[2] We consider the disclosure of God's personality in the Old and New Testaments.

I. The Biblical Disclosure of God's Personality in the Old Testament

No text in the Old Testament asserts the Trinity fully. Yet the Old Testament repeatedly intimates plurality in God's personality. It links this plurality with the Messiah and God's Spirit. It unfolds this plurality when God: (1) discloses his plural Name as Creator, (2) relates his interpersonal communion, (3) sends a divine messenger, (4) appoints a divine Messiah, and (5) calls his Spirit a distinct person.

A. God's Plural Name[3]

The name, *'elohîm*, translated *"God,"* is plural. This divine name also has a singular form, *'eloah*. We study these in Topic 23. Scripture thus associates plurality with the Creator. Although people debate the significance of this plural, none can deny its frequent occurrence. Thus, Scripture sometimes uses a plural verb when it describes a divine action. Although English translations cannot capture this nuance, the Hebrew verbs in Genesis 20:13, 35:7 are plural.

B. God's Interpersonal Communion[4]

Plural pronouns describe God's interpersonal communion. God alone creates man, yet he says, "Let *us* make man." God alone redeems his people, yet he says, "whom will I send, and who will go *for us*." This does not fully

---

[2] Benjamin B. Warfield, *Biblical and Theological Studies* (Philadelphia: Presbyterian & Reformed Publishing, 1968), 22-59.

[3] *Gen. 1:1, 3*: God created the heavens and the earth . . . the Spirit of God moved upon the face of the waters. And God said: Let there be light

[4] *Gen. 1:26*: God said, Let us make man in our image, after our likeness. *Gen. 3:22*: And Jehovah God said, Behold, the man is become as one of us, to know good and evil. *Gen. 11:6, 7*: Jehovah said . . . Come, let us go down, and there confound their language. *Isa. 6:8*: And I heard the voice of the Lord, saying, Whom shall I send, and who will go for us? Then I said, Here am I; send me

prove the doctrine of the Trinity. Yet intimates that as Creator and Redeemer God experiences plurality in his personal consciousness.

C. The Deity of God's Messenger

Bavinck lists the texts that present "the angel of Jehovah" as the Supreme Being.[5] This mysterious messenger comes from God to bring his Word to men. This messenger is himself a divine Person. Scripture calls him the Supreme Being.[6] He speaks as the Supreme Being.[7] When men see him, they see the Supreme Being. He receives homage as the Supreme Being.[8] How can one Person be both a divine messenger and a divine Person? How can people see God himself when they see this messenger? For answers we must wait until God the Son incarnate says: "I am come down from heaven, not to do my own will, but the will of him who sent me" (John 6:38), and, "he that has seen me has seen the Father" (John 14:9). God the Son comes from heaven to earth as a divine messenger who is also a divine Person. Christ is God, sent by God, to bring God's Word to men. When men see him, they see the Supreme Being incarnate. Thus, the angel of Jehovah reveals divine plurality in generic terms, preparing the way for its full disclosure in the incarnation of God the Son.

D. The Deity of God's Messiah

From the time of the Davidic covenant and dynasty Scripture asserts the deity of David's heir, the Messiah. It explicitly calls the Messiah: "God,"[9]

---

[5] Bavinck, *Doctrine of God*, 257

[6] *Gen. 16:13*: And she called the name of Jehovah that spake unto her, You are a God that sees: for she said, Have I even here looked after him that sees me? *Exod. 3:2, 6*: the angel of Jehovah appeared unto him in a flame of fire out of the midst of a bush . . . Moses hid his face; for he was afraid to look upon God

[7] *Gen. 16:10*: And the angel of Jehovah said unto her, I will greatly multiply thy seed, that it shall not be numbered for multitude. *Gen. 22:15-16*: the angel of Jehovah called unto Abraham a second time out of heaven, and said, By myself I have sworn, says Jehovah. *Gen. 31:11, 13*: The angel of God said unto me in the dream . . . I am the God of Bethel

[8] *Judg. 13:20-23*: the angel of Jehovah ascended in the flame of the altar: and Manoah and his wife looked on; and they fell on their faces to the ground. But the angel of the Jehovah did no more appear to Manoah or to his wife. Then Manoah knew that he was the angel of Jehovah. And Manoah said to his wife, we shall surely die, because we have seen God. But his wife said unto him, If Jehovah were pleased to kill us, he would not have received a burnt-offering and a meal-offering at our hand, neither would he have showed us all these things, nor would at this time have told such things as these.

[9] *Ps. 45:6-7*: Your throne, O God, is for ever and ever: a sceptre of equity is the sceptre of your kingdom. You have loved righteousness, and hated wickedness: therefore God, your God, has anointed you with the oil of gladness above your fellows

"the Lord,"[10] "God with us,"[11] and the "Mighty God."[12] The New Testament underscores the importance and relevance of this testimony.[13] God anoints and speaks to the Messiah: "God, your God has anointed you," and, "Jehovah says unto my Lord." How can God anoint God? How can Jehovah speak to David's Lord? How can Messiah, David's son, be the Supreme Being? God clearly answers these questions when God the Son becomes human.[14] Again, the general disclosure of God's plurality in unity in the Old Testament paves the way for its specific disclosure through Jesus Christ.

God the Son is "the Word." The Messiah is God the Word incarnate.[15] Christ is the Wisdom of God.[16] The Old Testament intimates this relationship between the Father and Son when it personifies God's Word and wisdom. God's Word creates the universe.[17] The Word of God heals and delivers.[18] The Word of God accomplishes his will.[19] The Wisdom of God eternally rejoices before God and creates the universe.[20] Thus, these personifications of God's word and wisdom point to Jesus Christ, God's Word and Wisdom incarnate.

E. The Distinct Personality of God's Spirit

God the Spirit is a distinct Person, not an impersonal force. The Spirit speaks words, something persons do, "the Spirit of Jehovah spoke by me, and his word was upon my tongue" (2 Sam. 23:2). When his people rebel, they grieve him: "but they rebelled, and grieved his Holy Spirit" (Isa. 63:10). An

---

[10] *Ps. 110:1*: Jehovah says unto my Lord, Sit at my right hand until I make your enemies your footstool

[11] *Isa. 7:14*: a virgin shall conceive, and bear a son, and shall call his name Immanuel

[12] *Isa. 9:6*: unto us a son is given; and the government shall be upon his shoulder: and his name shall be called Wonderful, Counsellor, Mighty God, Everlasting Father, Prince of Peace.

[13] Matt. 1:23, 22:41-46; Heb.1:8-9

[14] *John 1:1, 2, 14*: the Word was with God, and the Word was God. The same was in the beginning with God . . . and the Word became flesh, and dwelt among us.

[15] Rev. 19:13

[16] 1 Cor. 1:24, 30

[17] *Ps. 33:6*: By the word of Jehovah were the heavens made, and all the host of them by the breath of his mouth

[18] *Ps. 107:20*: he sends his word, and heals them, and delivers them from their destructions

[19] *Isa. 55:11*: So shall my word be that goes forth out of my mouth: it shall not return unto me void, but shall accomplish that which I please

[20] *Prov. 8:12, 29, 30*: I wisdom have made prudence my dwelling . . . When he marked out the foundations of the earth; then I was by him, as a master workman; and I was daily his delight, rejoicing always before him.

impersonal force doesn't feel anger or anything else. The Old Testament also reveals that God's Spirit has a distinct role in creation,[21] anoints the Messiah,[22] speaks through his prophets,[23] and dwells with God's people.[24] Thus, the Old Testament associates plurality in God's personality, not only with the Messiah, but also with God's Spirit. God emphatically discloses Messiah's deity upon the advent of David's monarchy and his Spirit's distinct personality during the prophetic era. This paves the way for the complete unveiling of the Trinity in the New Testament.

II. The Biblical Disclosure of God's Personality in the New Testament

The New Testament explicitly unveils the Trinity. God reveals his triune personality when: (1) God the Father sends God the Son, (2) the Father and the Son send God the Spirit, and (3) the inspired writers declare their devotion to God the Father, God the Son, and God the Holy Spirit.

A. The Son Sent from the Father

Scripture discloses God's triunity through the incarnation, anointing, teaching, and prayer of God the Son.

1. The incarnation of God the Son

Scripture declares that Jesus is "the Son of the Most High," and "the Son of God."[25] He is not God the Father. Nor is Jesus the Holy Spirit. His conception occurs by "the Holy Spirit," by "the power of the Most High." Who then is Jesus? Jesus is a divine Person. He is God the Word incarnate:[26] "the Word became flesh." God the Word is a distinct person from God the Father: "the Word was *with God*." Yet, God the Word is the Supreme Being: "and *the Word was God*." God the Word always was: "the same was in the beginning with God." He created all things: "all things were made through

---

[21] Gen. 1:3

[22] Isa. 61:1: the Spirit of the Lord Jehovah is upon me, because Jehovah has anointed me

[23] Zech. 7: 12: Yea, they made their hearts as an adamant stone, lest they should hear the law, and the words that Jehovah of hosts had sent by his Spirit by the former prophets.

[24] Hag. 2:4-5: be strong, all you people of the land, says Jehovah, and work: for I am with you, says Jehovah of hosts, according to the word that I covenanted with you when you came out of Egypt, and my Spirit abode among you

[25] Luke 1:32, 35: he shall be great, and shall be called the Son of the Most High: and the Lord God shall give unto him the kingdom of his father David . . . the Holy Spirit shall come upon you, and the power of the Most High shall overshadow you: wherefore also the holy thing which is begotten shall be called the Son of God

[26] John 1:1-3, 14: In the beginning was the Word, and the Word was with God, and the Word was God. The same was in the beginning with God. All things were made through him . . . and the Word became flesh, and dwelt among us

him." Thus, there is only one God. The Father is that one God. The Word is that one God. Yet, the Father is not the Word. They are distinct, divine Persons. This reveals the general concept of the Trinity: distinct Persons, God the Father and God the Word, are the one and the same Supreme Being.

2. The anointing of God the Son

At Jesus' baptism the Father spoke from heaven and the Spirit descended upon him and anointed him to serve as Christ.[27] This demonstrates that they are distinct Persons, who communicate and commune with each other: "you are my beloved Son." When Christ reflects on his anointing, he distinguishes himself from the Holy Spirit:[28] "The Spirit of the Lord is upon me, because he anointed me." Thus, his anointing reveals that the Father, Son, and Spirit are distinct persons, not the same person.

3. The teaching of God the Son

Consider with me five passages in which Christ's teaching discloses the Trinity.

a. Matt. 28:19[29]

Christ epitomizes the biblical teaching on God's personality. Warfield says that this text furnishes the closest thing in the New Testament to a complete statement of the Trinity.[30] Christ teaches that Christians have a special relationship with the triune God. Baptism is the ceremonial ritual of admission to the society of disciples. It symbolizes their insertion into "the name of the Father and of the Son and of the Holy Spirit." Christ does not say, "the names," plural. He envisions, not three divine Beings, but one only. Nor does he say, "the name, Father, Son, Spirit." He does not envision only one divine Person. Rather, Christ teaches that three distinct Persons, the Father, the Son, and the Holy Spirit, have the same "name." What does Jesus mean by "name"? As I demonstrate in Topic 23, God's name in this

---

[27] *Luke 3:21-2*: Jesus, also having been baptized, and praying, the heaven was opened, and the Holy Spirit descended in a bodily form, as a dove, upon him, and a voice came out of heaven, You are my beloved Son; in you I am well pleased

[28] *Luke 4:1, 18, 21*: Jesus, full of the Holy Spirit, returned from the Jordan . . . The Spirit of the Lord is upon me, because he anointed me . . . To-day has this scripture been fulfilled in your ears

[29] *Matt. 28:19*: Go therefore, and make disciples of all the nations, baptizing them into the name of the Father, and of the Son, and of the Holy Spirit, teaching them to observe all things whatsoever I have commanded you: and lo, I am with you always, even unto the end of the world

[30] Warfield, *Biblical and Theological Studies*, 41-42

general sense can depict his unique Being,[31] or his divine authority,[32] or his divine glory, the whole set of essential attributes without which he would not be God.[33] Whether Christ stresses one of these, or combines them, we reach the same conclusion. If three Persons equally have one and the same divine Being, authority, or glory, then each must be the Supreme Being. Thus, Christ teaches that the Father, the Son, and the Holy Spirit equally are the Supreme Being.

b. *Luke 12:10*[34]

Christ engages in controversy with unbelievers. They attributed his miracles to the power of the devil. Christ in response affirms that the Holy Spirit is a distinct Person. He also teaches the deity of the Spirit. When people speak against the Holy Spirit, they commit blasphemy

c. *John 3:17*[35]

Jesus teaches us the remedial design and focus of his Messianic mission and commission. God the Son says that God the Father sent him into the world to save sinners. Thus, God the Son and God the Father are distinct persons, not the same person. And, God the Son existed *before* he came into the world and became human. The pre-incarnate life of the Son and his distinction from the Father are pillars that support the biblical disclosure of the Trinity.

d. *John 5:23, 37*[36]

Jesus teaches us his essential deity when he engages in Sabbath controversy with the Pharisees. His defense of healing on the Sabbath provoked his adversaries. He called God his "Father, making himself equal with God." In defense of his claim to equality with God the Father, he teaches that the Father wants humanity to honor and worship the Son in the very same way that they worship the Father. He adds that the Father has verbally testified from heaven that Jesus is God the Son incarnate.

---

[31] Pss. 79:6, 80:18, 86:11
[32] Deut. 18:19-20
[33] Exod. 33:19, 22, 34:14; Ps. 20:1; Isa. 57:15
[34] *Luke 12:10*: every one who shall speak a word against the Son of man, it shall be forgiven him: but unto him that blasphemes against the Holy Spirit it shall not be forgiven
[35] *John 3:17*: For God sent not the Son into the world to judge the world; but that the world should be saved through him
[36] *John 5:23, 37*: that all may honor the Son, even as they honor the Father. He that honors not the Son honors not the Father that sent him . . . the Father that sent me, he has borne witness of me

e. John 14:8-10[37]

On Jesus' last night on earth, his disciples asked him to show them God the Father. He taught them that to see him was to see the Father. He said that he was one with the Father: "I am in the Father and the Father in me." Thus, Scripture discloses both the distinctness of the Son from the Father and his unity with his Father as the Supreme Being.

4. The prayer of God the Son[38]

Christ repeatedly mentioned his personal communion with his Father. In his prayer of intercession he speaks with the Father about their personal communion before the creation of the world. In this way God the Son disclosed both his eternal deity and his personal distinctness from his Father.

B. The Spirit Sent from the Father and Son

The Father[39] and Son[40] send God the Spirit to God's people as the Holy Spirit to sanctify them,[41] as the Comforter, to comfort them,[42] as the Spirit of truth, to instruct them,[43] and as the Spirit of the Father and of the Son, the Spirit of adoption, to commune with them.[44] This coming of the Spirit reveals the personal communion of the Trinity. The Son is not the Father. He prays to him. The Son and the Father are not the Spirit. They send him to us. This discloses plainly that the Spirit of God is not an impersonal force, but a Person. The Spirit communicates verbally.[45] He intercedes for the saints.[46]

---

[37] *John 14:8-10*: show us the Father, and it suffices us. Jesus says unto him, Have I been so long time with you, and do you not know me Philip? he that has seen me has seen the Father. Do you not believe that I am in the Father and the Father in me?

[38] *John 17:5*: Father, glorify me with your own self with the glory I had with you before the world was.

[39] *John 14:16-17, 26*: I will pray the Father, and he shall give you another Comforter, that he may be with you forever, even the Spirit of truth . . . the Comforter, the Holy Spirit, whom the Father shall send in my name

[40] *John 15:26*: when the Comforter is come, whom I will send you from the Father, even the Spirit of truth, which proceeds from the Father, he shall bear witness of me. *Acts 2:33*: Being therefore by the right hand of God exalted, and having received of the Father the promise of the Holy Spirit, he has poured forth this which you see and hear

[41] Ezek. 36:27; 2 Thess. 2:13; Titus 3:5

[42] John 14:16-17; Rom. 14:17, 15:13

[43] John 16:13; 1 Cor. 2:12

[44] Rom. 8:9-11, 15; Gal. 4:6

[45] *Acts 10:19*: the Spirit said unto him, Behold three men seek you . . . I have sent them

[46] *Rom. 8:26-27*: the Spirit himself makes intercession for us . . . the mind of the Spirit, because he makes intercession for the saints according to the will of God

He searches, understands, and teaches the deep things of God.[47] He dispenses spiritual gifts at his personal discretion.[48] He feels anger when his people rebel against him.[49] Further, this redemptive mission of the Spirit reveals his deity. If people lie to him, they lie to the Supreme Being.[50] He has infinite understanding (1 Cor. 2:10-11, 13). He is Jehovah.[51] Thus, the coming of the Spirit to earth explicitly unveils that he is the Supreme Being, and yet, a Person distinct from the Father and Son.

C. Experiential Communion with God the Father, Son, and Spirit

The Trinitarian consciousness and devotion of the apostles discloses God's triune personality. True Christianity is experiential knowledge of the Father, of the Son,[52] and of the Holy Spirit.[53] The Trinity has accomplished salvation in Christ.[54] The Trinity applies salvation[55] in conversion.[56] The Trinity secures the perseverance of believers.[57] The Trinity will complete salvation in the resurrection of the body.[58] The work of the Trinity supports and ensures the proclamation of Christ to the Gentiles.[59] Trinitarian fellowship

---

[47] *1 Cor. 2:10-11, 13*: unto us God revealed them through the Spirit: for the Spirit searches all things, yea, the deep things of God . . . the things of God none knows, save the Spirit of God . . . which things also we speak . . . in words . . . which the Spirit teaches

[48] *1 Cor. 12:11*: all these works the one and the same Spirit, dividing to each one severally even as he will

[49] *Eph. 4:30*: grieve not the Holy Spirit of God, in whom you were sealed unto the day of redemption

[50] *Acts 5:3-4*: why has Satan filled your heart to lie to the Holy Spirit . . . you have not lied unto men, but unto God

[51] *2 Cor. 3:17*: the Lord is the Spirit: and where the Spirit of the Lord is, there is liberty

[52] *1 John 1:3*: our fellowship is with the Father, and with his Son Jesus Christ

[53] *1 John 4:13-14*: we know that we abide in him and he in us, because he has given us his Spirit. And we have beheld and bear witness that the Father has sent the Son to be the Savior of the world

[54] *Heb. 2:3-4*: at the first spoken by the Lord, was confirmed unto us by them that heard; God also bearing witness with them . . . by the gifts of the Holy Spirit, according to his will

[55] 2 Thess. 2:13-14; 1 Pet. 1:2

[56] *Titus 3:4-6*: when the kindness of God our Savior . . . appeared . . . he saved us . . . through the . . . renewing of the Holy Spirit, which he poured out upon us richly through Jesus Christ our Savior

[57] *Jude 20-21*: praying in the Holy Spirit, keep yourselves in the love of God, looking for the mercy of our Lord Jesus Christ unto eternal life

[58] *Rom. 8:11*: But if the Spirit of him that raised up Jesus from the dead dwelleth in you, he that raised up Christ Jesus from the dead shall give life also to your mortal bodies through his Spirit that dwelleth in you

[59] Eph. 3:2-5

mandates the inclusion of Gentile believers in Christ's saved society.[60] Accordingly, spiritual communion with the Trinity governs and pervades every aspect of the Christian life and experience. Communion with the Trinity diversifies and unifies the conveyance of spiritual gifts.[61] Spiritual blessing from the Trinity constitutes the Christian experience of divine favor.[62] Communion with the Trinity regulates Christian worship.[63] Experiential knowledge of the Trinity undergirds and fosters Christian unity.[64] In these ways Scripture reveals the manifold riches of the Trinity through the experience of Trinitarian salvation and personal communion with the triune God.

Unit 2. The Biblical Doctrine of God's Personality

When Jesus speaks of "the name of the Father and of the Son and of the Holy Spirit," he affirms both the concept and personal relations of God's triune personality, *the Trinity*. Accordingly, I present the *concept* and *personal relations* of the Trinity exegetically, historically, and practically.

I. The Concept of the Trinity

I present a biblical definition of the Trinity, survey the historical confession of the Trinity, and summarize its practical applications.

A. Biblical Definition of the Trinity

Based on the biblical disclosure of God's triune personality in the Old and New Testaments, I offer the following definition of the Trinity, God's triune personality:

> *God's triune personality is*: God's triune personal consciousness and tri-personal life: in which three distinct, divine Persons or Subsistences, the Father, the Son, and the Holy Spirit, with unique interpersonal relations, are the one and only Supreme Being, equally have the same divine authority, equally possess each divine attribute, the one and the same divine nature, or essence, or substance, and equally manifest the divine glory.

---

[60] *Acts 11:15, 17*: the Holy Spirit fell on them, even as on us at the beginning . . . If then God gave unto them the same gift as he did also unto us, when we believed on the Lord Jesus Christ, who was I, that I could withstand God

[61] *1 Cor. 12:4-6*: there are diversity of gifts, but the same Spirit. And there are diversities of ministrations, and the same Lord. And there are diversity of workings, but the same God

[62] *2 Cor. 13:14*: the grace of the Lord Jesus Christ, and the love of God, and the communion of the Holy Spirit, be with you all

[63] *Eph. 2:18*: through him we both have our access in one Spirit unto the Father

[64] *Eph. 4:4-6*: there is one body, and one Spirit, even as you were called in one hope of your calling; one Lord, one faith, one baptism, one God and Father of all

My definition specifies the *general idea*, the *threeness,* and the *unity* of the Trinity. I now expound and support this definition and collate its biblical support.

1. The general idea of the Trinity: God's triune personal consciousness and tri-personal life

Triune combines oneness with threeness. God's personal consciousness involves both unity and triunity. The Supreme Being expresses unity in his personal consciousness with the singular, personal pronoun: "look unto me, and be ye saved, all the ends of the earth; for I am God, and there is none else (Isa. 45:22). He expresses plurality generally with the plural, personal pronoun: "let us make man in our image" (Gen. 1:26). He expresses triunity in his personal consciousness when the Father, the Son, and the Spirit relate using the second person pronoun: "Father, glorify me with your own self with the glory I had with you before the world was" (John 17:5), and the third person pronoun: "I will pray the Father, and he shall give you another Comforter, that he may be with you forever, even the Spirit of truth" (John 14:16-17). Thus, the personal consciousness of the Supreme Being is unique, mysterious, and incomprehensible. Triune personality also entails "tri-personal life." I demonstrated in Topic 12 that God's life always consists in his Trinitarian fellowship. Thus, God's triune personality is inherently living and active. His self-awareness necessarily involves personal communication and interpersonal communion.[65]

2. The threeness of the Trinity: "three distinct, divine Persons or Subsistences, the Father, the Son, and the Holy Spirit, with unique interpersonal relations"

I define God's personal threeness with the words, "Person" and "Subsistence." Divine *"Person"* means, not a separate divine being, but a distinct, divine self-awareness: "glorify thou me, with *your own self*" (John 17:5). Divine *"Subsistence"* means a distinct personal consciousness which is living, actively communing and communicating: "the life, the eternal life, which was with the Father" (1 John 1:2). Next, I identify the three divine Persons as: "the Father, the Son, and the Holy Spirit." Each is a divine personal consciousness with distinct self-awareness. I conclude with the distinct expressions of this threeness: "unique personal relations." Their names, "Father," "Son," and "Holy Spirit" express their unique personal relations. These are not arbitrary, reversible, or transferable, but eternal, inherent, essential, and immutable. They necessarily relate as they do, because they invariably are who they are. God's work displays these

---

[65] *John 1:1, 17:5; 1 John 1:2*: and the Word was with God ... Father, glorify me with your own self with the glory I had with you before the world was ... the life, the eternal life, which was with the Father.

relations: "And the Word became flesh" (John 1:14). Neither the Father nor the Spirit became human, only God the Word.

Scripture commends using both *Person* and *Subsistence* to describe God's personal distinctness and relations. Both words are transliterations of Latin words. "Person" comes from the Latin, *persona*, and "subsistence," from the Latin *subsistentia*. These Latin words have a rich theological history and close ties with Greek terms. The Council of Chalcedon published a creed in Greek that displays these ties:[66]

> Christ, Son, Lord, Only-begotten, to be acknowledged in two natures inconfusedly, unchangeably, indivisibly, inseparably; the distinction of natures [φυσεων] {naturarum}, by no means being taken away by the union, but rather the property of each nature being preserved, and concurring in one Person [προσωπον] {personam} and one Subsistence [ὑποστασιν] {subsistentiam}, not parted or divided into two persons [προσωπα] {personas}, but one and the same Son, and only begotten, God the Word, the Lord Jesus Christ.

They affirm that Christ is one divine Person, one Subsistence, who has both human and divine natures:

English: Person (transliteration of Latin)   English: Subsistence (transliteration of Latin)
Latin: Persona (translation of Greek)   Latin: Subsistentia (translation of Greek)
Greek: προσωπον (prosopon)   Greek: ὑποστασις (hupostasis)

The Latin and Greek fathers chose these terms, not arbitrarily, but based on their use in the New Testament. Note the biblical use of *person* (prosopon) and *subsistence* (hupostasis).

a. Three Persons

The Greek word for person is *prosopon*. It is translated, "face," "presence," or "person," with various nuances. It literally describes the face or countenance: "who, seeing Jesus, fell on his *face*," "they were affrighted and bowed down their *faces* to the earth" (Luke 5:12, 24:5). It also depicts personal presence, being "face to face": "they departed from the *presence* of the council" (Acts 5:41). It also explicitly refers to personal distinctness, "thanks may be given by many *persons* on our behalf" (2 Cor. 1:11). Thus, personal distinctness centers in the face and presence. With their faces human beings have personal communication and communion. *Prosopon* also describes God's personal distinctness. It can denote God's special

---

[66] Philip Schaff, *Creeds of Christendom* (3 Vols.; Grand Rapids: Baker Book House, 1990), 2:62-63

presence in general.[67] It explicitly depicts the Father's personal distinctness: "their angels do always behold *the face* of my Father" (Matt. 18:10), and, "now to appear in *the presence* of God for us" (Heb. 9:24). It also explicitly depicts the personal distinctness of God the Son: "for your sakes I have forgiven it in *the presence* [person, KJV] of Christ" (2 Cor. 2:10), and, "the glory of God in *the face* of Jesus Christ" (2 Cor. 4:6). Further, the phrase, "and the Word was *with God*" depicts "face to face" communion implicitly. Thus, Scripture supports using *person* to depict God's personal distinctness.

b. Three Subsistences

The Greek word for subsistence is *hupostasis* or *hypostasis*. It is translated, "confidence," "person" (KJV), "subsistence" (YLT), "substance," or "assurance." It occurs 5 times in Scripture.[68] According to Strong[69] it connotes "setting under," "standing beneath," or, "that which gives support." Its use displays various nuances. It depicts Paul's confidence that supports him when he publishes the Corinthians' pledge of benevolence.[70] It also depicts confidence that supports boasting.[71] With sarcasm Paul seems to mean that cocksure bragging is foolish because it lacks valid grounds or solid support. Further, *hupostasis* characterizes faith as: *"the assurance* [substance KJV] of things hoped for, a conviction of things not seen." (Heb. 11:1). It depicts confidence that future events will really happen. Thus, saving faith supports Christians in regard to unseen blessings that God promises us in his Word. *Hupostasis* also depicts our *"confidence"* in Christ (Heb. 3:14). Thus, in its usage *hupostasis* depicts *that which gives support* and provides security, stability, and certainty, especially regarding the future. This general use of *hupostasis* frames its explicit use to depict the personal distinctness of the Father and Son:

> Heb. 1:2-3: his Son, whom he appointed heir of all things, through whom also he made the worlds; who being the effulgence of his glory, and the very image of his *hupostasis* [*subsistence* Young's Literal Translation] [*person* KJV], and upholding all things by the word of his power, when he had made purification of sins, sat down on the right hand of the Majesty on high.

This text explicitly presents the Son as the Supreme Being, "through whom he made the worlds . . . upholding all things." It explicitly describes the

---

[67] Acts 3:19; 2 Thess. 1:9-10; 1 Pet. 3:12
[68] 2 Cor. 9:4; 11:17; Heb. 1:3, 3:14, 11:1.
[69] Strong, *Lexicon*, 74
[70] 2 Cor. 9:4
[71] 2 Cor. 11:17

personal relation of the Son and the Father with the word *hupostasis*: "the very image of his *hupostasis*." In accord with the usage of *hupostasis*, this signifies, "the very image of his [support]." What supports the Father? The Father himself supports his life and continued existence. He has "life in himself" (John 5:26). Thus, the *hupostasis* of the Father is his own living personal consciousness. The word, *subsistence*, in English signifies, "the condition of remaining in existence."[72] Therefore, subsistence is a good term to depict the personal distinctness of the Father, Son, and Spirit. Note that *hupostasis* in this text cannot mean "divine nature." If it did, Christ would have a divine nature "exactly like" the Father's divine nature. This would imply two separate divine natures, two separate divine beings. For this reason I am wary of the ASV's translation of *hupostasis* as "substance." Yet, if substance refers to the Father's *personal substance*, I won't quibble over it. That would amount to his personal distinctness or subsistence. Regarding this text Owen observes:[73]

> The apostle adds that he is χαραχτηρ ὑποστασεως αὐτου, 'the express figure' (or 'image') 'of his person;' that is, of the person of God the Father. I shall not enter into any dispute about the meaning of the word ὑποστασεως, or the difference between it and οὐσια. Many controversies about these words there were of old. And Jerome was very cautious about acknowledging three hypostases in the Deity, and that because he thought the word in this place to denote 'substantia;' and of that mind are many still, it being so rendered by the Vulgate translation. But the consideration of these vexed questions tending not to the opening of the design of the apostle and meaning of the Holy Ghost in this place, I shall not insist upon them. 1. The hypostasis of the Father is the Father himself. Hereof, or of him, is the Son said to be the 'express image.'

I agree with Owen: "the hypostasis of the Father is the Father himself." The Son is the very image of the Father himself. Thus, Scripture confirms that the Father, Son, and Spirit are distinct Subsistences. This supports using *subsistence* to describe God's personal distinctness.

3. The unity or oneness of the Trinity: "are the one and only Supreme Being, equally have the same divine authority, equally possess each divine attribute, the one and the same divine nature, or essence, or substance, and equally manifest the divine glory"

Divine oneness consists in unity and singularity of being, authority, nature, and glory. When I say, "the one and only Supreme Being," I mean that

---

[72] *WNC Dictionary*, 1153

[73] John Owen, *An Exposition of the Epistle to the Hebrews* (7 vols.; Grand Rapids: Baker Book House, 1960), 2:95

numerically there is only one Supreme Being and that the Father, the Son, and the Spirit are the Supreme Being. When I say: "equally have the same divine authority," I mean that each Person has every right and prerogative of the Supreme Being. When I say, "equally possess each divine attribute, the one and the same divine nature, or essence, or substance," I mean that numerically, there is only one divine nature, essence, or substance, one set of divine attributes, and that the Father, the Son, and the Holy Spirit equally have every divine attribute. God is radically unlike man. Human nature consists in a human body and soul. Distinct human beings each have a human nature, so that numerically there are as many human natures as human beings. Yet the Father, Son, and Spirit are not three divine beings, each having a divine nature, so that numerically there are three divine natures. That would be polytheism, three separate but equal gods. When I say, "equally manifest the divine glory," I mean that each Person of the Trinity equally manifests divine majesty and equally deserves the honor, devotion, worship, and praise that are due to God alone.

Scripture repeatedly affirms the deity of the Father, of the Son, and of the Spirit. I expound the evidence for deity of the Son in the Doctrine of Christ. I support the deity of the Spirit in detail the Doctrine of the Holy Spirit. I commend the presentations of this evidence that John Calvin[74] and Morton Smith[75] set forth in their works. I catalogue below the major categories of biblical support for the deity of the Father, of the Son, and of the Holy Spirit.

a. The deity of the Father (5 texts)

John 6:27: him the Father, even God, has sealed
Rom. 1:1, 2: the gospel of God . . . concerning his Son
1 Cor. 8:6: to us there is one God, the Father, of whom are all things
1 Cor. 15:24: he shall deliver up the kingdom to God, even the Father
Eph. 1:3: Blessed be the God and Father of our Lord Jesus Christ.

b. The deity of the Son (five categories)

[1] Scripture calls Christ the Supreme Being.[76]
[2] He possesses and manifests the attributes of the Supreme Being.[77]

---

[74] Calvin, *Institutes*, 1:129-140
[75] Morton Smith, *Systematic Theology*, 1:341-358. Biblical support for Spirit's deity was in the original syllabus: 1: 215-217
[76] John 1:1-3, 14, 5:18, 20:28; Rom. 9:5; Titus 2:13; Heb. 1:8, 10; 2 Pet. 1:1; 1 John 5:20.
[77] Matt. 11:27, 18:20, 28:20; John 1:1,2, 8:30, 12:41, 21:17; Phil. 2:6, 3:21; Heb. 1:11, 12, 7:26; Rev. 2:23, 19:11.

[3] He performs all the works of the Supreme Being.[78]
[4] He deserves and receives worship due to the Supreme Being alone.[79]
[5] Scripture describes him with the names and titles of the Supreme Being.[80]

c. *The deity of the Holy Spirit* (five categories)

[1] Scripture calls him the Supreme Being: Acts 5:3-4
[2] He has the attributes of the Supreme Being: Ps. 139:7-10; Isa. 40:13-14; 1 Cor. 2:10-11, 12:11; Heb. 9:14
[3] He performs the works of the Supreme Being: Gen. 1:2; Job 33:4; Ps. 104:30; Titus 3:5; Rom. 8:11
[4] He deserves reverence and devotion due to the Supreme Being alone: Luke 12:10; 2 Cor. 13:14; Rev. 4:8-9
[5] Scripture describes him with the name of the Supreme Being.[81]

Conclusion: collation of biblical support

The biblical evidence for the Trinity is threefold: (1) there is only one God; (2) the Father, the Son, and the Holy Spirit are God; and (3) the Father, the Son, and the Holy Spirit are distinct Persons or Subsistences. I proved in Topic 2 that only one God exists. Using my definition, I now collate biblical evidence for the *distinctness* and *deity* of the Father, the Son, and the Holy Spirit:

> *God's triune personality is*: God's triune personal consciousness and tri-personal life: in which three distinct, divine Persons or Subsistences, the Father, the Son, and the Holy Spirit, with unique interpersonal relations,[1] are the one and only Supreme Being, equally have the same divine authority, equally possess each divine attribute, the one and the same divine nature, or essence, or substance, and equally manifest the divine glory.[2]
>
> *1. The distinctness*: Matt. 28:19; Luke 1:35, 3:21, 22, 4:18, 21, 12:10; John 1:1-3, 14, 5:23,37, 14:16, 17, 26, 15:26, 16:13, 17:5; Acts 2:33, 11:15-17; Eph. 2:18; Titus 3:4-6; Heb. 2:3, 4; Rev. 1:4, 5.
>
> *2. The deity*: The Father: John 6:27, etc. : The Son: John 1:1, etc. : The Spirit: Acts 5:3-4, etc. [see above]

---

[78] Matt. 28:18; John 1:1-3, 5:19, 20, 24; Eph. 1:22; Col. 1:15-17; Titus 2:13; Heb. 1:3, 11, 12

[79] Matt. 4:9; John 5:21-23, 20:28, 29; Heb. 1:6; Rev. 19:10

[80] Isa. 9:6, 7; Isa. 6:1-8, w/John 12:41; Isa. 8:13, 14, w/1 Pet. 2:5-8; Isa. 7:14, w/Matt. 1:23; John 8:58.

[81] Isa. 6:8-10, w/Acts 28:25-27; Ps. 95:7-9, w/Heb. 3:7-9; 2 Cor. 3:17

Finally, all human effort to illustrate the Trinity falls short, for God's personality is unique. We catch a faint glimpse of the Trinity in creation, but we must use caution, for all our analogies break down. For example, distinct human beings with a common human nature would illustrate polytheism, not the Trinity. Again, some compare the Trinity to the three states of matter. Water has the same molecular structure (H_2O) as a liquid, gas (steam), or solid (ice). Yet this better illustrates modalism, because steam, ice, and liquid water don't naturally exist together. They only exist simultaneously at the triple point. The *triple point* is the temperature and pressure on the phase diagram at which water has no latent heat of vaporization or fusion, so that it is a gas, solid, and liquid simultaneously. Yet this too falls short, for water is rarely at its triple point, but the Father, Son, and Spirit are ever God.

B. The Historical Confession of the Trinity

All orthodox Christians affirm the Trinity. Only heretics deny it. We consider three creeds. First, from the circle of the English Puritans, we consider the 1689 London Confession (LCF). Second, from circle of Dutch Calvinism, we look at the Belgic Confession (BLC). Finally, we consider the Athanasian Creed (AC). We conclude with two prominent heresies that deny the Trinity.

1. The 1689 London Confession

> LCF 2:3: In this divine and infinite Being there are three subsistences, the Father, the Word or Son, and Holy Spirit, of one substance, power, and eternity, each having the whole divine essence, yet the essence undivided: the Father is of none, neither begotten nor proceeding; the Son is eternally begotten of the Father; the Holy Spirit proceeding from the Father and the Son; all infinite, without beginning, therefore but one God, who is not to be divided in nature and being, but distinguished by several peculiar relative properties and personal relations; which doctrine of the Trinity is the foundation of all our communion with God, and comfortable dependence on him.

The Confession defines God's triune personality: "In this divine and infinite Being there are three Subsistences, the Father, the Word or Son, and Holy Spirit, of one substance, power, and eternity, each having the whole divine essence, yet the essence undivided." Next, it specifies their personal relations: "the Father is of none, neither begotten nor proceeding; the Son is eternally begotten of the Father; the Holy Spirit proceeding from the Father and the Son." Third, it, summarizes the doctrine of the Trinity generically: "all infinite, without beginning, therefore but one God, who is not to be divided in nature and being, but distinguished by several peculiar relative properties and personal relations." Finally, it applies the Trinity to experiential religion: "which doctrine of the Trinity is the foundation of all our communion with God, and comfortable dependence on him." The Baptist fathers confess the biblical doctrine of the Trinity clearly and precisely. They define God's threeness as: "one God . . . distinguished by several peculiar relative properties and personal relations, and as: "three subsistences, the Father, the Word or Son, and Holy Spirit." They define God's oneness as: "one God, who is not to be divided in nature and being," and as, "of one substance, power, and eternity, each having the whole divine essence, yet the essence undivided." They thus confirm our faith.

2. The Belgic Confession (Articles 8-11)

The Belgic Confession defines and supports the Trinity in four articles. First they define the Trinity (Article 8). Next they present its biblical and historical support (Article 9). Next they confess the deity and personal distinctness of God the Son (Article 10). They conclude with the deity and personal distinctness of the Holy Spirit (Article 11).

a. Definition of the Trinity

ARTICLE 8: GOD ONE IN ESSENCE, YET DISTINGUISHED IN THREE PERSONS

> According to this truth and this Word of God, we believe in one only God, who is the one single essence, in which are three persons, really, truly, and eternally distinct according to their incommunicable properties; namely, the Father, and the Son, and the Holy Spirit. The Father is the cause, origin, and beginning of all things visible and invisible; the Son is the word, wisdom, and image of the Father; the Holy Spirit is the eternal power and might, proceeding from the Father and the Son. Nevertheless, God is not by this distinction divided into three, since the Holy Scriptures teach us that the Father, and the Son, and the Holy Spirit have each His personality, distinguished by their properties; but in such wise that these three persons are but one only God.
>
> Hence, then, it is evident that the Father is not the Son, nor the Son the Father, and likewise that the Holy Spirit is neither the Father nor the Son. Nevertheless, these persons thus distinguished are not divided, nor intermixed; for the Father has not assumed flesh, nor has the Holy Spirit, but the Son only. The Father has never been without His Son, or without His Holy Spirit. For these three are co-eternal and co-essential. There is neither first nor last; for They are all three one, in truth, in power, in goodness, and in mercy.

The first paragraph defines the doctrine of the Trinity. The second traces out its implications. The first paragraph has three complete sentences. The first sentence defines God's triune personality: "According to this truth and this Word of God, we believe in one only God, who is the one single essence, in which are three persons, really, truly, and eternally distinct according to their incommunicable properties; namely, the Father, and the Son, and the Holy Spirit." The second sentence defines the personal distinctness of each divine Person: "The Father is the cause, origin, and beginning of all things visible and invisible; the Son is the word, wisdom, and image of the Father; the Holy Spirit is the eternal power and might, proceeding from the Father and the Son." The third sentence reaffirms both divine triunity and unity: "Nevertheless, God is not by this distinction divided into three, since the Holy Scriptures teach us that the Father, and the Son, and the Holy Spirit have each His personality, distinguished by their properties; but in such wise that these three persons are but one only God." Observe that they define divine oneness with the word, "essence." In Article 11 they say again: "of one and the same essence, majesty, and glory with the Father and the Son." Note they define divine threeness with the word, "person," and speak of incommunicable "personal properties." In Article 9 they reaffirm: "there are three persons in only one divine essence."

b. Support for the Trinity

ARTICLE 9: THE PROOF OF THE FOREGOING ARTICLE OF THE TRINITY OF PERSONS IN ONE GOD

> All this we know as well from the testimonies of Holy Writ as from their operations, and chiefly by those we feel in ourselves. The testimonies of the Holy Scriptures that teach us to believe this Holy Trinity are written in many places of the Old Testament, which are not so necessary to enumerate as to choose them with discretion and judgment.
>
> In Gen.1:26,27, God says: *Let us make man in our image, after our likeness,* etc. *And God created man in his own image, male and female created he them.* And Gen.3:22, *Behold, the man is become as one of us.* From this saying, Let *us* make man in *our* image, it appears that there are more persons than one in the Godhead; and when He says, *God* created, He signifies the unity. It is true, He does not say how many persons there are, but that which appears to us somewhat obscure in the Old Testament, is very plain in the New. For when our Lord was baptized in Jordan, the voice of the Father was heard saying, *This is my beloved Son*; the Son was seen in the water, and the Holy Spirit appeared in the shape of a dove. This form is also instituted by Christ in the baptism of all believers: *Make disciples of all the nations, baptizing them into the name of the Father and of the Son and of the Holy Spirit.* In the Gospel of Luke the angel Gabriel thus

> addressed Mary, the mother of our Lord: *The Holy Spirit shall come upon thee, and the power of the Most High shall overshadow thee; wherefore also the holy thing which is begotten shall be called the Son of God.* Likewise: *The grace of the Lord Jesus Christ, and the love of God, and the communion of the Holy Spirit, be with you all.* And: *there are three that bear record in heaven, the Father, the Word, and the Holy Ghost: and these three are one.*
>
> In all these places we are fully taught that there are three persons in only one divine essence. And although this doctrine far surpasses all human understanding, nevertheless we now believe it by means of the Word of God, but expect to enjoy perfect knowledge and benefit thereof in heaven.
>
> Moreover, we must observe the particular offices and operations of these three persons toward us. The Father is called our Creator, by His power; the Son is our Savior and Redeemer, by His blood; the Holy Spirit is our Sanctifier, by his dwelling in our hearts.
>
> This doctrine of the Holy Trinity has always been affirmed and maintained by the true Church since the time of the apostles to this very day against the Jews, Mohammedans, and some false Christians and heretics, as Marcion, Manes, Praxeas, Sabellius, Samosatenus, Arius, and such like, who have been justly condemned by the orthodox fathers. Therefore, in this point, we do willingly receive the three creeds, namely, that of the Apostles, of Nicea, and of Athanasius; likewise that which, conformable thereunto, is agreed upon by the ancient fathers

This remarkable statement of faith supports the Trinity from its disclosure in the Old and New Testaments. It cites several of the texts we have considered. This article also supports the Trinity by appealing to its historical confession in church creeds and by exposing by name heretics that have denied it.

c. The deity and personal distinctness of the Son

> ARTICLE 10: JESUS CHRIST IS TRUE AND ETERNAL GOD
>
> We believe that Jesus Christ according to His divine nature is the only begotten Son of God, begotten from eternity, not made, nor created (for then He would be a creature), but co-essential and co-eternal with the Father, *the very image of his substance and the effulgence of his glory,* equal unto Him in all things. He is the Son of God, not only from the time that He assumed our nature, but from all eternity, as these testimonies, when compared together, teach us. Moses says that God created the world; and St. John says that all things were made by that Word which he calls God. The apostle says that God made the world by his Son;

likewise, that God created all things by Jesus Christ. Therefore, it must needs follow that he who is called God, the Word, the Son, and Jesus Christ, did exist at that time when all things were created by Him. Therefore the prophet Micah says: *His goings forth are from of old, from everlasting.* And the apostle: *He hath neither beginning of days nor end of life.* He therefore is that true, eternal, and almighty God whom we invoke, worship, and serve.

d. The deity and personal distinctness of the Holy Spirit

ARTICLE 11: THE HOLY SPIRIT IS TRUE AND ETERNAL GOD

We believe and confess also that the Holy Spirit from eternity proceeds from the Father and the Son; and therefore neither is made, created, nor begotten, but only proceeds from both; who in order is the third person of the Holy Trinity; of one and the same essence, majesty, and glory with the Father and the Son; and therefore is the true and eternal God, as the Holy Scriptures teach.

In sum, Dutch Calvinism and English Puritanism supply us with a rich heritage. The Belgic Confession speaks of three divine "Persons." The LCF confesses three divine "Subsistences." Both terms are firmly rooted in Scripture and in the formula of Chalcedon. Accordingly, I use both *person* and *subsistence*.

3. The Athanasian Creed

THE ATHANASIAN CREED: (ARTICLES 1-28)

1. Whosoever will be saved: before all things it is necessary that he hold the catholic faith:
2. Which faith except every one do keep whole and undefiled: without doubt he shall perish everlastingly.
3. And the catholic faith is this: that we worship one God in Trinity, and Trinity in Unity;
4. Neither confounding the Persons [personas], nor dividing the Substance [substantiam].
5. For there is one Person of the Father: another of the Son: another of the Holy Spirit.
6. But the Godhead of the Father, and of the Son, and of the Holy Spirit is one: the glory equal, the majesty coeternal.
7. Such as the Father is: such is the Son: and such is the Holy Spirit.
8. The Father uncreated [increatus]: the Son uncreated: and the Holy Spirit uncreated.
9. The Father infinite [immensus]: the Son infinite: and the Holy Spirit infinite.
10. The Father eternal: The Son eternal: and the Holy Spirit eternal.
11. And yet they are not three eternals: but one eternal.
12. As also there are not three uncreateds: nor three infinites: but one uncreated: and one infinite.
13. Similarly the Father is all-powerful [omnipotens]: the Son all-powerful: and the Holy Spirit all-powerful.
14. And yet there are not three all-powerfuls: but one all-powerful.
15. So the Father is God: the Son is God: and the Holy Spirit is God.
16. And yet there are not three Gods: but one God.
17. So likewise the Father is Lord: the Son is Lord: and the Holy Spirit is Lord.
18. And yet there are not three Lords: but one Lord.

19. For like as we are compelled by the Christian verity, to acknowledge every Person by himself to be God and Lord:
20. So we are forbidden by the catholic religion, to say, there are three Gods, or three Lords.
21. The Father is made of none: neither created nor begotten.
22. The Son is of the Father alone: not made [factus], nor created [creatus]: but begotten [genitus].
23. The Holy Spirit is of the Father and of the Son: neither made, nor created, nor begotten: but proceeding [procedens].
24. So there is one Father, not three Fathers: one Son, not three Sons: one Holy Spirit, not three Holy Spirits.
25. And in this Trinity nothing is before, or after: nothing greater or lesser. [Et in hac Trinitate nihil prius, aut posterus: nihil majus, aut minus.]
26. But the whole three Persons are coeternal [coaeternae], and coequal [coaequales].
27. So that in all things, as aforesaid: the Unity [Unitas] in Trinity, and the Trinity [Trinitas] in Unity, is to be worshipped [veneranda].
28. Therefore whoever wants to be saved, let him thus think of the Trinity

This section of the Athanasian Creed defines Christian faith in the Trinity. Its remainder defines Christian faith in Christ. Schaff relates the history and use of this creed.[82] Regarding this statement of the Trinity he says: "If the mystery of the Trinity can be logically defined, it is done here."[83]

Conclusion: Denial of the Trinity

The Athanasian Creed warns that faith in the Trinity is essential for heaven. The Belgic Confession identifies heretics by name. Accordingly, I close by identifying two major heresies that deny the Trinity: *Arianism* and *Sabellianism* or *Modalism*.

a. Sabellianism (Modalism)

Modalism claims that God is uni-personal. It alleges that one divine person has three different "modes of manifestation." Sometimes this person acts as the Father, sometimes as the Son, and sometimes as the Spirit. For example, I am one person. Yet, in some situations I act as a father, in others, as a son. Though I have fatherly and filial modes of manifestation, I am only one personal consciousness. So also, say Modalists, is God. Their heresy rejects Trinitarian personal communion. They seem to forget that to be a son I must relate to another person as father. I cannot be my own father, or my own son. Thus, the Father and the Son relate to each other because they are not the same Person. Modalism can never adequately account for the biblical testimony. Jesus didn't pray to himself: "I will pray the Father." He didn't ask himself to send himself: "and he will send you another Comforter." At Jordan, whose voice said from heaven: "you are my beloved Son"? Was

---

[82] Schaff, *Creeds of Christendom*, 1:34-42
[83] Ibid., 1:38

Jesus a ventriloquist? Did he throw his voice and talk to himself? Did he descend as a dove and land on himself? These absurdities arise when people reject Scripture and fashion a god in their own image. A god who is "Jesus only" is not the true God.

b. Arianism

Arians also see God as uni-personal. They admit that God the Father and Christ are distinct persons. Yet they deny that Jesus Christ is the Supreme Being. Arianism claims that Christ is an angel, or a lesser god. It alleges that he is not equal with the Father. It also claims that the Spirit of God is not a person, but an impersonal force. When a Jehovah's Witness knocks on your door, this heresy comes with him.

C. Practical Application of the Trinity

We consider two practical implications of the Trinity for genuine religion.

1. Faith in the Trinity is essential for genuine religion.

No Trinity, no Christianity! The creeds affirm this: "which doctrine of the Trinity is the foundation of all our communion with God, and comfortable dependence on him" (LCF 2:3), and, "Therefore whoever wants to be saved, let him thus think of the Trinity" (AC: 28). Christians have one God: the Father, the Son, and the Spirit. We give our religious loyalty, service, and devotion to him alone (Deut. 6:13; Matt. 4:9). Jehovah our God is the triune God. In communion with him we live in the world.[84] To deny the Trinity is idolatry and blasphemy. Either people worship the triune God, or they serve another god and practice another religion: "whosoever denies the Son, the same has not the Father (1 John 2:23), and, "if any man has not the Spirit of Christ, he is none of his" (Rom. 8:9).

2. Experiential communion with the Trinity is the soul of genuine religion.

Fellowship with the Trinity is eternal life. It frames Christian faith in creation and redemption. It fuels acceptable worship and ministry. Accordingly, Berkhof says: "it is, of course, of the greatest importance to maintain the personality of God, for without it there can be no religion in the real sense of the word: no prayer, no personal communion, no trustful reliance and no confident hope."[85] The Christian religion is thoroughly Trinitarian. Baptism is Trinitarian. We are baptized "into the name of the Father and of the Son and of the Holy Spirit" (Matt. 28:19). Christian ministry is Trinitarian: "there are diversity of gifts, but the same Spirit. And

---

[84] 2 Cor. 13:14; 1 John 1:3
[85] Berkhof, *Systematic Theology*, 84

there are diversities of ministrations, and the same Lord. And there are diversity of workings, but the same God" (1 Cor. 12:4-6). Christian fellowship with God is Trinitarian: "the grace of the Lord Jesus Christ, and the love of God, and the communion of the Holy Spirit, be with you all" (2 Cor. 13:14). Christian devotion is Trinitarian: "through him we both have our access in one Spirit unto the Father" (Eph. 2:18). Christian unity is Trinitarian: "there is one body, and one Spirit, even as you were called in one hope of your calling; one Lord, one faith, one baptism, one God and Father of all" (Eph. 4:4-6). Christian conversion is Trinitarian: "when the kindness of God our Savior . . . appeared . . . he saved us . . . through the . . . renewing of the Holy Spirit, which he poured out upon us richly through Jesus Christ our Savior" (Titus 3:4-6). Christian perseverance is Trinitarian: "praying in the Holy Spirit, keep yourselves in the love of God, looking for the mercy of our Lord Jesus Christ unto eternal life" (Jude 20-21). Thus, communion with the Trinity is the earmark of genuine Christianity.

II. The Personal Relations of the Trinity

I now expound the personal relations of the Father, Son, and Spirit. I address *biblical definition*, *historical confession*, and *practical application* of their personal relations.

A. A Biblical Definition of the Personal Relations of the Trinity

Scripture reveals the personal distinctness and relations of Persons of the Trinity. It defines the *identity*,[86] *foundation*,[87] and *display*[88] of these personal relations of the Trinity. I present these relations accordingly.

1. The identity of the personal relations of the Trinity

In accord with the biblical emphasis,[89] I first consider the personal distinctness and relation of the Father and Son, then the personal distinctness and relations of the Spirit.[90]

a. The personal relation of the Father and the Son: Pattern and Representation: Eternal Generation

The relationship of the Father and Son is necessary, permanent, and irreversible. It is not arbitrary, optional, or mutable. The Father is never without the Son. The Son is never without the Father. The Son is the "very

---

[86] Matt. 28:19; John 5:26, 14:8-10, 15:26; Rom. 8:9
[87] John 1:3, 14, 17:5; 1 John 1:3
[88] John 5:23, 14:16, 17, 26, 15:26; Acts 2:23; 1 Cor. 8:6
[89] John 1:1-3; 1 Cor. 8:6; 1 John 1:3
[90] Rom. 8:9

image," the exact representation, of the Father himself.[91] Thus Jesus says, "he that has seen me has seen the Father" (John 14:9). Therefore, the Father is *"the Pattern,* the Son is his *"Representation."* The Pattern is not the Representation, but never exists without it. The Pattern and Representation never reverse roles. This helps to clarify the concept of *eternal generation.* The Father, the Pattern, is a divine Person, a living personal consciousness. God the Son, his Representation, is a divine Person, a living personal consciousness. Both live eternally, always. Yet, the Representation does not generate its Pattern, nor does it generate itself without the Pattern. Every representation, by definition, is drawn from some pattern. Thus, the Father, the Pattern, eternally gives rise to, generates, the Son, his exact Representation: "as the Father has life in himself, even so he gave to the Son to have life in himself" (John 5:26). Thus, the Son is not made, or created, but *eternally begotten,* the eternal Representation of the eternal Pattern. Thus, the Father and Son are co-eternal and equal: "he called God his own Father, making himself equal with God" (John 5:18), and, "who, being in the form of God, did not count equality with God as robbery [stolen property]" (Phil. 2:6). Thus, Scripture stresses the Son's uniqueness: "the *only begotten* Son, who is in the bosom of the Father, he has declared Him" (John 1:18). This word, μομογενης (monogenes) translated, "only begotten," uniformly and exclusively describes an only child.[92] It oft denotes the Son.[93] Further, the Pattern reveals himself through his Representation. The Son declares and displays the Father. Thus, Scripture calls the Pattern, "God." It calls his Representation, "the Word of God" (John 1:1-3). Thus, all things are "of" the Pattern "through" his Representation.[94] Thus, we draw near "through" the Son "unto" the Father (Eph. 2:18).

b. *The personal relation of the Spirit to the Father and the Son: Procession, Exhalation*

Scripture calls the Holy Spirit the "Spirit *of* God" and the "Spirit *of* Christ."[95] He is the Spirit of the Pattern and of his Representation. Here is a profound mystery. In general Scripture connects "spirit" with life, animation, power,

---

[91] *Heb. 1:3*: who being the effulgence of his glory, the very image of his subsistence
[92] Luke 7:12, 8:42, 9:38; Heb. 11:17
[93] John 1:14, 3:16,18; 1 John 4:9
[94] *1 Cor. 8:6*: to us there is one God, the Father, of whom are all things, and we unto him; and one Lord, Jesus Christ, through whom are all things, and we through him
[95] *Rom. 8:9*: the Spirit of God dwells in you. But if any man have not the Spirit of Christ, he is none of his

and breath.[96] Thus, it connects God's Spirit with God's breath and power.[97] Accordingly, the Spirit is the breath of the Father and of the Son.[98] Thus, Christ "breathed on them and said, Receive the Holy Spirit" (John 20:22). In this way Scripture depicts the Spirit as going forth, proceeding, from God: "the Spirit of truth, *which proceeds* from the Father" (John 15:26). The word translated "proceeds" is ἐκπορευομαι (ekporeuomai), which means, "to go out," "to go forth," "to come out," in a wide variety of nuances. It can mean to emanate, emerge, issue from, radiate from, flow forth, gush, spurt, or depart. Thus God's breath proceeds from him. When a man breathes, he exhales his breath. It proceeds from his mouth. Thus God's breath, his Spirit, proceeds from him. Second, the Spirit, God's Breath, implements his power: "the Spirit of God has made me, and the breath of the Almighty has given me life" (Job 33:4), and, "the Holy Spirit shall come upon you, and the power of the Most High shall overshadow you" (Luke 1:35). A man's breath is hot air. Though it can warm cold hands, it is inanimate. God's breath, however, is living and powerful, a divine Person. The living Exhalation of the Father and the Son executes all God's will, effects all his designs, and implements his capacity to act deliberately (Ps. 104:30). The Holy Spirit is the living and powerful Exhalation of the Father and the Son, who proceeds from them and puts God's will into effect. The Supreme Being has no physical mouth from which his living Exhalation proceeds. Yet he created man after his likeness to furnish this true picture of himself. A man's breath conveys his words. Similarly, the living Exhalation of the Father and the Son conveys their inspired[99] Word.[100] A man's breath exhibits his life and presence. Similarly, the Spirit manifests the special presence and eternal life of the Father and the Son. Where he goes, they go; where he is, they are.

In sum, three divine Persons ever relate as the living Pattern, the Father, as his exact Representation, the Son, patterned after him and generated by him, and as their powerful Exhalation, the Holy Spirit, proceeding from them. God reveals this mystery that we may know him and worship him in truth.

---

[96] Gen. 2:7; James 2:26

[97] Job 33:4, 14; Luke 1:35; 1 Cor. 2:4

[98] *Job 33:4, 14*: the Spirit of God has made me, and the breath of the Almighty has given me life . . . if he gather unto himself his Spirit and his breath; all flesh shall perish together, and man shall turn again unto dust

[99] God-breathed (2 Tim. 3:16)

[100] *John 16:13*: the Spirit of truth . . . shall guide you into all the truth: for he shall not speak from himself; but what things soever he shall hear, these shall he speak

2. The eternal foundation of the personal relations of the Trinity: The Ontological Trinity

Theologians call the Trinity, relating in eternity, the "Ontological" Trinity. *Ontological* means, "related to existence or being." The personal distinctness and relations of the Trinity are inherent and irreversible.[101] The Word "was the Word" "in the beginning." The Son always was "with the Father." Thus, the Spirit ever was their Exhalation. Accordingly, Warfield rightly observes:[102]

> Question has even been raised whether the very designations of Father and Son may not be expressive of these new relations, and therefore without significance with respect to the eternal relations of the Persons so designated. This question must certainly be answered in the negative. Although, no doubt, in many instances in which the terms 'Father' and 'Son' occur, it would be possible to take them of merely economical relations, there ever remain some which are intractable to this treatment, and we may be sure that 'Father' and 'Son' are applied to their eternal and necessary relations.

3. The historical display of the personal relations of the Trinity: The "Economic" Trinity

Some theologians call the Trinity, relating in their works, the *"Economic"* [related to work] Trinity. The economic relations are not arbitrary, but rooted in the eternal and irreversible relations. We consider how God displays his personal relations in his works of creation and redemption.

a. The personal relations of the Trinity in creation

In creation the Father makes and preserves the world and all things in it, through God the Word, by God the Spirit. Scripture defines the Son's role in creation: "All things were made through Him" (John 1:3) and, "in him were all things created, in the heavens and upon the earth, whether visible or invisible . . . all things were created through him, and unto him; and he is before all things, and in him all things consist" (Col. 1:15-17). It also defines the Spirit's role in creation: "the Spirit of God has made me, and the breath of the Almighty has given me life . . . if he gather unto himself his Spirit and his breath; all flesh shall perish together, and man shall turn again unto dust" (Job 33:4, 14), and, "you send forth your Spirit, they are created; and you renew the face of the ground" (Ps. 104:30). The Father works through his Representation to reveal himself in creation. The Father and Son "send

---

[101] John 1:1-3, 14, 17:5; 1 John 1:3
[102] Warfield, *Biblical and Theological Studies*, 54-55

forth" their Exhalation, the Spirit, to effectuate the creation and preservation of the world and everything in it.

b. *The personal relations of the Trinity in redemption*

In redemption the Father sends the Son to save his people. The Son reveals and declares the Father and accomplishes his decision to save (Matt. 11:27; John 1:18; John 6:38-39). The Word becomes flesh, lives a perfect life for our acceptance, dies on the cross for our pardon, is raised from the dead, and returns to heaven. Then the Father and Son send their Exhalation to abide with Christians on earth, manifest his special presence, intercede for his saints, and give a foretaste of heaven.[103] Their Exhalation proceeds from them as the Holy Spirit, Comforter, Spirit of truth, and Spirit of adoption.[104] As the Holy Spirit he imparts spiritual life,[105] every grace,[106] and strength to obey God's law and mortify sin.[107] As the Spirit of truth he inspires the apostles[108] and illumines the saints.[109] As the Comforter he gives peace, hope, and joy.[110] As the Spirit of adoption he assures of God's favor and gives filial communion with God (Rom. 8:15; Gal. 4:6). When Christ returns, he will resurrect us (Rom. 8:11).

In sum, the Father, Son, and Spirit do what they do, because God is who he is. Creation and redemption are the design "of" the living Pattern, accomplished "through" his exact Representation, effectuated "by" their powerful Exhalation. Accordingly Calvin observes:[111]

> It is not fitting to suppress the distinction that we observe to be expressed in Scripture. It is this: to the Father is attributed the beginning of activity, and the fountain and wellspring of all things; to the Son, wisdom, counsel, and the ordered disposition of all things; but to the Spirit is assigned the power and efficacy of the activity.

---

[103] Acts 2:33; Rom. 8:26-27; Eph. 1:13-14
[104] John 14:16, 17, 26, 15:26, 16:13
[105] John 3:3, 5; Titus 3:5
[106] Gal. 5:22
[107] Ezek. 36:27; Rom. 8:13
[108] John 16:13
[109] Eph. 3:16-19; 1 John 2:26-27, 4:13
[110] Acts 9:31; Rom. 14:17, 15:13
[111] Calvin, *Institutes*, 1:142-143

In the work of redemption the Son accomplishes the decision of the Father.[112] The Spirit implements the decision of the Father and of the Son.[113] Persons equally divine, who are the Supreme Being, relate in this remarkable way when they undertake this remedial work.

B. Historical Confession of the Relations of the Trinity

The 1689 London Confession, the Belgic Confession, and the Athanasian Creed affirm the eternal generation of the Son and the eternal procession of the Spirit. We should confess these biblical truths even though we can't fully comprehend them. They too are part of the fence around the mystery.

1. The London Confession

LCF 2:3: the Father is of none, neither begotten nor proceeding; the Son is eternally begotten of the Father; the Holy Spirit proceeding from the Father and the Son.

2. The Belgic Confession

BLC 8: three persons, really, truly, and eternally distinct according to their incommunicable properties; namely, the Father, and the Son, and the Holy Spirit. The Father is the cause, origin, and beginning of all things visible and invisible; the Son is the word, wisdom, and image of the Father; the Holy Spirit is the eternal power and might, proceeding from the Father and the Son.

BLC 10: We believe that Jesus Christ according to His divine nature is the only begotten Son of God, begotten from eternity, not made, nor created (for then He would be a creature), but co-essential and co-eternal with the Father, *the very image of his substance and the effulgence of his glory*, equal unto Him in all things. He is the Son of God, not only from the time that He assumed our nature, but from all eternity, as these testimonies, when compared together, teach us

BLC 11: We believe and confess also that the Holy Spirit from eternity proceeds from the Father and the Son; and therefore neither is made, created, nor begotten, but only proceeds from both.

3. The Athanasian Creed

AC: 21-24:
21. The Father is made of none: neither created nor begotten.
22. The Son is of the Father alone: not made [factus], nor created [creatus]: but begotten [genitus].
23. The Holy Spirit is of the Father and of the Son: neither made, nor created, nor begotten: but proceeding [procedens].
24. So there is one Father, not three Fathers: one Son, not three Sons: one Holy Spirit, not three Holy Spirits.

---

[112] John 6:38-39; Eph. 1:3; Heb. 1:2
[113] John 14:26, 15:26, 16:13

C. Practical Application of the Personal Relations of the Trinity

God has revealed these relations, not to encourage many "evanescent" [as Calvin calls them] speculations about the Trinity. He wants us to relate to him in accord with his personal distinctness. We pray unto the Father, through and in the name of the Son, in and by the aid of the Spirit.[114] This does not mean that we should never address the Spirit[115] or the Son.[116] Rather, we should always address the Supreme Being with a Trinitarian awareness. We should never say: "thank you Father for becoming a man and for dying on the cross." Only the Son became human. We should praise our triune Creator: the Father for the design of creation, the Son for its mediation, and the Spirit for its effectuation. We should bless our triune Redeemer: the Father, for his plan and application of salvation, the Son for its accomplishment and mediation, and the Spirit for its effectuation. Let us sing from our hearts: "Glory to God the Father, Son, and Holy Spirit, Three in One. To thee, O blessed Trinity, be praise throughout eternity! Amen."

---

[114] Matt. 6:9; Jude 20-21
[115] Eph. 4:30
[116] Rom. 10:9-15

Topic 23. The Names of God

"by faith in his name has his name made this man strong" (Acts 3:16); "Jehovah, that is my name" (Isa. 42:8); "I appeared unto Abraham . . . as God Almighty" (Exod. 6:3); "You shall not take the name of Jehovah your God in vain" (Exod. 20:7)

Part 4: The Names of God

Introduction to Part 4: We now consider the personal designations by which we should address God. On this topic I highly recommend the work of Gill,[1] Kersten,[2] Thornwell[3] and Morton Smith.[4] Our epitomizing texts uncover biblical categories of thought on this topic. First, these texts reveal the *general concept* of God's names. Generically, God's name denotes his Being and attributes: "by faith in his name has his name made this man strong." Specifically, God's names are his personal designations: "Jehovah, that is my name." Second, these texts display the *progressive disclosure* of God's names: "I appeared unto Abraham, unto Isaac, and unto Jacob, as God Almighty; but by my name Jehovah I was not known to them." Third, these texts require the *appropriate use* of God's names: "you shall not take the name of Jehovah your God in vain; for Jehovah will not hold him guiltless who takes his name in vain." I present God's names in these categories.

Unit 1. The General Concept of God's Names

We consider the *foundation* and *features* of God's names.

I. The Foundation of God's Names: *The Name of God*[5]

God's name generically signifies: (1) God himself, his being; (2) his attributes, his nature; (3) his personal authorization; (4) his personal reputation, his renown; and (5) his self-disclosure, his holy Word.

A. God's Name is God Himself, his Being.

God's name is his supreme being, God himself.[6] When people love his name, they love him.[7] When people give thanks[8] and sing praises[9] to his

---

[1] Gill, *Body of Divinity*, 1:37-43
[2] Kersten, *Reformed Dogmatics*, 1:43-50
[3] J.H. Thornwell, *The Collected Writings of James Henley Thornwell*, (4 Vols.; Edinburgh: Banner of Truth, 1974), 1:143-157
[4] Smith, *Systematic Theology*, 1:07-120
[5] In Appendix 1 to this topic I catalogue the use of the biblical terms for God's name in both testaments, *shēm* and *onoma*.
[6] *Ps. 44:5*: through you we will push down our adversaries: through your name will we tread them under
[7] *Ps. 5:11*: let them also that love your name be joyful in you
[8] *Ps. 100:4*: Give thanks unto him, and bless his name
[9] *Ps. 68:4*: Sing unto God, sing praises to his name

name, they worship him. When people fear his name, they fear him.[10] When God's name delivers his people, God himself answers and helps them.[11] His holy name is the holy God himself.[12] Similarly, the name of Christ, God incarnate, in which we believe,[13] which healed the lame man,[14] is Christ himself.

B. God's Name is his Attributes, his Nature.

Sometimes Scripture identifies God's name with a divine attribute, such as his goodness,[15] jealousy,[16] power,[17] or holiness.[18] In this sense, his name is his nature, his attributes. When Christ says, "I have made known your name, and will make it known," he means that he has disclosed God's nature, especially as his work of redemption from sin displays it.[19]

C. God's Name is his Personal Authorization.

God's name can also signify the authority by which he commissions someone to speak his words to mankind.[20] Thus, when God authorizes and sends someone to speak his Word, they come *in his name*.[21] When Jesus comes "in his Father's name," he comes with his authorization, to act on his

---

[10] *Ps. 86:11*: Unite my heart to fear your name. *Mal. 4:2*: unto you that fear my name shall the sun of righteousness arise

[11] *Ps. 20:1*: Jehovah answer you in the day of trouble; the name of the God of Jacob set you up on high

[12] *Ps. 111:9*: Holy and reverend is his name

[13] *John 1:12*: but as many as received him, to them he gave the right to became children of God, even to then that believe on his name

[14] Acts 3:16

[15] *Exod. 33:19*: I will make all my goodness pass before you, and will proclaim the name of Jehovah

[16] *Exod. 34:14*: Jehovah, whose name is Jealous, is a jealous God

[17] *Ps. 54:1*: Save me, O God, by your name, and judge me in your might

[18] *Isa. 57:15*: the high and lofty One that inhabits eternity, whose name is holy

[19] *John 17:6, 26*: I manifested your name unto the men whom you gave me . . . I have made known unto them your name, and will make it known.

[20] *Deut. 18:18-20*: I will put my words in his mouth, and he shall speak all that I shall command him . . . my words which he shall speak in my name . . . but that prophet, that shall speak a word presumptuously in my name, which I have not commanded

[21] *Matt. 7:22*: Lord, did we not prophesy by your name. *Matt. 21:9*: Blessed is he that comes in the name of the Lord

behalf.[22] As his Father's delegate, he represents him. Thus, whoever receives him, receives his Father who sent him.[23]

D. God's Name is his Personal Reputation, his Renown.

Scripture sometimes identifies God's name with his fame,[24] reputation,[25] and renown.[26] In a closely related sense, it may also depict a memorial that commemorates his renown.[27]

E. God's Name is his Self-Disclosure, his Holy Word.

Sometimes Scripture identifies God's name with his self-disclosure.[28] Thus, Christ's name is the Christian faith, the sum of apostolic teaching about his person and work.[29] Thus, God's name can depict the verbal revelation by which he makes himself known.

In sum, God's name embraces himself, his attributes, his authorization, his reputation, and his special revelation. Thus, Hoeksema says judiciously:[30]

> The Name of God is His Being, not as He is in Himself, but as He is revealed to us. It is the implication of all His virtues and perfections as they are manifest in the works of His hands. 'Oh Lord, our Lord, how excellent is thy name in all the earth! who has set thy glory in the heavens!

II. The Features of God's Names

God's names display his attributes. Thus, Hoeksema presents God's attributes by expounding God's names. He aims to avoid difficulty occasioned by distinguishing God's attributes and proper names:[31]

---

[22] *John 5:43*: I am come in my Father's name, and you receive me not: if another shall come in his own name, him you will receive

[23] *John 13:20*: he that receives whomsoever I send receives me; and he that receives me receives him that sent me

[24] *Josh. 9:9*: your servants are come because of the name of Jehovah your God: for we have heard the fame of him

[25] *Neh. 9:10*: and did get you a name.

[26] *Josh. 7:9*: and what will you do for your great name?

[27] *Isa. 55:13*: and it shall be to the LORD for a name, for an everlasting sign *that* shall not be cut off.

[28] *Ps. 138:2*: you have magnified your word above all your name

[29] *Rev. 2:13*: you hold fast my name, and did not deny my faith.

[30] Hoeksema, *Reformed Dogmatics*, 64

[31] Ibid., 64-65

> a difficulty arises here at once, because we must needs make a distinction between the *nomina essentialia* and the *nomina propria* . . . the trouble with this distinction is that also the *nomina propria*, the names whereby we address God and speak about Him, very definitely are revelations of the virtues of God, so that, if we coordinate them with the attributes of God, we must either, in treating the names of God, limit ourselves to an etymological explanation of them, or necessarily fall into repetition. But the former is hardly possible, and the latter is not desirable.

His constructive criticism has some merit. I indeed present God's names with some truncation and repetition. Yet, his approach also has its problems. When he uses God's names to organize his nature and attributes, his treatment is somewhat difficult to follow. Some names reveal more than one attribute and several names reveal the same attribute. Thus, I prefer to suffer some repetition. We now unpack three features of God's names: their *definition, donation*, and *disclosure*.

A. *Definition of God's Names*

> God's names are: God's self-designations, by which he makes himself known in respect to his personal characteristics, his interpersonal relations, and his economic and official functions.

This definition of God's names highlights their *divine source, revelatory purpose*, and *comprehensive scope*. I now explain and support this definition accordingly.

1. *The divine source of God's names*

God's names are his "self-designations." Contrary to the claims of perverse men, God himself selects and divulges his names. He tells Abraham that his name is, "God Almighty."[32] He identifies himself to Moses as: "I AM THAT I AM," "I AM," and "Jehovah."[33] Abraham and Moses didn't name God, any more than they created God. A man-named god is a man-made god, no god at all.

---

[32] *Gen. 17:1*: Jehovah appeared to Abraham, and said to him, I am God almighty; walk before me, and be thou perfect

[33] *Exod. 3:13-15*: when I come to the children of Israel, and shall say to them, The God of your fathers has sent me unto you; and they shall say to me, What is his name? What shall I say unto them? And God said unto Moses, I AM THAT I AM: and he said, Thus shall you say unto the children of Israel, I AM has sent me unto you. And God said moreover unto Moses, Thus shall you say unto the children of Israel, Jehovah, the God of your fathers, the God of Abraham, the God of Isaac, and the God of Jacob, has sent me unto you: this is my name forever, and my memorial unto all generations.

2. The revelatory purpose of God's names

God's names are his "self-designations, by which he makes himself known." Thus, theologians call them "connotative," not merely "denotative." "God Almighty" connotes omnipotence. "Jehovah" connotes eternal self-existence and ever-presence. These attributes enable the God of Abraham, after some 400 years, to fulfill his pledge to save his people from Egypt and bring them to Canaan. Thus, Jehovah is "the faithful God, who keeps covenant and lovingkindness" (Deut. 7:9).

3. The comprehensive scope of God's names

God's names make him known, "in respect to his personal characteristics, his interpersonal relations, and his economic[34] and official functions." The names of Christ especially display this broad scope. Isaiah discloses names for Christ that display the whole spectrum of his person and work.[35] The name, "Jesus," signifies, "Jehovah our salvation," or, "Jehovah is salvation." Thus, *Jesus* connotes who he is, "Jehovah," and what he came to do, "save his people from their sins."[36] Further, "the Son" highlights his eternal Representation of the Father.[37] "The Word" highlights his personal distinctness as the Revelation of the Father.[38] "Our Lord" highlights his relation to us as our Supreme Provider and Master. "Christ," the "anointed One," highlights his Messianic office as the anointed prophet, priest, and king of God's people.[39]

B. Donation of God's Names

In remarkable grace God conveys his name to his people and identifies them with it.[40] When he places his name on them, they are called by his name and marked out as his special possession.[41] Under the old covenant God places his name, "*God*," on his people. He called Jacob, "Israel," "the one who strives with God," because he had striven with God and

---

[34] I use *economic* to mean "related to his work."
[35] *Isa. 9:6*: his name shall be called, Wonderful, Counselor, Mighty God, Everlasting Father, Prince of Peace
[36] *Matt. 1:21*: you shall call his name JESUS; for it is he that shall save his people from their sins
[37] *John 5:23*: that all may honor the Son, even as they honor the Father
[38] *John 1:1*: In the beginning was the Word
[39] *Rom. 1:3-4*: Concerning his Son . . . Jesus Christ our Lord.
[40] *Num. 6:27*: So shall they put my name upon the children of Israel, and I will bless them
[41] *2 Chron. 7:14*: if my people, who are called by my name, shall humble themselves

prevailed (Gen. 32:28). Thus, Israel, signifies "the people of God's favor," or, "the people that have prevailed with God." Thus, his name furnishes their distinctive identity. Further, God puts his name on his house, the place of his special presence with his people.[42] He selected that place in the days of David.[43] Solomon built the temple there.[44]

Under the new covenant these ideas coalesce. Now God's temple is his people.[45] As a man's children bear his name, so God's children, redeemed in Christ, created for his glory, bear his name.[46] Thus, God places his own name on his people that he redeemed from sin out of all the nations.[47] Under the new covenant he puts his names, "God," and "*Christ*," on his people. He calls his people under the new covenant, *Israel*, because in Christ they are the people of his gospel favor that have prevailed with him.[48] Further, he calls his new covenant people, "Christian,"[49] which means "little Christ." Christ's disciples are his little children, who belong to him and bear his likeness. Thus, our names, "Israel" and "Christian" come from God's own names. Further, Christ promises to write God's name and his new name[50] on his people in glory when we see him face to face.[51] This means that he will indelibly identify us forever as his beloved possession. This blessed conveyance of God's names promotes gratitude and godly fear. We should always be grateful for this privilege of bearing his name. We should always be careful never to bring shame on his name.

---

[42] *Deut. 12:5*: unto the place which Jehovah your God shall choose out of all your tribes, to put his name there, even unto his habitation shall you seek, and thither you shall come

[43] *1 Kings 3:2*: there was no house built for the name of Jehovah until those days

[44] *1 Kings 8:16, 17, 29*: I chose no city out of all the tribes of Israel to build a house, that my name should be there . . . a house for the name of Jehovah . . . this house night and day, even toward the place whereof you have said, My name shall be there

[45] 1 Cor. 3:16-17, 6:19; 2 Cor. 6:16; Eph. 2:21-22

[46] *Isa. 43:1, 5, 7*: O Israel: Fear not, for I have redeemed you . . . I will bring your seed from the east, and gather you from the west . . . bring my sons from far, and my daughters from the end of the earth; every one that is called by my name, whom I have created for my glory

[47] *Acts 15:14, 17*: God visited the Gentiles, to take out of them a people for his name . . . that the residue of men may seek after the Lord, and all the Gentiles, upon whom my name is called

[48] *Rom. 9:6-7*: But *it is* not as though the word of God has come to nought. For they are not all Israel, that are of Israel: 7 neither, because they are Abraham's seed, are they all children:

[49] *Acts 11:26*: the disciples were called Christians first in Antioch

[50] *Rev. 3:12*: he that overcomes . . . I will write upon him the name of my God . . . and mine own new name

[51] *Rev. 22:4*: they shall see his face; and his name shall be on their foreheads

C. Disclosure of God's Names

In accord with the unveiling of redemption God progressively discloses his names and their significance. He says to Abraham, "I am God Almighty" (Gen. 17:1). He says to Moses, "I am the God of your fathers." This establishes continuity. He ever remains "God Almighty." Yet adds, "but by my name Jehovah I was not known to them." This could mean that the patriarchs never heard of the name, Jehovah. Yet this is not likely. Eve knew God by this name. Believers called on God by this name from the days of Seth.[52] Further, Jehovah spoke to Abraham[53] and he built an altar to Jehovah[54] and "called upon the name of Jehovah."[55] Again, Sarah said: "Jehovah judge between me and you" (Gen. 16:5). It is possible to take these references as anachronisms. Yet it is far more likely that when God says that Abraham did not know him by this name, he means that he unfolds its rich significance progressively. When he redeems his people from Egypt, he unveils his self-existence, ever-presence, and faithfulness profoundly in ways that the patriarchs did not *know experientially*. Thus, when God incarnate accomplishes redemption from sin, he unveils through his person and work even greater riches of his name, Jehovah. Jesus is "Jehovah our salvation." Thus, Jehovah Jesus declares, "before Abraham was born, I AM" (John 8:58). Further, God divulges additional names in accord with his progressive unveiling of redemption from sin in Christ.[56]

Unit 2. The Progressive Revelation of God's Names

I am in debt to Pastor Steve Hofmaier, Manila, Philippines, whose work greatly assisted my labor. We consider names that God discloses in the Old Testament, then in the New Testament, then their relation to each other. We consider five divine names in each Testament:

---

[52] Gen. 4:1, 26
[53] Gen. 12:1, 13:14
[54] Gen. 12:8, 13:18
[55] Gen. 12:8
[56] Isa. 9:6-7; Rom. 1:3-4

OLD TESTAMENT NAMES	NEW TESTAMENT NAMES
1. אֱלֹהִים ('elohîm) "God"	6. θεος (theos) "God"
2. עֶלְיוֹן ('elyôn) "the Most High"	7. ὑψιστος (hupsistos) "Most High"
3. אֲדֹנָי ('adonay) "Lord"	8. δεσποτης (despotes) "Master,"
4. שַׁדַּי (shadday) "The Almighty"	9. παντοκρατωρ (pantokrator)
5. יהוה (yhvh): [yᵉhovah] "Jehovah," "the LORD"	10. κυριος (kurios) "Lord"

I. The Revelation of God's Names in the Old Testament

The first designation for the Supreme Being in the Bible is *'elohîm*, "*God*" (Gen. 1:1). Scripture uses only this name in the creation account (Gen. 1:1-31). Next, in Genesis 2 the name, *yᵉhovah*, "Jehovah," appears in conjunction with *'elohîm*. That combination is rendered, "Jehovah God," or, the "LORD God." Next, *yᵉhovah* appears by itself in Genesis 4. Next to appear is *'ēl 'elyôn*, "God most high" (Gen. 14:22). This name combines *'ēl*, "God," which is possibly a shorter form of *'elohîm*, with *'elyôn*, "Most High." Next is *'adonay*, "Lord" (Gen. 15:2, 8). Next, *'ēl* stands alone with no modifier (Gen. 16:13). Then comes *shadday*, "Almighty," in combination with *'ēl*. Thus, *'ēl shadday* is "God Almighty" (Gen. 17:1). In sum, God's names in order of appearance are: *'elohîm, yᵉhovah, 'ēl* and *'elyôn* together, *'adonay*, and *shadday*. Regarding frequency, Jehovah comes first, with 6,824[57] occurrences in both forms, *yᵉhovah* and *yehovih*. Second is *'elohîm* and its cognates. The plural form depicts God 2,344 times, the singular, *'elôah*, 52 times, and the Aramaic, *'elah*, 79 times, a total of 2,475. The shortened form, *'ēl*, depicts God an additional 213 times. This gives a total of 2,688 occurrences. Third is *'adonay*, which refers to God 432 times; its shortened form *'adôn*, 29 times, for a total of 461 uses. Fourth is *shadday*, which occurs 48 times. Fifth is, *'elyôn*, which depicts God 30 times, its cognates 16 times, a total of 46 uses. I begin with *'elohîm* and its cognates. Next I consider names introduced in the days of the patriarchs in order of appearance: *'elyôn, 'adonay*, and *shadday*. I conclude with *yᵉhovah* and its shortened form, *yah*, since it has preeminence as God's proper name in the Old Testament.

---

[57] A variant exists (Isa. 10:16): counting the text, 6,823, with the margin, 6,824. I include the margin in my collation.

A. *God*: 'elohîm,[58] 'elôah, 'elah, 'ēl[59]

1. אֱלֹהִים ('elohîm) "*God*"

We consider the derivation, form, significance, and use of *'elohîm*.

a. *The uncertain derivation of 'elohîm*

Its root is somewhat uncertain. It could come from, אוּל ('ûl), "to be strong," "the Mighty One." Or, it could come from אָלָה ('aliah), "to fear," "the One to be feared." BDB suggests other plausible derivations.[60]

b. *The plural form of 'elohîm*

People debate why *'elohîm* is plural. Some perversely say that this shows the influence of polytheism on the writers of Scripture. These forget that God himself chose this name, *'elohîm*. Surely he has never come under pagan influence! Some call it a "regal plural," as a queen might say, "we are not amused." I say simply, "we are not convinced." Some think that this plural name intimates plurality in God's personality. Thus, *'elohîm* says, "let us make man." Some call it a "quantitative," or "intensive," or "honorific" plural. Regarding the significance of this grammatical construction Waltke and O'Connor (IBHS § 7.4.3) say: "In this usage (sometimes called the *pluralis majestatis*) the referent is a singular individual, which is, however, so thoroughly characterized by the qualities of the noun that a plural is used."[61] Thus, without dogmatism I take this plural to convey both plurality in God's personality and that he is "thoroughly characterized by the qualities of the noun." This leads us naturally to consider the general meaning of *'elohîm*.

c. *The general significance of 'elohîm*

Its general use sheds light on its significance. Generically it connotes greatness[62] and might.[63] Accordingly, *'elohîm* sometimes depicts men so

---

[58] In Appendix 2 to this topic I catalogue the comprehensive use and relative frequency of *'elohîm*

[59] In Appendix 3 to this topic I catalogue the comprehensive use of *'elôah, 'elah,* and *'ēl*

[60] BDB, *Lexicon*, 41-42

[61] Bruce K. Waltke and M. O'Connor, *An Introduction to Biblical Hebrew Syntax* (Wynona Lake, IN: Eisenbrauns, 1990), 122

[62] *Gen. 23:6*: Hear us, my lord: you *are* a great ['elohîm] prince among us: in the choice of our sepulchers bury your dead; *Gen. 30:8*: And Rachel said: With great ['elohîm] wrestling have I wrestled with my sister; *Jonah 3:3*: So Jonah arose, and went unto Nineveh, according to the word of the LORD. Now Nineveh was an exceeding ['elohîm] great [gadôl] city of three days' journey

[63] *Exod. 9:28*: Entreat the LORD (for *it is* enough) that there be no *more* mighty ['elohîm] thundering and hail; *1 Sam. 14:15*: And there was trembling in the host, in the field, and

marked by greatness that they exercise authority and judgment.[64] Again, it once depicts angels, spiritual beings so marked by greatness that they inspire fear and awe in humans that encounter them.[65] Further it often (246 times) depicts false gods. Even though they don't in fact exist, humans ironically so endow them with greatness that they are the objects of human awe, devotion, and worship. Thus, the true God, the Creator, is "so thoroughly characterized" by greatness and might that he is their epitome, the Supreme Being. Thus, 'elohîm depicts the all-powerful Creator who is infinitely great, whose presence induces fear and awe in his creatures. Thus, 'elohîm highlights that the Creator is the only proper object of religious devotion and worship.

d. The biblical use of 'elohîm to denominate the Supreme Being

On average 'elohîm occurs 7.6 times per thousand words in the Old Testament. Its relative frequency in the Pentateuch is 9.1, 20% above average. Its relative frequency in the Psalms is 18.0, which is 2.4 times the average. In the Major Prophets its relative frequency is 4.0, only 52% of the average, roughly half. In the Minor Prophets it is 0.7, only 9.7% of the average, roughly one tenth. Eight books have a relative frequency more than 50% above the average (greater than 11.4): (1) Deuteronomy (23.3); (2) Jonah (20.3); (3) Psalms (18.0); (4) Ezra (13.9); (5) 2 Chronicles (13.6); (6) Ecclesiastes (13.4), (7) Nehemiah (12.9); and (8) Joel (11:4). Further, the first chapter of Genesis, the creation account, has a relative frequency of 72.7, almost ten times the average. This underscores that this divine name especially denotes God as the almighty Creator.

2. אֱלוֹהַּ ('elôah) "God"

This singular form of 'elohîm occurs only 52 times in the Old Testament. It occurs 41 times in Job. This emphasis is striking. Over 78 % of its uses are crammed into only 2.7% of the Old Testament. I offer no explanation for this remarkable emphasis. I report it in hope that some of you may investigate and eventually explain why Job so emphatically features the singular form of this divine name.

3 אֱלָהּ ('elah) "God"

This Aramaic form of 'elôah occurs 95 times. It depicts false gods 16 times. It depicts the Supreme Being 79 times, 43 times in Ezra and 36 times in Daniel. Thus Ezra uses both 'elohîm and its Aramaic cognate, 'elah. If we

---

among all the people: the garrison, and the spoilers, they also trembled, and the earth quaked: so it was a very great ['elohîm] trembling

[64] Exod. 21:6, 22:8, 9(2); 1 Sam. 2:25

[65] Ps. 8:5

add their uses, the relative frequency in Ezra becomes, 24.936, the highest of any book.

4. אֵל ('ēl) "God"

We consider the derivation, significance, and use of *'ēl*.

a. *The probable derivation of 'ēl*

This is probably a shorter form of *'elohîm* that comes from the verb אוּל ('ûl), "to be strong," "to be mighty." It occurs 245 times and depicts the Supreme Being 213 times.

b. *The general significance of 'ēl*

Like *'elohîm*, *'ēl* has a general meaning. Generically it signifies power, might, and strength with a variety of nuances.[66] It depicts physical strength, the capacity of a person to inflict physical harm,[67] or to prevent political subjugation,[68] or to accomplish acts of benevolence.[69] It depicts financial strength, the fiscal power to prevent the enslavement of your family.[70] It depicts metaphysical strength, the capacity to devise and implement moral good or evil.[71] It thus depicts other gods as "powers." This intimates that demonic power bolsters false religion.[72] Scripture affirms that Jehovah is highly exalted above all other so-called gods to which humans ascribe power.[73] It forbids God's people to recognize and honor any supernatural

---

[66] Gen. 31:29; Deut. 28:32; Neh. 5:5; Prov. 3:27; Ezek. 31:11, 32:21; Micah 2:1

[67] *Gen. 31:29*: It is in the power ['ēl] of my hand to do you hurt: but the God of your father spake unto me yesternight, saying, Take heed to yourself that you speak not to Jacob either good or bad.

[68] *Deut. 28:32*: Your sons and your daughters shall be given unto another people; and your eyes shall look, and fail with longing for them all the day: and there shall be nothing in the power ['ēl] of your hand.

[69] *Prov. 3:27*: Withhold not good from them to whom it is due, when it is in the power ['ēl] of your hand to do *it*.

[70] *Neh. 5:5*: we bring into bondage our sons and our daughters to be servants, and some of our daughters are brought into bondage *already*: neither is it in our power [*'ēl*] to help it; for other men have our fields and our vineyards.

[71] *Micah 2:1*: Woe to them that devise iniquity and work evil upon their beds! When the morning is light, they practise it, because it is in the power ['ēl] of their hand.

[72] *1 Cor. 10:19-20*: What say I then? that the idol is any thing, or that which is offered in sacrifice to idols is any thing? 20 But I *say*, that the things which the Gentiles sacrifice, they sacrifice to devils, and not to God: and I would not that you should have fellowship with devils.

[73] *Exod. 15:11*: Who *is* like unto thee, O LORD, among the gods ['ēl]? who *is* like you, glorious in holiness, fearful *in* praises, doing wonders

power other than Jehovah.[74] Isaiah with much irony exposes the folly of making your own god, ascribing power to it, asking it for help, and honoring it.[75] Accordingly, Scripture depicts God as "God of gods," the Supreme Power over every so-called god and supernatural power.[76] Therefore, *'ēl* highlights God's omnipotence.

c. The biblical use of *'ēl* to denominate the Supreme Being

In accord with this general significance, the use of *'ēl* features the contrast of God's absolute reliability and omnipotence with human fickleness and limitation,[77] and of divine impregnability with human vulnerability.[78] The use of *'ēl* also features God's infinite ability to let loose his compassion to help the needy and oppressed who trust him and call on him.[79] Similarly, *'ēl* features God's ability to impart strength to his people, to lead them safely to their blessed destiny, and to order every event in their lives for their good and his glory.[80] Finally, *'ēl* commonly occurs in compound names that

---

[74] *Exod. 34:14*: For you shall worship no other god ['ēl]: for the LORD, whose name *is* Jealous, *is* a jealous God

[75] *Isa. 44:10, 17*: Who has formed a god ['ēl], or molten a graven image that is profitable for nothing? . . . 17 And the residue thereof he makes a god ['ēl], even his graven image: he falls down unto it, and worships it, and prays unto it, and says, Deliver me; for you are my god ['ēl]

[76] *Dan. 11:36*: And the king shall do according to his will; and he shall exalt himself, and magnify himself above every god ['ēl], and shall speak marvellous things against the God ['ēl] of gods ['ēl]

[77] *Num. 23:19*: God ['ēl] *is* not a man, that he should lie; neither the son of man, that he should repent: has he said, and shall he not do *it*? or has he spoken, and shall he not make it good?

[78] *Ezek. 28:2, 9*: Son of man, say unto the prince of Tyrus, Thus saith the Lord GOD ['adonay yehovih]; Because your heart *is* lifted up, and you have said, I *am* a God ['ēl], I sit *in* the seat of God ['elohîm] , in the midst of the seas; yet you are a man, and not God ['ēl], though you set your heart as the heart of God ['elohîm] . . . 9 Will you still say before him that slays you, I *am* God ['elohîm] ? but you *shall be* a man, and no God ['ēl], in the hand of him that slays you.

[79] *Neh. 9:31-32*: Nevertheless for your great mercies' sake you did not utterly consume them, nor forsake them; for you *are* a gracious and merciful God ['ēl]. 32 Now therefore, our God ['elohîm], the great, the mighty, and the terrible God ['ēl], who keeps covenant and mercy, let not all the trouble seem little before you, that has come upon us, on our kings, on our princes, and on our priests, and on our prophets, and on our fathers, and on all your people, since the time of the kings of Assyria unto this day.

[80] *Ps. 18:30-34*: As for God ['ēl], his way is perfect: The word of Jehovah is tried. He is a shield unto all them that take refuge in him. 31 For who is God ['elôah], save Jehovah? And who is a rock, besides our God ['elohîm], 32 The God ['ēl] that girds me with strength, and makes my way perfect? 33 He maketh my feet like hinds' *feet*: and setteth me upon my high places. 34 He teaches my hands to war; so that mine arms do bend a bow of brass.

feature some aspect of God's supreme majesty, such as: *'ēl 'elyôn*, "God Most High" (Gen. 14:22); *'ēl shadday*, "God Almighty" (Gen. 17:1); *'ēl 'ôlam*, "the Everlasting God" (Gen. 21:33); and, *'ēl gibbôr*, "the Mighty God" (Isa. 9:6). This use evokes awe, reverence, and devotion.

B. *The Most High*[81]: *'elyôn, 'al, 'elyôn, 'illay*

We consider the use of *'elyôn*, "most high," and its cognates, *'al, 'elyôn,* and *'illay*.

1. עֶלְיוֹן ('elyôn): "Most High"

We consider its general significance and its use to depict the Supreme Being.

a. The general significance of 'elyôn

It comes from עָלָה ('alah), "to go up." In general it signifies "upper," "uppermost," "high." Thus it can depict elevation. It can signify a higher elevation in space: "the *uppermost* basket" (Gen. 40:17). It can also denote elevation in rank: "make you *high* above the nations" (Deut. 26:19) and "the *highest* of the kings of the earth (Ps. 89:27). In this sense it depicts God's attribute of transcendence: "you, whose name alone is Jehovah, are *most high* over all the earth (Ps. 83:18).

b. The use of 'elyôn to denote the Supreme Being

Accordingly, *'elyôn* features God's exaltation, his supremacy and sovereignty.[82] It occurs alone, "the Most High,"[83] and in combination with other names: "God Most High," *'ēl 'elyôn*;[84] "God Most High," *'elohîm 'elyôn*;[85] and "Jehovah Most High," *y^ehovah 'elyôn*.[86]

2. עַל ('al): "The High"

This shorter Hebrew form also comes from עָלָה ('alah). In general it signifies high or above. It twice depicts the Supreme Being in Hosea.[87]

---

[81] In Appendix 3 to this topic I catalogue the comprehensive use of *'elyôn* and its cognates

[82] *Deut. 32:8*: When the Most High ['elyôn] gave to the nations their inheritance, when he separated the children of men, he set the bounds of the peoples according to the number of the children of Israel

[83] Num. 24:16; Deut. 32:8; 2 Sam. 22:14; Pss. 9:2, 18:13, 21:7, 46:4, 50:14, 73:11, 77:10, 78:17, 82:6, 87:5, 91:1, 9, 92:1, 107:11; Isa. 14:14; Lam. 3:35, 38

[84] Gen. 14:18, 19, 20, 22; Ps. 78:35

[85] Pss. 57:2, 78:56

[86] Pss. 7:17, 47:2, 97:9

[87] Hos. 7:16, 11:7

3. עֶלְיוֹן ('elyôn): *"Most High"*

This Aramaic form corresponds to the Hebrew, *'elyôn*. It occurs in Daniel.[88] It always denotes the Supreme Being. It features his sovereignty and his special relation with his holy people, "the saints of the Most High."[89]

4. עִלָּי ('illay): *"Most High"*

This Aramaic form corresponds to the Hebrew, *'illiy*, "upper," from, עָלָה ('alah), "to go up." It occurs ten times in Daniel. It only depicts the Supreme Being. It occurs by itself, "the Most High,"[90] and with *'elah*, the Aramaic form of *'elôah*, "God Most High."[91] It features God's supremacy and sovereignty: "the Most High ['illay] rules in the kingdom of men, and gives it to whomsoever he will" (Dan. 4:32).

C. *Lord:* 'adôn, 'adonay[92]

We consider both 'adôn, "lord," "master," and its emphatic form 'adonay.

1. אָדוֹן ('adôn): "Lord": shortened form, אָדֹן ('adon)

'Adôn is translated "master," "sir," "owner," "lord," or "Lord." It occurs 335 times. It often occurs in direct address.[93] It sometimes (13 times) depicts angels or the angel of Jehovah.[94] It most often (293 times) depicts a human relationship that involves authority. Thus, an *'adon* can be a husband,[95] master,[96] parent,[97] or ruler.[98] Accordingly, it often occurs in polite speech to

---

[88] Dan. 7:18, 22, 25, 27

[89] *Dan. 7:27*: And the kingdom and the dominion, and the greatness of the kingdoms under the whole heaven, shall be given to the people of the saints of the Most High: his kingdom is an everlasting kingdom, and all dominions shall serve and obey him.

[90] Dan. 4:17, 24, 25, 32, 34, 7:25

[91] Dan. 3:26, 4:2, 5:18, 21

[92] In Appendix 3 to this topic I catalogue the comprehensive use of *'adôn* and *'adonay*.

[93] Gen. 19:2, 18, etc.

[94] Gen. 19:2, 18; Josh. 5:14; Judg. 6:13; Dan. 10:16, 17(2), 19; Zech. 1:9, 4:4, 5, 13, 6:4

[95] *Gen. 18:12*: Therefore Sarah laughed within herself, saying: After I am waxed old shall I have pleasure, my lord ['adôn] being old also?

[96] *Gen. 24:9*: And the servant put his hand under the thigh of Abraham his master ['adôn] and swore to him concerning that matter.

[97] *Gen. 31:35*: And she said to her father, Let it not displease my lord ['adôn] that I cannot rise up before you; for the custom of women *is* upon me. And he searched, but found not the images.

[98] *Gen. 42:33*: And the man, the lord ['adôn] of the country, said unto us: Hereby shall I know that you *are* true *men*;

express deference and respect.[99] Scripture uses *'adôn* 29 times to depict God as supreme Lord and Master of his people.[100] Accordingly, it compares and contrasts human lords and masters with Jehovah, the ultimate Master[101] and supreme Ruler[102] of the whole earth[103] and of all in authority.[104] Thus, God reproves those in his ministerial service who fail to show him due respect.[105] Thus, God's people thank and bless him[106] and look to him to provide for them and protect them.[107] Thus, Jehovah our God, as our Lord and Master, displays infinite wisdom and power in the way he governs us, takes care of us, and watches over us.[108]

2. אֲדֹנָי ('adonay): "Lord"

'Adonay is translated "lord," "Lord," and "God" (Hab. 3:19). It occurs 434 times. It is an emphatic form of *'adon*. Accordingly, it refers to humans only twice.[109] It denotes God 432 times with one variant.[110] This name depicts Jehovah our God as our supreme Master and Ruler, who provides for us, to whom we owe ultimate allegiance, to whom we must render account. In the Pentateuch *'adonay* denotes God 17 times, exclusively in direct address. For example, Abraham addresses God as, *'adonay yehovih,*

---

[99] Gen. 23:6, 11, 32: 4, 5, 18, 33:8,13, 14, 15, etc.

[100] *Neh. 10:29*: and to observe and do all the commandments of the LORD our Lord ['adôn] and his judgments and his statutes; *Ps. 8:9*: O LORD our Lord ['adôn], how excellent *is* your name in all the earth!

[101] *Ps. 123:2*: Behold, as the eyes of servants look unto the hand of their masters ['adôn], and as the eyes of a maiden unto the hand of her mistress; so our eyes *wait* upon the LORD our God, until that he have mercy upon us.

[102] *Isa. 26:13*: O LORD our God, other lords ['adôn] beside you have had dominion over us: *but* by you only will we make mention of your name.

[103] *Josh. 3:11*: Behold, the ark of the covenant of the Lord ['adôn] of all the earth passes over before you into Jordan.

[104] *Deut. 10:17*: For the LORD your God *is* God of gods, and Lord ['adôn] of lords ['adôn], a great God, a mighty, and a terrible, which regards not persons, nor takes reward:

[105] *Mal. 1:6*: A son honors *his* father, and a servant his master ['adôn]: if then I *be* a father, where *is* mine honor? And if I *be* a master ['adôn], where *is* my fear? Says the LORD of hosts unto you, O priests that despise my name. And you say: Wherein have we despised your name?

[106] *Ps. 136:3*: O give thanks to the Lord ['adôn] of lords ['adôn]: for his mercy *endures* forever.

[107] Ps. 123:2

[108] *Ps. 147:5*: Great *is* our Lord ['adôn], and of great power: his understanding *is* infinite

[109] Ezr. 10:3; Isa. 21:8

[110] A variant occurs in Isa. 10:16. The text reads *'adonay*, the margin, *y^ehovah*. I include this text with both names.

his Provider, Protector, and Master.[111] Again, when he sees the angel of Jehovah, he intercedes with the Supreme Ruler of mankind on behalf of Sodom.[112] Again, Moses addresses Jehovah as his supreme Ruler when he intercedes with him for his people.[113] In the historical narrative (Joshua-Job) *'adonay* denotes God 21 times, often, but not exclusively,[114] in direct address. Upon the defeat of Israel at Ai, Joshua addresses Jehovah as the Ruler of the universe and implores him to give aid.[115] When Gideon sees the angel of Jehovah, he addresses Jehovah as his supreme Master and pours out his amazement.[116] When God enters covenant with David to preserve his house forever, David addresses Jehovah as his supreme Ruler, expresses his wonder and gratitude, and asks him to fulfill his promise.[117] In the Psalms it denotes God 53 times, in Isaiah 47 times, in Jeremiah 14 times, in Lamentations 14 times. In the minor prophets it denotes God 45 times, 12 of these are in Daniel and 25 are in Amos. In Amos 21 times it occurs as *'adonay yehovih*; four times it stands alone.[118] In sum, from Genesis to Lamentations *'adonay* denotes God as supreme Master and Ruler 166 times, in the minor prophets 45 times, a total of 211. This brings us to Ezekiel. In Ezekiel *'adonay* denotes God 221 times, more than in the rest of the Old Testament combined. This emphasis is striking. Of these 221 uses in Ezekiel, 217 occur as *'adonay yehovih*. In the other four texts it occurs in the phrase: "the way of the Lord ['adonay] is not equal."[119]

The average relative frequency of *'adonay* to denote God per 1000 words in the Old Testament is 1.4. In Daniel its relative frequency is 2.0. In Lamentations it is 8.6. In Ezekiel it is 11.7. In Amos it is 12.1. Thus, Amos,

---

[111] *Gen. 15:2*: And Abram said, Lord GOD ['adonay yehovih], what will you give me, seeing I go childless, and the steward of my house *is* this Eliezer of Damascus?

[112] Gen. 18:3, 27, 30, 31, 32

[113] *Deut. 9:26*: I prayed therefore unto the LORD, and said, O Lord GOD ['adonay yehovih], destroy not your people and your inheritance, which you have redeemed through your greatness, which you have brought forth out of Egypt with a mighty hand.

[114] 1 Kings 2:26, 3:10, 22:6

[115] *Josh. 7:7*: And Joshua said, Alas, O Lord GOD ['adonay yehovih], wherefore have you at all brought this people over Jordan, to deliver us into the hand of the Amorites,

[116] *Judges 6:22*: And when Gideon perceived that he *was* the angel of the LORD, Gideon said, Alas, O Lord GOD! ['adonay yehovih] for because I have seen the angel of the LORD face to face

[117] *2 Sam. 7:29*: Therefore now let it please you to bless the house of your servant, that it may continue for ever before you: for you, O Lord GOD ['adonay yehovih], have spoken *it*: and with your blessing let the house of your servant be blessed forever.

[118] Amos 5:16, 7:7, 8, 9:1

[119] Ezek. 18:25, 29, 33:17, 20

Ezekiel, and Lamentations especially feature God's identity as the supreme Master of masters and Ruler of rulers. Possibly this emphasis reflects the fact that in times of sorrow (Lamentations) and oppression by worldly rulers and masters (Ezekiel) it comforts God's people to know and contemplate that their God is in control. Further, I am confident that its emphasis in Amos involves more than a statistical anomaly occasioned by the relatively small size of the data sample. Regarding the historical context of Amos, Keith Mathison observes:[120]

> The prophet Amos ministered during the overlapping reigns of Jeroboam II in Israel (793-753) and Uzziah in Judah (792-740)... During this time, Jeroboam II was able to expand the borders of Israel, and his successes created economic prosperity for many and a sense of security as well. During these years, Israel prospered and a powerful and wealthy upper class emerged who exploited the poor and perverted justice. Although a native of Judah, Amos prophesied to the northern kingdom of Israel. He preached to an affluent society that was deeply involved in false worship and in the mistreatment of the poor. These wealthy and powerful Israelites were confident and secure. Into the midst of this complacent society comes Amos, declaring that Israel has broken God's covenant.

And, Amos comes emphasizing that *'adonay yehovih* is in control, the supreme Lord and Master. Thus, this emphasis reminds us that especially in times of relative security and economic prosperity God's people must never forget that he is in contol. In our ease we must always remember our Lord and Master, to whom we owe ultimate loyalty and allegience, to whom we will give account for our behavior.

In conclusion, both *'adôn* and *'adonay* highlight God's rule over all lands, peoples, and authorities. They feature the accountability to him of all humanity, especially of those who rule others and of those who minister in spiritual things. These names also feature his tender care for and protection of his people.

D. שַׁדַּי (shadday): *The Almighty*[121]

We consider the significance of shadday and its use to depict the Supreme Being.

1. The significance of shadday

Shadday comes from שָׁדַד (shadad), "to overpower." This verb has a

---

[120] Keith Mathison, Ligioner Ministries: 02/07/09: http://www.ligonier.org/blog/top-5-commentaries-on-the-book-of-amos/

[121] In Appendix 3 to this topic I catalogue the comprehensive use of *shadday* and *shadad*.

variety of nuances: to devastate, to ruin, to destroy, to despoil. It occurs 56 times; 26 times in Jeremiah. It often depicts humans sinfully despoiling[122] and overpowering[123] others. Accordingly, *shadad* describes God in just vengeance destroying Babylon.[124] Thus, *shadday* denotes God's ability to overpower whatever opposes him.

2. The use of *shadday* to depict the Supreme Being

Shadday occurs 48 times. It exclusively depicts the Supreme Being. It occurs alone, "the Almighty," 41 times. It occurs 7 times in combination with *'ēl*, as *'ēl shadday*, "God Almighty."[125] It highlights that God's power is incomprehensible.[126] It depicts God's boundless capacity to bless,[127] to afflict and chasten,[128] and to destroy.[129] It emphasizes his sovereign control over everything that happens in the universe[130] and in our lives.[131] Thus, the Almighty evokes both our fear[132] and our trust.[133] Scripture especially associates this divine name with the patriarchs[134] and Job.[135]

---

[122] *Job 12:6*: The tabernacles of robbers [shadad] prosper, and they that provoke God are secure; into whose hand God brings *abundantly*.

[123] *Ps. 17:9*: From the wicked that oppress [shadad] me, *from* my deadly enemies, *who* compass me about.

[124] *Jer. 51:55, 56*: Because the LORD has spoiled [shadad] Babylon, and destroyed out of her the great voice . . . . 56 Because the spoiler [shadad] is come upon her, *even* upon Babylon, and her mighty men are taken, every one of their bows is broken: for the LORD God of recompences shall surely requite.

[125] Gen. 17:1, 28:3, 35:11, 43:14, 48:3; Exod. 6:3; Ezek. 10:5

[126] *Job 11:7*: Can you by searching find out God? can you find out the Almighty [shadday] unto perfection?

[127] *Gen. 28:3*: And God Almighty ['ēl shadday] bless you, and make you fruitful, and multiply you, that you may be a multitude of people

[128] *Job 5:17*: Behold, happy *is* the man whom God corrects: therefore do not despise the chastening of the Almighty [shadday]

[129] *Isa. 13:6*: Howl; for the day of the LORD *is* at hand; it shall come as a destruction from the Almighty [shadday]

[130] Job 34:12-15, 37:14-23

[131] Job 8:3, 33:4

[132] *Job 37:23-24*: *Touching* the Almighty [shadday], we cannot find him out: *he is* excellent in power, and in judgment, and in plenty of justice: he will not afflict. 24 Men do therefore fear him: he respecteth not any *that are* wise of heart.

[133] *Ps. 91:1-2*: He that dwells in the secret place of the most High shall abide under the shadow of the Almighty [shadday]. 2 I will say of the LORD, *He is* my refuge and my fortress: my God; in him will I trust

[134] *Exod. 6:3*: And I appeared unto Abraham, unto Isaac, and unto Jacob, by the name of God Almighty ['ēl shadday], but by my name JEHOVAH [yᵉhovah] was I not known to them.

[135] Of the 41 uses of *shadday*, 31 occur in Job, a striking emphasis.

E. יהוה (yhvh) [yᵉhovah, yehovih]: *Jehovah, the LORD*[136]

Note its pronunciation, significance, use, combination, transliteration, short form, and relation to *'elohîm*.

1. The pronunciation of yhvh

The exact pronunciation of *yhvh* is obscure because the Jews so feared taking this name in vain that they never audibly said it. Accordingly, in the pointed [with vowels] Hebrew Bible, the vowels of *'adonay*, which are "ᵉ, o, a," appear with the consonants of this name. Thus, they created, "*yᵉhovah*," which is not a word, but a reminder that they should never pronounce this name. Thus, when they saw *yᵉhovah* written in the text, they said, *'adonay*. Further, *yhvh* sometimes occurs in combination with *'adonay*, as *'adonay yhvh*. On these 305 occasions they pointed *yhvh* with the vowels of *'elohîm*, which are "e, o, i," Thus they created and wrote, *yehovih*. On those occasions they apparently said, *'adonay 'elohîm*.

This remarkable situation gives rise to various renderings of this divine name in English. The ASV uses, "Jehovah," a transliteration of *yᵉhovah*, to render both *yᵉhovah* and *yehovih*. The KJV almost always uses the "LORD" for *yᵉhovah* and "GOD" for *yehovih*. In the KJV the capital letters, "LORD," distinguish *yᵉhovah* from *'adonay*, which the KJV translates as "Lord." Similarly, in the KJV capital letters, "GOD," distinguish *yehovih* from other names that the KJV translates as "God." The KJV approach closely resembles what the Hebrews *said* when they read the text. Some modern scholars guess at the actual pronunciation of *yhvh*. Thus, some come up with "*Yahveh*," or, "*Yahweh*," which they say represents, יִהְיֶה (yihyeh), the third person singular Qal imperfect of *hayah*, "he was, is, will be." Accordingly, the New Jerusalem Bible renders both *yᵉhovah* and *yehovih* as, "Yahweh."

2. The significance of yhvh

The Hebrews singled out *yhvh* for reverence because it is God's proper name. *Yᵉhovah* comes from הָיָה (hayah), "*to be*." Accordingly, God's proper name signifies his abiding self-existence. He denotes himself as: the "One Who Is," in the first person, "I Am" (Exod. 3:13-15). Thus, God's personal denotation highlights that he is self-existent, ever existent, eternal, and immutable. Thus, his self-existence and permanent existence undergird his ability faithfully to keep his promises.[137]

---

[136] In Appendix 4 to this topic I catalogue the comprehensive use and relative frequency of *yhvh, yᵉhovah and yehovih*.

[137] Exod. 3:13-15; Deut. 7:9; Mal. 3:6

3. The use of yhvh [yᵉhovah and yehovih]

The pointed form, *yᵉhovah*, occurs 6,519 times; the pointed form, *yehovih*, 305 times, of which 217 are in Ezekiel. This reflects the emphasis that Ezekiel places on *'adonay*. The Supreme Being himself emphasizes that *yᵉhovah* is his proper, personal, and abiding, or memorial, name.[138] When Elijah brought the Israelites to recognize the personal identity of the Supreme Being, they cried out, "Yᵉhovah, he is God."[139] They affirm that a personal Being named, *yᵉhovah*, is the "Superlative Being," the "Ultimate Arbiter." Again, through Isaiah Scripture underscores the special place of God's self-designation, *yᵉhovah*.[140] Accordingly, Scripture speaks of "Jehovah thy God" [yᵉhovah 'eloheyka] in the singular, and, "Jehovah our God" [yᵉhovah 'eloheynû] in the plural. These expressions mean that *yᵉhovah* is the ultimate object of the devotion and loyalty of his people. Similarly, God's people address him as, *'adonay yehovih*, "Lord Jehovah."[141] This signifies that *yᵉhovah* is the Supreme Master and Ruler of his people. Similarly, Scripture declares that three times in a year all the males of Israel are to appear before "the Lord Jehovah, the God of Israel."[142] This expression signifies that their Master and Ruler, whose proper name is *yᵉhovah*, is the ultimate object of the religious devotion of Israel. Similarly, Scripture says: "thus says your Lord ['adôn], Jehovah [yᵉhovah], and your God ['elohîm] that pleads the cause of his people" (Isa. 51:22). Again, this signifies that a personal Being named, *yᵉhovah*, is their Master and their God, the object of their ultimate loyalty, devotion, and reverence and their final Arbiter and Judge.

On average *yhvh* occurs 22.1 times per thousand words in the Old Testament. Its relative frequency in the Pentateuch is 22.5, statistically average. Its relative frequency in the major prophets is 27.6, 25% above the average. In the minor prophets it is 25.2, 14% above average. Nine books have a relative frequency more than 50% above the average (greater than 33.2): (1) Haggai (57.7); (2) Malachi (53.2); (3) Zephaniah (44.0); (4)

---

[138] *Exod. 3:15*: And God said moreover unto Moses, Thus shall you say unto the children of Israel, Jehovah [yᵉhovah] God ['elohîm] of your fathers, the God ['elohîm] of Abraham, the God ['elohîm] of Isaac, and the God ['elohîm] of Jacob, has sent me unto you: this *is* my name forever, and this *is* my memorial unto all generations.

[139] *1 Kings 18:39*: And when all the people saw *it*, they fell on their faces: and they said, Jehovah [yᵉhovah], he *is* God ['elohîm]; Jehovah [yᵉhovah], he *is* God ['elohîm].

[140] *Isa. 42:8*: I *am* Jehovah [yᵉhovah]: that *is* my name: and my glory will I not give to another, neither my praise to graven images.

[141] Gen. 15:2, etc.

[142] *Exod. 34:23*: Thrice in the year shall all your males appear before *the Lord, Jehovah, the God of Israel* [ha 'adôn yᵉhovah 'elohēy yiśra'ēl].

Zechariah (42.0); (5) Amos (39.1); (6) Deuteronomy (38.0); (7) Jonah (37.6); (8) Psalms (35.5); and (9) Joel (34.3).

4. The combination of yhvh: y^{e}hovah of hosts

Scripture uses God's proper name in a number of combinations. Most are used only once or twice. Sometimes believers use God's proper name in combination to commemorate their personal experience of his power and blessing: *Jehovah-jireh* (Jehovah sees),[143] *Jehovah-nissi* (Jehovah my banner),[144] and *Jehovah-shalom* (Jehovah is peace).[145] Further, Jeremiah predicts that Christ and his church will be denoted as, *Jehovah-tsidqēnû* (Jehovah our righteousness).[146] Again, Ezekiel predicts that a city's name will become, *Jehovah-shammah* (Jehovah is there).[147]

The combination, יְהוָה צְבָאוֹת (y^{e}hovah ts^{e}ba'ôth), "Jehovah of hosts," deserves special attention. Scripture frequently combines *y^{e}hovah*, occasionally *yehovih*, with *ts^{e}ba'ôth*, the plural of, צָבָא (tsaba'). The root of *tsaba'* is the verb *tsaba'*, which occurs 13 times in the Old Testament.[148] This verb signifies "to assemble for service," with a variety of nuances. Thus, the KJV translates this verb as, "assemble," "muster," "fight," "to war," "to perform," "to wait." The noun, *tsaba'* occurs 485 times in the Old Testament with a variety of nuances. Thus, KJV translates this noun, *tsaba'* as, "host," "war," "army," "battle," "service," and in other ways. It can signify the entire collection of living things that fill and inhabit heaven and earth: "and the heaven and earth were finished, and all *the host* [tsaba'] of them."[149] Similarly, it can signify "the host of heaven," which in some contexts depicts the entire assemblage of angelic beings,[150] and in other contexts depicts the

---

[143] *Gen. 22:14*: And Abraham called the name of that place Jehovah-jireh: as it is said *to* this day, In the mount of Jehovah it shall be seen.

[144] *Exod. 17:15*: And Moses built an altar, and called the name of it Jehovah-nissi:

[145] *Judg. 6:24*: Then Gideon built an altar there unto Jehovah, and called it Jehovah-shalom: unto this day it *is* yet in Ophrah of the Abiezrites.

[146] *Jer. 23:6*: In his days Judah shall be saved, and Israel shall dwell safely: and this *is* his name whereby he shall be called, Jehovah our righteousness [y^{e}hovah tsidqēnû]. *Jer. 33:16*: In those days shall Judah be saved, and Jerusalem shall dwell safely: and this *is the name* wherewith she shall be called, Jehovah our righteousness [y^{e}hovah tsidqēnû].

[147] *Ezek. 48:35*: *It was* round about eighteen thousand *measures*: and the name of the city from *that* day *shall be*, Jehovah-shammah.

[148] Exod. 38:8(2); Num. 4:23, 8:24, 31:7, 42; 1 Sam. 2:22; 2 Kings 25:19; Isa. 29:7, 8, 31:4; Jer. 52:25; Zech. 14:12.

[149] Gen. 2:1; Neh. 9:6; Ps. 33:6

[150] 1 Kings 22:19; 2 Chron. 18:18; Ps. 148:2

entire collection of heavenly bodies that fill the sky and serve their King.[151] Again, it can signify the entire society of people that serve Jehovah and the service that God's servants render to their King.[152] Most often, it signifies an army, the entire assemblage of men that fill a battlefield and wage war in the service of their king.[153] Accordingly, it often signifies the army of Israel that assembles to serve their heavenly King and his anointed king by waging war.[154] Similarly, it also depicts the "host of Jehovah," the spiritual army of the Supreme Ruler and King of heaven and earth.[155]

This usage reveals its significance. In general, King $y^e hovah$ commands many hosts. He rules over every creature that inhabits the universe and over every heavenly body in the sky. More specifically, King $y^e hovah$ commands two armies. He commands his heavenly army of angels and his earthly army composed of the men of Israel. Thus, he is King, not merely of a host, but of *hosts*. Thus, *Jehovah of hosts* features God's invincible might as the King of glory, mighty in battle,[156] who commands the army of heaven and the army of Israel.[157] It highlights his regal glory as the Sovereign who rules over all. Even now, King $y^e hovah$ Jesus commands his army of angels[158] and his ecclesiastical army of disciples that fight spiritually with the Spirit's sword, the word of God.[159]

This name, $y^e hovah\ ts^e ba'ôth$ occurs these 265 times in the Old Testament, with one variant (Isa. 10:16): 1 Sam. 1:3, 11, 4:4, 15:2, 17:45; 2 Sam. 6:2, 18, 7:8, 26, 27; 1 Kings 18:15, 19:10, 14; 2 Kings 3:14; 1 Chron. 11:9, 17:7, 24; Pss.

---

[151] Deut. 4:19, 17:3; 2 Kings 17:16, 21:3, 5, 23:4, 5; 2 Chron. 33:3, 5; Isa. 34:4, 45:12; Jer. 8:2, 19:13, 33:22; Zeph. 1:5

[152] Exod. 12:17, 41; Num. 4:23; Pss. 68:11, 103:21.

[153] Gen. 21:22, 32, 26:26; Exod. 6:26, 7:4; Judg. 4:7, 9:29; Isa. 34:2, etc.

[154] Num. 1:3; Deut. 24:5; 2 Chron. 25:7; Ps. 44:9, etc.

[155] *Josh. 5:14*: And he said, Nay; but *as* captain of the host [tsaba'] of the LORD [y^ehovah] am I now come. And Joshua fell on his face to the earth, and did worship, and said unto him, What says my lord unto his servant?

[156] *Ps. 24:8-10*: Who *is* this King of glory? Jehovah [y^ehovah] strong and mighty, Jehovah [y^ehovah] mighty in battle. 9 Lift up your heads, O ye gates; even lift *them* up, ye everlasting doors; and the King of glory shall come in. 10 Who is this King of glory? The Jehovah [y^ehovah] of hosts [ts^eba'ôth], he *is* the King of glory. Selah

[157] *1 Sam. 17:45*: Then said David to the Philistine, Thou comest to me with a sword, and with a spear, and with a shield: but I come to thee in the name of the LORD of hosts [y^ehovah ts^eba'ôth], the God of the armies of Israel, whom you have defied.

[158] Rev. 19:11-16

[159] Matt. 16:18; and *Ps. 68:11*: The Lord gave the word: great *was* the company [tsaba'] of those that published *it*. Note the Christian context: Ps. 68:18, "you have ascended on high, you have lead captivity captive" (Eph. 4:7).

24:10, 46:7, 11, 48:8, 69:6, 80:4, 7, 14, 19, 84:1, 3, 12; Isa. 1:9, 24, 2:12, 3:1, 15, 5:7, 9, 16, 24, 6:3, 5, 8:13, 18, 9:7, 13, 19, 10:16, 23 [yehovih], 24 [yehovih], 26, 33, 13:4, 13, 14:22, 23, 24, 27, 17:3, 18:7(2), 19:4, 12, 16, 17, 18, 20, 25, 21:10, 22:5 [yehovih], 12 [yehovih], 14(2), 15 [yehovih], 25, 23:9, 24:23, 25:6, 28:5, 22 [yehovih], 29, 29:6, 31:4, 5, 37:16, 32, 39:5, 44:6, 45:13, 47:4, 48:2, 51:15, 54:5; Jer. 2:19 [yehovih], 6:6, 9, 7:3, 21, 8:3, 9:7, 15, 17, 10:16, 11:17, 20, 22, 15:16, 16:9, 19:3, 11, 15, 20:12, 23:15, 16, 36, 25:8, 27, 28, 29, 32, 26:18, 27:4, 18, 19, 21, 28:2, 14, 29:4, 8, 17, 21, 25, 30:8, 31:23, 35, 32:14, 15, 18, 33:11, 12, 35:13, 18, 19, 39:16, 42:15, 18, 43:10, 44:2, 11, 25, 46:10(2) [yehovih], 18, 25, 48:1, 15, 49:5 [yehovih], 7, 26, 35, 50:18, 25 [yehovih], 31 [yehovih], 33, 34, 51:5, 14, 19, 33, 57, 58; Micah 4:4; Nah. 2:13, 3:5; Hab. 2:13; Zeph. 2:9, 10; Hag. 1:2, 5, 7, 9, 14, 2:4, 6, 7, 8, 9(2), 11, 23(2); Zech. 1:3(3), 4, 6, 12, 14, 16, 17, 2:8, 9, 11, 3:7, 9, 10, 4:6, 9, 5:4, 6:12, 15, 7:3, 4, 9, 12(2), 13, 8:1, 2, 3, 4, 6(2), 7, 9(2), 11, 14(2), 18, 19, 20, 21, 22, 23, 9:15, 10:3, 12:5, 13:2, 7, 14:16, 17, 21(2); Mal. 1:4, 6, 8, 9, 10, 11, 13, 14, 2:2, 4, 7, 8, 12, 16, 3:1, 5, 7, 10, 11, 12, 14, 17, 4:1, 3.

The sister expression, "Jehovah God of hosts" [y^{e}hovah 'elohēy ts^{e}ba'ôth], occurs 19 times: 2 Sam. 5:10; Pss. 59:5, 84:8, 89:8; Jer. 5:14, 15:16, 35:17, 38:17, 44:7; Hos. 12:5; Amos 3:13, 4:13, 5:14, 15, 16, 27, 6:8, 14, 9:5.

Scripture closely relates these two forms of this name.[160] Thus, I combine them (284 uses) to calculate the relative frequency. On average in the Old Testament they occur 0.920 times per 1000 words, or, once every 1087 words. These names never occur in the Pentateuch. In accord with their significance, their use commences at the time of the inception of the mediatorial kingdom. They occur 18 times in the historical narrative, 15 times in the Psalms, and 251 times in the prophets. Their relative frequency in the prophets is 3.19, once every 313 words, over three times the average use. Their relative frequency in the minor prophets is 5.23, once every 191 words, over five times the average. Accordingly, the books with the highest relative frequency are: (1) Malachi (27.2, once every 37 words); (2) Haggai (23.1, once every 43 words); (3) Zechariah (16.7, once every 65 words); Amos (4.3, once every 230 words); (5) Jeremiah (3.7, once every 270 words); and Isaiah (3.6, once every 276 words).

This name, y^{e}hovah ts^{e}ba'ôth, appears twice in the New Testament as kurios sabaoth (Rom. 9:29; James 5:4). This striking form transliterates ts^{e}ba'ôth as σαβαωθ (sabaoth) and renders y^{e}hovah as κυριος (kurios). It also appears once in the New Testament as κυριος παντοκρατωρ (kurios pantokrator), "y^{e}hovah almighty" (2 Cor. 6:18). Both of these forms reflect LXX

---

[160] *Jer. 51:19*: The portion of Jacob *is* not like them; for he *is* the former of all things: and *Israel is* the rod of his inheritance: the LORD of hosts [y^{e}hovah ts^{e}ba'ôth] *is* his name. *Amos 5:27*: Therefore will I cause you to go into captivity beyond Damascus, says the LORD [y^{e}hovah], whose name *is* The God of hosts ['elohēy ts^{e}ba'ôth].

renderings of *yᵉhovah tsᵉba'ôth*.[161]

5. Transliteration of yhvh

I take time to consider the remarkable circumstances regarding the transliteration of יהוה into Greek. The transliteration of יהוה into English is straightforward, *yhvh*.[162] The transliteration of יהוה into Greek is quite another matter. The rendering of יְהֹוָה צְבָאוֹת (*yᵉhovah tsᵉba'ôth*) as κυριος σαβαωθ (kurios sabaoth) drew my attention to this. At first glance, κυριος σαβαωθ didn't make sense to me. We commonly transliterate proper names. For example, when Paul quotes Isaiah 1:9, he transliterates Sodom and Gomorrah.[163] Thus, I would expect Paul and James to transliterate *tsᵉba'ôth* as σαβαωθ (sabaoth) and also to transliterate, *yhvh*, the rest of the name. Yet Paul and James didn't transliterate *yhvh*. They rendered it as *kurios*. In this they followed the LXX, which renders *yᵉhovah tsᵉba'ôth* in Isaiah 1:9 as κυριος σαβαωθ.[164] Why didn't LXX and the apostles also transliterate *yhvh* into Greek? The reason, quite remarkably, is that the Greek language *has no consonants* equivalent to the Hebrew, י [*yod*] ("y"), or ה [*hē*] ("h"), or ו [*vav*] ("v"). So it would be nearly impossible and very impractical to transliterate יהוה (*yhvh*) into Greek. So apparently, since the Hebrews said, *'adonay*, when they saw *yhvh* written in the text, the LXX rendered *yhvh* with the best Greek translation of *'adonay*, κυριος (kurios). Apparently the apostles did the same.[165] Thus, *kurios* became the Greek equivalent of *yhvh*.

6. The shortened form of yhvh: יָהּ (yah)

The shortened form of *yhvh*, is יָהּ (yah or jah), more precisely, *yahh or jahh*. The KJV usually renders it, "LORD," but once transliterates it as JAH (Ps. 68:4). It occurs these 49 times in the Old Testament:

---

[161] I summarize in Appendix 5 the LXX renderings and uses of *yhvh tsᵉba'ôth* and *yhvh 'elohēy tsᵉba'ôth*.

[162] Or, as is more popular today, a *vav* is transliterated with a "w" rather than with a "v," yielding, *yhwh*.

[163] Sodom in Hebrew is סְדֹם (*sᵉdom*), which LXX transliterated into Greek as σοδομα (sodoma). Again, Gomorrah (KJV) in Hebrew is עֲמֹרָה ('amorah), which LXX transliterated as γομορρα (gomorra). Paul quoted and used these transliterations.

[164] *Isa. 1:9*: Except the LORD of hosts [*yᵉhovah tsᵉba'ôth*] [κυριος σαβαωθ in LXX] had left unto us a very small remnant, we should have been as Sodom, and we should have been like unto Gomorrah. *Rom. 9:29* [NKJV]: And as Isaiah said before: "Unless the LORD of Sabaoth [κυριος σαβαωθ (kurios sabaoth)] had left us a seed, We would have become like Sodom, And we would have been made like Gomorrah."

[165] *James 5:4*: Behold, the hire of the labourers who have reaped down your fields, which is of you kept back by fraud, cries: and the cries of them which have reaped are entered into the ears of Jehovah of hosts [κυριου σαβαωθ (kuriou sabaoth)].

Exod. 15:2, 17:16; Pss. 68:4, 18, 77:11, 89:8, 94:7, 12, 102:18, 104:35, 105:45, 106:1, 48, 111:1, 112:1, 113:1, 9, 115:17, 18(2), 116:19, 117:2, 118:5(2), 14, 17, 18, 19, 122:4, 130:3, 135:1, 3, 4, 21, 146:1, 10, 147:1, 20, 148:1, 14, 149:1, 9, 150:1, 6(2); Isa. 12:2, 26:4, 38:11(2).

It occurs twice in Exodus, 4 times in Isaiah, and 43 times in Psalms. It mostly expresses the religious devotion of God's people. Thus, it occurs with terms for blessing him[166] and praising him.[167] Scripture features an exhortation to praise *yah* that occurs 23 times in Psalms.[168] This exhortation to praise, הַלְלוּ (hal^{e}lû), is the masculine plural imperative in the Piel stem of the verb, הָלַל (halal). In its Piel stem *halal* signifies "to praise" or to "boast in." This imperative, *hal^{e}lû*, occurs three times in Psalm 135:1.[169] Its first use calls Jehovah's servants to praise, "yah." Its second use calls them to praise, "the name of y^{e}hovah." In its third use it stands alone: "praise, O you servants of y^{e}hovah." This exhortation to praise *yah* appears in three forms. On 7 occasions, as in Psalm 135:1, it occurs as two words, הַלְלוּ יָהּ (hal^{e}lû yahh).[170] On 15 occasions it appears as a hyphenated word, הַלְלוּ־יָהּ (hal^{e}lû-yahh).[171] Once it appears as one word, הַלְלוּיָהּ (hal^{e}lûyahh).[172] We typically transliterate this into English as, "hallelujah," using the English "j" rather than "y," to transliterate the Hebrew, י (yod). Thus, this transliteration, *hallelujah*, exceedingly common in our English hymnody, is an exhortation to praise and boast in the Supreme Being, a personal Being named, *y^{e}hovah*, whose proper name in short, is *yah*.

This exhortation, *hal^{e}lûyahh*, appears 4 times in the New Testament *transliterated* as, ἀλληλουια.[173] Again, the Greek alphabet has no "h" consonant equivalent to the Hebrew, ה (hē), and no "y" or "j" consonant equivalent to the Hebrew, י (yod). This limitation occasioned the Greek transliteration, ἀλληλουια. Since the Greek has a rough breathing mark, one

---

[166] Ps. 115:18: But we will bless the LORD [n^{e}barēk yahh] from this time forth and for evermore. Praise the LORD [hal^{e}lû-yahh].

[167] Ps. 102:18: This shall be written for the generation to come: and the people which shall be created shall praise the LORD [y^{e}hallel-yahh].

[168] Pss. 104:35, 105:45, 106:1, 48, 111:1, 112:1, 113:1, 9, 115:18, 116:19, 117:2, 135:1, 21, 146:1, 10, 147:1, 20, 148:1, 14, 149:1, 9, 150:1, 6.

[169] Ps. 135:1: Praise [hal^{e}lû] Yah. Praise [hal^{e}lû] the name of Y^{e}hovah. Praise [hal^{e}lû], O you servants of Y^{e}hovah.

[170] Pss. 111:1, 112:1, 113:1, 135:1, 148:1, 149:1, 150:1.

[171] Pss. 104:35, 105:45, 106:48, 113:9, 115:18, 116:19, 117:2, 135:21, 146:1, 10, 147:1, 20, 148:14, 149:9, 150:6.

[172] Ps. 106:1

[173] Rev. 19:1, 3, 4, 6.

could transliterate ἀλληλουια into English as *hallelouia*. Yet, the KJV transliterated ἀλληλουια into English in these 4 verses as *alleluia*.[174] Now then, since we have the "h" consonant and the "y" or "j" consonant in English, our hymnody sometimes transliterates directly from the Hebrew and uses, *hallelujah*. Yet sometimes, our English hymnody uses *alleluia*, the KJV transliteration of the Greek transliteration. I supply this information because over the years quite a few Christians have asked me to explain these different forms that we sing in our hymns.

7. The relation of yhvh to 'elohîm

These two primary names for the Supreme Being in the Old Testament denote him over 9,000 times, 9,168 to be precise. Often they occur alone, sometimes together. How do they relate to each other?

Only *'elohîm* occurs in the Creation account (Gen. 1:1-2:3). Thus, *'elohîm* highlights the identity of the Supreme Being as the Originator of the universe and everything in it. Further, the Originator of the universe rules and owns all he made. The apostle underscores this.[175] Thus, *'elohîm* is the *Originator*, "of him," the *Controller*, "through him," and the *Owner*, "unto him," of all things. In the first history, the primeval history of the cosmos, only *y^{e}hovah 'elohîm* occurs in the second account of creation, which describes the setting of the fall (Gen. 2:4-25). Again, in the account of the fall, again only *y^{e}hovah 'elohîm* occurs, except for Satan's use of *'elohîm* (Gen. 3:1-24). This underscores that both names, *y^{e}hovah* and *'elohîm,* depict the one and only Supreme Being. This discloses that the Supreme Being, the Originator, Controller, and Owner of the universe, is a Personal Being named, *y^{e}hovah*, who relates personally and verbally to man. In the account of the spiritual struggle that characterizes cosmic history, only *y^{e}hovah* occurs (Gen. 4:1-26). This underscores that when the Supreme Being rescues sinners, he relates to them personally and communes with them verbally in his Word: "then began men to call on the name of *y^{e}hovah*" (Gen. 4:26). Thus, when God redeems Israel, he features his personal identity as *y^{e}hovah*.[176] Further, Scripture stresses that this Personal Being named *y^{e}hovah*, the Redeemer of

---

[174] KJV: *Rev 19:6*: And I heard as it were the voice of a great multitude, and as the voice of many waters, and as the voice of mighty thunderings, saying, Alleluia: for the Lord God omnipotent reigneth. ASV, RSV, NASV, and NIV use, *hallelujah*.

[175] *Rom. 11:36*: For of him, and through him, and unto him, are all things. To him *be* the glory for ever. Amen.

[176] *Exod. 3:15*: And God said moreover unto Moses, Thus shall you say unto the children of Israel, Jehovah, God of your fathers, the God of Abraham, the God of Isaac, and the God of Jacob, has sent me unto you: this *is* my name forever, and this *is* my memorial unto all generations.

his people, is their *'elohîm*—Originator, Controller, and Owner.[177] Thus, Elijah brought Israel to confess, "Jehovah [y^{e}hovah], he is God ['elohîm]" (1 Kings 18:39).

Thus, God's people confess that a Personal Being named, *Jehovah*, who rescued us from sin, is our *God*, our *'elohîm*. We are "of him." He is our *Originator*. From our *'elohîm* we came into existence. From him we have value, meaning, and purpose. We are "through him." He is our *Controller*. By our *'elohîm* we live, have, and act. We are "unto him." He is our Owner, our Ultimate. Unto our *'elohîm* we live. He is our reason for being, the focus of our rationality, vision, and destiny. Unto our *'elohîm* we give account. He is the focus of our responsibility, our Arbiter and Judge. Unto our *'elohîm* we pledge allegiance. He is the focus of our loyalty, devotion, and adoration.[178]

In the account of the flood (Gen. 6:13-7:5), Scripture discloses a remarkable contrast between *'elohîm* and *y^{e}hovah*. First, *'elohîm* commands Noah to bring two of every kind into the ark.[179] Then *y^{e}hovah* commands Noah to bring seven of every clean animal.[180] Scripture records that Noah did what *'elohîm* commanded him and what *y^{e}hovah* commanded him.[181] Thus, the Supreme Being, denominated as *'elohîm*, preserves life as Creator; denominated as *y^{e}hovah*, regulates worship as Redeemer.

In sum, the name, *'elohîm*, features the identity of the Supreme Being as Creator, Preserver, and Owner of all things. All things are "of him," "through him," and "unto him." The name, *y^{e}hovah*, features the personal identity of the Supreme Being as the Redeemer, who saves his people, regulates their lives and worship, rules over them, draws near to them, and communes with them by his Word. The combination, *y^{e}hovah 'elohîm*, underscores that there is only one Supreme Being who is both Creator and Redeemer.

II. The Revelation of God's Names in the New Testament

We consider their *identity*, their *use*, and their *relation* to the Persons of the Trinity.

---

[177] *Deut 28:58*: If thou wilt not observe to do all the words of this law that are written in this book, that thou mayest fear this glorious and fearful name, THE LORD THY GOD [y^{e}hovah 'eloheyka]

[178] *Deut. 10:17*: For Jehovah your God *is* God of gods, and Lord of lords, a great God, a mighty, and a terrible, who regards not persons, nor takes reward:

[179] Gen. 6:13, 19, 22

[180] Gen. 7:1, 2, 3, 5

[181] Gen. 6:22, 7:5

A. The Identity of God's New Testament Names

God's names in order of appearance in the New Testament are: *kurios* (Matt. 1:20), *theos* (Matt. 1:23), *hupsistos* (Mark 5:7), *despotes* (Luke 2:29), and *pantokrator* (2 Cor. 6:18). In order of frequency, *theos* is first. It denotes God some 1,329 times. Next is *kurios*, which denotes the Supreme Being some 321 times. It also denotes Christ some 367 times, many of which depict him as the Supreme Being. The other three names occur a total of 24 times: *pantokrator* (10 times), *hupsistos* (9 times), and *despotes* (5 times).

B. The Use of God's New Testament Names

We consider the use of these names in the order of their frequency of occurrence.

1. God: θεος (theos)[182]

This divine name occurs 1,343 times in BYZ Greek text of the New Testament. It is the primary Greek name for the Supreme Being. We derive *theology*, literally, "a discourse about God," from *theos* and *logos*. We consider the *significance* and *relative frequency* of *theos*.

a. The significance of theos

Generically *theos* signifies deity, superlative greatness, the focus of ultimate devotion. It once functions adverbially, *"superlatively* fair," to depict superlative greatness in appearance.[183] It occasionally depicts great persons that act as arbiters of their fellow men. This significance of *theos* clearly reflects the general significance of *'elohîm*.[184] Similarly, like *'elohîm*,[185] it sometimes signifies objects of human devotion, false gods.[186] Most often, 1,329 times in the BYZ Greek text, it depicts the true God as the Superlative Being, the Creator, Controller, and Owner of the universe.

b. The relative frequency of theos

The average relative frequency of *theos* per 1000 words in the New Testament is 9.47. In the gospels the relative frequency is 4.73, about half

---

[182] In Appendix 6 I present the significance, occurrences, and relative frequency of *theos* in the New Testament

[183] *Acts 7:20*: In which time Moses was born, and was exceeding [theos] fair, and nourished up in his father's house three months

[184] *John 10:34*: Jesus answered them, Is it not written in your law, I said, You are gods [theos]? *Ps. 82:6*: I said, You are gods ['elohîm], and all of you sons of the Most High

[185] *Acts 7:40*: saying unto Aaron, Make us gods [theos] that shall go before us. *Exod. 32:23*: For they said unto me, Make us gods ['elohîm], which shall go before us

[186] *1 Cor. 8:5*: For though there be that are called gods [theos], whether in heaven or on earth; as there are gods [theos] many, and lords many

of the average. In Paul's letters it is 12.58, 1.3 times the average. The following nine books have a relative frequency 50% or more above the average (greater than or equal to 14.22): (1) 1 John (29.23); (2) 1 Thess. (24.72); (3) 2 Thess. (22.78); (4) 1 Peter (22.73); (5) Romans (21.23); (6) Titus (19.55); (7) 2 Cor. (17.31); (8) 1 Cor. (15.02); and (9) 1 Timothy (14.22).

2. *Lord, LORD*: κυριος (kurios)[187]

This name occurs some 767 times[188] in the New Testament. In general it signifies someone that has control or rule with various nuances. Consider three major uses in the New Testament.

First, some 79 times *kurios* denotes a created lord with various nuances. It can depict a civil ruler,[189] a master of a household and of domestic servants,[190] or an owner of property.[191] Accordingly, it sometimes occurs in direct address to express respect or deference to a human[192] or to an angel.[193]

Second, some 321 times *kurios* denotes the Supreme Being. It often depicts God's proper name, Jehovah, "the LORD."[194] It also depicts God as the supreme ruler and master, "Lord," of the universe.[195]

Third, some 367 times *kurios* denotes Christ with various nuances. Jesus is divine and human; and he is the Christ, the ruler and king of God's people.

---

[187] In Appendix 7 I catalogue the use and variant readings of *kurios* in the New Testament

[188] This includes 748 references in the BYZ text and an additonal 19 references from the Majority and UBS Greek texts.

[189] *Acts 25:26*: Of whom I have no certain thing to write unto my lord [kurios]

[190] *Eph. 6:5*: Servants, be obedient unto them that according to the flesh are your masters [kurios]

[191] *Luke 19:33*: And as they were loosing the colt, the owners [kurios] thereof said unto them, Why loose ye the colt?

[192] *John 12:21*: these therefore came to Philip . . . and asked him, saying, Sir [kurios], we would see Jesus.

[193] *Acts 10:4*: And he, fastening his eyes upon him, and being affrighted, said, What is it, Lord [kurios]?

[194] *Luke 20:42*: For David himself says in the book of Psalms, The LORD [kurios] said unto my Lord [kurios], Sit thou on my right hand. *Ps 110:1*: The LORD [y^{e}hovah] says unto my Lord ['adôn], Sit thou at my right hand: *Matt. 3:3*: For this is he that was spoken of through Isaiah the prophet, saying, The voice of one crying in the wilderness, Make ye ready the way of the Lord [kurios]. *Isa. 40:3*: The voice of one that crieth, Prepare ye in the wilderness the way of the LORD [y^{e}hovah]

[195] *Acts 17:24*: The God [theos] that made the world and all things therein, he, being Lord [kurios] of heaven and earth, dwells not in temples made with hands

Accordingly, *kurios* at times depicts Jesus as a religious leader or dignitary,[196] at other times as the Supreme Ruler of all, God incarnate,[197] and at other times as the Messiah, the anointed ruler of God's people.[198] And, when Paul saw Christ exalted in glory, he addressed him as a heavenly dignitary.[199] In some contexts the specific nuance difficult to discern.

3. The Almighty: παντοκρατωρ (pantokrator)

In the New Testament *pantokrator* only denotes the Supreme Being. It occurs 10 times, 9 in Revelation. It stresses God's omnipotence and sovereignty. It occurs once by itself: "*ho pantokrator*": *The Almighty*: Rev. 1:8. It occurs twice with *theos*: "*ho theos ho pantokrator*": "*God Almighty*": Rev. 16:14, 19:15. It occurs 6 times with *kurios ho theos*: "*kurios ho theos, ho pantokrator*": "*y^{e}hovah God, the Almighty*": Rev. 4:8, 11:17, 15:3, 16:7, 19:6, 21:22. It occurs once with *kurios*: "*kurios pantokrator*": "y^{e}hovah almighty."[200] These last two uses reflect the Hebrew *y^{e}hovah 'elohēy ts^{e}ba'ôth* and *y^{e}hovah ts^{e}ba'ôth*.

4. The Most High, The Highest: ὕψιστος (hupsistos):

This name comes from, ὕψος (hupsos), "height." It occurs 13 times in the New Testament. Generically it denotes the highest place or degree (Matt. 21:9; Mark 11:10; Luke 2:14, 19:28). It denotes the Supreme Being 9 times. It occurs by itself, *The Highest*, these 5 times: Luke 1:32, 35, 76, 6:35; Acts 7:48. It occurs in combination with θεος (theos), *God Most High, ho theos ho hupsistos*, these 4 times: Mark 5:7; Luke 8:28; Acts 16:17; Heb. 7:1. Thus, Luke accounts for 7 of its 9 uses: 5 in his gospel; 2 in Acts. Scripture explicitly connects *hupsistos* with the Hebrew, *'ēl 'elyôn*[201] and with God's

---

[196] *John 4:11*: The woman says unto him, Sir [kurios], you have nothing to draw with, and the well is deep

[197] *Acts 10:36*: The word which he sent unto the children of Israel, preaching good tidings of peace by Jesus Christ—He is Lord [kurios] of all

[198] *Acts 2:36*: Let all the house of Israel therefore know assuredly, that God has made him both Lord [kurios] and Christ, this Jesus whom you crucified

[199] *Acts 9:5*: And he said, Who are you, Lord [kurios]? And he *said*, I am Jesus whom you persecute

[200] *2 Cor. 6:18*: And will be to you a Father, and you shall be to me sons and daughters, says the Lord Almighty [kurios pantokrator]

[201] *Heb. 7:1*: For this Melchizedek, king of Salem, priest of the most high God [tou theou tou hupsistou], who met Abraham returning from the slaughter of the kings, and blessed him; *Gen. 14:18*: And Melchizedek king of Salem brought forth bread and wine: and he was priest of God Most High [*'ēl 'elyôn*].

proper name, *y^{e}hovah*.[202] This name, *hupsistos*, highlights God's sovereignty,[203] supreme power,[204] infinite goodness,[205] and transcendence.[206]

5. *Master, Lord*: δεσποτης (despotes)

This name occurs 10 times in the New Testament. It can depict an earthly master (1 Tim. 6:1, 2; Titus 2:9; 1 Pet. 2:18). It denotes God as Lord and Master 5 times: Luke 2:29; Acts 4:24; 2 Pet. 2:1; Jude 4; Rev. 6:10. It possibly also refers to Christ or God as Master (2 Tim. 2:21). It features God's sovereign control over all the affairs of men. Thus, *despotes* reflects the significance of the Hebrew *'adonay* and its shortened form, *'adôn*. Accordingly the LXX sometimes used *despotes* to translate both.[207]

C. *The Relation of God's New Testament Names to the Persons of the Trinity*

> 1 Cor. 8:5-6: For though there be that are called gods, whether in heaven or on earth, as indeed there are gods many, and lords many; yet to us there is one God [theos], the Father, of whom are all things, and we unto him; and one Lord [kurios], Jesus Christ, through whom are all things, and we through him.

Paul affirms plainly that the two primary divine names, *theos* and *kurios*, have a pronounced Trinitarian emphasis. *Theos* emphatically denotes God the Father. God the Father is emphatically our Originator, and Owner. *Kurios* emphatically denotes God the Son. God the Son incarnate is emphatically our Supreme Master through whom we have both animate life and also spiritual life. He redeems his people from sin, regulates our lives and worship, rules over us, draws near to us, and communes with us. This distinction is not absolute. It is merely a matter of emphasis. Scripture also denotes God the Son as *theos*[208] and God the Father as *kurios*.[209] Further, the Holy Spirit, the Spirit of the Father and of the Son, is both *theos* (Acts 5:3-4) and *kurios* (2 Cor. 3:17-18).

---

[202] *Gen. 14:22*: And Abram said to the king of Sodom, I have lifted up my hand unto Jehovah, God Most High [y^{e}hovah, 'ēl 'elyôn], possessor of heaven and earth

[203] Luke 1:32

[204] Luke 1:35

[205] Luke 6:35

[206] Acts 7:48

[207] Gen. 15:2, 8; Jer. 1:6, 4:10; Dan. 9:8, 15, 16, etc.

[208] *John 1:1*: In the beginning was the Word, and the Word was with God, and the Word was God [theos].

[209] Acts 4:29-30

Respecting the other divine names, *hupsistos* seems at times to emphasize God the Father.[210] *Pantokrator* appears not to feature any specific divine Person. *Despotes* refers specifically both to the Father (Acts 4:24) and to the Son (Jude 4).

III. The Relationship between God's New Testament and Old Testament Names

When the New Testament quotes the Old Testament and translates various divine names, it reveals this relationship. This is our most reliable source. A secondary source is the LXX. We consider both renderings of the Hebrew Names into Greek and uses of Greek names to render various Hebrew names.

A. Hebrew Names into Greek

1. 'elohîm and its cognates: 'ēl, 'elôah, 'elah

a. *'elohîm*: The primary term that translates *'elohîm* is *theos*. Scripture makes this connection explicitly[211] and repeatedly.[212] Occasionally LXX renders *'elohîm* with *kurios*, "Jehovah,"[213] or with *kurios ho theos*, "Jehovah God,"[214] or with *despotes*.[215]

b. *'ēl*: Scripture also uses *theos* for the shorter form, *'ēl*. Matthew transliterates the Hebrew, אֵלִי (*'ēlî*), "my God," with, *Eli*, and uses *theos* to translate *'ēl*.[216] The writer to Hebrews also uses *theos* for *'ēl*.[217]

---

[210] Luke 1:32, 35; Heb. 7:1

[211] *Gen. 1:27*: So God ['elohîm] created man in his own image, in the image of God ['elohîm] created he him; male and female created he them. *Mark 10:6*: But from the beginning of the creation God [theos] made them male and female.

[212] *Exod. 3:6*: Moreover he said, I am the God ['elohîm] of thy father, the God ['elohîm] of Abraham, the God ['elohîm] of Isaac, and the God ['elohîm] of Jacob. And Moses hid his face; for he was afraid to look upon God ['elohîm]. *Acts 7:32*: Saying, I am the God [theos] of thy fathers, the God [theos] of Abraham, and the God [theos] of Isaac, and the God [theos] of Jacob. Then Moses trembled, and durst not behold.

[213] Gen. 19:6, 21:2

[214] Gen. 8:15, 9:12

[215] Dan. 9:17

[216] *Ps. 22:1*: My God ['ēl], my God ['ēl], why hast thou forsaken me? *Matt. 27:46*: And about the ninth hour Jesus cried with a loud voice, saying, Eli, Eli, lama sabachthani? That is to say, My God [theos], my God [theos], why hast thou forsaken me?

[217] Heb. 7:1

c. *'elôah*: LXX often uses *theos* to translate *'elôah*.[218] However, in Job LXX typically renders *'elôah* with *ho kurios*, "the Lord,"[219] or just with *kurios*, "Jehovah."[220]

d. *'elah*: LXX most often uses *theos* to translate the Aramaic *'elah*.[221] Occasionally, it uses *ho kurios*[222] or *kurios ho theos*.[223] However, when *'elah* depicts "gods," LXX occasionally uses *angelos*, "angels,"[224] "or *eidolon*, "idols."[225]

2. *'elyôn* and its cognates: *'illay*, *'al*

a. *'elyôn*: The writer to Hebrews uses *hupsistos* to translate *'elyôn* when he renders *'ēl 'elyôn*, "God Most High," as *theos hupsistos* (Heb. 7:1). Accordingly, LXX uses *ho hupsistos*, "the Most High," for *'elyôn*,[226] *kurios hupsistos*, "Jehovah Most High," for *yᵉhovah 'elyôn*,[227] and *theos hupsistos*, "God Most High," for *'ēl 'elyôn*[228] and *'elohîm 'elyôn*.[229]

b. *'illay*: LXX translates this Aramaic form with *hupsistos* when it occurs alone, "the Most High,"[230] and when it occurs as *'elah 'illay*, "God Most High."[231]

c. *'al*: LXX does not render *'al* in Hosea 7:16 and renders it with *theos* in Hosea 11:7.

d. *'elyôn*: LXX also renders this Aramaic form with *hupsistos*: Dan. 7:18, 22, 25, 27.

---

[218] Deut. 32:15, 17; Neh. 9:17; Job 3:23; Pss. 18:31, 50:22, 114:7; Prov. 30:5; Isa. 44:8; Dan. 11:38, 39; Hab. 1:11, 3:3.

[219] For Example: Job 3:4, 5:17, 6:8, 9, 11:5

[220] For example: Job 4:9, 17, 10:2, 11:7

[221] For example: Ezr. 4:24, 5:1, 2(2), 5, 8, 11, 12, 13, 14, 16, 17, 6:3, 5(2), 7(2), 8, 9, 10, 12(2), 14, 16, 17, 18, 7:12, 14, 15, 16, 17, 18, 19(2), 20, 21, 23(2), 24, 25(2), 26; Jer. 10:11; Dan. 2:28, 44, 45, 47(3), 3:14, 15, 17, 25, 26, 28(2), 29, 5:23, 6:7, 12, 16, 20, 22, 23, 26(2).

[222] Dan. 2:18, 19, 20, 23, 37

[223] Dan. 3:28, 29, 6:5

[224] Dan. 2:11

[225] Dan. 3:12, 18, 5:4, 23

[226] Num. 24:16; Deut. 32:8; 2 Sam. 22:14; Pss. 9:2, 18:13, 21:7, 46:4, 50:14, 73:11, 77:10, 78:17, 82:6, 87:5, 91:1, 9, 92:1, 107:11; Isa. 14:14; Lam. 3:35, 38

[227] Pss. 7:17, 47:2

[228] Gen. 14:18, 19, 20, 22; Ps. 78:35

[229] Pss. 57:2, 78:56

[230] Dan. 4:24, 7:25

[231] Dan. 3:26

3. *'adôn* and *'adonay*

a. *'adôn*: Most often LXX translates *'adôn* with *kurios*.[232] Sometimes it uses *despotes*.[233]

b. *'adonay*: LXX occasionally transliterates using αδωναι (adonai).[234] Most often it translates *'adonay* with *kurios*.[235] Sometimes, but rarely, it uses *despotes*[236] or *theos*.[237] Further, on occasion it uses θεοσεβια (theosebeia), "godliness," to translate, *yir'ah 'adonay*, "fear of the Lord."[238] The rendering of *'adonay* in Ezekiel deserves special notice. Of the 221 uses of *'adonay* in Ezekiel, 217 are *'adonay yehovih*. I consider these momentarily with the renderings of *yhvh*.

4. *shadday* and *'ēl shadday*

a. *'ēl shadday*: "God Almighty": LXX renders *'ēl shadday* two ways: (1) 6 times LXX translates *'ēl* with *theos* and renders *shadday* with a possessive: "my," or "thy," or, "being of them": *ho theos sou*, "thy God," or, *ho theos mou*, "my God," or, *ho theos on auton*, "the God being of them," or "their God":[239] and (2) once, LXX translates *'ēl* with *theos* and transliterates *shadday* as, Σαδδαι (Saddai).[240]

b. *shadday*: "The Almighty": LXX renders *shadday* in various ways: (1) with *theos* and a possessive: *ho theos ho emos*: "my God"[241]; (2) with *theos*:

---

[232] Exod. 23:17, 34:23; Deut. 10:17(2); Josh. 3:11, 13; Neh. 8:10; Pss. 8:1 9, 45:11, 97:5, 110:1, 114:7, 135:5, 136:3(2), 147:5; Isa. 19:4; Dan. 12:8; Hos. 12:14; Micah 4:13; Zech. 4:14, 6:5; Mal. 3:1.

[233] Isa. 1:24, 3:1, 10:33

[234] Judg. 13:8, 16:28

[235] Gen. 18:3, 27, 30, 31, 32, 20:4; Exod. 4:10, 13, 5:22, 15:17, 34:9, Num. 14:17; Deut. 3:24, 9:26; Judg. 6:15, 22, 2 Sam. 7:18, 19(2), 20, 28, 29; 1 Kings 3:10, 8:53, 22:6; 2 Kings 7:6, 19:23; Neh. 1:11; Pss. 2:4, 16:2, 22:30, 35:17, 22, 23, 37:13, 38:9, 15, 22, 39:7, 40:17, 44:23, 51:15, 54:4, 55:9, 57:9, 59:11, 62:12, 66:18, 68:11, 17, 19, 20, 22, 26, 32, 69:6, 71:5, 16, 73:20, 77:7, 78:65, 79:12, 86:3, 4, 5, 8, 9, 12, 15, 89:49, 50, 90:1, 109:21, 110:5, 130:2, 3, 6, 140:7, 141:8; Isa. 3:18, 4:4, 6:1, 8, 11, 7:14, 20, 8:7, 9:8. 10:12, 11:11, 21:6, 16, 28:2, 29:13, 30:20, 37:24, 38:16, 49:14; Jer. 2:19, 44:26, 46:10, 50:25; Lam. 1:14, 15(2), 2:1, 2, 5, 7, 18, 19, 20, 3:31, 36, 37, 58; Ezek. 18:25, 29, 33:17, 20; Dan. 1:2, 9:3, 4, 7, 9, 17, 19(2); Amos 7:7, 8, 9:1; Obad. 1:1; Micah 1:2; Zeph. 1:7; Zech. 9:4; Mal. 1:14

[236] Gen. 15:2, 8; Jer. 1:6, 4:10; Dan. 9:8, 15, 16

[237] Neh. 4:14; Ps. 77:2; Isa. 3:17, 9:17

[238] Job 28:28

[239] Gen. 17:1, 28:3, 35:11, 43:14, 48:3; Exod. 6:3

[240] Ezek. 10:5

[241] Gen. 49:25

"God"[242]; (3) with ἱκανος (hikanos): "The Sufficient," or, "The Able"[243]; (4) with *pantokrator*: "the Almighty"[244]; (5) with *ho kurios* or *kurios*: "the Lord," or "y^{e}hovah"[245]; (6) with *kurios pantokrator*: "Y^{e}hovah Almighty"[246]; (7) with, *ho epouranios*, "the Heavenly"[247]; (8) with *ho theos tou ouranou*: "the God of heaven"[248]; (8) with a personal pronoun, *autos*: "him"[249]; (9) with paraphrases: LXX translates, "when the Almighty [shadday] was yet with me," as: ὅτε ἤμην ὑλώδης λιαν (hote emen hulodes lian): literally: "when I was very wooded"[250]; again, LXX translates "touching the Almighty [shadday] we cannot find him out," as, και ουχ ευρισκομεν αλλον ομοιον (kai ouk heuriskomen allon homoion): "and we do not find another similar"[251]; and (10) with no rendering at all.[252]

The most common renderings are *pantokrator* (14 times), *kurios* (11 times), and *hikanos* (5 times). These account for 30 of the 41 occurrences of *shadday*.

5. *yhvh*: *with cognates and combinations*

a. *y^{e}hovah*: "Jehovah": For reasons that I have previously explained, the most common Greek rendering for *yhvh* pointed as *y^{e}hovah* is *kurios*. However, LXX sometimes renders *y^{e}hovah* as, *ho theos*,[253] or as, *kurios ho theos*.[254]

b. *'adonay yehovih*: "Lord Jehovah": LXX renders this combination in a variety of ways: (1) *despotes* alone:[255] LXX translates *'adonay* with *despotes* and does not render *yehovih*; (2) *despotes kurios*:[256] LXX translates *'adonay*

---

[242] Num. 24:4, 16; Isa. 13:6
[243] Ruth 1:20, 21; Job 21:15, 31:2, 40:2
[244] Job 5:17, 8:5, 11:7, 22:17, 25, 23:16, 27:11, 13, 32:8, 33:4, 34:10, 12, 35:13
[245] Job 6:4, 14, 8:3, 13:3, 21:20, 22:3, 23, 26, 24:1, 27:2, 31:35
[246] Job 15:25
[247] Ps. 68:14
[248] Ps. 91:1
[249] Job. 27:10
[250] Job 29:5
[251] Job 37:23
[252] Ezek. 1:24; Joel 1:15
[253] Deut. 9:26; Isa. 8:18, 10:26, 44:6(2)
[254] Gen. 7:16
[255] Gen. 15:2
[256] Gen. 15:8; Jer. 1:6, 4:10

with *despotes* and renders *yehovih* with *kurios*; (3) *kurios kurios*:[257] LXX translates *'adonay* with *kurios* and also renders *yehovih* with *kurios*; (4) Αδωναιε κυριε (adonaie kurie):[258] LXX transliterates *'adonay* and renders *yehovih* with *kurios*; (5) *theos*:[259] LXX renders *'adonay yehovih* and *'adonay yehovih ts^{e}ba'ôth* as *ho theos*, "GOD"; (6) *kurios*:[260] LXX simply uses *kurios*. It is difficult to know whether *kurios* is a translation of *'adonay* or a rendering of *yehovih*; (7) *kurios theos*:[261] LXX translates *'adonay* with *kurios* and renders *yehovih* with *theos*. This reflects how the KJV renders *'adonay yehovih* in English, "Lord GOD"; (8) κυριος παντοκρατωρ (*kurios pantokrator*): "Lord ALMIGHTY," or "almighty Jehovah":[262] The explanation for this rendering is difficult to discern; (9) *kurios sabaoth*: "Lord sabaoth," or "Jehovah sabaoth":[263] The explanation for this rendering is also difficult to discern; (10) no rendering at all.[264]

Most often for *'adonay yehovih* LXX uses *kurios* (184 times), *kurios kurios* (76 times), and *kurios theos* (29 times). These account for 289 of the 305 occurrences.

---

[257] These 76 times: Deut. 3:24, 9:26; Judg. 6:22; 2 Sam. 7:18, 19(2), 20, 28, 29; 1 Kings 8:53; Pss. 68:20, 69:6, 71:5, 16, 109:21, 140:7, 141:8; Jer. 44:26; Ezek. 12:10, 13:20, 14:6, 20:39, 40, 47, 49, 21:7, 13, 22:3, 31, 23:28, 46, 26:15, 19, 21, 28:12, 25, 29:19, 20, 30:10, 13, 22, 31:15, 18, 32:8, 16, 31, 32, 33:25, 34:2, 8, 10, 15, 17, 20, 31, 35:3, 6, 36:2, 3, 5, 13, 14, 15, 32, 37:21, 38:3, 10, 17, 18, 39:8, 25, 29; Amos 5:3, 7:2, 5, 9:5

[258] Judg. 16:28

[259] Isa. 10:23, 25:8

[260] These 184 times: Josh. 7:7; 1 Kings 2:26; Ps. 73:28; Isa. 10:24, 22:5, 12, 15, 28:16, 22, 30:15, 40:10, 48:16, 49:22, 50:4, 5, 7, 9, 52:4, 56:8, 61:1, 11, 65:13, 15; Jer. 2:22, 7:20, 14:13, 32:17, 46:10, 49:5, 50:31; Ezek. 2:4, 3:11, 27, 5:5, 7, 8, 11, 6:3(2), 11, 7:2, 8:1, 9:8, 11:7, 8, 13, 16, 17, 21, 12:19, 23, 25, 28(2), 13:3, 8(2), 9, 13, 16, 18, 14:4, 11, 14, 16, 18, 20, 21, 23, 15:6, 8, 16:3, 8, 14, 19, 23, 30, 36, 43, 48, 59, 63, 17:3, 9, 16, 19, 22, 18:3, 9, 23, 30, 32, 20:3(2), 5, 27, 30, 31, 33, 36, 44, 21:24, 26, 28, 22:12, 19, 28, 23:22, 32, 34, 35, 49, 24:3, 6, 9, 14, 21, 24, 25:3(2), 6, 8, 12, 13, 14, 15, 16, 26:3, 5, 7, 14, 27:3, 28:2, 6, 10, 22, 24, 29:3, 8, 13, 16, 30:2, 6, 31:10, 32:3, 11, 14, 33:11, 34:11, 30, 35:11, 14, 36:4(2), 6, 22, 33, 37, 37:3, 5, 9, 12, 19, 38:14, 21, 39:1, 5, 10, 13, 17, 20, 43:27; Amos 1:8, 3:13, 4:2, 6:8, 7:1, 4(2), 6, 8:1, 3, 11; Micah 1:2

[261] These 29 times: Jer. 2:19, 46:10, 50:25; Ezek. 4:14, 43:18, 19, 44:6, 9, 12, 15, 27, 45:9(2), 15, 18, 46:1, 16, 47:13, 23, 48:29; Amos 3:7, 8, 11, 4:5, 8:9, 9:8; Obad. 1:1; Hab. 3:19; Zeph. 1:7

[262] Zech. 9:14

[263] Isa. 7:7

[264] Jer. 32:25; Ezek. 33:27, 36:7, 23

c. *yhvh tsᵉba'ôth*: "Jehovah of hosts":²⁶⁵ LXX renders this combination in four primary ways: (1) transliteration of *tsᵉba'ôth*: κυριος σαβαωθ (*kurios sabaoth*): "Jehovah Sabaoth" ²⁶⁶ ; (2) κυριος παντοκρατωρ (*kurios pantokrator*): "Jehovah almighty"²⁶⁷; (3) κυριος των δυναμεων (*kurios ton dunameon*): "Jehovah of the powers"²⁶⁸; and (4) κυριος (*kurios*): "Jehovah": no rendering of *tsᵉba'ôth*.²⁶⁹ These account for 237 of the 265 occurrences.

I observe the following features of this usage: (1) *In Psalms*: LXX exclusively uses *kurios ton dunameon*. (2) *In Isaiah*: when LXX renders *tsᵉba'ôth*, it almost always uses, *kurios sabaoth*, with a couple of noteworthy exceptions (Isa. 14:27, 44:6). (3) *In Jeremiah*: LXX most often simply uses *kurios* with no rendering of *tsᵉba'ôth*. When it renders *tsᵉba'ôth*, it most often uses *pantokrator*. When it renders *tsᵉba'ôth* in "yᵉhovah God of hosts," it uses *kurios pantokrator*. (4) *In Haggai*: LXX only uses *kurios pantokrator*. (5) *In Zechariah*: when LXX renders *tsᵉba'ôth*, it renders it with *pantokrator*, with one exception, Zech. 7:4, where it uses *ton dunameon*. (6) *In Malachi*: LXX always renders *tsᵉba'ôth* with *pantokrator*. (7) *In the minor prophets*: LXX never transliterates *tsᵉba'ôth* as *sabaoth*. It always either translates it with *pantokrator* or *ton dunameon* or omits it.

Further, LXX renders the sister combination, *yᵉhovah 'elohēy tsᵉba'ôth*, "Jehovah God of hosts" as follows: (1) *kurios ho theos ton dunameon*: "Jehovah God of the powers": Pss. 59:5, 84:8, 89:8; (2) *kurios ho theos ho pantokrator*: Jehovah God the almighty": Hos. 12:5; Amos 4:13, 5:14, 15, 16, 27; (3) *kurios pantokrator*: "Jehovah almighty": 2 Sam. 5:10; Jer. 5:14, 15:16, 44:7; (4) *kurios*: "Jehovah": Jer. 35:17, 38:17; and (5) complete

---

²⁶⁵ In Appendix 5 I present a complete catalogue of the LXX renderings of *yhvh tsᵉbaôth* and *yhvh 'elohēy tsᵉba'ôth*

²⁶⁶ These 50 times: 1 Sam. 15:2, 17:45; Isa. 1:9, 24, 2:12, 3:1, 5:7, 9, 16, 24, 6:3, 5, 8:18, 9:7, 10:16, 24, 33, 13:4, 13, 14:22, 24, 17:3, 18:7(2), 19:4, 12, 16, 25, 21:10, 22:5, 12, 14, 15, 25, 23:9, 25:6, 28:5, 22, 29, 29:6, 31:4, 37:16, 32, 39:5, 45:13, 47:4, 48:2, 51:15, 54:5; Jer. 46:10

²⁶⁷ These 105 times: 2 Sam. 7:8, 27; 1 Kings 19:10, 14; 1 Chron. 11:9, 17:7, 24; Jer. 23:16, 25:27, 31:35, 32:14, 33:11, 50:34, 51:5, 57; Micah 4:4; Nah. 2:13; Hab. 2:13; Zeph. 2:10; Hag. 1:2, 5, 7, 9, 14, 2:4, 6, 7, 8, 9(2), 11, 23(2); Zech. 1:3, 4, 6, 12, 14, 16, 17, 2:8, 9, 11, 3:7, 9, 10, 4:6, 9, 5:4, 6:12, 15, 7:3, 9, 12(2), 13, 8:1, 2, 3, 4, 6(2), 7, 9(2), 11, 14(2), 18, 19, 20, 21, 22, 23, 9:15, 12:5, 13:7, 14:16, 17, 21(2); Mal. 1:4, 6, 8, 9, 10, 11, 13, 14, 2:2, 4, 7, 8, 12, 16, 3:1, 5, 7, 10, 11, 12, 14, 17, 4:1, 3

²⁶⁸ These 19 times: 2 Sam. 6:2, 18; 1 Kings 18:15; 2 Kings 3:14; Pss. 24:10, 46:7, 11, 48:8, 69:6, 80:4, 7, 14, 19, 84:1, 3, 12; Jer. 33:12; Zeph. 2:9; Zech. 7:4

²⁶⁹ These 63 times: 1 Sam. 4:4; Isa. 8:13, 9:13, 19, 19:17, 18, 20, 24:23, 31:5; Jer. 6:6, 9, 7:3, 21, 9:7, 15, 17, 10:16, 11:17, 20, 16:9, 19:3, 11, 15, 20:12, 23:15, 25:8, 28, 32, 26:18, 27:4, 19, 28:2, 14, 29:4, 8, 21, 30:8, 31:23, 32:15, 35:13, 18, 39:16, 42:15, 18, 43:10, 44:2, 11, 25, 46:10, 48:1, 49:5, 7, 26, 35, 50:18, 31, 33, 51:14, 19, 33, 58; Zech. 1:3, 13:2

omission: Amos 6:8, 14. Similarly, LXX renders: *'adonay yehovih 'elohîm ts^{e}ba'ôth*, "Lord Jehovah God of hosts," as *kurios ho theos ho pantokrator* in Amos 3:13 and as *kurios kurios ho theos ho pantokrator* in Amos 9:5.

d. *y^{e}hovah 'elohîm*: "Jehovah God": In this combination Scripture renders *y^{e}hovah* with *kurios* and *'elohîm* with *theos*.[270] Accordingly, LXX also uses *kurios ho theos*.[271] Yet, sometimes LXX simply uses *ho theos*.[272]

e. *yah*: "Jah"

Sometimes LXX doesn't render Jah.[273] Once it uses θεος (theos): "God": Isa. 38:11. It uses two major renderings. First, 17 times it transliterates, יָהּ הַלְלוּ (hal^{e}lû yahh), as αλληλουια (allelouia): Pss. 104:35, 106:1, 48, 111:1, 112:1, 113:1, 9, 115:18, 117:2, 135:1, 21, 146:1, 147:1, 148:1, 149:1, 150:1, 6. Second, 20 times it renders *yahh* with κυριος (*kurios*): Pss. 68:4, 18, 77:11, 89:8, 94:7, 12, 102:18, 115:17, 18, 118:5, 14, 17, 18, 19, 122:4, 130:3, 135:3, 4, 150:6; Isa. 12:2. These two renderings account for 37 of its 49 occurrences.

B. Greek Names into Hebrew

1. theos

The name *theos* in its significance primarily correlates to *'elohîm* and its cognates, *'ēl*, *'elôah*, and *'elah*. It also renders, *'al*, the cognate of *'elyôn*. It also occasionally renders both *yhvh* and *yah*.

2. kurios

The name *kurios* in its significance primarily correlates to *'adôn* and *'adonay*. Further, through the remarkable circumstances we have noted, it became the primary Greek equivalent for *yhvh* and *yah*. In addition, LXX occasionally employed it to render both *'elohîm* and *shadday*.

3. pantokrator

The name *pantokrator* in its significance primarily correlates with *shadday* and with *ts^{e}ba'ôth*.

4. hupsistos

The name *hupsistos* in its significance primarily correlates with *'elyôn* and its cognates *'illay* and *'al*.

---

[270] *Deut. 6:16*: You shall not tempt the LORD [y^{e}hovah] your God ['elohîm]; *Matt. 4:7*: You shall not tempt the Lord [kurios] your God [theos]

[271] For example: Gen. 2:18, 22, 3:1, 8(2), 9, 13, 14, 21, 23

[272] For example: Gen. 2:19, 21, 3:22

[273] Exod. 15:2, 17:16; Pss. 105:45, 116:19, 146:10, 147:20, 148:14, 149:9; Isa. 26:4

5. despotes

The name *despotes* in its significance primarily correlates with *'adôn* and *'adonay*. LXX also occasionally used it to render *'elohîm*.

Unit 3. The Appropriate Use of God's Names

We begin with our Christian duty, based on the third commandment, to use God's names reverently. We then consider our Christian privilege, based on the teaching and practice of the apostles, to address God in a manner consistent with the gospel of Christ.

I. Our Christian Duty to Honor God's Names[274]

In the third commandment God's name specifically refers to his proper name, Jehovah. Again, *"to take"* his name, means to it lift up, to use it, or utter it verbally.[275] The word, *"vain"* can mean "pointless,"[276] "futile,"[277] "foolish,"[278] or "false."[279] Thus, this commandment explicitly forbids us to speak God's proper names, his distinctive designations, frivolously, falsely, trivially, pointlessly or rashly. This commandment also embodies a general moral principle, namely, the sanctity of God's name. Thus, we consider three aspects of our duty to reverence or honor his name: first, its *broad scope*, second, its *detailed substance*, and third, its *inspired enforcement*.

A. The Broad Scope of our Duty to Honor God's Name

The sanctity of God's name embraces not only his proper names, but also everything Scripture identifies with his name: his being, attributes, authority, reputation, and Word. Further, reverencing God's name requires more than just not swearing. God forbids whatever dishonors his name. He forbids profaning it,[280] blaspheming it,[281] despising or lightly esteeming it,[282] polluting it,[283] and defiling it.[284]

---

[274] *Exod. 20:7*: You shalt not take the name of Jehovah your God in vain; for Jehovah will not hold him guiltless that takes his name in vain.
[275] Exod. 23:11; Pss. 15:3, 16:4
[276] Mal. 3:14
[277] Ps. 127:1-2
[278] Lam. 2:14
[279] Prov. 30:8
[280] Lev. 19:12; Ezek. 36:20
[281] Lev. 24:16; Rom. 2:4
[282] Mal. 1:6
[283] Isa. 48:11; Jer. 34:16
[284] Ezek. 43:7-8

B. The Detailed Substance of our Duty to Honor God's Name

The sanctity of God's name has broad moral implications. We consider seven. The first two come from the narrower sense of God's name, his personal designations; the last five from its broader sense.

First, to honor God's name we must never misuse his personal designations. Rather, we must revere them. This precludes all profanity. It precludes all frivolous swearing in oaths, curses, or exclamations, whether spoken plainly or in euphemisms.[285] It precludes all false[286] and idolatrous[287] swearing. It precludes all blasphemy with the lips[288] and in the heart.[289]

Second, to honor God's name, we must honor the place and people called by his name.[290]

Third, to honor God's name we must never detest and shun God, but personally fellowship with him. If we would sanctify his name, then we must love him,[291] believe and trust him,[292] revere him,[293] remember him,[294] bless him,[295] call on him,[296] and fear him.[297]

Fourth, to honor God's name we must delight in, proclaim, and magnify his divine attributes.[298]

Fifth, to honor God's name we must never reject or demean those that the Lord authorizes and sends to us, but highly esteem them.[299]

Sixth, to honor God's name we must never bring reproach on God's reputation, but enhance it. Those who profess Christianity can bring

---

[285] Matt. 5:33-37; James 5:12
[286] Lev. 19:12
[287] Deut. 6:13, 10:20
[288] Rev. 16:9, 11
[289] Mark 7:22; Col. 3:8
[290] 1 Cor. 6:16-20; Heb. 6:10
[291] Ps. 5:10-11
[292] Acts 3:16
[293] Ps. 29:2
[294] Ps. 44:20
[295] Ps. 100:4
[296] Pss. 79:6, 80:18
[297] Ps. 86:11
[298] Exod. 33:18-19; John 17:6, 26
[299] Matt. 21:9, John 13:20; 1 Thess. 5:12-13

reproach on God's name by hypocrisy,[300] materialism and theft,[301] sexual scandal,[302] Liberation Theology,[303] and militant feminism.[304]

Seventh, to honor God's name we must never disrespect his Word. We must never deny his Word, add to it, or subtract from it. Nor should we ever make light of it. Rather we must respect and revere it.[305]

C. The Inspired Enforcement of our Duty to Honor God's Name

The Lord himself enforces this commandment: "the Lord will not hold him guiltless that takes his name in vain." God takes his name very seriously. The unpardonable sin is not rape, or murder, but blasphemy against the Holy Spirit (Matt. 12:32). Therefore, let us take this to heart. Let us honor his name. Let us honor his being, attributes, authorization, reputation, and Word. Let us avoid anything that would show disrespect for his great and holy name. Let us flee from everything that would bring reproach upon his name. May the Lord be pleased more and more to write love and reverence for his name on our hearts.

II. Our Christian Privilege to Speak God's Names

We conclude, not with God's law, but with his gospel. Hebrew Israel so feared breaking this commandment that they never uttered God's proper name, not even when they read Scripture. Now through Christ we have the privilege of access to God that is personal and familial. Scripture features three blessed traits of Christian address to God. First, because Christians are God's spiritual children, we address him in a *filial* manner. Second, because Christians call on Christ as Savior and Lord, we draw near in an *evangelical* manner. Third, since Christians worship the triune God, our prayer is *Trinitarian*.

A. Christians Address God in a Filial Manner.

Through Christ Christians address God as beloved children. Jesus brings Gentiles and Jews that believe into his spiritual family.[306] Thus, he teaches us to address God personally by name as our "Father."[307] Precisely because

---

[300] Rom. 2:24
[301] Prov. 30:10
[302] Amos 2:7
[303] 1 Tim. 6:1
[304] Titus 2:5
[305] Ps. 138:2; Rev. 2:13
[306] *Eph. 2:18*: for through him we both have our access in one Spirit unto the Father
[307] *Matt. 6:9*: After this manner therefore pray, Our Father, who is in heaven, hallowed be your name

we are God's spiritual children, he has given us the Spirit of his Son, so that we address him as our beloved "Father" with tender affection.[308] Yet, filial access does not promote disrespect, but rather filial reverence, because our Father is an impartial judge.[309] Yet, filial reverence does not kill assurance of our Father's favor: "*knowing* that you were redeemed . . . with precious blood." This blessed privilege of filial access calls for constant gratitude and praise to our heavenly Father.[310] The prayer of the church in Jerusalem to God the Father displays the richness of filial access.[311] Our heavenly Father is our God [theos], who made us, sustains us, and owns us. He is our Master [despotes], who governs the universe by his will. He is our Lord [kurios], who rules us, protects us, provides for us, and delivers us from every enemy. Therefore, it would be a tragedy for any who identify with the Christian faith to refuse to address God as their Father. Worse yet, it would be a travesty if they were to think themselves better men for their lack of that filial disposition that is a distinctive privilege of Christians.

B. Christians Address God in an Evangelical Manner.

Through Christ Christians also address God as evangelically as Savior. The prophet Joel predicts that whoever calls on the name of y^{e}hovah shall be saved.[312] When Peter quotes Joel, he renders y^{e}hovah with *kurios*, "*Lord*."[313] Paul too quotes Joel and renders y^{e}hovah with *kurios*.[314] God saves sinners when they call on y^{e}hovah. To "call on him" signifies to rely on him alone for rescue from sin and death. It signifies to trust him and depend on him

---

[308] *Gal. 4:6*: because you are sons, God sent forth the Spirit of his Son into our hearts, crying, Abba Father

[309] *1 Pet. 1:17-19*: if you call on him as Father, who without respect of persons judges according to each man's work, spend the time of your sojourning in fear: knowing that you were redeemed . . . with precious blood

[310] *Eph. 5:20*: giving thanks always for all things in the name of our Lord Jesus Christ to God [theos], even the Father

[311] *Acts 4:24-29*: lifted up their voice to God [theos] with one accord, and said, O Lord [despotes], you that did make heaven and earth . . . who by the Holy Spirit, by the mouth of our father David did say . . . for of a truth in this city against your holy Servant Jesus, whom you did anoint, both Herod and Pontius Pilate . . . were gathered together, to do whatsoever your hand and your counsel foreordained to come to pass. And now, Lord [kurios], look on their threatenings

[312] *Joel 2:32 [3:5 Heb]*: and it will be that whoever will call on the name of Jehovah [y^{e}hovah] will be saved: for in mount Zion and in Jerusalem will be deliverance: as Jehovah [y^{e}hovah] has said: and in the remnant that Jehovah [y^{e}hovah] will call.

[313] *Acts 2:21*: whoever shall call the name of the Lord [kurios] shall be saved

[314] *Rom. 10:9, 13*: If you shall confess with your mouth Jesus as Lord [kurios], and shall believe in your heart that God raised him from the dead, you shall be saved . . . for, Whosoever shall call upon the name of the Lord [kurios] shall be saved.

for provision, protection, and deliverance from every enemy. Yet, on whom do sinners call? Paul tells us, *"if you shall confess with your mouth Jesus as Lord."* Accordingly, Christians come to God the Son incarnate, Jehovah Jesus our Redeemer, to save us from our sins.[315] Jehovah Jesus regulates our lives, protects us, delivers us, communes with us, and provides for all our needs. Thus, Paul pleads three times with our Provider and Protector about his thorn in the flesh.[316] In like manner, we pour out hearts and cares before Jehovah Jesus, the Supreme Being incarnate, our Lord [kurios] and our God [theos].

C. *Christians Address God in a Trinitarian Manner.*

The name of the Supreme Being is the name of the Father, of the Son, and of the Holy Spirit.[317] Each Person of the Trinity is *'elohîm-theos*. Each Person of the Trinity is *'adonay/Jehovah-kurios*. Thus, the Father is our Lord and our God. The Son is our Lord and our God.[318] The Spirit is our Lord[319] and our God.[320] Accordingly, in our prayer and worship we address and commune with the triune God. We pray unto the Father, through the Son, in and by the Holy Spirit.[321] Our personal fellowship is with the Father and the Son[322] in and with the Holy Spirit who dwells in us.[323]

---

[315] *Acts 22:16*: wash away your sins, calling on his name

[316] *2 Cor. 12:8-9*: I besought the Lord [kurios] thrice, that it might depart from me. And he has said unto me, My grace is sufficient for you: for my power is made perfect in weakness . . . that the power of Christ may rest upon me.

[317] *Matt. 28:19*: Go therefore, and make disciples of all the nations, baptizing them into the name of the Father, and of the Son, and of the Holy Spirit

[318] *John 20:28-29*: And Thomas answered and said unto him, My Lord [kurios] and my God [theos]. 29 Jesus says unto him, Thomas, because you have seen me, you have believed

[319] *Y^{e}hovah*: Isa. 6:8-10, w/Acts 28:25-27; Ps. 95:7-9, w/Heb. 3:7-9; *'adonay:* 2 Cor. 3:17

[320] *Acts 5:3-4*: But Peter said, Ananias, why has Satan filled your heart to lie to the Holy Spirit, and to keep back *part* of the price of the land? 4 While it remained, was it not your own? and after it was sold, was it not in your own power? Why have you conceived this thing in your heart? You have not lied unto men, but unto God [theos].

[321] *Eph. 2:18*: For through him we both have access by one Spirit unto the Father.

[322] *1 John 1:3*: That which we have seen and heard we declare unto you, that you also may have fellowship with us: and truly our fellowship *is* with the Father, and with his Son Jesus Christ.

[323] *2 Cor. 13:14*: The grace of the Lord Jesus Christ, and the love of God, and the fellowship of the Holy Spirit, *be* with you all.

Under the new covenant we worship, *kurios ho theos*, "the LORD God," the Greek equivalent of *yᵉhovah 'elohîm*, "Jehovah God," both in heaven[324] and on earth.[325] We bless the triune God, Jehovah our Creator and our Redeemer. Christ the Lamb, God incarnate, is the special focus of our worship of Jehovah our Redeemer.[326] Thus, we sing, "*hallelujah*," praise Jehovah our God, the Father, Son, and Spirit. When we thus draw near to the Father, through the Son, in the Spirit, we have a foretaste of the glorious praise above. Therefore, let us magnify the great and holy name of our triune God.

---

[324] *Rev. 4:8*: Holy, holy, holy, is the Lord [kurios] God [theos], the Almighty [pantokrator], who was, who is, and who is to come: *Rev. 4:11*: You are worthy our Lord [kurios] and our God [theos], to receive the glory and the honor and the power: for you did create all things

[325] *Rev. 19:6*: Hallelujah: for the Lord [kurios] our God [theos], the Almighty [pantokrator] reigns.

[326] *Rev. 5:13*: unto him that sits on the throne, and unto the Lamb, be the blessing, and the honor, and the glory, and the dominion, for ever and ever

APPENDIX 1: BIBLICAL TERMINOLOGY FOR GOD'S NAME

OLD TESTAMENT

שֵׁם (shēm): "name": can connote designation, affiliation, recognition, reputation, remembrance, authorization: with a wide variety of nuances: occurs 864 times: depicts a designation that characterizes, distinguishes, and identifies: a river (Gen. 2:11, etc.), an animal (Gen. 2:19, etc.), a person (Gen. 3:20, 4:19, 21, 25, etc.), a city (Gen. 4:17, 19:22, 26:33, etc.), mankind (Gen. 5:2), a place (Gen. 22:14, 28:19, 31:48, 32:2, 30, 35:15; Num. 11:3, 34, etc.), a well (Gen. 26:18, etc.), bread from heaven (Exod. 16:21), an altar (Exod. 17:15), other gods (Exod. 23:13; Josh. 23:7, etc.), the tribes of Israel (Exod. 28:9,10, 12, 21, 29, 39:14), a monument (1 Sam. 7:12), and many other aspects of created reality: Depicts affiliation with a person that involves a right of inheritance (Gen. 48:6,16; Deut. 25:6; Ruth 4:5, 10(2), etc.): Depicts recognition, knowing someone personally, "by name" (Exod. 33:12. 17, etc.): Depicts reputation, renown, fame (Gen. 6:4, 11:4, 12:2; Num. 16:2; Deut. 22:14, 19, 26:19; Ruth 4:11; 1 Sam. 18:30; 2 Sam. 7:9(2), 8:13, 23:18, 22; 1 Kings 1:47(2), 4:31; 1 Chron. 5:24, 14:17, 22:5; Prov. 22:1; Ezek. 16:14, 15, etc.), or infamy (Ezek. 22:5): Depicts remembrance (Deut. 7:24, 9:14, 12:3, 25:7, 29:20; 1 Sam. 24:21; 2 Sam. 14:7; 2 Kings 14:27; Job 18:17; Ps. 41:5; Prov. 10:7; Isa. 14:22, etc.): Depicts authorization (Deut. 18:20; 1 Sam. 25:5, 9; 1 Kings 21:8; Esth. 8:8(2), etc.): Refers to the Supreme Being at least these 379 times: It has at least the following seven nuances: [1] *God's personal Being, God himself*, at least 77 times: Gen. 4:26, 12:8, 13:4, 21:33, 26:25; Deut. 10:8; 2 Sam. 22:50; 1 Kings 18:24; 2 Kings 5:11; 1 Chron. 16:8, 35, 29:13; Neh. 1:11; Job 1:21; Pss. 5:11, 7:17, 9:2, 10, 18:49, 20:1, 33:21, 34:3, 44:5, 8, 20, 52:9, 54:6, 61:5, 8, 66:4, 68:4, 69:30, 36, 74:21, 79:6, 80:18, 83:16, 86:11, 92:1, 99:6, 102:15, 103:1, 105:1, 106:47, 113:1, 3, 115:1, 116:4, 13, 17, 122:4, 135:1, 3, 138:2, 140:13, 142:7, 145:1, 2, 21, 148:5, 13, 149:3; Isa. 24:15, 25:1, 50:10, 59:19, 64:7; Jer. 10:25; Lam. 3:55; Joel 2:26, 32; Zeph. 3:9, 12; Zech. 13:9; Mal. 2:2, 5, 4:2: [2] *God's personal designation* at least 38 times: Gen. 16:13, 32:29(2); Exod. 3:13, 15, 6:3, 15:3, 20:7(2); Lev. 24:11, 24:16(2); Deut. 5:11(2), 28:58; Ps. 83:18; Isa. 7:14, 9:6, 42: 8, 47:4, 48:2, 51:15, 54:5; Jer. 10:16, 16:21, 23:6, 31:35, 32:18, 33:2, 46:18, 48:15, 50:34, 51:19, 57; Amos 4:13, 5:8, 27, 9:6: [3] *God's authorization*, "in God's name," at least 27 times: Exod. 5:23; Deut. 18:5, 7, 19, 18:20, 22; 1 Sam. 17:45; 1 Kings 22:16; 2 Kings 2:24; 1 Chron. 21:19; 2 Chron. 18:15, 33:18; Ps. 118:26; Jer. 11:21, 14:14, 15, 20:9, 23:25, 26:9, 16, 20, 29:9, 21, 23, 44:16; Dan. 9:6; Zech. 13:3: [4] *God's renown, reputation* at least 11 times: Exod. 9:16; Josh. 7:9, 9:9; 1 Sam. 12:22; 2 Sam. 7:23; 1 Chron. 17:21; Neh. 9:10; Isa. 63:12, 14; Jer. 32:20; Dan. 9:15: [5] *God's nature and attributes* at least 7 times: Exod. 33:19, 34:5, 14; Ps. 22:22, 54:1, 111:9; Isa. 57:15: [6] *God's self-disclosure, Word*, at least 1 time: Ps. 138:2: [7] *God's memorial, monument*, at least 1 time: Isa. 55:13: I have not categorized more specifically the following 217 references to God's name: these texts could have one of the above nuances, or combine some of them, or possibly convey additional nuances: these texts include such expressions as: "swearing by," "profaning," "despising," "being called by," "walking in," "seeing," and "thinking upon" his name; as "his name being one"; and as his "name being in" a place: Exod. 20:24, 23:21; Lev. 18:21, 19:12(2), 20:3, 21:6, 22:2, 32; Num. 6:27; Deut. 6:13, 10:20, 12:5, 11, 21, 14:23, 24, 16:2, 6, 11, 21:5, 26:2, 28:10, 32:3; Judg. 13:6, 17, 18; 1 Sam. 20:42; 2 Sam. 6:2, 6:18, 7:13, 26; 1 Kings 3:2, 5:3, 5:5(2), 8:16, 17, 18, 19, 20, 29, 33, 35, 41, 42, 43(2), 44, 48, 9:3, 7, 10:1, 11:36, 14:21, 18:32; 2 Kings 21:4, 7, 23:27; 1 Chron. 13:6, 16:10, 29, 17:24, 22:7, 8, 10, 19, 23:13, 28:3, 29:16; 2 Chron. 2:1, 4, 6:5, 6, 7, 8, 9, 10, 20, 24, 26, 32, 33(2), 34, 38, 7:14, 16, 20, 14:11, 20:8, 9, 33:4, 7; Neh. 1:9, 9:5; Pss. 8:1, 9, 20:5, 7, 23:3, 25:11, 29:2, 31:3, 45:17[1], 48:10, 63:4, 66:2, 72:17, 19, 74:7, 10, 18, 75:1, 76:1, 79:9, 86:9, 12, 89:12, 16, 24, 91:14, 96:2, 8, 99:3, 100:4, 102:21, 105:3, 106:8, 109:13, 113:2, 118:10, 11, 12, 119:55, 132, 124:8, 129:8, 135:13, 143:11, 148:13; Prov. 18:10, 30:4(2)[2], 9; Isa. 12:4(2), 18:7, 26:8, 13, 29:23, 30:27, 41:25, 43:7, 48:1, 9, 52:5, 6, 56:6, 60:9, 63:16, 19, 64:2, 65:1, 66:5; Jer. 3:17, 7:10, 11, 12, 14, 30, 10:6, 12:16, 13:11, 14:7, 9, 21, 15:16, 23:27, 25:29, 32:34, 33:9, 34:15, 16, 44:26(2); Ezek. 20:9, 14, 22, 20:39, 44, 36:20, 21, 22, 23, 39:7(2), 25, 43:7, 8; Dan. 9:18, 19; Amos 2:7, 6:10, 9:12; Micah 4:5, 5:4, 6:9; Zech. 5:4, 10:12, 14:9; Mal. 1:6, 11(2), 14, 3:16.

Notes:

1. Ps. 45:17: "I will make your name to be remembered in all generations: therefore shall the people praise you for ever and ever." I include this text because it probably refers to the name of God the Son incarnate.

2. Prov. 30:4: "Who has ascended up into heaven, or descended? Who has gathered the wind in his fists? Who has bound the waters in a garment? Who has established all the ends of the earth? What *is* his name, and what *is* his son's name, if you can tell?" These two occurrences probably refer to God's name.

NEW TESTAMENT

ὄνομα (onoma): "name": like *shēm*, *onoma* can connote designation (Matt. 10:2, etc.); authorization (Matt. 10:41, 42, etc.); reputation (Mark 6:14, etc.); person, distinguishing characteristics (Acts 4:7; 1 Cor. 1:13, 15); title, rank (Eph. 1:21): occurs 229 times: Depicts the Supreme Being at least these 120 times: Depicts the name of the triune God, or of God the Father specifically, with nuances similar to the OT, at least these 42 times: Matt. 6:9, 7:22(2), 21:9, 23:39, 28:19; Mark 11:9, 10; Luke 1:49, 11:2, 13:35, 19:38; John 5:43, 10:25, 12:13, 28, 17:6, 11, 12, 26; Acts 2:21, 15:14, 17; Rom. 1:5, 2:24, 9:17, 10:13, 15:9; 1 Tim. 6:1; Heb. 2:12, 6:10, 13:15; James 2:7, 5:10; Rev. 3:12, 11:18, 13:6, 14:1, 15:4, 16:9, 22:4: Depicts the name of Christ, God the Son incarnate specifically, with nuances similar to the OT, at least these 78 times: Matt. 1:21, 23, 25, 10:22, 12:21, 18:5, 18:20, 19:29, 24:5, 9; Mark 6:14, 9:37, 38, 39, 41, 13:6, 13, 16:17; Luke 1:31, 2:21, 9:48, 49, 10:17, 21:8, 12, 17, 24:47; John 1:12, 2:23, 3:18, 14:13, 14, 26, 15:16, 21, 16:23, 24, 26, 20:31; Acts 2:38, 3:6, 16(2), 4:10, 12, 17, 18, 30, 5:28, 40, 41, 8:12, 16, 9:14, 15, 16, 21, 27, 29, 10:43, 48, 15:26, 16:18, 19:5, 13, 17, 21:13, 22:16, 26:9; 1 Cor. 1:2, 10, 5:4, 6:11; Eph. 5:20; Phil. 2:9, 10; Col. 3:17; 2 Thess. 1:12; 2 Thess. 3:6; 2 Tim. 2:19; Heb. 1:4; James 5:14; 1 Pet. 4:14; 1 John 2:12, 3:23, 5:13(2); 3 John 7; Rev. 2:3, 13, 3:8, 12, 19:12, 13, 16.

APPENDIX 2: USE AND RELATIVE FREQUENCY OF THE DIVINE NAME: 'elohîm

אֱלֹהִים ('elohîm): "God": occurs 2,602[1] times in the Hebrew: Used generally 12 times: Generically it denotes majesty, might, greatness, that which is marked by the superlative: Gen. 23:6, 30:8; Exod. 9:28; 1 Sam. 14:15; Jonah 3:3: also 1 time may depict what is divine, or godlike, "godly": Mal. 2:15.[2] In this general sense it depicts *judges* 5 times (Exod. 21:6, 22:8, 9(2); 1 Sam. 2:25) and *angels* 1 time (Ps. 8:5). These 246 times it depicts objects of veneration and devotion, a god, gods (244), or goddess (2: 1 Kings 11:5, 33): Gen. 3:5, 31:30, 32, 35:2, 4; Exod. 7:1, 12:12, 18:11, 20:3, 23(2), 22:20, 28,[3] 23:13, 24, 32, 33, 32:1, 4, 8, 23, 31, 34:15(2), 16(2), 17; Lev. 19:4; Num. 25:2(2), 33:4; Deut. 4:28, 5:7, 6:14(2), 7:4, 16, 25, 8:19, 10:17, 11:16, 28, 12:2, 3, 30(2), 31(2), 13:2, 6, 7, 13, 17:3, 18:20, 20:18, 28:14, 36, 64, 29:18, 26(2), 30:17, 31:16, 18, 20, 32:17, 37, 39; Jos. 22:22(2), 23:7, 16, 24:2, 14, 15(2), 16, 20, 23; Judg. 2:3, 12(2), 17, 19, 3:6, 5:8, 6:10, 31, 8:33, 9:27, 10:6(5), 13, 14, 16, 11:24, 16:23(2), 24(2), 17:5, 18:24; Ruth 1:15; 1 Sam. 5:7, 6:5, 7:3, 8:8, 17:43, 26:19, 28:13; 2 Sam. 7:23; 1 Kings 9:6, 9, 11:2, 4, 5, 11:8, 10, 33(3), 12:28, 14:9, 18:24, 25, 27, 19:2, 20:10, 23(2);[4] 2 Kings 1:2, 3, 6, 16, 5:17, 17:7, 29, 31, 33, 35, 37, 38, 18:33, 34(2), 35, 19:12, 18(2), 37, 22:17; 1 Chron. 5:25, 10:10, 14:12, 16:25, 26; 2 Chron. 2:5, 7:19, 22, 13:8, 9, 25:14(2), 15, 20, 28:23(2), 24, 32:13, 14, 15, 17, 19, 21, 33:15, 34:25; Ezra 1:7; Pss. 82:1, 6, 86:8, 95:3, 96:4, 5, 97:7, 9, 135:5, 136:2, 138:1; Isa. 21:9, 36:18, 19(2), 20, 37:12, 19(2), 38, 41:23, 42:17; Jer. 1:16, 2:11(2), 28, 5:7, 19, 7:6, 9, 18, 11:10, 12, 13, 13:10, 16:11, 13, 20(2), 19:4, 13, 22:9, 25:6, 32:29, 35:15, 43:12, 13, 44:3, 5, 8, 15, 46:25, 48:35; Dan. 1:2(2), 11:8; Hos. 3:1, 13:4, 14:3; Amos 2:8, 5:26, 8:14; Jonah 1:5; Micah 4:5; Nah. 1:14; Zeph. 2:11: It depicts the Supreme Being: translated "God" or "Godward" (Exod. 18:19): these *2,348* times (2,344[1] in the Hebrew): Gen. 1:1, 2, 3, 4(2), 5, 6, 7, 8, 9, 10(2), 11, 12, 14, 16, 17, 18, 20, 21(2), 22, 24, 25(2), 26, 27(2), 28(2), 29, 31, 2:2, 3(2), 4, 5, 7, 8, 9, 15, 16, 18, 19, 21, 22, 3:1(2), 3, 5, 8(2), 9, 13, 14, 21, 22, 23, 4:25, 5:1(2), 22, 24(2), 6:2, 4, 9, 11, 12, 13, 22, 7:9, 16, 8:1(2), 15, 9:1, 6, 8, 12, 16, 17, 26, 27, 17:3, 7, 8, 9, 15, 18, 19, 22, 23, 19:29(2), 20:3, 6, 11, 13, 17(2), 21:2, 4, 6, 12, 17(3), 19, 20, 22, 23, 22:1, 3, 8, 9, 12, 24:3(2), 7, 12, 27, 42, 48, 25:11, 26:24, 27:20, 28, 28:4, 12, 13(2), 17, 20, 21, 22, 30:2, 6, 17, 18, 20, 22(2), 23, 31:5, 7, 9, 11, 16(2), 24, 29, 42(3), 50, 53(3), 32:1, 2, 9(2), 28, 30, 33:5, 10, 11, 35:1, 5, 7, 9, 10, 11, 13, 15, 39:9, 40:8, 41:16, 25, 28, 32(2), 38, 39, 51, 52, 42:18, 28, 43:23(2), 29, 44:16, 45:5, 7, 8, 9, 46:1, 2, 3, 48:9, 11, 15(2), 20, 21, 50:17, 19, 20, 24, 25; Exod. 1:17, 20, 21, 2:23, 24(2), 25(2), 3:1, 4, 6(5), 11, 12, 13(2), 14, 15(5), 16(2), 18(2), 4:5(4), 16, 20, 27, 5:1, 3(2), 8, 6:2, 7(2), 7:16, 8:10, 19, 25, 26, 27, 28, 9:1, 13, 30, 10:3, 7, 8, 16, 17, 25, 26, 13:17(2), 18, 19, 14:19, 15:2, 26, 16:12, 17:9, 18:1, 4, 5, 12(2), 15, 16, 19(3), 21, 23, 19:3, 17, 19, 20:1, 2, 5, 7, 10, 12, 19, 20, 21, 21:13, 23:19, 25, 24:10, 11, 13, 29:45, 46(2), 31:3, 18, 32:11, 16(2), 27, 34:23, 24, 26, 35:31; Lev. 2:13, 4:22, 11:44, 45, 18:2, 4, 21, 30, 19:2, 3, 4, 10, 12, 14, 25, 31, 32, 34, 36, 20:7, 24, 21:6(3), 7, 8, 12(2), 17, 21, 22, 22:25, 33, 23:14, 22, 23:28, 40, 43, 24:15, 22, 25:17(2), 36, 38(2), 43, 55, 26:1, 12, 13, 44, 45; Num.

6:7, 10:9, 10(2), 15:40, 41(3), 16:9, 22, 21:5, 22:9, 10, 12, 18, 20, 22, 38, 23:4, 21, 27, 24:2, 25:13, 27:16; Deut. 1:6, 10, 11, 17, 19, 20, 21(2), 25, 26, 30, 31, 32, 41, 2:7(2), 29, 30, 33, 36, 37, 3:3, 18, 20, 21, 22, 4:1, 2, 3, 4, 5, 7(2), 10, 19, 21, 23(2), 24, 25, 29, 30, 31, 32, 33, 34(2), 35, 39, 40, 5:2, 6, 9, 11, 12, 14, 15(2), 16(2), 24(2), 25, 26, 27(2), 32, 33, 6:1, 2, 3, 4, 5, 10, 13, 15(2), 16, 17, 20, 24, 25, 7:1, 2, 6(2), 9(2), 12, 16, 18, 19(2), 20, 21, 22, 23, 25, 8:2, 5, 6, 7, 10, 11, 14, 18, 19, 20, 9:3, 4, 5, 6, 7, 10, 16, 23, 10:9, 12(3), 14, 17(2), 20, 21, 22, 11:1, 2, 12(2), 13, 22, 25, 27, 28, 29, 31, 12:1, 4, 5, 7(2), 9, 10, 11, 12, 15, 18(3), 20, 21, 27(2), 28, 29, 31, 13:3(2), 4, 5(2), 10, 12, 16, 18(2), 14:1, 2, 21, 23(2), 24(2), 25, 26, 29, 15:4, 5, 6, 7, 10, 14, 15, 18, 19, 20, 21, 16:1(2), 2, 5, 6, 7, 8, 10(2), 11(2), 15(2), 16, 17, 18, 20, 21, 22, 17:1(2), 2(2), 8, 12, 14, 15, 19, 18:5, 7, 9, 12, 13, 14, 15, 16(2), 19:1(2), 2, 3, 8, 9, 10, 14, 20:1, 4, 13, 14, 16, 17, 18, 21:1, 5, 10, 23(2), 22:5, 23:5(3), 14, 18(2), 20, 21(2), 23, 24:4, 9, 13, 18, 19, 25:15, 16, 18, 19(2), 26:1, 2(2), 3, 4, 5, 7, 10(2), 11, 13, 14, 16, 17, 19, 27:2, 3(2), 5, 6(2), 7, 9, 10, 28:1(2), 2, 8, 9, 13, 15, 45, 47, 52, 53, 58, 62, 29:6, 10, 12(2), 13, 15, 18, 25, 29, 30:1, 2, 3(2), 4, 5, 6(2), 7, 9, 10(2), 16(2), 20, 31:3, 6, 11, 12, 13, 17, 26, 32:3, 33:1, 27; Josh. 1:9, 11, 13, 15, 17, 2:11(2), 3:3, 9, 4:5, 23(2), 24, 7:13, 19, 20, 8:7, 30, 9:9, 18, 19, 23, 24, 10:19, 40, 42, 13:14, 33, 14:6, 8, 9, 14, 18:3, 6, 22:3, 4, 5, 16, 19, 24, 29, 33, 34, 23:3(2), 5(2), 8, 10, 11, 13(2), 14, 15(2), 16, 24:1, 2, 17, 18, 19, 23, 24, 26, 27; Judg. 1:7, 2:12, 3:7, 20, 4:6, 23, 5:3, 5, 6:8, 10, 20, 26, 36, 39, 40, 7:14, 8:3, 34, 9:7, 9, 13, 23, 56, 57, 10:10, 11:21, 23, 24, 13:5, 6(2), 7, 8, 9(2), 22, 15:19, 16:17, 28, 18:5, 10, 31, 20:2, 18(2),[1] 26,[1] 27, 31,[1] 21:2(2),[1] 3; Ruth 1:16(2), 2:12; 1 Sam. 1:17, 2:2, 27, 30, 3:3(2), 17, 4:4, 7, 8*(2), 11, 13, 17, 18, 19, 21, 22, 5:1, 2, 7, 8(3), 10(3), 11(2), 6:3, 5, 20, 7:8, 9:6, 7, 8, 9, 10, 27, 10:3, 5, 7, 9, 10, 18, 19, 26, 11:6, 12:9, 12, 14, 19, 13:13, 14:18(2), 36, 37, 41, 44, 45, 15:15, 21, 30, 16:15, 16, 23, 17:26, 36, 45, 46, 18:10, 19:20, 23, 20:12, 22:3, 13, 15, 23:7, 10, 11, 14, 16, 25:22, 29, 32, 34, 26:8, 28:15, 29:9, 30:6, 15; 2 Sam. 2:27, 3:9, 35, 5:10, 6:2, 3, 4, 6, 7(2), 12(2), 7:2, 22(2), 23, 24, 25, 26, 27, 28, 9:3, 10:12, 12:7, 16, 14:11, 13, 14, 16, 17(2), 20, 15:24(2), 25, 29, 32, 16:23, 18:28, 19:13, 27, 21:14, 22:3, 7, 22, 30, 32, 47, 23:1, 3(2), 24:3, 23, 1 Kings 1:17, 30, 36, 47, 48, 2:3, 23, 3:5, 7, 11, 28, 4:29, 5:3, 4, 5, 8:15, 17, 20, 23(2), 25, 26, 27, 28, 57, 59, 60, 61, 65, 9:9, 10:9, 24, 11:4, 9, 23, 31, 12:22(2), 13:1, 4, 5, 6(3), 7, 8, 11, 12, 14(2), 21(2), 26, 29, 31, 14:7, 13, 15:3, 4, 30, 16:13, 26, 33, 17:1, 12, 14, 18, 20, 21, 24, 18:10, 21, 24(2), 36(2), 37, 39(2), 19:8, 10, 14, 20:28(3), 21:10, 13, 22:53; 2 Kings 1:3, 6, 9, 10, 11, 12(2), 13, 16, 2:14, 4:7, 9, 16, 21, 22, 25(2), 27(2), 40, 42, 5:7, 8, 11, 14, 15(2), 20, 6:6, 9, 10, 15, 31, 7:2, 17, 18, 19, 8:2, 4, 7, 8, 11, 9:6, 10:31, 13:19, 14:25, 16:2, 17:7, 9, 14, 16, 19, 26(2), 27, 39, 18:5, 12, 22, 19:4(3), 10, 15(2), 16, 19(2), 20, 20:5, 21:12, 22, 22:15, 18, 23:16, 17, 21; 1 Chron. 4:10(2), 5:20, 22, 25(2), 26, 6:48, 49, 9:11, 13, 26, 27, 11:2, 19, 12:17, 18, 22, 13:2, 3, 5, 6, 7, 8, 10, 12(2), 14, 14:10, 11, 14(2), 15, 16, 15:1, 2(2), 12, 13, 14, 15, 24, 26, 16:1(2), 4, 6, 14, 35, 36, 42, 17:2, 3, 16, 17(2), 20, 21, 22, 24(2), 25, 26, 19:13, 21:7, 8, 15, 17(2), 30, 22:1, 2, 6, 7, 11, 12, 18, 19(3), 23:14, 25, 28, 24:5, 19, 25:5(2), 6, 26:5, 20, 32, 28:2, 3, 4, 8(2), 9, 12, 20(2), 21, 29:1(2), 2, 3(2), 7, 10, 13, 16, 17, 18, 20(2); 2 Chron. 1:1, 3, 4, 7, 8, 9, 11, 2:4(2), 5, 12, 3:3, 4:11, 19, 5:1, 14, 6:4, 7, 10, 14(2), 16, 17, 18, 19, 40, 41(2), 42, 7:5, 22, 8:14, 9:8(3),

23, 10:15, 11:2, 16(2), 13:5, 10, 11, 12(2), 15, 16, 18, 14:2, 4, 7, 11(3), 15:1, 3, 4, 6, 9, 12, 13, 18, 16:7, 17:4, 18:5, 13, 31, 19:3, 4, 7, 20:6(2), 7, 12, 15, 19, 20, 29, 30, 33, 21:10, 12, 22:7, 12, 23:3, 9, 24:5, 7, 9, 13, 16, 18, 20(2), 24, 27, 25:7, 8(2), 9(2), 16, 20, 24, 26:5(3), 7, 16, 18, 27:6, 28:5, 6, 9, 10, 24, 25, 29:5, 6, 7, 10, 36, 30:1, 5, 6, 7, 8, 9, 12, 16, 19(2), 22, 31:6, 13, 14, 20, 21(2), 32:8, 11, 14, 15, 16, 17(2), 19, 29, 31, 33:7(2), 12(2), 13, 16, 17, 18(2), 34:3, 8, 9, 23, 26, 27, 32(2), 33(2), 35:3, 8, 21(2), 22, 36:5, 12, 13(2), 15, 16, 18, 19, 23(2); Ezra 1:2, 3(3), 4, 5, 2:68, 3:2(2), 8, 9, 4:1, 2, 3(2), 6:21, 22(2), 7:6(2), 9, 27, 28, 8:17, 18, 21, 22, 23, 25, 28, 30, 31, 33, 35, 36, 9:4, 5, 6(2), 8(2), 9(2), 10, 13, 15, 10:1, 2, 3(2), 6, 9, 11, 14; Neh. 1:4, 5, 2:4, 8, 12, 18, 20, 4:4, 9, 15, 20, 5:9, 13, 15, 19, 6:10, 12, 14, 16, 7:2, 5, 8:6, 8, 9, 16, 18, 9:3(2), 4, 5, 7, 18, 32, 10:28, 29(2), 32, 33, 34(2), 36(2), 37, 38, 39, 11:11, 16, 22, 12:24, 36, 40, 43, 45, 46, 13:1, 2, 4, 7, 9, 11, 14(2), 18, 22, 25, 26(2), 27, 29, 31; Job 1:1, 5, 6, 8, 9, 16, 22, 2:1, 3, 9, 10, 5:8, 20:29, 28:23, 32:2, 34:9, 38:7; Pss. 3:2, 7, 4:1, 5:2, 10, 7:1, 3, 9, 10, 11, 9:17, 10:4, 13, 13:3, 14:1, 2, 5, 18:6, 21, 28, 29, 31, 46, 20:1, 5, 7, 22:2, 24:5, 25:2, 5, 22, 27:9, 30:2, 12, 31:14, 33:12, 35:23, 24, 36:1, 7, 37:31, 38:15, 21, 40:3, 5, 8, 17, 41:13, 42:1, 2(2), 3, 4, 5, 6, 10, 11(2), 43:1, 2, 4(3), 5(2), 44:1, 4, 8, 20, 21, 45:2, 6, 7(2), 46:1, 4, 5(2), 7, 10, 11, 47:1, 5, 6, 7, 8(2), 9(2), 48:1, 3, 8(2), 9, 10, 14(2), 49:7, 15, 50:1, 2, 3, 6, 7(2), 14, 16, 23, 51:1, 10, 14(2), 17(2), 52:7, 8(2), 53:1, 2(2), 4, 5(2), 6, 54:1, 2, 3, 4, 55:1, 14, 16, 19, 23, 56:1, 4(2), 7, 9, 10, 11, 12, 13, 57:1, 2, 3, 5, 7, 11, 58:6, 11, 59:1, 5(2), 9, 10(2), 13, 17(2), 60:1, 6, 10(2), 12, 61:1, 5, 7, 62:1, 5, 7(2), 8, 11(2), 63:1, 11, 64:1, 7, 9, 65:1, 5, 9, 66:1, 3, 5, 8, 10, 16, 19, 20, 67:1, 3, 5, 6(2), 67:7, 68:1, 2, 3, 4, 5, 6, 7, 8(3), 9, 10, 15, 16, 17, 18, 21, 24, 26, 28(2), 31, 32, 34, 35(2), 69:1, 3, 5, 6, 13, 29, 30, 32, 35, 70:1, 4, 5, 71:4, 11, 12(2), 17, 18, 19(2), 22, 72:1, 18(2), 73:1, 26, 28, 74:1, 10, 12, 22, 75:1, 7, 9, 76:1, 6, 9, 11, 77:1(2), 3, 13(2), 16, 78:7, 10, 19, 22, 31, 35, 56, 59, 79:1, 9, 10, 80:3, 4, 7, 14, 19, 81:1(2), 4, 10, 82:1, 8, 83:1, 12, 13, 84:3, 7, 8(2), 9, 10, 11, 85:4, 86:2, 10, 12, 14, 87:3, 88:1, 89:8, 90:1, 17, 91:2, 92:13, 94:7, 22, 23, 95:7, 98:3, 99:5, 8, 9(2), 100:3, 104:1, 33, 105:7, 106:47, 48, 108:1, 5, 7, 11(2), 13, 109:1, 26, 113:5, 115:2, 3, 116:5, 118:28, 119:115, 122:9, 123:2, 135:2, 136:2, 143:10, 144:9, 15, 145:1, 146:2, 5, 10, 147:1, 7, 12; Prov. 2:5, 17, 3:4, 25:2, 30:9; Eccles. 1:13, 2:24, 26, 3:10, 11, 13, 14(2), 15, 17, 18, 5:1, 2(2), 4, 6, 7, 18, 19(2), 20, 6:2(2), 7:13, 14, 18, 26, 29, 8:2, 12, 13, 15, 17, 9:1, 7, 11:5, 9, 12:7, 13, 14; Isa. 1:10, 2:3, 7:11, 13, 8:19, 21, 13:19, 17:6, 10, 21:10, 17, 24:15, 25:1, 9, 26:13, 28:26, 29:23, 30:18, 35:2, 4(2), 36:7, 37:4(3), 10, 16(2), 17, 20, 21, 38:5, 40:1, 3, 8, 9, 27, 28, 41:10, 13, 17, 43:3, 44:6, 45:3, 5, 14, 15, 18, 21, 46:9, 48:1, 2, 17, 49:4, 5, 50:10, 51:15, 20, 22, 52:7, 10, 12, 53:4, 54:5, 6, 55:5, 7, 57:21, 58:2(2), 59:2, 13, 60:9, 19, 61:2, 6, 10, 62:3, 5, 64:4, 65:16(2), 66:9; Jer. 2:17, 19, 3:13, 21, 22, 23, 25(2), 5:4, 5, 14, 19, 24, 7:3, 21, 23, 28, 8:14, 9:15, 10:10(2), 11:3, 4, 13:12, 16, 14:22, 15:16, 16:9, 10, 19:3, 15, 21:4, 22:9, 23:2, 23(2), 36(2), 24:5, 7, 25:15, 27, 26:13, 16, 27:4, 21, 28:2, 14, 29:4, 8, 21, 25, 30:2, 9, 22, 31:1, 6, 18, 23, 33, 32:14, 15, 27, 36, 38, 33:4, 34:2, 13, 35:4, 13, 17(2), 18, 19, 37:3, 7, 38:17(2), 39:16, 40:2, 42:2, 3, 4, 5, 6(2), 9, 13, 15, 18, 20(3), 21, 43:1(2), 2, 10, 44:2, 7(2), 11, 25, 45:2, 46:25, 48:1, 50:4, 18, 28, 40, 51:5, 10, 33; Ezek. 1:1, 8:3, 4, 9:3, 10:19, 20, 11:20, 22, 24, 14:11, 20:5, 7, 19, 20, 28:2(2), 6, 9, 13, 14, 16,

26, 31:8(2), 9, 34:24, 30, 31, 36:28, 37:23, 27, 39:22, 28, 40:2, 43:2, 44:2; Dan. 1:2, 9, 17, 9:3, 4, 9, 10, 11, 13, 14, 15, 17, 18, 19, 20(2), 10:12, 11:32, 37; Hos. 1:7, 2:23, 3:5, 4:1, 6, 12, 5:4, 6:6, 7:10, 8:2, 6, 9:1, 8(2), 17, 12:3, 5, 6(2), 9, 13:4, 16, 14:1, 3; Joel 1:13(2), 14, 16, 2:13, 14, 17, 23, 26, 27, 3:17; Amos 3:13, 4:11, 12, 13, 5:14, 15, 16, 27, 6:8, 14, 9:15; Jonah 1:6(2), 9, 2:1, 6, 3:5, 8, 9, 10(2), 4:6, 7, 8, 9; Micah 3:7, 4:2, 5, 5:4, 6:6, 8, 7:7(2), 10, 17; Hab. 1:12, 3:18; Zeph. 2:7, 9, 3:2, 17; Hag. 1:12(2), 14; Zech. 6:15, 8:8, 23, 9:7, 16, 10:6, 11:4, 12:5, 8, 13:9, 14:5; Mal. 2:16, 17, 3:8, 14, 15, 18

Notes:

1. Judg. 20:18, 26, 31, 21:2: The *Bible Works* search of Strong's 430 ('elohîm) yields 2,606 uses; yet the Hebrew search of 'elohîm yields 2,602 uses. These four verses in Judges explain this difference. These verses in Hebrew each contain, בֵּית־אֵל (bēyth-el), "house of God," which *Bible Works* search of Strong's 430 catalogues as uses of 'elohîm. Yet the *Bible Works* Hebrew search of 'elohîm does not include them. For this reason two of these texts, Judg. 20:26, 31, do not appear in this Hebrew search, because the word, 'elohîm does not occur in these texts in the Hebrew. Nevertheless, this Hebrew search for 'elohîm does include two of these texts, Judg. 20:18, 21:2, because both bēyth-el and 'elohîm occur in these verses in the Hebrew. *Strong's Concordance*, page 400, confirms this. It categorizes each of these four listings as occurrences of 1008 (bēyth-el), not of 430 ('elohîm). Therefore, I use the Hebrew count of 2,602 with 2,344 references to the Supreme Being, 47 in Judges, to calculate relative frequency.

2. Mal. 2:15: "And did not he make one? Yet had he the residue of the spirit. And wherefore one? That he might seek a godly ['elohîm] seed." This could possibly depict the Supreme Being, "a seed of God," his spiritual child.

3. Exod. 22:28: "you shall not revile the gods, nor curse the ruler of your people." This could be a reference to the Supreme Being: "you shall not revile God."

4. 1 Kings 20:23: "And the servants of the king of Syria said unto him, Their gods *are* gods of the hills; therefore they were stronger than we; but let us fight against them in the plain, and surely we shall be stronger than they." In this text *'elohîm* refers to Jehovah. Thus, it could be: "Their God is a God of the hills."

5. Hab. 1:11: *Strong's Concordance*, page 406, cites this text as an instance of *'elohîm* (430); but the *Bible Works* search does not include this verse in its list of Strong's 430 (*'elohîm*). Rather it includes this verse in its list of the uses of *'elôah* (433). The Hebrew in Hab. 1:11 reads: לֵאלֹהוֹ (lē'lohô): "unto his god." Therefore, I have included this text in Appendix 3 with my catalogue of the uses of *'elôah*, rather than with *'elohîm*.

Relative Frequency of 'Elohîm to depict the Supreme Being: Uses /1000 Words in the Hebrew OT

Scripture	Uses	Words	Rel. Freq.	Scripture	Uses	Words	Rel. Freq.
Old Testament	2,344 (48)	308,691	7.593	Psalms	353	19,595	18.015
Pentateuch	736	80,676	*9.123*	Proverbs	5	6,967	0.7177
Genesis	211	20,706	10.190	Ecclesiastes	40	2,991	13.373
Genesis 1	32	440	72.727	Song of Sol.	0	1,270	0
Exodus	112	16,878	6.636	*Maj. Prophets*	*232*	*58,200*	*3.986*
Leviticus	52	12,054	4.314	Isaiah	83	17,141	4.842
Numbers	24	16,575	1.448	Jeremiah	113	22,143	5.103
Deuteronomy	337	14,463	23.301	Lamentations	0	1,629	0
Deut. 12	20	522	38.314	Ezekiel	36	18,916	1.903
Deut. 16	20	340	58.824	*Min. Prophets*	*115*	*20,449*	*0.734*
Joshua	65	10,146	6.406	Daniel[3]	19	5,951	3.193
Judges	47 (51)	9,977	4.711	Hosea	24	2,401	9.996
Ruth	3	1,297	2.313	Joel	11	963	11.423
1 Samuel	91	13,433	6.774	Amos	11	2,072	5.309
2 Samuel	54	11,188	4.827	Obadiah	0	291	0
1 Kings	88	13,248	6.643	Jonah	14	691	20.260
2 Kings	77	12,366	6.227	Micah	10	1412	7.082
1 Chronicles	114	11,007	10.357	Nahum	0	561	0
2 Chronicles	183	13,479	13.577	Habakkuk	2	680	2.941
Ezra[1]	54	3,890	13.882	Zephaniah	4	772	5.181
Nehemiah	70	5,433	12.884	Haggai	3	607	4.942
Esther	0	3,068	0	Zechariah	11	3,165	3.476
Job[2]	17	8,382	2.028	Malachi	6	883	6.795

Table Notes:

1. Ezra: if we add the 43 uses of the Aramaic cognate, 'elah, this becomes 24.936.
2. Job: if we add the 41 uses of the singular, 'elôah, this becomes 6.920
3. Daniel: if we add the 36 uses of the Aramaic cognate, 'elah, this becomes 9.242.

APPENDIX 3 : BIBLICAL USE OF THE DIVINE NAMES:
'ēl, 'elôah, 'elah; 'elyôn, 'illay, 'al; 'adonay, 'adôn; shadday; yahh

אֵל ('ēl) "God": probably from: אוּל ('ûl), "to be strong," "the mighty One": occurs 245 times: depicts "might" or "strength" with a variety of nuances these 11 times according to the KJV translation: Gen. 31:29; Deut. 28:32; Neh. 5:5; Pss. 29:1,[1] 50:1,[2] 82:1,[3] 89:6;[4] Prov. 3:27; Ezek. 31:11, 32:21; Micah 2:1: Similarly, could depict grandeur and stability, "great": Pss. 36:6,[5] 80:10[6]: depicts false gods and idols these 17 times: Exod. 15:11, 34:14; Deut. 32:12; Judg. 9:46; Pss. 44:20, 81:9(2); Isa. 44:10, 15, 17(2), 45:20, 46:6, 57:5; Dan. 11:36(2); Mal. 2:11: Depicts God incarnate, "Immanuel," 2 times: Isa. 7:14, 8:8: Primarily depicts the Supreme Being as mighty, great, the only proper object of devotion and worship, these 213 times: Gen. 14:18, 19, 20, 22, 16:13, 17:1, 21:33, 28:3, 31:13, 35:1, 3, 11, 43:14, 46:3, 48:3, 49:25; Exod. 6:3, 15:2, 20:5, 34:6, 34:14; Num. 12:13, 16:22, 23:8, 19, 23:22, 23, 24:4, 8, 16, 23; Deut. 3:24, 4:24, 31, 5:9, 6:15, 7:9, 21, 10:17, 32:4, 18, 21, 33:26; Josh. 3:10, 22:22(2), 24:19; 1 Sam. 2:3; 2 Sam. 22:31, 32, 33, 48, 23:5; Neh. 1:5, 9:31, 32; Job 5:8, 8:3, 5, 13, 20, 9:2, 12:6, 13:3, 7, 8, 15:4, 11, 13, 25, 16:11, 18:21, 19:22, 20:15, 29, 21:14, 22, 22:2, 13, 17, 23:16, 25:4, 27:2, 9, 11, 13, 31:14, 23, 28, 32:13, 33:4, 6, 14, 29, 34:5, 10, 12, 23, 31, 37, 35:2, 13, 36:5, 22, 26, 37:5, 10, 14, 38:41, 40:9, 19; Pss. 5:4, 7:11, 10:11, 12, 16:1, 17:6, 18:2, 30, 32, 47, 19:1, 22:1(2), 10, 29:3, 31:5, 42:2, 8, 9, 43:4, 52:1, 5, 55:19, 57:2, 63:1, 68:19, 20(2), 24, 35, 73:11, 17, 74:8, 77:9, 13, 14, 78:7, 8, 18, 19, 34, 35, 41, 83:1, 84:2, 85:8, 86:15, 89:7, 26, 90:2, 94:1(2), 95:3, 99:8, 102:24, 104:21, 106:14, 21, 107:11, 118:27, 28, 136:26, 139:17, 23, 140:6, 146:5, 149:6, 150:1; Isa. 5:16, 8:10, 9:6, 10:21, 12:2, 14:13, 31:3, 40:18, 42:5, 43:10, 12, 45:14, 15, 21, 22, 46:9; Jer. 32:18, 51:56; Lam. 3:41; Ezek. 10:5, 28:2(2), 9; Dan. 9:4, 11:36; Hos. 1:10, 11:9, 12; Jonah 4:2; Micah 7:18; Nah. 1:2; Zech. 7:2; Mal. 1:9, 2:10

---

[1] *Ps. 29:1*: Ascribe unto Jehovah, O you sons of the mighty ['ēl] Ascribe unto Jehovah glory and strength. It is possible that this could be "sons of God." If so this text could be an additional use of 'ēl to depict the Supreme Being.

[2] *Ps. 50:1*: The mighty ['ēl] God ['elohîm], even the LORD [yᵉhovah] has spoken. ASV translates it, "The Mighty One, God, Jehovah, has spoken." If ASV is correct, then 'ēl in this text denominates God as "The Mighty."

[3] *Ps. 82:1*: God ['elohîm] stands in the congregation of the mighty ['ēl]; he judgeth among the gods ['elohîm]. ASV translates this: "the congregation of God": If this is correct, then 'ēl also denominates the Supreme Being in this text.

[4] *Ps. 89:6*: For who in the heaven can be compared unto the LORD? *who* among the sons of the mighty ['ēl] can be likened unto the LORD? This could also be "sons of God" and an additonal use of 'ēl to denominate the Supreme Being.

[5] *Ps. 36:6*: Your righteousness is like the great ['ēl] mountains; your judgments are a great deep: O Jehovah. ASV translates this: "Your righteousness is like the mountains of God." If this is correct, then 'ēl denominates the Supreme Being.

[6] *Ps. 80:10*: The hills were covered with the shadow of it, and the boughs thereof *were like* the goodly ['ēl] cedars. The ASV translates this "the cedars of God." If this is correct, then 'ēl also denominates the Supreme Being in this text.

אֱלוֹהַּ ('elôah) "God": singular of 'elohîm: possibly emphatic form of אֵל ('ēl): translated "God," or "god": Occurs 57 times: depicts false gods 5 times: 2 Chr. 32:15, Dan. 11:37, 38, 39; Hab. 1:11: depicts the Supreme Being these 52 times (41 times in Job): Deut. 32:15, 17; Neh. 9:17; Job 3:4, 23, 4:9, 17, 5:17, 6:4, 8, 9, 9:13, 10:2, 11:5, 6, 7, 12:4, 6, 15:8, 16:20, 21, 19:6, 21, 26, 21:9, 19, 22:12, 26, 24:12, 27:3, 8, 10, 29:2, 4, 31:2, 6, 33:12, 26, 35:10, 36:2, 37:15, 22, 39:17, 40:2; Pss. 18:31, 50:22, Ps. 114:7, 139:19; Prov. 30:5; Isa. 44:8; Dan. 11:38; Hab. 3:3

אֱלָהּ ('elah): "God": Aramaic form of 'elôah: translated "God," or "god": used in Ezra and Daniel, once in Jeremiah: occurs 95 times: Depicts gods 16 times: Jer. 10:11; Dan. 2:11, 47, 3:12, 14, 3:18, 28, 4:8(2), 9, 18, 5:4, 11(2), 14, 23: Depicts the Supreme Being 79 times: Ezr. 4:24, 5:1, 2(2), 5, 8, 11, 12, 13, 14, 15, 16, 17, 6:3, 5(2), 7(2), 8, 9, 10, 12(2), 14, 16, 17, 18, 7:12, 14, 15, 16, 17, 18, 19(2), 20, 21, 23(2), 24, 25(2), 26; Dan. 2:18, 19, 20, 23, 28, 37, 44, 45, 47(2), 3:15, 17, 25, 26, 28(2), 29(2), 4:2, 5:3, 18, 21, 23, 26, 6:5, 7, 10, 11, 12, 16, 20(2), 22, 23, 26(2)

עֶלְיוֹן ('elyôn): "The Most High": from עָלָה ('alah), "to go up": Occurs 53 times: Can depict elevation generally: "upper," "uppermost," "high": Used in this generic sense these 22 times: Gen. 40:17; Deut. 26:19, 28:1; Josh. 16:5; 1 Kings 9:8; 2 Kings 15:35, 18:17, 1 Chron. 7:24; 2 Chron. 7:21, 8:5, 23:20, 27:3, 32:30; Neh. 3:25; Ps. 89:27; Isa. 7:3, 36:2; Jer. 20:2, 36:10; Ezek. 9:2, 41:7, 42:5: In this use it signifies a higher elevation in space, "the *uppermost* basket" (Gen. 40:17), or in rank, "make you *high* above the nations" (Deut. 26:19), and "the *highest* of the kings of the earth (Ps. 89:27): it once denotes God's attribute of transcendence: "you, whose name alone is Jehovah, are *most high* over all the earth (Ps. 83:18): It depicts the Supreme Being these 30 times: both by itself, "the Most High," and in combination with *'ēl*, with *'elohîm*, and with *y{"e"}hovah* as follows: *The Most High*: *'elyôn*: 20 times: Num. 24:16; Deut. 32:8; 2 Sam. 22:14; Pss. 9:2, 18:13, 21:7, 46:4, 50:14, 73:11, 77:10, 78:17, 82:6, 87:5, 91:1, 9, 92:1, 107:11; Isa. 14:14; Lam. 3:35, 38: *God Most High*: *'ēl 'elyôn*: 5 times: Gen. 14:18, 19, 20, 22; Ps. 78:35: *God Most High*: *'elohîm 'elyôn*: 2 times: Pss. 57:2, 78:56: *Jehovah Most High*: *y{"e"}hovah 'elyôn*: 3 times: Pss. 7:17, 47:2, 97:9.[7]

עֶלְיוֹן ('elyôn): "The Most High": Aramaic form: corresponds to Hebrew *'elyôn*: Used in Daniel. Only depicts the Supreme Being: Occurs 4 times: Dan. 7:18, 22, 25, 27

עִלַּי ('illay): "The Most High": Aramaic form: corresponds to the Hebrew, עֲלִי ('illiy), "upper," from, עָלָה ('alah), "to go up": Used in Daniel: Only depicts the Supreme Being: Occurs 10 times: by itself, *the Most High*: Dan. 4:17, 24, 25, 32, 34, 7:25: with *'elah*, "God": *God Most High*: Dan. 3:26, 4:2, 5:18, 21.

---

[7] I include this text based on the translation: "you, Jehovah Most High [*y{"e"}hovah 'elyôn*] are above all the earth; you are exalted above the gods." Some translate this text: "you, LORD, are *high* above all the earth; you are exalted above the gods." If this is correct, then this text also denotes God's transcendence. But this text reads, *y{"e"}hovah 'elyôn*. Whereas Ps. 83:18 [19 Heb.] does not say *y{"e"}hovah 'elyôn*, but says: יְהוָה לְבַדְּךָ עֶלְיוֹן (*y{"e"}hovah l{"e"}baddeka 'elyôn*).

עַל ('al): "The High": high, above: from עָלָה ('alah), "to go up": Occurs 6 times: Gen. 27:39, 49:25; 2 Sam. 23:1; Ps. 50:4: depicts the Supreme Being 2 times in Hosea: Hos. 7:16, 11:7.

אֲדֹנָי ('adonay): "Lord": emphatic form of אָדוֹן ('adôn): translated: "lord," "God," "Lord": occurs 434 times: depicts men 2 times: Ezr. 10:3; Isa. 21:8: Depicts God as Supreme Master and Ruler these 432 times (221 times in Ezekiel) with one variant (Isa. 10:16), margin (qere) reads $y^e hovah$: Gen. 15:2, 8, 18:3, 27, 30, 31, 32, 20:4; Exod. 4:10, 13, 5:22, 15:17, 34:9(2); Num. 14:17; Deut. 3:24, 9:26; Josh. 7:7, 8; Judg. 6:15, 6:22, 13:8, 16:28; 2 Sam. 7:18, 19(2), 20, 28, 29; 1 Kings 2:26, 3:10, 8:53, 22:6; 2 Kings 7:6, 19:23; Neh. 1:11, 4:14; Job 28:28; Pss. 2:4, 16:2, 22:30, 35:17, 22, 23, 37:13, 38:9, 15, 22, 39:7, 40:17, 44:23, 51:15, 54:4, 55:9, 57:9, 59:11, 62:12, 66:18, 68:11, 17, 19, 20, 22, 26, 32, 69:6, 71:5, 16, 73:20, 28, 77:2, 7, 78:65, 79:12, 86:3, 4, 5, 8, 9, 12, 15, 89:49, 50, 90:1, 109:21, 110:5, 130:2, 3, 6, 140:7, 141:8; Isa. 3:15, 17, 18, 4:4, 6:1, 8, 11, 7:7, 14, 20, 8:7, 9:8, 17, 10:12, 16, 23, 24, 11:11, 21:6, 16, 22:5, 12, 14, 15, 25:8, 28:2, 16, 22, 29:13, 30:15, 20, 37:24, 38:16, 40:10, 48:16, 49:14, 22, 50:4, 5, 7, 9, 52:4, 56:8, 61:1, 11, 65:13, 15; Jer. 1:6, 2:19, 22, 4:10, 7:20, 14:13, 32:17, 25, 44:26, 46:10(2), 49:5, 50:25, 31; Lam. 1:14, 15(2), 2:1, 2, 5, 7, 18, 19, 20, 3:31, 36, 37, 58; Ezek. 2:4, 3:11, 27, 4:14, 5:5, 7, 8, 11, 6:3(2), 11, 7:2, 5, 8:1, 9:8, 11:7, 8, 13, 16, 17, 21, 12:10, 19, 23, 25, 28(2), 13:3, 8(2), 9, 13, 16, 18, 20, 14:4, 6, 11, 14, 16, 18, 20, 21, 23, 15:6, 8, 16:3, 8, 14, 19, 23, 30, 36, 43, 48, 59, 63, 17:3, 9, 16, 19, 22, 18:3, 9, 23, 25, 29, 30, 32, 20:3(2), 5, 27, 30, 31, 33, 36, 39, 40, 44, 47, 49, 21:7, 13, 24, 26, 28, 22:3, 12, 19, 28, 31, 23:22, 28, 32, 34, 35, 46, 49, 24:3, 6, 9, 14, 21, 24, 25:3(2), 6, 8, 12, 13, 14, 15, 16, 26:3, 5, 7, 14, 15, 19, 21, 27:3, 28:2, 6, 10, 12, 22, 24, 25, 29:3, 8, 13, 16, 19, 20, 30:2, 6, 10, 13, 22, 31:10, 15, 18, 32:3, 8, 11, 14, 16, 31, 32, 33:11, 17, 20, 25, 27, 34:2, 8, 10, 11, 15, 17, 20, 30, 31, 35:3, 6, 11, 14, 36:2, 3, 4(2), 5, 6, 7, 13, 14, 15, 22, 23, 32, 33, 37, 37:3, 5, 9, 12, 19, 21, 38:3, 10, 14, 17, 18, 21, 39:1, 5, 8, 10, 13, 17, 20, 25, 29, 43:18, 19, 27, 44:6, 9, 12, 15, 27, 45:9(2), 15, 18, 46:1, 16, 47:13, 23, 48:29; Dan. 1:2, 9:3, 4, 7, 8, 9, 15, 16, 17, 19(3); Amos 1:8, 3:7, 8, 11, 13, 4:2, 5, 5:3, 16, 6:8, 7:1, 2, 4(2), 5, 6, 7, 8, 8:1, 3, 9, 11, 9:1, 5, 8; Obad. 1:1; Micah 1:2(2); Hab. 3:19; Zeph. 1:7; Zech. 9:4, 14; Mal. 1:14

אָדוֹן ('adôn): "Lord": shortened to אָדֹן ('adon): translated: "master," "sir," "owner," "lord," "Lord": occurs 335 times: often used in direct address: depicts a human master, lord, ruler, prince, or husband these 293 times: Gen. 18:12, 23:6, 11, 15, 24:9, 10(2), 12(2), 14, 18, 27(3), 35, 36(2), 37, 39, 42, 44, 48(2), 49, 51, 54, 56, 65, 31:35, 32:4, 5, 18, 33:8, 13, 14(2), 15, 39:2, 3, 7, 8(2), 16, 19, 20, 40:1, 7, 42:10, 30, 33, 43:20, 44:5, 7, 8, 9, 16(2), 18(2), 19, 20, 22, 24, 33, 45:8, 9, 47:18(3), 25; Exod. 21:4(2), 5, 6(2), 8, 32, 32:22; Num. 11:28, 12:11, 32:25, 27, 36:2(2); Deut. 10:17, 23:15(2); Judg. 3:25, 4:18, 19:11, 12, 26, 27; Ruth 2:14; 1 Sam. 1:15, 26(2), 16:16, 20:38, 22:12, 24:6, 8, 10, 25:10, 14, 17, 24, 25(2), 26(2), 27(2), 28(2), 29, 30, 31(3), 41, 26:15(2), 16, 17, 18, 19, 29:4, 8, 10, 30:13, 15; 2 Sam. 1:10, 2:5, 7, 3:21, 4:8, 9:9, 10(2), 11, 10:3, 11:9, 11(2), 13, 12:8(2), 13:32, 33, 14:9, 12, 15, 17(2), 18, 19(2), 20, 22, 15:15, 21(2), 16:3, 4, 9, 18:28, 31, 32, 19:19(2), 20, 26, 27(2), 28, 30, 35, 37, 20:6, 24:3(2), 21, 22; 1 Kings 1:2(2), 11, 13, 17, 18, 20(2), 21, 24, 27(2), 31, 33, 36, 37(2), 43, 47, 2:38, 3:17, 26, 11:23, 12:27, 16:24, 18:7, 8, 10, 11, 13, 14,

20:4, 9, 22:17; 2 Kings 2:3, 5, 16, 19, 4:16, 28, 5:1, 3, 4, 18, 20, 22, 25, 6:5, 12, 15, 22, 23, 26, 32, 8:5, 12, 14, 9:7, 11, 31, 10:2, 3(2), 6, 9, 18:23, 24, 27(2), 19:4, 6; 1 Chron. 12:19, 21:3(3), 23; 2 Chron. 2:14, 15, 13:6, 18:16; Job 3:19; Pss. 12:4, 105:21, 123:2, 136:3; Prov. 25:13, 27:18, 30:10; Isa. 19:4, 22:18, 24:2, 26:13, 36:8, 9, 12(2), 37:4, 6; Jer. 22:18, 27:4(2), 34:5, 37:20, 38:9; Dan. 1:10; Amos 4:1; Zeph. 1:9; Mal. 1:6(2): Refers to angels or the angel of Jehovah at least these 13 times: Gen. 19:2, 18; Josh. 5:14; Judg. 6:13; Dan. 10:16, 17(2), 19; Zech. 1:9, 4:4, 5, 13, 6:4: Depicts God as Supreme Master and Lord of the universe 29 times: Exod. 23:17, 34:23; Deut. 10:17; Josh. 3:11, 13; Neh. 3:5, 8:10, 10:29; Pss. 8:1, 9, 45:11, 97:5, 110:1, 114:7, 135:5, 136:3, 147:5; Isa. 1:24, 3:1, 10:16, 33, 19:4, 51:22; Dan. 12:8; Hos. 12:14; Micah 4:13; Zech. 4:14, 6:5; Mal. 3:1.

שַׁדַּי (shadday): "The Almighty": from שָׁדַד (shadad), "to overpower": Translated, "Almighty": Occurs **48** times (31 times in Job): Exclusively depicts the Supreme Being both by itself and in combination with *'el* as follows: God Almighty: *'ēl shadday*: 7 times: Gen. 17:1, 28:3, 35:11, 43:14, 48:3; Exod. 6:3; Ezek. 10:5: The Almighty: *shadday*: 41 times (31 times in Job): Gen. 49:25; Num. 24:4, 16; Ruth 1:20, 21; Job 5:17, 6:4, 14, 8:3, 5, 11:7, 13:3, 15:25, 21:15, 20, 22:3, 17, 23, 25, 26, 23:16, 24:1, 27:2, 10, 11, 13, 29:5, 31:2, 35, 32:8, 33:4, 34:10, 12, 35:13, 37:23, 40:2; Pss. 68:14, 91:1; Isa. 13:6; Ezek. 1:24; Joel 1:15.

שָׁדַד shadad: "to overpower": with a variety of nuances: to devastate, to ruin, to destroy, to despoil: occurs at least these 56 times in these 47 verses (26 times in Jeremiah): Judg. 5:27; Job 12:6, 15:21; Pss. 17:9, 137:8; Prov. 11:3, 19:26, 24:15; Isa. 15:1(2), 16:4, 21:2(2), 23:1, 14, 33:1(4); Jer. 4:13, 20(2), 30, 5:6, 6:26, 9:19, 10:20, 12:12, 15:8, 25:36, 47:4(2), 48:1, 8, 15, 18, 20, 32, 49:3, 10, 28, 51:48, 53, 55, 56; Ezek. 32:12; Hos. 10:2, 14; Joel 1:10(2); Obad. 1:5; Micah 2:4; Nah. 3:7; Zech. 11:2, 3(2): often depicts men overpowering and despoiling others wickedly: depicts God destroying a pasture (Jer. 25:36); overpowering [despoiling KJV] the Philistines (Jer. 47:4); sending destroyers [spoilers KJV] upon Babylon (Jer. 51:53); and overpowering and devastating [despoiling KJV] Babylon (Jer. 51:55) in his righteous vengeance (Jer. 51:56).

יָהּ (yahh): shortened form of *yhvh*: in KJV rendered "LORD," and transliterated, JAH (Ps. 68:4): occurs these 49 times: Exod. 15:2, 17:16; Pss. 68:4, 18, 77:11, 89:8, 94:7, 12, 102:18, 104:35, 105:45, 106:1, 48, 111:1, 112:1, 113:1, 9, 115:17, 18(2), 116:19, 117:2, 118:5(2), 14, 17, 18, 19, 122:4, 130:3, 135:1, 3, 4, 21, 146:1, 10, 147:1, 20, 148:1, 14, 149:1, 9, 150:1, 6(2); Isa. 12:2, 26:4, 38:11(2).

APPENDIX 4: RELATIVE FREQUENCY AND USE OF GOD'S NAME: *yhvh*

Relative Frequency of yhvh: Uses /1000 Words in the Hebrew Old Testament
[relative frequency combines both pointed forms: yᵉhovah and yehovih]

Scripture	Form		Words	Rel. Freq.	Scripture	Form		Words	Rel. Freq.
	vah	vih				vah	vih		
Old Testament	6,519	305	308,691	22.106	Ecclesiastes	0		2,991	0
Pentateuch	1814	4	80,676	22.534	Song of Sol.	0		1,270	0
Genesis	162	2	20,706	7.920	Maj. Prophets	1353	256	58,200	27.646
Exodus	397		16,878	23.522	Isaiah	426	25	17,141	26.311
Leviticus	311		12,054	25.801	Jeremiah	710	14	22,143	32.697
Numbers	396		16,575	23.891	Lamentations	32		1,629	19.644
Deuteronomy	548	2	14,463	38.028	Ezekiel	217	217	18,916	22.944
Joshua	223	1	10,146	22.078	Min. Prophets	489	26	20,449	25.185
Judges	172	2	9,977	17.440	Daniel	7		5,951	1.176
Ruth	18		1,297	13.878	Hosea	46		2,401	19.159
1 Samuel	320		13,433	23.822	Joel	33		963	34.268
2 Samuel	146	6	11,188	13.586	Amos	60	21	2,072	39.093
1 Kings	256	2	13,248	19.475	Obadiah	6	1	291	24.055
2 Kings	277		12,366	22.400	Jonah	26		691	37.627
1 Chronicles	174		11,007	15.808	Micah	39	1	1412	28.329
2 Chronicles	384		13,479	28.489	Nahum	13		561	23.173
Ezra	37		3,890	6.810	Habakkuk	12	1	680	19.118
Nehemiah	17		5,433	3.129	Zephaniah	33	1	772	44.041
Esther	0		3,068	0	Haggai	35		607	57.661
Job	32		8,382	3.818	Zechariah	132	1	3,165	42.022
Psalms	688	8	19,595	35.519	Malachi	47		883	53.228
Proverbs	87		6,967	12.487					

USE OF YHVH (6824 uses):
Yehovih (305) and Yᵉhovah (6519)

Both pointing forms occur together in Deut. 9:26: "I prayed therefore unto the LORD [yᵉhovah], and said, O Lord ['adonay] GOD [yehovih], destroy not your people and your inheritance."

Yehovih (305 uses)

יהוה (yhvh): pointed as, יֱהֹוִה (yehovih), with the vowels of *'elohîm*: rendered in the KJV as "GOD," once as LORD (Hab. 3:19): used when *yhvh* occurs in conjunction with *'adonay*: denominates the Supreme Being these 305 times, 217 times in Ezekiel where *'adonay* is featured: Gen. 15:2, 8; Deut. 3:24, 9:26; Josh. 7:7; Judg. 6:22,

16:28; 2 Sam. 7:18, 19(2), 20, 28, 29; 1 Kings 2:26, 8:53; Pss. 68:20, 69:6, 71:5, 16, 73:28, 109:21, 140:7, 141:8; Isa. 3:15, 7:7, 10:23, 24, 22:5, 12, 14, 15, 25:8, 28:16, 22, 30:15, 40:10, 48:16, 49:22, 50:4, 5, 7, 9, 52:4, 56:8, 61:1, 11, 65:13, 15; Jer. 1:6, 2:19, 22, 4:10, 7:20, 14:13, 32:17, 25, 44:26, 46:10(2), 49:5, 50:25, 31; Ezek. 2:4, 3:11, 27, 4:14, 5:5, 7, 8, 11, 6:3(2), 11, 7:2, 5, 8:1, 9:8, 11:7, 8, 13, 16, 17, 21, 12:10, 19, 23, 25, 28(2), 13:3, 8(2), 9, 13, 16, 18, 20, 14:4, 6, 11, 14, 16, 18, 20, 21, 23, 15:6, 8, 16:3, 8, 14, 19, 23, 30, 36, 43, 48, 59, 63, 17:3, 9, 16, 19, 22, 18:3, 9, 23, 30, 32, 20:3(2), 5, 27, 30, 31, 33, 36, 39, 40, 44, 47, 49, 21:7, 13, 24, 26, 28, 22:3, 12, 19, 28, 31, 23:22, 28, 32, 34, 35, 46, 49, 24:3, 6, 9, 14, 21, 24, 25:3(2), 6, 8, 12, 13, 14, 15, 16, 26:3, 5, 7, 14, 15, 19, 21, 27:3, 28:2, 6, 10, 12, 22, 24, 25, 29:3, 8, 13, 16, 19, 20, 30:2, 6, 10, 13, 22, 31:10, 15, 18, 32:3, 8, 11, 14, 16, 31, 32, 33:11, 25, 27, 34:2, 8, 10, 11, 15, 17, 20, 30, 31, 35:3, 6, 11, 14, 36:2, 3, 4(2), 5, 6, 7, 13, 14, 15, 22, 23, 32, 33, 37, 37:3, 5, 9, 12, 19, 21, 38:3, 10, 14, 17, 18, 21, 39:1, 5, 8, 10, 13, 17, 20, 25, 29, 43:18, 19, 27, 44:6, 9, 12, 15, 27, 45:9(2), 15, 18, 46:1, 16, 47:13, 23, 48:29; Amos 1:8, 3:7, 8, 11, 13, 4:2, 5, 5:3, 6:8, 7:1, 2, 4(2), 5, 6, 8:1, 3, 9, 11, 9:5, 8; Obad. 1:1; Micah 1:2; Hab. 3:19; Zeph. 1:7; Zech. 9:14

Y^{e}hovah (6519 uses)

יהוה (yhvh): pointed as, יְהֹוָה (y^{e}hovah)[1], with the vowels of *'adonay*: transliterated, "Jehovah": rendered in the KJV as the "LORD," "GOD," (Gen. 6:5; Exod. 23:17, 34:23; 2 Sam. 12:22), and JEHOVAH (Exod. 6:3; Ps. 83:18; Isa. 12:2, 26:4): derived from הָיָה (hayah), "to be": "the One Who Is": denominates the Supreme Being these 6,519 times with one variant (Isa. 10:16)[2]:

Gen. 2:4, 5, 7, 8, 9, 15, 16, 18, 19, 21, 22, 3:1, 8(2), 9, 13, 14, 21, 22, 23, 4:1, 3, 4, 6, 9, 13, 15(2), 16, 26, 5:29, 6:3, 5, 6, 7, 8, 7:1, 5, 16, 8:20, 21(2), 9:26, 10:9(2), 11:5, 6, 8, 9(2), 12:1, 4, 7(2), 8(2), 17, 13:4, 10(2), 13, 14, 18, 14:22, 15:1, 4, 6, 7, 18, 16:2, 5, 7, 9, 10, 11(2), 13, 17:1, 18:1, 13, 14, 17, 19(2), 20, 22, 26, 33, 19:13(2), 14, 16, 24(2), 27, 20:18, 21:1(2), 33, 22:11, 14, 15, 16, 24:1, 3, 7, 12, 21, 26, 27(2), 31, 35, 40, 42, 44, 48(2), 50, 51, 52, 56, 25:21(2), 22, 23, 26:2, 12, 22, 24, 25, 28, 29, 27:7, 20, 27, 28:13(2), 16, 21, 29:31, 32, 33, 35, 30:24, 27, 30, 31:3, 49, 32:9, 38:7(2), 10, 39:2, 3(2), 5(2), 21, 23(2), 49:18;

Exod. 3:2, 4, 7, 15, 16, 18(2), 4:1, 2, 4, 5, 6, 10, 11(2), 14, 19, 21, 22, 24, 27, 28, 30, 31, 5:1, 2(2), 3, 17, 21, 22, 6:1, 2, 3, 6, 7, 8, 10, 12, 13, 26, 28, 29(2), 30, 7:1, 5, 6, 8, 10, 13, 14, 16, 17(2), 19, 20, 22, 25, 8:1(2), 5, 8(2), 10, 12, 13, 15, 16, 19, 20(2), 22, 24, 26, 27, 28, 29(2), 30, 31, 9:1(2), 3, 4, 5(2), 6, 8, 12(2), 13(2), 20, 21, 22, 23(2), 27, 28, 29(2), 30, 33, 35, 10:1, 2, 3, 7, 8, 9, 10, 11, 12, 13, 16, 17, 18, 19, 20, 21, 24, 25, 26(2), 27, 11:1, 3, 4, 7, 9, 10, 12:1, 11, 12, 14, 23(2), 25, 27, 28, 29, 31, 36, 41, 42(2), 43, 48, 50, 51, 13:1, 3, 5, 6, 8, 9(2), 11, 12(2), 14, 15(2), 16, 21, 14:1, 4, 8, 10, 13, 14, 15, 18, 21, 24, 25, 26, 27, 30, 31(3), 15:1(2), 3(2), 6(2), 11, 16, 17, 18, 19, 21, 25(2), 26(2), 16:3, 4, 6, 7(2), 8(3), 9, 10, 11, 12, 15, 16, 23(2), 25, 28, 29, 32, 33, 34, 17:1, 2, 4, 5, 7(2), 14, 16, 18:1, 8(2), 9, 10, 11, 19:3, 7, 8(2), 9(2), 10, 11, 18, 20(2), 21(2), 22(2), 23, 24(2), 20:2, 5, 7(2), 10, 11(2), 12, 22, 22:11, 20, 23:17, 19, 25, 24:1, 2, 3(2), 4, 5, 7, 8, 12, 16, 17, 25:1, 27:21, 28:12, 29, 30(2), 35, 36, 38, 29:11, 18(2), 23, 24, 25(2), 26, 28, 41, 42, 46(2), 30:8, 10, 11, 12, 13, 14,

15, 16, 17, 20, 22, 34, 37, 31:1, 12, 13, 15, 17, 32:5, 7, 9, 11(2), 14, 26, 27, 29, 30, 31, 33, 35, 33:1, 5, 7, 11, 12, 17, 19, 21, 34:1, 4, 5(2), 6(3), 10, 14, 23, 24, 26, 27, 28, 32, 34, 35:1, 2, 4, 5(2), 10, 21, 22, 24, 29(2), 30, 36:1(2), 2, 5, 38:22, 39:1, 5, 7, 21, 26, 29, 30, 31, 32, 42, 43, 40:1, 16, 19, 21, 23(2), 25(2), 27, 29, 32, 34, 35, 38;

Lev. 1:1, 2, 3, 5, 9, 11, 13, 14, 17, 2:1, 2, 3, 8, 9, 10, 11(2), 12, 14, 16, 3:1, 3, 5, 6, 7, 9, 11, 12, 14, 16, 4:1, 2, 3, 4, 6, 7, 13, 15(2), 17, 18, 22, 24, 27, 31, 35, 5:6, 7, 12, 14, 15(2), 17, 19, 6:1, 2, 6, 7, 8, 14, 15, 18, 19, 20, 21, 22, 24, 25, 7:5, 11, 14, 20, 21, 22, 25, 28, 29(2), 30(2), 35(2), 36, 38(2), 8:1, 4, 5, 9, 13, 17, 21(2), 26, 27, 28, 29(2), 34, 35, 36, 9:2, 4(2), 5, 6(2), 7, 10, 21, 23, 24, 10:1, 2(2), 3, 6, 7, 8, 11, 12, 13, 15(2), 17, 19(2), 11:1, 44, 45, 12:1, 7, 13:1, 14:1, 11, 12, 16, 18, 23, 24, 27, 29, 31, 33, 15:1, 14, 15, 30, 16:1(2), 2, 7, 8, 9, 10, 12, 13, 18, 30, 34, 17:1, 2, 4(2), 5(2), 6(2), 9, 18:1, 2, 4, 5, 6, 21, 30, 19:1, 2, 3, 4, 5, 8, 10, 12, 14, 16, 18, 21, 22, 24, 25, 28, 30, 31, 32, 34, 36, 37, 20:1, 7, 8, 24, 26, 21:1, 6, 8, 12, 15, 16, 21, 23, 22:1, 2, 3(2), 8, 9, 15, 16, 17, 18, 21, 22(2), 24, 26, 27, 29, 30, 31, 32, 33, 23:1, 2, 3, 4, 5, 6, 8, 9, 11, 12, 13, 16, 17, 18(2), 20(2), 22, 23, 25, 26, 27, 28, 33, 34, 36(2), 37(2), 38(2), 39, 40, 41, 43, 44, 24:1, 3, 4, 6, 7, 8, 9, 12, 13, 16(2), 22, 23, 25:1, 2, 4, 17, 38, 25:55, 26:1, 2, 13, 44, 45, 46, 27:1, 2, 9(2), 11, 14, 16, 21, 22, 23, 26(2), 28(2), 30(2), 32, 34;

Num. 1:1, 19, 48, 54, 2:1, 33, 34, 3:1, 4(2), 5, 11, 13, 14, 16, 39, 40, 41, 42, 44, 45, 51(2), 4:1, 17, 21, 37, 41, 45, 49(2), 5:1, 4, 5, 6, 8, 11, 16, 18, 21(2), 25, 30, 6:1, 2, 5, 6, 8, 12, 14, 16, 17, 20, 21, 22, 24, 25, 26, 7:3, 4, 11, 8:1, 3, 4, 5, 10, 11(2), 12, 13, 20, 21, 22, 23, 9:1, 5, 7, 8, 9, 10, 13, 14, 18(2), 19, 20(2), 23(4), 10:1, 9, 10, 13, 29(2), 32, 33(2), 34, 35, 36, 11:1(3), 2, 3, 10, 11, 16, 18(2), 20, 23(2), 24, 25, 29(2), 31, 33(2), 12:2(2), 4, 5, 6, 8, 9, 13, 14, 13:1, 3, 14:3, 8, 9(2), 10, 11, 13, 14(2), 16, 18, 20, 21, 26, 28, 35, 37, 40, 41, 42, 43(2), 44, 15:1, 3(2), 4, 7, 8, 10, 13, 14, 15, 17, 19, 21, 22, 23(2), 24, 25(2), 28, 30, 31, 35, 36, 37, 39, 41(2), 16:3(2), 5, 7(2), 9, 11, 15, 16, 17, 19, 20, 23, 28, 29, 30(2), 35, 36, 38, 40(2), 41, 42, 44, 46, 17:1, 7, 9, 10, 11, 13, 18:1, 6, 8, 12, 13, 15, 17, 19(2), 20, 24, 25, 26, 28(2), 29, 19:1, 2, 13, 20, 20:3, 4, 6, 7, 9, 12, 13, 16, 23, 27, 21:2, 3, 6, 7(2), 8, 14, 16, 34, 22:8, 13, 18, 19, 22, 23, 24, 25, 26, 27, 28, 31(2), 32, 34, 35, 23:3, 5, 8, 12, 16, 17, 21, 26, 24:1, 6, 11, 13(2), 25:3, 4(3), 10, 16, 26:1, 4, 9, 52, 61, 65, 27:3, 5, 6, 11, 12, 15, 16, 17, 18, 21, 22, 23, 28:1, 3, 6, 7, 8, 11, 13, 15, 16, 19, 24, 26, 27, 29:2, 6, 8, 12, 13, 36, 39, 40, 30:1, 2, 3, 5, 8, 12, 16, 31:1, 3, 7, 16(2), 21, 25, 28, 29, 30, 31, 37, 38, 39, 40, 41(2), 47(2), 50(2), 52, 54, 32:4, 7, 9, 10, 12, 13(2), 14, 20, 21, 22(3), 23, 27, 29, 31, 32, 33:2, 4(2), 38, 50, 34:1, 13, 16, 29, 35:1, 9, 34, 36:2(2), 5, 6, 10, 13;

Deut. 1:3, 6, 8, 10, 11, 19, 20, 21(2), 25, 26, 27, 30, 31, 32, 34, 36, 37, 41(2), 42, 43, 45(2), 2:1, 2, 7(2), 9, 12, 14, 15, 17, 21, 29, 30, 31, 33, 36, 37, 3:2, 3, 18, 20(2), 21(2), 22, 23, 26(2), 4:1, 2, 3(2), 4, 5, 7, 10(2), 12, 14, 15, 19, 20, 21(2), 23(2), 24, 25, 27(2), 29, 30, 31, 34, 35, 39, 40, 5:2, 3, 4, 5(2), 6, 9, 11(2), 12, 14, 15(2), 16(2), 22, 24, 25, 27(2), 28(2), 32, 33, 6:1, 2, 3, 4(4), 5, 10, 12, 13, 15(2), 16, 17, 18(2), 19, 20, 21, 22, 24(2), 25, 7:1, 2, 4, 6(2), 7, 8(2), 9, 12, 15, 16, 18, 19(2), 20, 21, 22, 23, 25, 8:1, 2, 3, 5, 6, 7, 10, 11, 14, 18, 19, 20(2), 9:3(2), 4(3), 5(2), 6, 7(2), 8(2), 9, 10(2), 11, 12, 13, 16(2), 18(2), 19(2), 20, 22, 23(2), 24, 25(2), 26, 28, 10:1, 4(2), 5, 8(3), 9(2), 10(2), 11, 12(3), 13, 14, 15, 17, 20, 22, 11:1, 2, 4, 7, 9, 12(2), 13, 17(2),

21, 22, 23, 25, 27, 28, 29, 31, 12:1, 4, 5, 7(2), 9, 10, 11(2), 12, 14, 15, 18(3), 20, 21(2), 25, 26, 27(2), 28, 29, 31(2), 13:3(2), 4, 5(2), 10, 12, 16, 17, 18(2), 14:1, 2(2), 21, 23(2), 24(2), 25, 26, 29, 15:2, 4(2), 5, 6, 7, 9, 10, 14, 15, 18, 19, 20(2), 21, 16:1(2), 2(2), 5, 6, 7, 8, 10(3), 11(2), 15(3), 16(2), 17, 18, 20, 21, 22, 17:1(2), 2(2), 8, 10, 12, 14, 15, 16, 19, 18:1, 2, 5(2), 6, 7(2), 9, 12(2), 13, 14, 15, 16, 17, 21, 22(2), 19:1(2), 2, 3, 8, 9, 10, 14, 17, 20:1, 4, 13, 14, 16, 17, 18, 21:1, 5(2), 8, 9, 10, 23, 22:5, 23:1, 2(2), 3(2), 5(3), 8, 14, 18(2), 20, 21(2), 23, 24:4(2), 9, 13, 15, 18, 19, 25:15, 16, 19(2), 26:1, 2(2), 3(2), 4, 5, 7(2), 8, 10(3), 11, 13, 14, 16, 17, 18, 19, 27:2, 3(2), 5, 6(2), 7, 9, 10, 15, 28:1(2), 2, 7, 8(2), 9(2), 10, 11(2), 12, 13(2), 15, 20, 21, 22, 24, 25, 27, 28, 35, 36, 37, 45, 47, 48, 49, 52, 53, 58, 59, 61, 62, 63(2), 64, 65, 68, 29:1, 2, 4, 6, 10, 12(2), 15, 18, 20(3), 21, 22, 23, 24, 25, 27, 28, 29, 30:1, 2, 3(2), 4, 5, 6(2), 7, 8, 9(2), 10(2), 16(2), 20(2), 31:2, 3(2), 4, 5, 6, 7, 8, 9, 11, 12, 13, 14, 15, 16, 25, 26, 27, 29, 32:3, 6, 9, 12, 19, 27, 30, 36, 48, 33:2, 7, 11, 12(2), 13, 21, 23, 29, 34:1, 4, 5(2), 9, 10, 11;

Josh. 1:1(2), 9, 11, 13(2), 15(3), 17, 2:9, 10, 11, 12, 14, 24, 3:3, 5, 7, 9, 13, 17, 4:1, 5, 7, 8, 10, 11, 13, 14, 15, 18, 23(2), 24(2), 5:1, 2, 6(3), 9, 14, 15, 6:2, 6, 7, 8(2), 11, 12, 13(2), 16, 17, 19(2), 24, 26, 27, 7:1, 6, 10, 13, 14(3), 15, 19, 20, 23, 25, 26, 8:1, 7, 8, 18, 27, 30, 31(2), 33(2), 9:9, 14, 18, 19, 24, 27, 10:8, 10, 11, 12(2), 14(2), 19, 25, 30, 32, 40, 42, 11:6, 8, 9, 12, 15(2), 20(2), 23, 12:6(2), 13:1, 8, 14, 33, 14:2, 5, 6, 7, 8, 9, 10(2), 12(3), 14, 15:13, 17:4(2), 14, 18:3, 6, 7(2), 8, 10, 19:50, 51, 20:1, 21:2, 3, 8, 43, 44(2), 45, 22:2, 3, 4(2), 5(2), 9, 16(3), 17, 18(2), 19(4), 22(3), 23(2), 24, 25(3), 27(2), 28, 29(3), 31(3), 34, 23:1, 3(2), 5(2), 8, 9, 10, 11, 13(2), 14, 15(3), 16(2), 24:2, 7, 14(2), 15(2), 16, 17, 18(2), 19, 20, 21, 22, 23, 24, 26, 27, 29, 31(2);

Judg. 1:1, 2, 4, 19, 22, 2:1, 4, 5, 7(2), 8, 10, 11, 12(2), 13, 14, 15(3), 16, 17, 18(3), 20, 22, 23, 3:1, 4, 7(2), 8, 9(2), 10(2), 12(3), 15, 28, 4:1, 2, 3, 6, 9, 14(2), 15, 5:2, 3(2), 4, 5(2), 9, 11(2), 13, 23(3), 31, 6:1(2), 6, 7, 8(2), 10, 11, 12(2), 13(3), 14, 16, 21(2), 22(2), 23, 24, 25, 26, 27, 34, Jdg. 7:2, 4, 5, 7, 9, 15, 18, 20, 22, 8:7, 19, 23, 34, 10:6(2), 7, 10, 11, 15, 16, 11:9, 10, 11, 21, 23, 24, 27, 29, 30, 31, 32, 35, 36(2), 12:3, 13:1(2), 3, 8, 13, 15, 16(3), 17, 18, 19, 20, 21(2), 23, 24, 25, 14:4, 6, 19, 15:14, 18, 16:20, 28, 17:2, 3, 13, 18:6, 19:18, 20:1, 18, 23(3), 26(2), 27, 28, 35, 21:3, 5(2), 7, 8, 15, 19;

Ruth 1:6, 8, 9, 13, 17, 21(2), 2:4(2), 12(2), 20, 3:10, 13, 4:11, 12, 13, 14;

1 Sam. 1:3(2), 5, 6, 7, 9, 10, 11(2), 12, 15, 19(2), 20, 21, 22, 23, 24, 26, 27, 28(3), 2:1(2), 2, 3, 6, 7, 8, 10(2), 11, 12, 17(2), 18, 20(2), 21(2), 24, 25(2), 26, 27, 30(2), 3:1(2), 3, 4, 6, 7(2), 8(2), 9, 10, 11, 15, 18, 19, 20, 21(3), 4:3(2), 4, 5, 6, 5:3, 4, 6, 9, 6:1, 2, 8, 11, 14, 15(2), 17, 18, 19(2), 20, 21, 7:1(2), 2, 3(2), 4, 5, 6(2), 8, 9(3), 10, 12, 13, 17, 8:6, 7, 10, 18, 21, 22, 9:15, 17, 10:1, 6, 17, 18, 19, 22(2), 24, 25, 11:7, 13, 15(2), 12:3, 5, 6, 7(2), 8(2), 9, 10(2), 11, 12, 13, 14(3), 15(3), 16, 17(2), 18(3), 19, 20(2), 22(2), 23, 24, 13:12, 13(2), 14(3), 14:3, 6(2), 10, 12, 23, 33, 34, 35(2), 39, 41, 45, 15:1(2), 2, 10, 11, 13(2), 15, 16, 17, 18, 19(2), 20(2), 21, 22(2), 23, 24, 25, 26(2), 28, 30, 31, 33, 35, 16:1, 2(2), 4, 5, 6, 7(2), 8, 9, 10, 12, 13, 14(2), 18, 17:37(2), 45, 46, 47(2), 18:12, 14, 17, 28, 19:5, 6, 9, 20:3, 8, 12, 13(2), 14, 15, 16, 21, 22, 23, 42(2), 21:6, 7, 22:10, 17(2), 21, 23:2(2), 4(2), 10, 11(2), 12, 18, 21, 24:4, 6(3), 10(2), 12(2), 15, 18, 19, 21, 25:26(2), 28(2), 29, 30, 31, 32, 34, 38, 39(2), 26:9,

10(2), 11(2), 12, 16(2), 19(3), 20, 23(3), 24, 28:6(2), 10(2), 16, 17(2), 18(2), 19(2), 29:6, 30:6, 8, 23, 26;

2 Sam. 1:12, 14, 16, 2:1(2), 5, 6, 3:9, 18, 28, 39, 4:8, 9, 5:2, 3, 10, 12, 19(2), 20, 23, 24, 25, 6:2, 5, 7, 8, 9(2), 10, 11(2), 12, 13, 14, 15, 16(2), 17(2), 18, 21(3), 7:1, 3, 4, 5, 8, 11, 18, 22, 24, 25, 26, 27, 8:6, 11, 14, 10:12, 11:27, 12:1, 5, 7, 9, 11, 13(2), 14, 15, 20, 22, 24, 25, 14:11(2), 17, 15:7, 8(2), 21, 25, 31, 16:8(2), 10, 11, 12(2), 18, 17:14(2), 18:19, 28, 31, 19:7, 21, 20:19, 21:1(2), 3, 6(2), 7, 9, 22:1(2), 2, 4, 7, 14, 16, 19, 21, 22, 25, 29(2), 31, 32, 42, 47, 50, 23:2, 10(2), 12, 16, 17, 24:1, 3, 10, 11, 12, 14, 15, 16(2), 17, 18, 19, 21, 23, 24, 25(2);

1 Kings 1:17, 29, 30, 36, 37, 48, 2:3, 4, 8, 15, 23, 24, 27(2), 28, 29, 30, 32, 33, 42, 43, 44, 45, 3:1, 2, 3, 5, 7, 15, 5:3(2), 4, 5(2), 7, 12, 6:1, 2, 11, 19, 37, 7:12, 40, 45, 48, 51(2), 8:1, 4, 6, 9, 10, 11(2), 12, 15, 17, 18, 20(3), 21, 22, 23, 25, 28, 44, 54(2), 56, 57, 59(2), 60, 61, 62, 63(2), 64(2), 65, 66, 9:1, 2, 3, 8, 9(2), 10, 15, 25(2), 10:1, 5, 9(2), 12, 11:2, 4, 6(2), 9(2), 10, 11, 14, 31, 12:15(2), 24(3), 27, 13:1, 2(2), 3, 5, 6(2), 9, 17, 18, 20, 21(3), 26(3), 32, 14:5, 7, 11, 13, 14, 15(2), 18, 21, 22, 24, 26, 28, 15:3, 4, 5, 11, 14, 15, 18, 26, 29, 30, 34, 16:1, 7(2), 12, 13, 19, 25, 26, 30, 33, 34, 17:1, 2, 5, 8, 12, 14(2), 16, 20(2), 21(2), 22, 24, 18:1, 3, 4, 10, 12(2), 13(2), 15, 18, 21, 22, 24, 30, 31, 32, 36, 37(2), 38, 39(2), 46, 19:4, 7, 9, 10, 11(5), 12, 14, 15, 20:13(2), 14, 28(3), 35, 36, 42, 21:3, 17, 19(2), 20, 23, 25, 26, 28, 22:5, 7, 8, 11, 12, 14(2), 15, 16, 17, 19(2), 20, 21, 22, 23(2), 24, 28, 38, 43, 52, 53;

2 Kings 1:3, 4, 6, 15, 16, 17, 2:1, 2(2), 3, 4(2), 5, 6(2), 14, 16, 21, 24, 3:2, 10, 11(2), 12, 13, 14, 15, 16, 17, 18, 4:1, 27, 30, 33, 43, 44, 5:1, 11, 16, 17, 18(2), 20, 6:17(2), 18, 20(2), 27, 33(2), 7:1(2), 2, 16, 19, 8:1, 8, 10, 13, 18, 19, 27, 9:3, 6(2), 7, 12, 25, 26(3), 36, 10:10(3), 16, 17, 23, 30, 31, 32, 11:3, 4(2), 7, 10, 13, 15, 17(2), 18, 19, 12:2, 4(2), 9(2), 10, 11(2), 12, 13(2), 14, 16, 18, 13:2, 3, 4(2), 5, 11, 17, 23, 14:3, 6, 14, 24, 25, 26, 27, 15:3, 5, 9, 12, 18, 24, 28, 34, 35, 37, 16:2, 3, 8, 14(2), 18, 17:2, 7, 8, 9, 11(2), 12, 13, 14, 15, 16, 17, 18, 19, 20, 21, 23, 25(2), 28, 32, 33, 34(2), 35, 36, 39, 41, 18:3, 5, 6(2), 7, 12(2), 15, 16, 22, 25(2), 30(2), 32, 35, 19:1, 4(2), 6, 14(2), 15(2), 16(2), 17, 19(2), 20, 21, 31, 32, 33, 35, 20:1, 2, 3, 4, 5(2), 8(2), 9(2), 11, 16, 17, 19, 21:2(2), 4(2), 5, 6, 7, 9, 10, 12, 16, 20, 22(2), 22:2, 3, 4, 5(2), 8, 9, 13(2), 15, 16, 18(2), 19(2), 23:2(2), 3(2), 4, 6, 7, 9, 11, 12, 16, 21, 23, 24, 25, 26, 27, 32, 37, 24:2(2), 3, 4, 9, 13(3), 19, 20, 25:9, 13(2), 16;

1 Chron. 2:3, 6:15, 31, 32, 9:19, 20, 23, 10:13(2), 14, 11:2, 3(2), 9, 10, 14, 18, 23, 13:2, 6, 10, 11, 14, 14:2, 10, 14:17, 15:2, 3, 12, 13, 14, 15, 25, 26, 28, 29, 16:2, 4(2), 7, 8, 10, 11, 14, 23, 25, 26, 28(2), 29(2), 31, 33, 34, 36(2), 37, 39, 40(2), 41, 17:1, 4, 7, 10, 16(2), 17, 19, 20, 22, 23, 24, 26, 27, 18:6, 11, 13, 19:13, 21:3, 9, 10, 11, 12(2), 13, 14, 15(2), 16, 17, 18(2), 19, 22, 24, 26(2), 27, 28, 29, 30, 22:1, 5, 6, 7, 8, 11(2), 12(2), 13, 14, 16, 18(2), 19(4), 23:4, 5, 13, 24, 25, 28, 30, 31(2), 32, 24:19(2), 25:3, 6, 7, 26:12, 22, 27, 30, 27:23, 28:2, 4, 5(2), 8(2), 9, 10, 12, 13(2), 18, 19, 20(2), 29:1, 5, 8, 9, 10(2), 11(2), 16, 18, 20(3), 21(2), 22(2), 23, 25;

2 Chron. 1:1, 3, 5, 6, 9, 2:1, 4(2), 11, 12(2), 3:1, 4:16, 5:1, 2, 7, 10, 13(2), 14, 6:1, 4, 7, 8, 10(3), 11, 12, 14, 16, 17, 19, 41(2), 42, 7:1, 2(3), 3(2), 4, 6(2), 7, 10, 11(2), 12, 21, 22, 8:1, 11, 12(2), 16(2), 9:4, 8(2), 11, 10:15, 11:2, 4(2), 14, 16(2), 12:1, 2, 5, 6, 7(2), 9, 11, 12, 13, 14, 13:5, 8, 9, 10(2), 11(2), 12, 14, 18, 20, 14:2, 4, 6, 7,

11(4), 12, 13, 14, 15:2, 4, 8(2), 9, 11, 12, 13, 14, 15, 16:2, 7, 8, 9, 12, 17:3, 5, 6, 9, 10, 16, 18:4, 6, 7, 10, 11, 13, 15, 16, 18(2), 19, 20(2), 22(2), 23, 27, 31, 19:2(2), 4, 6, 7(2), 8, 9, 10, 11(2), 20:3, 4(2), 5, 6, 13, 14, 15, 17(2), 18(2), 19, 20, 21(2), 22, 26, 27, 28, 29, 32, 37, 21:6, 7, 10, 12, 14, 16, 18, 22:4, 7, 9, 23:3, 5, 6(2), 12, 14, 16, 18(3), 19, 20, 24:2, 4, 6, 7, 8, 9, 12(3), 14(2), 18, 19, 20(2), 21, 22, 24(2), 25:2, 4, 7, 9, 15, 27, 26:4, 5, 16(2), 17, 18(2), 19, 20, 21, 27:2(2), 3, 6, 28:1, 3, 5, 6, 9(2), 10, 11, 13, 19(2), 21, 22, 24, 25, 29:2, 3, 5, 6(2), 8, 10, 11, 15(2), 16(3), 17(2), 18, 19, 20, 21, 25(2), 27, 30, 31(2), 32, 35, 30:1(2), 5, 6, 7, 8(2), 9(2), 12, 15, 17, 18, 19, 20, 21(2), 22(2), 31:2, 3, 4, 6, 8, 10(2), 11, 14, 16, 20, 32:8, 11, 16, 17, 21, 22, 23, 24, 26, 33:2(2), 4(2), 5, 6, 9, 10, 11, 12, 13, 15(2), 16(2), 17, 18, 22, 23, 34:2, 8, 10(2), 14(2), 15, 17, 21(3), 23, 24, 26(2), 27, 30(2), 31(2), 33(2), 35:1, 2, 3(2), 6, 12, 16(2), 26, 36:5, 7, 9, 10, 12(2), 13, 14, 15, 16, 18, 21, 22(2), 23(2);

Ezra 1:1(2), 2, 3, 5, 7, 2:68, 3:3, 5(2), 6(2), 8, 10(2), 11(3), 4:1, 3, 6:21, 22, 7:6(2), 10, 11, 27(2), 28, 8:28(2), 29, 35, 9:5, 8, 15, 10:11;

Neh. 1:5, 5:13, 8:1, 6(2), 9, 10, 14, 9:3(2), 4, 5, 6, 7, 10:29, 34, 35;

Job 1:6, 7(2), 8, 9, 12(2), 21(3), 2:1(2), 2(2), 3, 4, 6, 7, 12:9, 38:1, 40:1, 3, 6, 42:1, 7(2), 9(2), 10(2), 11, 12;

Pss. 1:2, 6, 2:2, 7, 11, 3:1, 3, 4, 5, 7, 8, 4:3(2), 5, 6, 8, 5:1, 3, 6, 8, 12, 6:1, 2(2), 3, 4, 8, 9(2), 7:1(2), 3, 6, 8(2), 17(2), 8:1, 9, 9:1, 7, 9, 10, 11, 13, 16, 19, 20, 10:1, 3, 12, 16, 17, 11:1, 4(2), 5, 7, 12:1, 3, 5, 6, 7, 13:1, 3, 6, 14:2, 4, 6, 7, 15:1, 4, 16:2, 5, 7, 8, 17:1, 13, 14, 18:1(4), 2, 3, 6, 13, 15, 18, 20, 21, 24, 28, 30, 31, 41, 46, 49, 19:7(2), 8(2), 9(2), 14, 20:1, 5, 6, 7, 9, 21:1, 7, 9, 13, 22:8, 19, 23, 26, 27, 28, 23:1, 6, 24:1, 3, 5, 8(2), 10, 25:1, 4, 6, 7, 8, 10, 11, 12, 14, 15, 26:1(2), 2, 6, 8, 12, 27:1(2), 4(3), 6, 7, 8, 10, 11, 13, 14(2), 28:1, 5, 6, 7, 8, 29:1(2), 2(2), 3(2), 4(2), 5(2), 7, 8(2), 9, 10(2), 11(2), 30:1, 2, 3, 4, 7, 8(2), 10(2), 12, 31:1, 5, 6, 9, 14, 17, 21, 23(2), 24, 32:2, 5, 10, 11, 33:1, 2, 4, 5, 6, 8, 10, 11, 12, 13, 18, 20, 22, 34:1, 2, 3, 4, 6, 7, 8, 9, 10, 11, 15, 16, 17, 18, 19, 22, 35:1, 5, 6, 9, 10, 22, 24, 27, 36:1, 5, 6, 37:3, 4, 5, 7, 9, 17, 18, 20, 23, 24, 28, 33, 34, 39, 40, 38:1, 15, 21, 39:4, 12, 40:1, 3, 4, 5, 9, 11, 13(2), 16, 41:1, 2, 3, 4, 10, 13, 42:8, 46:7, 8, 11, 47:2, 5, 48:1, 8, 50:1, 54:6, 55:16, 22, 56:10, 58:6, 59:3, 5, 8, 64:10, 68:16, 69:13, 16, 31, 33, 70:1, 5, 71:1, 72:18, 74:18, 75:8, 76:11, 78:4, 21, 79:5, 80:4, 19, 81:10, 15, 83:16, 18, 84:1, 2, 3, 8, 11(2), 12, 85:1, 7, 8, 12, 86:1, 6, 11, 17, 87:2, 6, 88:1, 9, 13, 14, 89:1, 5, 6(2), 8, 15, 18, 46, 51, 52, 90:13, 17, 91:2, 9, 92:1, 4, 5, 8, 9, 13, 15, 93:1(2), 3, 4, 5, 94:1, 3, 5, 11, 14, 17, 18, 22, 23, 95:1, 3, 6, 96:1(2), 2, 4, 5, 7(2), 8, 9, 10, 13, 97:1, 5, 8, 9, 10, 12, 98:1, 2, 4, 5, 6, 9, 99:1, 2, 5, 6, 8, 9(2), 100:1, 2, 3, 5, 101:1, 8, 102:1(2), 12, 15, 16, 19, 21, 22, 103:1, 2, 6, 8, 13, 17, 19, 20, 21, 22(2), 104:1(2), 16, 24, 31(2), 33, 34, 35, 105:1, 3, 4, 7, 19, 106:1, 2, 4, 16, 25, 34, 40, 47, 48, 107:1, 2, 6, 8, 13, 15, 19, 21, 24, 28, 31, 43, 108:3, 109:14, 15, 20, 26, 27, 30, 110:1, 2, 4, 111:1, 2, 4, 10, 112:1, 7, 113:1(2), 2, 3, 4, 5, 115:1, 9, 10, 11(2), 12, 13, 14, 15, 16, 116:1, 4(2), 5, 6, 7, 9, 12, 13, 14, 15, 16, 17, 18, 19, 117:1, 2, 118:1, 4, 6, 7, 8, 9, 10, 11, 12, 13, 15, 16(2), 20, 23, 24, 25(2), 26(2), 27, 29, 119:1, 12, 31, 33, 41, 52, 55, 57, 64, 65, 75, 89, 107, 108, 126, 137, 145, 149, 151, 156, 159, 166, 169, 174, 120:1, 2, 121:2, 5(2), 7, 8, 122:1, 4, 9, 123:2, 3, 124:1, 2, 6, 8, 125:1, 2, 4, 5, 126:1, 2, 3, 4, 127:1(2), 3, 128:1, 4, 5, 129:4, 8(2), 130:1, 5, 7(2), 131:1, 3, 132:1, 2, 5, 8, 11, 13, 133:3,

Part 4: The Names of God | **641**

134:1(3), 2, 3, 135:1(2), 2, 3, 5, 6, 13(2), 14, 19(2), 20(3), 21, 136:1, 137:4, 7, 138:4, 5(2), 6, 8(2), 139:1, 4, 21, 140:1, 4, 6(2), 8, 12, 141:1, 3, 142:1(2), 5, 143:1, 7, 9, 11, 144:1, 3, 5, 15, 145:3, 8, 9, 10, 14, 17, 18, 20, 21, 146:1, 2, 5, 7, 8(3), 9, 10, 147:2, 6, 7, 11, 12, 148:1, 5, 7, 13, 149:1, 4;

Prov. 1:7, 29, 2:5, 6, 3:5, 7, 9, 11, 12, 19, 26, 32, 33, 5:21, 6:16, 8:13, 22, 35, 9:10, 10:3, 22, 27, 29, 11:1, 20, 12:2, 22, 14:2, 26, 27, 15:3, 8, 9, 11, 16, 25, 26, 29, 33, 16:1, 2, 3, 4, 5, 6, 7, 9, 11, 20, 33, 17:3, 15, 18:10, 22, 19:3, 14, 17, 21, 23, 20:10, 12, 22, 23, 24, 27, 21:1, 2, 3, 30, 31, 22:2, 4, 12, 14, 19, 23, 23:17, 24:18, 21, 25:22, 28:5, 25, 29:13, 25, 26, 30:9, 31:30;

Isa. 1:2, 4, 9, 10, 11, 18, 20, 24, 28, 2:2, 3(2), 5, 10, 11, 12, 17, 19, 21, 3:1, 8, 13, 14, 16, 17, 4:2, 5, 5:7, 9, 12, 16, 24, 25, 6:3, 5, 12, 7:3, 10, 11, 12, 17, 18, 8:1, 3, 5, 11, 13, 17, 18(2), 9:7, 11, 13, 14, 19, 10:16², 20, 26, 33, 11:2(2), 3, 9, 15, 12:1, 2, 4, 5, 13:4, 5, 6, 9, 13, 14:1, 2, 3, 5, 22(2), 23, 24, 27, 32, 16:13, 14, 17:3, 6, 18:4, 7(2), 19:1, 4, 12, 14, 16, 17, 18, 19(2), 20(2), 21(3), 22(2), 25, 20:2, 3, 21:10, 17, 22:14, 17, 25(2), 23:9, 11, 17, 18(2), 24:1, 3, 14, 15(2), 21, 23, 25:1, 6, 8, 9, 10, 26:4(2), 8, 10, 11, 12, 13, 15, 16, 17, 21, 27:1, 3, 12, 13, 28:5, 13, 14, 21, 29, 29:6, 10, 15, 19, 22, 30:1, 9, 18(2), 26, 27, 29, 30, 31, 32, 33, 31:1, 3, 4(2), 5, 9, 32:6, 33:2, 5, 6, 10, 21, 22(3), 34:2, 6(2), 8, 16, 35:2, 10, 36:7, 10(2), 15(2), 18, 20, 37:1, 4(2), 6, 14(2), 15, 16, 17(2), 18, 20(2), 21, 22, 32, 33, 34, 36, 38:1, 2, 3, 4, 5, 7(2), 14, 20(2), 22, 39:5, 6, 8, 40:2, 3, 5(2), 7, 13, 27, 28, 31, 41:4, 13, 14, 16, 17, 20, 21, 42:5, 6, 8, 10, 12, 13, 19, 21, 24, 43:1, 3, 10, 11, 12, 14, 15, 16, 44:2, 5(2), 6(2), 23(2), 24(2), 45:1, 3, 5, 6, 7, 8, 11, 13, 14, 17, 18(2), 19, 21, 24, 25, 47:4, 48:1, 2, 14, 17(2), 20, 22, 49:1, 4, 5(2), 7(2), 8, 13, 14, 18, 23, 25, 26, 50:1, 10(2), 51:1, 3(2), 9, 11, 13, 15(2), 17, 20, 22, 52:3, 5(2), 8, 9, 10, 11, 12, 53:1, 6, 10(2), 54:1, 5, 6, 8, 10, 13, 17(2), 55:5, 6, 7, 8, 13, 56:1, 3(2), 4, 6(2), 57:19, 58:5, 8, 9, 11, 13, 14(2), 59:1, 13, 15, 19(2), 20, 21(2), 60:1, 2, 6, 9, 14, 16, 19, 20, 22, 61:1, 2, 3, 6, 8, 9, 10, 62:2, 3, 4, 6, 8, 9, 11, 12, 63:7(3), 14, 16, 17, 64:8, 9, 12, 65:7, 8, 11, 23, 25, 66:1, 2, 5(2), 6, 9, 12, 14, 15, 16(2), 17, 20(3), 21, 22, 23;

Jer. 1:2, 4, 7, 8, 9(2), 11, 12, 13, 14, 15, 19, 2:1, 2, 3(2), 4, 5, 6, 8, 9, 12, 17, 19, 29, 31, 37, 3:1, 6, 10, 11, 12(2), 13(2), 14, 16(2), 17(2), 20, 21, 22, 23, 25(2), 4:1, 2, 3, 4, 8, 9, 17, 26, 27, 5:2, 3, 4, 5, 9, 10, 11, 12, 14, 15, 18, 19, 22, 24, 29, 6:6, 9, 10, 11, 12, 15, 16, 21, 22, 30, 7:1, 2(3), 3, 4(3), 11, 13, 19, 21, 28, 29, 30, 32, 8:1, 3, 4, 7, 8, 9, 12, 13, 14(2), 17, 19, 9:3, 6, 7, 9, 12, 13, 15, 17, 20, 22, 23, 24(2), 25, 10:1, 2, 6, 10, 16, 18, 21, 23, 24, 11:1, 3, 5, 6, 9, 11, 16, 17, 18, 20, 21(2), 22, 12:1, 3, 12, 13, 14, 16, 17, 13:1, 2, 3, 5, 6, 8, 9, 11, 12, 13, 14, 15, 16, 17, 25, 14:1, 7, 9, 10(2), 11, 14, 15, 20, 22, 15:1, 2, 3, 6, 9, 11, 15, 16, 19, 20, 16:1, 3(2), 5, 9, 10(2), 11, 14(2), 15, 16, 19, 21, 17:5(2), 7(2), 10, 13(2), 14, 15, 19, 20, 21, 24, 26, 18:1, 5, 6, 11, 13, 19, 23, 19:1, 3(2), 6, 11, 12, 14(2), 15, 20:1, 2, 3, 4, 7, 8, 11, 12, 13(2), 16, 21:1, 2(2), 4, 7, 8, 10, 11, 12, 13, 14, 22:1, 2, 3, 5, 6, 8, 9, 11, 16, 18, 24, 29, 30, 23:1, 2(2), 4, 5, 7(2), 8, 9, 11, 12, 15, 16(2), 17, 18, 19, 20, 23, 24(2), 28, 29, 30, 31, 32(2), 33(2), 34, 35(2), 36(2), 37(2), 38(4), 24:1(2), 3, 4, 5, 7, 8, 25:3, 4, 5, 7, 8, 9, 12, 15, 17(2), 27, 28, 29, 30, 31(2), 32, 33, 36, 37, 26:1, 2(3), 4, 7, 8, 9(2), 10(2), 12, 13(2), 15, 16, 18, 19(3), 20, 27:1, 2, 4, 8, 11, 13, 15, 16(2), 18(3), 19, 21(2), 22, 28:1, 2, 3, 4, 5, 6(3), 9, 11, 12, 13, 14, 15, 16(2), 29:4, 7, 8, 9, 10, 11, 14(2), 15, 16,

17, 19(2), 20, 21, 22, 23, 25, 26(2), 30, 31, 32(3), 30:1, 2, 3(2), 4, 5, 8, 9, 10, 11, 12, 17, 18, 21, 23, 24, 31:1, 2, 3, 6, 7(2), 10, 11, 12, 14, 15, 16(2), 17, 18, 20, 22, 23(2), 27, 28, 31, 32, 33, 34(2), 35(2), 36, 37(2), 38(2), 40, 32:1, 3, 5, 6, 8(2), 14, 15, 16, 18, 26, 27, 28, 30, 36, 42, 44, 33:1, 2(3), 4, 10, 11(4), 12, 13, 14, 17, 19, 20, 23, 24, 25, 34:1, 2(2), 4(2), 5, 8, 12(2), 13, 17(2), 22, 35:1, 2, 4, 12, 13(2), 17, 18, 19, 36:1, 4, 5, 6(2), 7(2), 8(2), 9, 10(2), 11, 26, 27, 29, 30, 37:2, 3, 6, 7, 9, 17, 38:2, 3, 14, 16, 17, 20, 21, 39:15, 16, 17, 18, 40:1, 2, 3(2), 41:5, 42:2, 3, 4(2), 5(2), 6(2), 7, 9, 11, 13, 15(2), 18, 19, 20(3), 21, 43:1(2), 2, 4, 7, 8, 10, 44:2, 7, 11, 16, 21, 22, 23(2), 24, 25, 26(2), 29, 30, 45:2, 3, 4, 5, 46:1, 5, 13, 15, 18, 23, 25, 26, 28, 47:1, 2, 4, 6, 7, 48:1, 8, 10, 12, 15, 25, 26, 30, 35, 38, 40, 42, 43, 44, 47, 49:1, 2(2), 6, 7, 12, 13, 14, 16, 18, 20, 26, 28, 30, 31, 32, 34, 35, 37, 38, 39, 50:1, 4(2), 5, 7(2), 10, 13, 14, 15, 18, 20, 21, 24, 25, 28, 29, 30, 33, 34, 35, 40, 45, 51:1, 5, 6, 7, 10(2), 11(2), 12, 14, 19, 24, 25, 26, 29, 33, 36, 39, 45, 48, 50, 51, 52, 53, 55, 56, 57, 58, 62, 52:2, 3, 13, 17(2), 20;

Lam. 1:5, 9, 11, 12, 17, 18, 20, 2:6, 7, 8, 9, 17, 20, 22, 3:18, 22, 24, 25, 26, 40, 50, 55, 59, 61, 64, 66, 4:11, 16, 20, 5:1, 19, 21;

Ezek. 1:3(2), 28, 3:12, 14, 16, 22, 23, 4:13, 5:13, 15, 17, 6:1, 7, 10, 13, 14, 7:1, 4, 9, 19, 27, 8:12(2), 14, 16(3), 9:4, 9(2), 10:4(2), 18, 19, 11:1, 5(2), 10, 12, 14, 15, 23, 25, 12:1, 8, 15, 16, 17, 20, 21, 25, 26, 13:1, 2, 5, 6(2), 7, 14, 21, 23, 14:2, 4, 7, 8, 9, 12, 15:1, 7, 16:1, 35, 58, 62, 17:1, 11, 21, 24(2), 18:1, 20:1, 2, 5, 7, 12, 19, 20, 26, 38, 42, 44, 45, 47, 48, 21:1, 3, 5, 8, 9, 17, 18, 32, 22:1, 14, 16, 17, 22, 23, 28, 23:1, 36, 24:1, 14, 15, 20, 27, 25:1, 5, 7, 11, 17, 26:1, 6, 14, 27:1, 28:1, 11, 20, 22, 23, 26, 29:1, 6, 9, 17, 21, 30:1, 3, 6, 8, 12, 19, 20, 25, 26, 31:1, 32:1, 15, 17, 33:1, 22, 23, 29, 30, 34:1, 7, 9, 24(2), 27, 30, 35:1, 4, 9, 10, 12, 15, 36:1, 11, 16, 20, 23, 36(2), 38, 37:1(2), 4, 6, 13, 14(2), 15, 28, 38:1, 23, 39:6, 7, 22, 28, 40:1, 46, 41:22, 42:13, 43:4, 5, 24(2), 44:2(2), 3, 4(2), 5(2), 45:1, 4, 23, 46:3, 4, 9, 12, 13, 14, 48:9, 10, 14;

Dan. 9:2, 4, 10, 13, 14(2), 20;

Hos. 1:1, 2(3), 4, 7, 2:13, 16, 20, 21, 3:1(2), 5(2), 4:1(2), 10, 15, 16, 5:4, 6, 7, 6:1, 3, 7:10, 8:1, 13, 9:3, 4(2), 5, 14, 10:3, 12, 11:10, 11, 12:2, 5(2), 9, 13, 13:4, 15, 14:1, 2, 9;

Joel 1:1, 9(2), 14(2), 15, 19, 2:1, 11(2), 12, 13, 14, 17(2), 18, 19, 21, 23, 26, 27, 31, 32(3), 3:8, 11, 14, 16(2), 17, 18, 21;

Amos 1:2, 3, 5, 6, 9, 11, 13, 15, 2:1, 3, 4(2), 6, 11, 16, 3:1, 6, 10, 12, 15, 4:3, 6, 8, 9, 10, 11, 13, 5:4, 6, 8, 14, 15, 16, 17, 18(2), 20, 27, 6:8, 10, 11, 14, 7:3(2), 6, 8, 15(2), 16, 17, 8:2, 7, 11, 12, 9:6, 7, 8, 12, 13, 15;

Obad. 1:1, 4, 8, 15, 18, 21;

Jonah 1:1, 3(2), 4, 9, 10, 14(3), 16(2), 17, 2:1, 2, 6, 7, 9, 10, 3:1, 3, 4:2(2), 3, 4, 6, 10;

Micah 1:1, 3, 12, 2:3, 5, 7, 13, 3:4, 5, 8, 11(2), 4:1, 2(2), 4, 5, 6, 7, 10, 12, 13, 5:4(2), 7, 10, 6:1, 2(2), 5, 6, 7, 8, 9, 7:7, 8, 9, 10, 17;

Nah. 1:2(3), 3(2), 7, 9, 11, 12, 14, 2:2, 13, 3:5;

Hab. 1:2, 12(2), 2:2, 13, 14, 16, 20, 3:2(2), 8, 18;

Zeph. 1:1, 2, 3, 5, 6(2), 7(2), 8, 10, 12, 14(2), 17, 18, 2:2(2), 3(2), 5, 7, 9, 10, 11, 3:2, 5, 8, 9, 12, 15(2), 17, 20;

Hag. 1:1, 2(2), 3, 5, 7, 8, 9, 12(3), 13(3), 14(2), 2:1, 4(3), 6, 7, 8, 9(2), 10, 11, 14, 15, 17, 18, 20, 23(3);

Zech. 1:1, 2, 3(3), 4(2), 6, 7, 10, 11, 12(2), 13, 14, 16(2), 17(2), 20, 2:5, 6(2), 8, 9, 10, 11(2), 12, 13, 3:1, 2(3), 5, 6, 7, 9, 10, 4:6(2), 8, 9, 10, 5:4, 6:9, 12(2), 13, 14, 15(3), 7:1, 2, 3, 4, 7, 8, 9, 12(2), 13, 8:1, 2, 3(2), 4, 6(2), 7, 9(2), 11, 14(2), 17, 18, 19, 20, 21(2), 22(2), 23, 9:1(2), 14, 15, 16, 10:1(2), 3, 5, 6, 7, 12(2), 11:4, 5, 6, 11, 13(2), 15, 12:1(2), 4, 5, 7, 8(2), 13:2, 3, 7, 8, 9, 14:1, 3, 5, 7, 9(2), 12, 13, 16, 17, 18, 20(2), 21(2);

Mal. 1:1, 2(2), 4(2), 5, 6, 7, 8, 9, 10, 11, 12, 13(2), 14, 2:2, 4, 7, 8, 11, 12(2), 13, 14, 16(2), 17(2), 3:1, 3, 4, 5, 6, 7, 10, 11, 12, 13, 14, 16(3), 17, 4:1, 3, 5.

Notes:

1. Hebrew pointing: The Hebrew Old Testament (British and Foreign Bible Society) points *yhvh* as: יְהֹוָה (yᵉhôah or yᵉhovah). Strong's dictionary points it יְהֹוָה (yᵉhovah). The online Hebrew Old Testament (WTT) in *Bible Works* software points it as יְהוָה (yᵉhvah), completely leaving out any form of the "o" vowel. These differences could engender confusion. I use the transliteration, "yᵉhovah," since it most closely mirrors the English, "Jehovah," and comports well the pointing in the Hebrew OT and in Strong's dictionary.

2. Variant: Isa. 10:16: "Therefore shall the Lord ['adôn], the *Lord* [variant] of hosts, send among his fat ones leanness; and under his glory he shall kindle a burning like the burning of a fire." The variant for "*Lord*" is as follows: the text reads, *'adonay* and the margin reads, *yᵉhovah*.

APPENDIX 5: USE AND LXX RENDERING OF GOD'S NAME: *yhvh ts^{e}ba'ôth*

yhvh ts^{e}ba'ôth: "Jehovah of hosts": occurs these **265** times in the Old Testament, with one variant (Isa. 10:16): 1 Sam. 1:3, 11, 4:4, 15:2, 17:45; 2 Sam. 6:2, 18, 7:8, 26, 27; 1 Kings 18:15, 19:10, 14; 2 Kings 3:14; 1 Chron. 11:9, 17:7, 24; Pss. 24:10, 46:7, 11, 48:8, 69:6, 80:4, 7, 14, 19, 84:1, 3, 12; Isa. 1:9, 24, 2:12, 3:1, 15, 5:7, 9, 16, 24, 6:3, 5, 8:13, 18, 9:7, 13, 19, 10:16, 23 [yehovih], 24 [yehovih], 26, 33, 13:4, 13, 14:22, 23, 24, 27, 17:3, 18:7(2), 19:4, 12, 16, 17, 18, 20, 25, 21:10, 22:5 [yehovih], 12 [yehovih], 14(2), 15 [yehovih], 25, 23:9, 24:23, 25:6, 28:5, 22 [yehovih], 29, 29:6, 31:4, 5, 37:16, 32, 39:5, 44:6, 45:13, 47:4, 48:2, 51:15, 54:5; Jer. 2:19 [yehovih], 6:6, 9, 7:3, 21, 8:3, 9:7, 15, 17, 10:16, 11:17, 20, 22, 15:16, 16:9, 19:3, 11, 15, 20:12, 23:15, 16, 36, 25:8, 27, 28, 29, 32, 26:18, 27:4, 18, 19, 21, 28:2, 14, 29:4, 8, 17, 21, 25, 30:8, 31:23, 35, 32:14, 15, 18, 33:11, 12, 35:13, 18, 19, 39:16, 42:15, 18, 43:10, 44:2, 11, 25, 46:10(2) [yehovih], 18, 25, 48:1, 15, 49:5 [yehovih], 7, 26, 35, 50:18, 25 [yehovih], 31 [yehovih], 33, 34, 51:5, 14, 19, 33, 57, 58; Micah 4:4; Nah. 2:13, 3:5; Hab. 2:13; Zeph. 2:9, 10; Hag. 1:2, 5, 7, 9, 14, 2:4, 6, 7, 8, 9(2), 11, 23(2); Zech. 1:3(3), 4, 6, 12, 14, 16, 17, 2:8, 9, 11, 3:7, 9, 10, 4:6, 9, 5:4, 6:12, 15, 7:3, 4, 9, 12(2), 13, 8:1, 2, 3, 4, 6(2), 7, 9(2), 11, 14(2), 18, 19, 20, 21, 22, 23, 9:15, 10:3, 12:5, 13:2, 7, 14:16, 17, 21(2); Mal. 1:4, 6, 8, 9, 10, 11, 13, 14, 2:2, 4, 7, 8, 12, 16, 3:1, 5, 7, 10, 11, 12, 14, 17, 4:1, 3.

y^{e}hovah 'elohēy ts^{e}ba'ôth: "Jehovah God of hosts": occurs these 19 times: 2 Sam. 5:10; Pss. 59:5, 84:8, 89:8; Jer. 5:14, 15:16, 35:17, 38:17, 44:7; Hos. 12:5; Amos 3:13, 4:13, 5:14, 15, 16, 27, 6:8, 14, 9:5.

LXX RENDERINGS:
yhvh ts^{e}ba'ôth and *yhvh 'elohēy ts^{e}ba'ôth*

LXX RENDERING: *yhvh ts^{e}ba'ôth*

1. *transliteration of ts^{e}ba'ôth*:

κυριος σαβαωθ: *kurios sabaoth*: "Jehovah sabaoth": 1 Sam. 15:2, 17:45; Isa. 1:9, 24, 2:12, 3:1, 5:7, 9, 16, 24, 6:3, 5, 8:18, 9:7, 10:16, 24, 33, 13:4, 13, 14:22, 24, 17:3, 18:7(2), 19:4, 12, 16, 25, 21:10, 22:5, 12, 14, 15, 25, 23:9, 25:6, 28:5, 22, 29, 29:6, 31:4, 37:16, 32, 39:5, 45:13, 47:4, 48:2, 51:15, 54:5; Jer. 46:10;

κυριος θεος σαβαωθ: *kurios theos sabaoth*: "Jehovah God sabaoth": 1 Sam. 1:3

κυριος ελωαι σαβαωθ: *kurios eloai sabaoth*: "Jehovah my God sabaoth": 1 Sam. 1:11: LXX transliterates Hebrew for "my God," even though no Hebrew equivalent, אֱלֹהַי ('elohay) [Greek transliteration, eloai] appears in the Masoretic Hebrew text;

θεος σαβαωθ: *theos sabaoth*: "GOD sabaoth": Isa. 44:6.

2. κυριος παντοκρατωρ: *kurios pantokrator*: "Jehovah almighty": 2 Sam. 7:8, 27; 1 Kings 19:10, 14; 1 Chron. 11:9, 17:7, 24; Jer. 23:16, 25:27, 31:35, 32:14, 33:11, 50:34, 51:5, 57; Micah 4:4; Nah. 2:13; Hab. 2:13; Zeph. 2:10; Hag. 1:2, 5, 7, 9, 14, 2:4, 6, 7, 8, 9(2), 11, 23(2); Zech. 1:3, 4, 6, 12, 14, 16, 17, 2:8, 9, 11, 3:7, 9, 10, 4:6, 9, 5:4, 6:12, 15, 7:3, 9, 12(2), 13, 8:1, 2, 3, 4, 6(2), 7, 9(2), 11, 14(2), 18, 19, 20, 21, 22, 23, 9:15, 12:5, 13:7, 14:16, 17, 21(2); Mal. 1:4, 6, 8, 9, 10, 11, 13, 14, 2:2, 4, 7, 8, 12, 16, 3:1, 5, 7, 10, 11, 12, 14, 17, 4:1, 3;

kurios ho theos ho pantokrator: "Jehovah God almighty": Nah. 3:5; Zech. 10:3.

3. κυριος των δυναμεων: *kurios ton dunameon*: "Jehovah of the powers": 2 Sam. 6:2, 18; 1 Kings 18:15; 2 Kings 3:14; Pss. 24:10, 46:7, 11, 48:8, 69:6, 80:4, 7, 14, 19, 84:1, 3, 12; Jer. 33:12; Zeph. 2:9; Zech. 7:4.

4. no rendering of *ts^{e}ba'ôth*

κυριος: *kurios*: "Jehovah": with no rendering of *ts^{e}ba'ôth*: 1 Sam. 4:4; Isa. 8:13, 9:13, 19, 19:17, 18, 20, 24:23, 31:5; Jer. 6:6, 9, 7:3, 21, 9:7, 15, 17, 10:16, 11:17, 20, 16:9, 19:3, 11,

15, 20:12, 23:15, 25:8, 28, 32, 26:18, 27:4, 19, 28:2, 14, 29:4, 8, 21, 30:8, 31:23, 32:15, 35:13, 18, 39:16, 42:15, 18, 43:10, 44:2, 11, 25, 46:10, 48:1, 49:5, 7, 26, 35, 50:18, 31, 33, 51:14, 19, 33, 58; Zech. 1:3, 13:2; LXX also uses kurios for *'adonay yehovih ts^{e}ba'ôth*: Jer. 50:31; θεος: *theos*: "GOD": with no rendering of *ts^{e}ba'ôth*: Isa. 10:23, 26.

ho kurios theos: "the Lord GOD": LXX uses sometimes uses this for: *'adonay yehovih ts^{e}ba'ôth*: Jer. 50:25.

5. paraphrases, possibly with variant Hebrew original: for example: in Isa. 14:27: *ho theos ho hagios*, "the holy God"; and in Jer. 46:18 [26:18 LXX]: *kurios ho theos*: "Jehovah God."

6. complete omission: for example: Jer. 46:25 [26:25 LXX], 48:15 [31:15 LXX].

LXX RENDERING: *y^{e}hovah 'elohēy ts^{e}ba'ôth*

1. kurios ho theos ton dunameon: " Jehovah God of the powers": Pss. 59:5, 84:8, 89:8; *2. kurios ho theos ho pantokrator*: Jehovah God the almighty": Hos. 12:5; Amos 3:13, 4:13, 5:14, 15, 16, 27, 9:5; *3. kurios pantokrator*: "Jehovah almighty": 2 Sam. 5:10; Jer. 5:14, 15:16, 44:7; *4. kurios*: "Jehovah": Jer. 35:17, 38:17; *5.* complete omission: Amos 6:8, 14.

Note the following patterns: (1) in Psalms: LXX exclusively uses *kurios ton dunameon*; (2) in Isaiah: when LXX renders *ts^{e}ba'ôth*, it almost always uses, *kurios sabaoth*, with a couple of noteworthy exceptions (Isa. 14:27, 44:6); (3) in Jeremiah: LXX most often simply uses *kurios* with no rendering of *ts^{e}ba'ôth*; when it renders *ts^{e}ba'ôth*, it most often uses *pantokrator*; and when it renders *ts^{e}ba'ôth* in "y^{e}hovah God of hosts," it uses *kurios pantokrator*; (4) in Haggai: LXX only uses *kurios pantokrator*; (5) in Zechariah: when LXX renders *ts^{e}ba'ôth*, it renders it with *pantokrator*, with one exception, Zech. 7:4, where it uses *ton dunameon*; (6) in Malachi, LXX always renders *ts^{e}ba'ôth* with *pantokrator*; (7) in the minor prophets: LXX never transliterates *ts^{e}ba'ôth* as *sabaoth*. It always either translates it with *pantokrator* or *ton dunameon* or omits it.

APPENDIX 6: USE AND RELATIVE FREQUENCY OF GOD'S NAME:
Theos

θεος (theos): "God": also translated in KJV as, "Godward," "godly," "gods," "exceeding": Occurs 1,343 times in BYZ text: some variants exist: used generically, "exceeding," once: Acts 7:20[1]: depicts a god or gods these 13 times: John 10:34, 35; Acts 7:40, 43, 12:22 14:11, 19:26, 28:6; 1 Cor. 8:5(2); 2 Cor. 4:4; Gal. 4:8; Phil. 3:19[2]: depicts the Supreme Being these 1,329 times in the BYZ text: Of these twice translated, "Godward" (2 Cor. 3:4; 1 Thess. 1:8)[3]; and seven times translated, "godly" (2 Cor. 1:12, 7:9, 10, 11, 11:2; 1 Tim. 1:4; 3 John 6)[4]: I include these 9 references since they denote the Supreme Being: Matt. 1:23, 3:9, 16, 4:3, 4, 6, 7, 10, 5:8, 9, 34, 6:24, 30, 33, 8:29, 9:8, 12:4, 28(2), 14:33, 15:3, 4, 6, 31, 16:16, 23, 19:6, 17, 24, 26, 21:12, 31, 43, 22:16, 21(2), 29, 30, 31, 32(5), 37, 23:22, 26:61, 63(2), 27:40, 43(2), 46(2), 54; Mark 1:1, 14, 15, 24, 2:7, 12, 26, 3:11, 35, 4:11, 26, 30, 5:7(2), 7:8, 9, 13, 8:33, 9:1, 47, 10:6, 9, 14, 15, 18, 23, 24, 25, 27(2), 11:22, 12:14, 17(2), 24, 26(4), 27(2), 29, 30, 32, 34, 13:19, 14:25, 15:34(2), 39, 43, 16:19; Luke 1:6, 8, 16, 19, 26, 30, 32, 35, 37, 47, 64, 68, 78, 2:13, 14, 20, 28, 40, 52, 3:2, 6, 8, 38, 4:3, 4, 8, 9, 12, 34, 41, 43, 5:1, 21, 25, 26, 6:4, 12, 20, 7:16(2), 28, 29, 30, 8:1, 10, 11, 21, 28, 39, 9:2, 11, 20, 27, 43, 60, 62, 10:9, 11, 27, 11:20(2), 28, 42, 49, 12:6, 8, 9, 20, 21, 24, 28, 31, 13:13, 18, 20, 28, 29, 14:15, 15:10, 16:13, 15(2), 16, 17:15, 18, 20(2), 21, 18:2, 4, 7, 11, 13, 16, 17, 19, 24, 25, 27, 29, 43(2), 19:11, 37, 20:21, 25(2), 36, 37(3), 38, 21:4, 31, 22:16, 18, 69, 70, 23:35, 40, 47, 51, 24:19, 53; John 1:1(2), 2, 6, 12, 13, 18, 29, 34, 36, 49, 51, 3:2(2), 3, 5, 16, 17, 18, 21, 33, 34(3), 36, 4:10, 24, 5:18, 25, 42, 44, 6:27, 28, 29, 33, 45, 46, 69, 7:17, 8:40, 41, 42(2), 47(3), 54, 9:3, 16, 24, 29, 31(2), 33, 35, 10:33, 35, 36, 11:4(2), 22(2), 27, 40, 52, 12:43, 13:3(2), 31, 32(2), 14:1, 16:2, 27, 30, 17:3, 19:7, 20:17(2), 28, 31, 21:19; Acts 1:3, 2:11, 17, 22(2), 23, 24, 30, 32, 33, 36, 39, 47, 3:8, 9, 13(2), 15, 18, 21, 22, 25, 26, 4:10, 19(2), 21, 24(2), 31, 5:4, 29, 30, 31, 32, 39, 6:2, 7, 11, 7:2, 6, 7, 9, 17, 25, 32(4), 35, 37, 42, 45, 46(2), 55(2), 56, 8:10, 12, 14, 20, 21, 22, 37, 9:20, 10:2, 3, 4, 15, 22(2), 28, 31, 33(2), 34, 38(2), 40, 41, 42, 46, 11:1, 9, 17(2), 18(2), 23, 12:5, 23, 24, 13:5, 7, 16, 17, 21, 23, 26, 30, 33, 36, 37, 43, 44, 46, 14:15, 22, 26, 27, 15:4, 7, 8, 10, 12, 14, 18, 19, 40, 16:14, 17, 25, 34, 17:13, 23, 24, 29, 30, 18:7, 11, 13, 21, 26, 19:8, 11, 20:21, 24, 25, 27, 28, 32, 21:19, 22:3, 14, 23:1, 3, 4, 24:14, 15, 16, 26:6, 8, 18, 20, 22, 29, 27:23, 24, 25, 35, 28:15, 23, 28, 31; Rom. 1:1, 4, 7(2), 8, 9, 10, 16, 17, 18, 19(2), 21(2), 23, 24, 25, 26, 28(2), 32, 2:2, 3, 4, 5, 11, 13, 16, 17, 23, 24, 29, 3:2, 3, 4, 5(2), 6, 7, 11, 18, 19, 21, 22, 23, 25(2), 29, 30, 4:2, 3, 6, 17, 20(2), 5:1, 2, 5, 8, 10, 11, 15, 6:10, 11, 13(2), 17, 22, 23, 7:4, 22, 25(2), 8:3, 7(2), 8, 9, 14(2), 16, 17, 19, 21, 27, 28, 31, 33(2), 34, 39, 9:5, 6, 8, 11, 14, 16, 20, 22, 26, 10:1, 2, 3(2), 9, 17, 11:1, 2(2), 8, 21, 22, 23, 29, 30, 32, 33, 12:1(2), 2, 3, 13:1(2), 2, 4(2), 6, 14:3, 4, 6(2), 11, 12, 17, 18, 20, 22, 15:5, 6, 7, 8, 9, 13, 15, 16, 17, 19, 30, 32, 33, 16:20, 26, 27; 1 Cor. 1:1, 2, 3, 4(2), 9, 14, 18, 20, 21(3), 24(2), 25(2), 27(2), 28, 30, 2:1, 5, 7(2), 9, 10(2), 11(2), 12(2), 14, 3:6, 7, 9(3), 10, 16(2), 17(3), 19, 23, 4:1, 5, 9, 20, 5:13, 6:9, 10, 11, 13, 14, 19, 20(2), 7:7, 15, 17, 19, 24, 40, 8:3, 4, 6, 8, 9:9, 21, 10:5, 13, 20, 31, 32, 11:3, 7, 12, 13, 16, 22, 12:3, 6, 18, 24, 28, 14:2, 18, 25(2), 28, 33, 36, 15:9, 10(2), 15(2), 24, 28, 34, 38, 50, 57; 2 Cor. 1:1(2), 2, 3(2), 4, 9, 12(2), 18, 19, 20(2), 21, 23, 2:14, 15, 17(3), 3:3, 4, 5, 4:2(2), 4, 6(2), 7, 15, 5:1, 5,

11, 13, 18, 19, 20(2), 21, 6:1, 4, 7, 16(4), 7:1, 6, 9, 10, 11, 12, 8:1, 5, 16, 9:7, 8, 11, 12, 13, 14, 15, 10:4, 5, 13, 11:2, 7, 11, 31, 12:2, 3, 19, 21, 13:4(2), 7, 11, 14; Gal. 1:1, 3, 4, 10, 13, 15, 20, 24, 2:6, 19, 20, 21, 3:6, 8, 11, 17, 18, 20, 21, 26, 4:4, 6, 7, 8, 9(2), 14, 5:21, 6:7, 16; Eph. 1:1, 2, 3, 17, 2:4, 8, 10, 16, 19, 22, 3:2, 7, 9, 10, 19, 4:6, 13, 18, 24, 30, 32, 5:1, 2, 5, 6, 20, 21, 6:6, 11, 13, 17, 23; Phil. 1:2, 3, 8, 11, 28, 2:6(2), 9, 11, 13, 15, 27, 3:3, 9, 14, 15, , 4:6, 7, 9, 18, 19, 20; Col. 1:1, 2, 3, 6, 10, 15, 25(2), 27, 2:2, 12, 19, 3:1, 3, 6, 12, 15, 17, 22, 4:3, 11, 12; 1 Thess. 1:1(2), 2, 3, 4, 8, 9(2), 2:2(2), 4(2), 5, 8, 9, 10, 12, 13(3), 14, 15, 3:2, 9(2), 11, 13, 4:1, 3, 5, 7, 8, 14, 16, 5:9, 18, 23; 2 Thess. 1:1, 2, 3, 4, 5(2), 6, 8, 11, 12, 2:4(4), 11, 13(2), 6, 3:5; 1 Tim. 1:1, 2, 4, 11, 17, 2:3, 5(2), 3:5, 15(2), 16, 4:3, 4, 5, 10, 5:4, 5, 21, 6:1, 11, 13, 17; 2 Tim. 1:1, 2, 3, 6, 7, 8, 2:9, 15, 19, 25, 3:17, 4:1; Tit. 1:1(2), 2, 3, 4, 7, 16, 2:5, 10, 11, 13, 3:4, 8; Philem. 3, 4; Heb. 1:1, 6, 8, 9(2), 2:4, 9, 13, 17, 3:4, 12, 4:4, 9, 10, 12, 14, 5:1, 4, 10, 12, 6:1, 3, 5, 6, 7, 10, 13, 17, 18, 7:1, 3, 19, 25, 8:10, 9:14(2), 20, 24, 10:7, 9, 12, 21, 29, 31, 36, 11:3, 4(2), 5(2), 6, 10, 16(2), 19, 25, 40, 12:2, 7, 15, 22, 23, 28, 29, 13:4, 7, 15, 16, 20; Jas. 1:1, 5, 13(2), 20, 27, 2:5, 19, 23(2), 3:9(2), 4:4(2), 6, 7, 8; 1 Pet. 1:2, 3, 5, 21(2), 23, 2:4, 5, 10, 12, 15, 16, 17, 19, 20, 3:4, 5, 15, 17, 18, 20, 21, 22, 4:2, 6, 10, 11(3), 14, 16, 17(2), 19, 5:2, 5, 6, 10, 12; 2 Pet. 1:1, 2, 17, 21, 2:4, 3:5, 12; 1 John 1:5, 2:5, 14, 17, 3:1, 2, 8, 9(2), 10(2), 17, 20, 21, 4:1, 2(2), 3, 4, 6(3), 7(3), 8(2), 9(2), 10, 11, 12(2), 15(3), 16(4), 20(2), 21, 5:1, 2(2), 3, 4, 5, 9(2), 10(3), 11, 12, 13(2), 18(2), 19, 20(2); 2 John 3, 9; 3 John 6, 11(2); Jude 1, 4(2), 21, 25; Rev. 1:1, 2, 6, 9, 2:7, 18, 3:1, 2, 12(4), 14, 4:5, 8, 5:6, 9, 10, 6:9, 7:2, 3, 10, 11, 12, 15, 17, 8:2, 4, 9:4, 13, 10:7, 11:1, 4, 11, 13, 16(2), 17, 19, 12:5, 6, 10(2), 17, 13:6, 14:4, 5, 7, 10, 12, 19, 15:1, 2, 3(2), 7, 8, 16:1, 7, 9, 11, 14, 19, 21, 17:17(2), 18:5, 8, 20, 19:1, 4, 5, 6, 9, 10, 13, 15, 17, 20:4, 6, 9, 12, 21:2, 3(3), 4, 7, 10, 11, 22, 23, 22:1, 3, 5, 6, 9, 18, 19.

Notes:

1. Acts 7:20: "In which time Moses was born, and was *exceeding* [theos] fair, and nourished up in his father's house three months": This generic use of *theos* could be a Hebraism that reflects the general use of *'elohîm* to denote what is great or superlative: "and was *superlatively* fair."

2. Phil. 3:19: "Whose end *is* destruction, whose *god* [theos] *is their* belly, and *whose* glory *is* in their shame, who mind earthly things." KJV translates this: "whose *God* is their belly." In the context Paul seems to be saying that they have made their belly a false god. Accordingly, ASV translates this phrase, "whose *god* is their belly." Therefore, I have included this verse with the references to "god," and have not used it to calculate the relative frequency of *theos* to depict the Supreme Being.

3. "Godward": In two texts, 2 Cor. 3:4; 1 Thess. 1:8, KJV translates *theos* as "Godward." In both texts the idiom is, *pros ton theon*, "to God." Therefore, I include these texts as references to the Supreme Being.

4. "godly": In seven texts, 2 Cor. 1:12, 7:9, 10, 11, 11:2; 1 Tim. 1:4; 3 John 6, KJV translates *theos* as "godly": These all denote the Supreme Being with various idioms as follows:

> *1. 2 Cor. 1:12*: "For our rejoicing is this, the testimony of our conscience, that in simplicity and *godly* sincerity": the idiom is: εἰλικρινεια του θεου (eilikrineia tou theou): literally: "sincerity of the God."
>
> *2. 2 Cor. 7:9*: "Now I rejoice, not that you were made sorry, but that you sorrowed to repentance: for you were made sorry after a *godly* manner": the idiom is: ἐλυπηθητε γαρ κατα θεον (elupethete gar kata theon): literally: "for you were made sorry according to God."
>
> *3. 2 Cor. 7:10*: "For *godly* sorrow works repentance": the idiom is: ἡ γαρ κατα θεον λυπη (he gar kata theon lupe): literally: "for the according to God sorrow."
>
> *4. 2 Cor. 7:11*: "For behold this selfsame thing, that you sorrowed after a *godly* sort": the idiom is: το κατα θεον λυπηθηναι (to kata theon lupethenai): literally, "the according to God to be made sorry."
>
> *5. 2 Cor. 11:2*: "For I am jealous over you with *godly* jealousy": the idiom is: ζηλω γαρ ὑμας θεου ζηλω (zelo gar humas theou zelo): literally: "for I am jealous of you with of God jealousy."
>
> *6. 1 Tim. 1:4*: "Neither give heed to fables and endless genealogies, which minister questions, rather than *godly* edifying which is in faith": the idiom is: μαλλον ἡ οἰκονομιαν θεου (mallon he oikonomian theou): literally: "rather than edifying of God."
>
> *7. 3 John 6*: "Which have borne witness of your love before the church: whom if you bring forward on their journey after a *godly* sort, you shall do well": the idiom is: ἀξιως του θεου (axios tou theou): literally, "worthily of the God."

Relative Frequency of *Theos* to Depict the Supreme Being
(Uses per 1000 words in the Majority Greek Text)

Scripture	Uses	Words	Rel. Freq.
New Testament	1,329	140,221	9.48
Gospels	*313*	*66,190*	*4.73*
Matthew	55	18,753	2.93
Mark	52	11,627	4.73
Luke	124	19,886	6.24
John	82	15,924	5.15
Acts	165	18,672	8.84
Paul's Letters	*547*	*43,487*	*12.58*
Romans	153	7,208	21.23
1 Corinthians	104	6,926	15.02
2 Corinthians	78	4,507	17.31
Galatians	30	2,252	13.32
Ephesians	32	2,454	13.04
Philippians	22	1,641	14.02
Colossians	22	1,608	13.68
1 Thessalonians	37	1,497	24.72
2 Thessalonians	19	834	22.78
1 Timothy	23	1,618	14.22
2 Timothy	12	1,250	9.60
Titus	13	665	19.55
Philemon	2	340	5.88
Hebrews	69	4,989	13.83
James	17	1,761	9.65
1 Peter	39	1,716	22.73
2 Peter	7	1,102	6.35
1 John	63	2,155	29.23
2 John	2	249	8.03
3 John	3	216	13.89
Jude	5	450	11.11
Revelation	99	9,921	9.98

APPENDIX 7: USE OF GOD'S NAME: kurios

κυριος (kurios): "Lord": translated in KJV, "LORD," "God," "Lord," "lord," "master," "sir," "owner": occurs these 767 times[1] with over 60 variants[2]:

1. *Denotes a human being or angel as ruler or dignitary with various nuances*: a civil ruler (Acts 25:26), a master of a household and of servants (Eph. 6:5), an owner of property (Luke 19:33), a direct address of respect and deference to a man (John 12:21) or to an angel (Acts 10:4; Rev. 7:14): reflects the primary use of the Hebrew, '*adôn*: translated, "lord," "master," "owner", "sir": these 79 times: Matt. 6:24, 10:24, 25, 13:27, 15:27, 18:25, 26[4], 27, 31, 32, 34, 20:8, 21:30, 40, 24:45, 46, 48, 50, 25:11(2), 18, 19, 20, 21(2), 22, 23(2), 24, 26, 27:63; Mark 12:9, 13:35; Luke 12:36, 37, 42, 43, 45, 46, 47, 13:8, 25(2)[14], 14:21, 22, 23, 16:3, 5(2), 8, 13, 19:16, 18, 20, 25, 33, 20:13, 15; John 12:21, 13:16, 15:15, 20, 20:15; Acts 10:4, 16:16, 19, 30, 25:26; Rom. 14:4; 1 Cor. 8:5; Gal. 4:1; Eph. 6:5, 9; Col. 3:22, 4:1; 1 Pet. 3:6; Rev. 7:14, 17:14, 19:16:

2. *Denotes God as the Supreme Ruler, and as y^{e}hovah, with various nuances*: reflects both the primary use of the Hebrew, '*adonay*, and God's proper name, *y^{e}hovah*: translated, "Lord," "LORD" (Matt. 22:44; Mark 12:36; Luke 20:42), "God" (Acts 19:20): these 321 times: Matt. 1:20, 22, 24, 2:13, 15, 19, 3:3, 4:7, 10, 5:33, 9:38, 11:25, 21:3, 9, 42, 22:37, 44, 23:39, 27:10, 28:2; Mark 1:3, 5:19, 11:3, 9, 10[7], 12:11, 29(2), 30, 36, 13:20, 16:20; Luke 1:6, 9, 11, 15, 16, 17, 25, 28, 32, 38, 45, 46, 58, 66, 68, 76, 2:9(2), 15, 22, 23(2), 24, 26, 38[8], 39, 3:4, 4:8, 12, 18, 19, 5:17, 10:2, 21, 27, 13:35, 19:31, 34, 38, 20:37, 42; John 1:23, 12:13, 38(2); Acts 1:24, 2:20, 21, 25, 34, 39, 47, 3:19[18], 22, 4:26, 29, 5:9, 14, 19, 7:30[19], 31, 33, 37[20], 49, 8:22[21], 24, 25, 26, 39, 9:31, 35, 42, 10:14, 33[25], 48[26], 11:8, 21(2), 23, 24, 12:7, 11, 17, 23, 13:2, 10, 11, 12, 44[27], 47, 48, 49, 14:3, 23, 15:17(2), 35, 36, 40[28], 16:10[29], 14, 15, 32, 17:24, 27[30], 18:8, 9, 25, 19:20, 20:19, 21:14, 20[33], 22:16[34], 23:11; Rom. 4:8, 9:28, 29, 10:13, 16, 11:3, 34, 12:11, 19, 14:4[38], 14:6(4)[39], 8(3), 11, 15:11; 1 Cor. 1:31, 3:5, 20, 4:4, 19, 7:17, 25(2), 32(2), 34, 35, 39, 10:22, 26, 28[41], 11:11, 32, 14:21, 37, 15:58(2), 16:7, 10, 19; 2 Cor. 2:12, 3:16, 17(2), 18(2), 5:11, 6:17, 18, 8:5, 19, 21, 10:8, 17, 18, 11:17, 12:1, 8, 13:10; Gal. 5:10; Eph. 2:21, 4:1, 17, 5:8, 10, 17, 19, 6:1, 4, 7, 8, 10, 21; Phil. 1:14, 2:24, 29, 3:1, 4:1, 2, 4, 10; Col. 1:10, 3:16[51], 20, 22[52], 23, 24, 4:7, 17; 1 Thess. 1:8, 3:8, 12, 4:6, 15, 5:12; 2 Thess. 2:13, 3:1, 3, 4, 5, 16(2); 1 Tim. 1:14, 6:15; 2 Tim. 1:16, 18(2), 2:7, 14[57], 19, 24, 3:11, 4:14, 17, 18; Philem. 16; Heb. 7:21, 8:2, 8, 9, 10, 11, 10:16, 30(2)[62], 12:5, 6, 14, 13:6; James 1:7, 12[63], 3:9[64], 4:10, 15, 5:4, 10, 11(2)[65], 14, 15; 1 Pet. 1:25, 2:3, 13, 3:12(2), 3:15; 2 Pet. 2:9, 11, 3:8, 9, 10, 15; Jude 5; Rev. 1:8, 4:8, 11, 11:4[68], 15, 17, 19[69], 14:13, 15:3, 4, 16:5[70], 7, 18:8, 19:1[71], 6, 21:22, 22:5, 6:

3. *Denotes Christ as the Supreme Ruler, as y^{e}hovah, as a ruler, or as a dignitary with various nuances*: reflects the Hebrew, '*adôn*, '*adonay*, and *y^{e}hovah*: translated, "the Lord," "Lord," "Master," "sir": these 367 times:

(1) Denotes Christ's office as the Ruler and King of God's people, the Heir of David: Luke 2:11; Acts 2:36.

(2) Denotes Christ's personal identity as Supreme Ruler, or as $y^e hovah$ incarnate, with various nuances: translated, "the Lord," "Lord": Matt. 12:8, 22:43, 44, 45, 24:42, 25:37, 44, 28:6[5]; Mark 2:28, 12:36, 37, 16:19; Luke 1:43, 6:5, 7:13, 19[9], 31[10], 10:1, 39[12], 41[13], 11:39, 12:42, 13:15, 17:6, 18:6, 19:8, 20:42, 44, 22:31[15], 61(2), 24:3, 34; John 4:1[17], 6:23, 11:2, 20:2, 13, 18, 20, 25, 28, 21:7(2), 12; Acts 1:21, 2:34, 4:33, 8:16, 9:1, 5[22], 6[23], 10, 11, 15, 17, 27, 29[24], 10:36, 11:16, 17, 20, 15:11, 26, 16:31, 18:25[31], 19:5, 10, 13, 17, 20:21, 24, 28[32], 35, 21:13, 22:10, 26:15[35], 28:31; Rom. 1:3[36], 7, 4:24, 5:1, 11, 21, 6:11[37], 23, 7:25, 8:39, 10:9, 12, 13:14, 14:14, 15:6, 30, 16:2, 8, 11, 12(2), 13, 18, 20, 22, 24[40]; 1 Cor. 1:2, 3, 7, 8, 9, 10, 2:8, 16, 4:5, 17, 5:4(2), 5, 6:11, 13(2), 14, 17, 7:10, 12, 22(2), 8:6, 9:1(2), 2, 5, 14, 10:21(2), 11:23(2), 26, 27(2)[42], 29[43], 12:3, 5, 15:31, 47[44], 57, 16:22, 23; 2 Cor. 1:2, 3, 14, 4:5, 10[45], 14, 5:6, 8, 8:9, 11:31, 13:14; Gal. 1:3, 19, 6:14, 17[46], 18; Eph. 1:2, 3, 15, 17, 3:11, 14[47], 4:5, 5:20, 22, 29[48], 6:9, 23, 24; Phil. 1:2, 2:11, 19, 3:8, 20, 4:5, 4:23; Col. 1:2[49], 3, 2:6, 3:13[50], 17, 18, 24, 4:1; 1 Thess. 1:1(2)[53], 3, 6, 2:15, 19, 3:11, 13, 4:1, 2, 15, 16, 17(2), 5:2, 9, 23, 27, 28; 2 Thess. 1:1, 2, 7, 8, 9, 12(2), 2:1, 2[54], 8, 14, 16, 3:6, 12, 18; 1 Tim. 1:1[55], 2, 12, 5:21[56], 6:3, 14; 2 Tim. 1:2, 8, 22, 2:19[58], 4:1[59], 8, 4:22; Tit. 1:4[60]; Philem. 3, 5, 20(2)[61], 25; Heb. 1:10, 2:3, 7:14, 13:20; James 1:1, 2:1, 5:7, 8; 1 Pet. 1:3; 2 Pet. 1:2, 8, 11, 14, 16, 2:20, 3:2, 18; 2 John 3[66]; Jude 4, 9, 14, 17, 21, 25[67]; Rev. 11:8, 17:14, 19:16, 22:20, 21:

(3) Occurs in direct address to Jesus with various nuances: KJV translates these vocatives as "Lord," "Sir": *(a) Jesus addressed by the general population*: denotes respect for him as a person, dignitary, and religious leader: Luke 13:23; John 4:11, 15, 19, 5:7: *(b) Jesus addressed by suppliants*: additionally denotes conviction that he has divine authority to heal and rule: Matt. 8:2, 6, 8, 9:28, 15:22, 25, 27, 17:15, 20:30, 31, 33; Mark 7:28, 9:24[6]; Luke 5:12, 7:6, 18:41; John 4:49, 6:34, 8:11: *(c) Jesus addressed by his disciples*: additionally denotes personal devotion him as Master and Messiah: Matt. 8:21, 25, 13:51[3], 14:28, 30, 16:22, 17:4, 18:21, 26:22; Luke 5:8, 9:54, 57[11], 59, 61, 10:17, 40, 11:1, 12:41, 17:5, 37, 19:8, 22:33, 38, 49, 23:42; John 6:68, 9:36, 38, 11:3, 12, 21, 27, 32, 34, 39, 13:6, 9, 25, 36, 37, 14:5, 8, 22, 21:15, 16, 17, 20, 21; Acts 1:6, 7:59, 60, 9:10, 13, 22:19: *(d) Christ exalted addressed by Paul as a supernatural dignitary*: Acts 9:5, 6[23], 22:8, 10; 26:15:

(4) In a closely related nuance, Jesus addresses those who address him as dignitary, ruler, or Master: Matt. 7:21(2), 22(2); Luke 6:46(2); John 13:13, 14.

Notes:

1. 767 uses: The *Bible Works* KJV search of *kurios* (Strong's number 2962), based on BYZ Greek Text, yields 748 uses; the MAJ text search (Robinson-Pierpont 1995 Majority Greek Text) yields 746 uses; the BNT search (United Bible Society/Nestle Aland 27 Greek Text) yields 717 uses. I include all 748 uses from the BYZ-KJV search and **19** additional verses from the BNT and MAJ searches that do not appear in the KJV-BYZ search list.

Part 4: The Names of God | 653

2. *Variant readings*: Due to the unusually high number of variants, I identify each variant with a note. The following table summarizes these variant readings:

Books	KJV/BYZ	MAJ	BNT	VARIANTS
Matthew	83	83	80	BNT omits: 13:51, 18:26, 28:6
Mark	20	20	18	BNT omits: 9:24, 11:10
Luke	107	106	104	BNT omits: 2:38, 7:31, 9:57, 13:25, 22:31, 23:42; adds: 7:19, 10:39, 41 MAJ omits: 7:31
John	53	53	52	BNT omits: 4:1
Acts	113	111	107	BNT omits: 7:30, 37, 9:5, 6(2), 10:48, 16:10, 17:27, 18:25, 21:20, 22:16; BNT adds: 8:22, 10:33, 13:44, 15:40, 26:15 MAJ omits: 8:16, 9:6(2); adds: 20:28
Romans	45	45	43	BNT omits: 6:11, 14:6, 16:24; adds: 14:4
1 Cor.	69	70	66	BNT omits: 10:28, 11:29, 15:47 MAJ adds: 11:27
2 Cor.	30	30	29	BNT omits: 4:10
Gal.-Col.	66	66	63	BNT omits: Gal. 6:17; Eph. 3:14, 5:29; Col. 1:2, 3:16; adds: Col. 3:13, 22
1, 2 Thess.	46	46	46	BNT omits 1 Thess. 1:1; adds: 2 Thess. 2:2
1 Tim-Jam	63	63	57	BNT omits: 1 Tim. 1:1, 5:21; 2 Tim. 2:14, 4:1; Titus 1:4; Philem. 20; Heb. 10:30; James 1:12; BNT adds: 2 Tim. 2:19; James 3:9 MAJ omits: James 5:11; adds: 2 Tim. 2:19
1 Pet-Rev	53	53	52	BNT omits: 2 John 3; Rev. 16:5, 19:1; adds: Jude 25; Rev. 11:4 MAJ omits: Rev. 16:5, 19:1; adds: Rev. 11:4, 19
Totals	748	746	717	

3. *Matt. 13:51*: "Jesus says unto them: have you understood all these things? They say unto him: yes, [*Lord*]." BNT omits *kurie*, the vocative singular of *kurios*.

4. *Matt. 18:26*: "The servant therefore fell down, and worshipped him, saying: [*lord*], have patience with me, and I will pay you all." BNT omits *kurie*, the vocative singular of *kurios*.

5. *Matt. 28:6*: "He is not here: for he is risen, as he said: come, see the place where [*the Lord*] lay." BNT omits, *ho kurios*. Thus, ASV translates it, "the place where he lay."

6. *Mark 9:24*: "And straightway the father of the child cried out, and said with tears, [*Lord*], I believe; help thou mine unbelief": BNT omits *kurie*, the vocative of *kurios*.

7. *Mark 11:10*: "Blessed *be* the kingdom of our father David, that cometh [*in the name of the Lord*]: Hosanna in the highest": BNT omits the phrase, "en onomati kuriou," "in yᵉhovah's name."

8. *Luke 2:38*: "And she coming in that instant gave thanks likewise unto [*the Lord*]": MAJ reads, "to kurio," "unto the Lord": BNT reads, "to theo," "unto God."

9. *Luke 7:19*: "And John calling *unto him* two of his disciples sent *them* [*to Jesus*]": BNT reads, "pros ton kurion": "to the Lord": MAJ reads, "pros ton Iesoun": "to Jesus."

10. *Luke 7:31*: "[*And the Lord said*], Whereunto then shall I liken the men of this generation? And to what are they like?" BNT and MAJ omit the phrase, "and the Lord said." BYZ reads: *eipe de ho kurios*.

11. *Luke 9:57*: "And it came to pass, that, as they went in the way, a certain *man* said unto him, [Lord], I will follow thee whithersoever you go": BNT omits *kurie*, the vocative singular of *kurios*.

12. *Luke 10:39*: "And she had a sister called Mary, which also sat [at *Jesus'*] feet, and heard his word." BNT reads "tou kuriou," "*the Lord's*"; KJV and MAJ read, "tou Iesou," "Jesus'."

13. *Luke 10:41*: "And [Jesus] answered and said unto her: Martha, Martha, you are careful and troubled about many things: BNT reads "ho kurios," "the Lord." BYZ and MAJ read, "ho Iesous," "Jesus."

14. *Luke 13:25*: "saying, Lord, [*Lord*], open unto us": BNT has only one use of *kurie*, the vocative of *kurios*. KJV and MAJ use *kurie* twice.

15. *Luke 22:31*: "[*And the Lord said*], Simon, Simon, behold, Satan hath desired *to have* you": BNT omits the phrase, "and the Lord said": MAJ reads, "eipen de ho kurios."

16. *Luke 23:42*: "And he said unto Jesus, [Lord], remember me when you come you're your kingdom": BNT omits *kurie*, the vocative singular of *kurios*.

17. *John 4:1*: "When therefore [*the Lord*] knew how the Pharisees had heard": MAJ reads, "ho kurios": BNT reads, "ho Iesous," "Jesus."

18. *Acts 3:19[20 BNT]*: The phrase, "when the times of refreshing shall come from the presence *of the Lord*," is in 3:19 in KJV and MAJ and in 3:20 in BNT.

19. *Acts 7:30*: "an angel [*of the Lord*] in a flame of fire": BNT omits *tou kuriou*, "of the Lord."

20. *Acts 7:37*: "A prophet shall [*the Lord your*] God raise up": BNT omits, "kurios hemon": BNT reads, "ho theos"; Thus ASV translates, "a prophet shall God raise up."

21. *Acts 8:22*: "Repent therefore of this thy wickedness, and pray [God]": BNT reads, *kurio*, the dative singular of *kurios*. Thus, ASV translates, "pray the Lord." BYZ and MAJ read, *theo*, the dative singular of *theos*, "God."

22. *Acts 9:5*: "Who are you, Lord? And [*the Lord*] said, I am Jesus": BNT omits "kurios eipen," "the Lord said": Thus, ASV translates it, "and he *said*."

23. *Acts 9:6*: "[And he trembling and astonished said, Lord, what wilt thou have me to do? And the Lord *said* unto him]": BNT and MAJ omit this entire phrase and both uses of *kurios*. BYZ reads: τρεμων τε και θαμβων ειτε κυριε τι με θελεις ποιησαι και ο κυριος προς αυτον: "and trembling and astonished he said, Lord,

what do you want me to do? And the Lord to him." KJV translates accordingly.

24. Acts 9:28 [29 KJV]: the phrase, "spoke boldly in the name of *the Lord* Jesus," occurs in 9:28 in BNT and MAJ and in 9:29 in BYZ and KJV.

25. Acts 10:33: "to hear all things that are commanded thee of [*God*]": BNT reads, *kuriou*, the genitive singular of *kurios*. Thus ASV translates, "that have been commanded thee of the Lord." BYZ and MAJ read, *theou*, the genitive singular of *theos*. KJV translates accordingly, "of God."

26. Acts 10:48: "And he commanded them to be baptized in the name [*of the Lord*]": BNT omits *kuriou*, "of the Lord." It reads, "Iesou Christou." Thus, ASV translates, "in the name of Jesus Christ."

27. Acts 13:44: "came almost the whole city together to hear the word of [God]": BNT reads, *kuriou*, the genitive singular of *kurios*, "of the Lord." ASV notes this variant in the margin. BYZ and MAJ read, *theou*, the genitive singular of *theos*. Thus, KJV translates it, "of God."

28. Acts 15:40: "And Paul chose Silas, and departed, being recommended by the brethren unto the grace of [*God*]": BNT reads, *kuriou*, the genitive singular of *kurios*, "of the Lord." Accordingly, ASV translates it, "of the Lord." BYZ and MAJ read, *theou*, the genitive singular of *theos*. Accordingly, KJV translates it, "of God."

29. Acts 16:10: "assuredly gathering that [*the Lord*] had called us for to preach the gospel unto them": BYZ and MAJ read, "kurios." BNT omits *kurios*: it reads "ho theos." Thus, ASV translates, "that God had called us."

30. Acts 17:27: "that they should seek [the Lord]": BNT reads, "ton theon," the accusative singular of *theos*, "God." BYZ and MAJ read, "kurion," the accusative singular of *kurios*.

31. Acts 18:25: "he spoke and taught diligently the things of [*the Lord*]": BNT reads, "tou Iesou," "the things of Jesus."

32. Acts 20:28: "feed the church of [*God*]": MAJ adds, "kuriou kai," "of the Lord and God." BYZ and BNT omit *kuriou kai*.

33. Acts 21:20: "And when they heard *it*, they glorified [*the Lord*]": BNT reads, "they glorified God," "ton theon," the accusative singular of *theos*. BYZ and MAJ read, "kurion," the accusative singular of *kurios*.

34. Acts 22:16: "calling on the name [*of the Lord*]": BNT reads, "autou," "of him," and omits "tou kuriou," "of the Lord." Thus, ASV translates this: "calling on his name." BYZ and MAJ read, "tou kuriou," "of the Lord."

35. Acts 26:15: "And I said: Who are you, Lord? And [he said], I am Jesus whom you persecute": BNT adds, "ho kurios": Thus ASV translates, "and the Lord said." BYZ and MAJ omit *ho kurios*.

36. Rom. 1:3 [1:4 BNT, MAJ, BYZ]: "Concerning his Son [*Jesus Christ our Lord*]": BNT, MAJ, and BYZ Greek texts include this phrase, "Jesus Christ our Lord," in 1:4: yet, KJV translates it in 1:3.

37. Rom. 6:11: "but alive unto God through Jesus Christ [*our Lord*]": BNT omits, "to kurio hemon," "our Lord."

38: Rom. 14:4: "Yea, he shall be holden up: for [*God*] is able to make him stand": BYZ and MAJ read, "ho theos": thus KJV translates accordingly, "God." BNT reads, "ho kurios": Thus, ASV translates accordingly, "the Lord."

39. Rom. 14:6: "He that regards the day, regards *it* unto the Lord; [*and he that regards not the day, to the Lord he does not regard it*]": BNT omits this use of *kurio*, the dative singular of *kurios*. BYZ and MAJ include it.

40. Rom. 16:24: "[*The grace of our Lord Jesus Christ be with you all. Amen*]": BNT omits this verse; BYZ and MAJ, and thus KJV, include it. ASV notes this verse as a variant in its margin.

41. 1 Cor. 10:28: "eat not for his sake that shewed it, and for conscience sake: [*for the earth is the Lord's, and the fullness thereof*]": BNT omits this phrase and its use of *kuriou*, the genitive singular of *kurios*: BYZ and MAJ include it, and KJV translates accordingly.

42. 1 Cor. 11:27: "Wherefore whosoever shall eat this bread, and drink *this* cup of the Lord, unworthily [MAJ adds: *of the Lord*], shall be guilty of the body and blood of the Lord": MAJ Greek Text adds, *tou kuriou*, "unworthily of the Lord": BYZ and BNT do not include this additional use of *kuriou*, the genitive singular of *kurios*, in the text. Thus, "unworthily *of the Lord*" does not appear either in the KJV or in the ASV.

43. 1 Cor. 11:29: "eateth and drinketh damnation to himself, not discerning [*the Lord's*] body": BNT omits *tou kuriou*, the genitive singular of *kurios*. BYZ and MAJ include it. Thus, "the Lord's" is not in the ASV.

44. 1 Cor. 15:47: "the second man *is* [*the Lord*] from heaven": BNT omits *ho kurios*; BYZ and MAJ include it:

45. 2 Cor. 4:10: "Always bearing about in the body the dying of [*the Lord*] Jesus": BNT omits *tou kuriou*, the genitive singular of *kurios*. Accordingly, ASV translates this phrase, "the dying of Jesus." BYZ and MAJ include "tou kuriou" and KJV translates accordingly.

46. Gal. 6:17: "From henceforth let no man trouble me: for I bear in my body the marks [*of the Lord*] Jesus": BNT omits *tou kuriou*, the genitive singular of *kurios*. Thus, ASV translates it, "the marks of Jesus." BYZ and MAJ include "tou kuriou" and KJV translates accordingly.

47. Eph. 3:14: "For this cause I bow my knees unto the Father [*of our Lord Jesus Christ*]": BNT omits this entire phrase and its use of the genitive singular of *kurios*, "tou kuriou." Thus, the phrase, "of our Lord Jesus Christ," is not in the ASV translation. BYZ and MAJ include this use of *kurios*. Thus, the KJV translates accordingly.

48. Eph. 5:29: "For no man ever yet hated his own flesh; but nourisheth and cherisheth it, even as [*the Lord*] the church": BNT reads "ho christos" rather than "ho kurios." Thus, ASV translates it, "even as Christ the church." BYZ and MAJ read, *ho kurios*, and KJV translates accordingly.

49. Col. 1:2: "Grace *be* unto you, and peace, from God our Father [*and the Lord Jesus Christ*]": BNT deletes this phrase and its use of *kuriou*, the genitive singular of *kurios*. Accordingly, the phrase, "and the Lord Jesus Christ," is not in the ASV translation. It appears in the KJV because both BYZ and MAJ contain this use of *kurios*.

50: Col. 3:13: "Forbearing one another, and forgiving one another, if any man have a quarrel against any: even as [Christ] forgave you, so also *do* ye": BYZ and MAJ read, *ho christos*. KJV translates accordingly, "Christ." BNT reads, *ho kurios*. Accordingly ASV translates the phrase, "even as the Lord forgave you."

51. Col. 3:16: "singing with grace in your hearts [*to the Lord*]": BYZ and MAJ read, *to kurio*, the dative singular of *kurios*. KJV translates accordingly. BNT has, *to theo*, the dative singular of *theos*. Thus, ASV has, "unto God."

52. Col. 3:22: "Servants, obey in all things *your* masters according to the flesh; not with eyeservice, as menpleasers; but in singleness of heart, fearing [*God*]": BYZ and MAJ read, *ton theon*, the accusative singular of *theos*. KJV translates accordingly. BNT has, *ton kurion*, the accusative singular of *kurios*. Thus, ASV has, "*fearing the Lord.*"

53. 1 Thess. 1:1: "Paul, and Silvanus, and Timotheus, unto the church of the Thessalonians *which is* in God the Father and *in* the Lord Jesus Christ: Grace *be* unto you, and peace, [*from God our Father, and the Lord Jesus Christ*]": BNT omits the phrase that contains *kuriou*, the genitive singular of *kurios*. ASV translates accordingly.

54. 2 Thess. 2:2: "That ye be not soon shaken in mind, or be troubled, neither by spirit, nor by word, nor by letter as from us, as that the day [*of Christ*] is at hand": BYZ and MAJ read, *tou christou*, the genitive singular of *christos*. KJV translates accordingly. BNT has, *tou kuriou*, the genitive singular of *kurios*, and ASV reads, "of the Lord."

55. 1 Tim. 1:1: "Paul, an apostle of Jesus Christ by the commandment of God our Saviour, and [*Lord*] Jesus Christ, *which is* our hope": BYZ and MAJ read *kuriou*, the genitive singular of *kurios*. BNT omits *kuriou*. ASV translates accordingly, "of God our Savior, and Christ Jesus our hope."

56. 1 Tim. 5:21: "I charge *thee* before God, and [*the Lord*] Jesus Christ": BYZ and MAJ read *kuriou* and KJV translates accordingly. BNT omits *kuriou*. Thus, ASV translates, "in the sight of God and Christ Jesus."

57. 2 Tim. 2:14: "Of these things put *them* in remembrance, charging *them* before [*the Lord*] that they strive not about words": BYZ and MAJ read, *tou kuriou* and

KJV translates accordingly. BNT reads *tou theou*, the genitive singular of *theos*, "charging *them* before God."

58. *2 Tim. 2:19*: "And, Let every one that nameth the name [*of Christ*] depart from iniquity": BYZ reads, *christou*, the genitive singular of *christos*, and KJV translates accordingly, "of Christ. BNT and MAJ read, *kuriou*, the genitive singular of *kurios*, and ASV translates accordingly, "of the Lord."

59. *2 Tim. 4:1*: "I charge *thee* therefore before God, and [*the Lord*] Jesus Christ": BYZ and MAJ read *kuriou* and KJV translates accordingly. BNT omits *kuriou*. Thus, ASV translates, "in the sight of God, and of Christ Jesus."

60. *Titus 1:4*: "Grace, mercy, *and* peace, from God the Father and [th*e Lord*] Jesus Christ our Saviour": BYZ and MAJ read *kuriou* and KJV translates accordingly. BNT omits *kuriou*": ASV reads, "and Christ Jesus our Savior."

61: *Philem. 20*: "Yea, brother, let me have joy of thee in the Lord: refresh my bowels in [*the Lord*]": BYZ and MAJ read, *kurio*, the dative singular of *kurios*. KJV translates accordingly. BNT reads, *christo*, the dative singular of *christos*. Thus, ASV translates, "in Christ."

62. *Heb. 10:30*: "For we know him that hath said, Vengeance *belongeth* unto me, I will recompense, [*saith the Lord*]": BNT omits, "legei kurios," translated, "says the Lord." ASV translation thus omits the phrase.

63. *James 1:12*: "the crown of life, which [*the Lord*] hath promised to them that love him": BYZ and MAJ read *ho kurios* and KJV translates accordingly. BNT omits *ho kurios*: ASV reads, "which *the Lord* has promised." It places "*the Lord*" in italics to indicate that it was not in the Greek text they used.

64. *James 3:9*: "Therewith bless we [*God*], even the Father": BYZ and MAJ have, *ton theon*, the accusative singular of *theos*. KJV translates accordingly, "God." BNT has *ton kurion*, the accusative singular of *kurios*. Thus, ASV has, "the Lord and Father."

65. *James 5:11*: "Ye have heard of the patience of Job, and have seen the end of the Lord; that [*the Lord*] is very pitiful, and of tender mercy": BYZ and BNT read, ho kurios. Thus ASV and KJV translate accordingly. MAJ omits *ho kurios*, "the end of the Lord, that he is very pitiful, and of tender mercy."

66. *2 John 3*: "Grace be with you, mercy, *and* peace, from God the Father, and from [*the Lord*] Jesus Christ, the Son of the Father, in truth and love": BYZ and MAJ read *kuriou* and KJV translates accordingly. BNT omits *kuriou*: ASV translates, "and from Jesus Christ."

67. *Jude 25*: "To the only wise God our Saviour, [BNT adds the phrase with *kuriou* here] *be* glory and majesty, dominion and power, both now and ever. Amen": BNT adds, "dia Iesou Christou tou kuriou hemon," which ASV translates, "through Jesus Christ our Lord."

68. *Rev. 11:4*: "These are the two olive trees, and the two candlesticks standing before [*the God*] of the earth": BYZ reads, to*u theou*, the genitive of *theos*. BNT

and MAJ read, *tou kuriou*. ASV translates, accordingly, "the Lord."

69. Rev. 11:19: "And the temple of God was opened in heaven, and there was seen in his temple the ark [*of his*] testament": BYZ and BNT read, *autou*, which KJV translates, "of his." MAJ reads, *tou kuriou*, the genitive of *kurios*, which is translated, "the testament of the Lord."

70. Rev. 16:5: "Thou art righteous, [*O Lord*], which art, and wast, and shalt be, because thou hast judged thus": BYZ reads, *kurie*, the vocative of *kurios*. BNT and MAJ omit *kurie*. ASV translates accordingly.

71. Rev. 19:1: "Alleluia; Salvation, and glory, and honour, and power, [*unto the Lord*] our God": BYZ reads, "kurio to theo," the dative singular of *kurios* and *theos*. KJV translates accordingly. BNT and MAJ omit *kurio*. They read, "tou theou," the genitive singular of *theos*. Thus, ASV translates, "belong to our God."

Topic 24. The Decree of God

"the purpose of him who works all things after the counsel of his will" (Eph. 1:11)

Part 5: The Decree of God

Introduction to Part 5: Our epitomizing text features three crucial distinctions that categorize our thinking. First, it identifies God's decree as an eternal determination his of will: "the counsel of his will." Second, it depicts predestination as a specific aspect of God's decree: "having been predestined according to the purpose of him who works all things after the counsel of his will." Third, it distinguishes the eternal formulation of God's decree from its historical execution: "who works all things after the counsel of his will." Thus, Scripture presents God's will and decree in concentric circles. Predestination, God's decree to save, is an aspect of God's eternal determination, which is an act of God's faculty of will. In accord with this testimony, I address God's will and decree both in Theology and in Christology. Bavinck comments on this order of presentation:[1]

> Many theologians of the early period discussed election in connection with the doctrine of salvation instead of in connection with the doctrine of God. In this they followed the example of the apostle Paul who in Romans 9-11 begins with the doctrine of sin and grace and reasons back to election, and who in Eph.1:3 makes the blessings in Christ his point of departure...Whether predestination is made part of the doctrine of God (the a priori order) or is treated at the beginning or in the middle of the doctrine of salvation (the a posteriori order) does not necessarily imply an essential difference in principle. Nevertheless, it is a significant fact that the a priori order is usually followed by Reformed theologians; while Lutherans, Arminians, Roman Catholics and most of the more recent dogmaticians, have gradually begun to adopt the a posteriori order...the synthetic, a priori order is rooted in a deeply religious motive...in dogmatics we do not discuss truth as it subjectively enters the consciousness of the believer but as God has objectively revealed it in his word. The synthetic method alone is able to do justice to the glorification of God, as a religious interest.

In keeping with this religious interest to honor God's Word, I expound the historical execution of God's decree when we study his works of creation and salvation. I begin the Doctrine of Christ by expounding predestination, God's decree to save. Now I expound God's eternal decree. In Topic 14 I expounded God's faculty of will. I defined God's faculty of will as: "his faculty of self-determination, his supreme capacity to act intentionally (on

---

[1] Bavinck, *Doctrine of God*, 358-359

purpose) and preferentially (as he pleases)." I introduced God's decree as the eternal act of his will: "by which, in its decretive function, he designed and determined in eternity, everything that happens in history." Now I expound this idea.

Our text features the *essential nature* of God's overall decree: "the purpose . . . the counsel." It also intimates its *internal order*: "having been foreordained according to the purpose." Finally, it commends its *practical application*: "the counsel of his will, to the end that we should be to the praise of his glory." I expound God's eternal decree accordingly.

Unit 1. The Essential Nature of God's Decree

Scripture highlights the concept,[2] qualifications,[3] and characteristics of God's decree.[4]

I. The Concept of God's Decree

> *God's decree is*: the eternal act of God's will, in which, the triune God, emphatically the Father, solely out of his good pleasure, designed and determined in eternity everything that happens in history, unto the praise of his glory.

I now explain and support this definition. We consider its *author, cause, occasion, scope,* and *goal*.

A. The Author of God's Decree: "the triune God, emphatically the Father"

The Triune God decreed to create. "Our Lord and our God" is the Father, Son, and Spirit.[5] Scripture declares repeatedly in the plainest terms that God the Father especially decreed salvation.[6] The Father decreed the redemptive mission of Christ[7] and the salvation of his elect in Christ.[8]

---

[2] Job 23:13-14; Ps. 135:6; Acts 13:48, 17:26; Rom. 8:29; Eph. 1:3-5, 11, 3:10, 11; 1 Thess. 5:9; 2 Tim. 1:9; 1 Pet. 2:8-9; Rev. 4:11

[3] Gen. 50:20; Prov. 16:33; Isa. 10:5-7; Acts 2:23, 4:28; Rom. 9:19-20

[4] Isa. 14:24, 27, 46:9-10; Rom. 9:19

[5] *Rev. 4:11*: Worthy you are, our Lord and our God, to receive the glory and the honor and the power: for you did create all things, and because of your will they were, and were created

[6] *Rom. 8:29*: whom he foreknew, he also foreordained to be conformed to the image of his Son. *1 Thess. 5:9*: for God appointed us not to wrath, but unto the obtaining of salvation through our Lord Jesus Christ

[7] *Acts 4:27-28*: against your holy Servant Jesus, whom you did anoint, both Herod and Pontius Pilate, with the Gentiles and the peoples of Israel, were gathered together, to do whatsoever your hand and your counsel foreordained to come to pass

[8] *Eph. 1:3-5*: Blessed be the God and Father of our Lord Jesus Christ . . . even as he chose us in him before the foundation of the world . . . having foreordained us unto adoption as sons .

B. The Cause of God's Decree: "solely out of his good pleasure"

The Bible says simply that God's decree rests in "the good pleasure of His will."[9] In Topic 14 we studied this passage in detail. God decided to create and save, without external constraint, only because he wanted to do so. God ordered all of history as seemed good to him,[10] in accord with his good pleasure.[11] He even ordered the sufferings of his saints as it pleased him.[12]

C. The Occasion of God's Decree: "in eternity"

Scripture asserts, explicitly[13] and by necessary implication,[14] that God's decree is eternal. He decided to create and save before the foundation of the world.

D. The Scope of God's Decree: "everything that happens in history"

In its scope God's decree includes "all things" (Eph. 1:11). Scripture emphatically affirms its universal extent. God's decree includes: creation,[15] all "random" events,[16] all the inter-workings of the universe,[17] every event in the history of every nation,[18] every event in each man's life,[19] every sin of

---

. . according to the good pleasure of his will. *2 Tim. 1:9*: who saved us and called us . . . according to his own purpose and grace, which was given us in Christ Jesus before times eternal

[9] Eph. 1:5, 11

[10] *Ps. 135:6*: Whatsoever Jehovah pleased, that has he done, in heaven and earth, in the seas and in all the deeps

[11] *Isa. 46:9-10*: I am God, and there is none like me; declaring the end from the beginning, and from ancient times things that are not yet done; saying, My counsel shall stand, and I will do all my pleasure

[12] *Job 23:13-14*: But he is of one mind, and who can turn him? And what his soul desires, even that he does. For he performs that which is appointed for me: and many such things are with him. Therefore I am terrified at his presence; when I consider, I am afraid of him

[13] Eph. 1:3-4, 3:10-11; 2 Tim. 1:9

[14] Rev. 4:11

[15] Rev. 4:11

[16] *Prov. 16:33*: The lot is cast into the lap; but the whole disposing thereof is of Jehovah

[17] *Ps. 135:6*: Whatsoever Jehovah pleased, that has he done, in heaven and earth, in the seas and in all the deeps

[18] *Acts 17:26*: having determined their appointed seasons, and the bounds of their habitations

[19] Job 23:13-14

every creature,[20] every event in every church in every generation,[21] the salvation of every elect saint,[22] and the damnation of every reprobate sinner.[23] No wonder Paul exclaims: "O the depth of the riches both of the wisdom and knowledge of God! How unsearchable are his judgments, and his ways past tracing out . . For of him, and through him, and unto him, are all things" (Rom. 11:33-36).

E. The Goal of God's Decree: "unto the praise of his glory"

God's decree aims to achieve "the praise of the glory of his grace" (Eph. 1:6). Here is the ultimate end of God's eternal counsel: "To whom be the glory forever, Amen" (Rom. 11:36). God, from all eternity, ordained creation, fall, and redemption for his own glory. God uses everything to honor and glorify his name. When men design evil, he employs their evil designs for good, to the praise of his glorious wisdom, goodness, grace, and justice.[24] In the final analysis, even sin does not overthrow God's design to magnify his name. God even ordained sin to display his glory in salvation and in damnation.

II. Qualifications of God's Decree

The 1689 London Confession affirms the biblical concept of God's decree:

> LCF 3:1: God has decreed in himself, from all eternity, by the most wise and holy counsel of his own will, freely and unchangeably, all things, whatsoever comes to pass:

It then adds qualifying remarks that highlight three striking corollaries or qualifications of God's decree:

> LCF 3:1: . . . yet so as thereby God is neither the author of sin, nor has any fellowship with any therein; nor is violence offered to the will of the creature, nor yet is the liberty or contingency of second causes taken away, but rather established.

They observe that God's decree is consistent with divine purity, moral free agency, and with instrumental liberty and contingency. We now consider these qualifications.

---

[20] *Acts 4:27-28*: against your holy Servant Jesus, whom you did anoint, both Herod and Pontius Pilate, with the Gentiles and the peoples of Israel, were gathered together, to do whatsoever your hand and your counsel foreordained to come to pass

[21] *Eph. 3:10-11*: might be made manifest through the church the manifold wisdom of God, according to the eternal purpose which he purposed in Jesus Christ our Lord

[22] *Acts 13:48*: and as many as were ordained to eternal life believed

[23] *1 Pet. 2:8-9*: for they stumble at the word, being disobedient; whereunto they were also appointed. But you are an elect race

[24] Gen. 50:20; Isa. 10:5-7; Acts 2:23, 4:28

A. God's Decree does not Contradict God's Impeccability.

LCF affirms this qualification: "yet so as thereby God is neither the author of sin nor has any fellowship therein." God's decree of sin does not make him its author. Nor does it erase human responsibility and culpability for sin.[25] Sinners purpose and perpetrate evil: "you meant evil against me." God purposes to use human evil for good: "but God meant it for good."[26] Sinners are exclusively to blame for sin. The holy God has neither fellowship with sin nor culpability for it. Rather, he hates and forbids it. Sin is transgression of his law, his revealed will. In Topic 14 I addressed the incomprehensible mystery associated with God's sovereignty over sin.[27]

B. God's Decree does not Contradict Moral Free Agency.

The 1689 Confession also affirms this qualification: "nor is violence offered to the will of the creature." Man is not a puppet: "howbeit he means not so."[28] God's decree does not cancel man's purposes, even his wicked ones. Rather, it uses them in ways man knows not. God does not force the Assyrian against his will to be the rod of his anger. The Assyrian has no intention whatsoever of serving God. The Assyrian freely pursues his own purposes and plans. Yet God before the foundation of the world determined and fixed for his own holy and just ends these free choices of the Assyrian. Such is the wisdom and power of the incomprehensible God with whom we have to do.

C. God's Decree does not Contradict Instrumental Liberty or Contingency.

The 1689 Confession also affirms this qualification: "nor yet is the liberty or contingency of second causes taken away, but rather established." God's decree is not fatalistic. The God who ordains the ends, also ordains the means. Thus Paul says: "except these abide in the ship you cannot be saved." (Acts 27:31). God decreed their deliverance but they still must remain in the ship. Further, God even decreed what appear to us as random events.[29] God controls chance, what people call "luck." Again, who can begin to fathom the depths of the wisdom and power of God? Thus, LCF concludes:

---

[25] *Acts 2:23*: him, being delivered up by the determinate counsel and foreknowledge of God, you by the hand of lawless men did crucify and slay

[26] *Gen. 50:20*: you meant evil against me; but God meant it for good, to bring to pass, as it is this day, to save much people alive

[27] *Rom. 9:19-20*: You will then say unto me, Why does he yet find fault? For who withstands his will? Nay but, O man, who are you that replies against God?

[28] *Isa. 10:5-7*: Ho Assyrian, the rod of mine anger . . . I will send him against a profane nation . . . Howbeit he means not so, neither does his heart think so; but it is in his heart to destroy

[29] *Prov. 16:33*: The lot is cast into the lap; but the whole disposing thereof is of Jehovah

"in which appears his wisdom in disposing all things, and power and faithfulness in accomplishing his decree."

III. Characteristics of God's Decree

God's decree has the stamp of his supremacy, especially, of his supreme power, virtue, and wisdom. It is unconditional, immutable, effectual, ideal, and incomprehensible.

A. God's Decree is Unconditional.

God's decree must be unconditional because he is self-existent. He decided as he did only because it pleased him: "*whatsoever Jehovah pleased*, that has he done."[30] God declares the future before it happens because God in his good pleasure ordained the future.[31] Jesus confirms that God's decree is unconditional. He affirms that God destroyed Sodom even though he foresaw that they would have repented at Christ's mighty works.[32] Paul affirms explicitly that God ordained our adoption, not according to our works or merit, but because it pleased him.[33] The London Confession stresses this remarkable trait of God's decree:

> LCF 3:2: Although God knows whatsoever may or can came to pass, upon all supposed conditions, yet he has not decreed anything, because he foresaw it as future, or as that which would come to pass upon such conditions"

The Confession stresses this truth to honor God's sovereignty in the salvation and damnation of sinners. We study reprobation and election in the Doctrine of Christ. We show that God determined to save some sinners and damn others, all equally condemned in Adam and justly deserving hell, solely because of his just good pleasure. We prove from Scripture that he decided to save unconditionally, not because he foresaw that some would cooperate with a moral ability he allegedly gives equally to all. Some may not find this distinctive of God's decree to their liking. Nevertheless, we should please God rather than men.

---

[30] *Ps. 135:6*: Whatsoever Jehovah pleased, that has he done, in heaven and earth, in the seas and in all the deeps.

[31] *Isa. 46:9-10*: I am God, and there is none like me; declaring the end from the beginning, and from ancient times things that are not yet done; saying: My counsel shall stand, and I will do all my pleasure

[32] *Matt. 11:21, 23*: if the mighty works had been done in Tyre and Sidon which were done in you, they would have repented . . . if the mighty works had been done in Sodom which were done in you, it would have remained until this day

[33] *Eph. 1:5*: having foreordained us unto adoption as sons . . . according to the good pleasure of his will.

B. God's Decree is Immutable and Irreversible.[34]

Whatever God decided in eternity is fixed, certain, and irreversible, because God is unchangeable. I supported this characteristic of God's decree in Topic 10 when I expounded God's immutability.

C. God's Decree is *Effectual and Invincible*.

God's eternal decree is his blueprint for history. History unfolds exactly as he designed it. Nothing is lacking, or out of sequence, or added that he failed to plan. He never alters his "blueprint" for reality during the "construction phase." No man or devil can reverse God's eternal decision, annul it,[35] withstand it,[36] prevent it, or overcome it. Everything God decided in eternity happens in history, exactly when he decided it would, and precisely how he decided it would.[37] His decree is effectual and invincible. Yet, his decree is not itself history. Creation, fall, and salvation happen, not in eternity, but when God implements the eternal plan that his will devised and resolved.[38]

D. God's Decree is *Ideal and Immaculate*.

God's decree, designed by his infinite wisdom and virtue, cannot be improved. It is infinitely perfect. Thus, when the apostles contemplate God's decree in general,[39] and his decision to create[40] and to save[41] in particular, they praise and bless his name. They extol its manifold display of his wisdom,[42] grace,[43] justice,[44] and glory.[45]

---

[34] *Job 23:13-14*: But he is of one mind, and who can turn him? And what his soul desires, even that he does. For he performs that which is appointed for me: and many such things are with him. Therefore I am terrified at his presence; when I consider, I am afraid of him.

[35] *Isa. 14:24, 27*: Jehovah of hosts has sworn saying, Surely, as I have thought, so shall it come to pass; and as I have purposed, so shall it stand . . . For Jehovah of hosts has purposed, and who shall annul it?

[36] *Rom. 9:19-20*: You will then say unto me, Why does he yet find fault? For who withstands his will? Nay but, O man, who are you that replies against God?

[37] Isa. 46:9-10

[38] Eph. 1:11

[39] *Rom. 11:36*: For of him, and through him, and unto him, are all things. To whom be the glory forever. Amen

[40] *Rev. 4:11*: Worthy you are, our Lord and our God, to receive the glory and the honor and the power: for you did create all things, and because of your will they were, and were created.

[41] *Eph. 1:3-5, 11*: Blessed be the God and Father of our Lord Jesus Christ . . . even as he chose us in him before the foundation of the world

[42] Rom. 11:33-36; Eph. 3:10-11

[43] Eph. 1:5-6, 9-11; 2 Tim. 1:9

[44] 1 Pet. 2:9

[45] Eph. 1:12

E. God's Decree is Incomprehensible.[46]

Who can fathom these things? God's decree leaves us gazing spellbound into the infinite expanse of divine wisdom. Thus, as we take up the internal order of decrees, remember that our finite minds cannot effectually restrain God's decree with the straightjacket of our logical schemes.

Unit 2. The Internal Order of God's Decree: *Its Unity and Diversity*

God's decree is one, indivisible. Paul speaks of God's plan as a unit, as single, all-embracing purpose, *"the counsel* of his will." All reality—everything that is, and all history—everything that happens, flow from one plan of God: "who works *all things after the counsel."* God's plan is indivisible. Nevertheless, it has various aspects. God, in his infinite wisdom weaves diverse decrees, each interdependent and coordinate, into one cohesive whole, his eternal decree.

God does not have the same relation to creation that he has to sin. Creation is God's work, inherently good; sin is man's work, inherently evil, which God hates and forbids. Thus, his eternal decision respecting creation differs from his eternal decision respecting sin. Nor does he have the same relationship to salvation that he has to damnation. He delights when sinners repent, but has no pleasure in the death and damnation of the wicked: "I have no pleasure in the death of the wicked; but that the wicked turn from his way and live" (Ezek. 33:11). Thus, election, his eternal decision respecting salvation, differs from reprobation, his eternal decision respecting damnation. God's decisions respecting sin and damnation involve tension, a seeming contradiction with God's revealed will. In this respect, they differ from his decree to create and to save. Thus, God's eternal decree displays both unity and diversity. Further, this unity and diversity raise the issue of priority. With what logical order or priority does God formulate his decree? To answer this question, some look at the end of all things. They behold eternal salvation and punishment. Then, they reason that since God plans the end from the beginning, the priority must lie with his decision respecting salvation and damnation. Others, however, look at the unfolding of all things. Then they reason that since God does in history exactly what he plans in eternity, the priority must lie with creation, since it begins the execution of God's decree. Thus, we consider first, *two major views* of its internal order, then, second, the *biblical concept* of its internal order.

---

[46] *Rom. 11:33, 36*: O the depth of the riches both of the wisdom and knowledge of God! How unsearchable are his judgments, and his ways past tracing out . . . For of him, and through him, and unto him, are all things. To whom be the glory forever. Amen.

I. The Two Major Views of the Internal Order of God's Decree

One major view of God's eternal plan assigns logical priority to God's decision respecting creation; the other assigns it to his decision respecting salvation and damnation. Their respective names come from the way they relate God's decision to save to his decision respecting the fall into sin. The view that assigns priority to God's decision to save is called "supralapsarian," since his decision to save has logical priority over, stands above [supra], his decision respecting the fall [lapse] of man. The view that assigns logical priority to creation is called, "infralapsarian," since his decision to save does not have logical priority over, but stands below [infra], his decision respecting the fall of man.

A. The Supralapsarian View

We take up their proposed order of decrees, stated concerns, and dangerous tendencies.

1. Proposed supralapsarian order of decrees

(1) A decree of God's glory in the final salvation and eternal damnation of possible men
(2) A decree to create these possible men thus elected and reprobated
(3) A decree to permit them to fall in Adam

Or, as an alternative order:

(1) A decree of God's glory in the final salvation and eternal damnation of possible men
(2) A decree to permit the fall of these possible men
(3) A decree to create them

In both cases God's decree of salvation and damnation logically precedes his decree of creation and the fall. The alternate order merely stresses that what is last in execution is first in design.

2. Stated supralapsarian concerns

First, they desire to uphold God's absolute sovereignty in salvation. They assert that sin is not the *ultimate cause* of God's decision to damn some sinners. Sin alone does not explain this decision because those God decides to save were equally sinful and hell-deserving. Indeed, Scripture affirms God's sovereignty in his eternal decision regarding damnation.[47] Second, they desire to make no excuses for God. Our supralapsarian brothers adamantly oppose the bashful spirit that drives many to dilute God's truth. Quite properly, they reject any notion that God must justify himself in men's eyes. They assert with unmistakable clarity that God is not accountable to

---
[47] Matt. 11:25-27; 1 Thess. 5:9; 1 Pet. 2:9

men, but vice versa. Again, this concern is biblical.[48] Third, they desire to honor the unity and indivisibility of God's eternal decree. It's unity resides in the fact that God's glory is the grand end of everything he decrees. Thus, they feature the truth that God uses everything, even sin, to bring glory to himself.[49]

3. Dangerous supralapsarian tendencies

First, they tend to minimize the inherent value and glory of creation. They seldom regard creation as worthwhile, with significance in and of itself. They tend to speak and live as though creation's chief worth is that it occasions the fall. This tends to foster a negative attitude toward culture, education, politics, sports, and all else associated with creation. *Second*, they tend to minimize or deny common grace. They tend to deny any genuine kindness or goodwill in God's heart toward those who perish in hell. Looking exclusively at the end, they oft acknowledge only justice and wrath, and deny any "well-meant" offer of pardon to the reprobate. Valuing human logic too highly, they try to explain away texts like Ezekiel 33:11, rather than submit to them. Thus, sadly, this view often fosters a harsh disposition towards lost sinners. *Third*, they tend to hold the error of eternal justification, which alleges that Christians were justified in eternity, not when we believe.[50] But Christian salvation is a transition from wrath to grace. When he saved us we were condemned in Adam and dead in sins, children of wrath even as the rest. What happens in history is precisely what God decided in eternity. Thus, God decided in eternity to emancipate us from our sin. He viewed us as fallen, under wrath, when he decided to save us. This truth is hard to harmonize with their order of decrees. How did God decide to save "someone" he had not yet decided to create from "something" he had not yet decided would happen? *Fourth*, they tend to stress the unity of the decree to such an extent that they deny its diversity. Thus, they tend to minimize the disruptive nature of sin. Sin is totally evil, not inherently God-honoring. God uses it for his glory in spite of itself. They typically fail to admit the tension associated with God's decrees respecting sin and damnation. Thus, they tend to force an exact parallel between reprobation and election. These four errors almost always infect those who espouse this scheme. These errors result when men try to impose one-dimensional human logic on God's decree. They skate on thin ice because they exclude God's historical order of implementation from their scheme of logic.

---

[48] Rom. 9:19-20
[49] Gen. 50:20; Eph. 1:12
[50] Rom. 5:1

B. The Infralapsarian View

1. Infralapsarian order of decrees

(1) A decree to create
(2) A decree to permit the fall.
(3) A decree of God's glory in the final salvation of some sinners and eternal damnation of others

2. Stated infralapsarian concerns

First, they desire to honor the fact that Scripture always presents salvation as deliverance from sin and wrath.[51] *Second*, they desire to honor the fact that Scripture connects salvation from sin with the indiscriminate offer of the gospel to sinners.[52]

3. Infralapsarian dangers

The infralapsarian view has two great strengths: it neither claims to resolve the seeming contradictions associated with God's decree, nor fails to recognize the logic of its historical sequence of execution. This does not mean that it is free of all danger. *First*, it faces the danger of obscuring the unity of God's decree. We must indeed call sin evil and disruptive, but not at the expense of the indivisibility of God's decree. *Second*, it faces the danger of obscuring the primacy of salvation. This view can encourage preoccupation with this life and a practical denial of the priority of spiritual things.[53] Since Adam himself was a type of Christ, this creation should never be our ultimate focus or priority. *Third*, it faces the danger of downplaying God's absolute sovereignty over sin and damnation. We must never act as if God is accountable to men. Truly, God's decision of reprobation expresses his justice. Yet, its determining cause is his sovereignty, not his justice, because he satisfies the demands of his justice both toward the saved and the damned.

In sum, both views have valid concerns and face dangers. Accordingly, Bavinck observes:[54]

> the fact that each of the two views leans for support on a certain group of texts without doing full justice to a different group indicates the one-sided character of both theories. Though infralapsarianism deserves praise because of its modesty- it abides by the historical, causal order- and though it *seems* to be less

---

[51] Eph. 2:1-3
[52] Matt. 11:28-30; 2 Thess. 2:13-15
[53] Matt. 6:33; Rom. 5:14; Eph. 5:22-31
[54] Bavinck, *Doctrine of God*, 386-387

offensive and though it shows greater consideration for the demands of practical life, it fails to give satisfaction... Reprobation can not be explained as an act of justice, for the first sinful deed was permitted by God's sovereignty. Reasoning backward, infralapsarianism finally arrives at the position of supralapsarianism.... supralapsarianism undoubtedly has in its favor the fact that it refrains from every attempt to justify God, and that both with respect to reprobation and with respect to election it rests in God's sovereign, incomprehensible, and yet wise and holy good pleasure.

II. The Biblical Concept of the Internal Order of God's Decree

We *survey* the biblical evidence and *summarize* the biblical teaching.

A. A Survey of the Biblical Evidence

We consider biblical testimony that supports the concerns of both perspectives.

1. Biblical evidence for an infralapsarian perspective

This evidence rests on the fact that what happens in history is precisely what God planned in eternity. In history Christ chooses his people out of the world.[55] In history Christ dies for the ungodly.[56] In history God loves children of wrath by nature and imparts spiritual life to dead sinners.[57] In history God justifies the ungodly by means of their faith.[58] Thus, in eternity this is exactly what God decided to do. He decided to choose his people out of the fallen world. He decided to send Christ to die for sinners. He decided to love sinners under his wrath and to make dead sinners alive in Christ. He decided to justify the ungodly by means of their faith in Christ.[59] Thus, God had already decided to create and to allow the fall when he decided to save. This demonstrates that his decisions respecting creation and the fall are logically prior to his decisions respecting salvation and damnation.

---

[55] *John 15:19*: because you are not to the world, but I chose you out of the world, therefore the world hates you

[56] *Rom. 5:6, 8*: While we were yet weak, in due season Christ died for the ungodly . . . But God commends his own love for us, in that, while we were yet sinners, Christ died for us

[57] *Eph. 2:3-5*: and were by nature children of wrath even as the rest:- But God, being rich in mercy, for his great love wherewith he loved us, even when we were dead, made us alive together with Christ

[58] *Rom. 4:5*: to him that works not, but believes on him who justifies the ungodly, his faith is reckoned for righteousness

[59] *2 Tim. 1:9*: who saved us and called us . . . according to his own purpose and grace, which was given us in Christ Jesus before times eternal.

2. Biblical evidence for a supralapsarian perspective

In history God brings the wicked into the world with the intent to bring evil upon them.[60] In history God uses evil as his means to achieve his purpose to preserve human life.[61] In history he uses wicked people to judge other sinners.[62] In history he uses the sins of wicked men to save his people from their sins through the death of Christ.[63] In history God hardens some sinners and shows mercy to others as it pleases him.[64] Thus, in eternity God decided to use sin to accomplish his purposes of grace and salvation. Thus, in eternity he decided to show mercy to sinners according to his sovereign good pleasure.[65] Therefore, the *ultimate cause* of salvation and damnation is God's sovereignty, not his justice. This evidence clearly supports the major supralapsarian concerns. Adam's creation provides even more compelling testimony. In history, God creates Adam as a type of Christ, so that Adam's headship typifies Christ's even before the fall.[66] Thus, in eternity, when God decided to create Adam, he decided to create him as a picture of Christ. Thus, God viewed the coming of Christ as absolutely certain when he decided to create Adam. Thus, God's decision to send Christ to save sinners is logically prior to his decision to create Adam. It is hard to harmonize this fact of revelation with infralapsarian logic. Shall infralapsarians resort to a "potentially send-able Christ" after whom Adam was created? I hope not. Rather, I hope we all abandon any effort to strap God's eternal decree with a one-dimensional scheme of human logic.

B. A Summary of the Biblical Teaching

Bavinck correctly asserts that each view is inadequate alone. Each view has noble concerns and compelling evidence. Both grasp and articulate an aspect of the truth to which they tenaciously cling. Supralapsarians will never relinquish the truth that God viewed salvation in Christ as certain

---

[60] *Prov. 16:4*: Jehovah has made everything for its own end; even the wicked for the day of evil

[61] *Gen. 50:20*: you meant evil against me; but God meant it for good, to bring to pass, as it is this day, to save much people alive

[62] *Isa. 10:5-7*: Ho Assyrian, the rod of mine anger . . . I will send him against a profane nation . . . Howbeit he means not so, neither does his heart think so; but it is in his heart to destroy

[63] *Acts 4:27-28*: against your holy Servant Jesus, whom you did anoint, both Herod and Pontius Pilate, with the Gentiles and the peoples of Israel, were gathered together, to do whatsoever your hand and your counsel foreordained to come to pass

[64] *Rom. 9:18*: he has mercy on whom he will, and whom he will he hardens

[65] *Rom. 9:11-12*: the children being not yet born, neither having done anything good or bad, that the purpose of God according to election might stand

[66] *Rom. 5:14*: Adam's transgression, who is a type of him that was to come

when he decided to create. As long as Romans 5:14 remains in Scripture, no argument will drive them from it. Infralapsarians will never relinquish the truth that God viewed condemnation in Adam as certain when he determined to save his people in Christ. As long as Ephesians 2:3 remains in the Bible, no argument will drive them from it. Yet each view galvanizes its own insight and rejects the other's. When we accept as valid the insights of both, we reach the biblical mystery of the internal order in God's decree. Every aspect of God's decree is coordinate, coincident, reciprocal, and correlative. No aspect has exclusive logical priority. Each presupposes the other. His decision to create presupposes his decision to save; and vice versa.[67] Salvation in Christ is God's ultimate; yet, creation has value in its own right. Salvation cancels, not creation's significance, but sin's influence. What God designs in eternity, he does in history. The historical sequence of execution—creation, fall, salvation—deserves the preeminence. We must emphasize this more friendly face of God's decree, but never deny its more solemn face. I hope this preserves you from the pitfalls of each view when it stands alone. Some may wonder what to call my position. You can call me an *infra-supralapsarian*.

Unit 3. The Practical Application of God's Decree

I summarized practical applications of God's decretive will in Topic 14. I listed warnings, comforts, and duties. I entreat you to return there and consider them again. I now apply only the internal order of God's decree. We should never overestimate human logic or impose one logical scheme on God's decree. We must not assign exclusive logical priority either to creation or salvation, for that will adversely influence our sense of priorities. At times we face difficult decisions, such as the relative priority of work or evangelism, or of our role in church or civil affairs, or of our loyalty to church members or family members. Sometimes men, influenced by a supralapsarian view, neglect their families thinking that "doing the Lord's work" of preaching is all that matters. Others, influenced by an infralapsarian view, pay little attention to spiritual things, thinking that the "creation mandate" to pursue an education, career, family, sports, music, social issues, and political concerns is all that matters. Let us avoid such extremes. Let us embrace in faith all he reveals about his incomprehensible decree.

---

[67] Rom. 5:14; Eph. 2:3-5

Topic 25. Conclusion to the Doctrine of God
"Behold your God!" (Isa. 40:9)

Isa. 40:9-11: O you that tell good tidings to Zion, get you up on a high mountain; O you that tell good tidings to Jerusalem, lift up your voice with strength; lift it up, be not afraid; say to the cities of Judah, Behold your God! Behold, the Lord Jehovah will come as a mighty one, and his arm will rule for him: Behold, his reward is with him, and his recompense before him. He will feed his flock like a shepherd, he will gather the lambs in his arm, and carry them in his bosom, and will gently lead those that have their young.

Conclusion to the Doctrine of God

In this final lecture I review the design and content of our studies. Isaiah furnishes an appropriate perspective with which to conclude. He foretells the coming of Christ. Those who proclaim salvation by grace should call on Christians to behold their God. Every gospel minister should recognize that when believers behold God incarnate, the sight of him greatly encourages them and strengthens their faith. Isaiah promises God's people that the Lord Jehovah will come. Now our Lord, Jehovah Jesus, has come. In him we behold all the fullness of the Godhead. Our great burden as faithful servants of Christ should be that God's people would come to know God better through our lives and labors. Our design in this study has been to gaze by faith on the triune God so that we can say to Christian Judah: "Behold your God." I earnestly hope and pray that these labors will, in God's kind providence, prove useful to that end.

Say to God's people: behold *the existence of God*. Behold the fact, revelation, uniqueness, denial, and importance of his existence. Again, say to God's people: behold *the knowledge of God*. Contemplate his knowability and incomprehensibility. Although we can know him truly, we can never know him exhaustively because he is incomprehensible. Again, let us say to the cities of spiritual Judah: behold *the nature of God*. Behold his spiritual, supreme, and simple nature. Behold his existential supremacy. Behold his ideality. Behold his self-existence. Behold his infinite, eternal, unchangeable Being. Behold his supreme spirituality. He is a non-material, living, Being with faculty, morality, and personality. Behold his supreme form. He dwells in light unapproachable. Behold his supreme life and power. Behold his supreme faculty, his infinite mind, sovereign will, and absolute affection. Behold his supreme morality, his infinitely perfect goodness, holiness, justice, and faithfulness. Behold his triune personality. He is the Father and the Son and the Holy Spirit. Again, let us lift up our voice, and say to God's people: behold *the names of God*. Behold the glory and honor of his great name, his being, attributes, authority, reputation, and Word. Behold his proper names: God, the Almighty, the Most High, the

Lord, Jehovah, I AM. Finally, say to God's people: behold *the decree of God*. Your God in eternity planned and decided for his own glory whatever happens in history. Here is the sum of all the lectures:

> IS THERE A GOD?
>
> CAN WE KNOW HIM?
>
> WHO AND WHAT IS HE?
>
> HOW SHOULD WE ADDRESS HIM?
>
> WHAT HAS HE PLANNED?

This work answers these basic questions. Thus, let us answer them boldly. Don't be afraid. Don't water it down. Lift up your voice. Never be ashamed. Be determined. Here is our solemn and glad duty. Stand up and proclaim these truths about God to his people in his name for his glory, so that Christians would behold their God, marvel at him, glory in him, and bless him forever. We have a blessed mission of mercy, goodwill, joy, and peace. Let us count it a great privilege to say to Christian Israel, "Behold your God!" This God, whom we behold, is "the blessed God" (1 Tim. 1:11). When all our studies are done, we must bless him and say: "to thee O blessed Trinity, be praise throughout eternity. Amen."

Made in the USA
Middletown, DE
23 February 2017